here i am, i am me

AN ILLUSTRATED GUIDE TO MENTAL HEALTH

CARA BEAN

Workman Publishing
New York

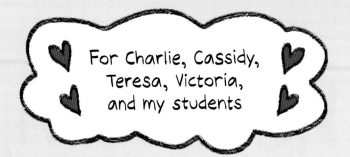

For Charlie, Cassidy, Teresa, Victoria, and my students

Library of Congress Cataloging-in-Publication Data is available

ISBN 978-1-5235-2438-9 (jacketed hardcover)
ISBN 978-1-5235-0805-1 (paperback)

Design by Molly Magnell and Sam Pun

Workman books are available at special discounts when purchased in bulk for premiums and sales promotions as well as for fundraising or educational use. Special editions or book excerpts can also be created to specification. For details, please contact special.markets@hbgusa.com.

Workman Publishing Co., Inc.
a subsidiary of Hachette Book Group, Inc.
1290 Avenue of the Americas
New York, NY 10104

workman.com

Distributed in Europe by Hachette Livre,
58 rue Jean Bleuzen, 92 178 Vanves Cedex, France.

Distributed in the United Kingdom by Hachette Book Group, UK,
Carmelite House, 50 Victoria Embankment, London EC4Y 0DZ.

WORKMAN is a registered trademark of Workman Publishing Co., Inc.,
a subsidiary of Hachette Book Group, Inc.

Printed in China on responsibly sourced paper.

First printing February 2024

10 9 8 7 6 5 4 3 2 1

FOREWORD

Hello, reader!

You've probably heard a lot about mental health lately. Society is finally recognizing how important mental health is—and I know from my own practice that teens are having a lot of complicated thoughts, feelings, and experiences that are worth exploring. Adolescence has always been known to be a time of strong emotions and identity development. We also know that the patterns and expectations you set for yourself and your well-being now will carry you into adulthood.

To the adolescent reading this: Many adults care about you, and while a lot of the talk may seem to center on how to keep you out of trouble, it's you who are the most powerful driver of your own mental health. Research tells us that people who know about how emotions, thoughts, and behaviors affect their mood and how they function . . .

- have concrete things to do when times get tough,

- can rely on trusted people for help,

- feel empowered and invested in their own well-being,

- and will be more likely to stay healthy and to feel happy with their life choices.

In this book, Cara Bean gives you all these tools in a fun, relatable way. As an art teacher, she has a ton of experience in talking with and helping teens, and it shows. She celebrates you, your abilities, and your agency, and helps you understand that you can care for your own well-being. Scientific information and technical language can sometimes feel overwhelming and hard to get through—but not in this book. Complex concepts and processes are made accessible through her illustrations. This isn't a textbook—Ms. Bean uses her art to convey emotions and reactions that go beyond words but are critical to understanding the depth of mental health experiences.

You may recognize yourself, your friends, and your family in these pages. Perhaps you have faced similar situations as described in this book and have wondered what to do. Ms. Bean doesn't simply present the doom and gloom and walk away—she gives you specific steps that show you how to take care of yourself and others. Because you can.

Dive in, explore, and take charge of your mental health.

Dr. Mandi

Mandi White-Ajmani, PhD
Clinical Psychologist
Small Brooklyn Psychology

TABLE OF CONTENTS

INTRODUCTION

Hello! I'm Cara Bean and I draw myself as a bean shape because my students have been calling me "Ms. Bean" in the classroom for years.

I am an art teacher who draws comics.

SPRING DANCE! TICKETS ON SALE

I love my students. They amaze me on a daily basis.

RRRRING!

I'm lucky to teach art because we get to have a lot of fun.

Being a teacher is also about paying attention to the sensitive issues that come up during art class.

Anxiety, depression, substance use issues, and confusing emotions are often under the surface and affecting me and my students in some way.

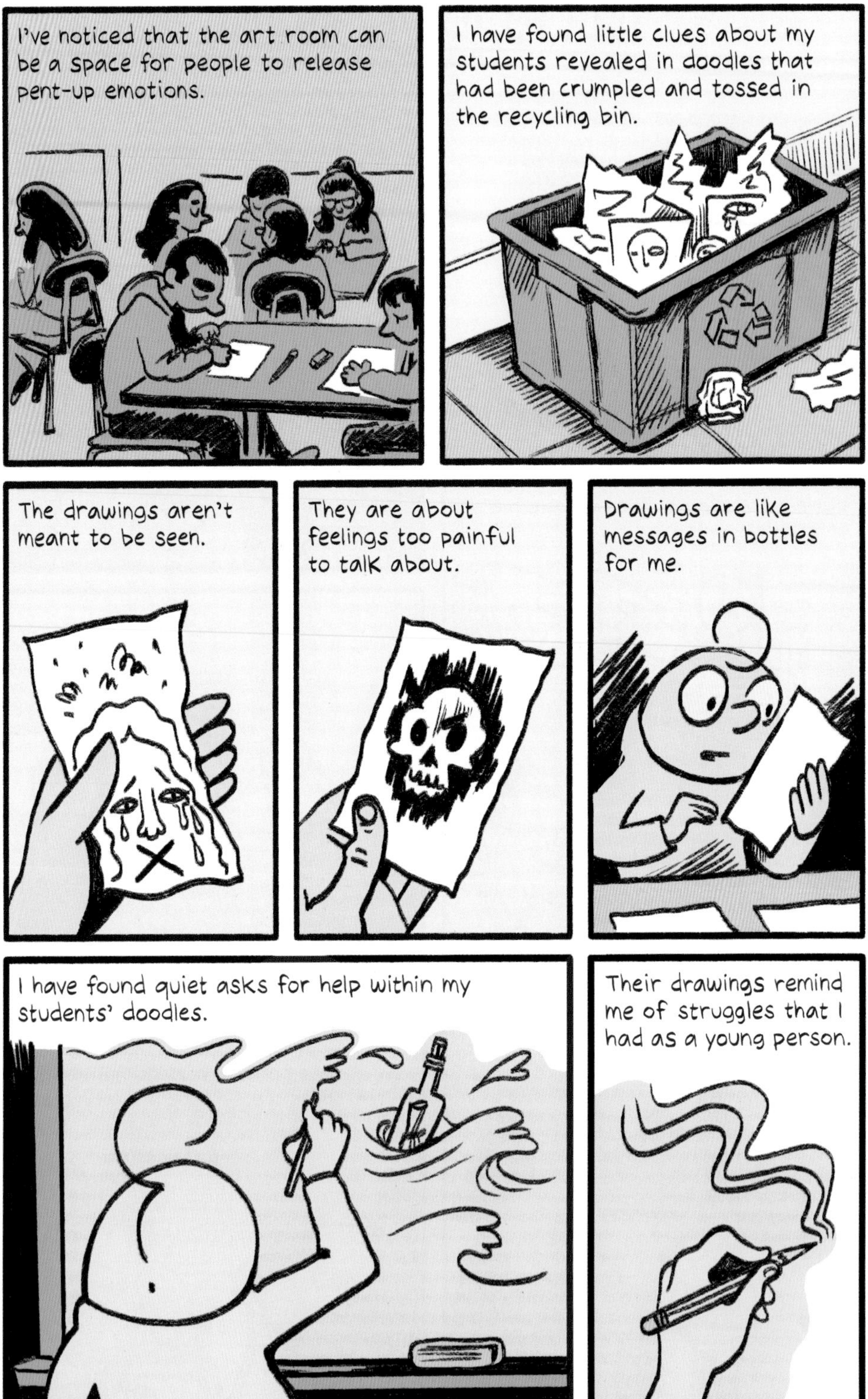
I've noticed that the art room can be a space for people to release pent-up emotions.
I have found little clues about my students revealed in doodles that had been crumpled and tossed in the recycling bin.
The drawings aren't meant to be seen.
They are about feelings too painful to talk about.
Drawings are like messages in bottles for me.
I have found quiet asks for help within my students' doodles.
Their drawings remind me of struggles that I had as a young person.

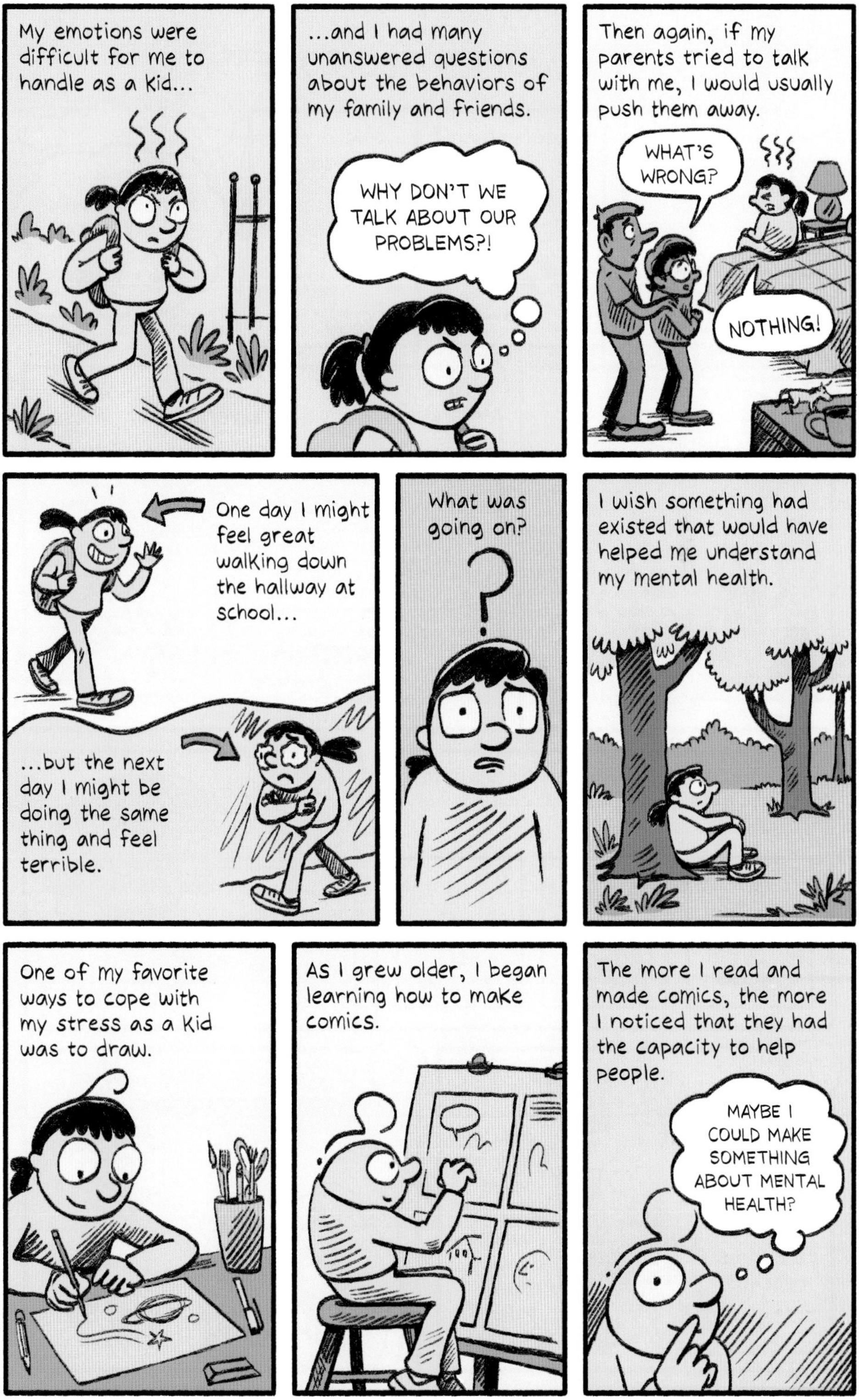
My emotions were difficult for me to handle as a kid...
...and I had many unanswered questions about the behaviors of my family and friends.
WHY DON'T WE TALK ABOUT OUR PROBLEMS?!
Then again, if my parents tried to talk with me, I would usually push them away.
WHAT'S WRONG?
NOTHING!
One day I might feel great walking down the hallway at school...
...but the next day I might be doing the same thing and feel terrible.
What was going on?
I wish something had existed that would have helped me understand my mental health.
One of my favorite ways to cope with my stress as a kid was to draw.
As I grew older, I began learning how to make comics.
The more I read and made comics, the more I noticed that they had the capacity to help people.
MAYBE I COULD MAKE SOMETHING ABOUT MENTAL HEALTH?

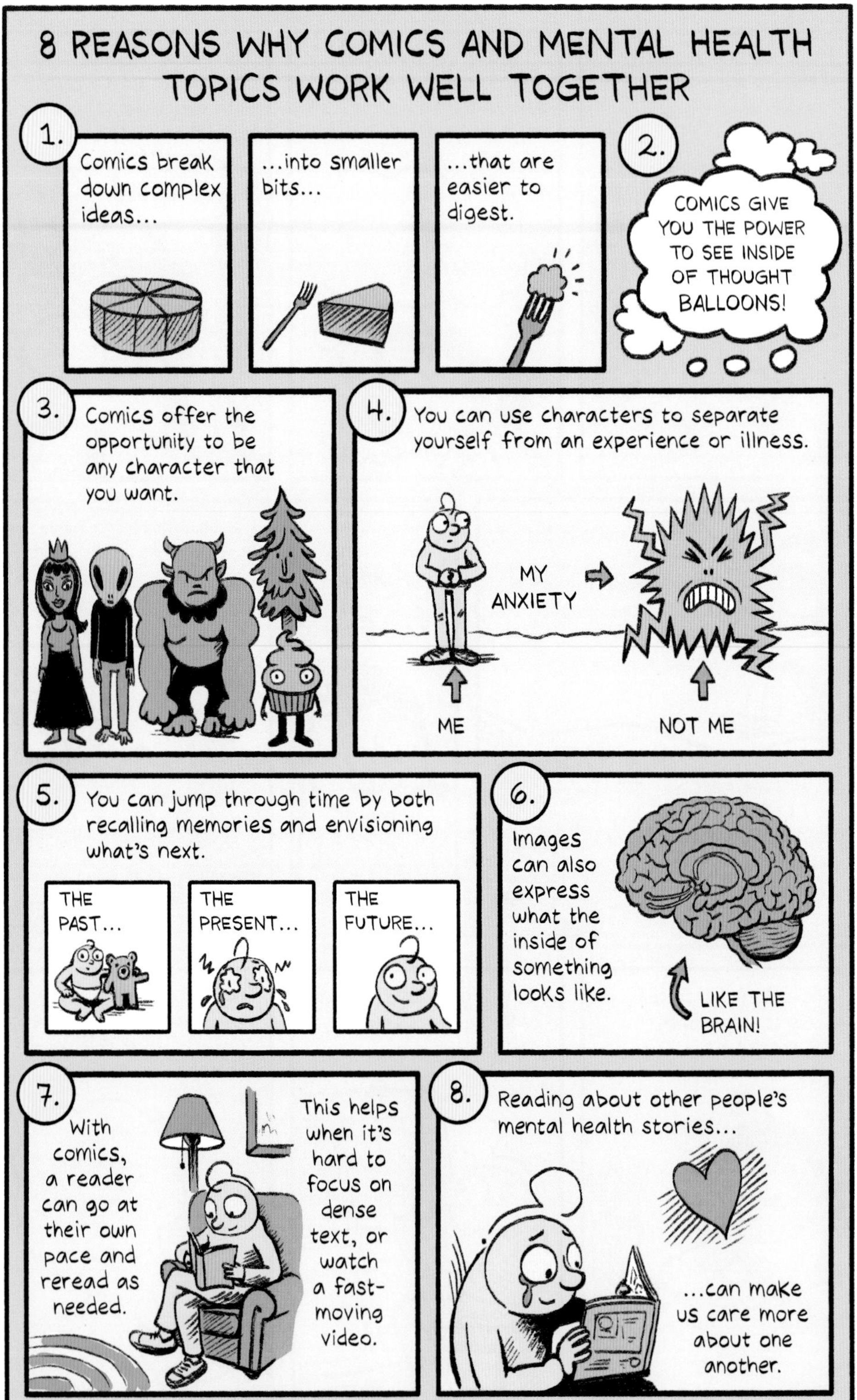
8 REASONS WHY COMICS AND MENTAL HEALTH TOPICS WORK WELL TOGETHER
1.
Comics break down complex ideas...
...into smaller bits...
...that are easier to digest.
2.
COMICS GIVE YOU THE POWER TO SEE INSIDE OF THOUGHT BALLOONS!
3.
Comics offer the opportunity to be any character that you want.
4.
You can use characters to separate yourself from an experience or illness.
MY ANXIETY
ME
NOT ME
5.
You can jump through time by both recalling memories and envisioning what's next.
THE PAST...
THE PRESENT...
THE FUTURE...
6.
Images can also express what the inside of something looks like.
LIKE THE BRAIN!
7.
With comics, a reader can go at their own pace and reread as needed.
This helps when it's hard to focus on dense text, or watch a fast-moving video.
8.
Reading about other people's mental health stories...
...can make us care more about one another.

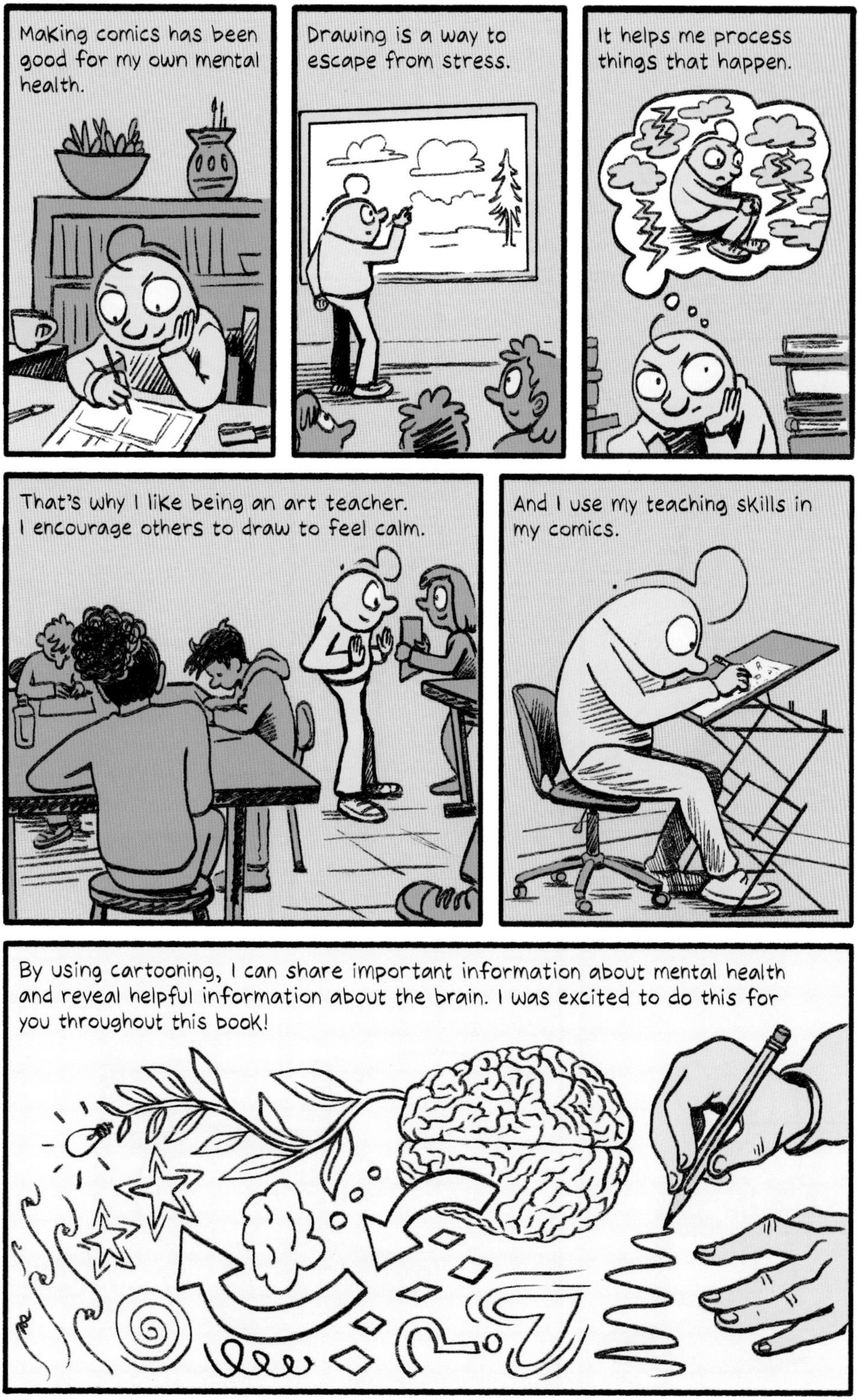
Making comics has been good for my own mental health.
Drawing is a way to escape from stress.
It helps me process things that happen.
That's why I like being an art teacher. I encourage others to draw to feel calm.
And I use my teaching skills in my comics.
By using cartooning, I can share important information about mental health and reveal helpful information about the brain. I was excited to do this for you throughout this book!

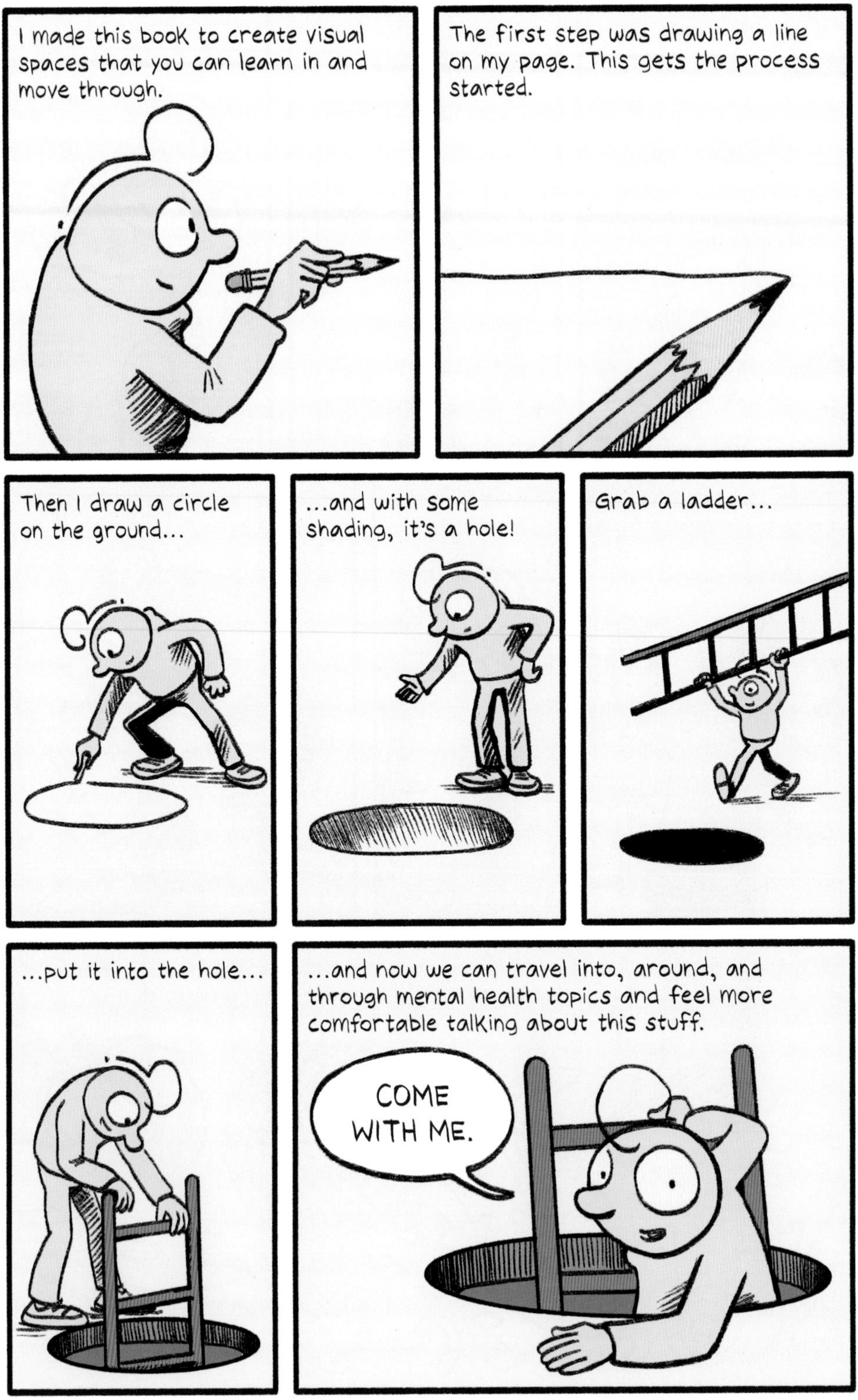
I made this book to create visual spaces that you can learn in and move through.
The first step was drawing a line on my page. This gets the process started.
Then I draw a circle on the ground...
...and with some shading, it's a hole!
Grab a ladder...
...put it into the hole...
...and now we can travel into, around, and through mental health topics and feel more comfortable talking about this stuff.
COME WITH ME.

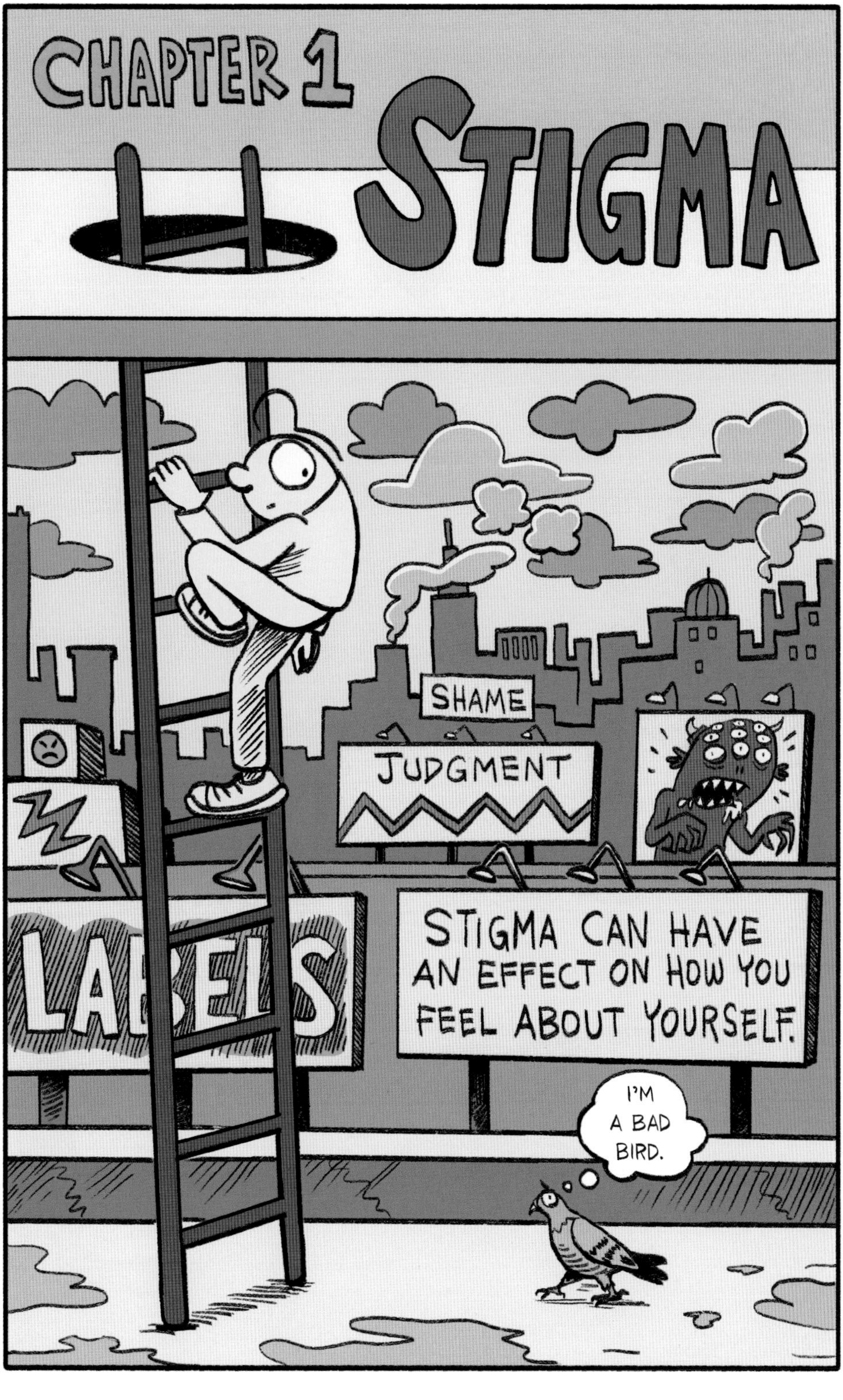
CHAPTER 1
STIGMA
SHAME
JUDGMENT
LABELS
STIGMA CAN HAVE AN EFFECT ON HOW YOU FEEL ABOUT YOURSELF.
I'M A BAD BIRD.

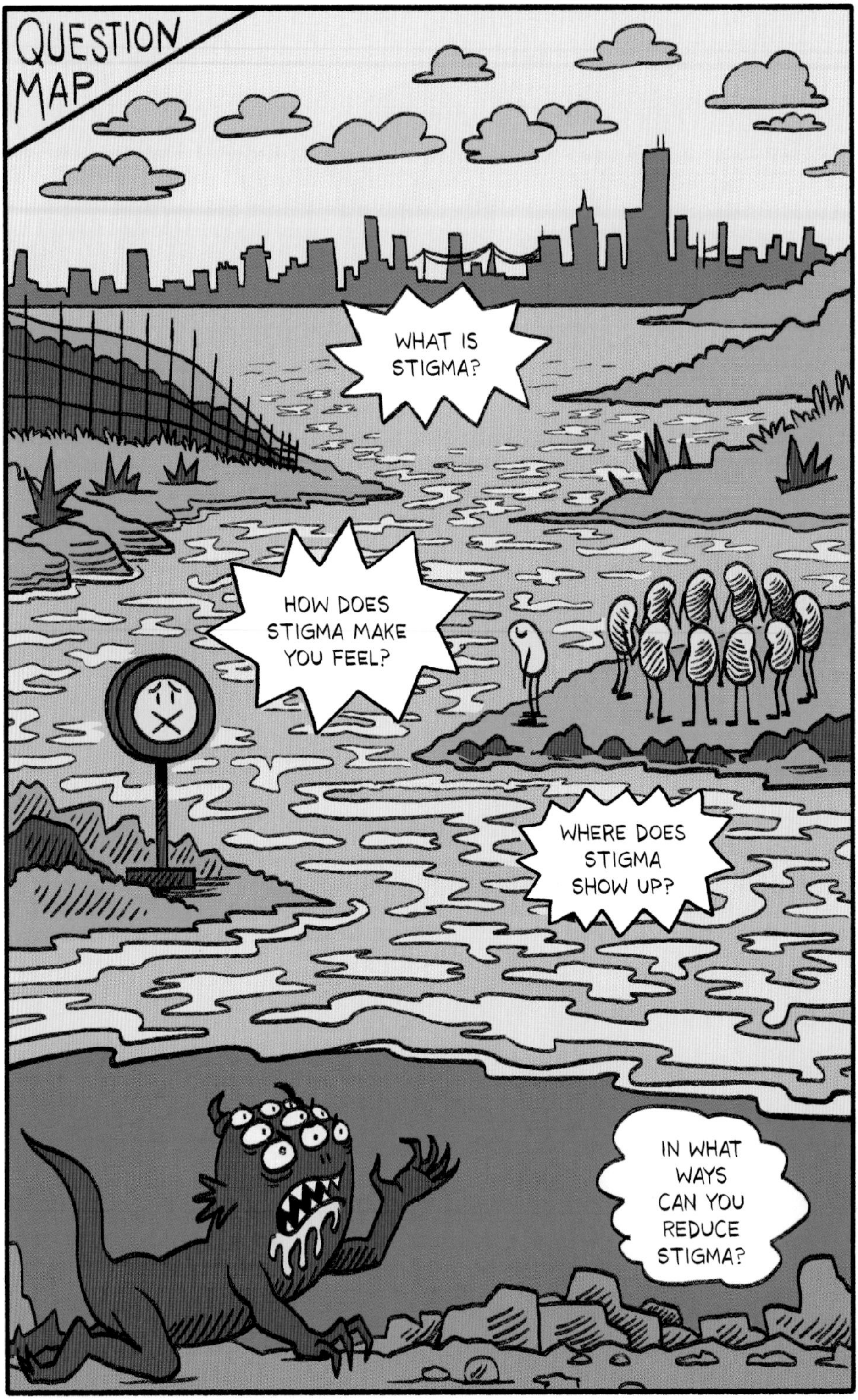
QUESTION MAP
WHAT IS STIGMA?
HOW DOES STIGMA MAKE YOU FEEL?
WHERE DOES STIGMA SHOW UP?
IN WHAT WAYS CAN YOU REDUCE STIGMA?

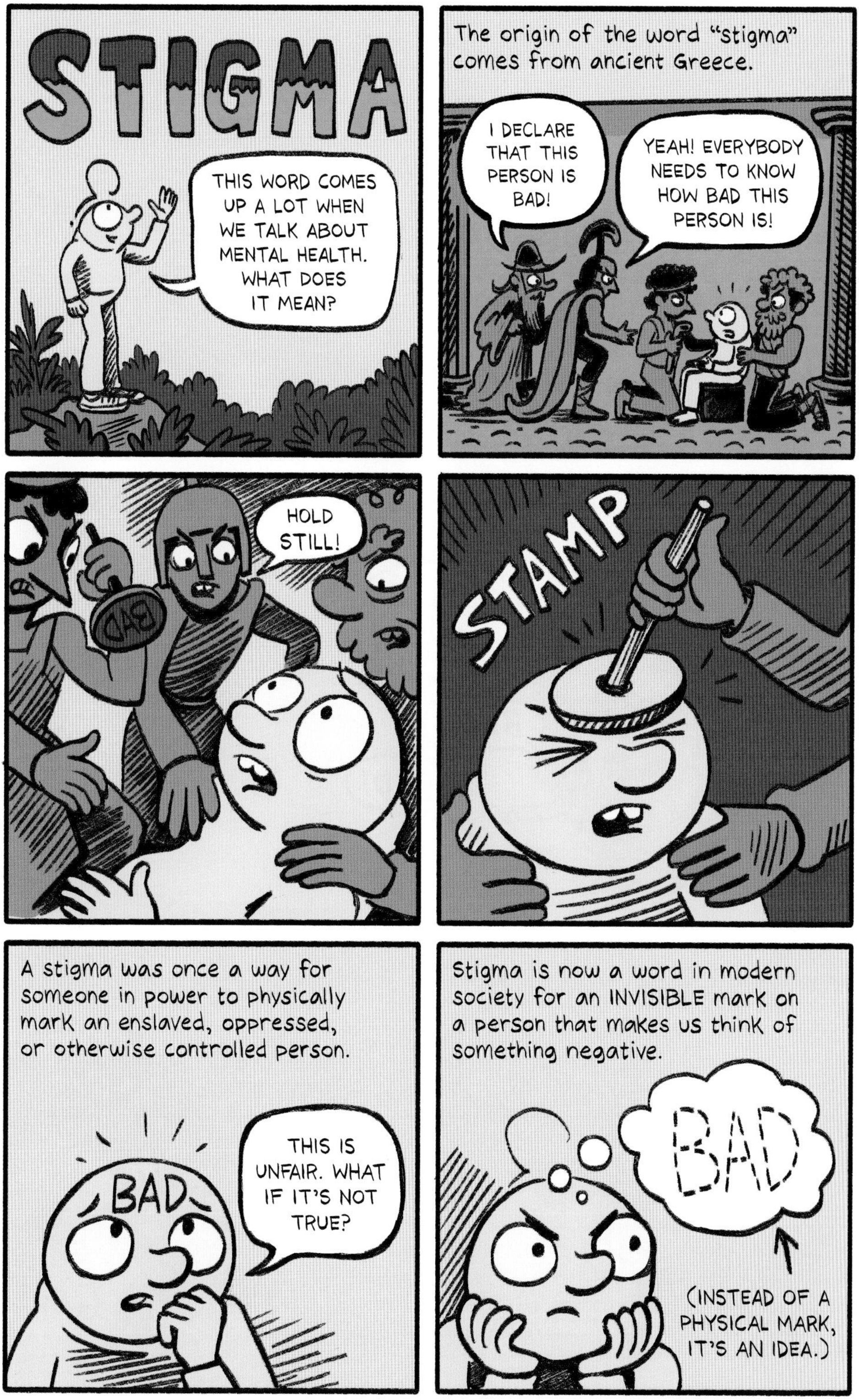
STIGMA
THIS WORD COMES UP A LOT WHEN WE TALK ABOUT MENTAL HEALTH. WHAT DOES IT MEAN?
The origin of the word "stigma" comes from ancient Greece.
I DECLARE THAT THIS PERSON IS BAD!
YEAH! EVERYBODY NEEDS TO KNOW HOW BAD THIS PERSON IS!
BAD
HOLD STILL!
STAMP
A stigma was once a way for someone in power to physically mark an enslaved, oppressed, or otherwise controlled person.
BAD
THIS IS UNFAIR. WHAT IF IT'S NOT TRUE?
Stigma is now a word in modern society for an INVISIBLE mark on a person that makes us think of something negative.
BAD
(INSTEAD OF A PHYSICAL MARK, IT'S AN IDEA.)

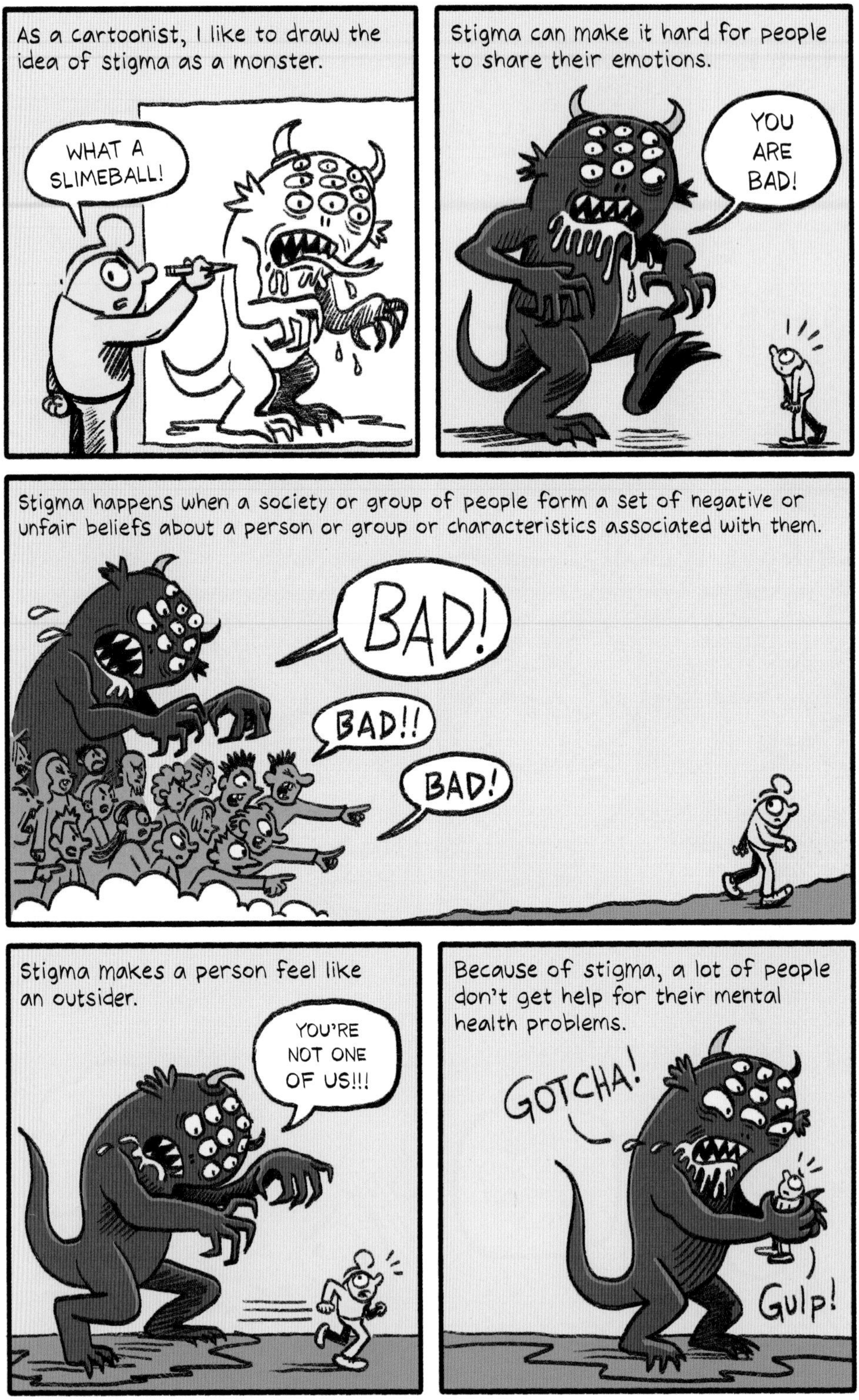
As a cartoonist, I like to draw the idea of stigma as a monster.
WHAT A SLIMEBALL!
Stigma can make it hard for people to share their emotions.
YOU ARE BAD!
Stigma happens when a society or group of people form a set of negative or unfair beliefs about a person or group or characteristics associated with them.
BAD!
BAD!!
BAD!
Stigma makes a person feel like an outsider.
YOU'RE NOT ONE OF US!!!
Because of stigma, a lot of people don't get help for their mental health problems.
GOTCHA!
Gulp!

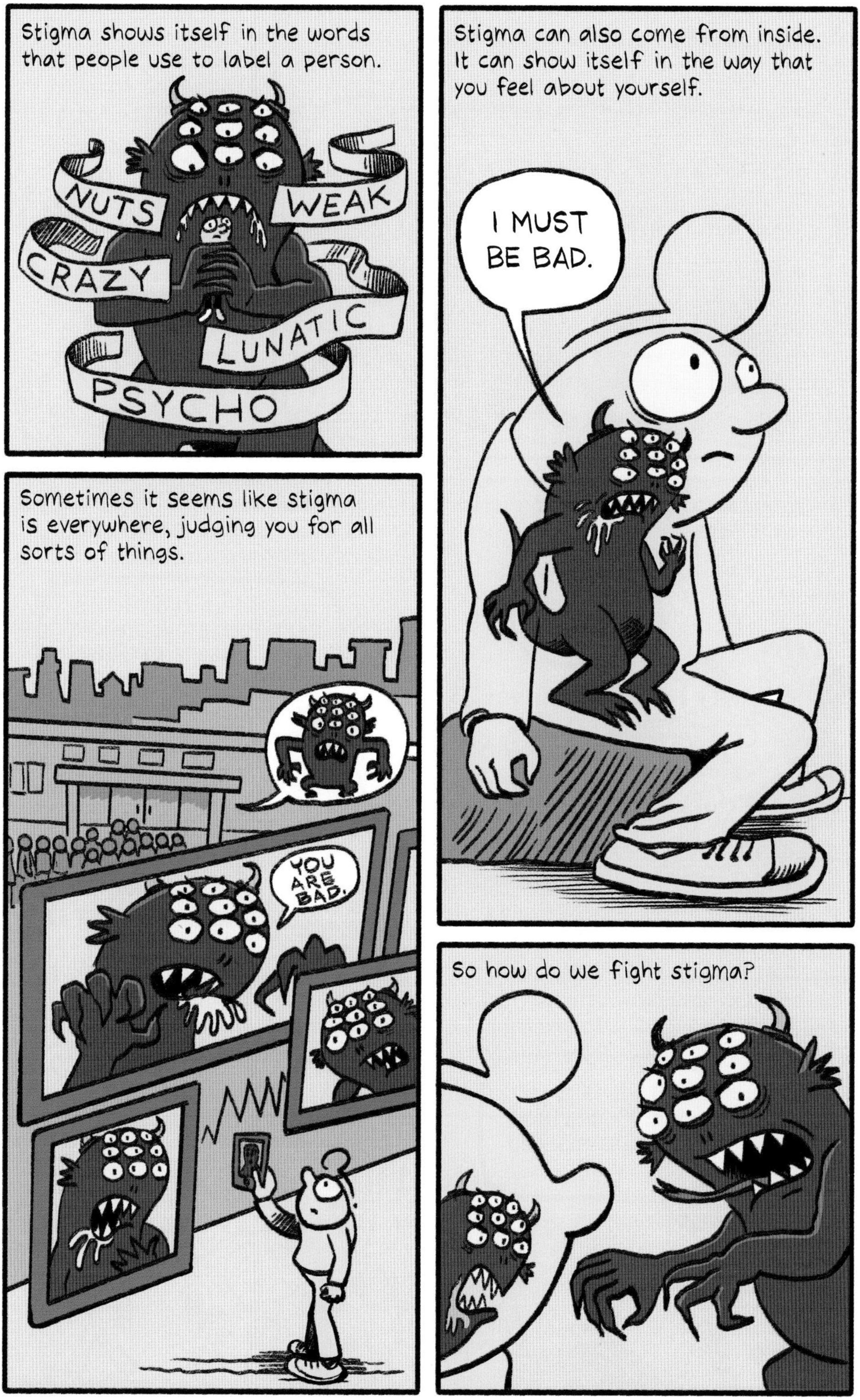
Stigma shows itself in the words that people use to label a person.
NUTS
WEAK
CRAZY
LUNATIC
PSYCHO
Stigma can also come from inside. It can show itself in the way that you feel about yourself.
I MUST BE BAD.
Sometimes it seems like stigma is everywhere, judging you for all sorts of things.
YOU ARE BAD.
So how do we fight stigma?

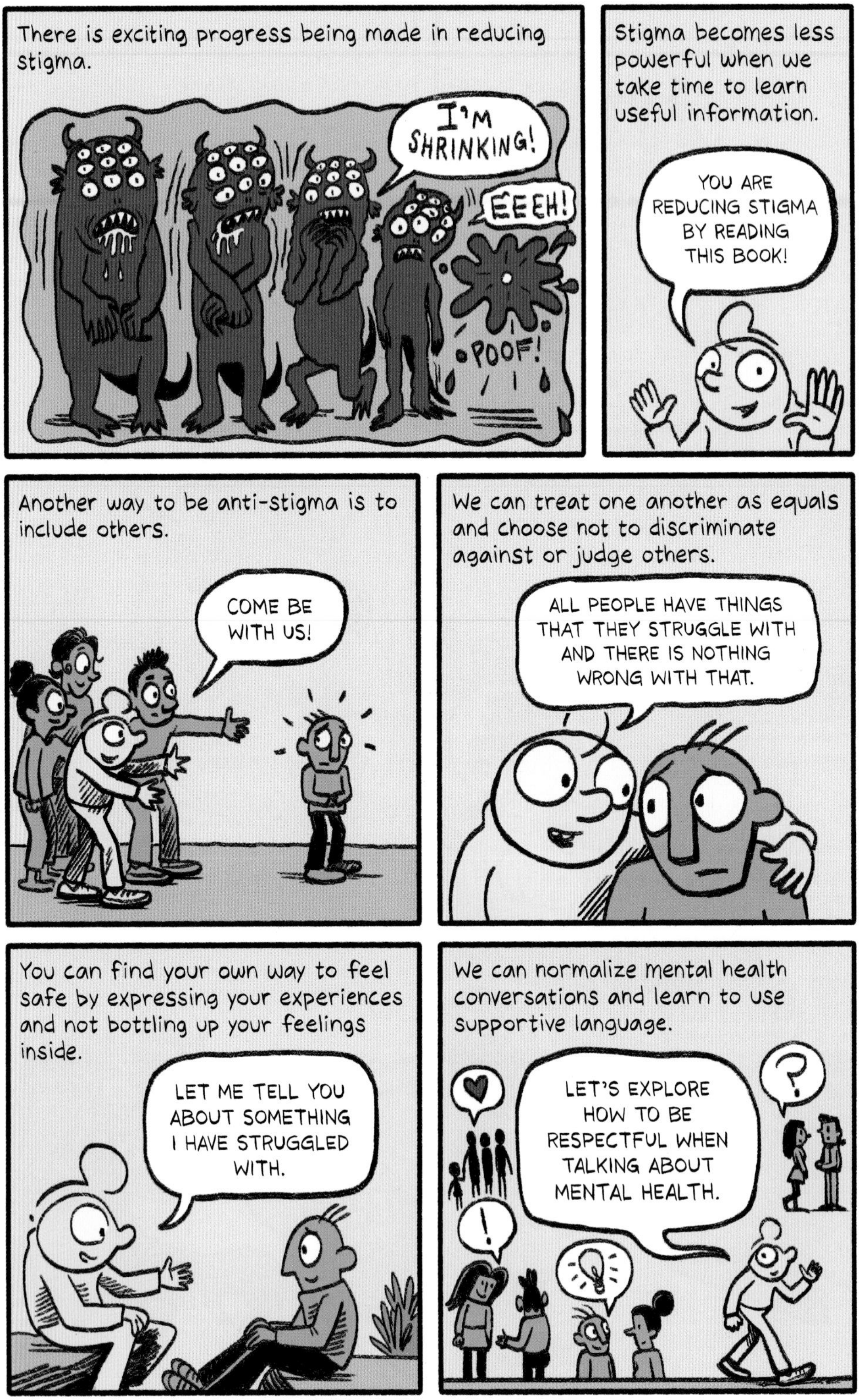
There is exciting progress being made in reducing stigma.
I'M SHRINKING!
EEEH!
POOF!
Stigma becomes less powerful when we take time to learn useful information.
YOU ARE REDUCING STIGMA BY READING THIS BOOK!
Another way to be anti-stigma is to include others.
COME BE WITH US!
We can treat one another as equals and choose not to discriminate against or judge others.
ALL PEOPLE HAVE THINGS THAT THEY STRUGGLE WITH AND THERE IS NOTHING WRONG WITH THAT.
You can find your own way to feel safe by expressing your experiences and not bottling up your feelings inside.
LET ME TELL YOU ABOUT SOMETHING I HAVE STRUGGLED WITH.
We can normalize mental health conversations and learn to use supportive language.
LET'S EXPLORE HOW TO BE RESPECTFUL WHEN TALKING ABOUT MENTAL HEALTH.
?
!

LANGUAGE MATTERS

When we focus on person-centered language, we can help people with a variety of conditions see that their health is valued and important.

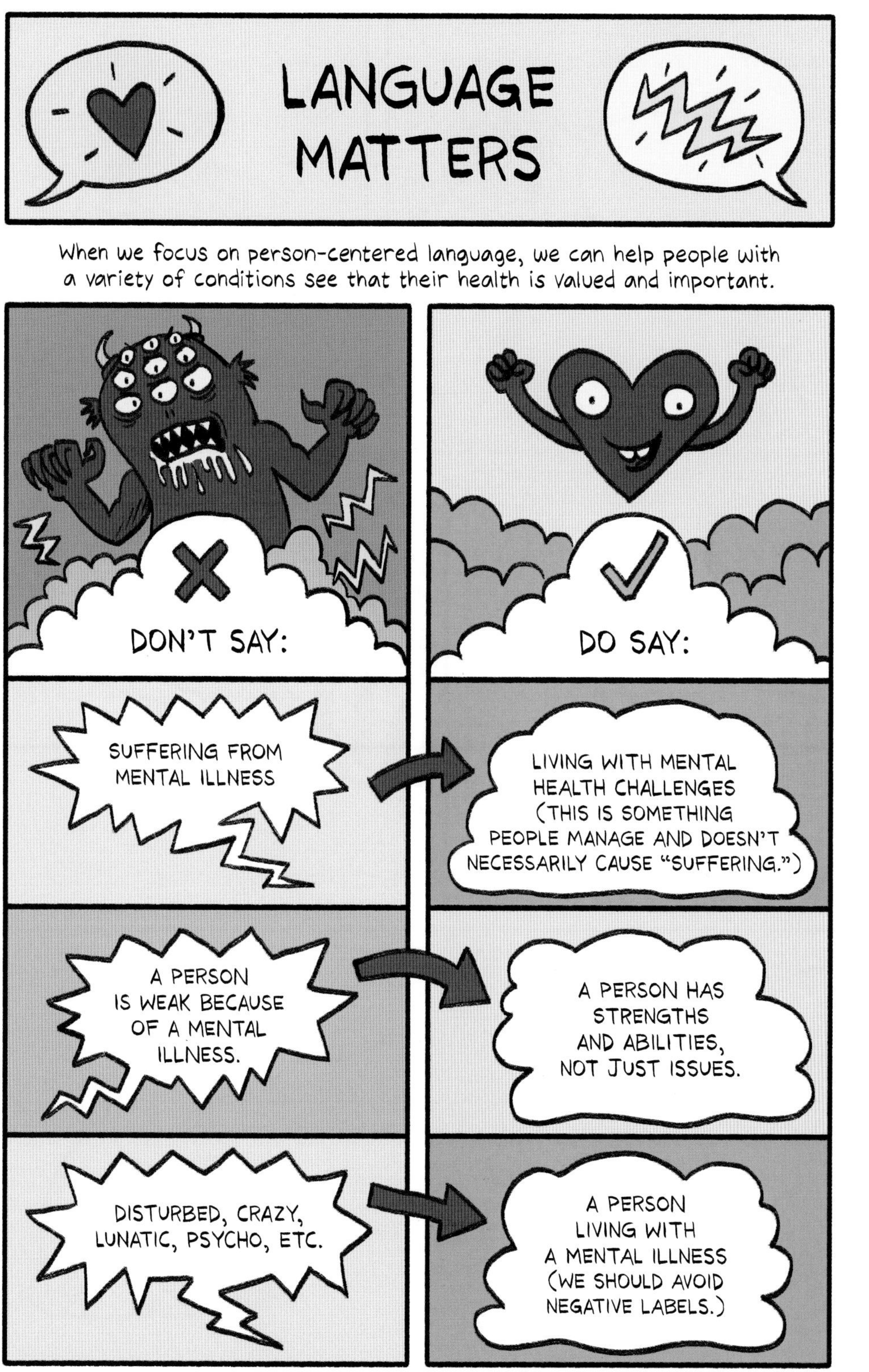
DON'T SAY:
DO SAY:
SUFFERING FROM MENTAL ILLNESS
LIVING WITH MENTAL HEALTH CHALLENGES (THIS IS SOMETHING PEOPLE MANAGE AND DOESN'T NECESSARILY CAUSE "SUFFERING.")
A PERSON IS WEAK BECAUSE OF A MENTAL ILLNESS.
A PERSON HAS STRENGTHS AND ABILITIES, NOT JUST ISSUES.
DISTURBED, CRAZY, LUNATIC, PSYCHO, ETC.
A PERSON LIVING WITH A MENTAL ILLNESS (WE SHOULD AVOID NEGATIVE LABELS.)

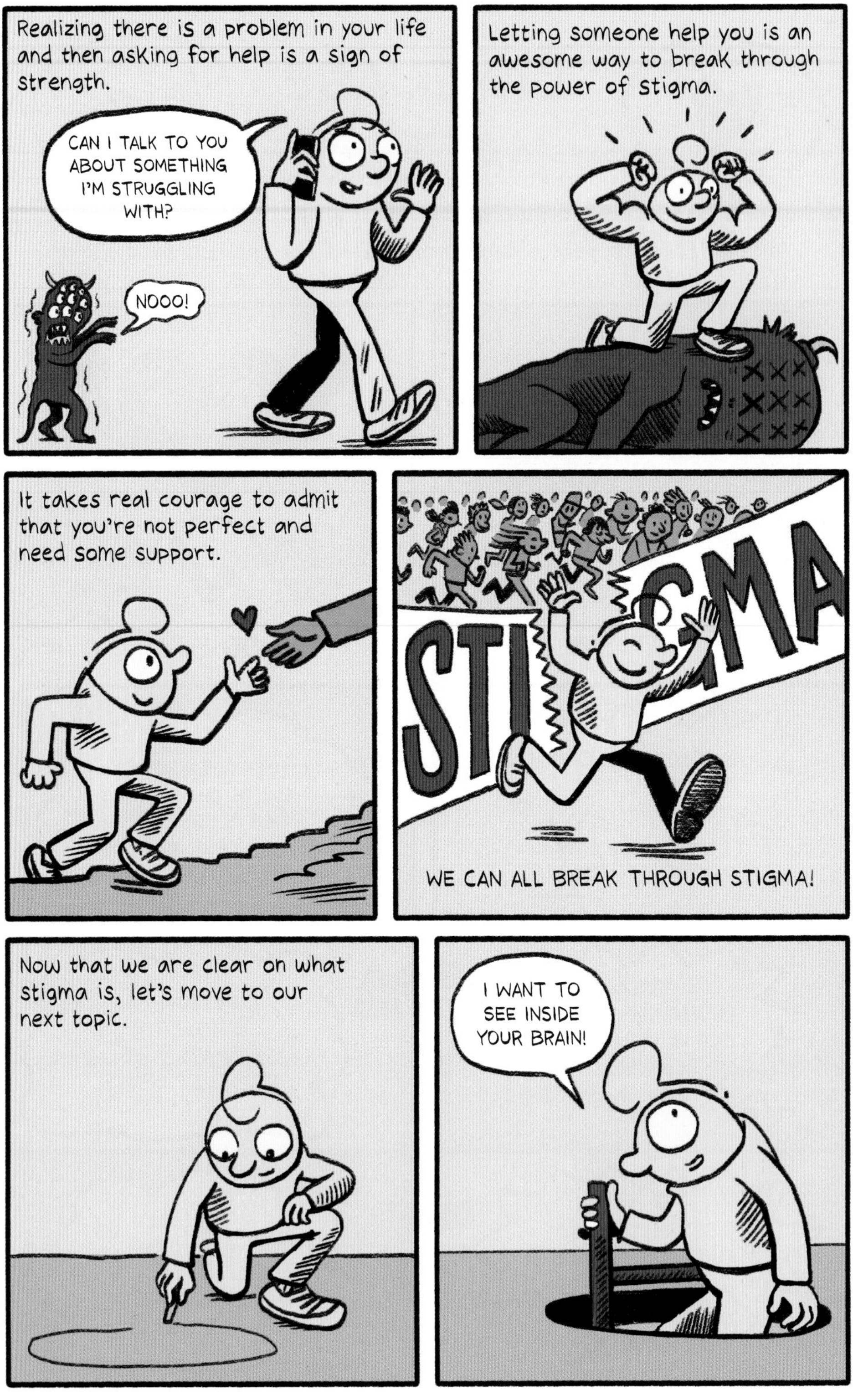
Realizing there is a problem in your life and then asking for help is a sign of strength.
CAN I TALK TO YOU ABOUT SOMETHING I'M STRUGGLING WITH?
NOOO!
Letting someone help you is an awesome way to break through the power of stigma.
It takes real courage to admit that you're not perfect and need some support.
STI
GMA
WE CAN ALL BREAK THROUGH STIGMA!
Now that we are clear on what stigma is, let's move to our next topic.
I WANT TO SEE INSIDE YOUR BRAIN!

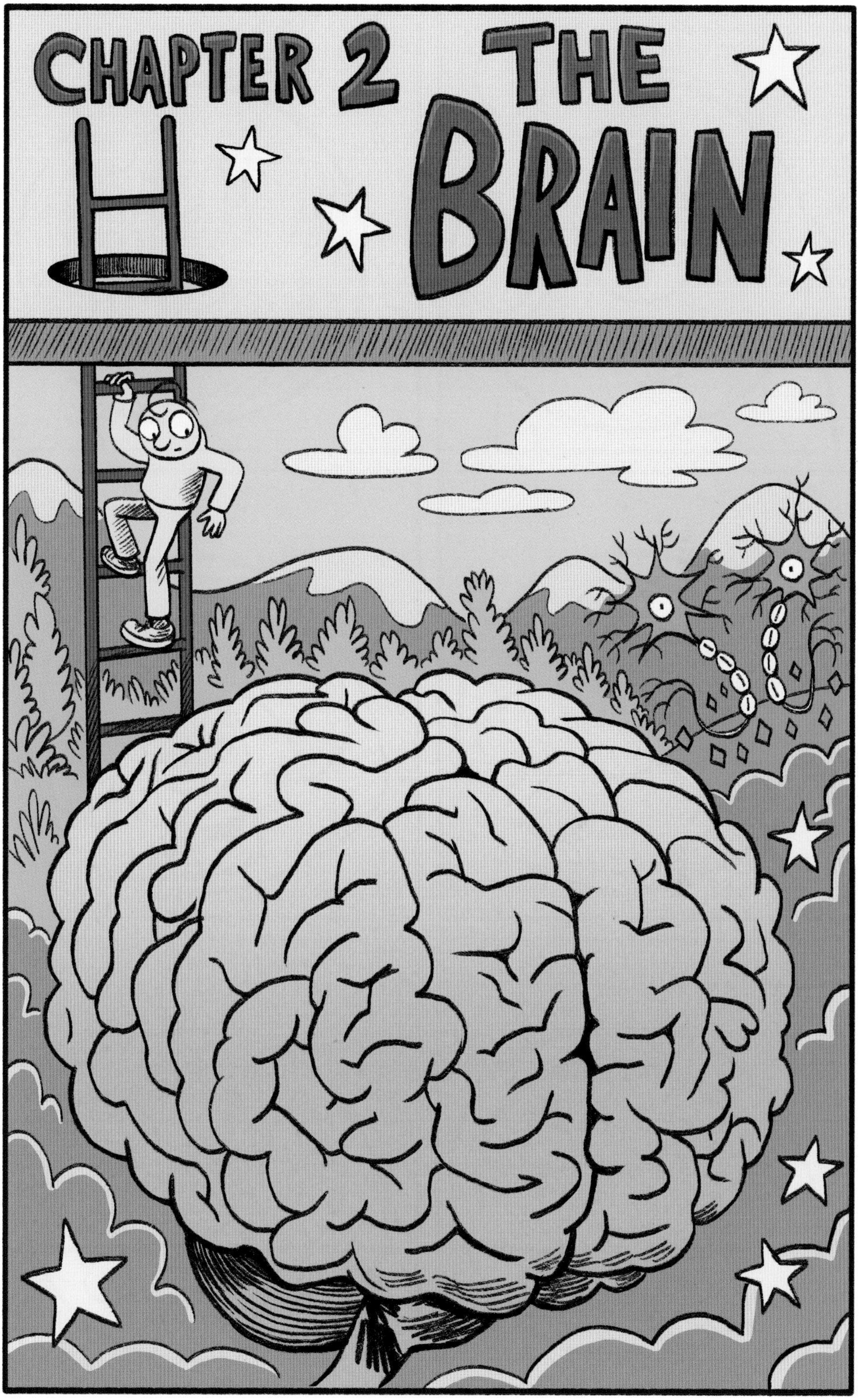

CHAPTER 2
THE BRAIN

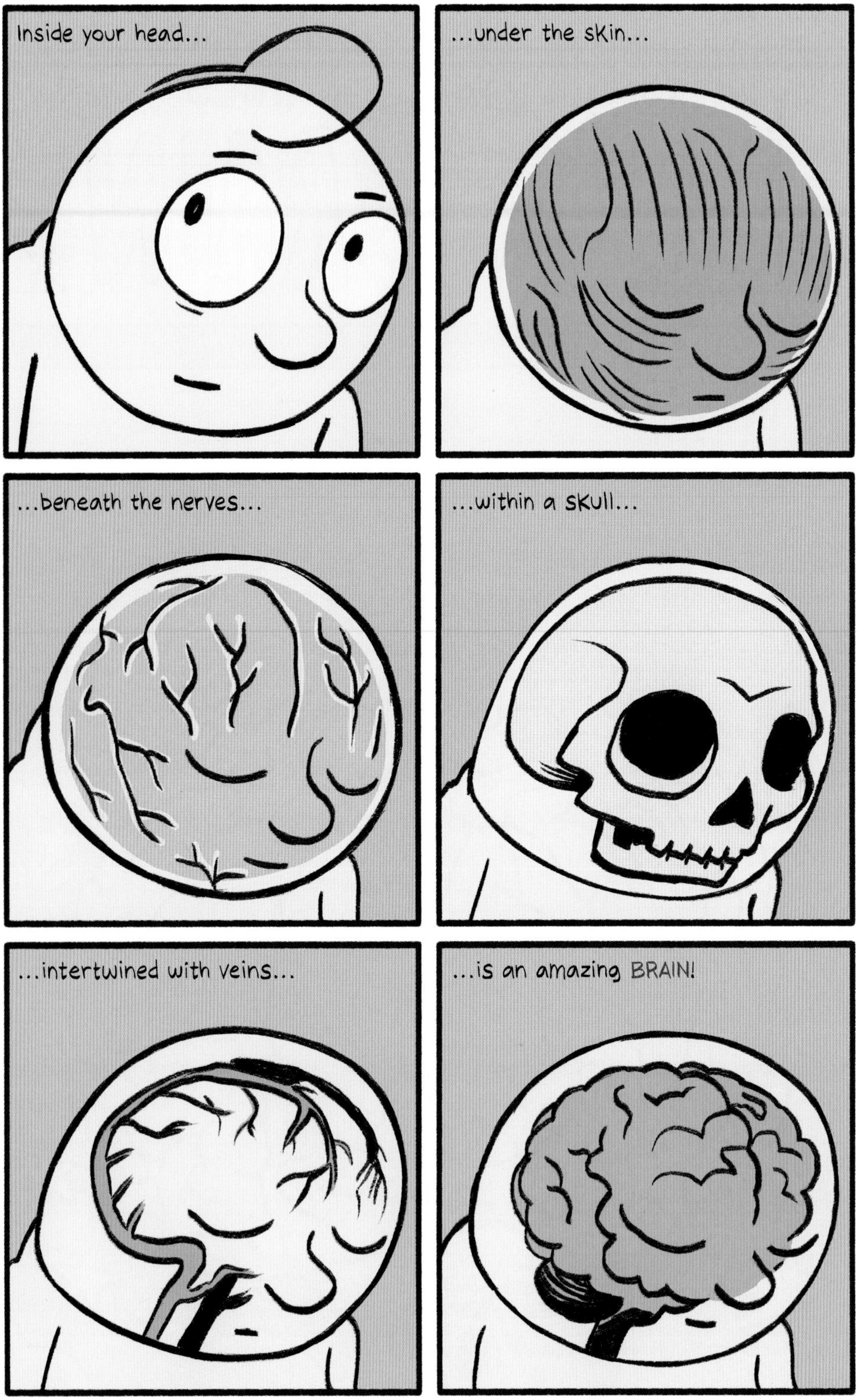
Inside your head...
...under the skin...
...beneath the nerves...
...within a skull...
...intertwined with veins...
...is an amazing BRAIN!

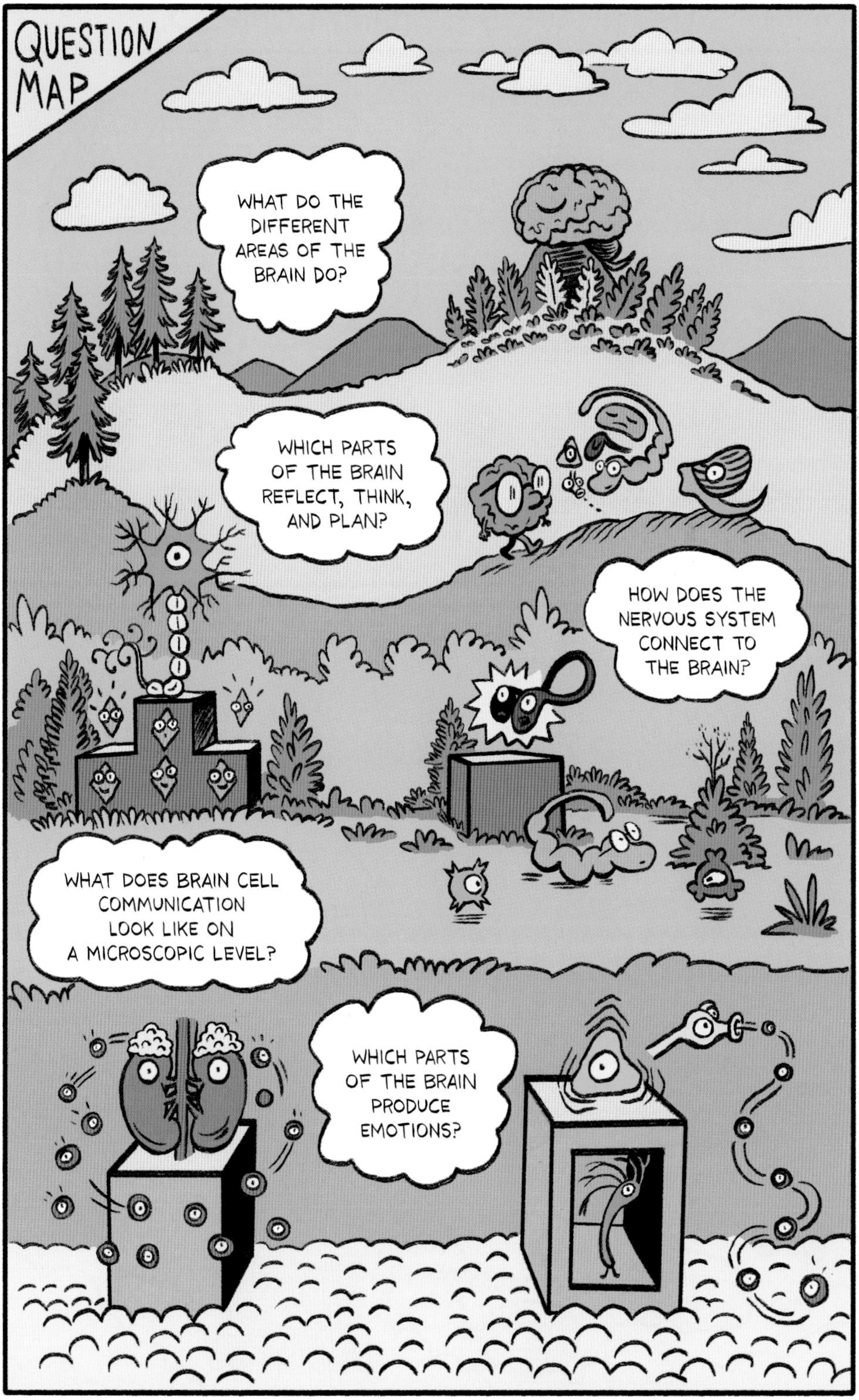
QUESTION MAP
WHAT DO THE DIFFERENT AREAS OF THE BRAIN DO?
WHICH PARTS OF THE BRAIN REFLECT, THINK, AND PLAN?
HOW DOES THE NERVOUS SYSTEM CONNECT TO THE BRAIN?
WHAT DOES BRAIN CELL COMMUNICATION LOOK LIKE ON A MICROSCOPIC LEVEL?
WHICH PARTS OF THE BRAIN PRODUCE EMOTIONS?

THE BRAIN IS BEYOND COMPLEX!

The human brain is like an orchestra!

Different regions perform different types of processing...

...much like the individual musicians who must read the music, play their instruments, and also listen and adapt to the sounds that others make.

The brain has many interconnected systems working in harmony with one another.

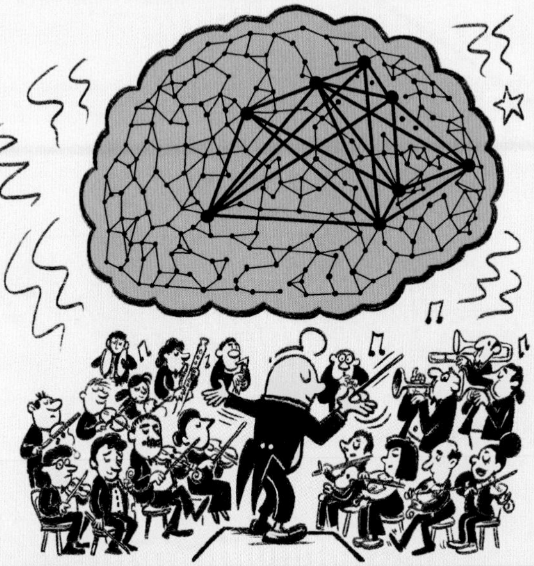

When we turn the brain to one side, we can view the left hemisphere and locate all the areas of its specific function.

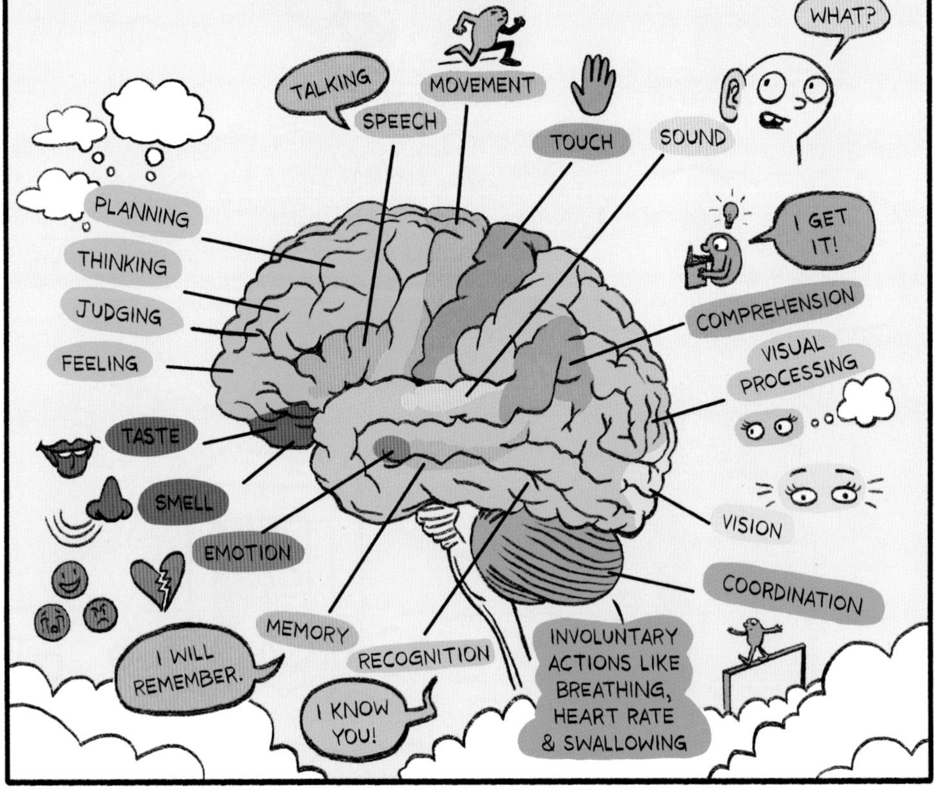
TALKING
MOVEMENT
SPEECH
TOUCH
SOUND
WHAT?
PLANNING
THINKING
JUDGING
FEELING
I GET IT!
COMPREHENSION
VISUAL PROCESSING
TASTE
SMELL
EMOTION
VISION
COORDINATION
MEMORY
RECOGNITION
INVOLUNTARY ACTIONS LIKE BREATHING, HEART RATE & SWALLOWING
I WILL REMEMBER.
I KNOW YOU!

SEE INSIDE YOUR BRAIN'S EMOTIONAL EQUIPMENT

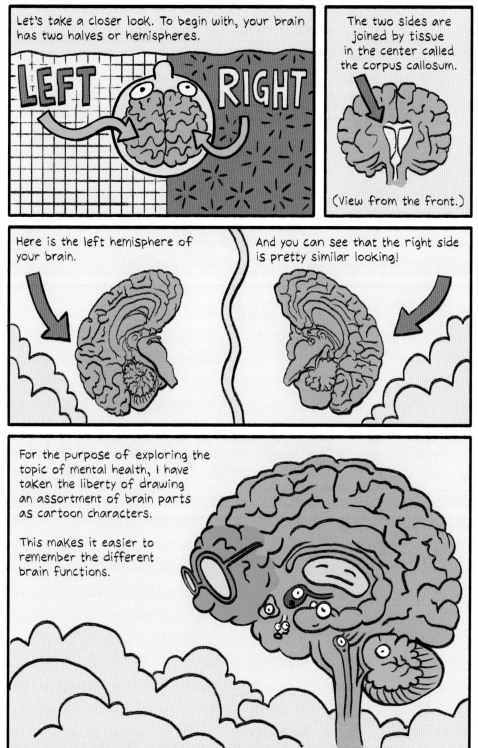

Let's take a closer look. To begin with, your brain has two halves or hemispheres.

LEFT RIGHT

The two sides are joined by tissue in the center called the corpus callosum.

(View from the front.)

Here is the left hemisphere of your brain.

And you can see that the right side is pretty similar looking!

For the purpose of exploring the topic of mental health, I have taken the liberty of drawing an assortment of brain parts as cartoon characters.

This makes it easier to remember the different brain functions.

THERE ARE THREE BASIC AREAS OF THE BRAIN

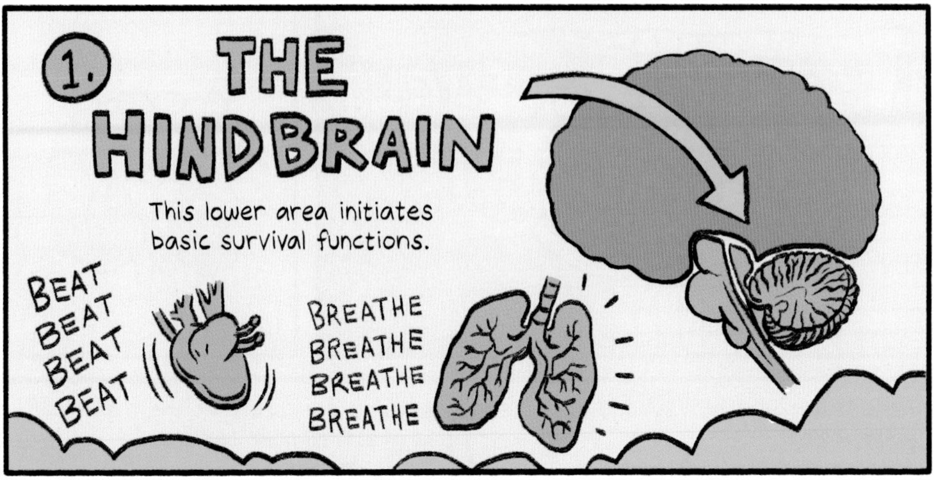
1. THE HINDBRAIN
This lower area initiates basic survival functions.
BEAT BEAT BEAT BEAT
BREATHE BREATHE BREATHE BREATHE

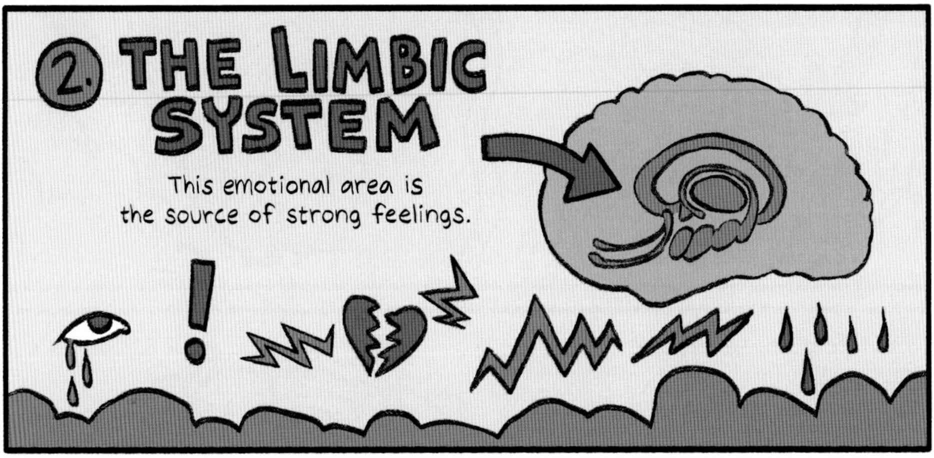
2. THE LIMBIC SYSTEM
This emotional area is the source of strong feelings.
!

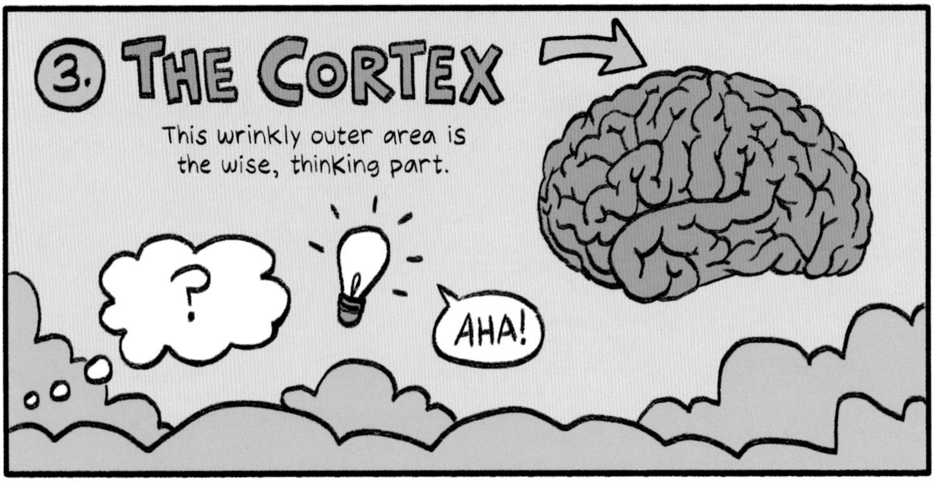
3. THE CORTEX
This wrinkly outer area is the wise, thinking part.
?
AHA!

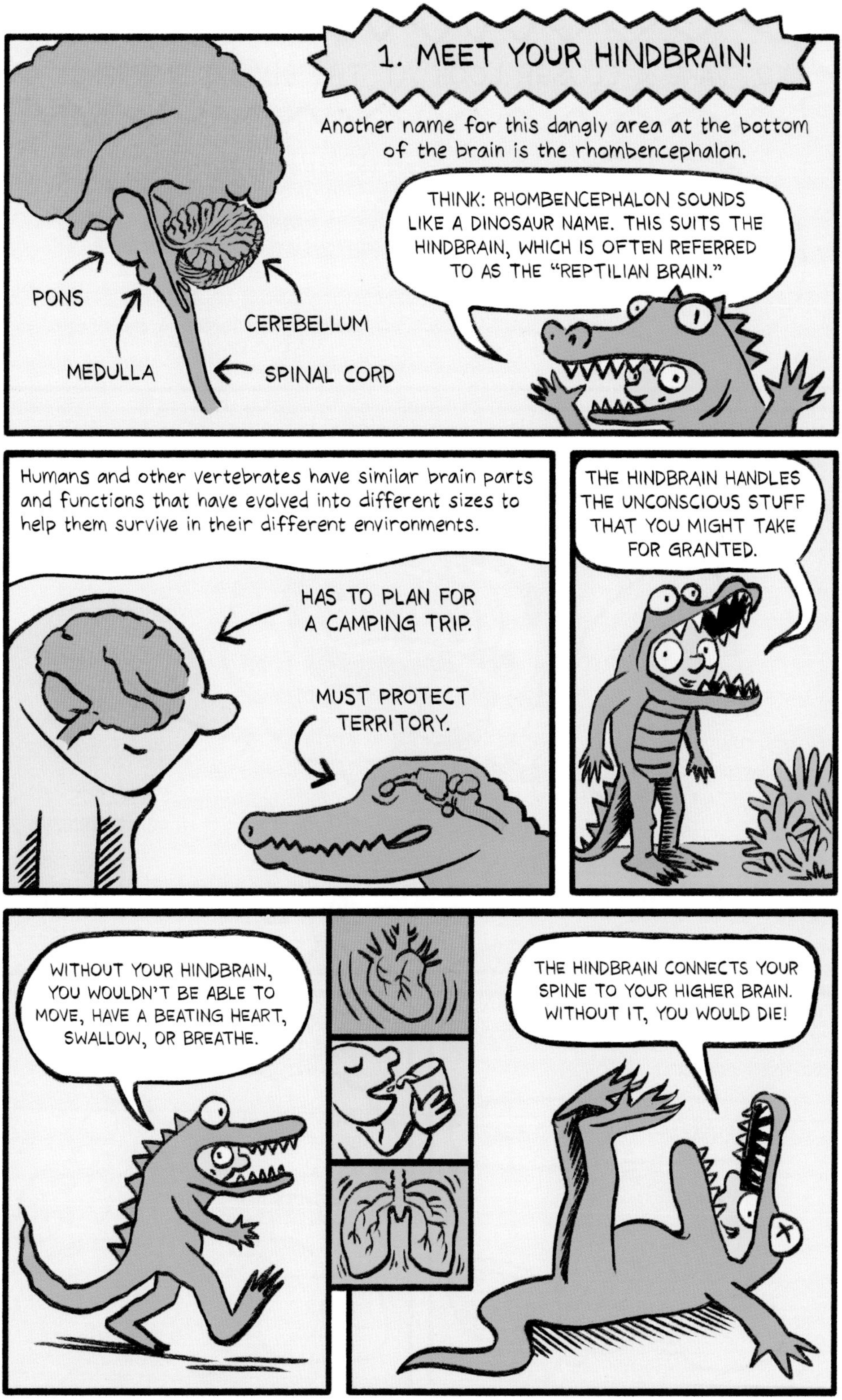
1. MEET YOUR HINDBRAIN!
Another name for this dangly area at the bottom of the brain is the rhombencephalon.
THINK: RHOMBENCEPHALON SOUNDS LIKE A DINOSAUR NAME. THIS SUITS THE HINDBRAIN, WHICH IS OFTEN REFERRED TO AS THE "REPTILIAN BRAIN."
PONS
MEDULLA
CEREBELLUM
SPINAL CORD
Humans and other vertebrates have similar brain parts and functions that have evolved into different sizes to help them survive in their different environments.
HAS TO PLAN FOR A CAMPING TRIP.
MUST PROTECT TERRITORY.
THE HINDBRAIN HANDLES THE UNCONSCIOUS STUFF THAT YOU MIGHT TAKE FOR GRANTED.
WITHOUT YOUR HINDBRAIN, YOU WOULDN'T BE ABLE TO MOVE, HAVE A BEATING HEART, SWALLOW, OR BREATHE.
THE HINDBRAIN CONNECTS YOUR SPINE TO YOUR HIGHER BRAIN. WITHOUT IT, YOU WOULD DIE!

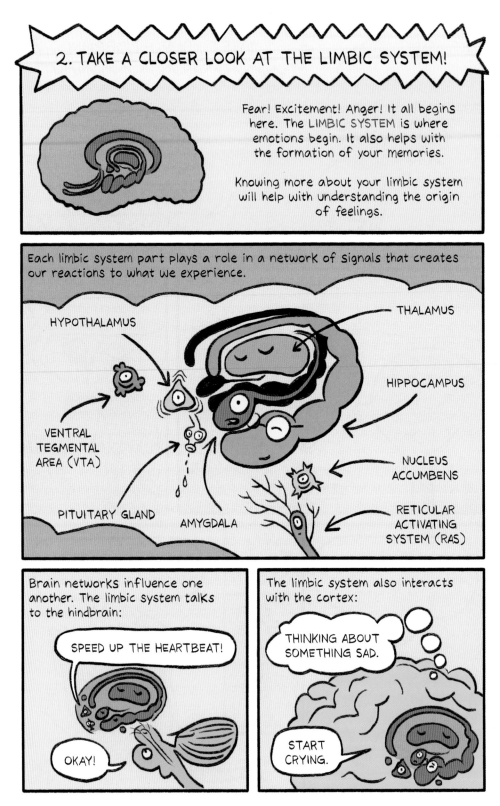

2. TAKE A CLOSER LOOK AT THE LIMBIC SYSTEM!

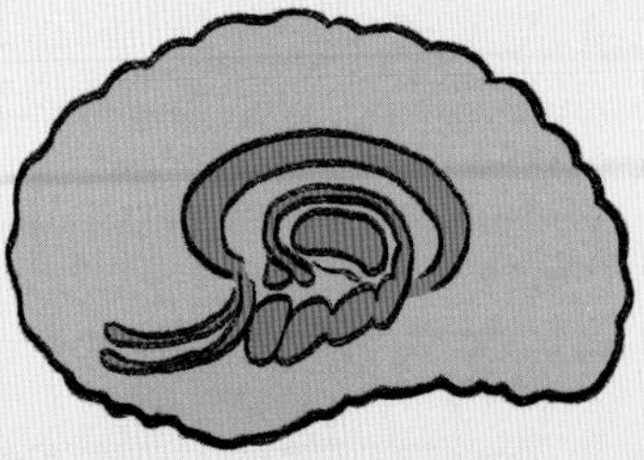

Fear! Excitement! Anger! It all begins here. The LIMBIC SYSTEM is where emotions begin. It also helps with the formation of your memories.

Knowing more about your limbic system will help with understanding the origin of feelings.

Each limbic system part plays a role in a network of signals that creates our reactions to what we experience.

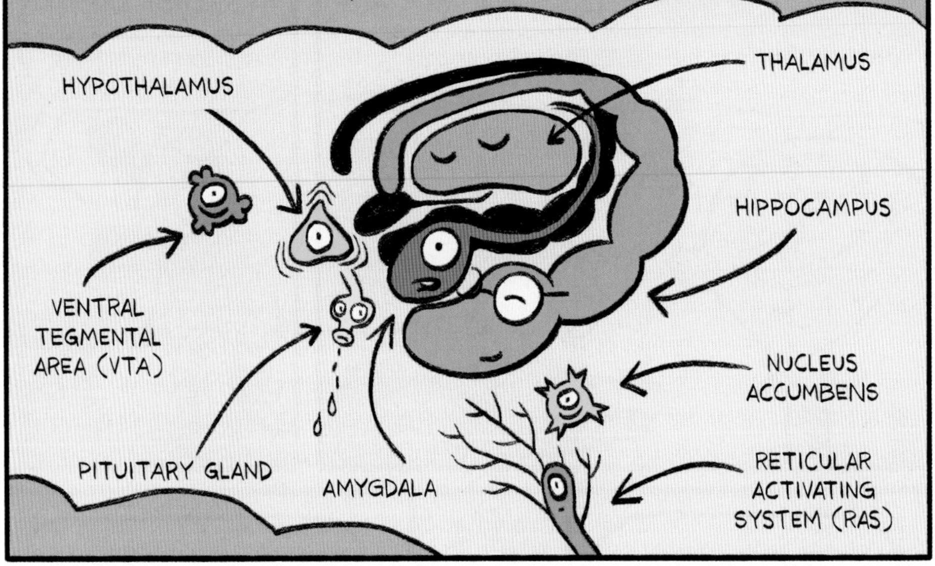
HYPOTHALAMUS
THALAMUS
HIPPOCAMPUS
VENTRAL TEGMENTAL AREA (VTA)
NUCLEUS ACCUMBENS
PITUITARY GLAND
AMYGDALA
RETICULAR ACTIVATING SYSTEM (RAS)

Brain networks influence one another. The limbic system talks to the hindbrain:

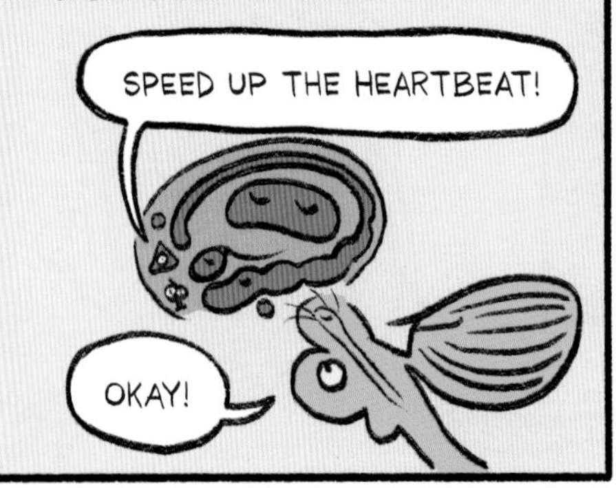
SPEED UP THE HEARTBEAT!
OKAY!

The limbic system also interacts with the cortex:

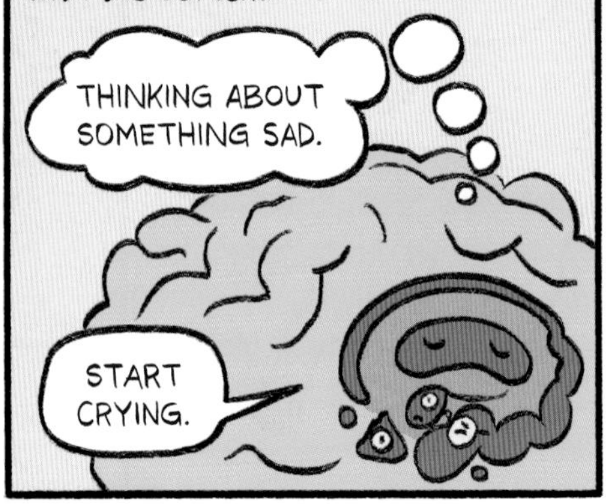
THINKING ABOUT SOMETHING SAD.
START CRYING.

GET TO KNOW YOUR LIMBIC SYSTEM PARTS!

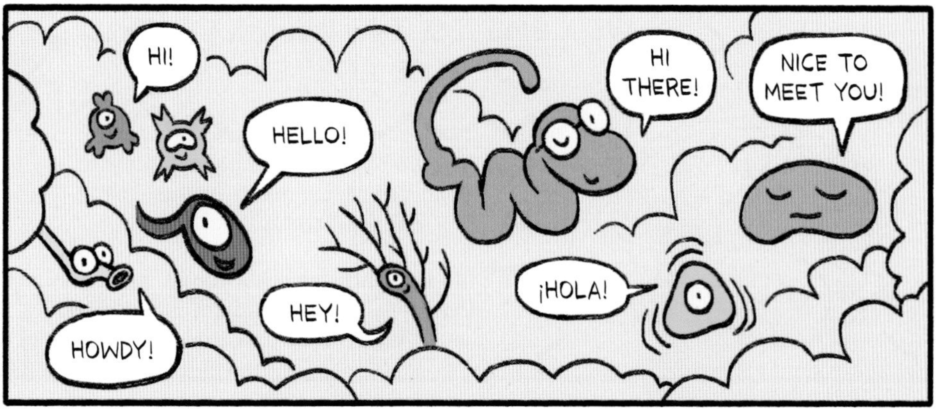
HI!
HELLO!
HI THERE!
NICE TO MEET YOU!
HOWDY!
HEY!
¡HOLA!

EACH ONE SERVES A SPECIAL FUNCTION

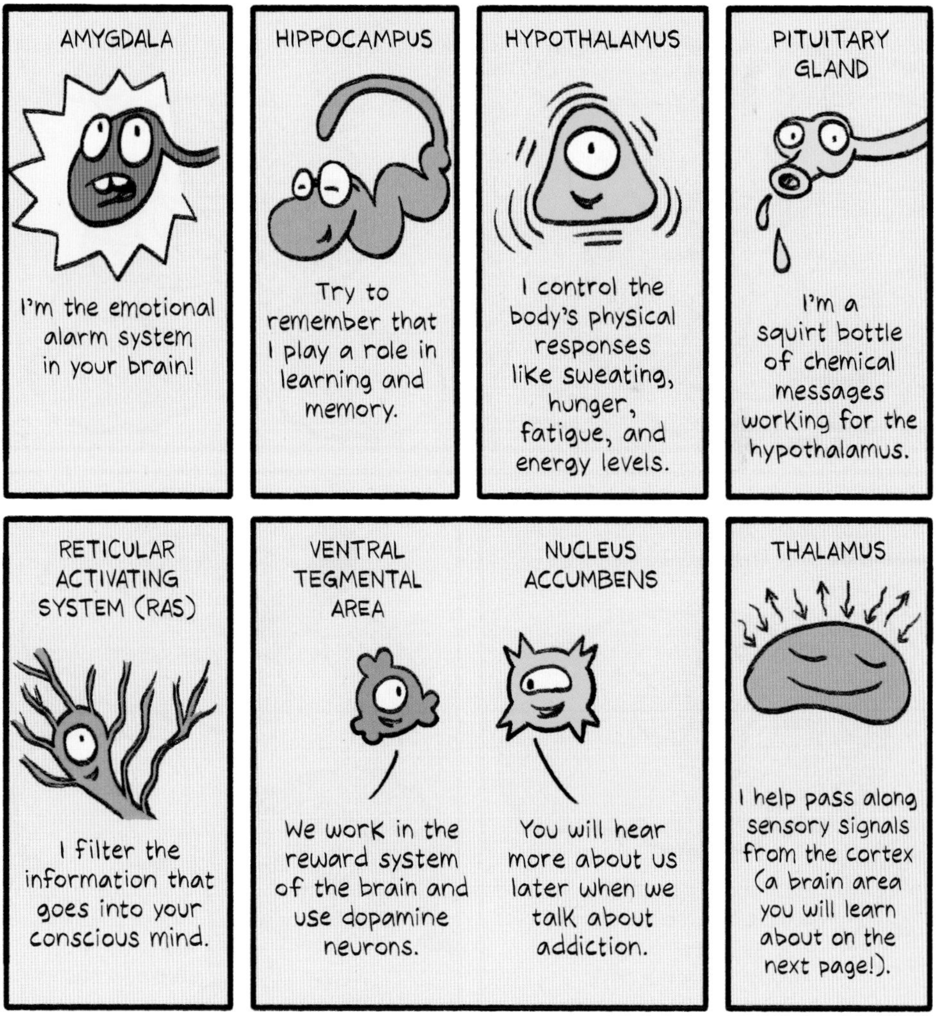
AMYGDALA
I'm the emotional alarm system in your brain!
HIPPOCAMPUS
Try to remember that I play a role in learning and memory.
HYPOTHALAMUS
I control the body's physical responses like sweating, hunger, fatigue, and energy levels.
PITUITARY GLAND
I'm a squirt bottle of chemical messages working for the hypothalamus.
RETICULAR ACTIVATING SYSTEM (RAS)
I filter the information that goes into your conscious mind.
VENTRAL TEGMENTAL AREA
NUCLEUS ACCUMBENS
We work in the reward system of the brain and use dopamine neurons.
You will hear more about us later when we talk about addiction.
THALAMUS
I help pass along sensory signals from the cortex (a brain area you will learn about on the next page!).

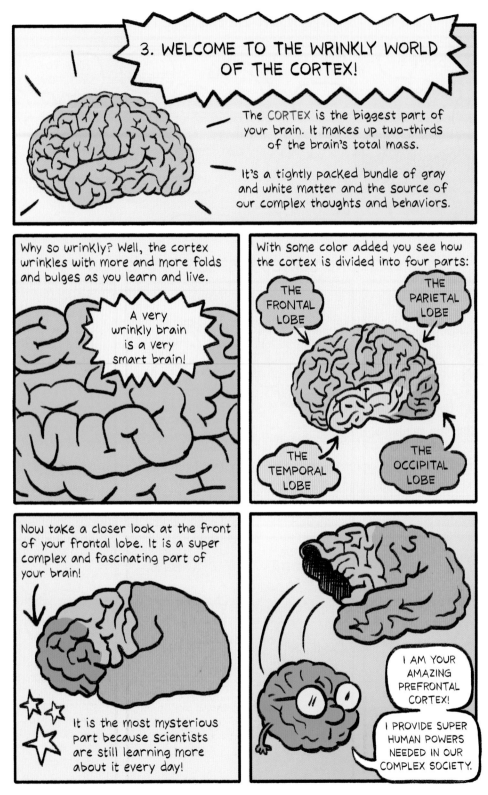

3. WELCOME TO THE WRINKLY WORLD OF THE CORTEX!

The CORTEX is the biggest part of your brain. It makes up two-thirds of the brain's total mass.

It's a tightly packed bundle of gray and white matter and the source of our complex thoughts and behaviors.

Why so wrinkly? Well, the cortex wrinkles with more and more folds and bulges as you learn and live.

A very wrinkly brain is a very smart brain!

With some color added you see how the cortex is divided into four parts:

THE FRONTAL LOBE

THE PARIETAL LOBE

THE TEMPORAL LOBE

THE OCCIPITAL LOBE

Now take a closer look at the front of your frontal lobe. It is a super complex and fascinating part of your brain!

It is the most mysterious part because scientists are still learning more about it every day!

I AM YOUR AMAZING PREFRONTAL CORTEX!

I PROVIDE SUPER HUMAN POWERS NEEDED IN OUR COMPLEX SOCIETY.

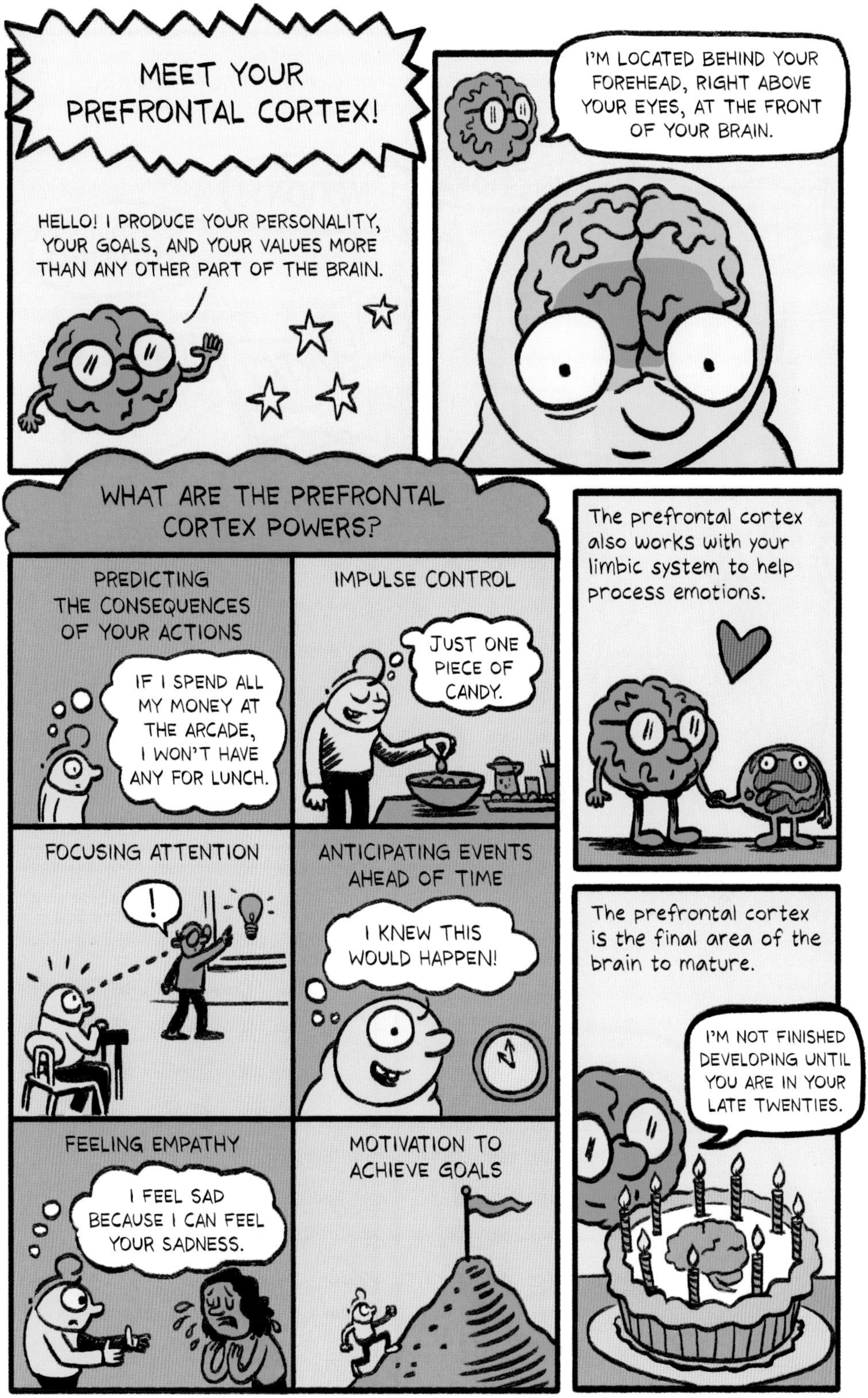
MEET YOUR PREFRONTAL CORTEX!
HELLO! I PRODUCE YOUR PERSONALITY, YOUR GOALS, AND YOUR VALUES MORE THAN ANY OTHER PART OF THE BRAIN.
I'M LOCATED BEHIND YOUR FOREHEAD, RIGHT ABOVE YOUR EYES, AT THE FRONT OF YOUR BRAIN.
WHAT ARE THE PREFRONTAL CORTEX POWERS?
PREDICTING THE CONSEQUENCES OF YOUR ACTIONS
IF I SPEND ALL MY MONEY AT THE ARCADE, I WON'T HAVE ANY FOR LUNCH.
IMPULSE CONTROL
JUST ONE PIECE OF CANDY.
FOCUSING ATTENTION
!
ANTICIPATING EVENTS AHEAD OF TIME
I KNEW THIS WOULD HAPPEN!
FEELING EMPATHY
I FEEL SAD BECAUSE I CAN FEEL YOUR SADNESS.
MOTIVATION TO ACHIEVE GOALS
The prefrontal cortex also works with your limbic system to help process emotions.
The prefrontal cortex is the final area of the brain to mature.
I'M NOT FINISHED DEVELOPING UNTIL YOU ARE IN YOUR LATE TWENTIES.

At this point, you have been introduced to a whole parade of brain parts. Now that you know them, many of these characters will come back in future chapters when we discuss fear, coping, addiction, and depression.

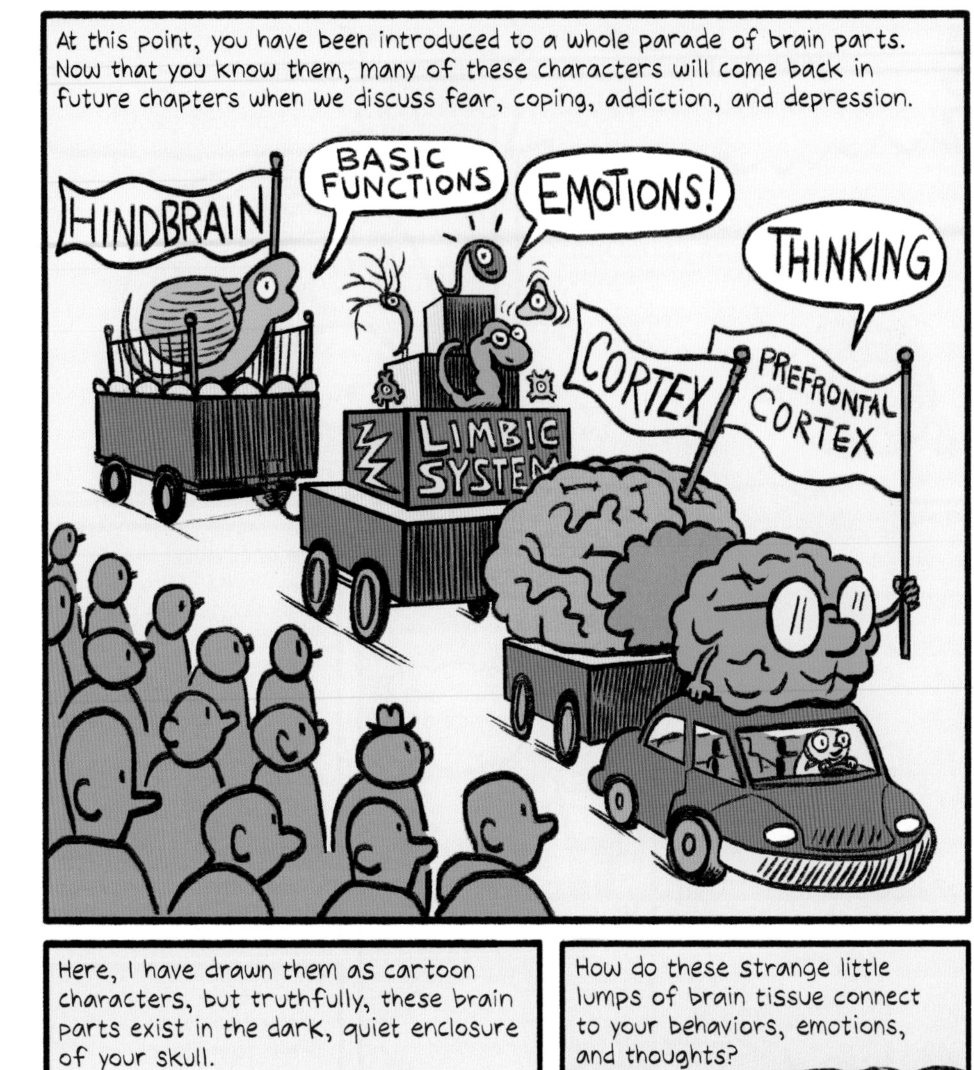
HINDBRAIN
BASIC FUNCTIONS
LIMBIC SYSTE
EMOTIONS!
CORTEX
THINKING
PREFRONTAL CORTEX

Here, I have drawn them as cartoon characters, but truthfully, these brain parts exist in the dark, quiet enclosure of your skull.

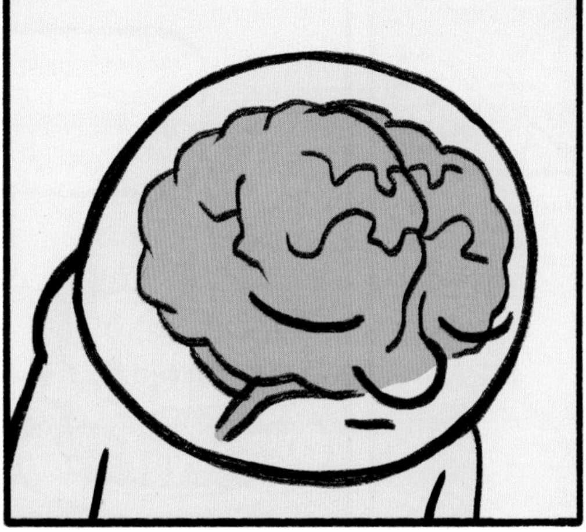

How do these strange little lumps of brain tissue connect to your behaviors, emotions, and thoughts?

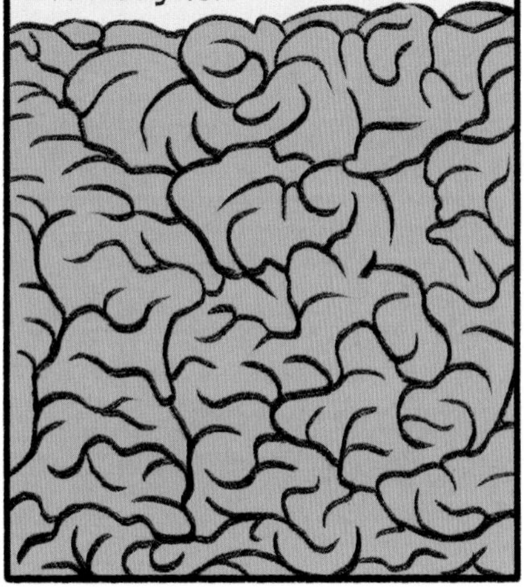

THE BRAIN BRANCHES OUT!

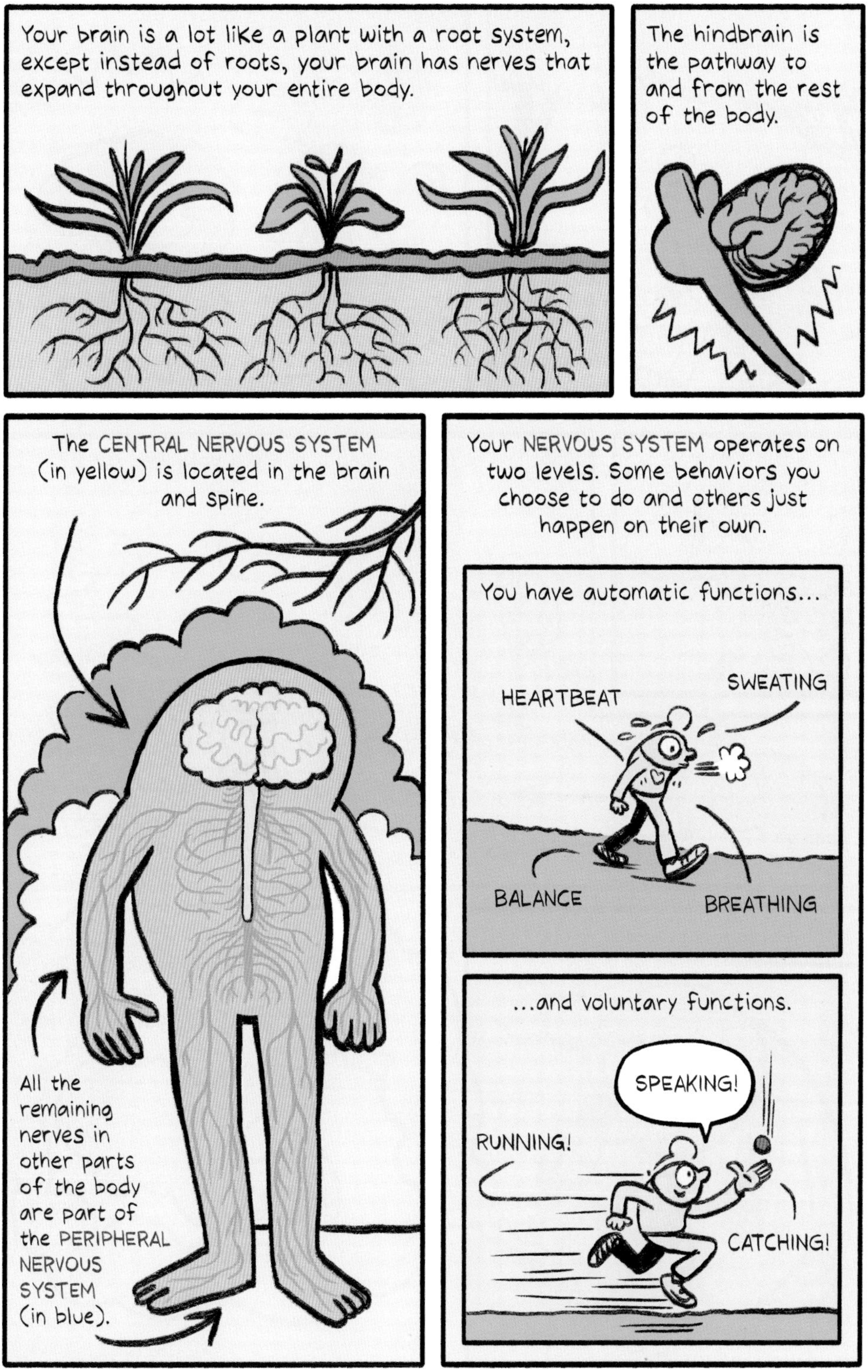
Your brain is a lot like a plant with a root system, except instead of roots, your brain has nerves that expand throughout your entire body.
The hindbrain is the pathway to and from the rest of the body.
The CENTRAL NERVOUS SYSTEM (in yellow) is located in the brain and spine.
All the remaining nerves in other parts of the body are part of the PERIPHERAL NERVOUS SYSTEM (in blue).
Your NERVOUS SYSTEM operates on two levels. Some behaviors you choose to do and others just happen on their own.
You have automatic functions...
HEARTBEAT
SWEATING
BALANCE
BREATHING
...and voluntary functions.
SPEAKING!
RUNNING!
CATCHING!

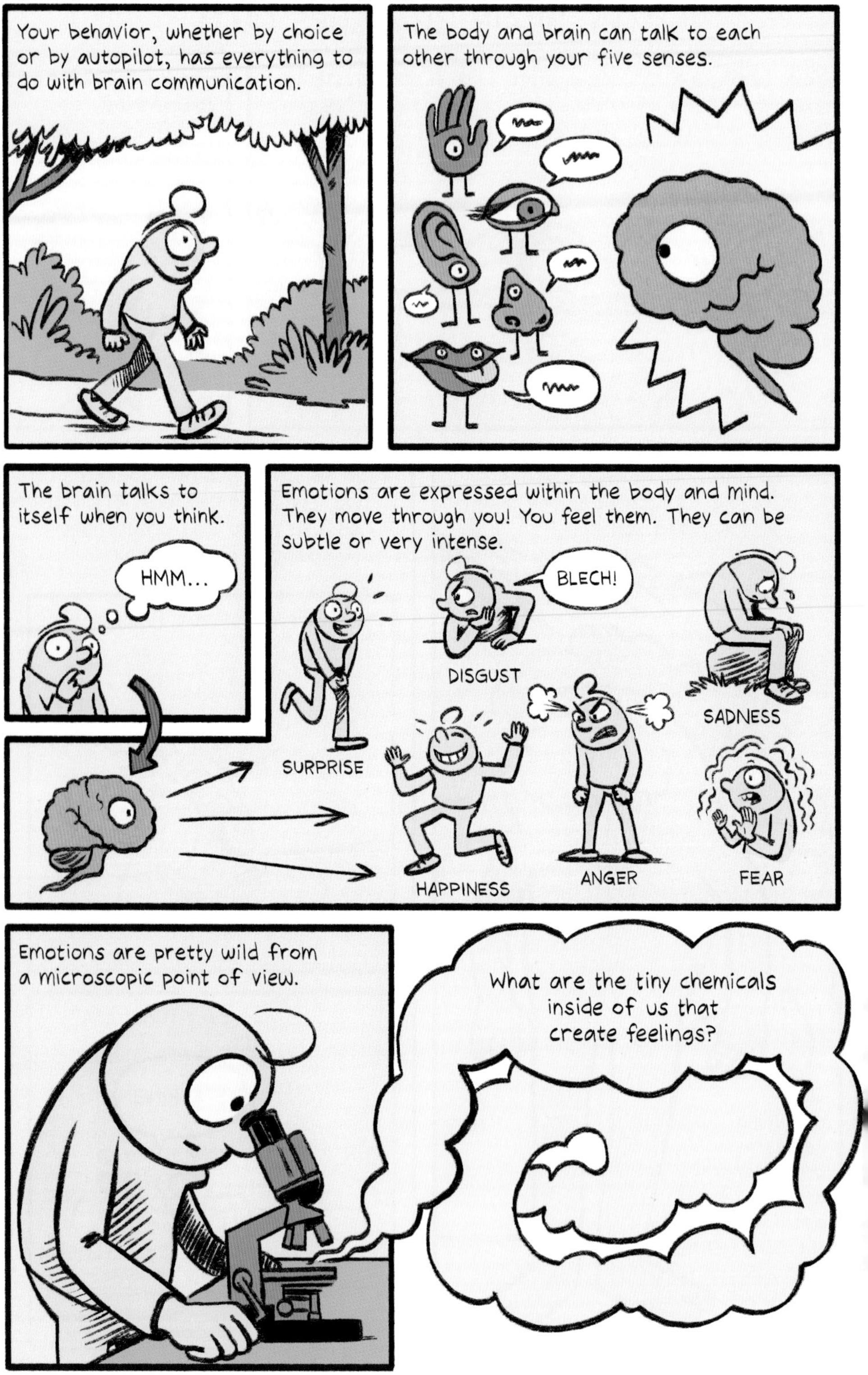
Your behavior, whether by choice or by autopilot, has everything to do with brain communication.
The body and brain can talk to each other through your five senses.
The brain talks to itself when you think.
HMM...
Emotions are expressed within the body and mind. They move through you! You feel them. They can be subtle or very intense.
BLECH!
DISGUST
SADNESS
SURPRISE
HAPPINESS
ANGER
FEAR
Emotions are pretty wild from a microscopic point of view.
What are the tiny chemicals inside of us that create feelings?

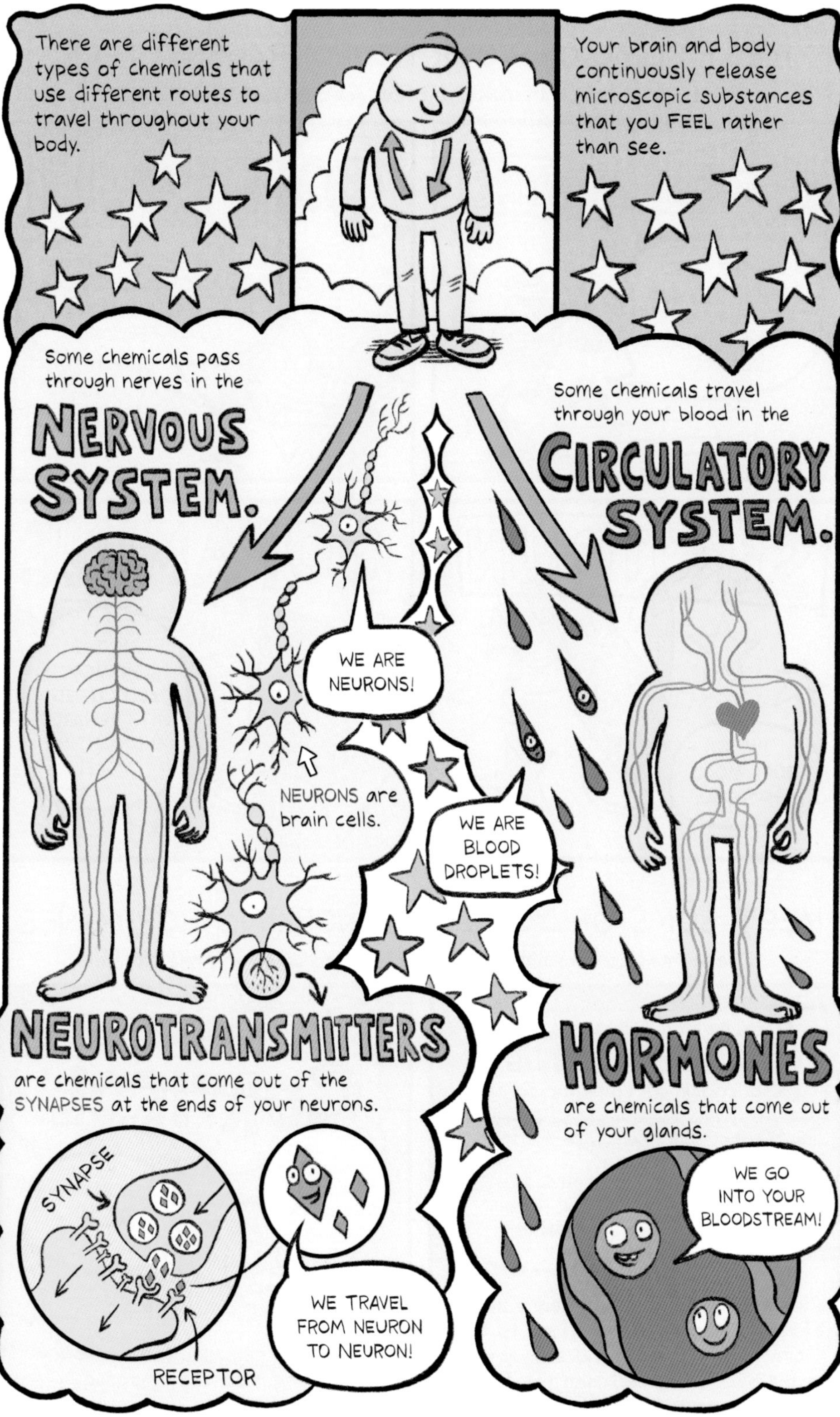

There are different types of chemicals that use different routes to travel throughout your body.
Your brain and body continuously release microscopic substances that you FEEL rather than see.
Some chemicals pass through nerves in the
NERVOUS SYSTEM.
Some chemicals travel through your blood in the
CIRCULATORY SYSTEM.
WE ARE NEURONS!
NEURONS are brain cells.
WE ARE BLOOD DROPLETS!
NEUROTRANSMITTERS
are chemicals that come out of the SYNAPSES at the ends of your neurons.
HORMONES
are chemicals that come out of your glands.
SYNAPSE
RECEPTOR
WE TRAVEL FROM NEURON TO NEURON!
WE GO INTO YOUR BLOODSTREAM!

MEET SOME OF YOUR NEUROTRANSMITTERS

These chemicals can make you feel good or motivate habits.

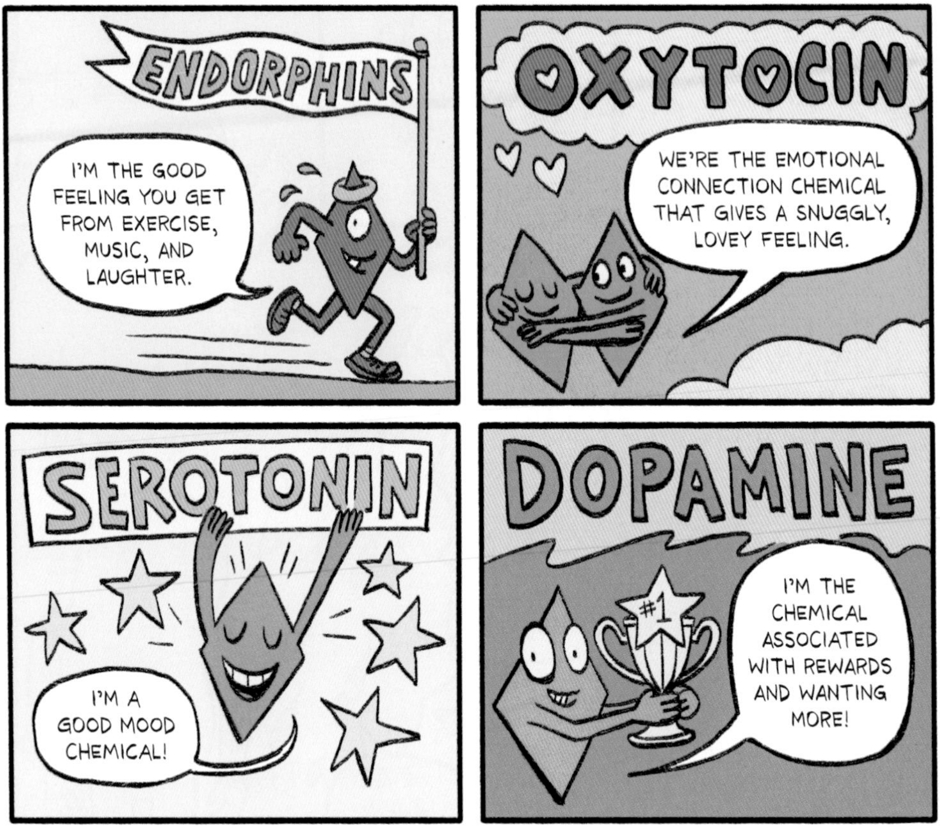
ENDORPHINS
I'M THE GOOD FEELING YOU GET FROM EXERCISE, MUSIC, AND LAUGHTER.
OXYTOCIN
WE'RE THE EMOTIONAL CONNECTION CHEMICAL THAT GIVES A SNUGGLY, LOVEY FEELING.
SEROTONIN
I'M A GOOD MOOD CHEMICAL!
DOPAMINE
#1
I'M THE CHEMICAL ASSOCIATED WITH REWARDS AND WANTING MORE!

MEET SOME OF YOUR HARDWORKING HORMONES

These reaction chemicals jump into action when you need them!

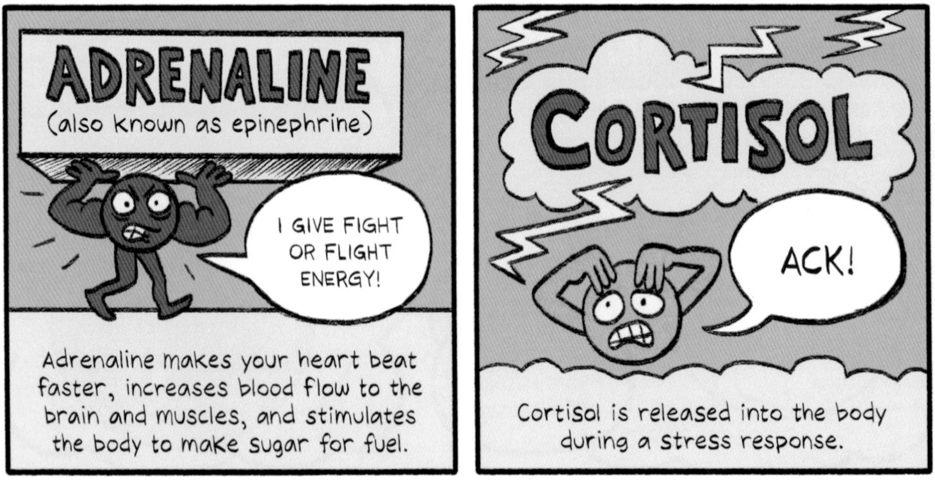
ADRENALINE
(also known as epinephrine)
I GIVE FIGHT OR FLIGHT ENERGY!
Adrenaline makes your heart beat faster, increases blood flow to the brain and muscles, and stimulates the body to make sugar for fuel.
CORTISOL
ACK!
Cortisol is released into the body during a stress response.

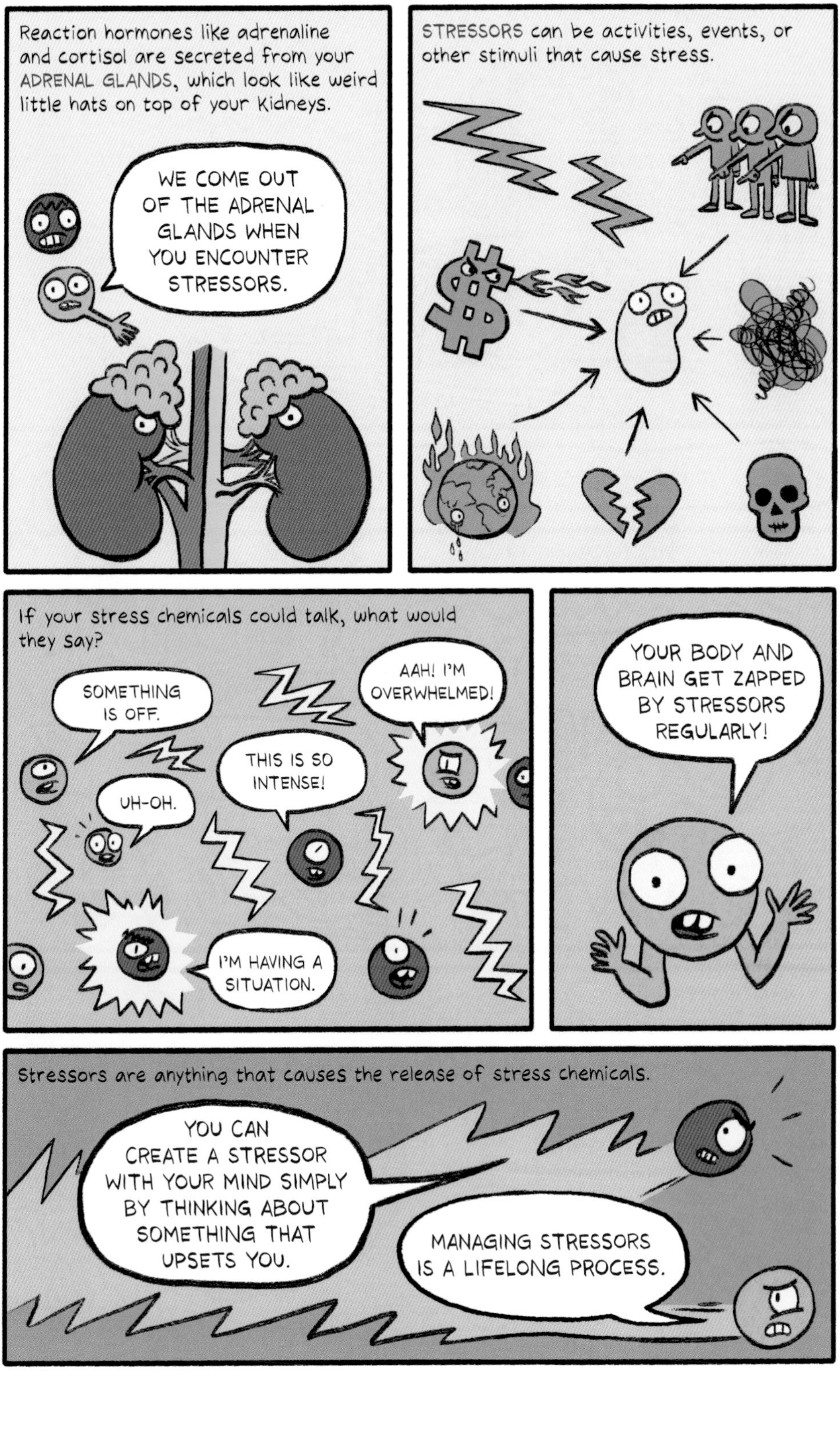
Reaction hormones like adrenaline and cortisol are secreted from your ADRENAL GLANDS, which look like weird little hats on top of your kidneys.
WE COME OUT OF THE ADRENAL GLANDS WHEN YOU ENCOUNTER STRESSORS.
STRESSORS can be activities, events, or other stimuli that cause stress.
If your stress chemicals could talk, what would they say?
SOMETHING IS OFF.
AAH! I'M OVERWHELMED!
THIS IS SO INTENSE!
UH-OH.
I'M HAVING A SITUATION.
YOUR BODY AND BRAIN GET ZAPPED BY STRESSORS REGULARLY!
Stressors are anything that causes the release of stress chemicals.
YOU CAN CREATE A STRESSOR WITH YOUR MIND SIMPLY BY THINKING ABOUT SOMETHING THAT UPSETS YOU.
MANAGING STRESSORS IS A LIFELONG PROCESS.

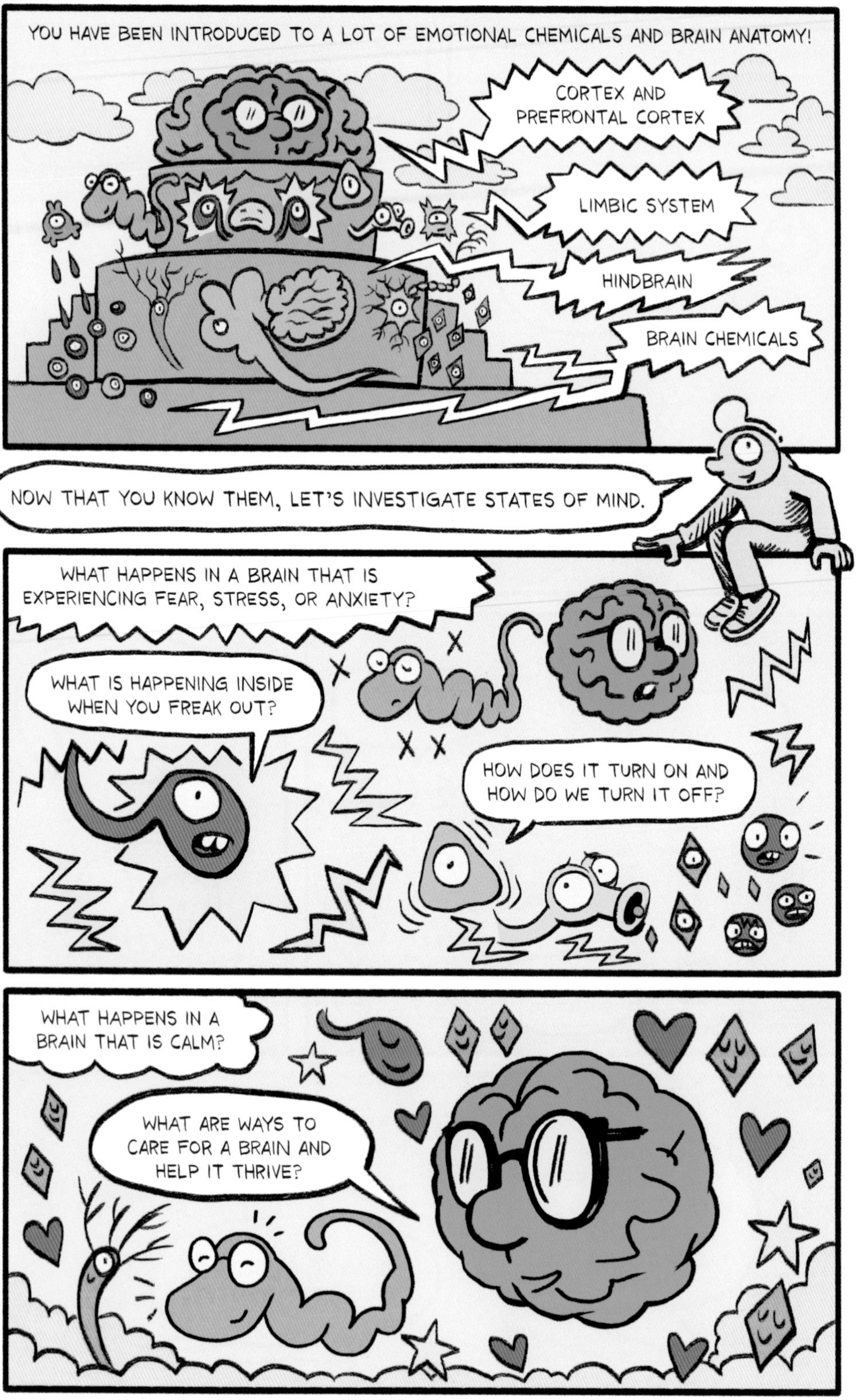

YOU HAVE BEEN INTRODUCED TO A LOT OF EMOTIONAL CHEMICALS AND BRAIN ANATOMY!
CORTEX AND PREFRONTAL CORTEX
LIMBIC SYSTEM
HINDBRAIN
BRAIN CHEMICALS
NOW THAT YOU KNOW THEM, LET'S INVESTIGATE STATES OF MIND.
WHAT HAPPENS IN A BRAIN THAT IS EXPERIENCING FEAR, STRESS, OR ANXIETY?
WHAT IS HAPPENING INSIDE WHEN YOU FREAK OUT?
HOW DOES IT TURN ON AND HOW DO WE TURN IT OFF?
WHAT HAPPENS IN A BRAIN THAT IS CALM?
WHAT ARE WAYS TO CARE FOR A BRAIN AND HELP IT THRIVE?

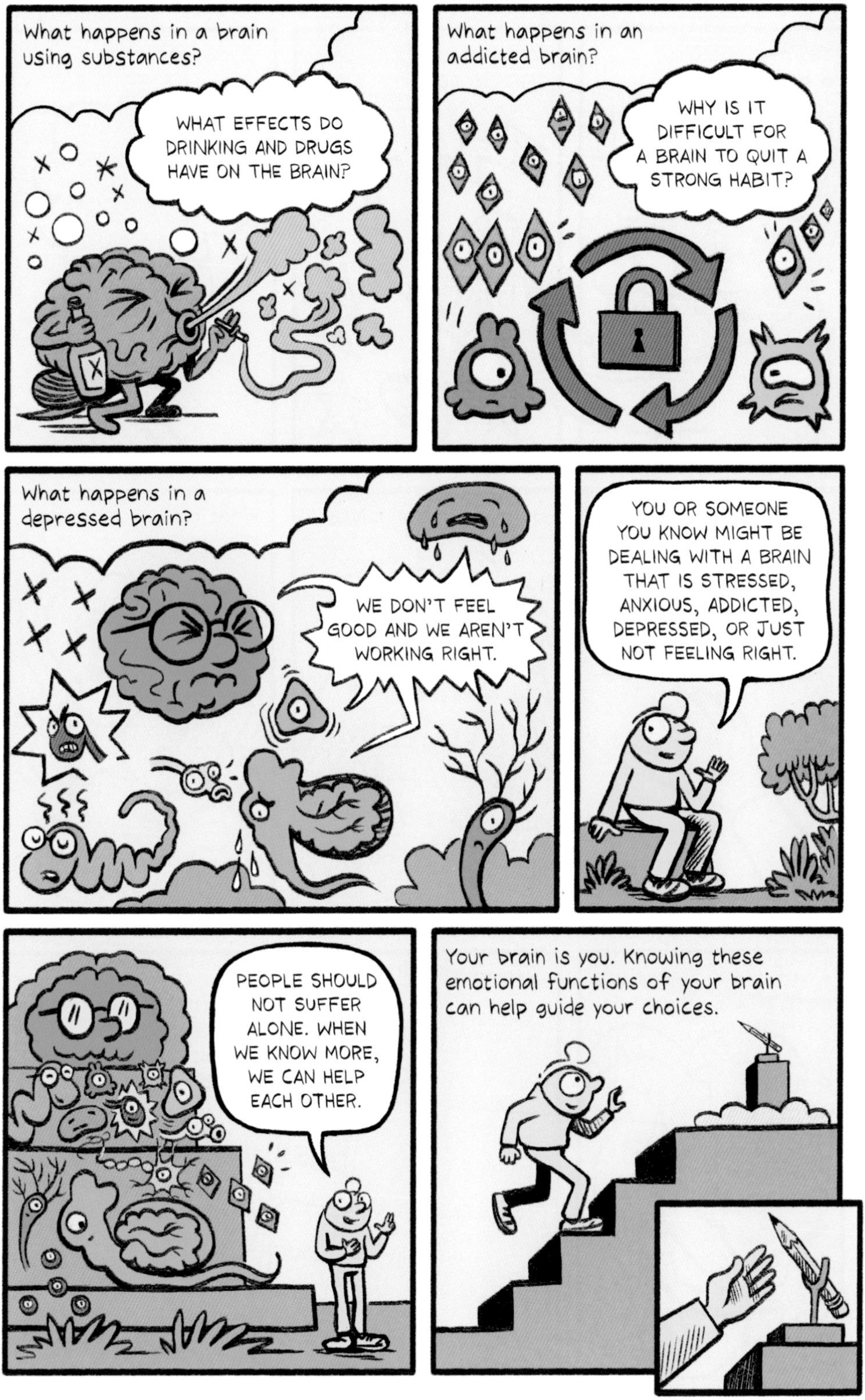

What happens in a brain using substances?
WHAT EFFECTS DO DRINKING AND DRUGS HAVE ON THE BRAIN?
What happens in an addicted brain?
WHY IS IT DIFFICULT FOR A BRAIN TO QUIT A STRONG HABIT?
What happens in a depressed brain?
WE DON'T FEEL GOOD AND WE AREN'T WORKING RIGHT.
YOU OR SOMEONE YOU KNOW MIGHT BE DEALING WITH A BRAIN THAT IS STRESSED, ANXIOUS, ADDICTED, DEPRESSED, OR JUST NOT FEELING RIGHT.
PEOPLE SHOULD NOT SUFFER ALONE. WHEN WE KNOW MORE, WE CAN HELP EACH OTHER.
Your brain is you. Knowing these emotional functions of your brain can help guide your choices.

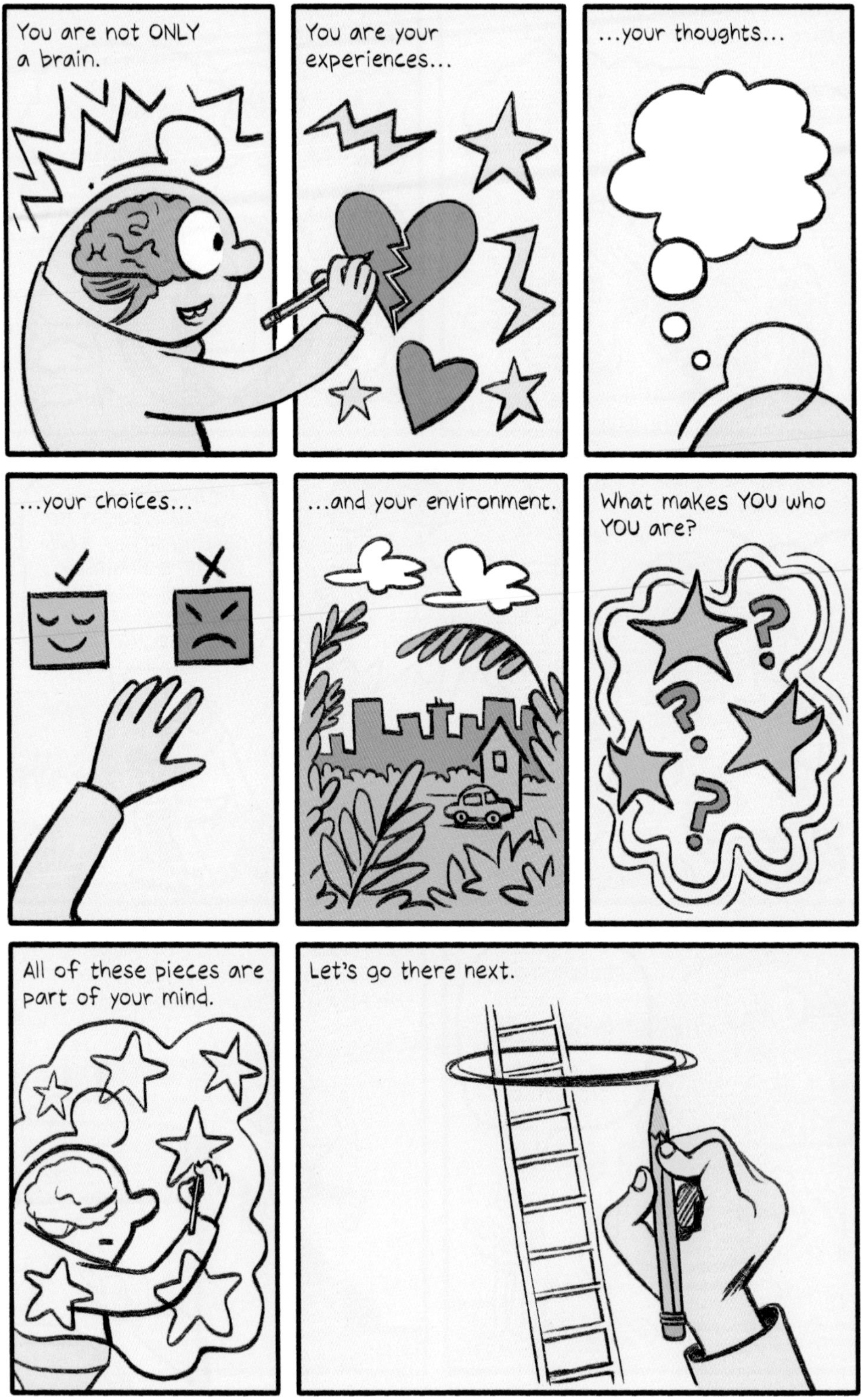
You are not ONLY a brain.
You are your experiences...
...your thoughts...
...your choices...
...and your environment.
What makes YOU who YOU are?
All of these pieces are part of your mind.
Let's go there next.

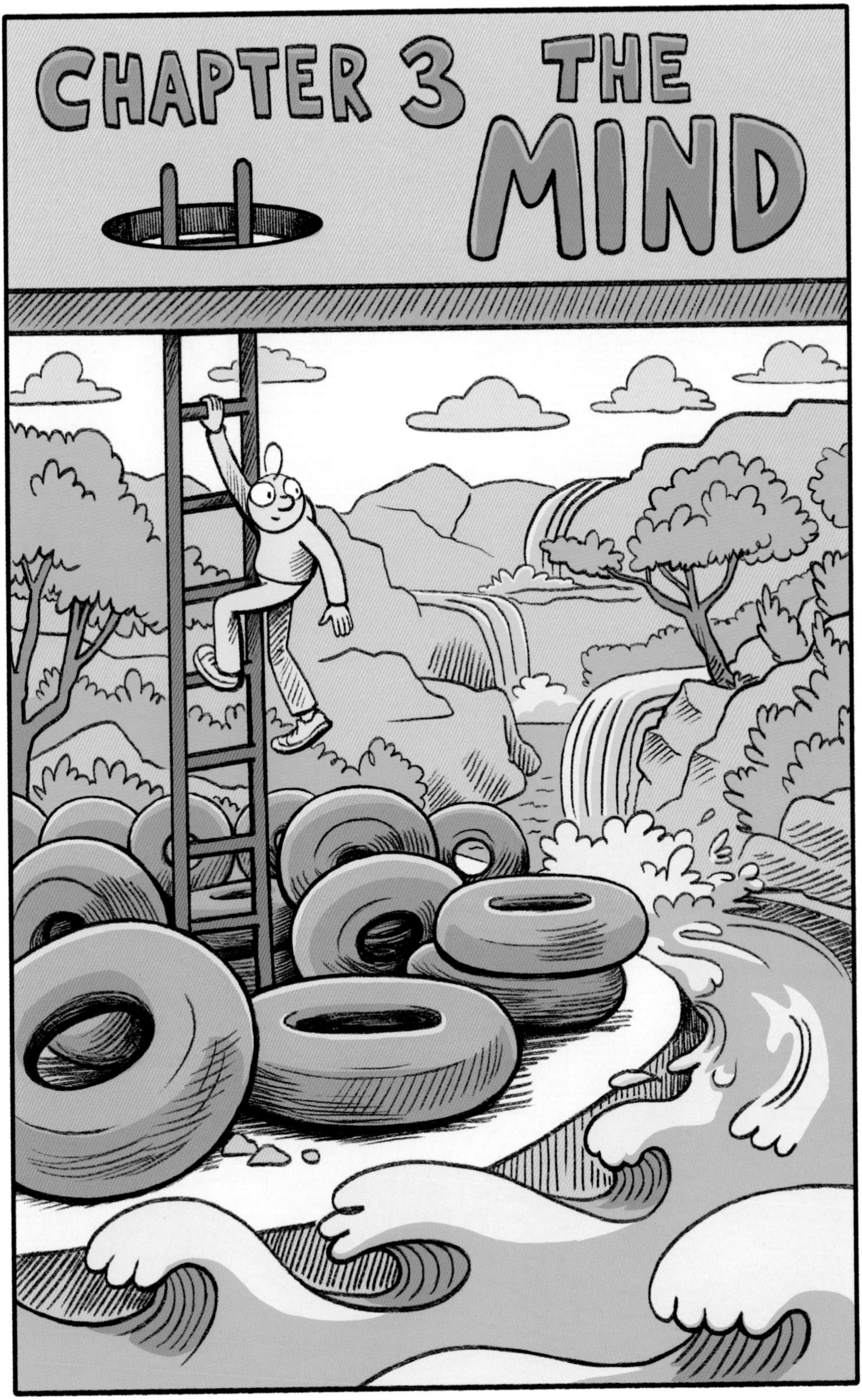
CHAPTER 3 THE MIND

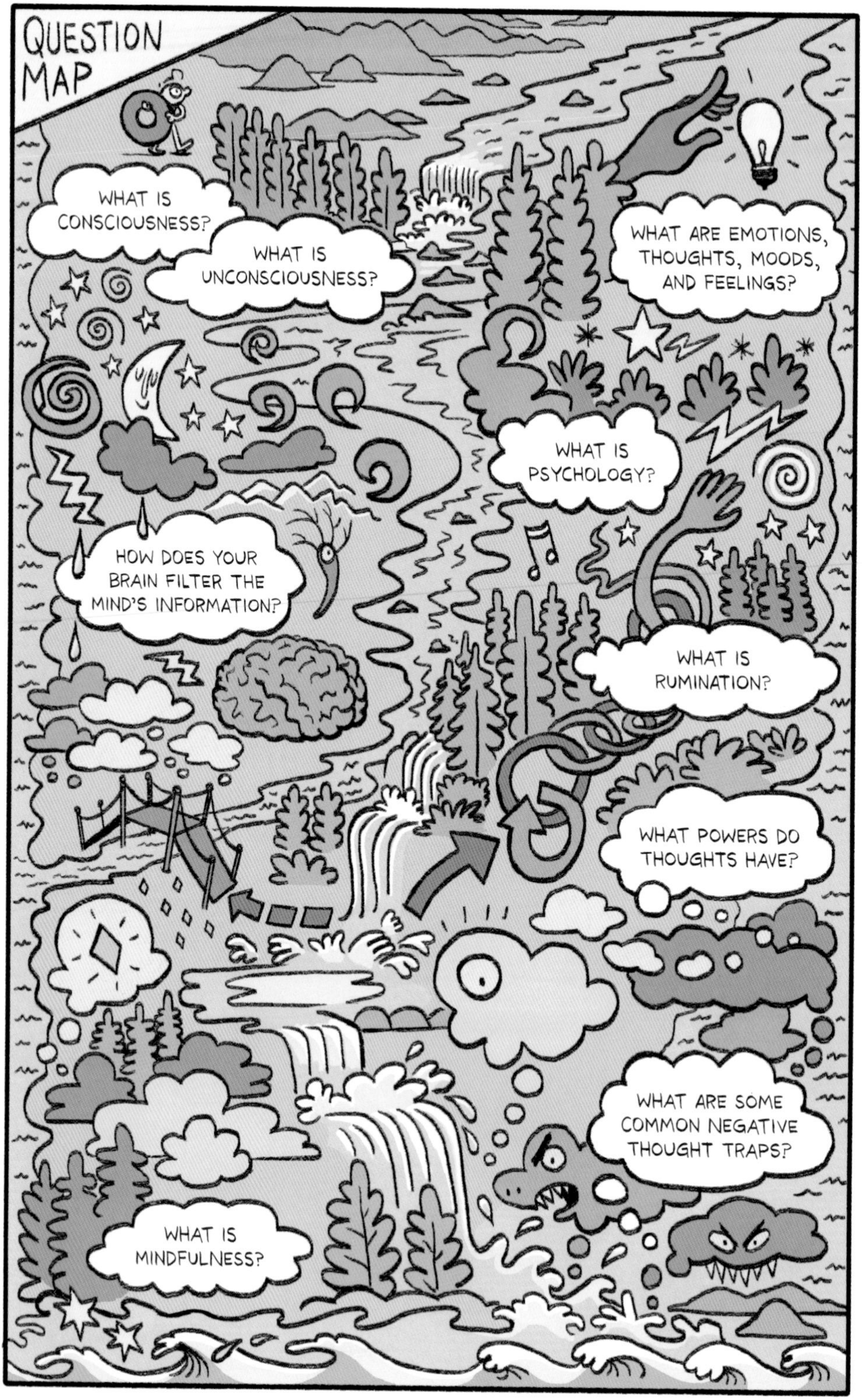
QUESTION MAP
WHAT IS CONSCIOUSNESS?
WHAT IS UNCONSCIOUSNESS?
WHAT ARE EMOTIONS, THOUGHTS, MOODS, AND FEELINGS?
WHAT IS PSYCHOLOGY?
HOW DOES YOUR BRAIN FILTER THE MIND'S INFORMATION?
WHAT IS RUMINATION?
WHAT POWERS DO THOUGHTS HAVE?
WHAT ARE SOME COMMON NEGATIVE THOUGHT TRAPS?
WHAT IS MINDFULNESS?

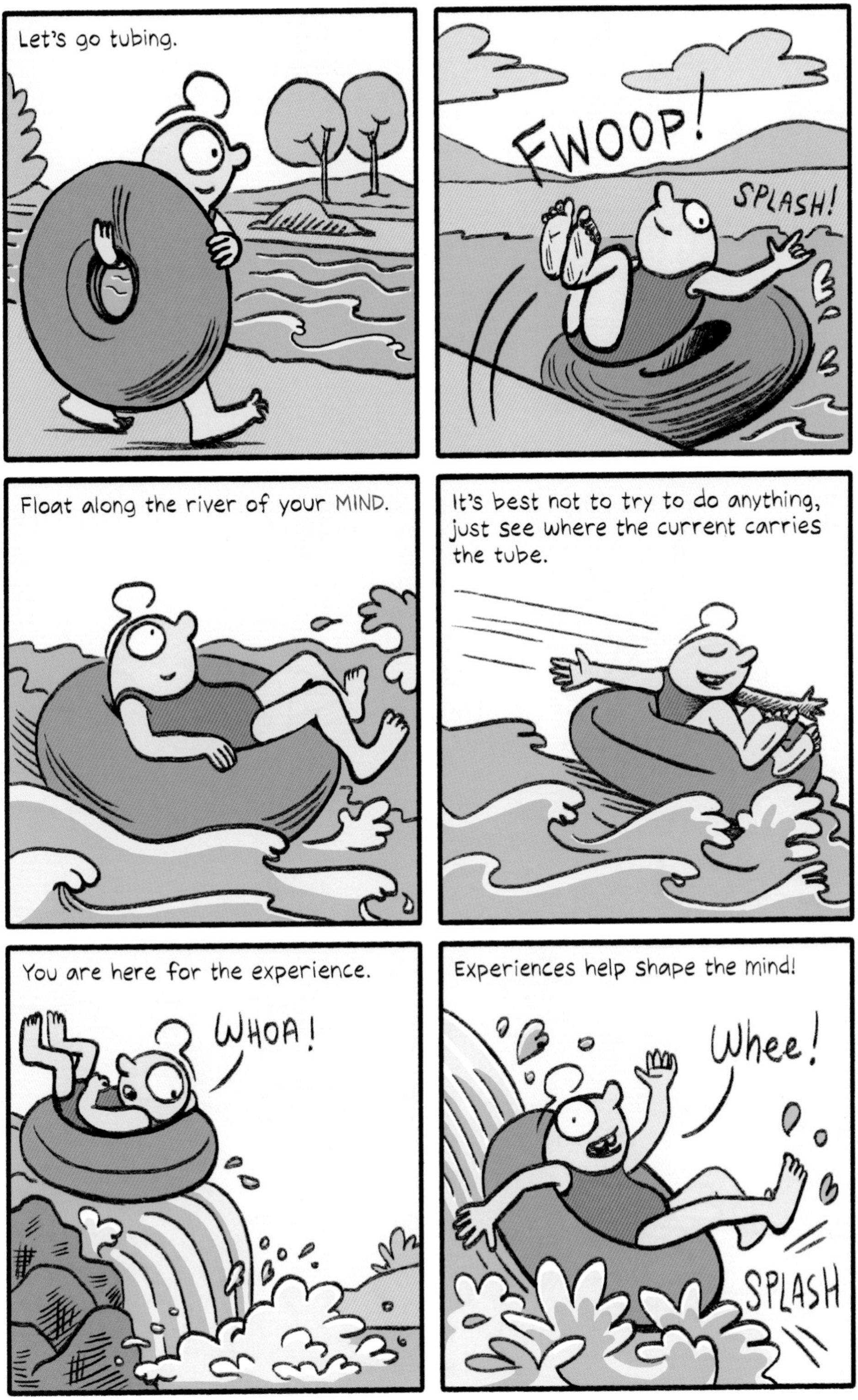
Let's go tubing.
FWOOP!
SPLASH!
Float along the river of your MIND.
It's best not to try to do anything, just see where the current carries the tube.
You are here for the experience.
WHOA!
Experiences help shape the mind!
Whee!
SPLASH

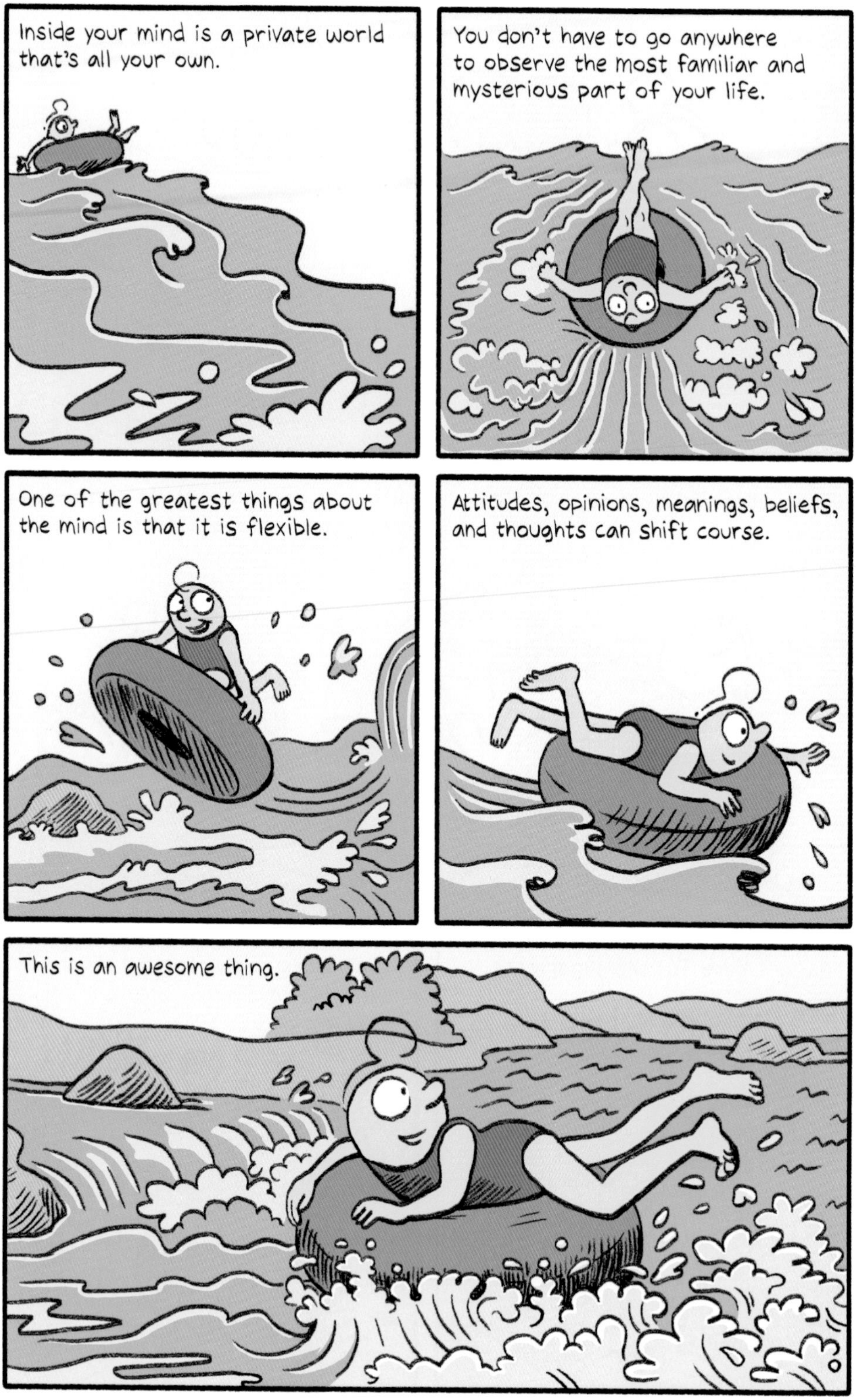
Inside your mind is a private world that's all your own.
You don't have to go anywhere to observe the most familiar and mysterious part of your life.
One of the greatest things about the mind is that it is flexible.
Attitudes, opinions, meanings, beliefs, and thoughts can shift course.
This is an awesome thing.

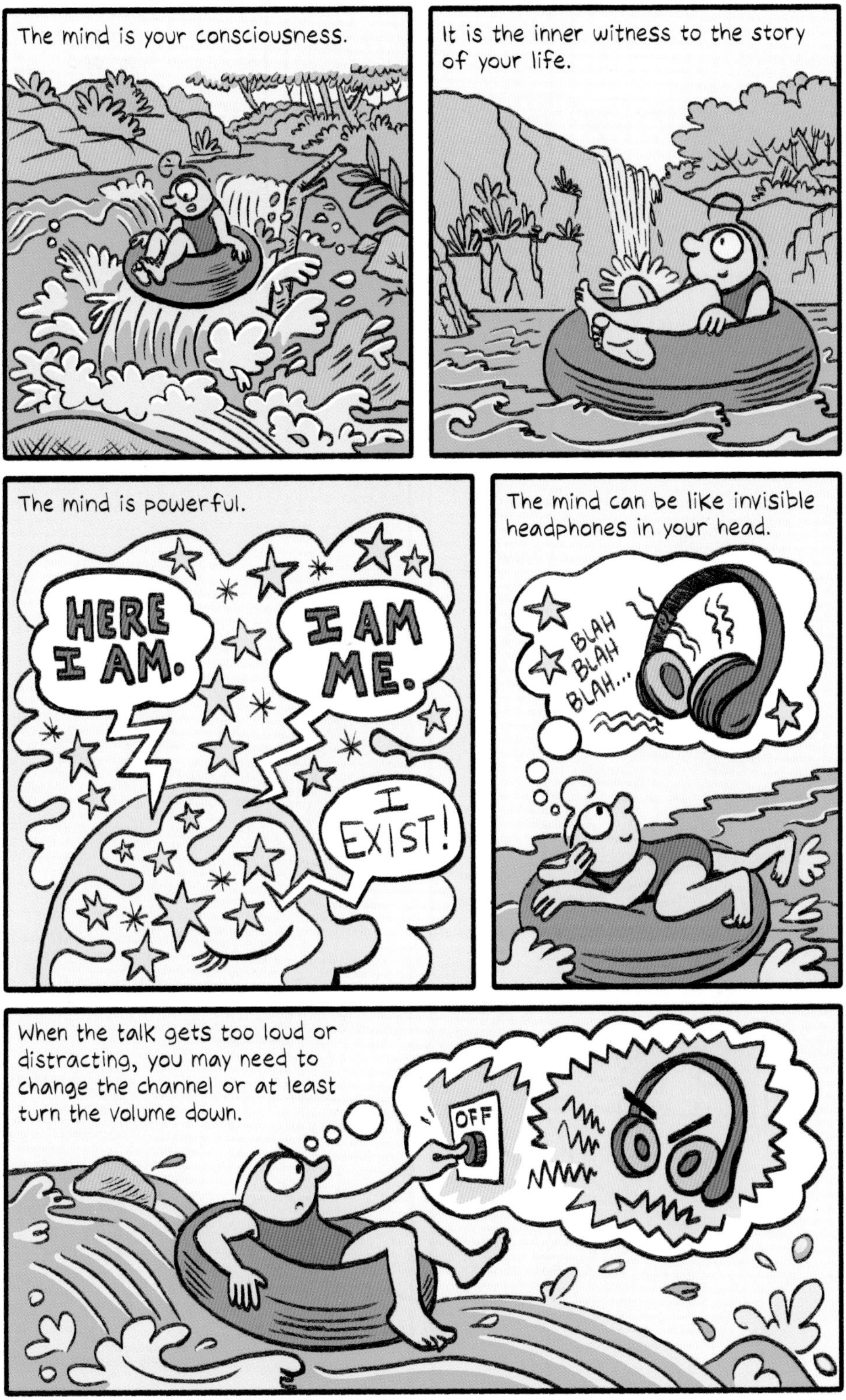
The mind is your consciousness.
It is the inner witness to the story of your life.
The mind is powerful.
HERE I AM.
I AM ME.
I EXIST!
The mind can be like invisible headphones in your head.
BLAH BLAH BLAH...
When the talk gets too loud or distracting, you may need to change the channel or at least turn the volume down.
OFF

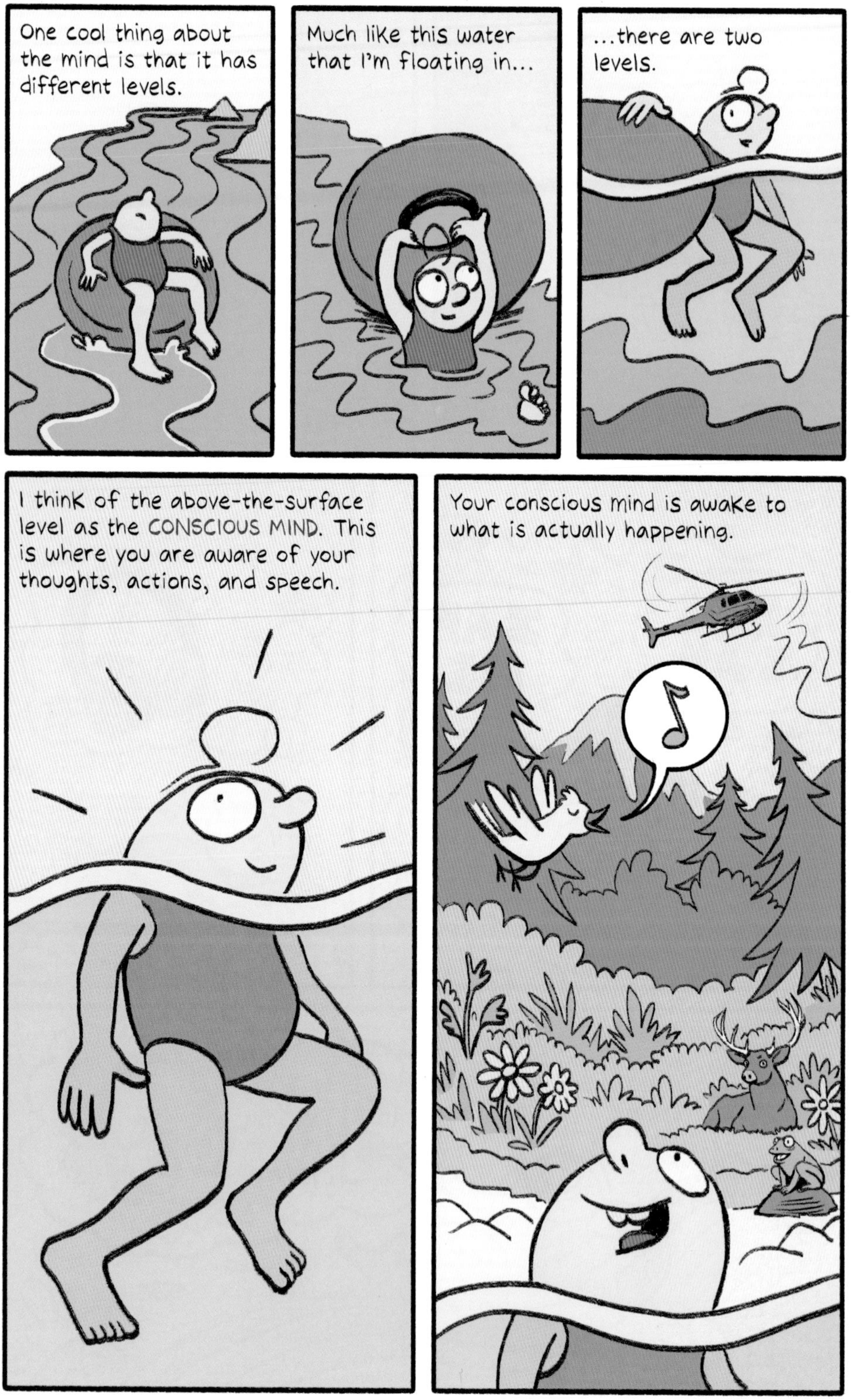
One cool thing about the mind is that it has different levels.
Much like this water that I'm floating in...
...there are two levels.
I think of the above-the-surface level as the CONSCIOUS MIND. This is where you are aware of your thoughts, actions, and speech.
Your conscious mind is awake to what is actually happening.

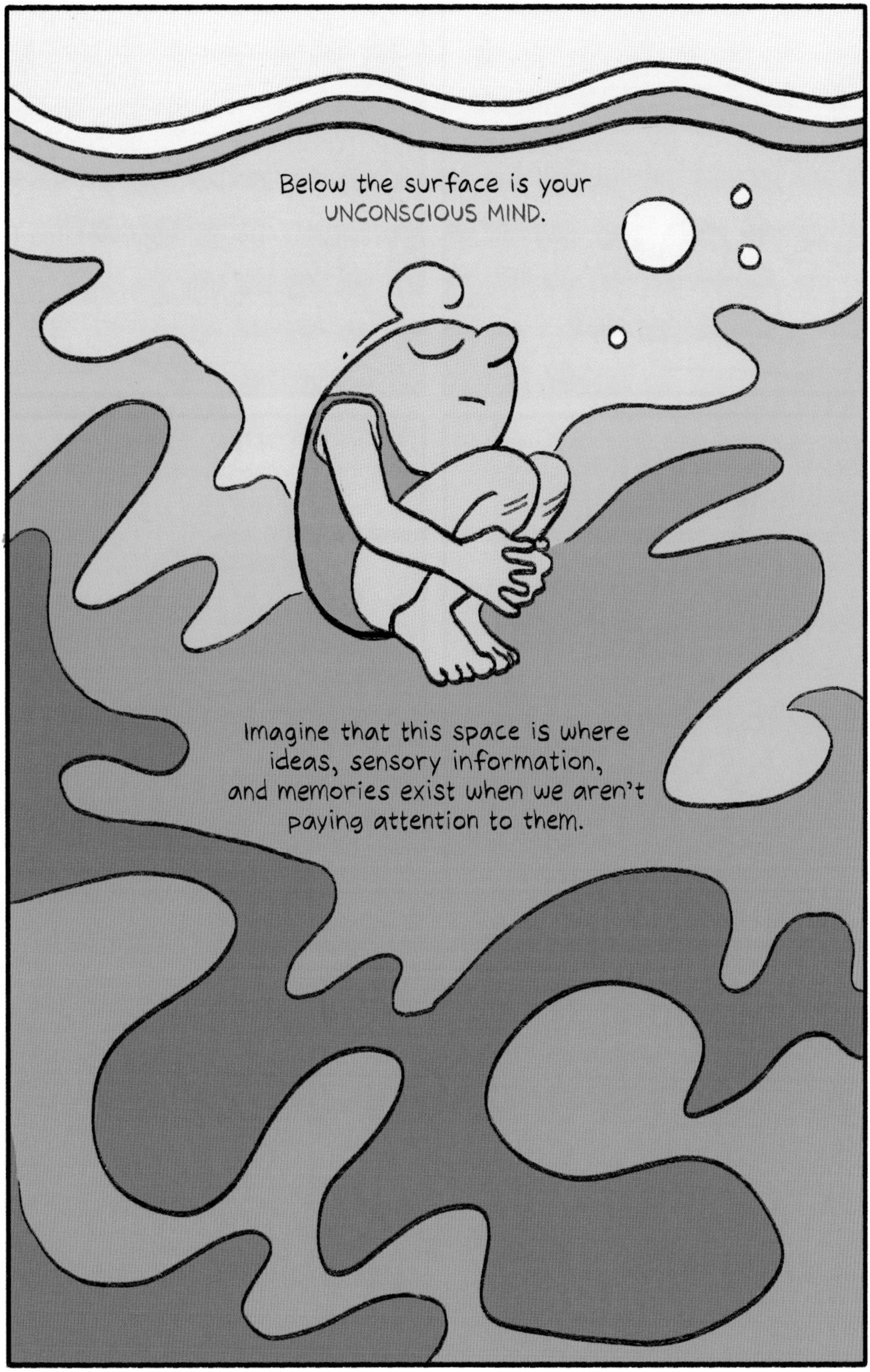
Below the surface is your UNCONSCIOUS MIND.
Imagine that this space is where ideas, sensory information, and memories exist when we aren't paying attention to them.

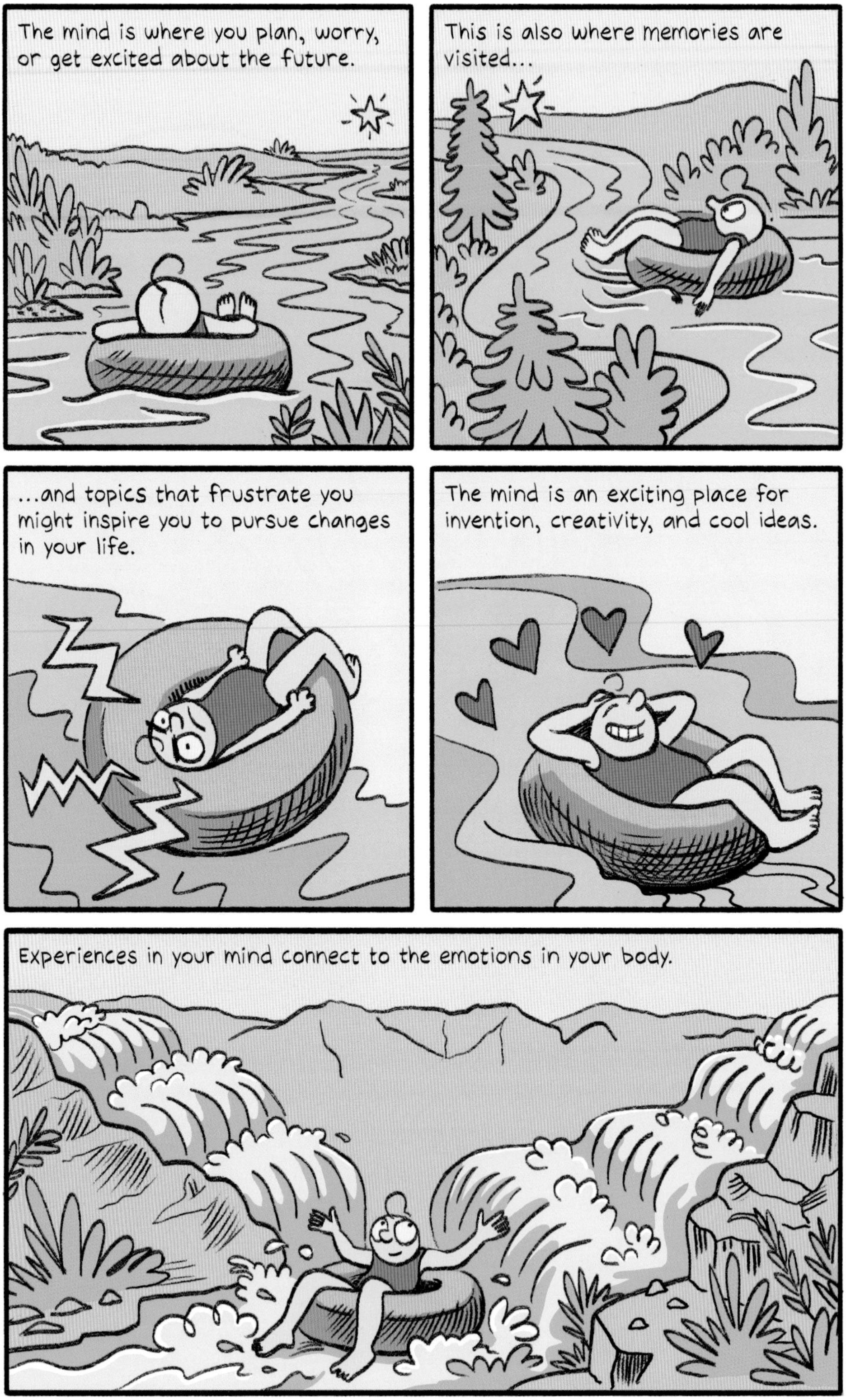
The mind is where you plan, worry, or get excited about the future.
This is also where memories are visited...
...and topics that frustrate you might inspire you to pursue changes in your life.
The mind is an exciting place for invention, creativity, and cool ideas.
Experiences in your mind connect to the emotions in your body.

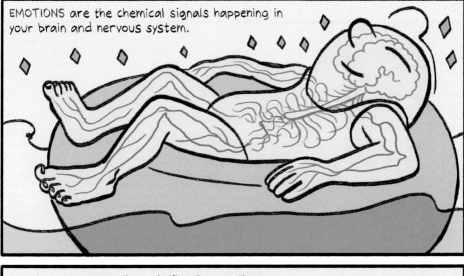

EMOTIONS are the chemical signals happening in your brain and nervous system.

Emotions can pass through like the weather.

Sometimes they stay longer, like seasons, and become moods.

Paying attention to emotions and moods can teach you more about yourself and your environment.

WHAT IS PSYCHOLOGY?

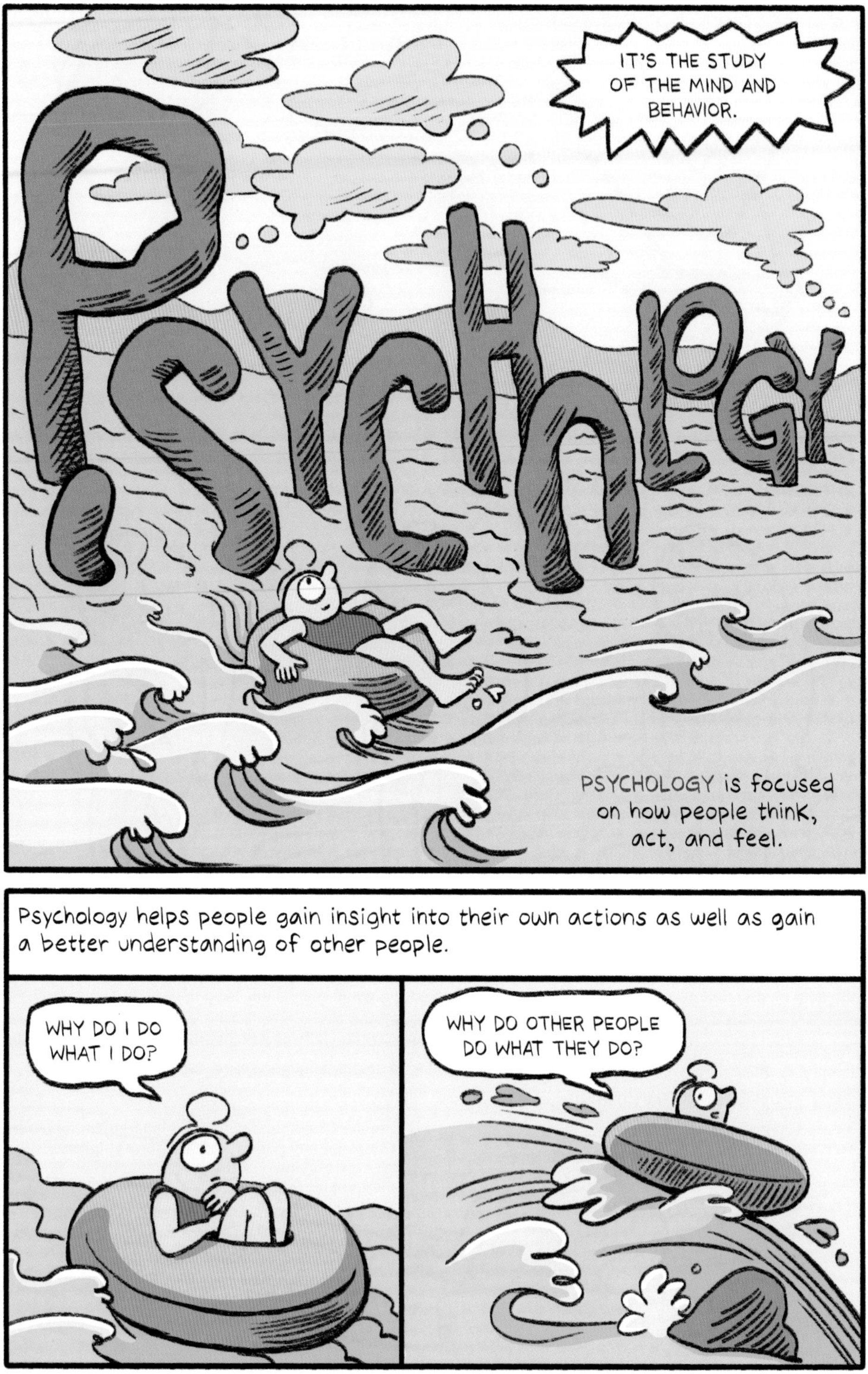
PSYCHOLOGY
IT'S THE STUDY OF THE MIND AND BEHAVIOR.
PSYCHOLOGY is focused on how people think, act, and feel.
Psychology helps people gain insight into their own actions as well as gain a better understanding of other people.
WHY DO I DO WHAT I DO?
WHY DO OTHER PEOPLE DO WHAT THEY DO?

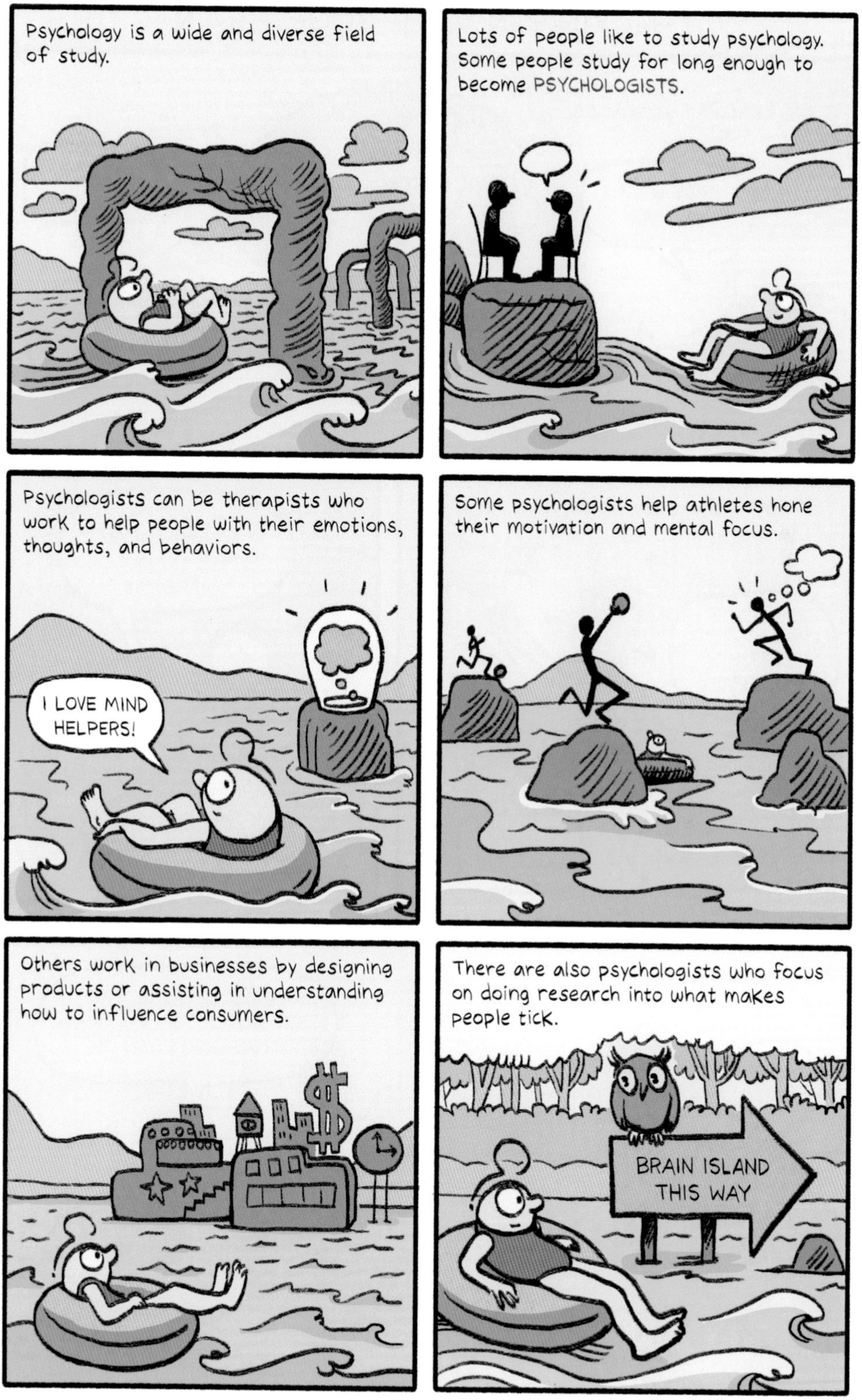
Psychology is a wide and diverse field of study.
Lots of people like to study psychology. Some people study for long enough to become PSYCHOLOGISTS.
Psychologists can be therapists who work to help people with their emotions, thoughts, and behaviors.
I LOVE MIND HELPERS!
Some psychologists help athletes hone their motivation and mental focus.
Others work in businesses by designing products or assisting in understanding how to influence consumers.
There are also psychologists who focus on doing research into what makes people tick.
BRAIN ISLAND THIS WAY

CHECKING IN WITH YOUR BRAIN

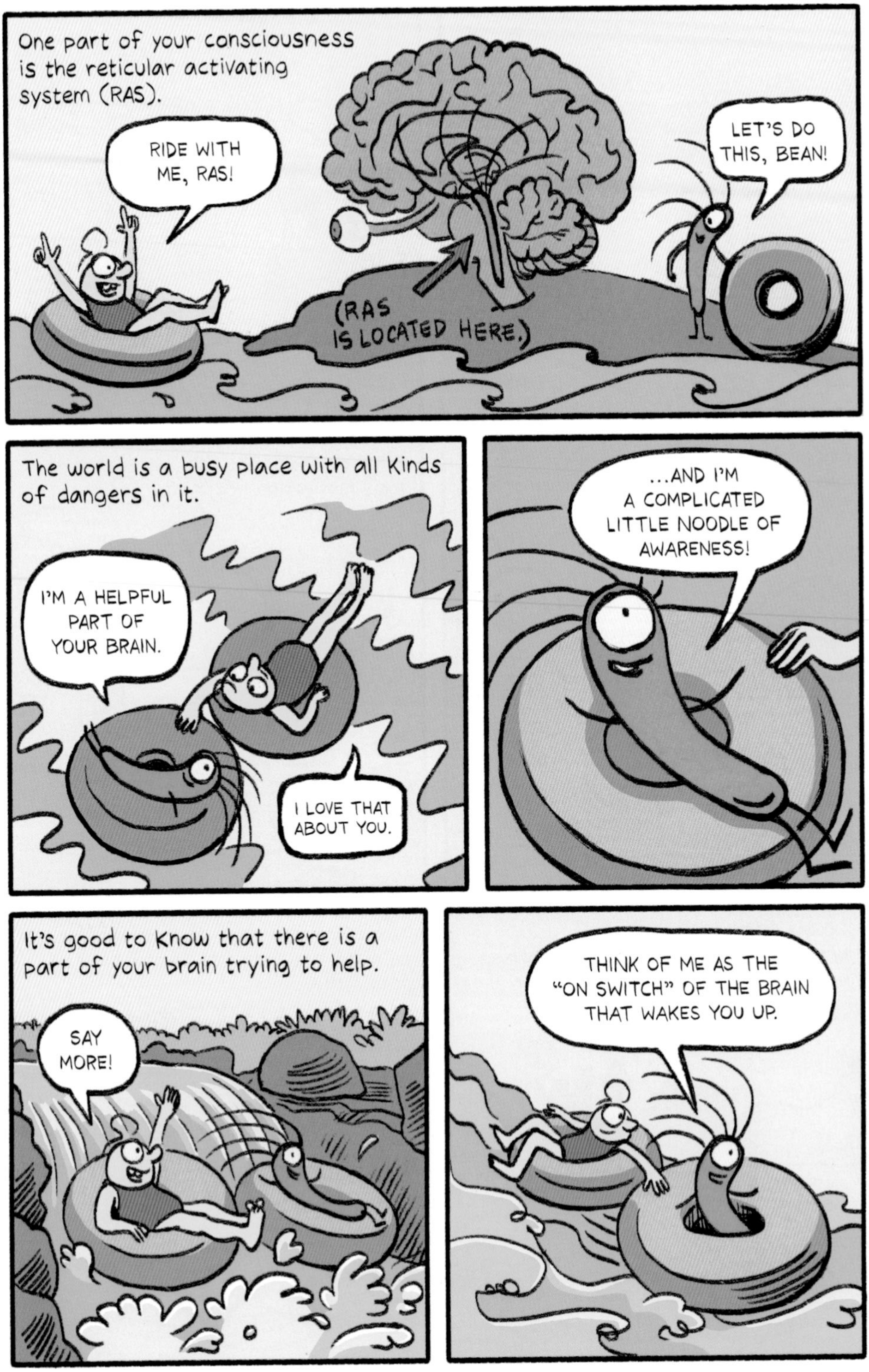

One part of your consciousness is the reticular activating system (RAS).
RIDE WITH ME, RAS!
(RAS IS LOCATED HERE.)
LET'S DO THIS, BEAN!
The world is a busy place with all kinds of dangers in it.
I'M A HELPFUL PART OF YOUR BRAIN.
I LOVE THAT ABOUT YOU.
...AND I'M A COMPLICATED LITTLE NOODLE OF AWARENESS!
It's good to know that there is a part of your brain trying to help.
SAY MORE!
THINK OF ME AS THE "ON SWITCH" OF THE BRAIN THAT WAKES YOU UP.

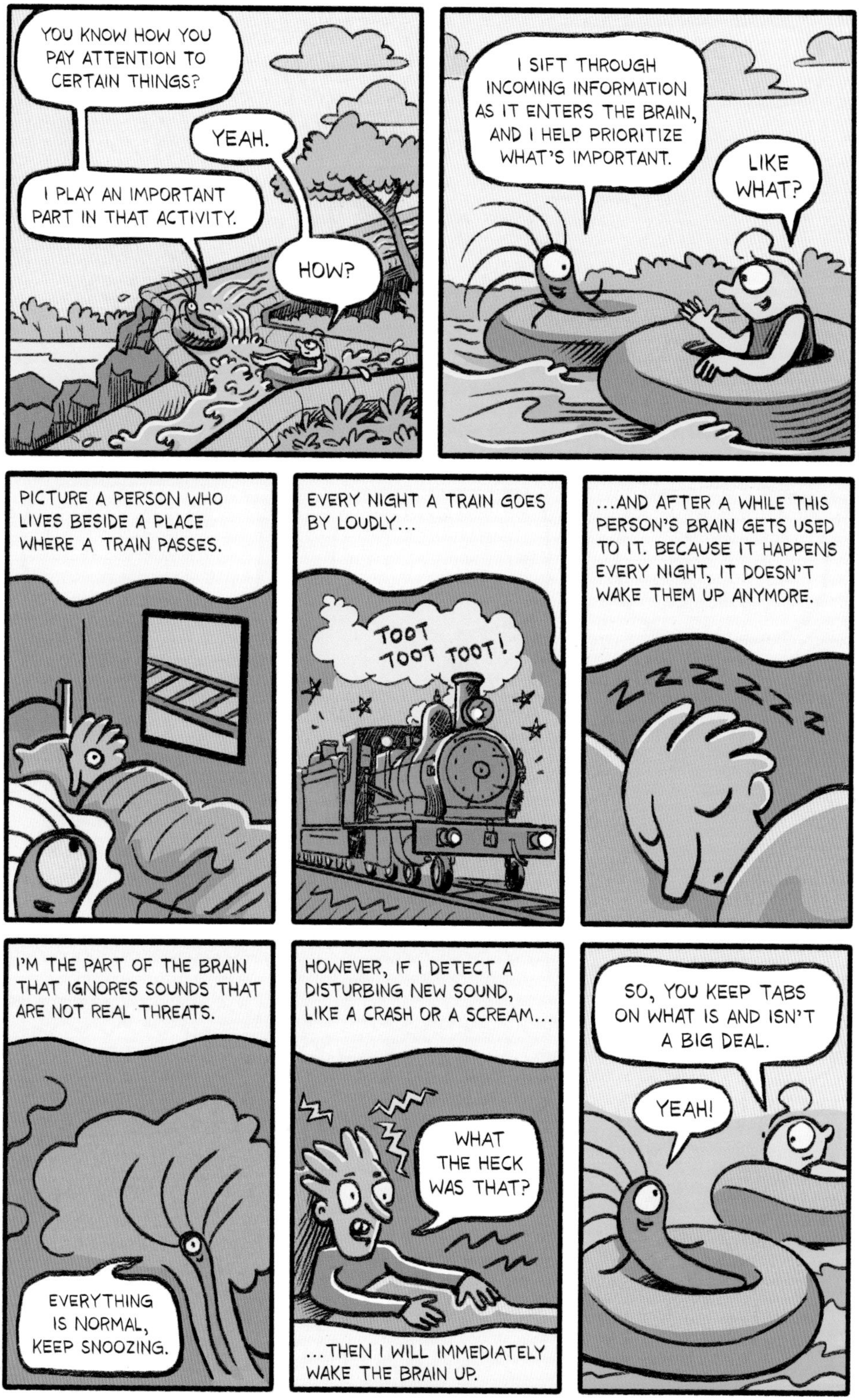
YOU KNOW HOW YOU PAY ATTENTION TO CERTAIN THINGS?
YEAH.
I PLAY AN IMPORTANT PART IN THAT ACTIVITY.
HOW?
I SIFT THROUGH INCOMING INFORMATION AS IT ENTERS THE BRAIN, AND I HELP PRIORITIZE WHAT'S IMPORTANT.
LIKE WHAT?
PICTURE A PERSON WHO LIVES BESIDE A PLACE WHERE A TRAIN PASSES.
EVERY NIGHT A TRAIN GOES BY LOUDLY...
TOOT TOOT TOOT!
...AND AFTER A WHILE THIS PERSON'S BRAIN GETS USED TO IT. BECAUSE IT HAPPENS EVERY NIGHT, IT DOESN'T WAKE THEM UP ANYMORE.
ZZZZZZZ
I'M THE PART OF THE BRAIN THAT IGNORES SOUNDS THAT ARE NOT REAL THREATS.
EVERYTHING IS NORMAL, KEEP SNOOZING.
HOWEVER, IF I DETECT A DISTURBING NEW SOUND, LIKE A CRASH OR A SCREAM...
WHAT THE HECK WAS THAT?
...THEN I WILL IMMEDIATELY WAKE THE BRAIN UP.
SO, YOU KEEP TABS ON WHAT IS AND ISN'T A BIG DEAL.
YEAH!

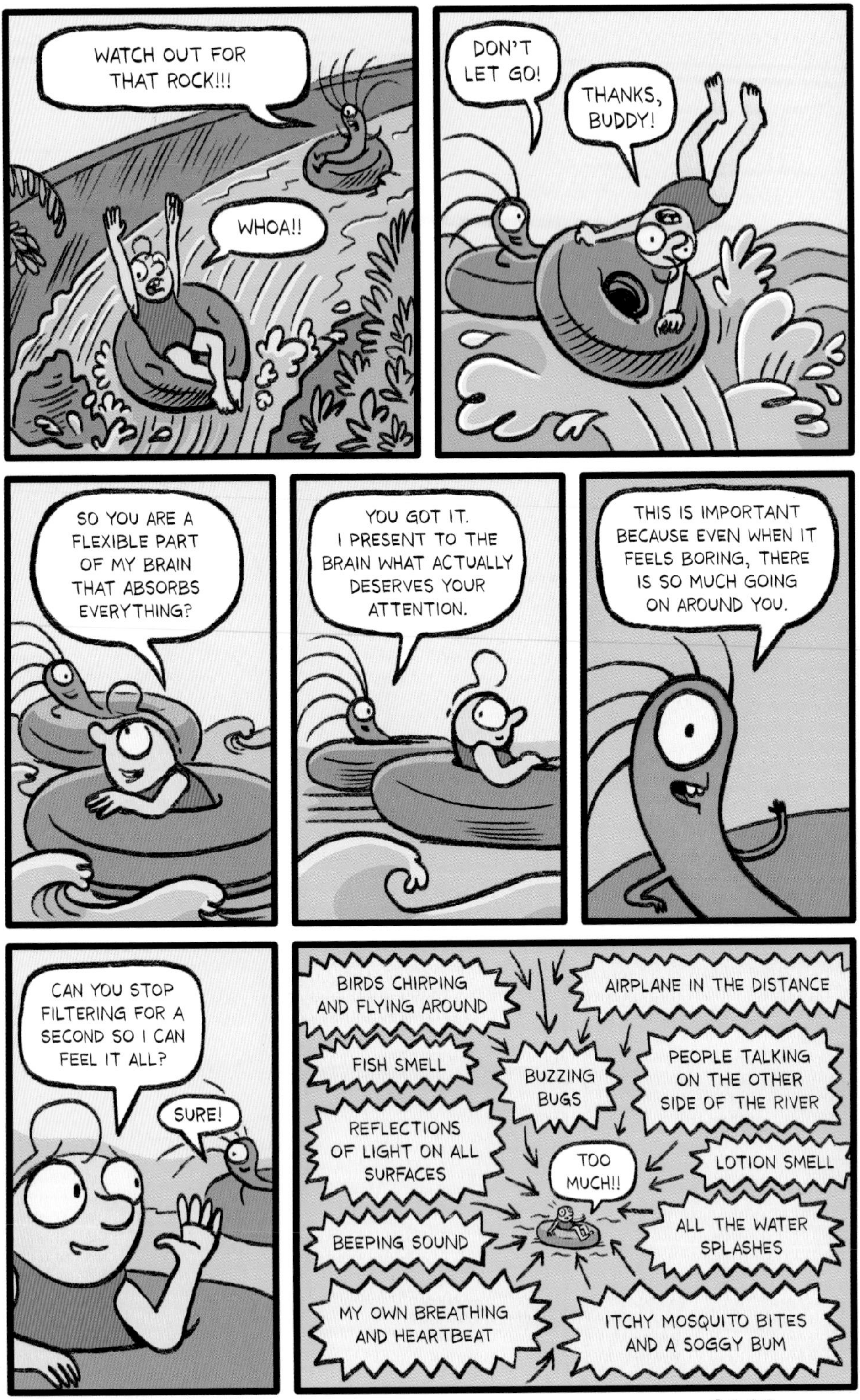
WATCH OUT FOR THAT ROCK!!!
WHOA!!
DON'T LET GO!
THANKS, BUDDY!
SO YOU ARE A FLEXIBLE PART OF MY BRAIN THAT ABSORBS EVERYTHING?
YOU GOT IT. I PRESENT TO THE BRAIN WHAT ACTUALLY DESERVES YOUR ATTENTION.
THIS IS IMPORTANT BECAUSE EVEN WHEN IT FEELS BORING, THERE IS SO MUCH GOING ON AROUND YOU.
CAN YOU STOP FILTERING FOR A SECOND SO I CAN FEEL IT ALL?
SURE!
BIRDS CHIRPING AND FLYING AROUND
AIRPLANE IN THE DISTANCE
FISH SMELL
BUZZING BUGS
PEOPLE TALKING ON THE OTHER SIDE OF THE RIVER
REFLECTIONS OF LIGHT ON ALL SURFACES
TOO MUCH!!
LOTION SMELL
BEEPING SOUND
ALL THE WATER SPLASHES
MY OWN BREATHING AND HEARTBEAT
ITCHY MOSQUITO BITES AND A SOGGY BUM

♥ THANK YOUR RAS FOR MAKING LIFE LESS OVERWHELMING! ♥ ♥

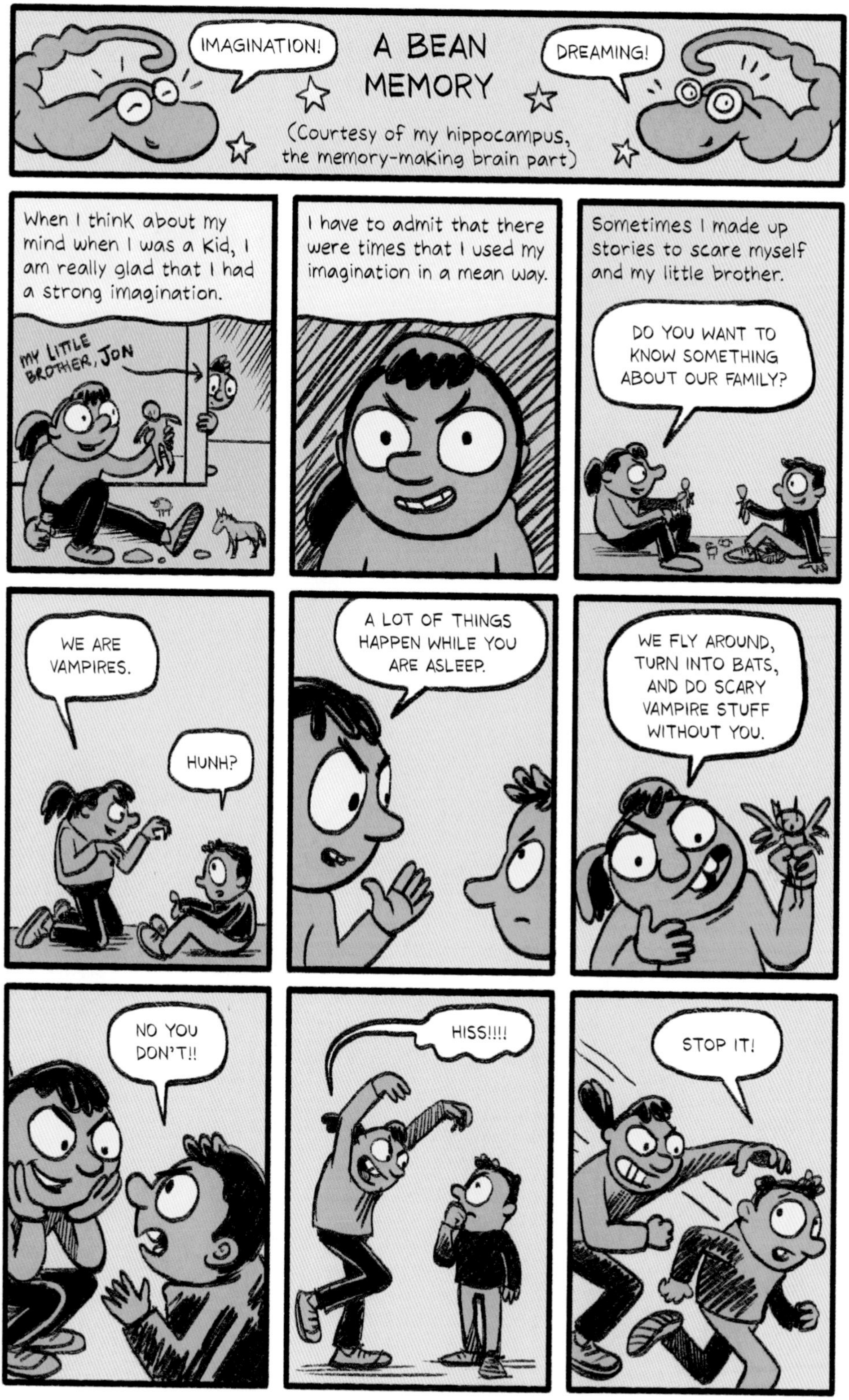
IMAGINATION!
A BEAN MEMORY
DREAMING!
(Courtesy of my hippocampus, the memory-making brain part)
When I think about my mind when I was a Kid, I am really glad that I had a strong imagination.
MY LITTLE BROTHER, JON
I have to admit that there were times that I used my imagination in a mean way.
Sometimes I made up stories to scare myself and my little brother.
DO YOU WANT TO KNOW SOMETHING ABOUT OUR FAMILY?
WE ARE VAMPIRES.
HUNH?
A LOT OF THINGS HAPPEN WHILE YOU ARE ASLEEP.
WE FLY AROUND, TURN INTO BATS, AND DO SCARY VAMPIRE STUFF WITHOUT YOU.
NO YOU DON'T!!
HISS!!!!
STOP IT!

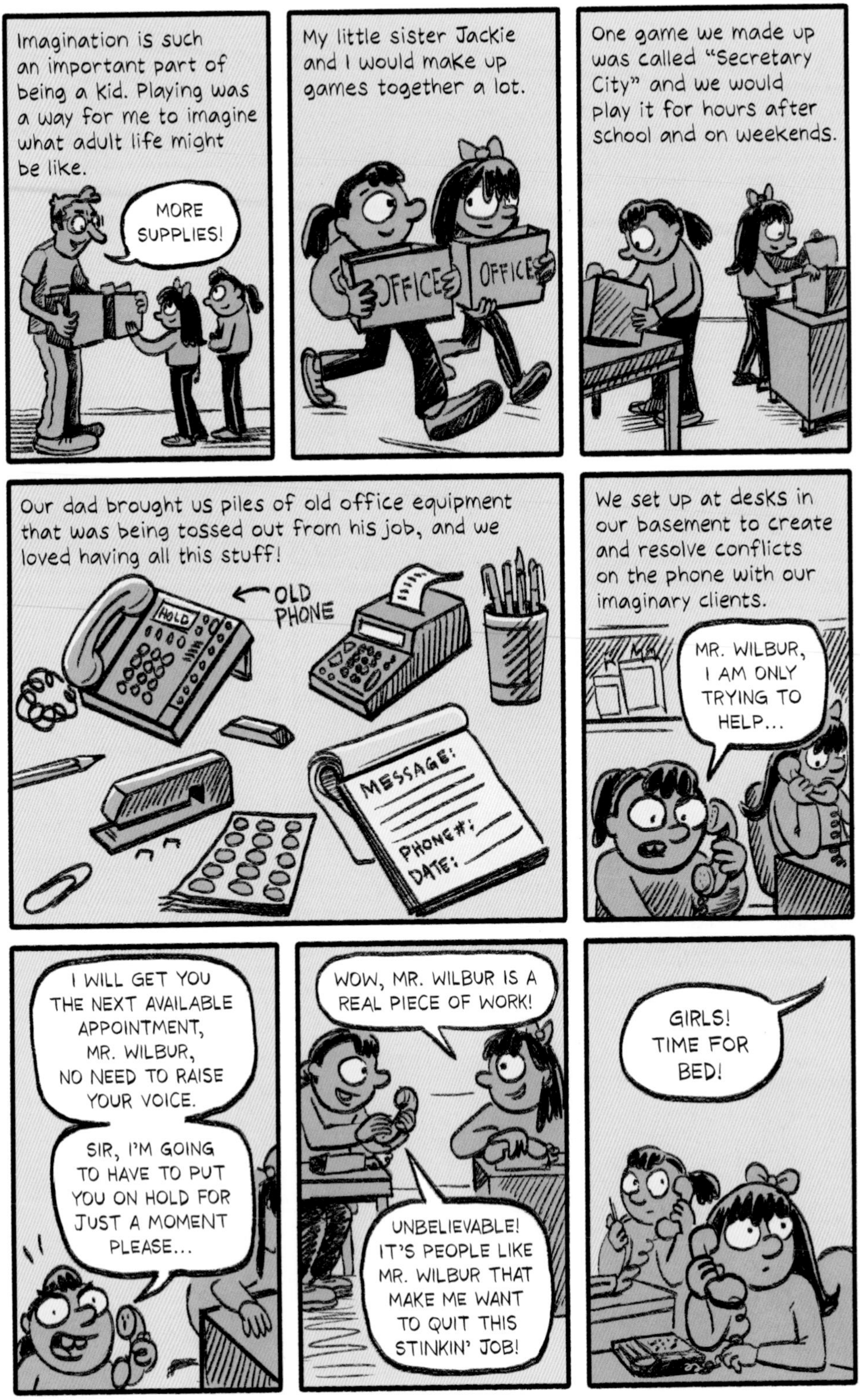
Imagination is such an important part of being a kid. Playing was a way for me to imagine what adult life might be like.
MORE SUPPLIES!
My little sister Jackie and I would make up games together a lot.
OFFICE
OFFICES
One game we made up was called "Secretary City" and we would play it for hours after school and on weekends.
Our dad brought us piles of old office equipment that was being tossed out from his job, and we loved having all this stuff!
HOLD
OLD PHONE
MESSAGE:
PHONE #:
DATE:
We set up at desks in our basement to create and resolve conflicts on the phone with our imaginary clients.
MR. WILBUR, I AM ONLY TRYING TO HELP...
I WILL GET YOU THE NEXT AVAILABLE APPOINTMENT, MR. WILBUR, NO NEED TO RAISE YOUR VOICE.
SIR, I'M GOING TO HAVE TO PUT YOU ON HOLD FOR JUST A MOMENT PLEASE...
WOW, MR. WILBUR IS A REAL PIECE OF WORK!
UNBELIEVABLE! IT'S PEOPLE LIKE MR. WILBUR THAT MAKE ME WANT TO QUIT THIS STINKIN' JOB!
GIRLS! TIME FOR BED!

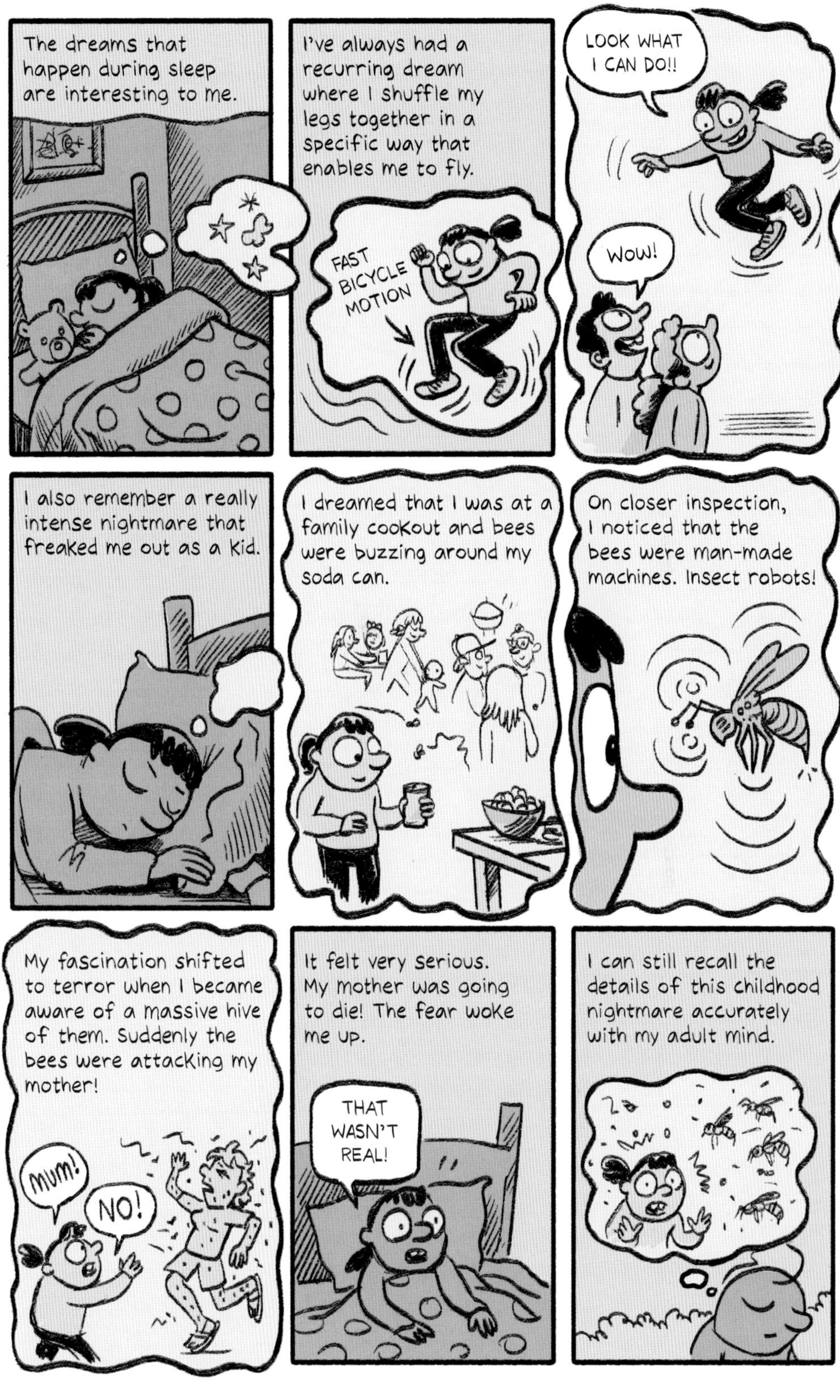
The dreams that happen during sleep are interesting to me.
I've always had a recurring dream where I shuffle my legs together in a specific way that enables me to fly.
FAST BICYCLE MOTION
LOOK WHAT I CAN DO!!
WOW!
I also remember a really intense nightmare that freaked me out as a kid.
I dreamed that I was at a family cookout and bees were buzzing around my soda can.
On closer inspection, I noticed that the bees were man-made machines. Insect robots!
My fascination shifted to terror when I became aware of a massive hive of them. Suddenly the bees were attacking my mother!
MUM!
NO!
It felt very serious. My mother was going to die! The fear woke me up.
THAT WASN'T REAL!
I can still recall the details of this childhood nightmare accurately with my adult mind.

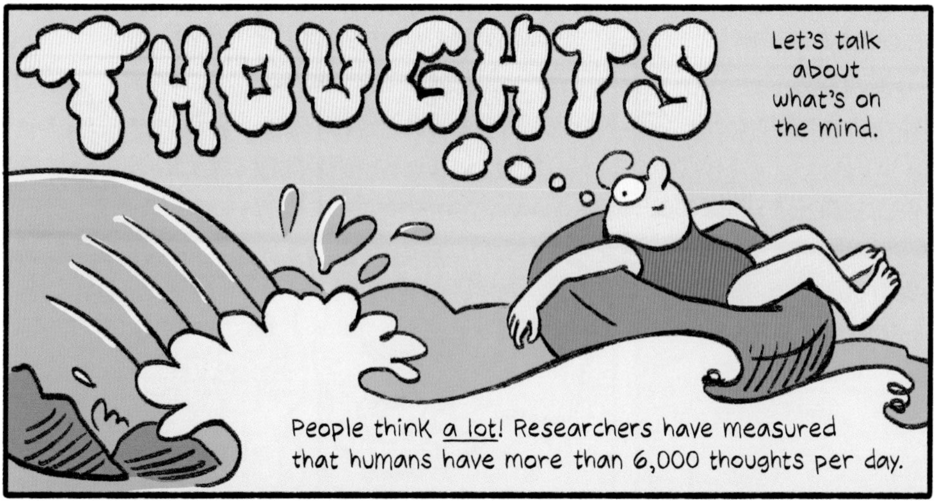
THOUGHTS
Let's talk about what's on the mind.
People think a lot! Researchers have measured that humans have more than 6,000 thoughts per day.

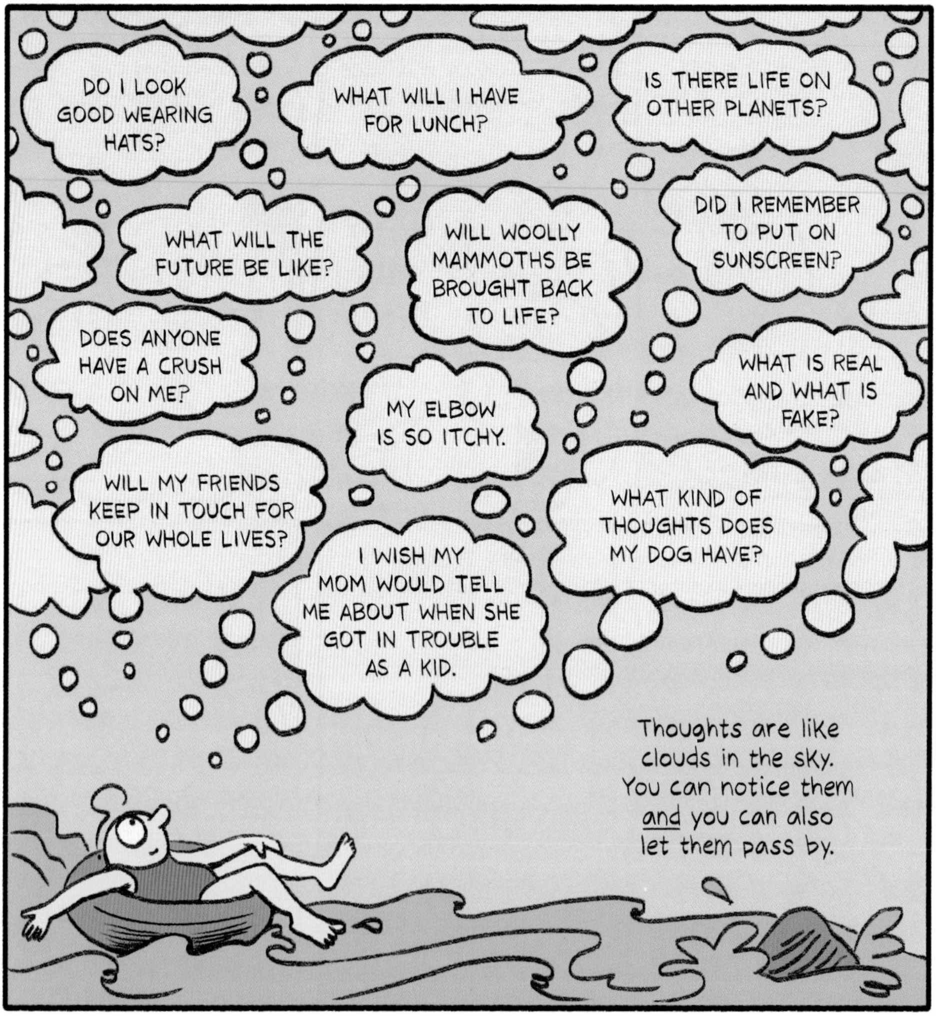
DO I LOOK GOOD WEARING HATS?
WHAT WILL I HAVE FOR LUNCH?
IS THERE LIFE ON OTHER PLANETS?
WHAT WILL THE FUTURE BE LIKE?
WILL WOOLLY MAMMOTHS BE BROUGHT BACK TO LIFE?
DID I REMEMBER TO PUT ON SUNSCREEN?
DOES ANYONE HAVE A CRUSH ON ME?
MY ELBOW IS SO ITCHY.
WHAT IS REAL AND WHAT IS FAKE?
WILL MY FRIENDS KEEP IN TOUCH FOR OUR WHOLE LIVES?
WHAT KIND OF THOUGHTS DOES MY DOG HAVE?
I WISH MY MOM WOULD TELL ME ABOUT WHEN SHE GOT IN TROUBLE AS A KID.
Thoughts are like clouds in the sky. You can notice them and you can also let them pass by.

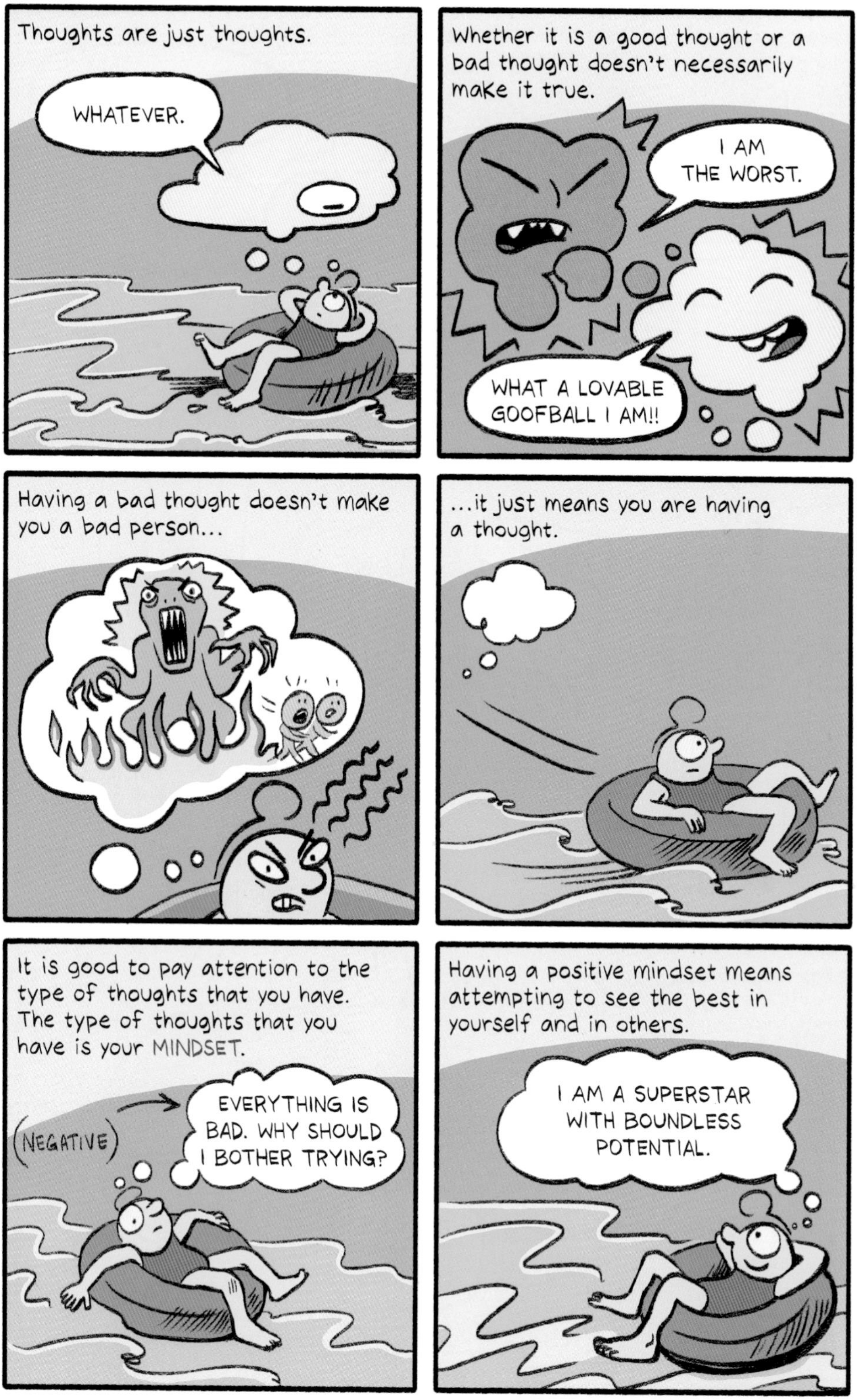
Thoughts are just thoughts.
WHATEVER.
Whether it is a good thought or a bad thought doesn't necessarily make it true.
I AM THE WORST.
WHAT A LOVABLE GOOFBALL I AM!!
Having a bad thought doesn't make you a bad person...
...it just means you are having a thought.
It is good to pay attention to the type of thoughts that you have. The type of thoughts that you have is your MINDSET.
(NEGATIVE)
EVERYTHING IS BAD. WHY SHOULD I BOTHER TRYING?
Having a positive mindset means attempting to see the best in yourself and in others.
I AM A SUPERSTAR WITH BOUNDLESS POTENTIAL.

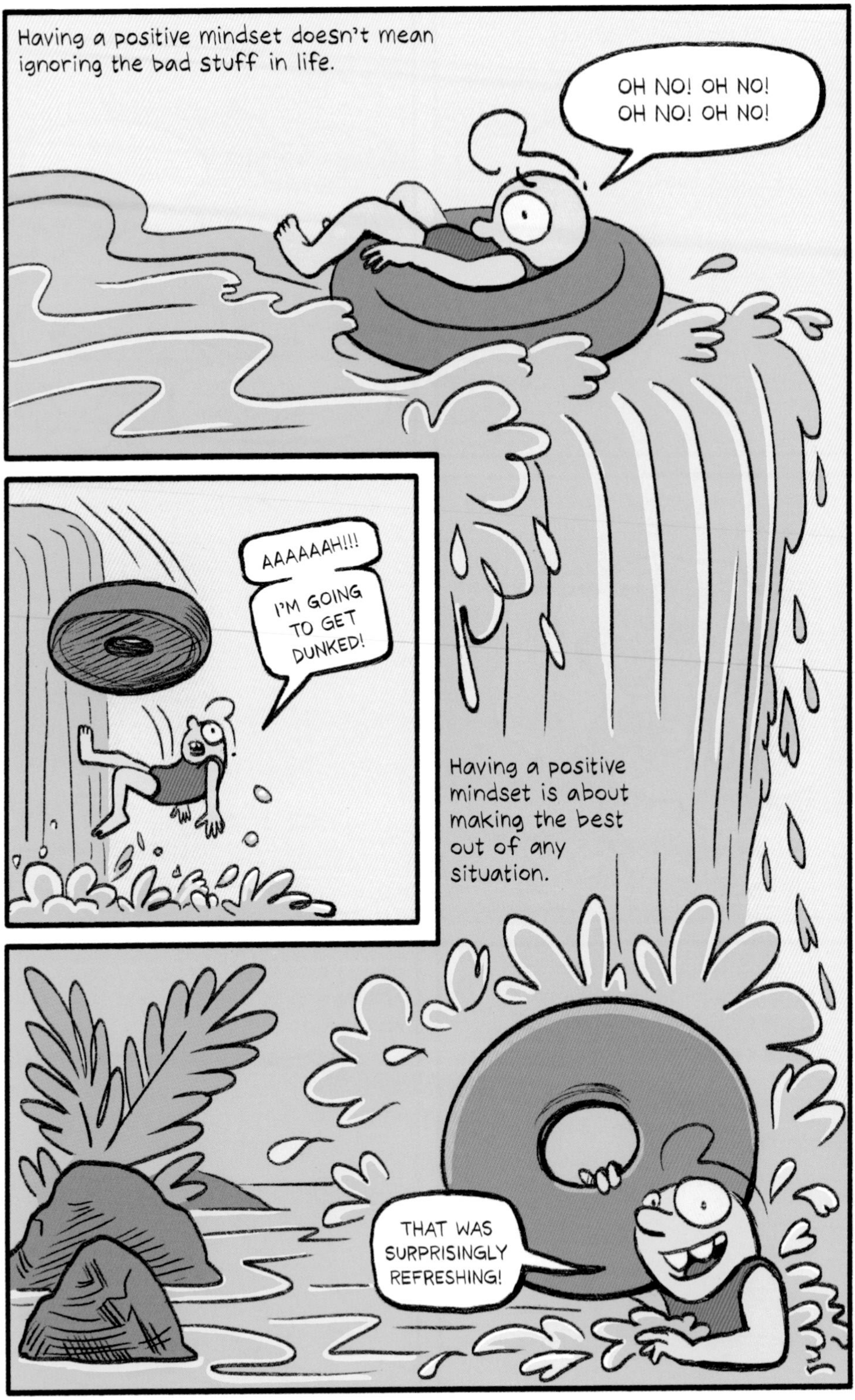
Having a positive mindset doesn't mean ignoring the bad stuff in life.
OH NO! OH NO! OH NO! OH NO!
AAAAAAH!!!
I'M GOING TO GET DUNKED!
Having a positive mindset is about making the best out of any situation.
THAT WAS SURPRISINGLY REFRESHING!

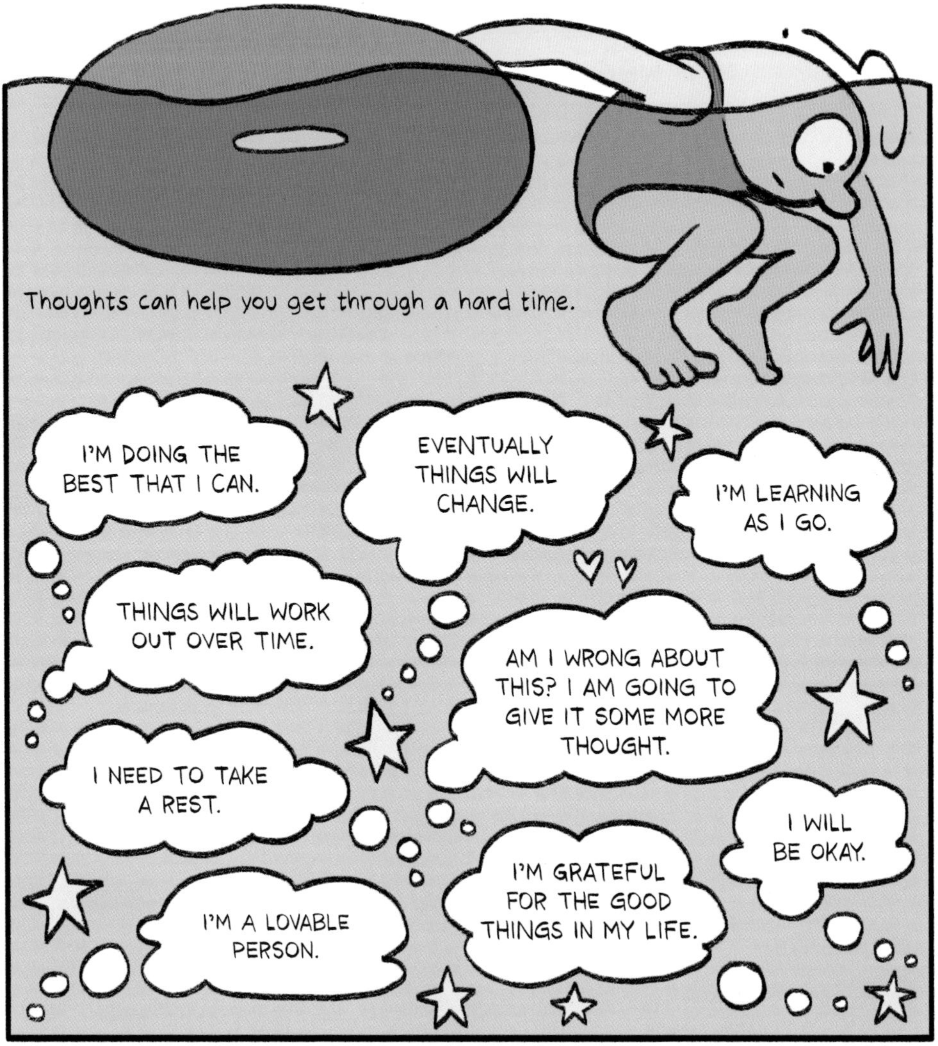
Thoughts can help you get through a hard time.
I'M DOING THE BEST THAT I CAN.
EVENTUALLY THINGS WILL CHANGE.
I'M LEARNING AS I GO.
THINGS WILL WORK OUT OVER TIME.
AM I WRONG ABOUT THIS? I AM GOING TO GIVE IT SOME MORE THOUGHT.
I NEED TO TAKE A REST.
I WILL BE OKAY.
I'M GRATEFUL FOR THE GOOD THINGS IN MY LIFE.
I'M A LOVABLE PERSON.

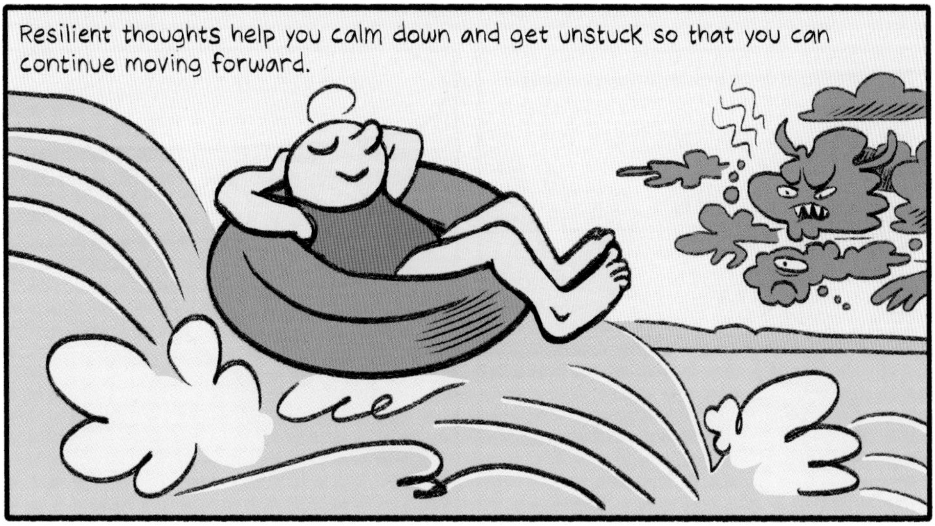
Resilient thoughts help you calm down and get unstuck so that you can continue moving forward.

NEGATIVE THOUGHTS

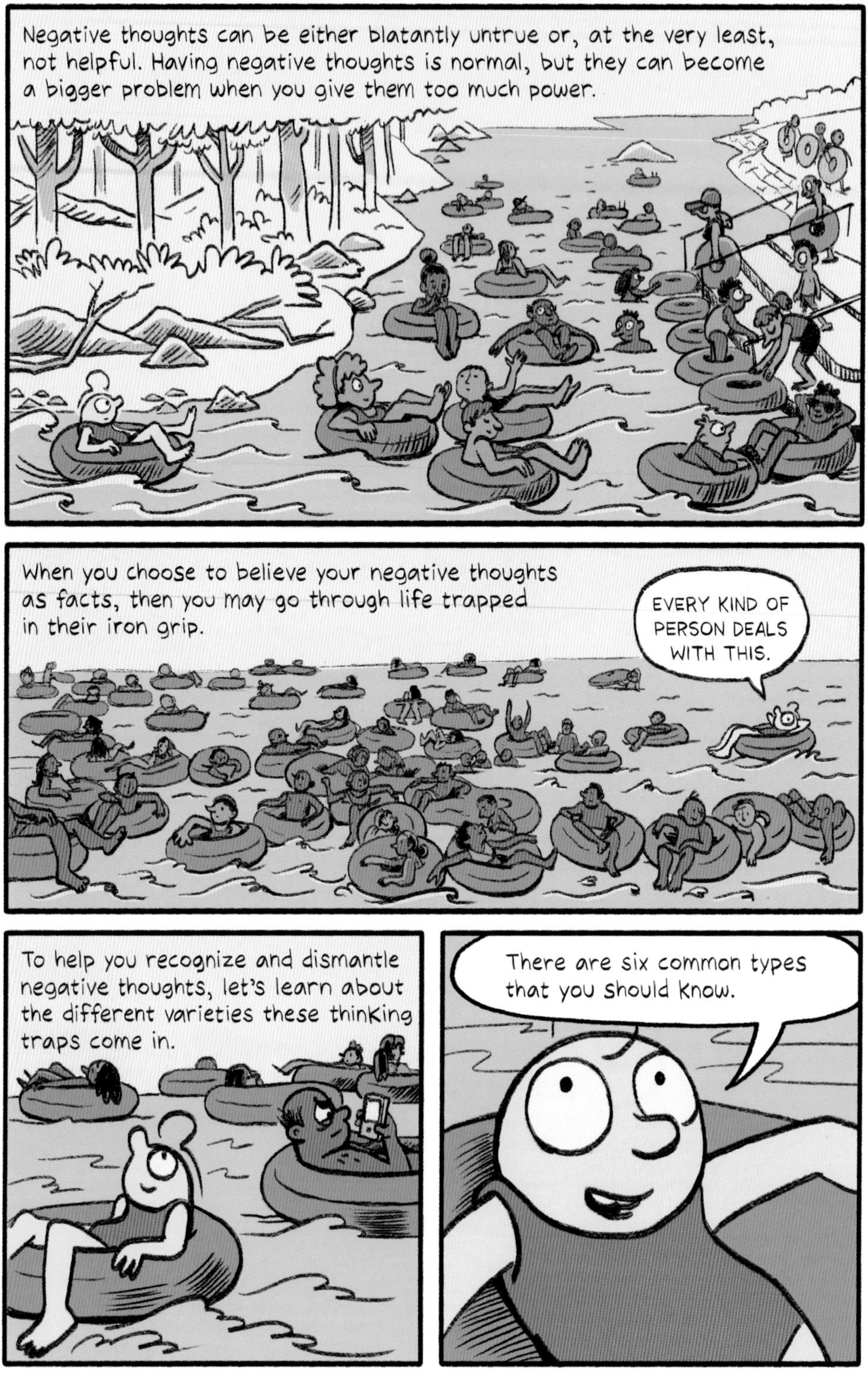
Negative thoughts can be either blatantly untrue or, at the very least, not helpful. Having negative thoughts is normal, but they can become a bigger problem when you give them too much power.
When you choose to believe your negative thoughts as facts, then you may go through life trapped in their iron grip.
EVERY KIND OF PERSON DEALS WITH THIS.
To help you recognize and dismantle negative thoughts, let's learn about the different varieties these thinking traps come in.
There are six common types that you should know.

1.) BLACK-AND-WHITE THINKING

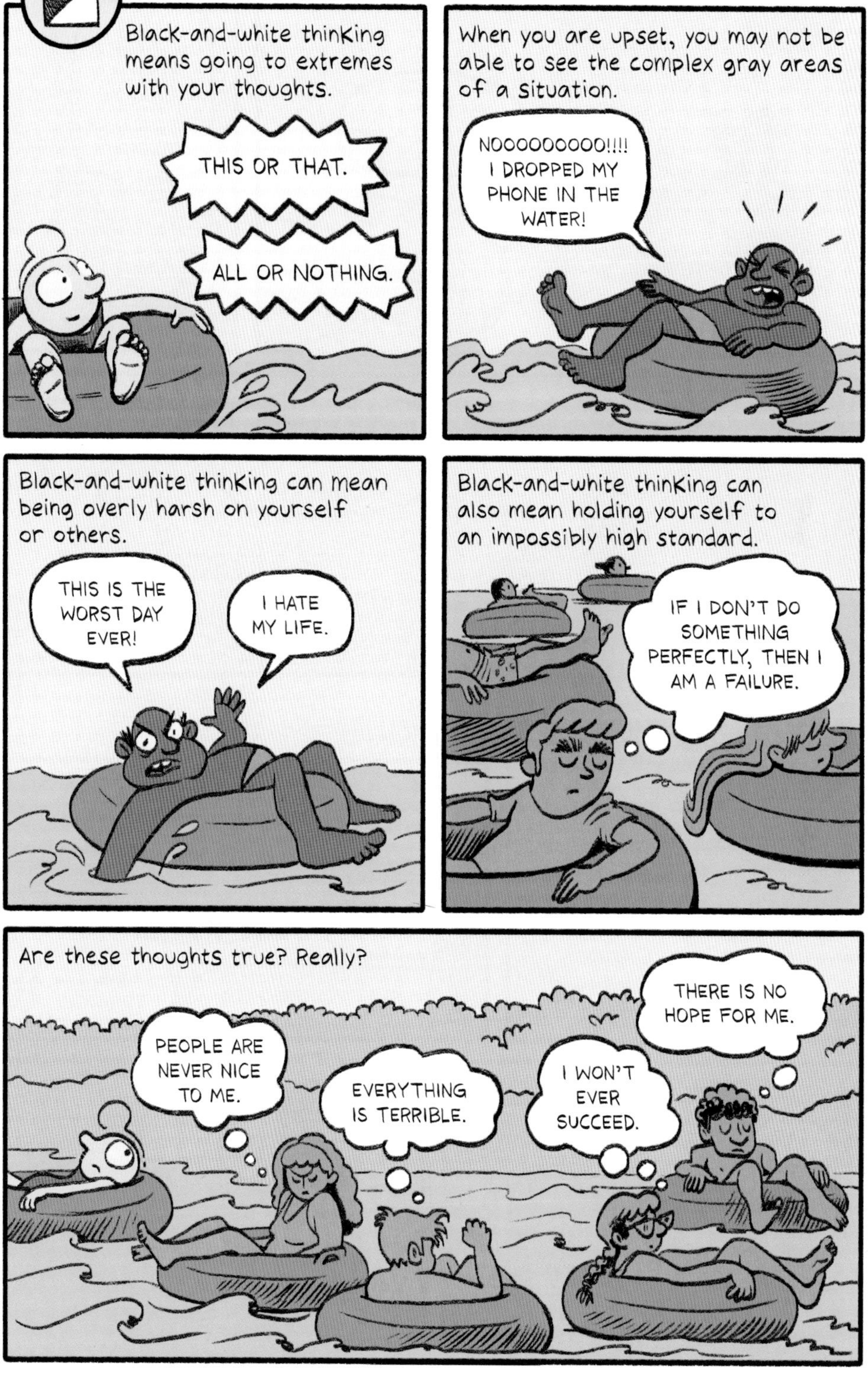
Black-and-white thinking means going to extremes with your thoughts.
THIS OR THAT.
ALL OR NOTHING.
When you are upset, you may not be able to see the complex gray areas of a situation.
NOOOOOOOOO!!!! I DROPPED MY PHONE IN THE WATER!
Black-and-white thinking can mean being overly harsh on yourself or others.
THIS IS THE WORST DAY EVER!
I HATE MY LIFE.
Black-and-white thinking can also mean holding yourself to an impossibly high standard.
IF I DON'T DO SOMETHING PERFECTLY, THEN I AM A FAILURE.
Are these thoughts true? Really?
PEOPLE ARE NEVER NICE TO ME.
EVERYTHING IS TERRIBLE.
I WON'T EVER SUCCEED.
THERE IS NO HOPE FOR ME.

2.) CATASTROPHIZING

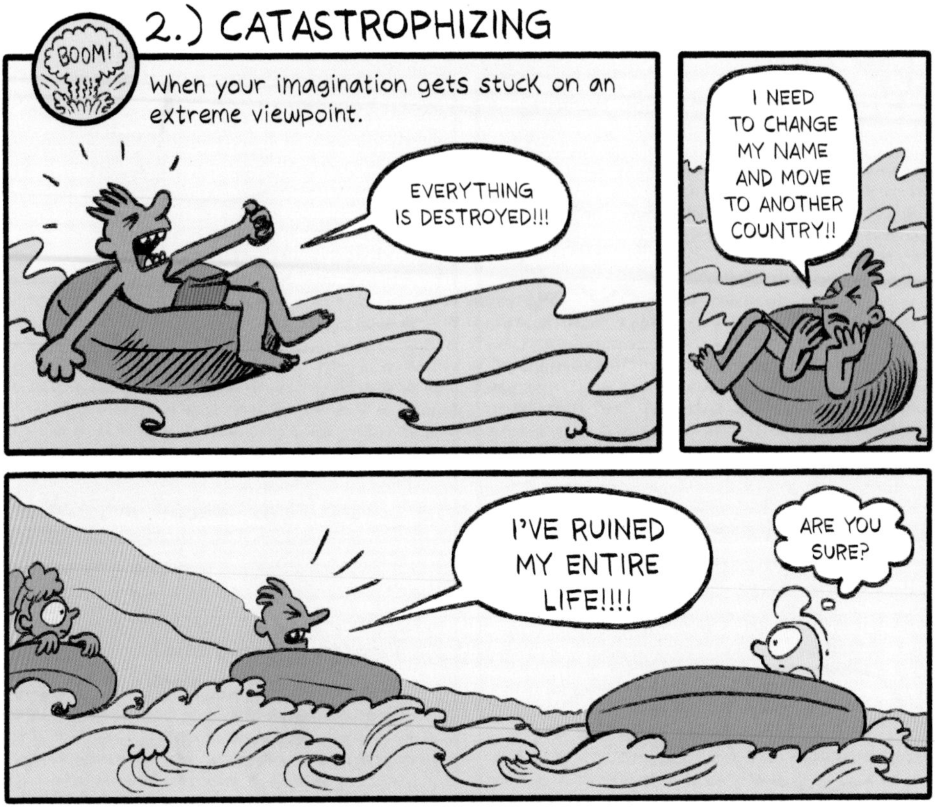
BOOM!
When your imagination gets stuck on an extreme viewpoint.
EVERYTHING IS DESTROYED!!!
I NEED TO CHANGE MY NAME AND MOVE TO ANOTHER COUNTRY!!
I'VE RUINED MY ENTIRE LIFE!!!!
ARE YOU SURE?

3.) FILTERED THINKING

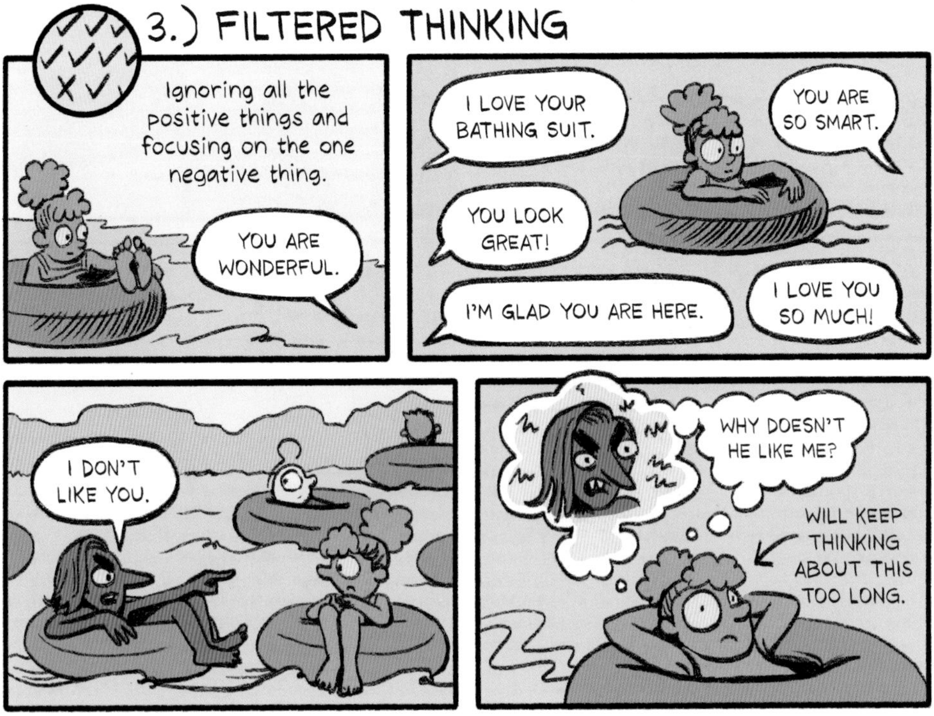
Ignoring all the positive things and focusing on the one negative thing.
YOU ARE WONDERFUL.
I LOVE YOUR BATHING SUIT.
YOU ARE SO SMART.
YOU LOOK GREAT!
I'M GLAD YOU ARE HERE.
I LOVE YOU SO MUCH!
I DON'T LIKE YOU.
WHY DOESN'T HE LIKE ME?
WILL KEEP THINKING ABOUT THIS TOO LONG.

4.) COMPARE AND DESPAIR

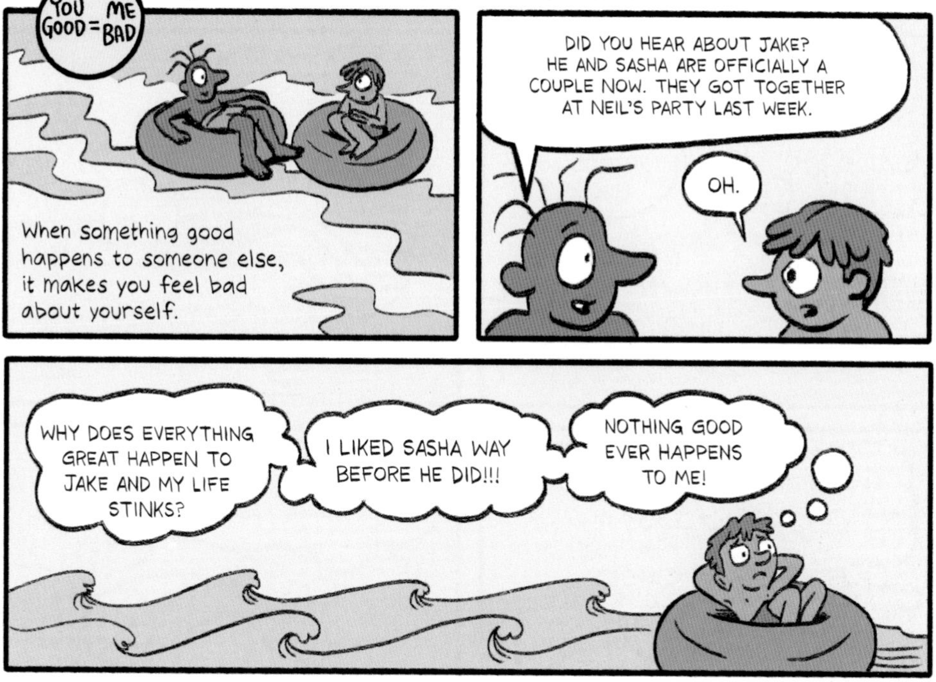
YOU GOOD = ME BAD
When something good happens to someone else, it makes you feel bad about yourself.
DID YOU HEAR ABOUT JAKE? HE AND SASHA ARE OFFICIALLY A COUPLE NOW. THEY GOT TOGETHER AT NEIL'S PARTY LAST WEEK.
OH.
WHY DOES EVERYTHING GREAT HAPPEN TO JAKE AND MY LIFE STINKS?
I LIKED SASHA WAY BEFORE HE DID!!!
NOTHING GOOD EVER HAPPENS TO ME!

5.) MIND READING

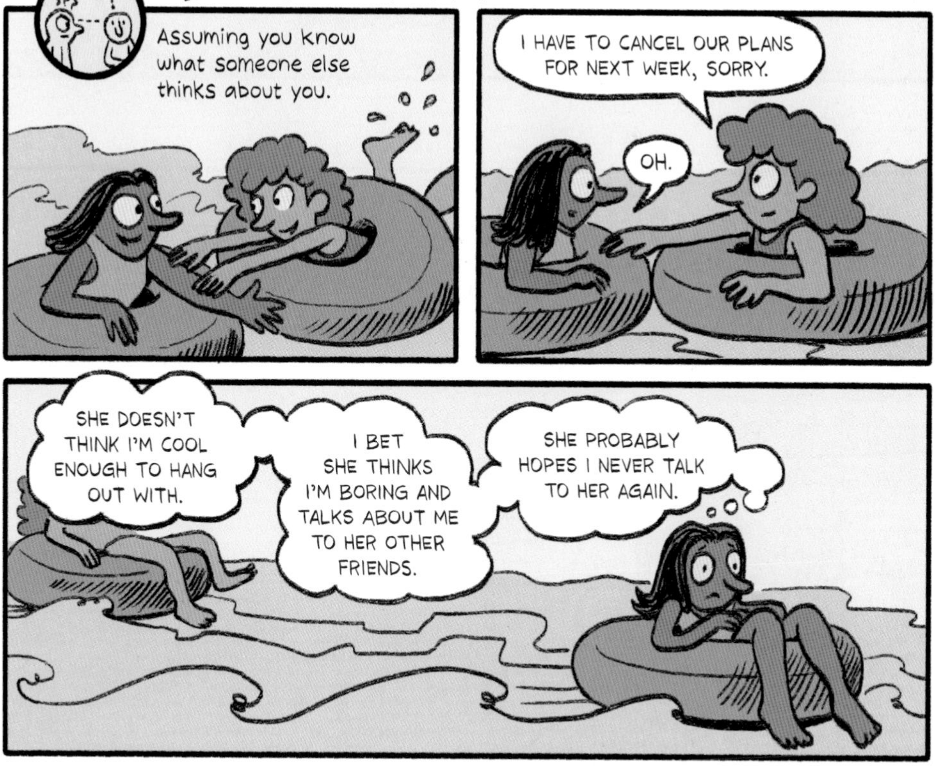
Assuming you know what someone else thinks about you.
I HAVE TO CANCEL OUR PLANS FOR NEXT WEEK, SORRY.
OH.
SHE DOESN'T THINK I'M COOL ENOUGH TO HANG OUT WITH.
I BET SHE THINKS I'M BORING AND TALKS ABOUT ME TO HER OTHER FRIENDS.
SHE PROBABLY HOPES I NEVER TALK TO HER AGAIN.

6.) FORTUNE TELLING

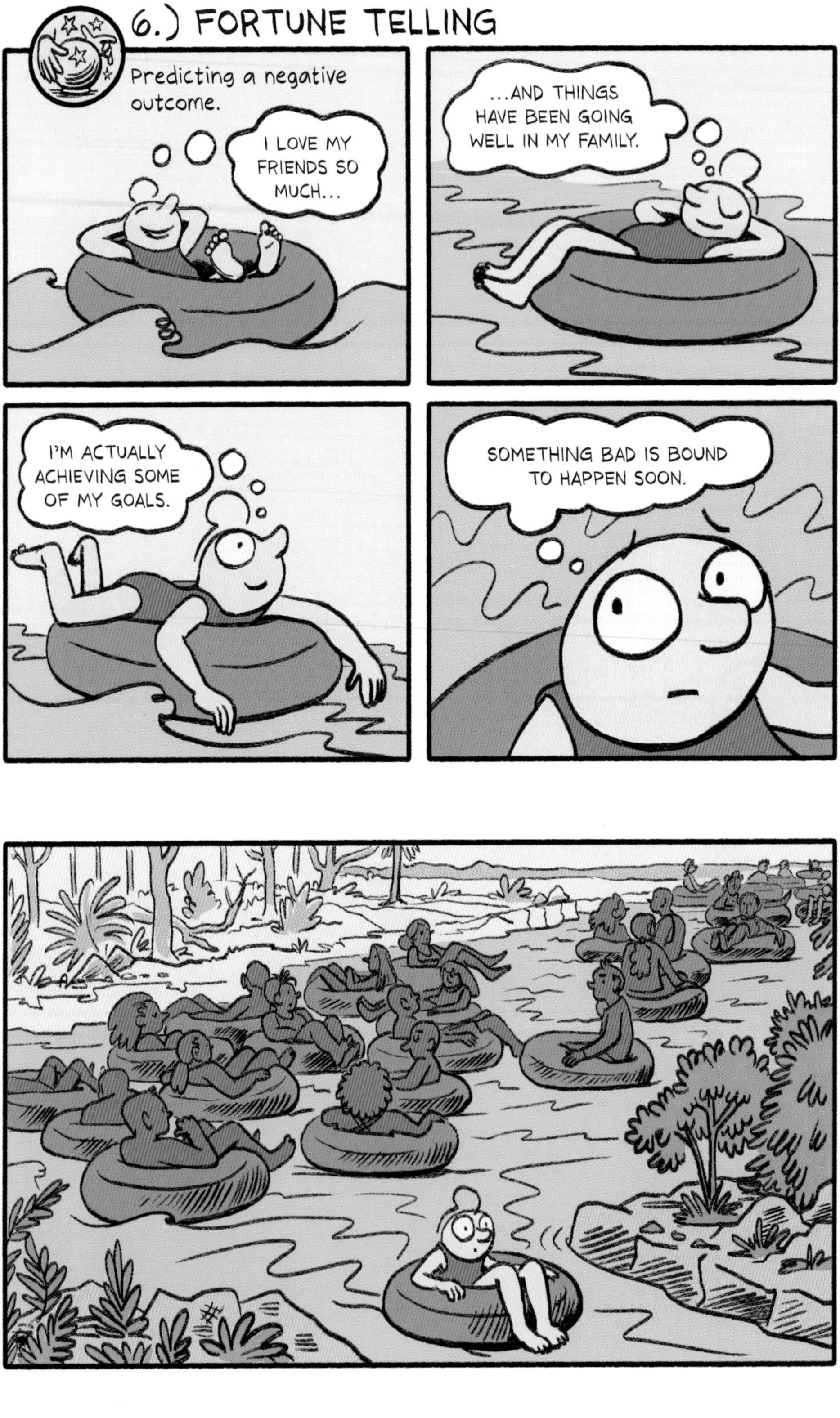
Predicting a negative outcome.
I LOVE MY FRIENDS SO MUCH...
...AND THINGS HAVE BEEN GOING WELL IN MY FAMILY.
I'M ACTUALLY ACHIEVING SOME OF MY GOALS.
SOMETHING BAD IS BOUND TO HAPPEN SOON.

THOUGHT REALITY

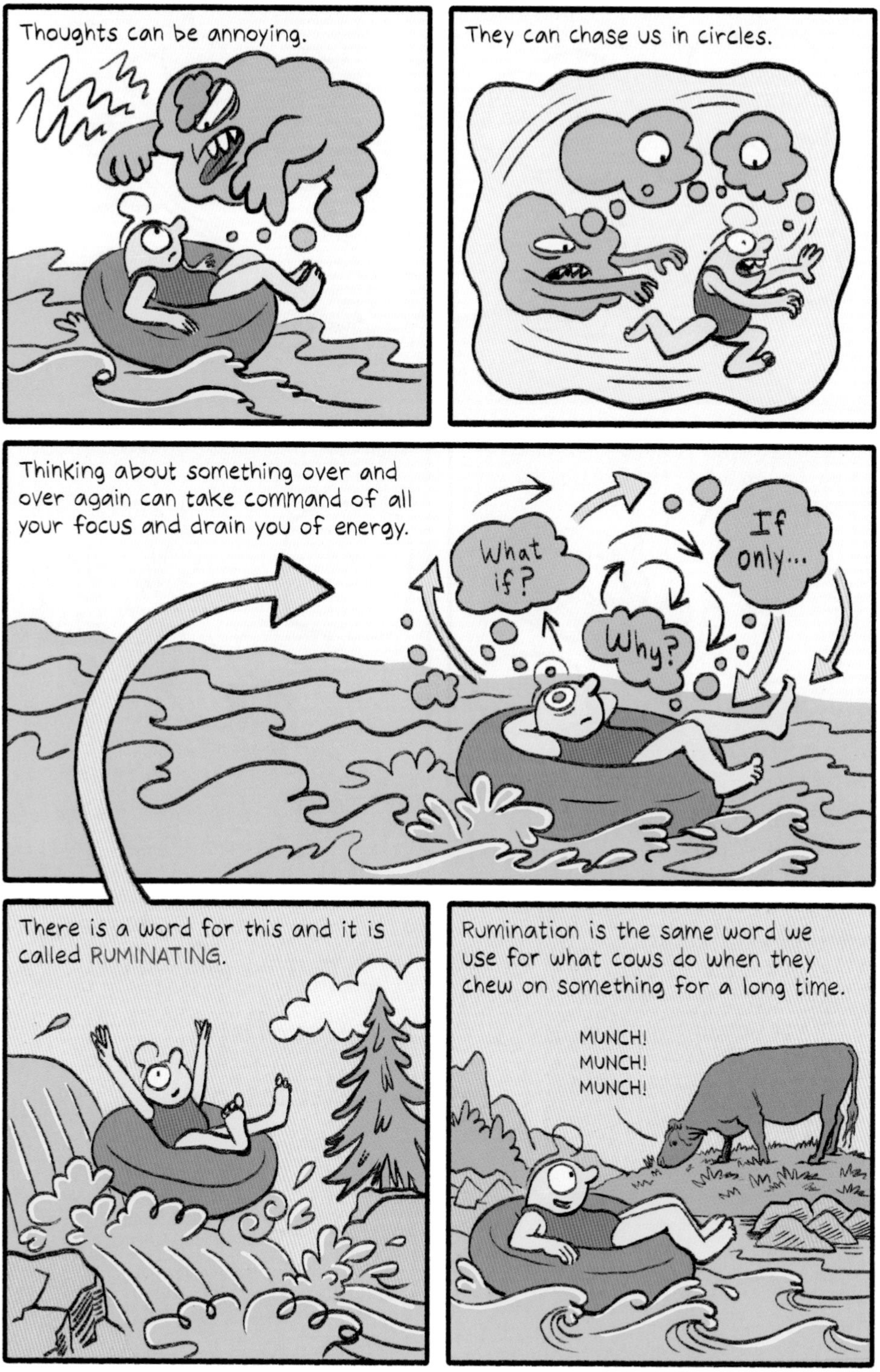
Thoughts can be annoying.
They can chase us in circles.
Thinking about something over and over again can take command of all your focus and drain you of energy.
What if?
If only...
Why?
There is a word for this and it is called RUMINATING.
Rumination is the same word we use for what cows do when they chew on something for a long time.
MUNCH!
MUNCH!
MUNCH!

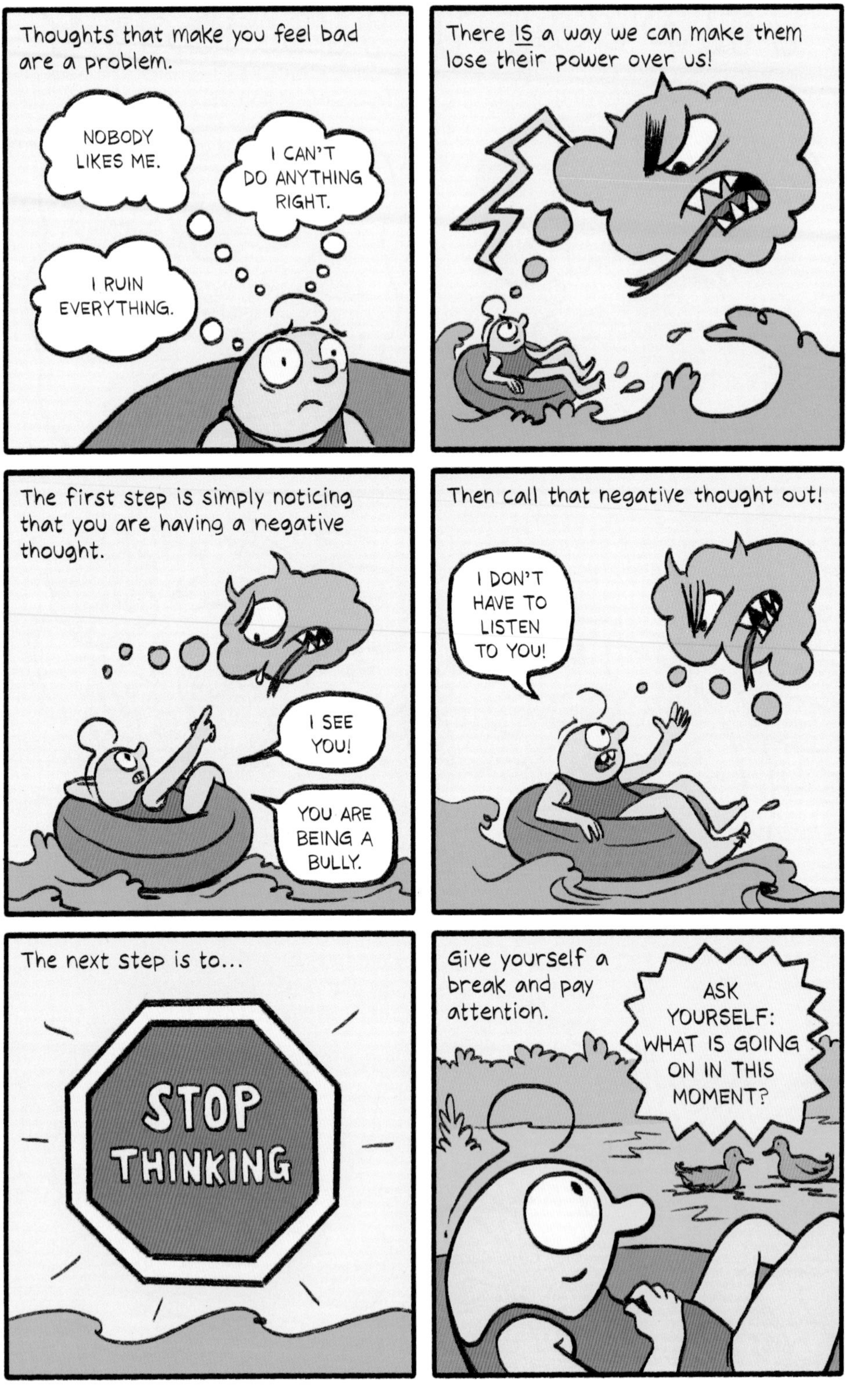
Thoughts that make you feel bad are a problem.
NOBODY LIKES ME.
I CAN'T DO ANYTHING RIGHT.
I RUIN EVERYTHING.
There IS a way we can make them lose their power over us!
The first step is simply noticing that you are having a negative thought.
I SEE YOU!
YOU ARE BEING A BULLY.
Then call that negative thought out!
I DON'T HAVE TO LISTEN TO YOU!
The next step is to...
STOP THINKING
Give yourself a break and pay attention.
ASK YOURSELF: WHAT IS GOING ON IN THIS MOMENT?

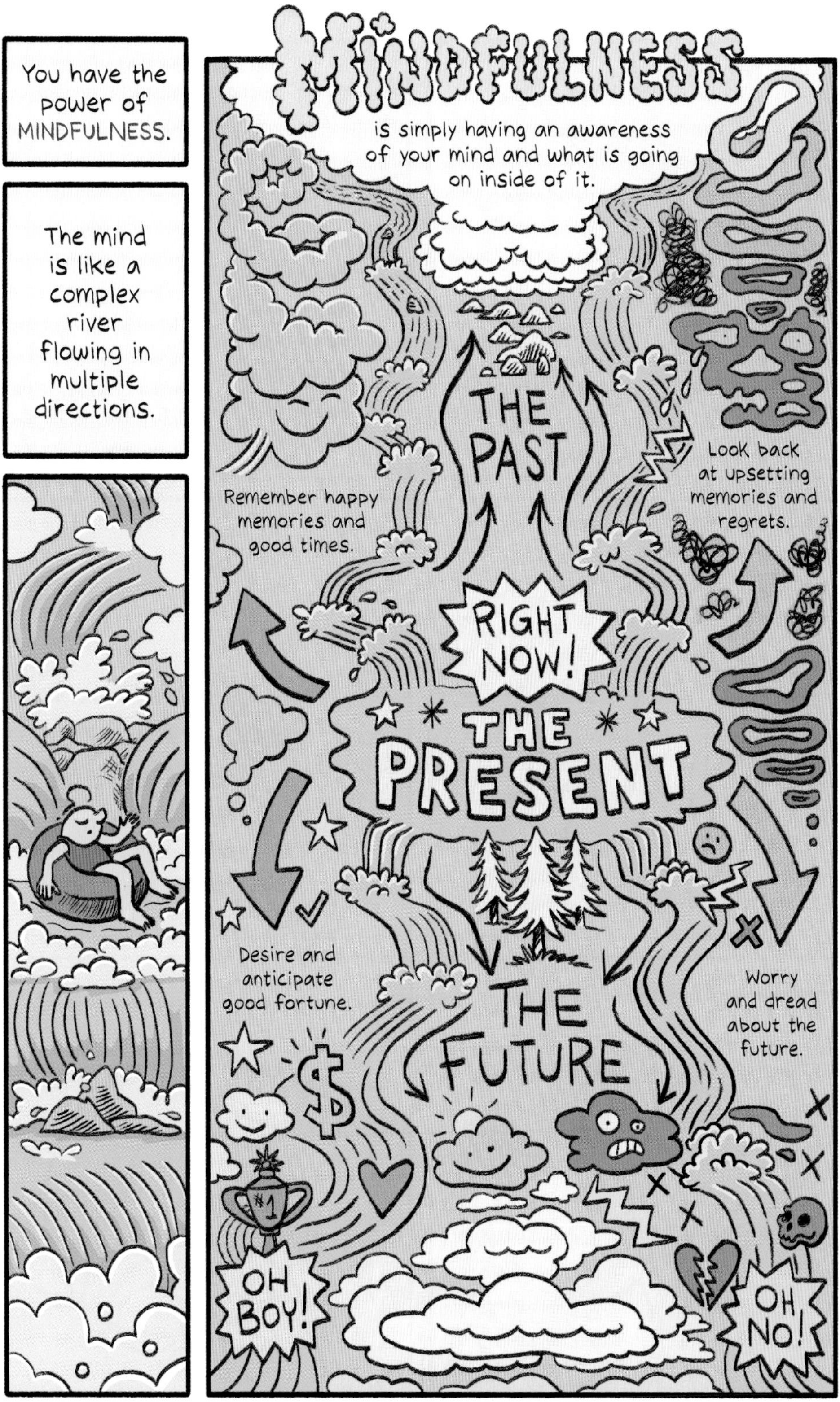
You have the power of MINDFULNESS.
The mind is like a complex river flowing in multiple directions.
MINDFULNESS
is simply having an awareness of your mind and what is going on inside of it.
THE PAST
Remember happy memories and good times.
Look back at upsetting memories and regrets.
RIGHT NOW!
THE PRESENT
Desire and anticipate good fortune.
Worry and dread about the future.
THE FUTURE
OH BOY!
OH NO!

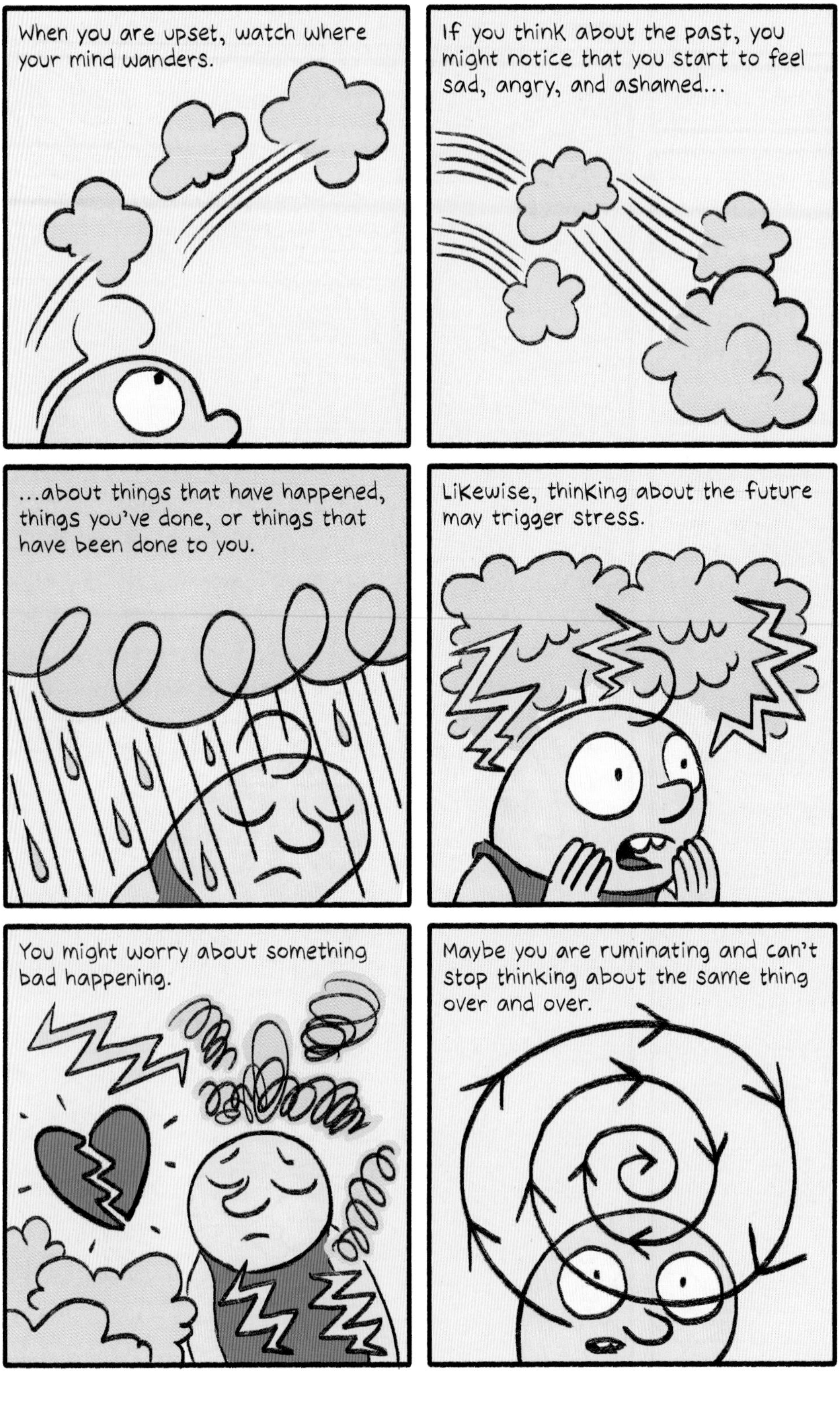
When you are upset, watch where your mind wanders.
If you think about the past, you might notice that you start to feel sad, angry, and ashamed...
...about things that have happened, things you've done, or things that have been done to you.
Likewise, thinking about the future may trigger stress.
You might worry about something bad happening.
Maybe you are ruminating and can't stop thinking about the same thing over and over.

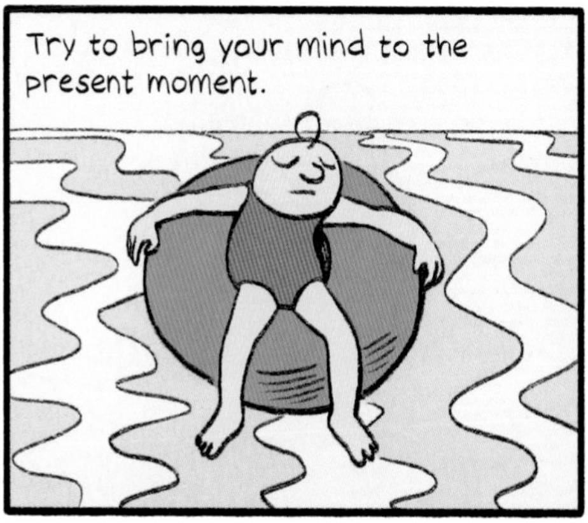
Try to bring your mind to the present moment.

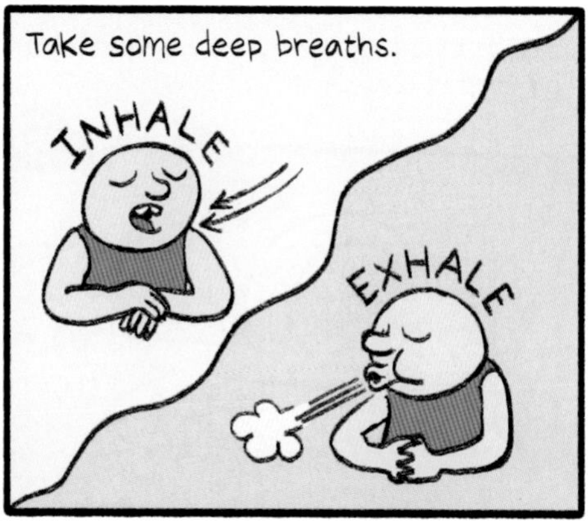
Take some deep breaths.
INHALE
EXHALE

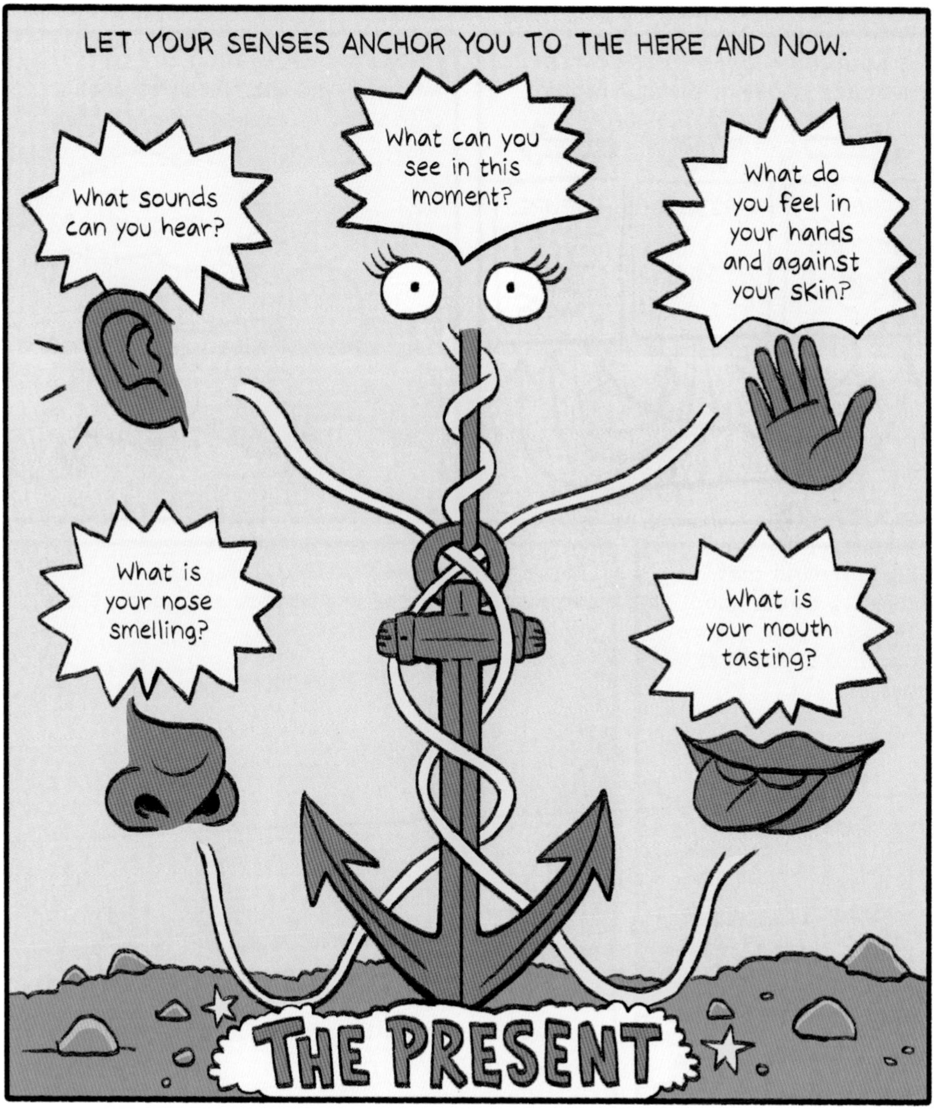
LET YOUR SENSES ANCHOR YOU TO THE HERE AND NOW.
What sounds can you hear?
What can you see in this moment?
What do you feel in your hands and against your skin?
What is your nose smelling?
What is your mouth tasting?
THE PRESENT

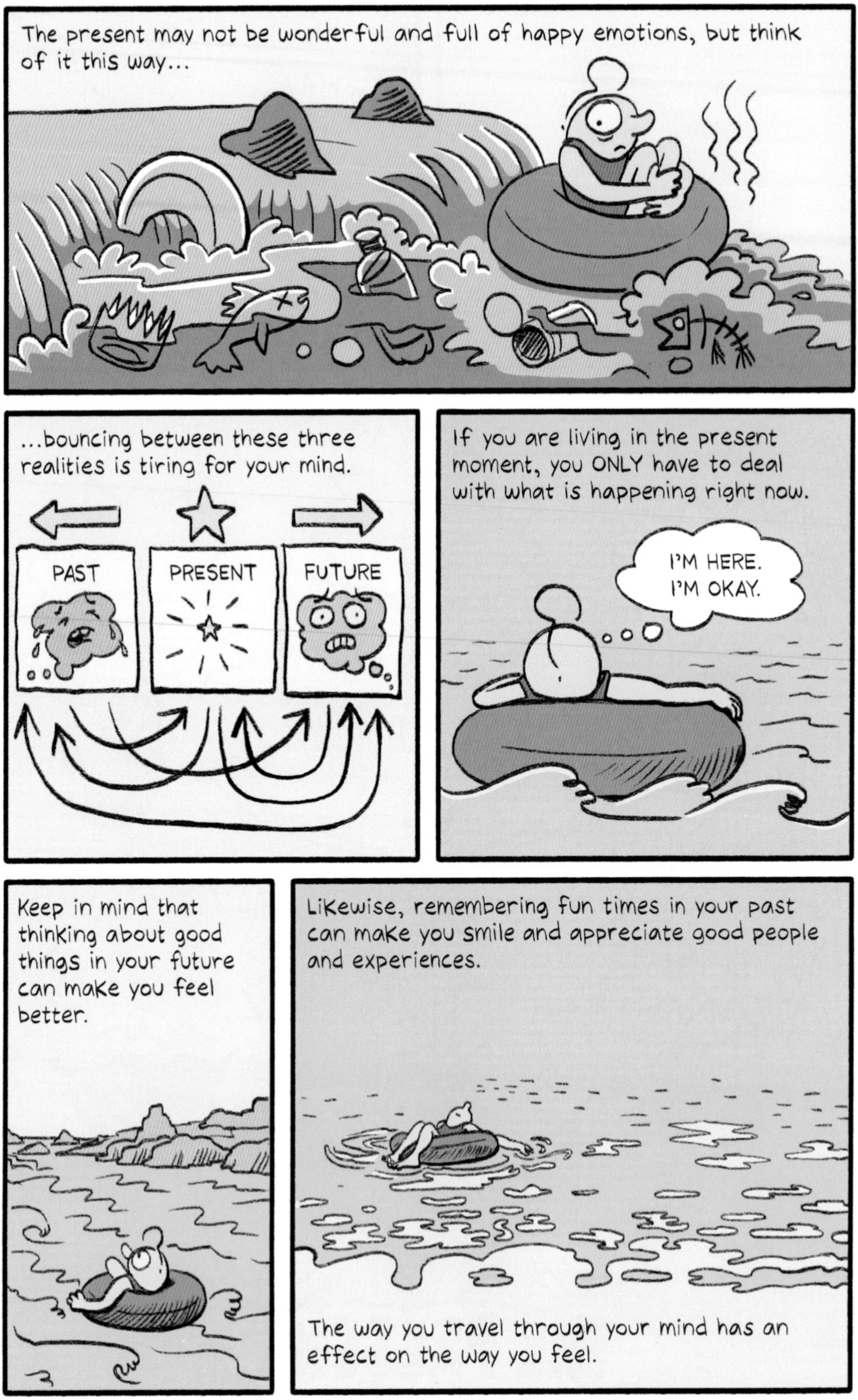
The present may not be wonderful and full of happy emotions, but think of it this way...
...bouncing between these three realities is tiring for your mind.
PAST
PRESENT
FUTURE
If you are living in the present moment, you ONLY have to deal with what is happening right now.
I'M HERE.
I'M OKAY.
Keep in mind that thinking about good things in your future can make you feel better.
Likewise, remembering fun times in your past can make you smile and appreciate good people and experiences.
The way you travel through your mind has an effect on the way you feel.

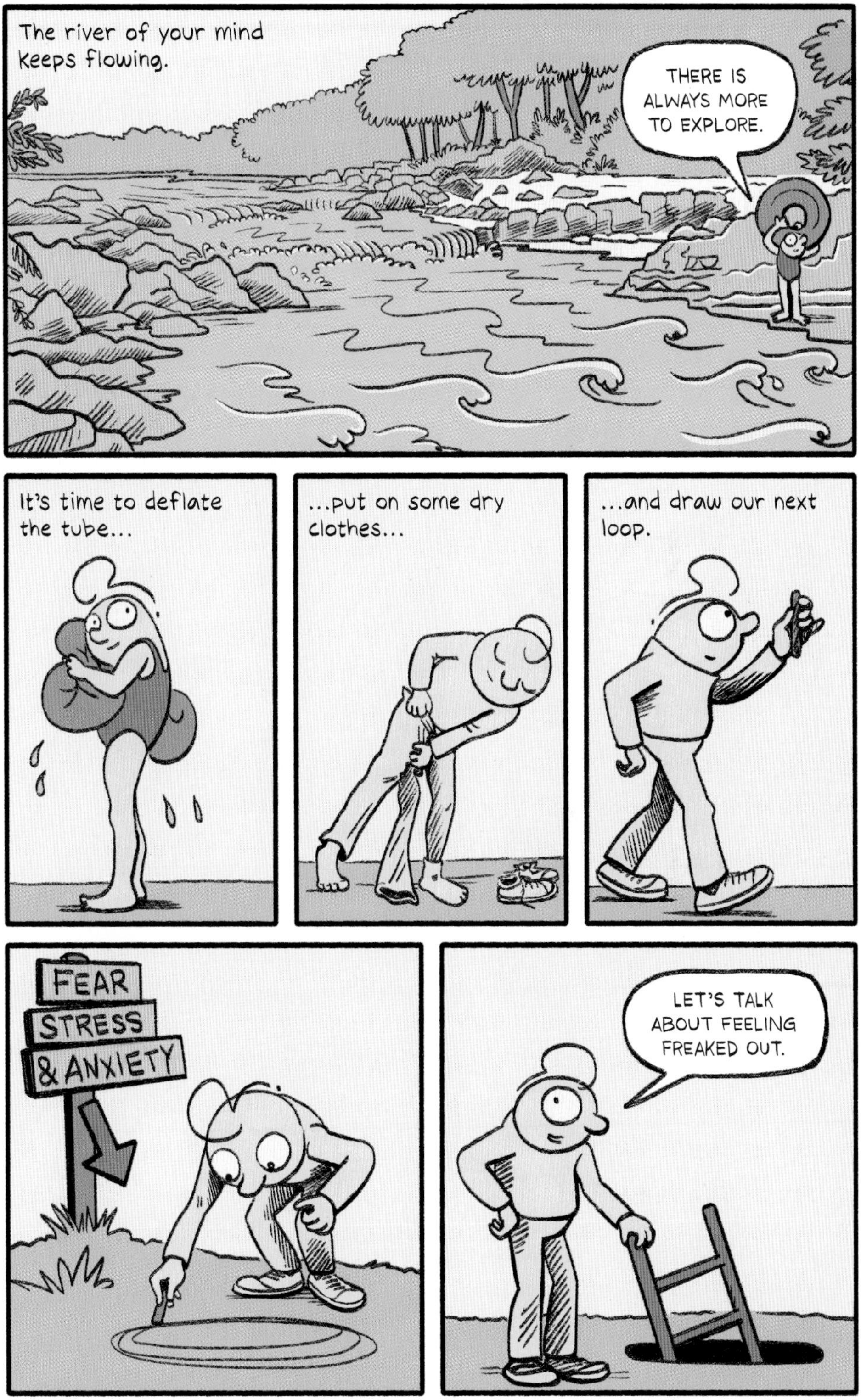
The river of your mind keeps flowing.
THERE IS ALWAYS MORE TO EXPLORE.
It's time to deflate the tube...
...put on some dry clothes...
...and draw our next loop.
FEAR
STRESS
& ANXIETY
LET'S TALK ABOUT FEELING FREAKED OUT.

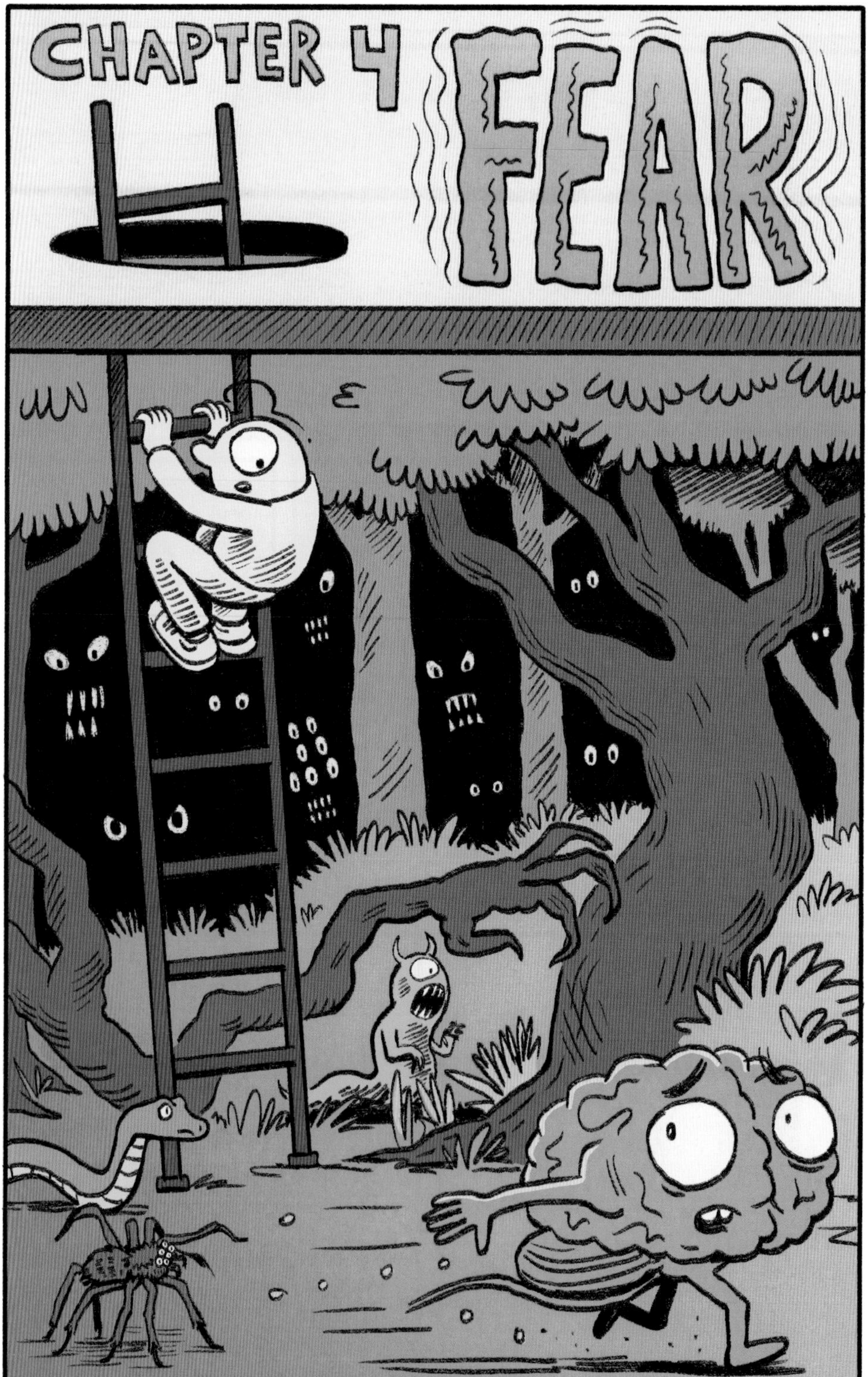
CHAPTER 4
FEAR

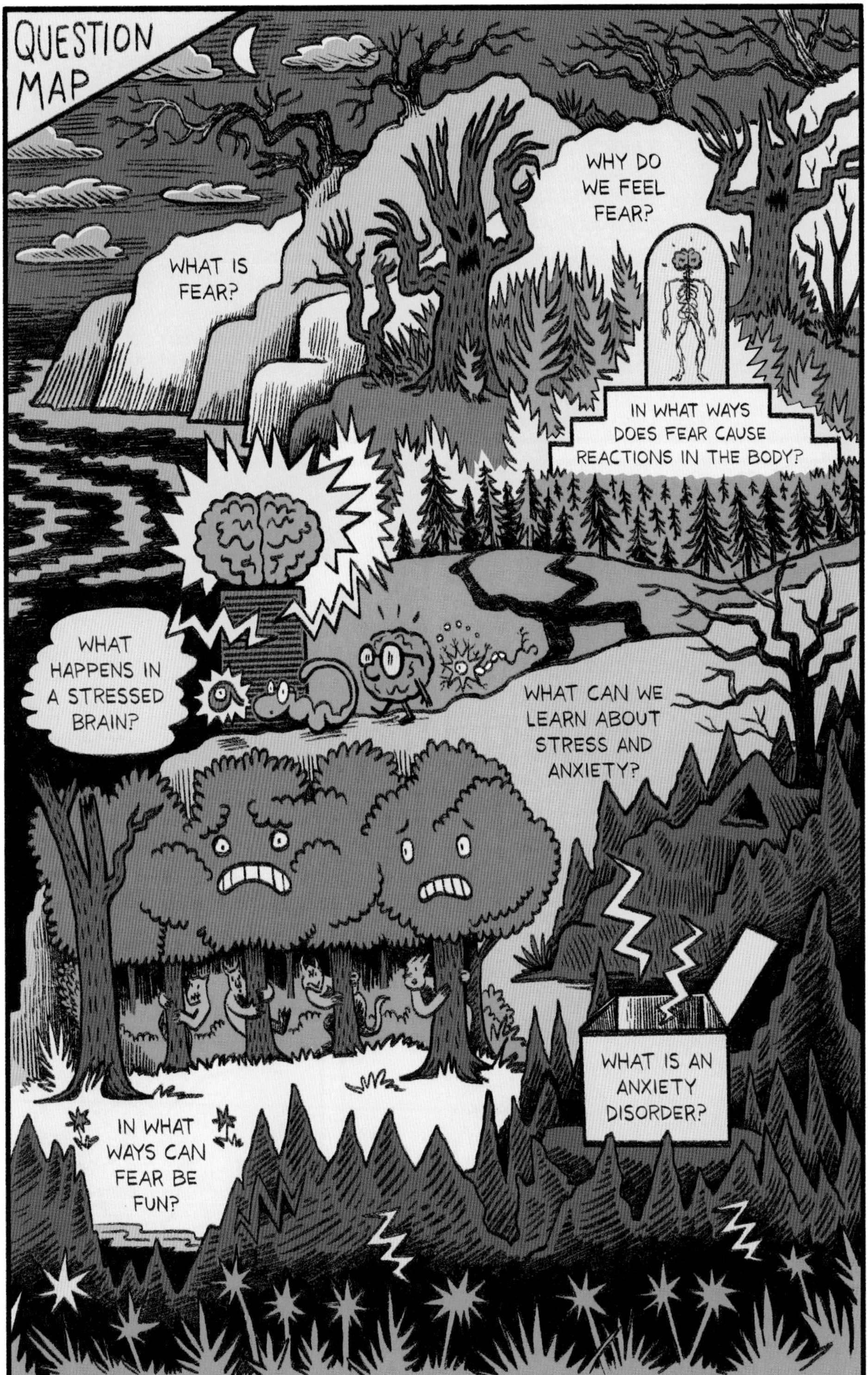
QUESTION MAP
WHAT IS FEAR?
WHY DO WE FEEL FEAR?
IN WHAT WAYS DOES FEAR CAUSE REACTIONS IN THE BODY?
WHAT HAPPENS IN A STRESSED BRAIN?
WHAT CAN WE LEARN ABOUT STRESS AND ANXIETY?
WHAT IS AN ANXIETY DISORDER?
IN WHAT WAYS CAN FEAR BE FUN?

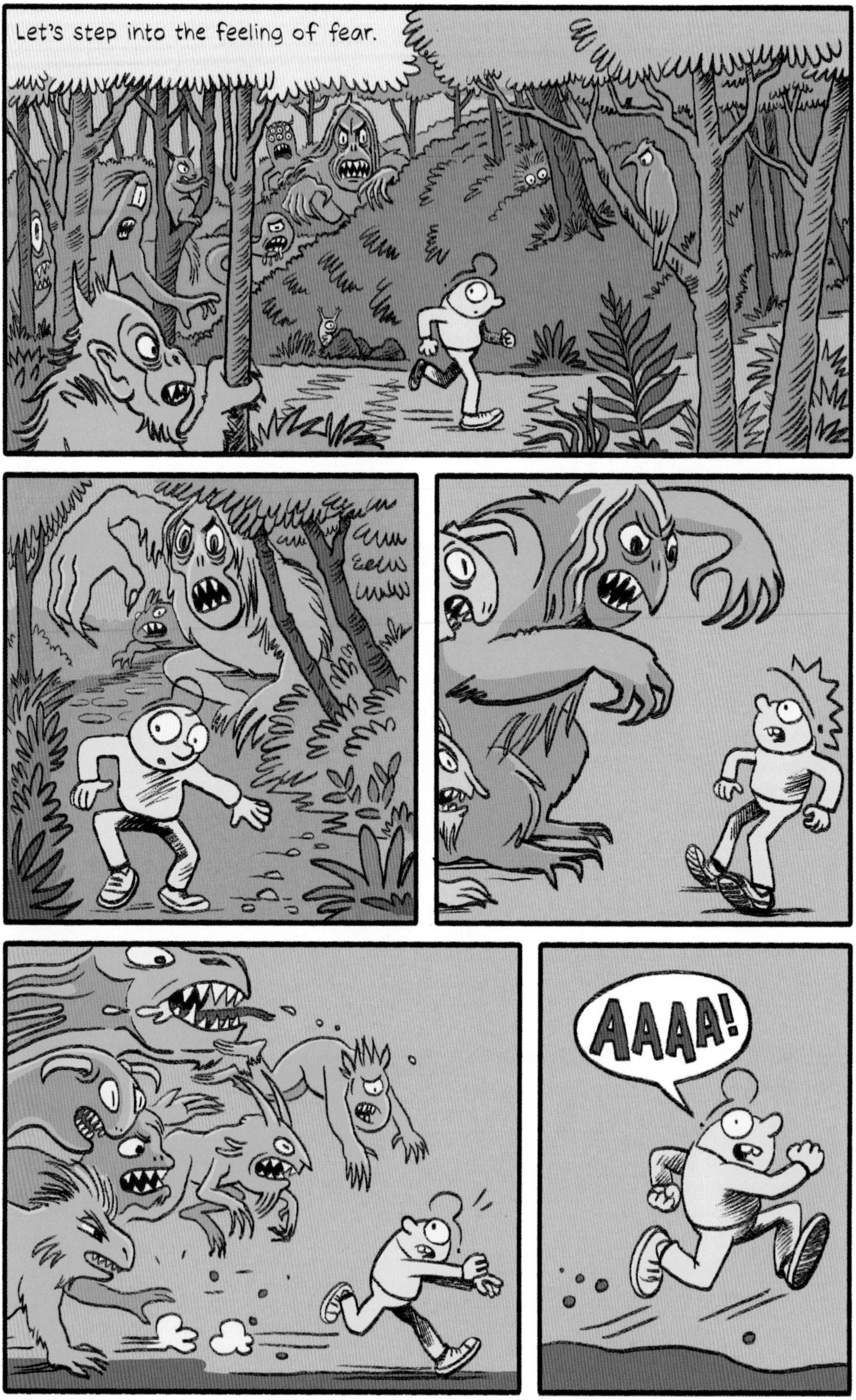
Let's step into the feeling of fear.
AAAA!

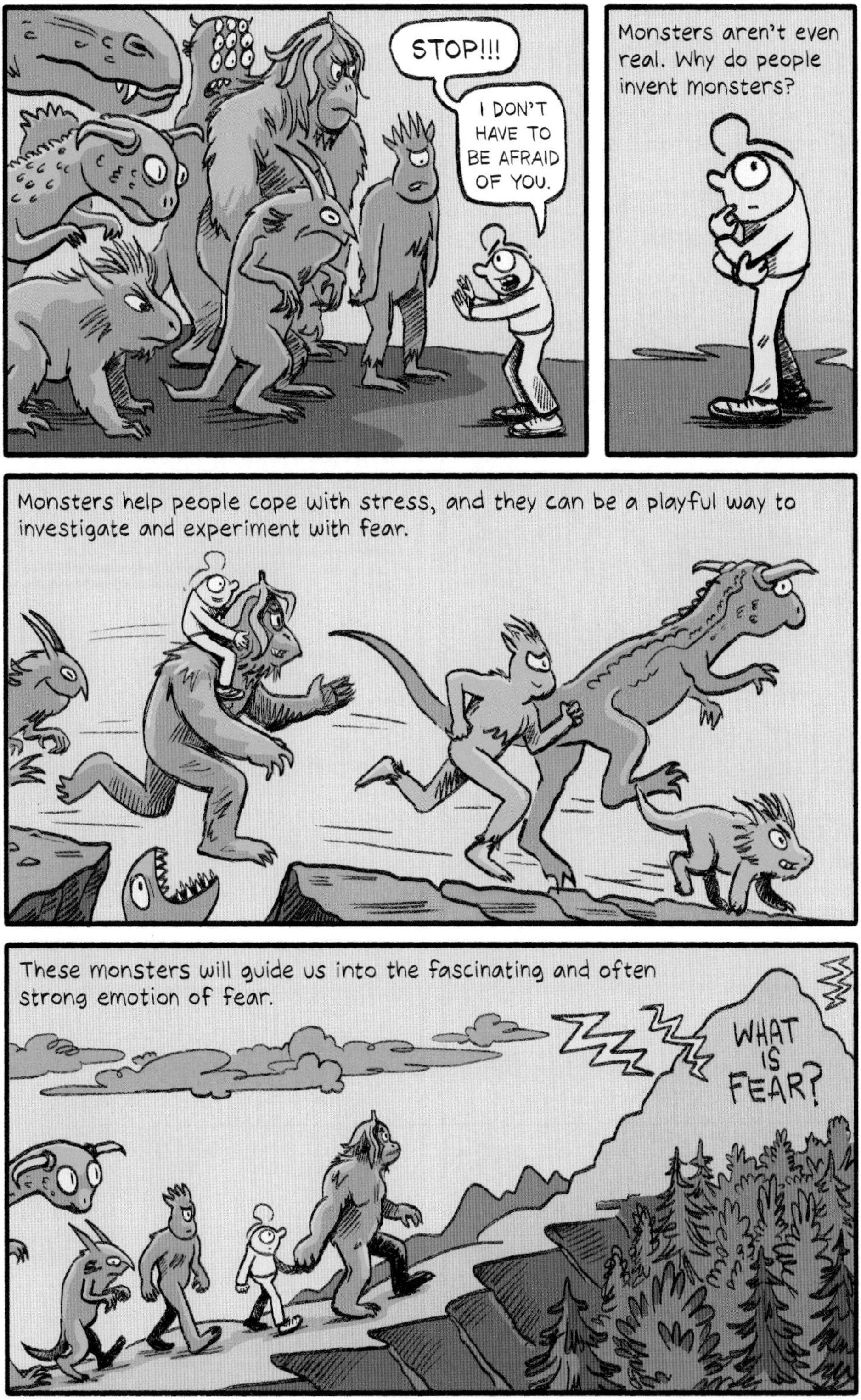
STOP!!!
I DON'T HAVE TO BE AFRAID OF YOU.
Monsters aren't even real. Why do people invent monsters?
Monsters help people cope with stress, and they can be a playful way to investigate and experiment with fear.
These monsters will guide us into the fascinating and often strong emotion of fear.
WHAT IS FEAR?

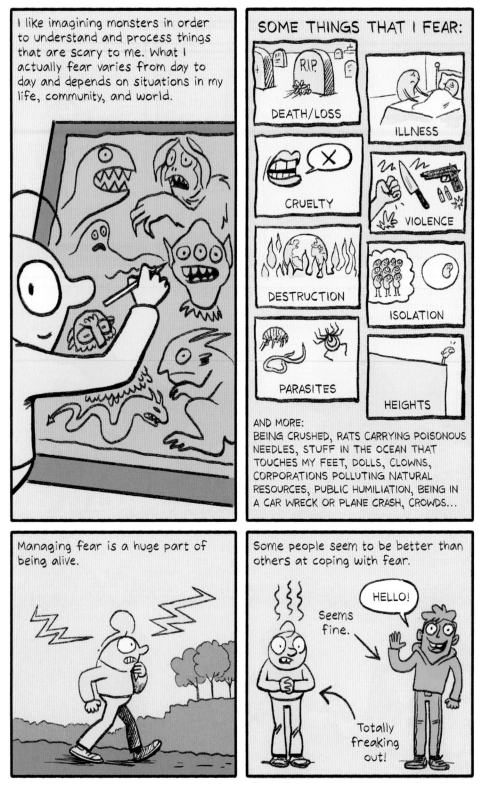

I like imagining monsters in order to understand and process things that are scary to me. What I actually fear varies from day to day and depends on situations in my life, community, and world.

SOME THINGS THAT I FEAR:

DEATH/LOSS

ILLNESS

CRUELTY

VIOLENCE

DESTRUCTION

ISOLATION

PARASITES

HEIGHTS

AND MORE:
BEING CRUSHED, RATS CARRYING POISONOUS NEEDLES, STUFF IN THE OCEAN THAT TOUCHES MY FEET, DOLLS, CLOWNS, CORPORATIONS POLLUTING NATURAL RESOURCES, PUBLIC HUMILIATION, BEING IN A CAR WRECK OR PLANE CRASH, CROWDS...

Managing fear is a huge part of being alive.

Some people seem to be better than others at coping with fear.

HELLO!

Seems fine.

Totally freaking out!

FEAR IS NECESSARY

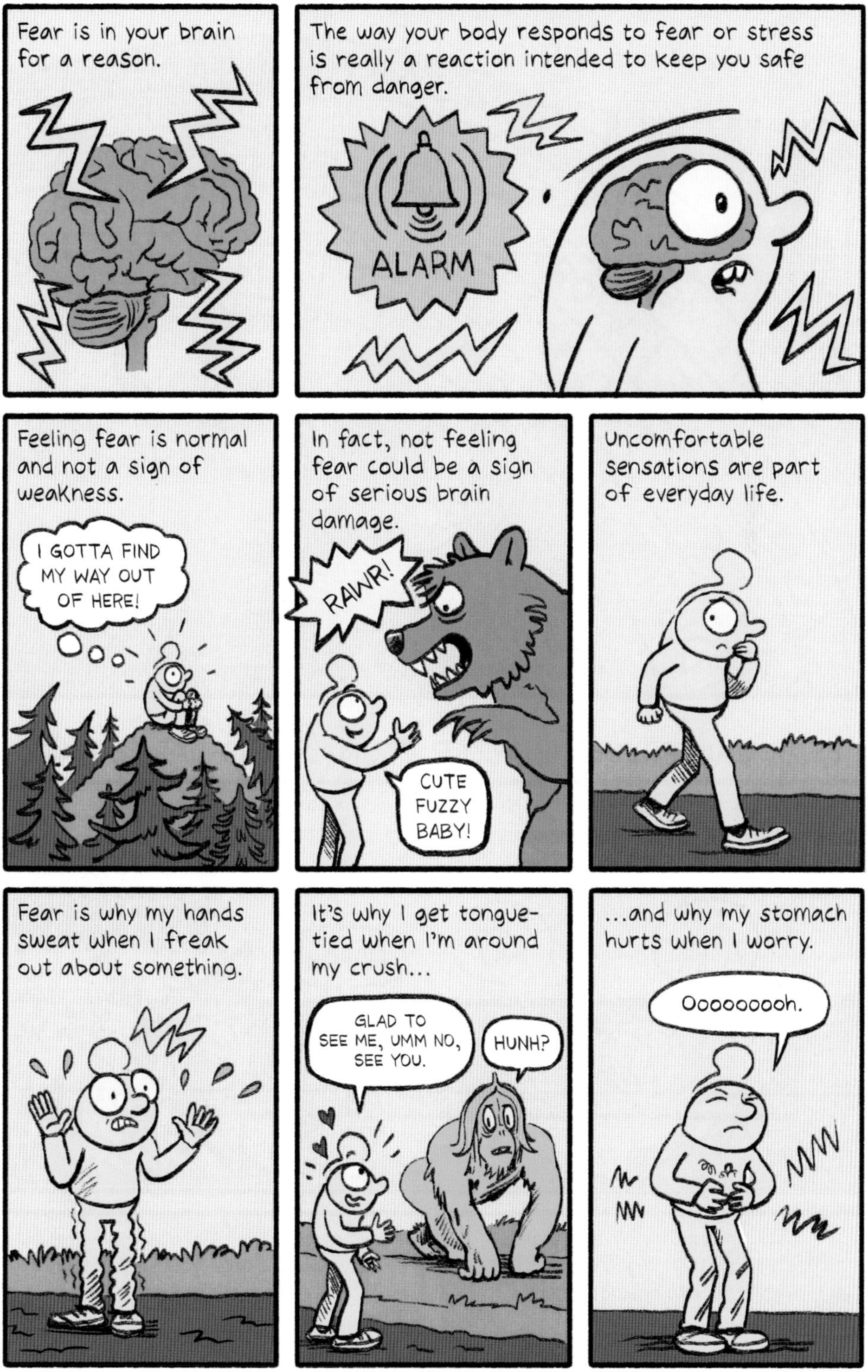

Fear is in your brain for a reason.
The way your body responds to fear or stress is really a reaction intended to keep you safe from danger.
ALARM
Feeling fear is normal and not a sign of weakness.
I GOTTA FIND MY WAY OUT OF HERE!
In fact, not feeling fear could be a sign of serious brain damage.
RAWR!
CUTE FUZZY BABY!
Uncomfortable sensations are part of everyday life.
Fear is why my hands sweat when I freak out about something.
It's why I get tongue-tied when I'm around my crush...
GLAD TO SEE ME, UMM NO, SEE YOU.
HUNH?
...and why my stomach hurts when I worry.
Oooooooh.

WHAT IS FEAR?

Fear represents a whole spectrum of emotions.

AWE | JITTERS | ALARM | PANIC | STU
EXCITEMENT | NERVES | TERROR | FRE
SURPRISE | WORRY | ANGER | TRAUMA | TR
ANTICIPATION | EXASPERATION | ME
DISTRESS | INSECURITY | ANXIETY | EM

FEAR CAN PRESENT ITSELF IN SMALL AND LARGE WAYS

You may be having a low-intensity feeling or a high-intensity feeling.

I'M ON ALERT.

OH NO!

AAAAH!

MAXIMUM FREAKED!

Even though many emotions feel bad, it is important to be able to experience them.

Emotions are signals that are trying to catch your attention for a reason.

FEAR TENDS TO FALL INTO TWO CATEGORIES

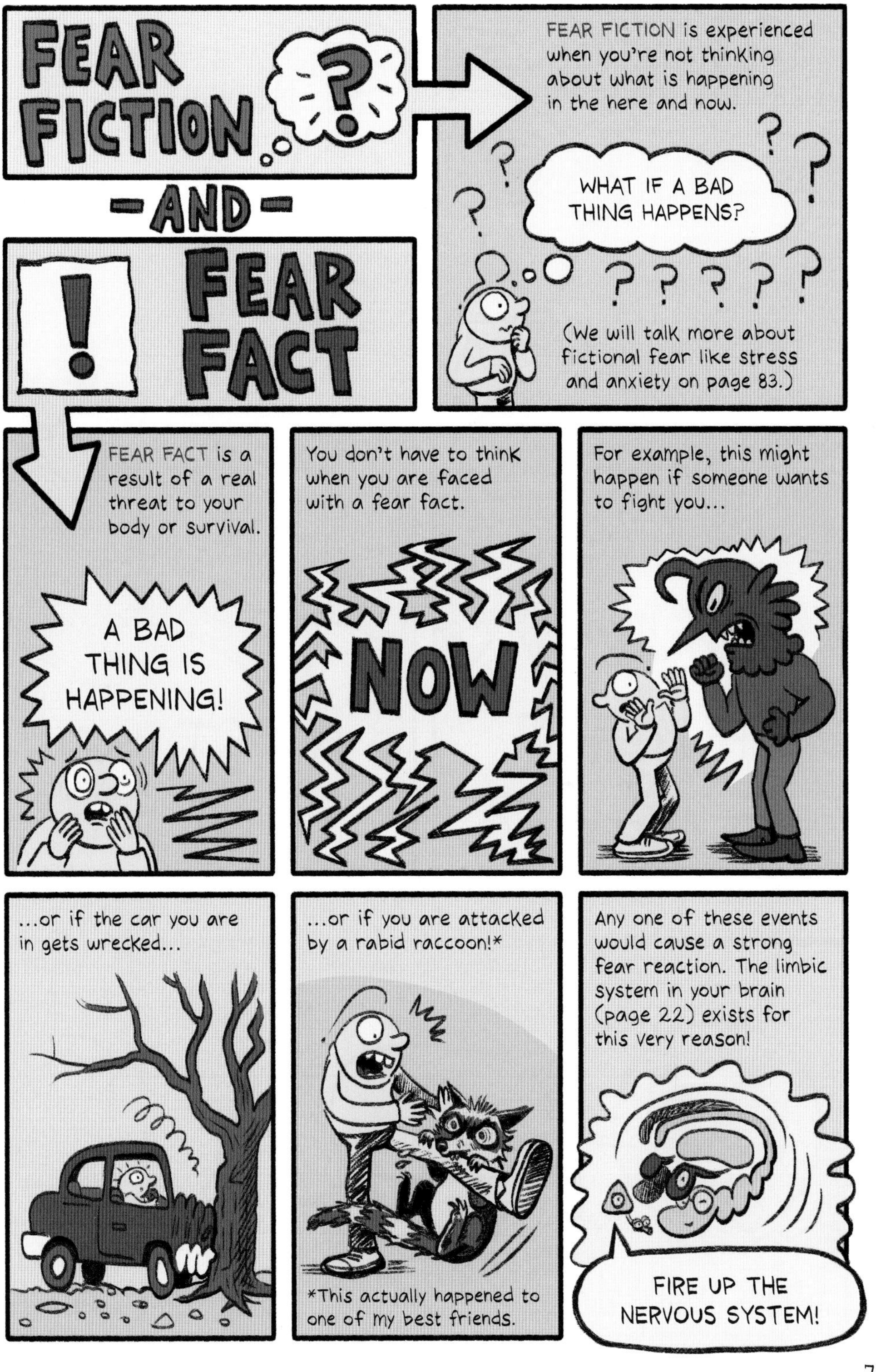
FEAR FICTION
?
-AND-
!
FEAR FACT
FEAR FICTION is experienced when you're not thinking about what is happening in the here and now.
WHAT IF A BAD THING HAPPENS?
(We will talk more about fictional fear like stress and anxiety on page 83.)
FEAR FACT is a result of a real threat to your body or survival.
A BAD THING IS HAPPENING!
You don't have to think when you are faced with a fear fact.
NOW
For example, this might happen if someone wants to fight you...
...or if the car you are in gets wrecked...
...or if you are attacked by a rabid raccoon!*
*This actually happened to one of my best friends.
Any one of these events would cause a strong fear reaction. The limbic system in your brain (page 22) exists for this very reason!
FIRE UP THE NERVOUS SYSTEM!

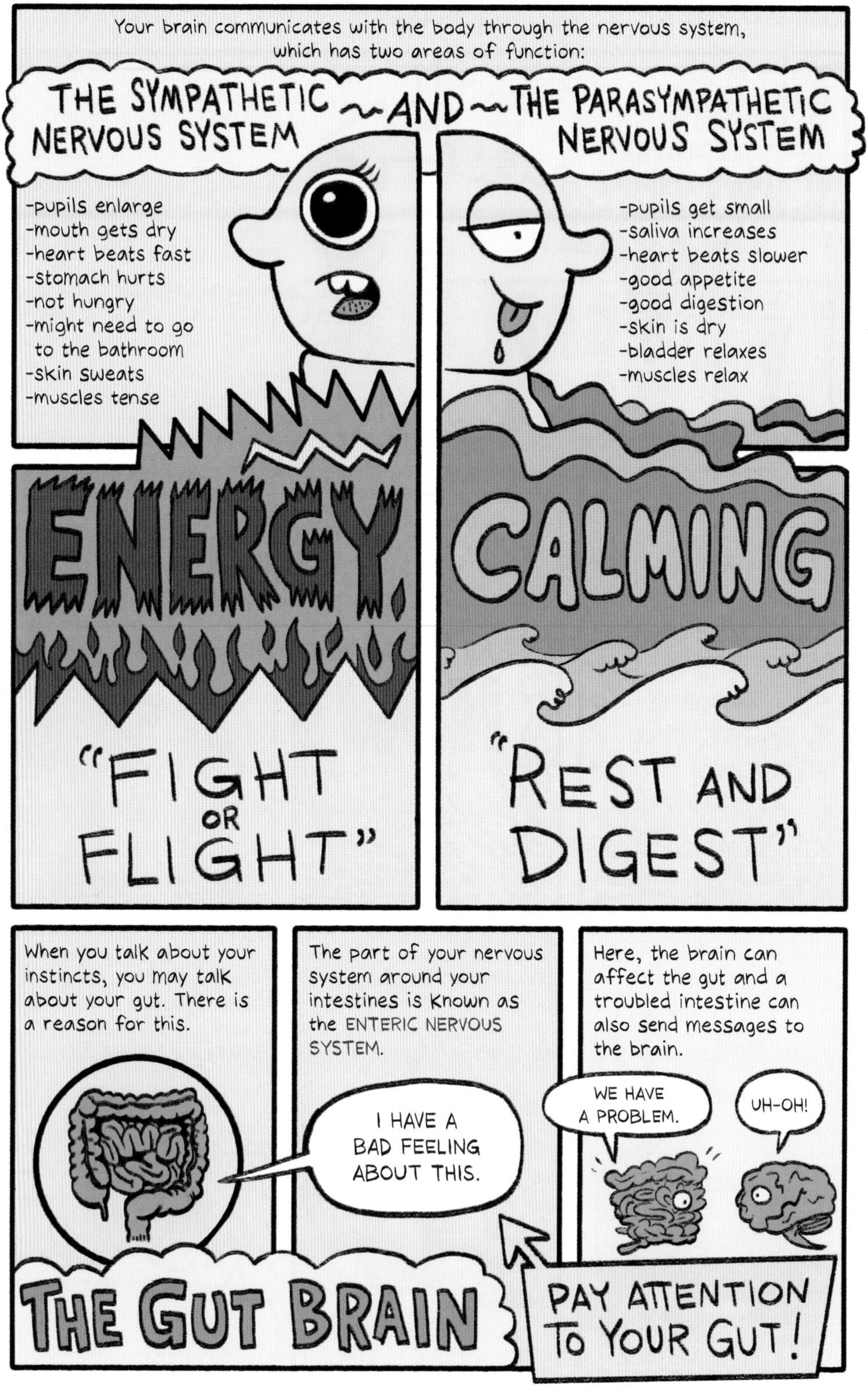

Your brain communicates with the body through the nervous system, which has two areas of function:
THE SYMPATHETIC NERVOUS SYSTEM
AND
THE PARASYMPATHETIC NERVOUS SYSTEM
-pupils enlarge
-mouth gets dry
-heart beats fast
-stomach hurts
-not hungry
-might need to go to the bathroom
-skin sweats
-muscles tense
-pupils get small
-saliva increases
-heart beats slower
-good appetite
-good digestion
-skin is dry
-bladder relaxes
-muscles relax
ENERGY
CALMING
"FIGHT OR FLIGHT"
"REST AND DIGEST"
When you talk about your instincts, you may talk about your gut. There is a reason for this.
The part of your nervous system around your intestines is known as the ENTERIC NERVOUS SYSTEM.
I HAVE A BAD FEELING ABOUT THIS.
Here, the brain can affect the gut and a troubled intestine can also send messages to the brain.
WE HAVE A PROBLEM.
UH-OH!
THE GUT BRAIN
PAY ATTENTION TO YOUR GUT!

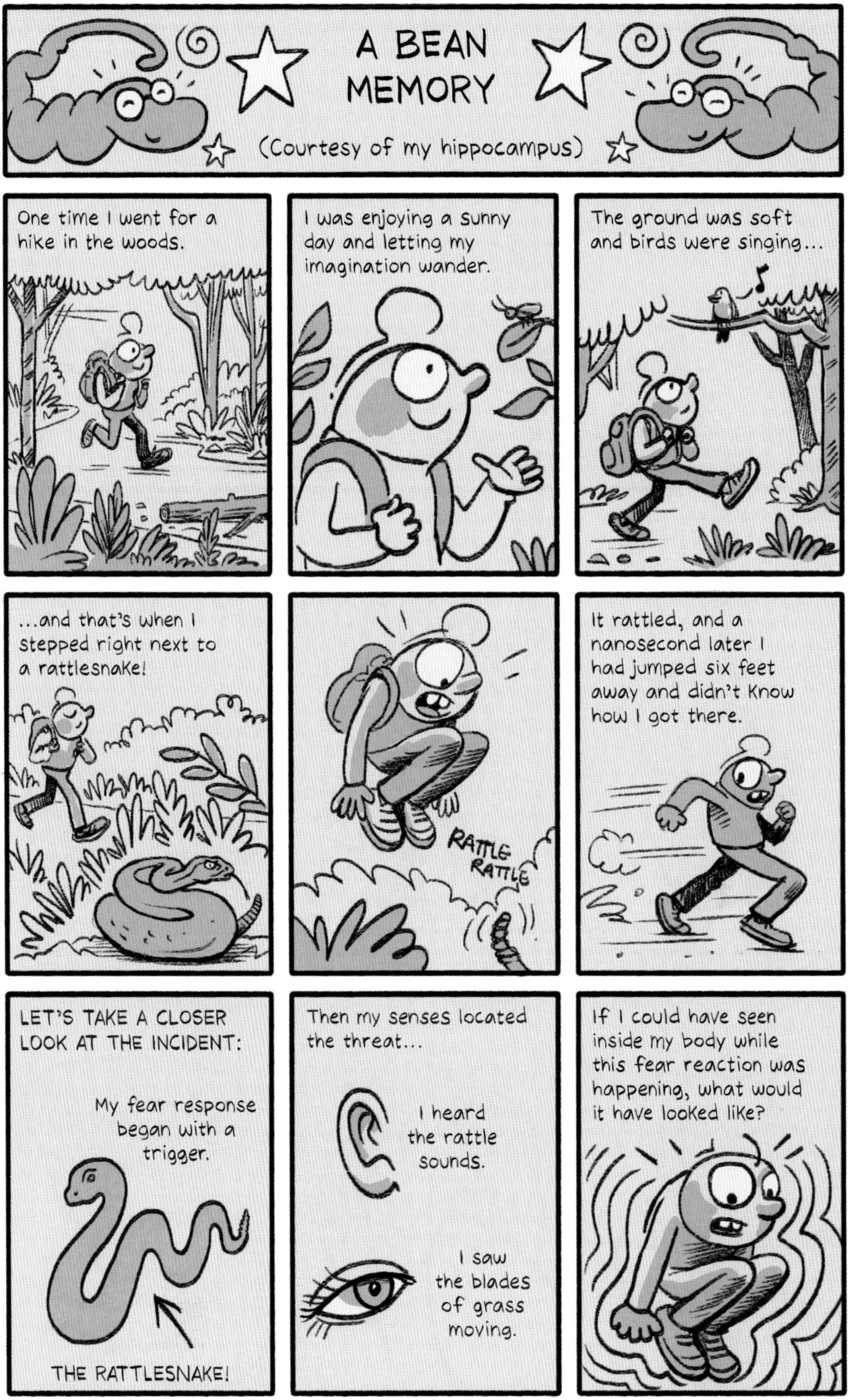
A BEAN MEMORY
(Courtesy of my hippocampus)
One time I went for a hike in the woods.
I was enjoying a sunny day and letting my imagination wander.
The ground was soft and birds were singing...
...and that's when I stepped right next to a rattlesnake!
RATTLE RATTLE
It rattled, and a nanosecond later I had jumped six feet away and didn't know how I got there.
LET'S TAKE A CLOSER LOOK AT THE INCIDENT:
My fear response began with a trigger.
THE RATTLESNAKE!
Then my senses located the threat...
I heard the rattle sounds.
I saw the blades of grass moving.
If I could have seen inside my body while this fear reaction was happening, what would it have looked like?

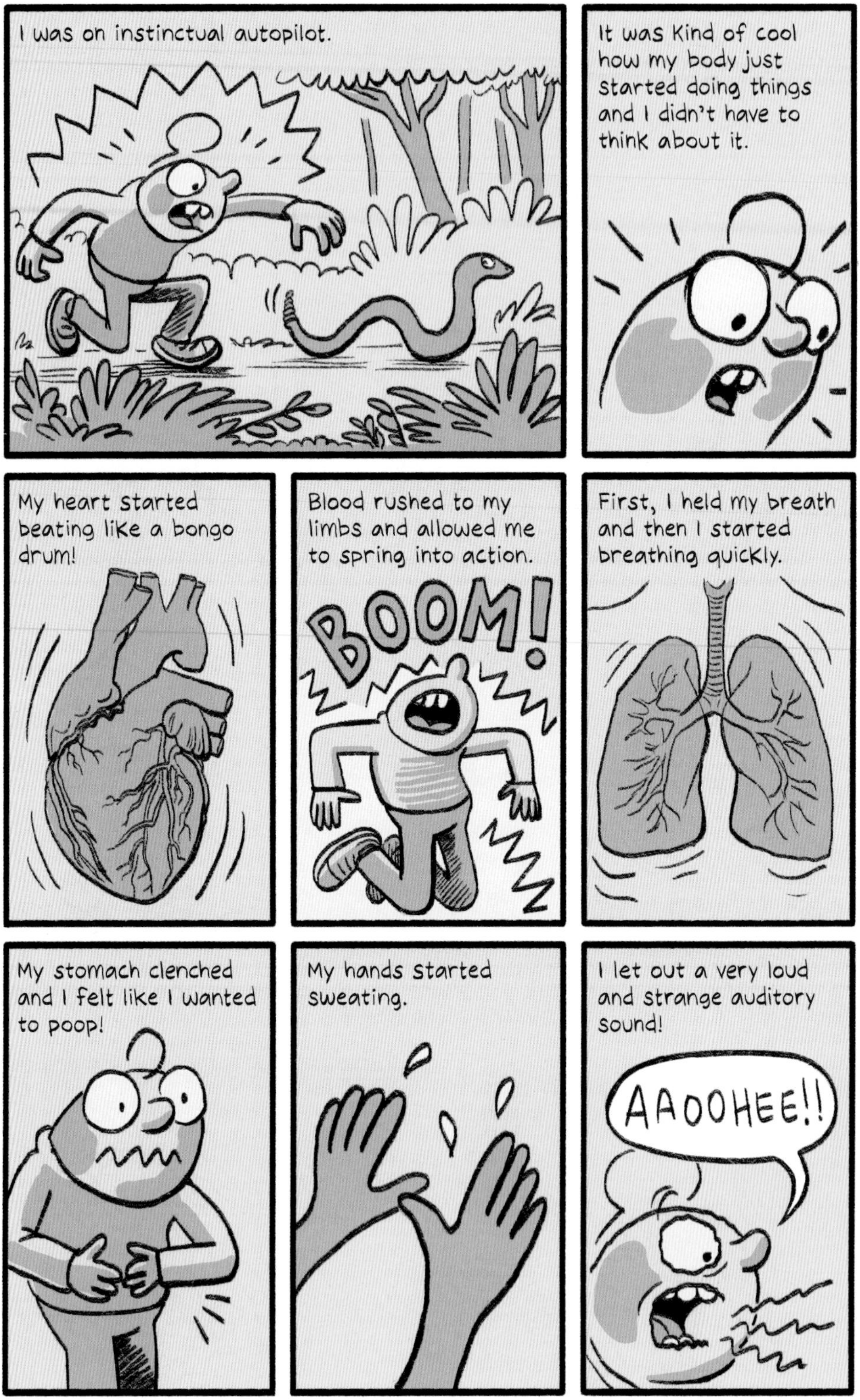
I was on instinctual autopilot.
It was kind of cool how my body just started doing things and I didn't have to think about it.
My heart started beating like a bongo drum!
Blood rushed to my limbs and allowed me to spring into action.
BOOM!
First, I held my breath and then I started breathing quickly.
My stomach clenched and I felt like I wanted to poop!
My hands started sweating.
I let out a very loud and strange auditory sound!
AAOOHEE!!

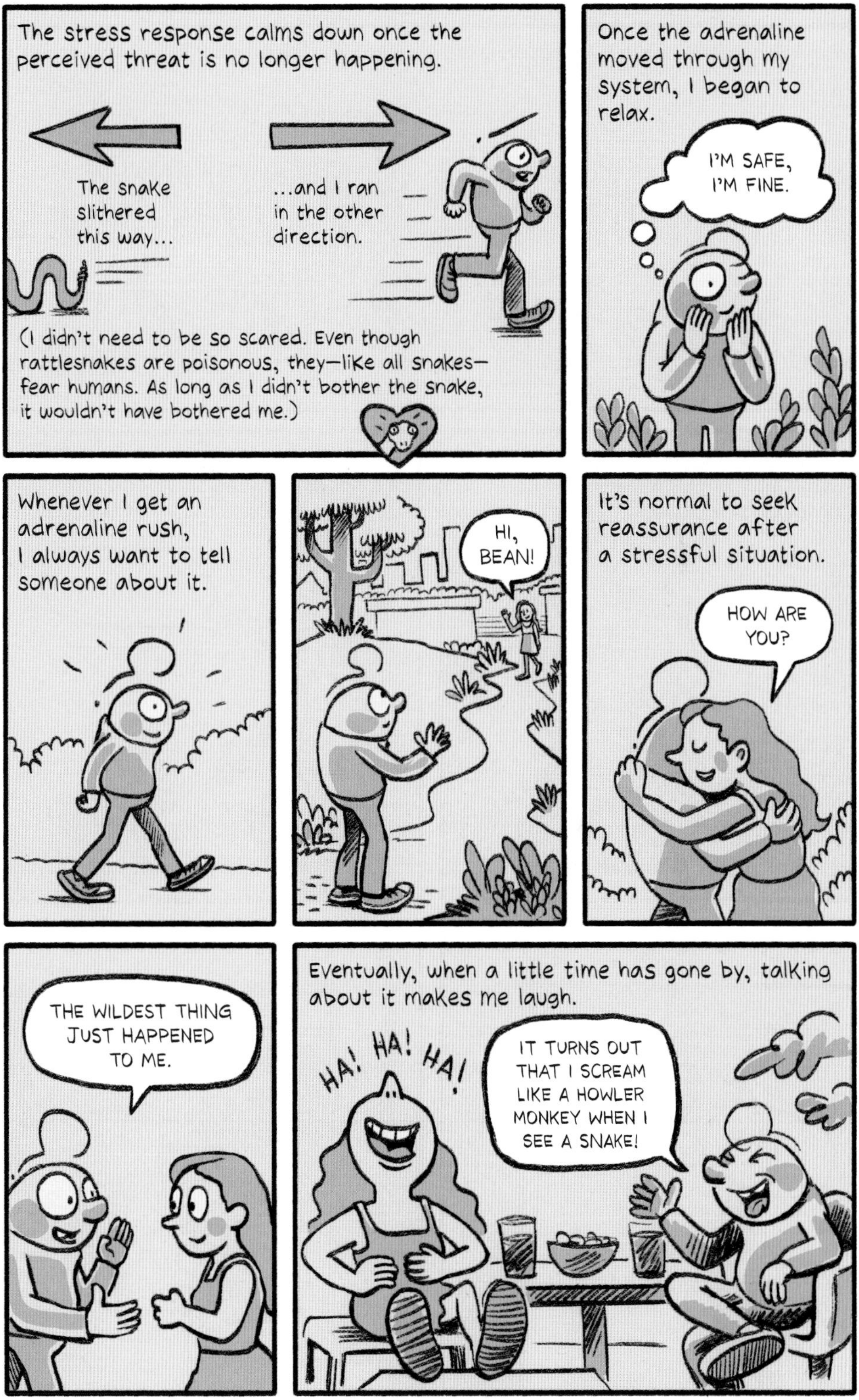

The stress response calms down once the perceived threat is no longer happening.
The snake slithered this way...
...and I ran in the other direction.
(I didn't need to be so scared. Even though rattlesnakes are poisonous, they—like all snakes—fear humans. As long as I didn't bother the snake, it wouldn't have bothered me.)
Once the adrenaline moved through my system, I began to relax.
I'M SAFE, I'M FINE.
Whenever I get an adrenaline rush, I always want to tell someone about it.
HI, BEAN!
It's normal to seek reassurance after a stressful situation.
HOW ARE YOU?
THE WILDEST THING JUST HAPPENED TO ME.
Eventually, when a little time has gone by, talking about it makes me laugh.
HA! HA! HA!
IT TURNS OUT THAT I SCREAM LIKE A HOWLER MONKEY WHEN I SEE A SNAKE!

FEAR AND EVOLUTION

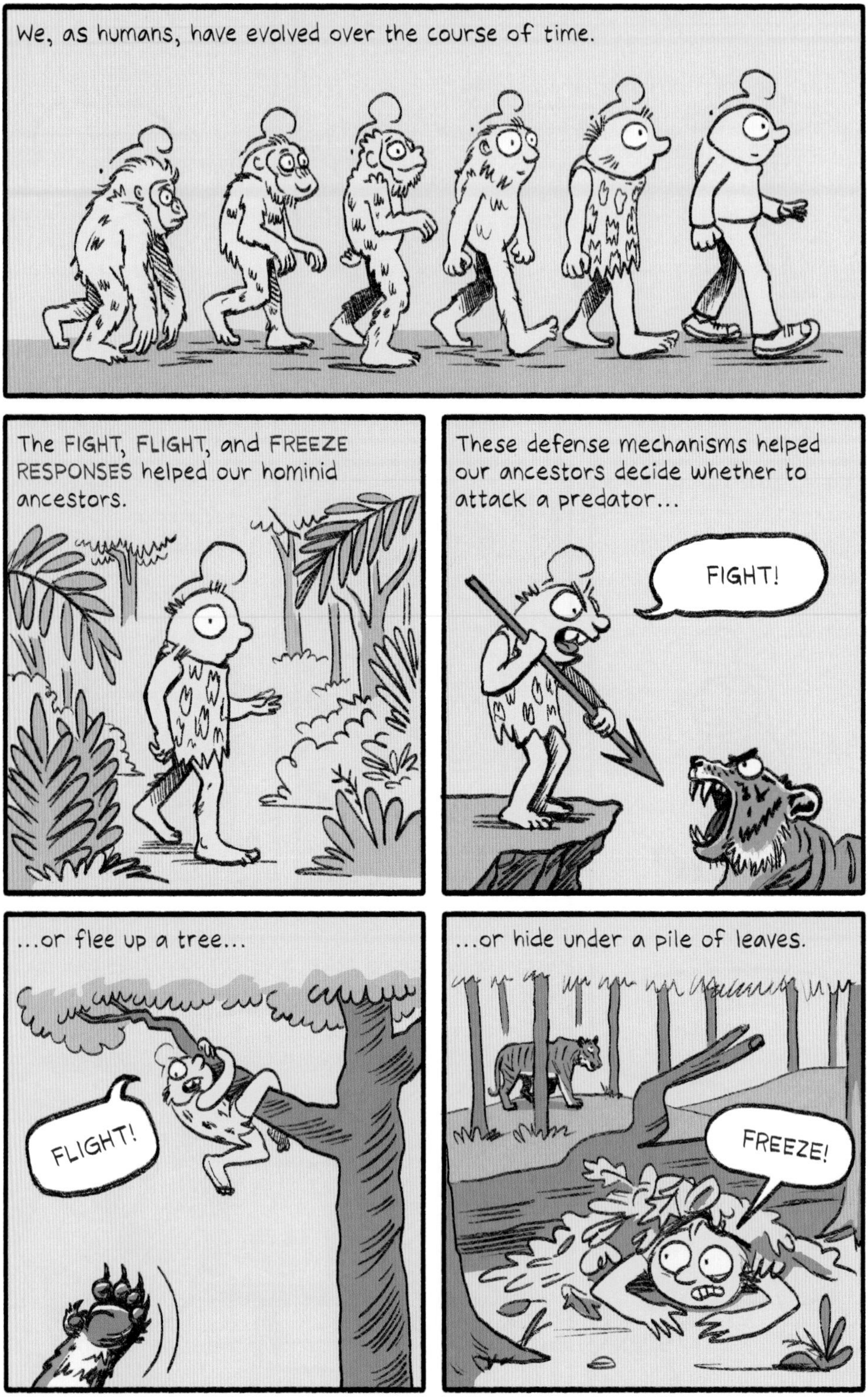
We, as humans, have evolved over the course of time.
The FIGHT, FLIGHT, and FREEZE RESPONSES helped our hominid ancestors.
These defense mechanisms helped our ancestors decide whether to attack a predator...
FIGHT!
...or flee up a tree...
FLIGHT!
...or hide under a pile of leaves.
FREEZE!

WHAT ARE THE NERVOUS SYSTEM'S GO-TO FUNCTIONS?

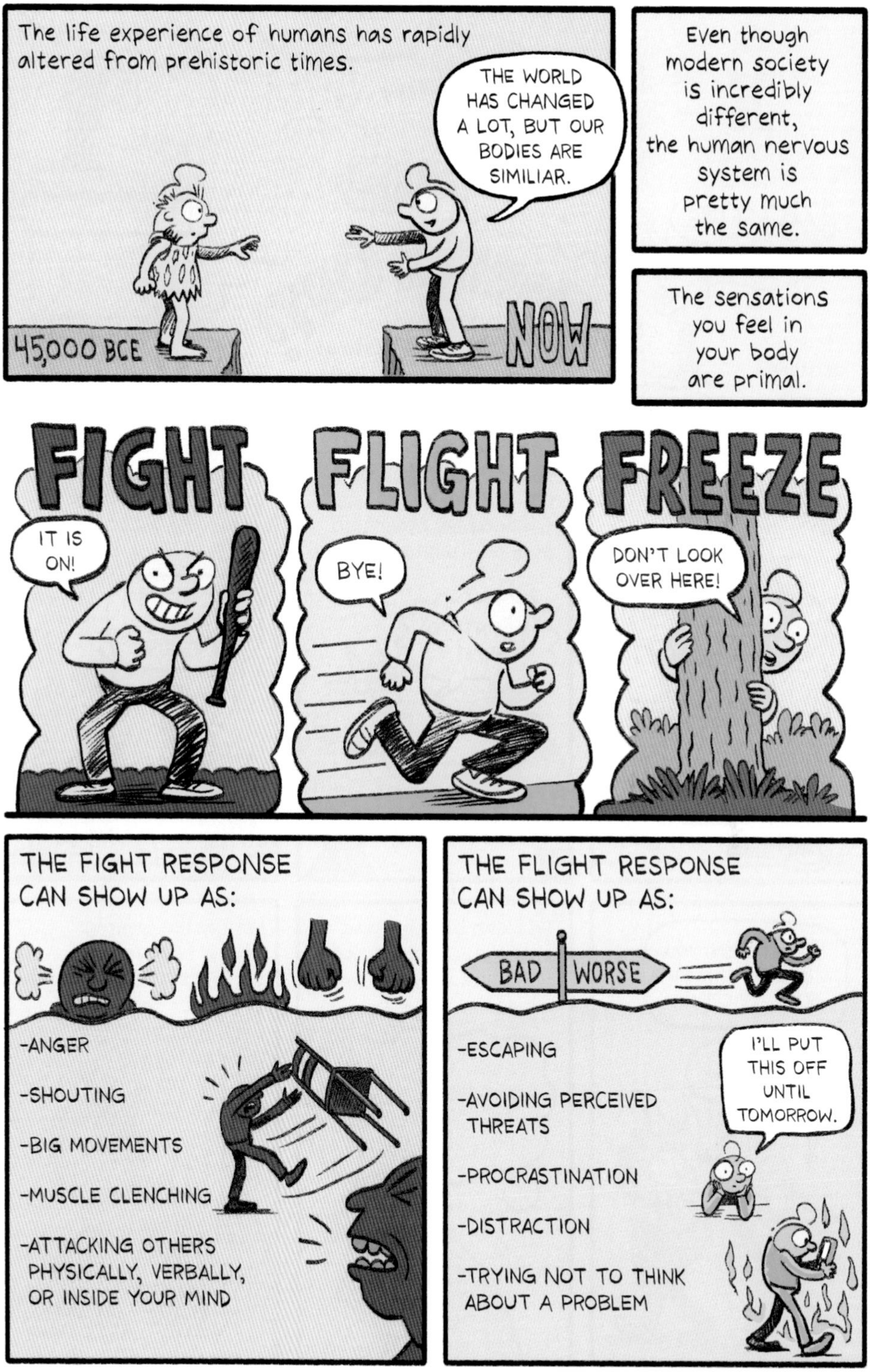

The life experience of humans has rapidly altered from prehistoric times.
THE WORLD HAS CHANGED A LOT, BUT OUR BODIES ARE SIMILIAR.
45,000 BCE
NOW
Even though modern society is incredibly different, the human nervous system is pretty much the same.
The sensations you feel in your body are primal.
FIGHT
IT IS ON!
FLIGHT
BYE!
FREEZE
DON'T LOOK OVER HERE!
THE FIGHT RESPONSE CAN SHOW UP AS:
-ANGER
-SHOUTING
-BIG MOVEMENTS
-MUSCLE CLENCHING
-ATTACKING OTHERS PHYSICALLY, VERBALLY, OR INSIDE YOUR MIND
THE FLIGHT RESPONSE CAN SHOW UP AS:
BAD
WORSE
-ESCAPING
-AVOIDING PERCEIVED THREATS
-PROCRASTINATION
-DISTRACTION
-TRYING NOT TO THINK ABOUT A PROBLEM
I'LL PUT THIS OFF UNTIL TOMORROW.

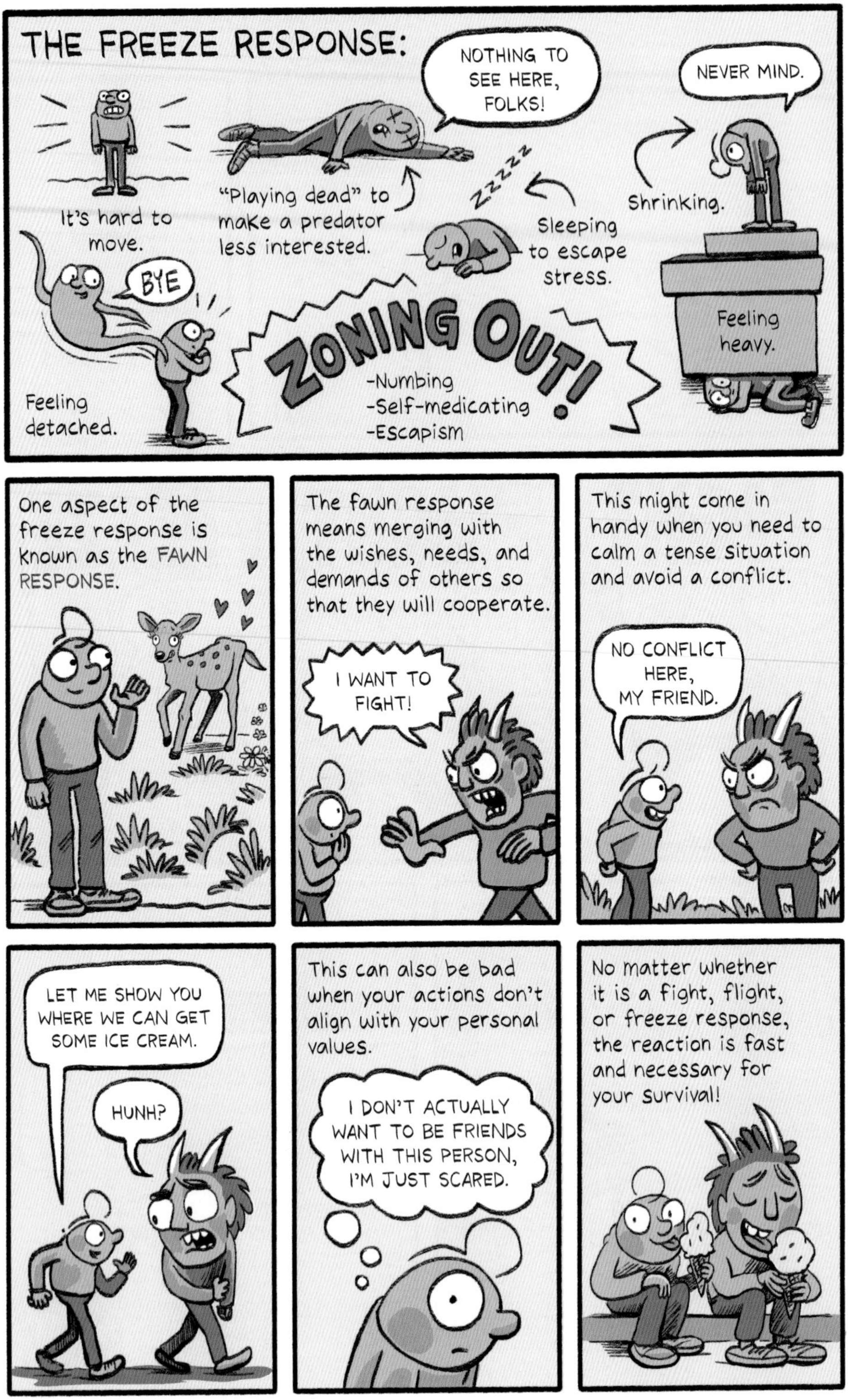
THE FREEZE RESPONSE:
It's hard to move.
"Playing dead" to make a predator less interested.
NOTHING TO SEE HERE, FOLKS!
ZZZZZ
Sleeping to escape stress.
Shrinking.
NEVER MIND.
BYE
Feeling detached.
ZONING OUT!
-Numbing
-Self-medicating
-Escapism
Feeling heavy.
One aspect of the freeze response is known as the FAWN RESPONSE.
The fawn response means merging with the wishes, needs, and demands of others so that they will cooperate.
I WANT TO FIGHT!
This might come in handy when you need to calm a tense situation and avoid a conflict.
NO CONFLICT HERE, MY FRIEND.
LET ME SHOW YOU WHERE WE CAN GET SOME ICE CREAM.
HUNH?
This can also be bad when your actions don't align with your personal values.
I DON'T ACTUALLY WANT TO BE FRIENDS WITH THIS PERSON, I'M JUST SCARED.
No matter whether it is a fight, flight, or freeze response, the reaction is fast and necessary for your survival!

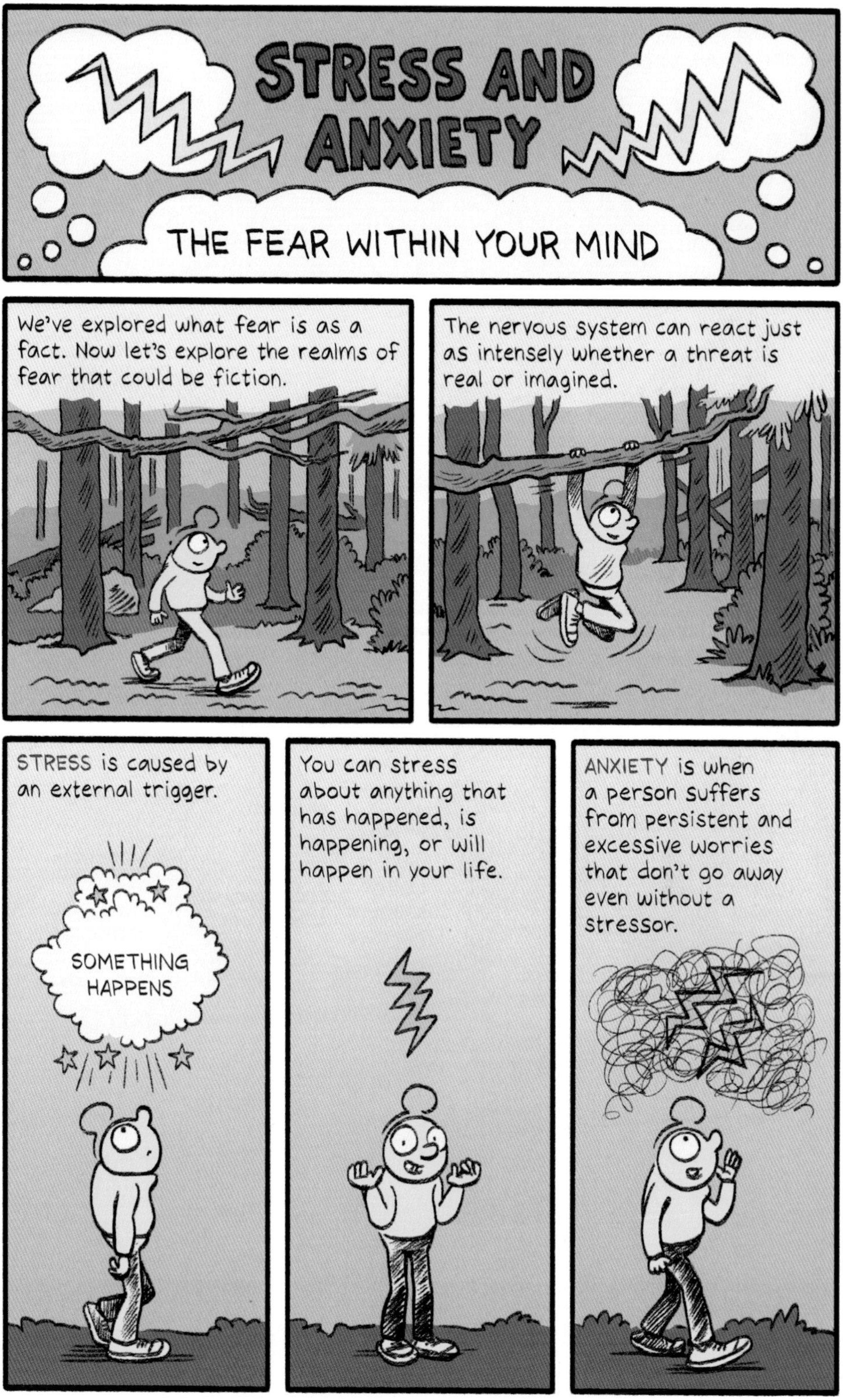
STRESS AND ANXIETY
THE FEAR WITHIN YOUR MIND
We've explored what fear is as a fact. Now let's explore the realms of fear that could be fiction.
The nervous system can react just as intensely whether a threat is real or imagined.
STRESS is caused by an external trigger.
SOMETHING HAPPENS
You can stress about anything that has happened, is happening, or will happen in your life.
ANXIETY is when a person suffers from persistent and excessive worries that don't go away even without a stressor.

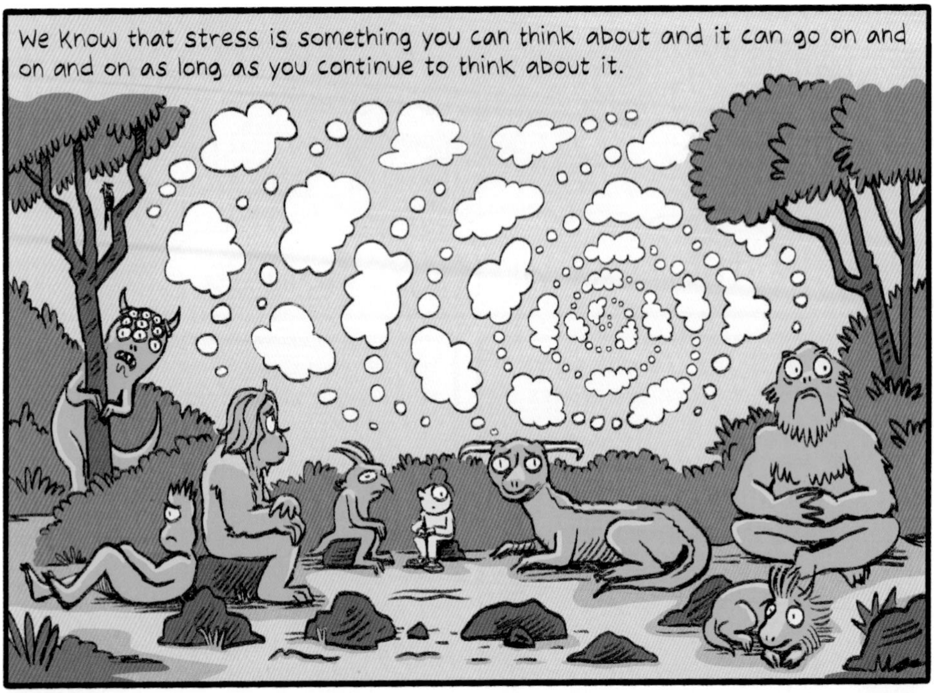
We know that stress is something you can think about and it can go on and on and on as long as you continue to think about it.

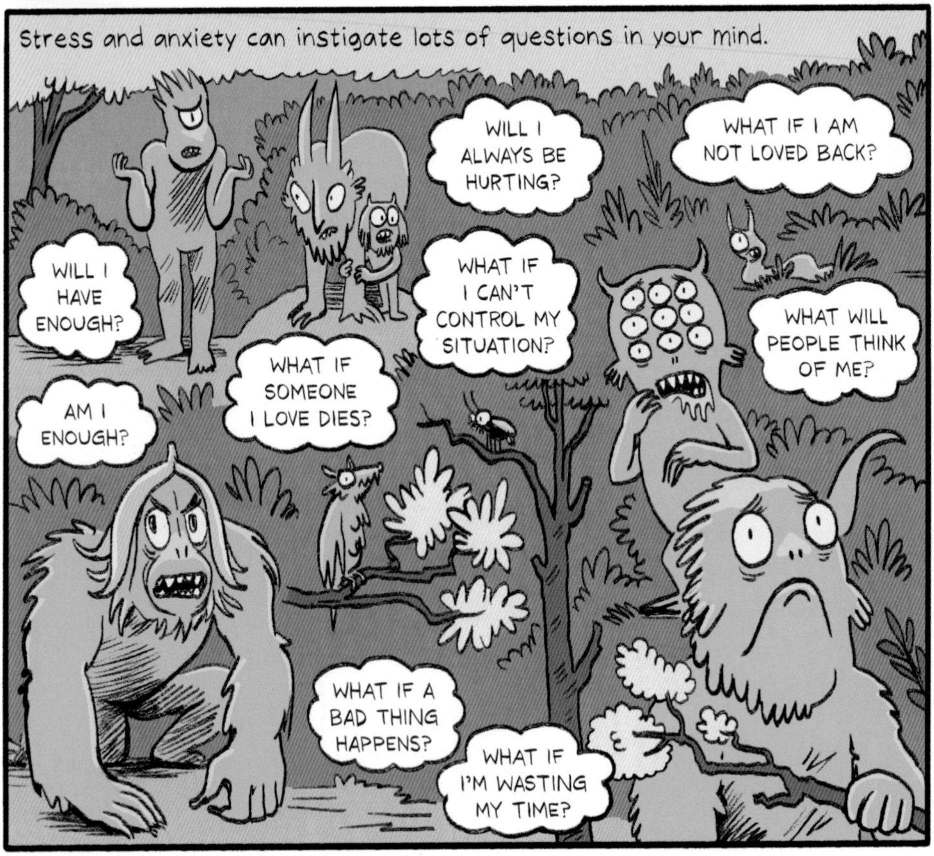
Stress and anxiety can instigate lots of questions in your mind.
WILL I ALWAYS BE HURTING?
WHAT IF I AM NOT LOVED BACK?
WILL I HAVE ENOUGH?
WHAT IF I CAN'T CONTROL MY SITUATION?
WHAT WILL PEOPLE THINK OF ME?
WHAT IF SOMEONE I LOVE DIES?
AM I ENOUGH?
WHAT IF A BAD THING HAPPENS?
WHAT IF I'M WASTING MY TIME?

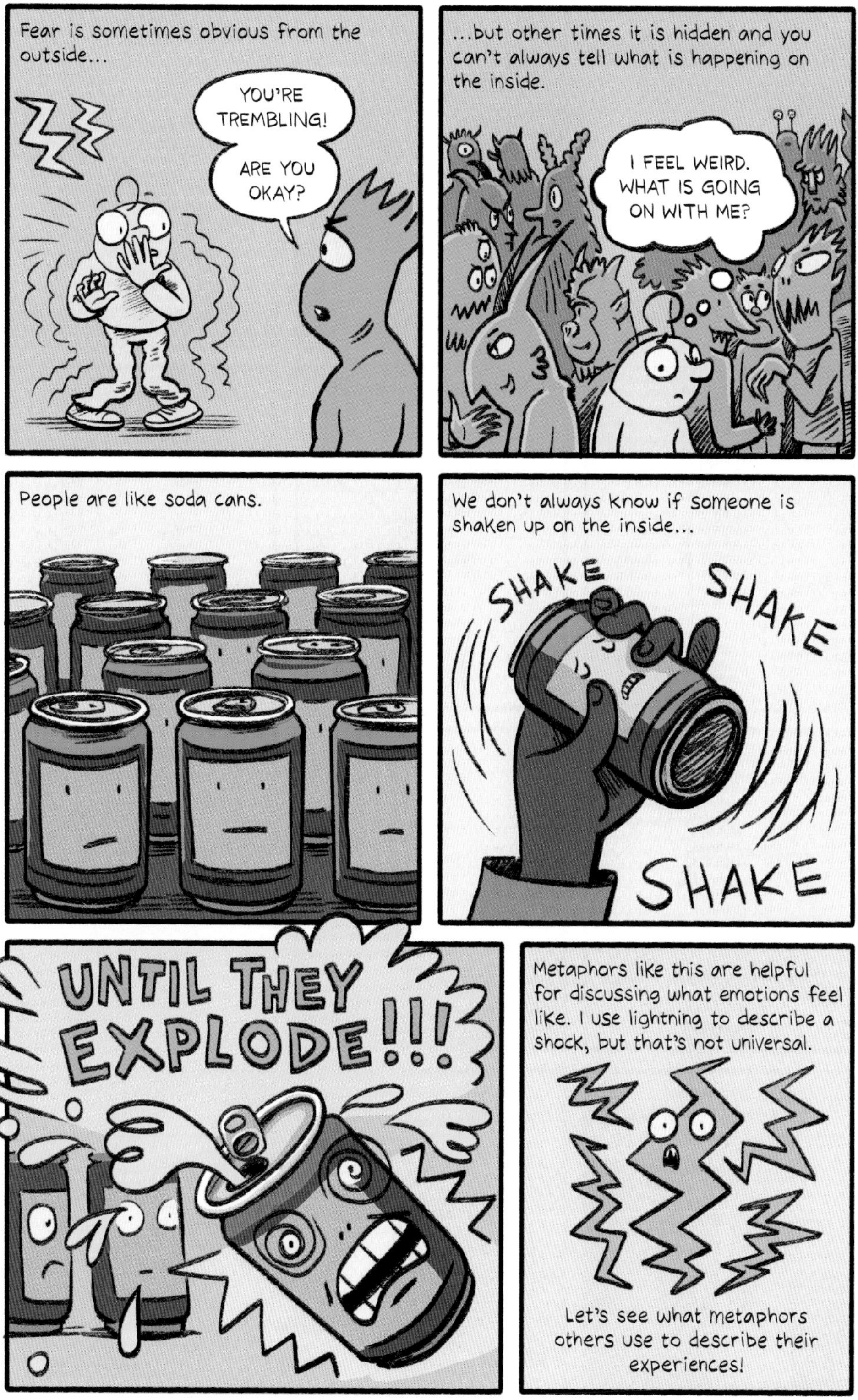
Fear is sometimes obvious from the outside...
YOU'RE TREMBLING!
ARE YOU OKAY?
...but other times it is hidden and you can't always tell what is happening on the inside.
I FEEL WEIRD. WHAT IS GOING ON WITH ME?
People are like soda cans.
We don't always know if someone is shaken up on the inside...
SHAKE
SHAKE
SHAKE
UNTIL THEY EXPLODE!!!
Metaphors like this are helpful for discussing what emotions feel like. I use lightning to describe a shock, but that's not universal.
Let's see what metaphors others use to describe their experiences!

WHAT DOES FEAR, STRESS, OR ANXIETY FEEL LIKE IN A BODY?

I asked this question to friends, family, and students. Here are some of their answers.

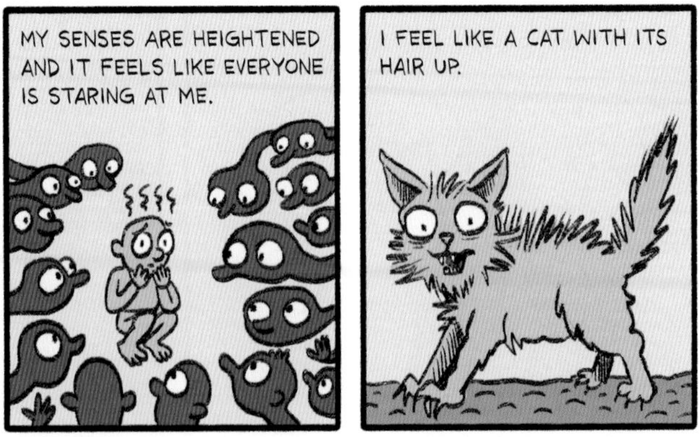

MY SENSES ARE HEIGHTENED AND IT FEELS LIKE EVERYONE IS STARING AT ME.
I FEEL LIKE A CAT WITH ITS HAIR UP.

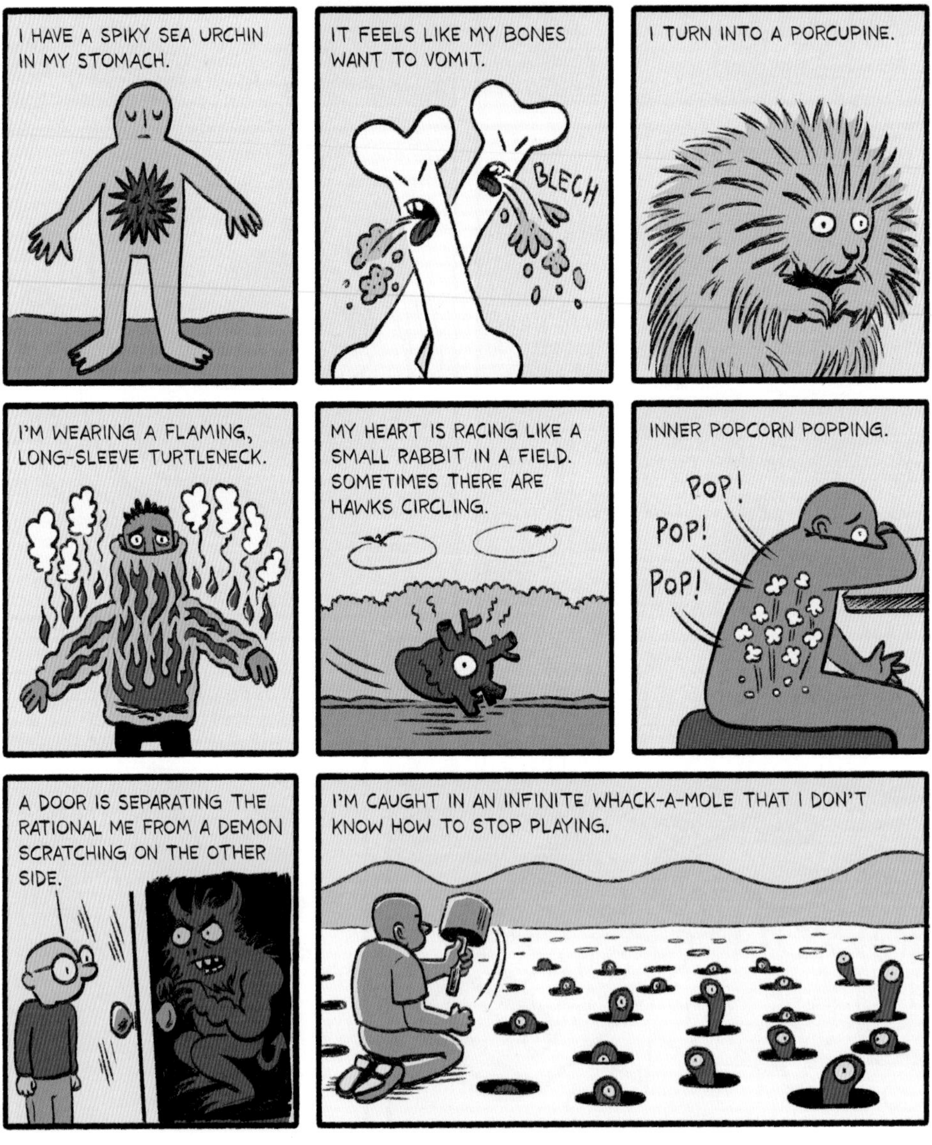

I HAVE A SPIKY SEA URCHIN IN MY STOMACH.
IT FEELS LIKE MY BONES WANT TO VOMIT.
BLECH
I TURN INTO A PORCUPINE.
I'M WEARING A FLAMING, LONG-SLEEVE TURTLENECK.
MY HEART IS RACING LIKE A SMALL RABBIT IN A FIELD. SOMETIMES THERE ARE HAWKS CIRCLING.
INNER POPCORN POPPING.
POP!
POP!
POP!
A DOOR IS SEPARATING THE RATIONAL ME FROM A DEMON SCRATCHING ON THE OTHER SIDE.
I'M CAUGHT IN AN INFINITE WHACK-A-MOLE THAT I DON'T KNOW HOW TO STOP PLAYING.

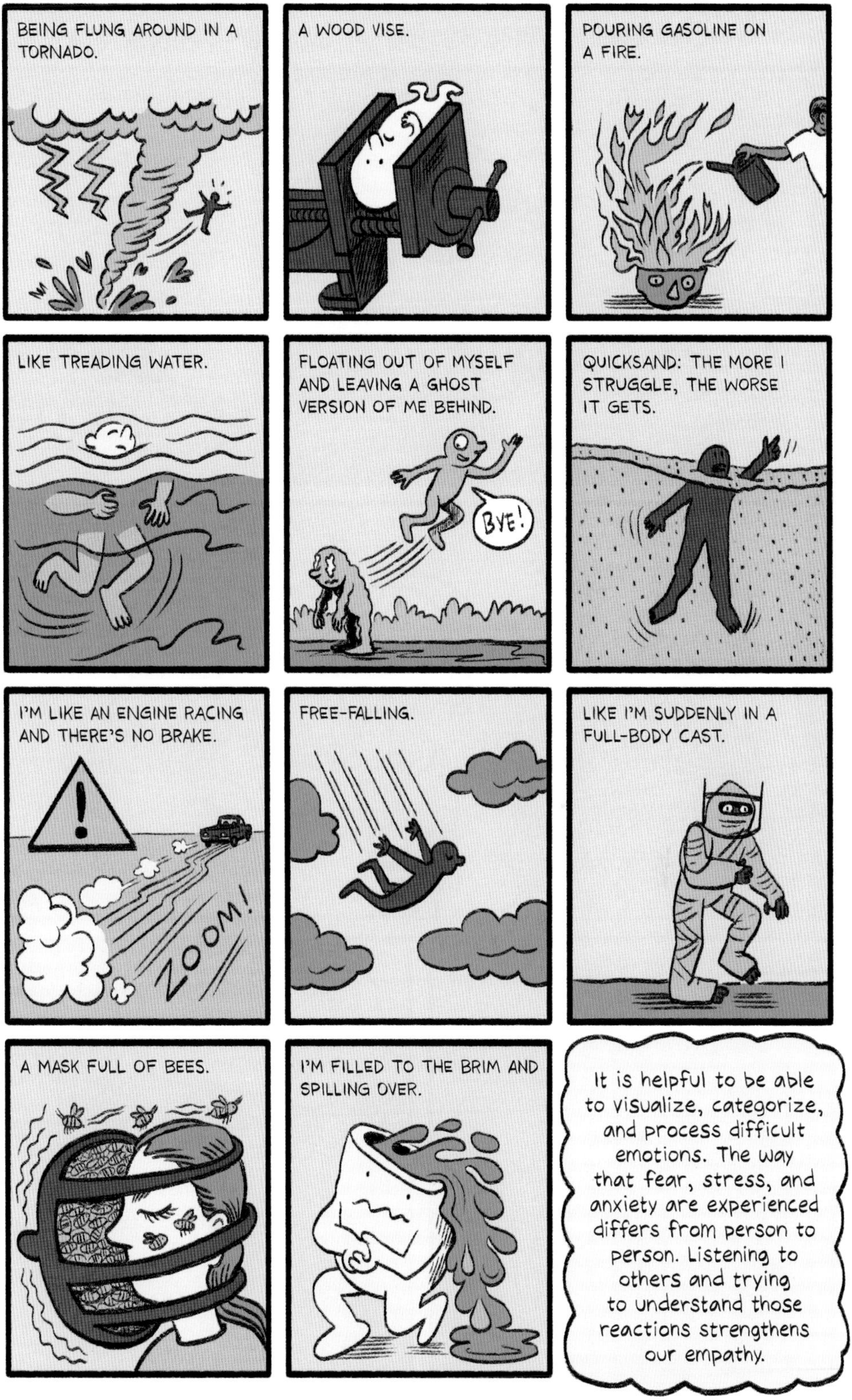
BEING FLUNG AROUND IN A TORNADO.
A WOOD VISE.
POURING GASOLINE ON A FIRE.
LIKE TREADING WATER.
FLOATING OUT OF MYSELF AND LEAVING A GHOST VERSION OF ME BEHIND.
BYE!
QUICKSAND: THE MORE I STRUGGLE, THE WORSE IT GETS.
I'M LIKE AN ENGINE RACING AND THERE'S NO BRAKE.
ZOOM!
FREE-FALLING.
LIKE I'M SUDDENLY IN A FULL-BODY CAST.
A MASK FULL OF BEES.
I'M FILLED TO THE BRIM AND SPILLING OVER.
It is helpful to be able to visualize, categorize, and process difficult emotions. The way that fear, stress, and anxiety are experienced differs from person to person. Listening to others and trying to understand those reactions strengthens our empathy.

HOW CAN STRESS BE A GOOD THING?

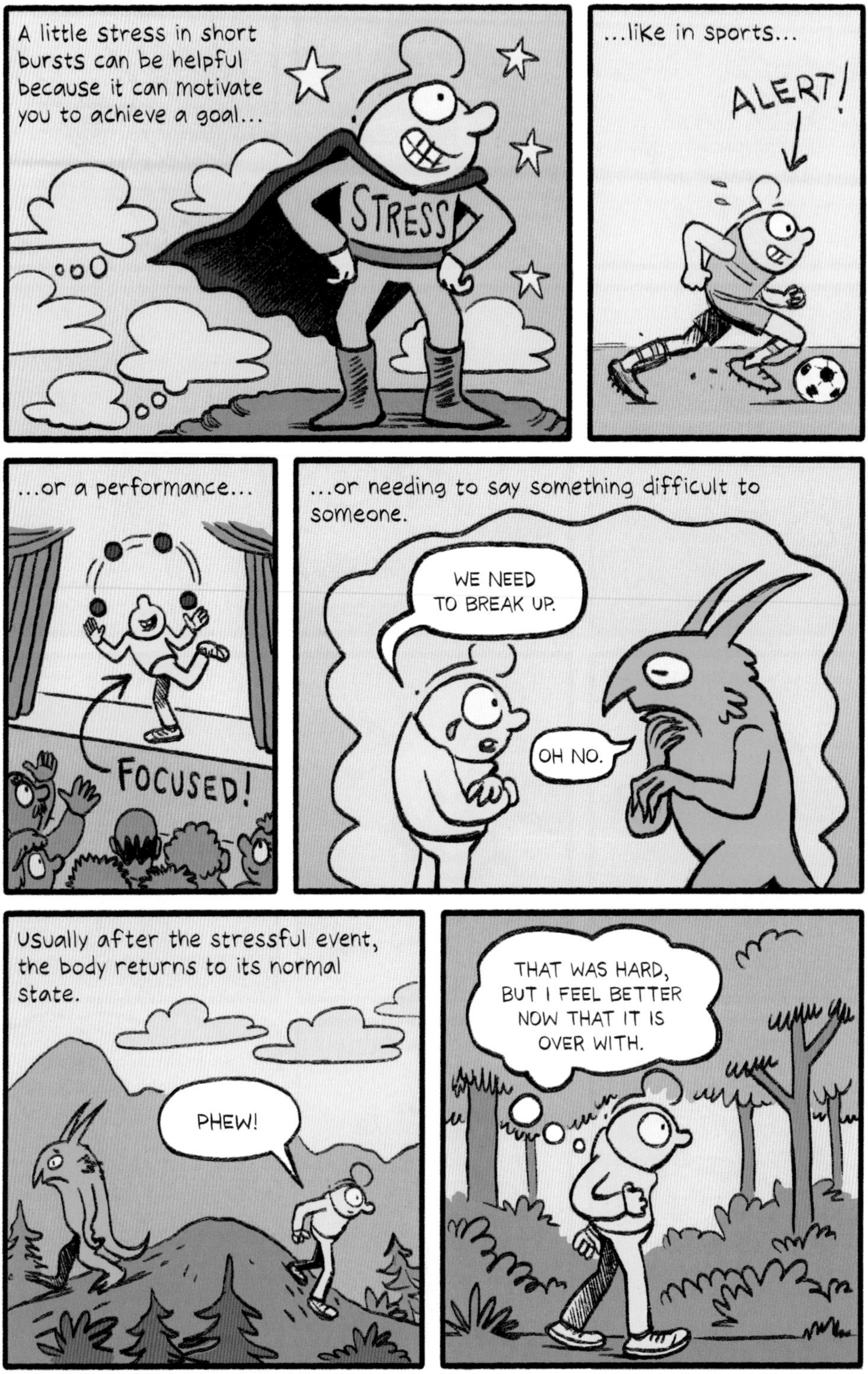

A little stress in short bursts can be helpful because it can motivate you to achieve a goal...
STRESS
...like in sports...
ALERT!
...or a performance...
FOCUSED!
...or needing to say something difficult to someone.
WE NEED TO BREAK UP.
OH NO.
Usually after the stressful event, the body returns to its normal state.
PHEW!
THAT WAS HARD, BUT I FEEL BETTER NOW THAT IT IS OVER WITH.

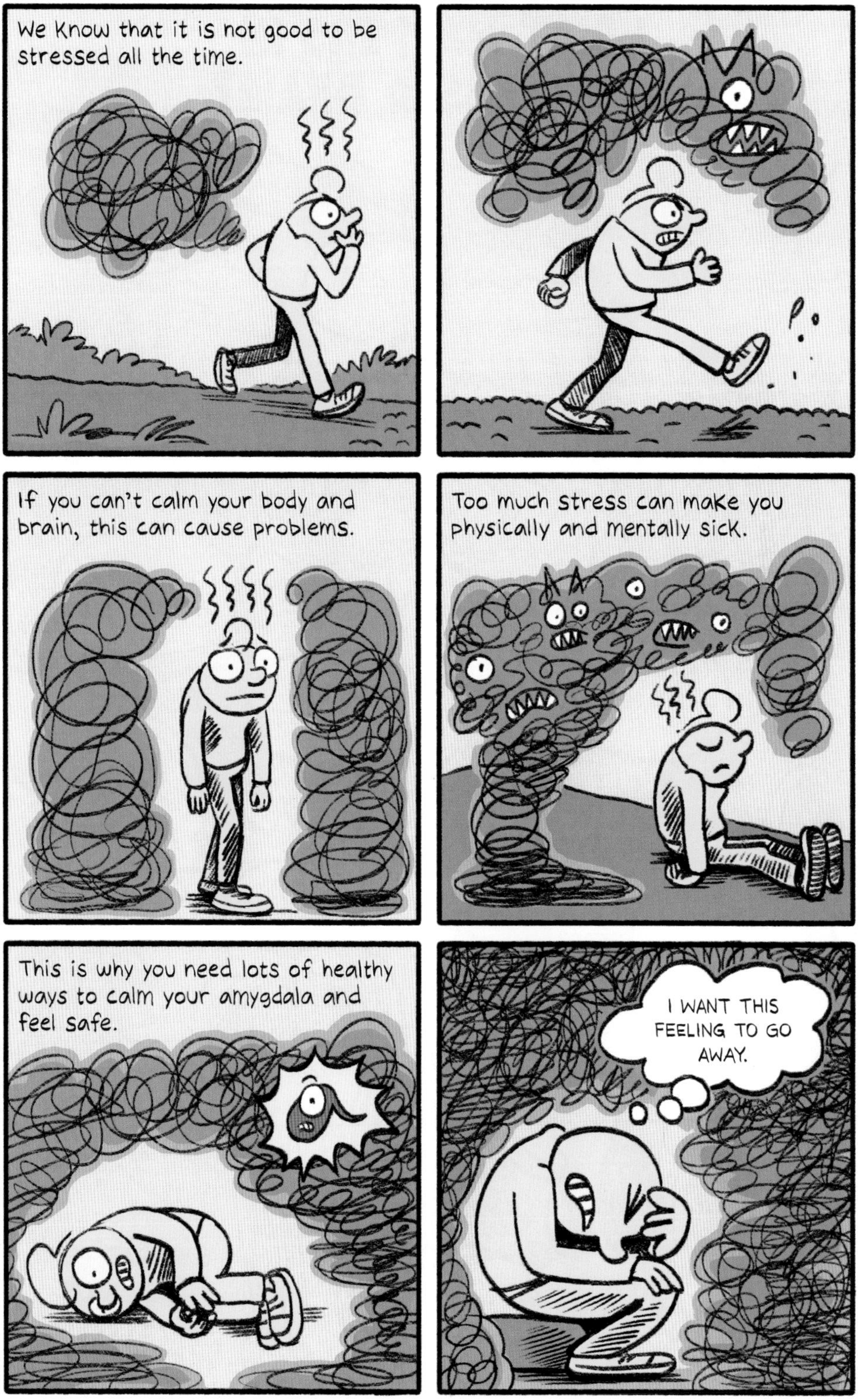
We Know that it is not good to be stressed all the time.
If you can't calm your body and brain, this can cause problems.
Too much stress can make you physically and mentally sick.
This is why you need lots of healthy ways to calm your amygdala and feel safe.
I WANT THIS FEELING TO GO AWAY.

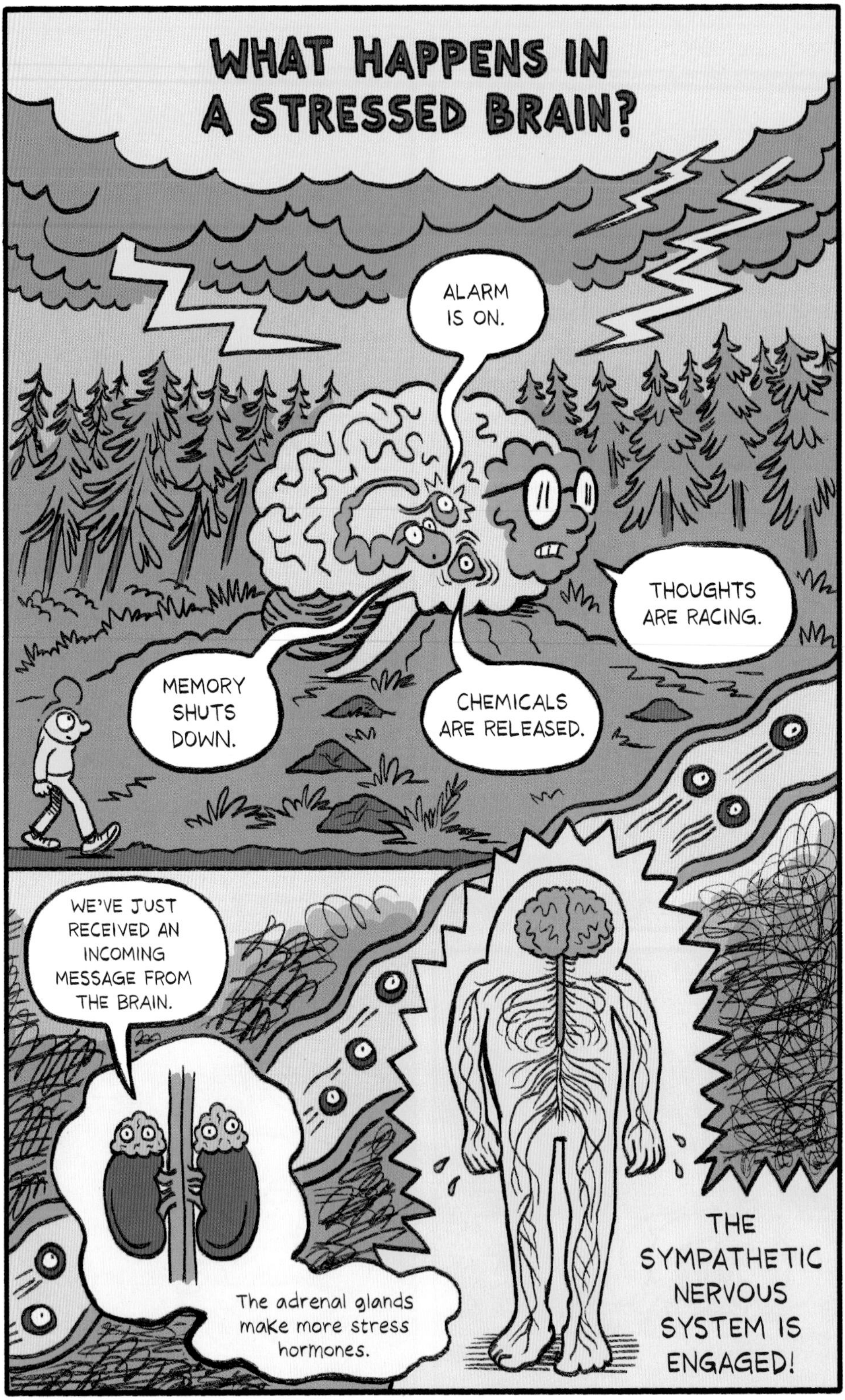
WHAT HAPPENS IN A STRESSED BRAIN?
ALARM IS ON.
THOUGHTS ARE RACING.
MEMORY SHUTS DOWN.
CHEMICALS ARE RELEASED.
WE'VE JUST RECEIVED AN INCOMING MESSAGE FROM THE BRAIN.
The adrenal glands make more stress hormones.
THE SYMPATHETIC NERVOUS SYSTEM IS ENGAGED!

THE AMYGDALA STRESS LOOP INSIDE THE BRAIN

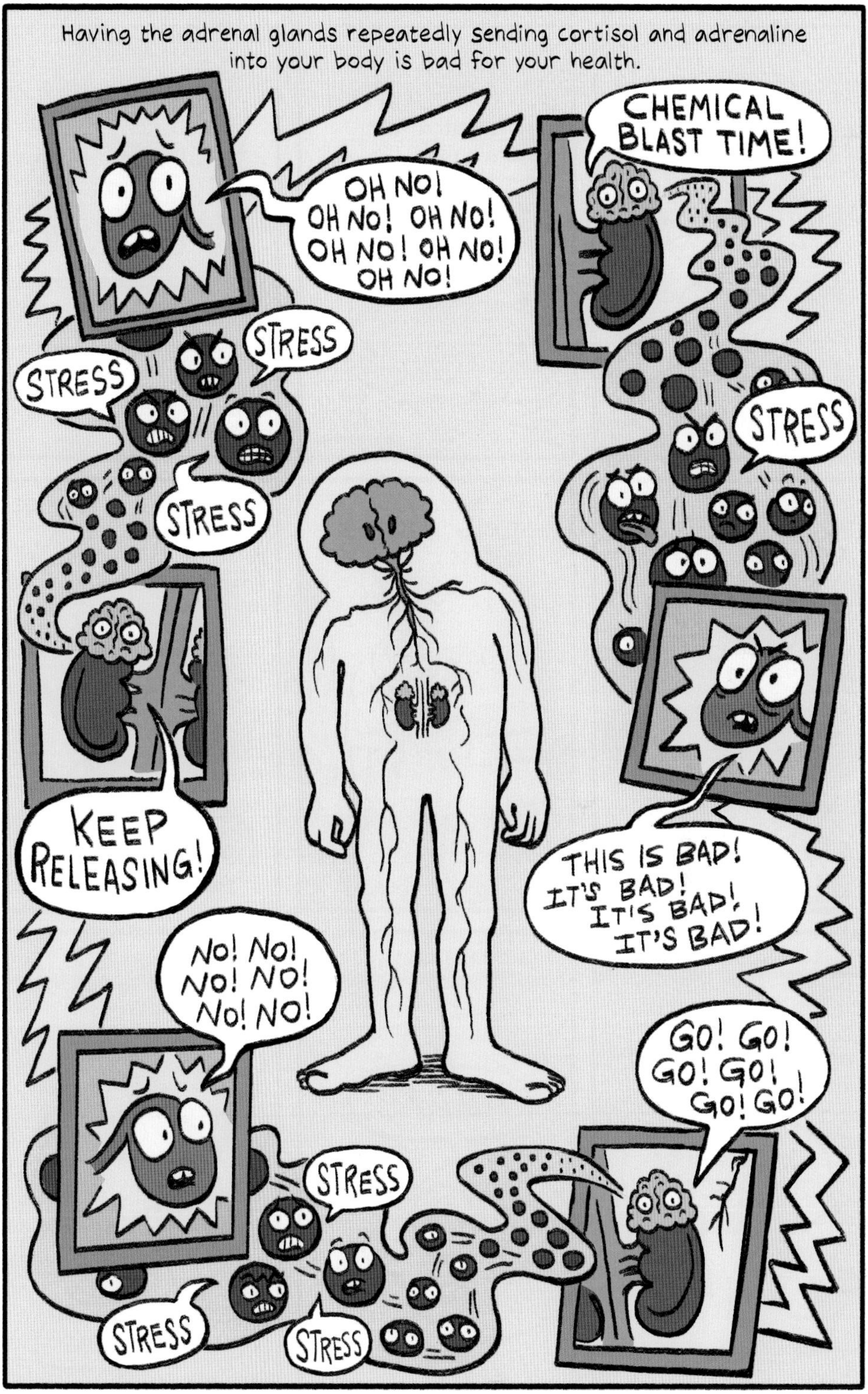

Having the adrenal glands repeatedly sending cortisol and adrenaline into your body is bad for your health.
OH NO! OH NO! OH NO! OH NO! OH NO! OH NO!
CHEMICAL BLAST TIME!
STRESS
STRESS
STRESS
STRESS
THIS IS BAD! IT'S BAD! IT'S BAD! IT'S BAD!
GO! GO! GO! GO! GO! GO!
STRESS
STRESS
STRESS
No! No! No! NO! No! NO!
KEEP RELEASING!

FEAR AND MEMORY

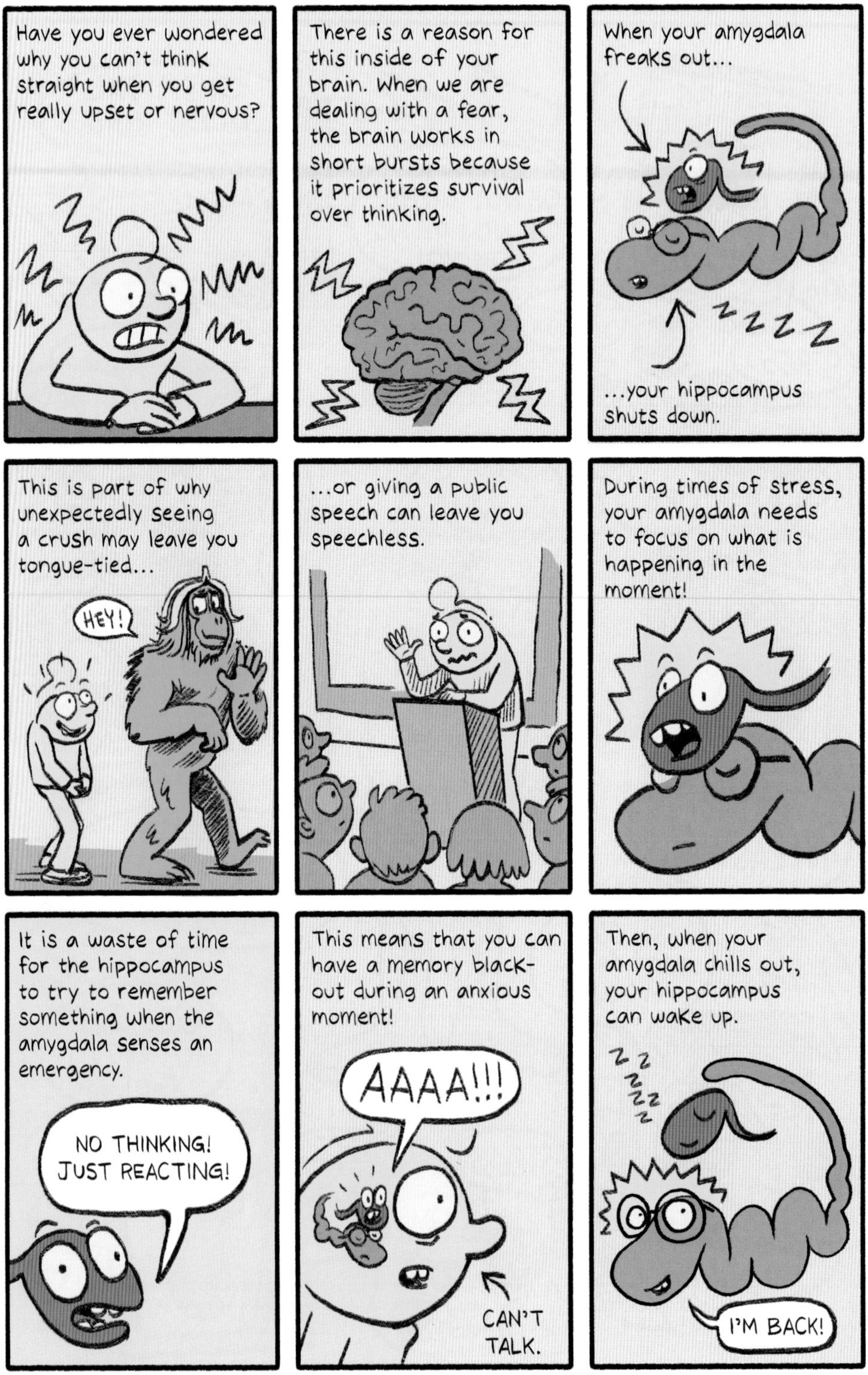
Have you ever wondered why you can't think straight when you get really upset or nervous?
There is a reason for this inside of your brain. When we are dealing with a fear, the brain works in short bursts because it prioritizes survival over thinking.
When your amygdala freaks out...
...your hippocampus shuts down.
This is part of why unexpectedly seeing a crush may leave you tongue-tied...
HEY!
...or giving a public speech can leave you speechless.
During times of stress, your amygdala needs to focus on what is happening in the moment!
It is a waste of time for the hippocampus to try to remember something when the amygdala senses an emergency.
NO THINKING! JUST REACTING!
This means that you can have a memory black-out during an anxious moment!
AAAA!!!
CAN'T TALK.
Then, when your amygdala chills out, your hippocampus can wake up.
I'M BACK!

CALMING YOURSELF DOWN

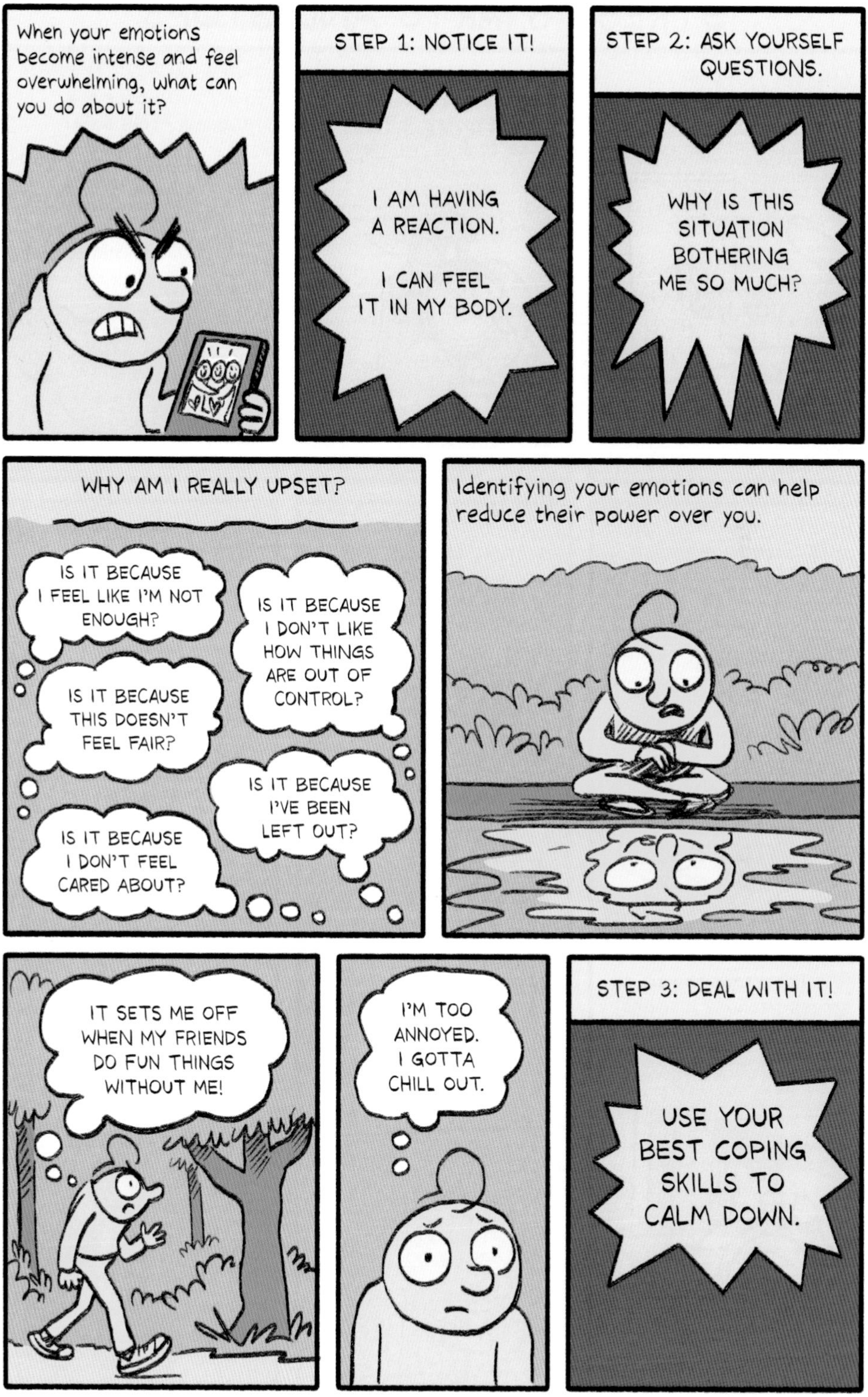
When your emotions become intense and feel overwhelming, what can you do about it?
STEP 1: NOTICE IT!
I AM HAVING A REACTION.
I CAN FEEL IT IN MY BODY.
STEP 2: ASK YOURSELF QUESTIONS.
WHY IS THIS SITUATION BOTHERING ME SO MUCH?
WHY AM I REALLY UPSET?
IS IT BECAUSE I FEEL LIKE I'M NOT ENOUGH?
IS IT BECAUSE I DON'T LIKE HOW THINGS ARE OUT OF CONTROL?
IS IT BECAUSE THIS DOESN'T FEEL FAIR?
IS IT BECAUSE I'VE BEEN LEFT OUT?
IS IT BECAUSE I DON'T FEEL CARED ABOUT?
Identifying your emotions can help reduce their power over you.
IT SETS ME OFF WHEN MY FRIENDS DO FUN THINGS WITHOUT ME!
I'M TOO ANNOYED. I GOTTA CHILL OUT.
STEP 3: DEAL WITH IT!
USE YOUR BEST COPING SKILLS TO CALM DOWN.

STRESS STARTS AND STOPS

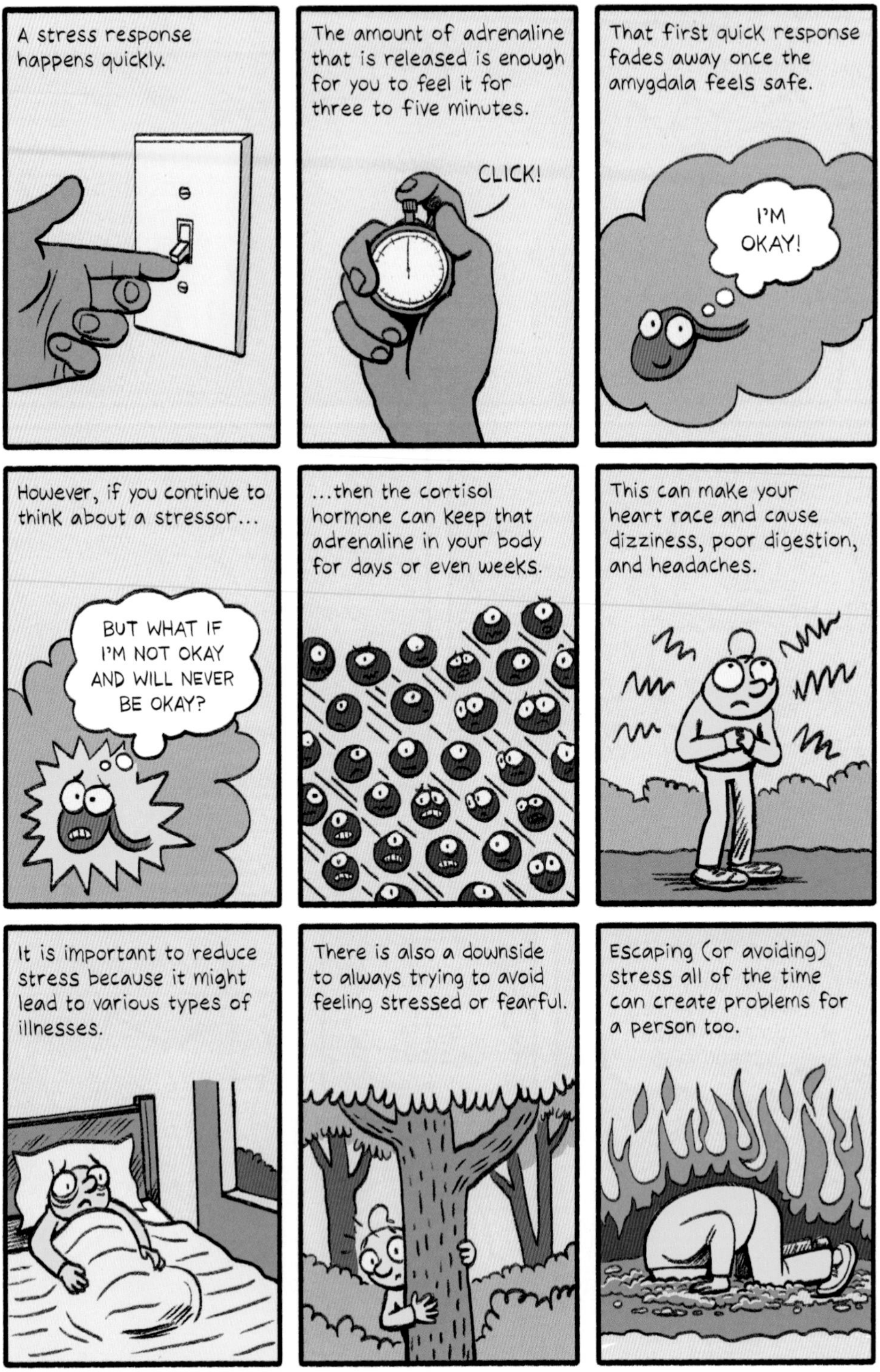
A stress response happens quickly.
The amount of adrenaline that is released is enough for you to feel it for three to five minutes.
CLICK!
That first quick response fades away once the amygdala feels safe.
I'M OKAY!
However, if you continue to think about a stressor...
BUT WHAT IF I'M NOT OKAY AND WILL NEVER BE OKAY?
...then the cortisol hormone can keep that adrenaline in your body for days or even weeks.
This can make your heart race and cause dizziness, poor digestion, and headaches.
It is important to reduce stress because it might lead to various types of illnesses.
There is also a downside to always trying to avoid feeling stressed or fearful.
Escaping (or avoiding) stress all of the time can create problems for a person too.

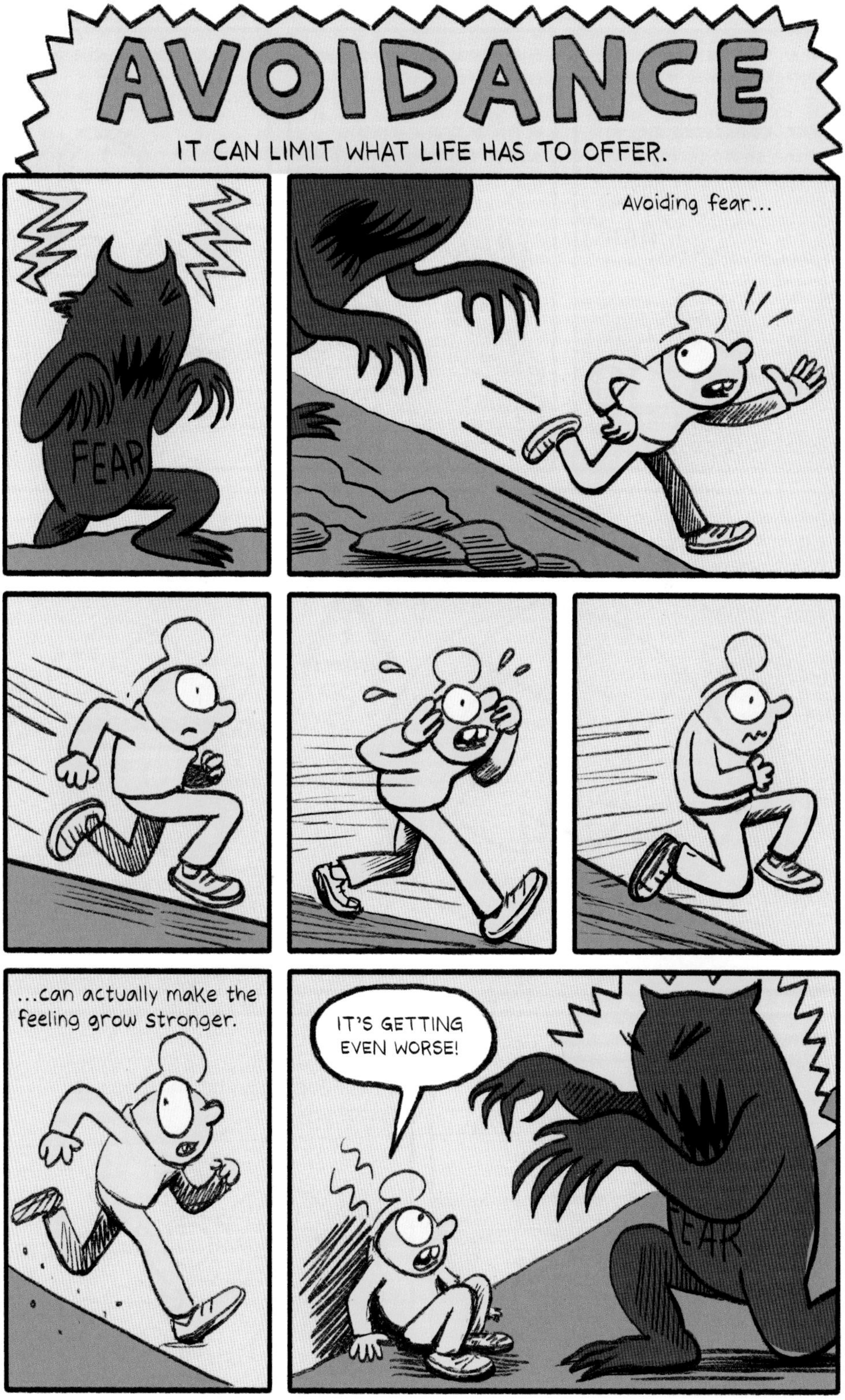
AVOIDANCE
IT CAN LIMIT WHAT LIFE HAS TO OFFER.
FEAR
Avoiding fear...
...can actually make the feeling grow stronger.
IT'S GETTING EVEN WORSE!
FEAR

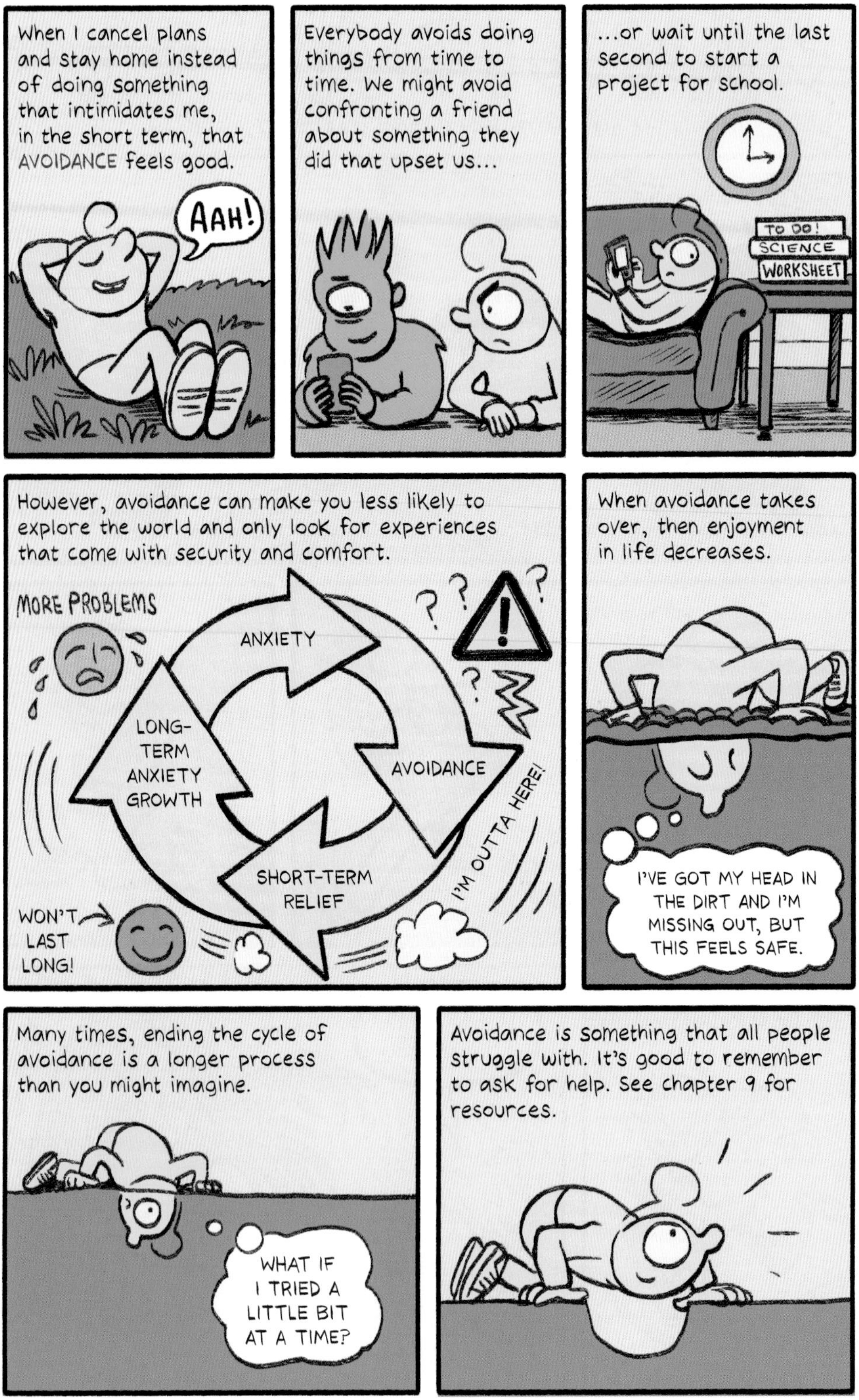

When I cancel plans and stay home instead of doing something that intimidates me, in the short term, that AVOIDANCE feels good.
AAH!
Everybody avoids doing things from time to time. We might avoid confronting a friend about something they did that upset us...
...or wait until the last second to start a project for school.
TO DO!
SCIENCE
WORKSHEET
However, avoidance can make you less likely to explore the world and only look for experiences that come with security and comfort.
MORE PROBLEMS
ANXIETY
AVOIDANCE
SHORT-TERM RELIEF
LONG-TERM ANXIETY GROWTH
I'M OUTTA HERE!
WON'T LAST LONG!
When avoidance takes over, then enjoyment in life decreases.
I'VE GOT MY HEAD IN THE DIRT AND I'M MISSING OUT, BUT THIS FEELS SAFE.
Many times, ending the cycle of avoidance is a longer process than you might imagine.
WHAT IF I TRIED A LITTLE BIT AT A TIME?
Avoidance is something that all people struggle with. It's good to remember to ask for help. See chapter 9 for resources.

LET'S TALK ABOUT THE INTENSE SIDE OF FEAR

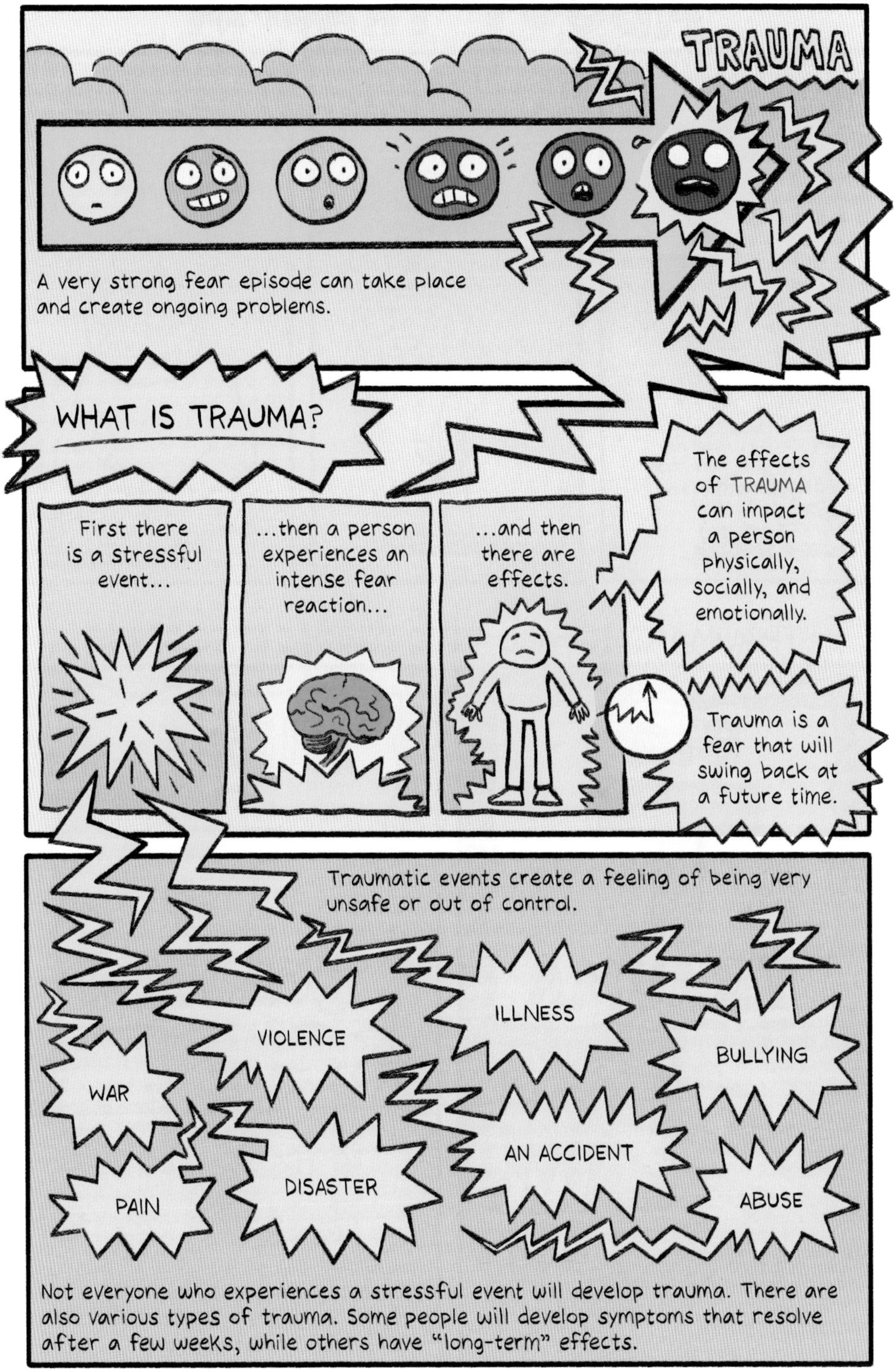

TRAUMA
A very strong fear episode can take place and create ongoing problems.
WHAT IS TRAUMA?
First there is a stressful event...
...then a person experiences an intense fear reaction...
...and then there are effects.
The effects of TRAUMA can impact a person physically, socially, and emotionally.
Trauma is a fear that will swing back at a future time.
Traumatic events create a feeling of being very unsafe or out of control.
VIOLENCE
ILLNESS
BULLYING
WAR
AN ACCIDENT
DISASTER
PAIN
ABUSE
Not everyone who experiences a stressful event will develop trauma. There are also various types of trauma. Some people will develop symptoms that resolve after a few weeks, while others have "long-term" effects.

ABOUT TRAUMA

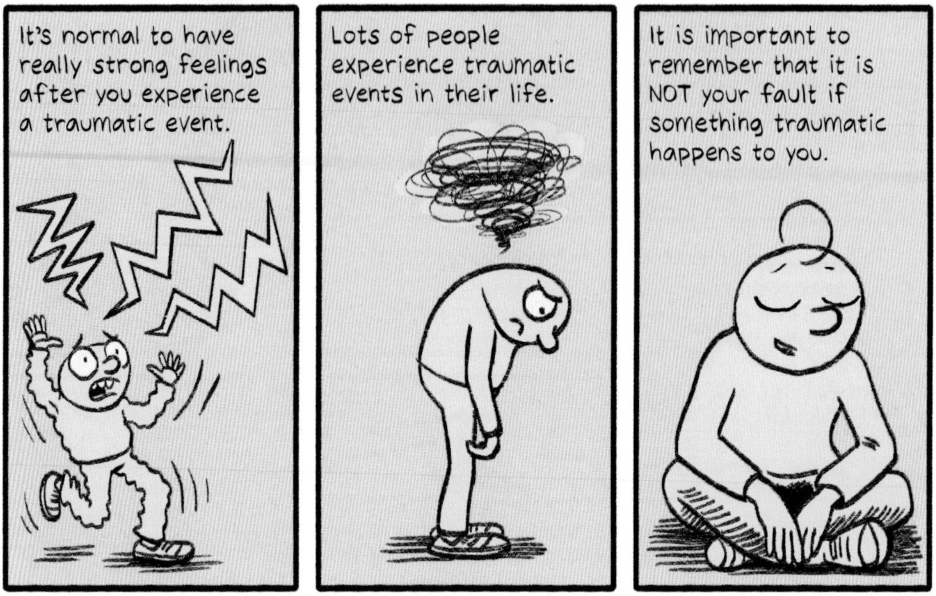
It's normal to have really strong feelings after you experience a traumatic event.
Lots of people experience traumatic events in their life.
It is important to remember that it is NOT your fault if something traumatic happens to you.

TRAUMA CAN FALL INTO TWO CATEGORIES

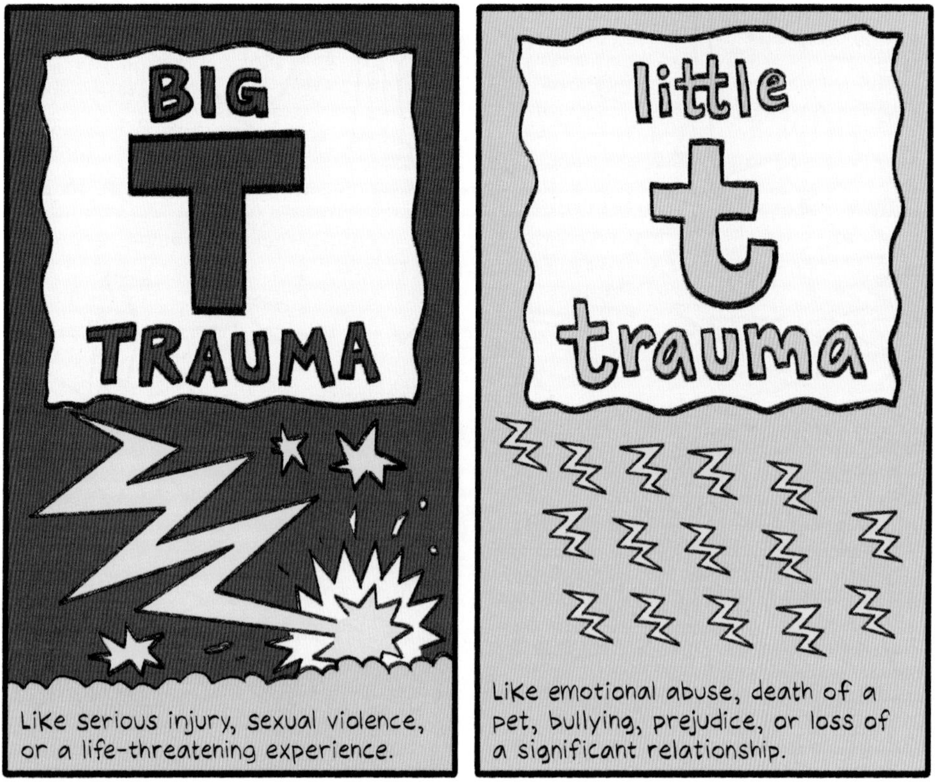
BIG T TRAUMA
Like serious injury, sexual violence, or a life-threatening experience.
little t trauma
Like emotional abuse, death of a pet, bullying, prejudice, or loss of a significant relationship.

WHAT ARE THE SIGNS THAT SOMEONE IS SUFFERING FROM TRAUMA?

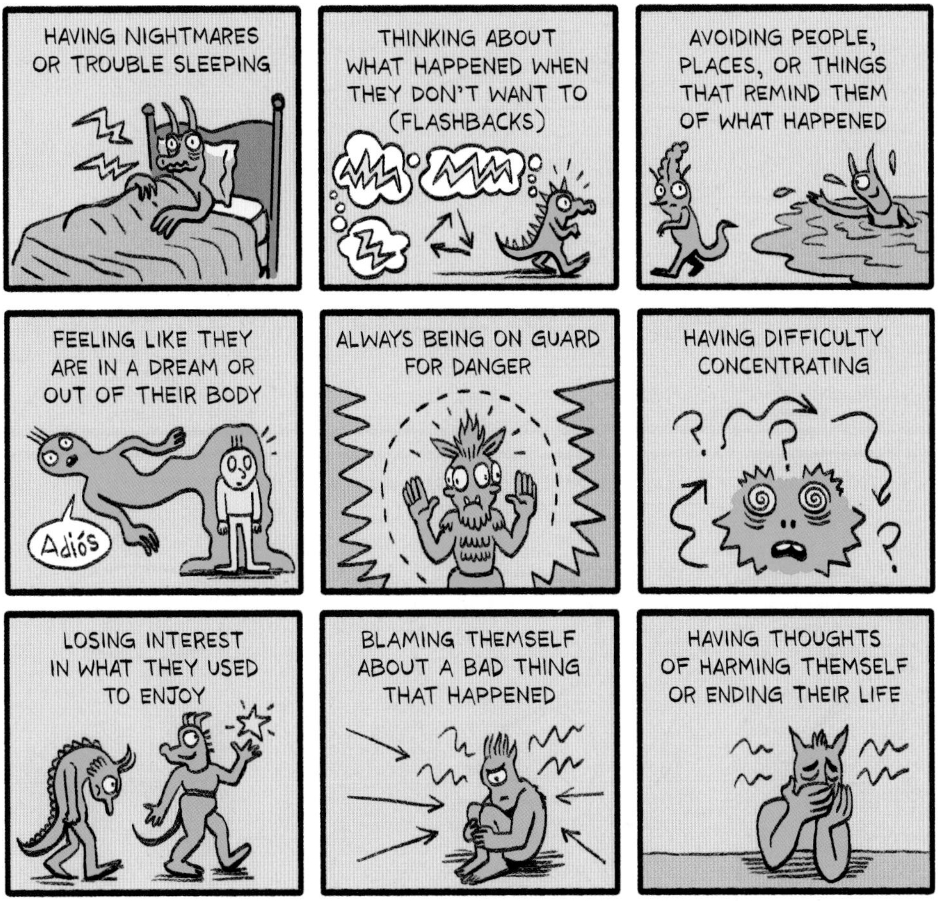
HAVING NIGHTMARES OR TROUBLE SLEEPING
THINKING ABOUT WHAT HAPPENED WHEN THEY DON'T WANT TO (FLASHBACKS)
AVOIDING PEOPLE, PLACES, OR THINGS THAT REMIND THEM OF WHAT HAPPENED
FEELING LIKE THEY ARE IN A DREAM OR OUT OF THEIR BODY
Adiós
ALWAYS BEING ON GUARD FOR DANGER
HAVING DIFFICULTY CONCENTRATING
LOSING INTEREST IN WHAT THEY USED TO ENJOY
BLAMING THEMSELF ABOUT A BAD THING THAT HAPPENED
HAVING THOUGHTS OF HARMING THEMSELF OR ENDING THEIR LIFE

TRAUMA NEEDS CARE

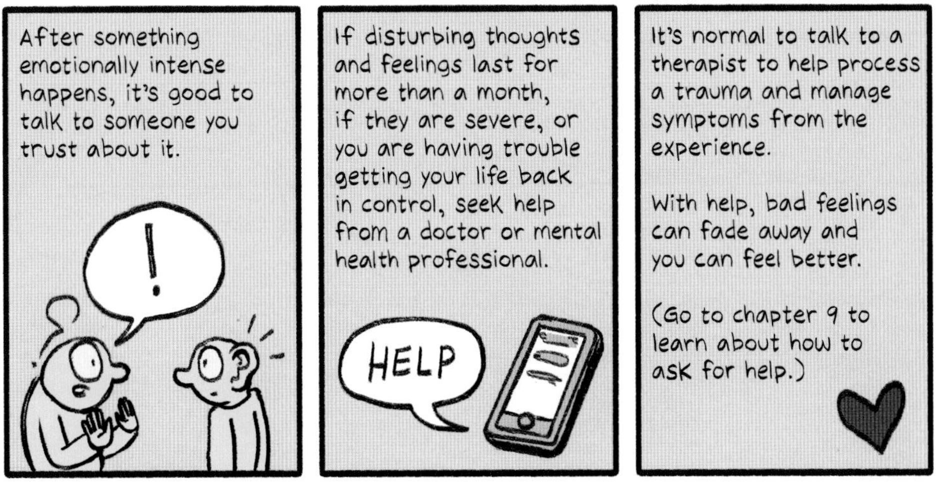
After something emotionally intense happens, it's good to talk to someone you trust about it.
!
If disturbing thoughts and feelings last for more than a month, if they are severe, or you are having trouble getting your life back in control, seek help from a doctor or mental health professional.
HELP
It's normal to talk to a therapist to help process a trauma and manage symptoms from the experience.
With help, bad feelings can fade away and you can feel better.
(Go to chapter 9 to learn about how to ask for help.)

WHAT IS A PANIC ATTACK?

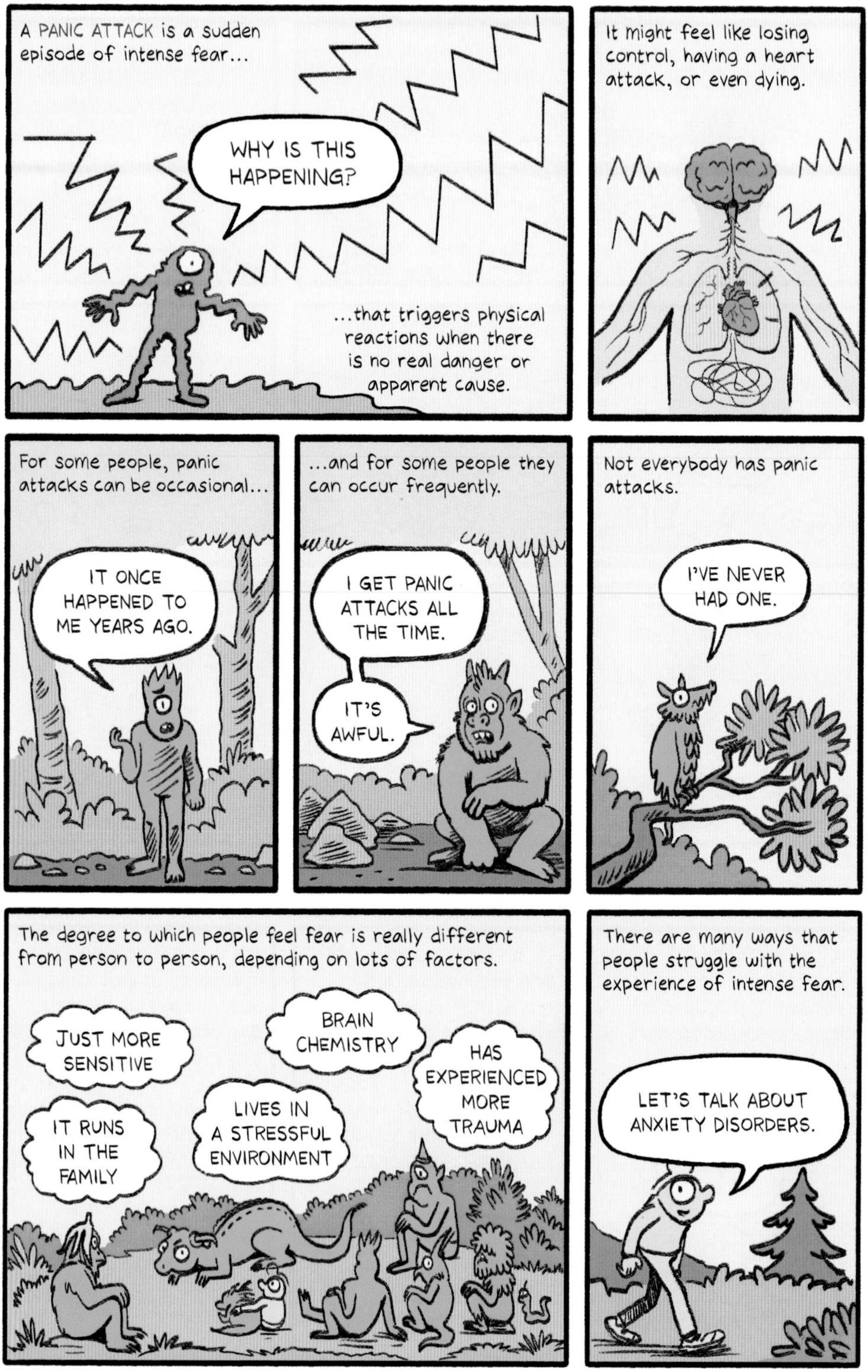
A PANIC ATTACK is a sudden episode of intense fear...
WHY IS THIS HAPPENING?
...that triggers physical reactions when there is no real danger or apparent cause.
It might feel like losing control, having a heart attack, or even dying.
For some people, panic attacks can be occasional...
IT ONCE HAPPENED TO ME YEARS AGO.
...and for some people they can occur frequently.
I GET PANIC ATTACKS ALL THE TIME.
IT'S AWFUL.
Not everybody has panic attacks.
I'VE NEVER HAD ONE.
The degree to which people feel fear is really different from person to person, depending on lots of factors.
JUST MORE SENSITIVE
BRAIN CHEMISTRY
HAS EXPERIENCED MORE TRAUMA
IT RUNS IN THE FAMILY
LIVES IN A STRESSFUL ENVIRONMENT
There are many ways that people struggle with the experience of intense fear.
LET'S TALK ABOUT ANXIETY DISORDERS.

ANXIETY DISORDERS

For some people, the fear response can really interfere with daily activities such as school, work, social engagements, and relationships. Here are some common anxiety disorders that set off the amygdala alarm in an overwhelming way.

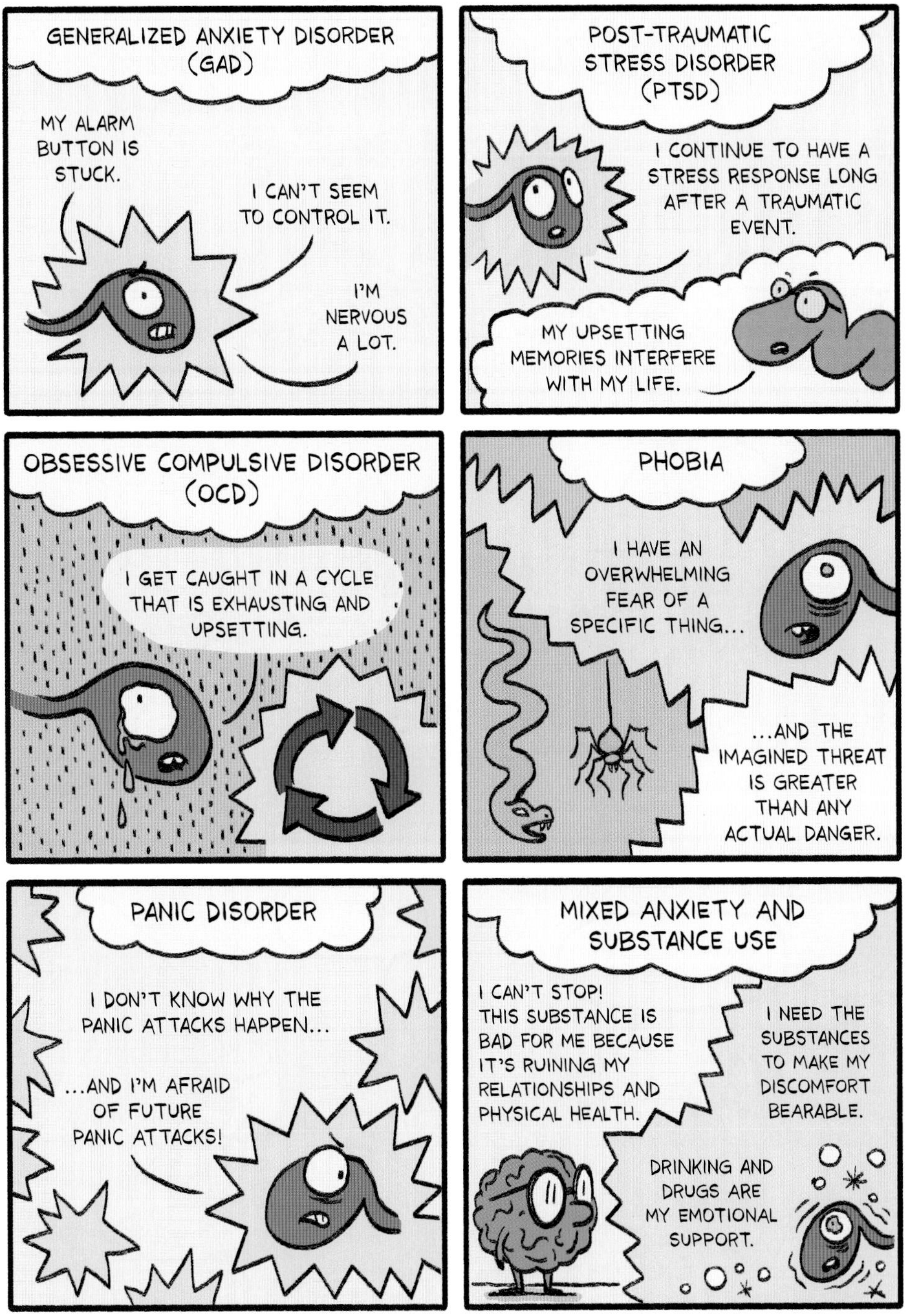
GENERALIZED ANXIETY DISORDER (GAD)
MY ALARM BUTTON IS STUCK.
I CAN'T SEEM TO CONTROL IT.
I'M NERVOUS A LOT.
POST-TRAUMATIC STRESS DISORDER (PTSD)
I CONTINUE TO HAVE A STRESS RESPONSE LONG AFTER A TRAUMATIC EVENT.
MY UPSETTING MEMORIES INTERFERE WITH MY LIFE.
OBSESSIVE COMPULSIVE DISORDER (OCD)
I GET CAUGHT IN A CYCLE THAT IS EXHAUSTING AND UPSETTING.
PHOBIA
I HAVE AN OVERWHELMING FEAR OF A SPECIFIC THING...
...AND THE IMAGINED THREAT IS GREATER THAN ANY ACTUAL DANGER.
PANIC DISORDER
I DON'T KNOW WHY THE PANIC ATTACKS HAPPEN...
...AND I'M AFRAID OF FUTURE PANIC ATTACKS!
MIXED ANXIETY AND SUBSTANCE USE
I CAN'T STOP! THIS SUBSTANCE IS BAD FOR ME BECAUSE IT'S RUINING MY RELATIONSHIPS AND PHYSICAL HEALTH.
I NEED THE SUBSTANCES TO MAKE MY DISCOMFORT BEARABLE.
DRINKING AND DRUGS ARE MY EMOTIONAL SUPPORT.

ANXIETY DISORDERS CAN BE TREATED

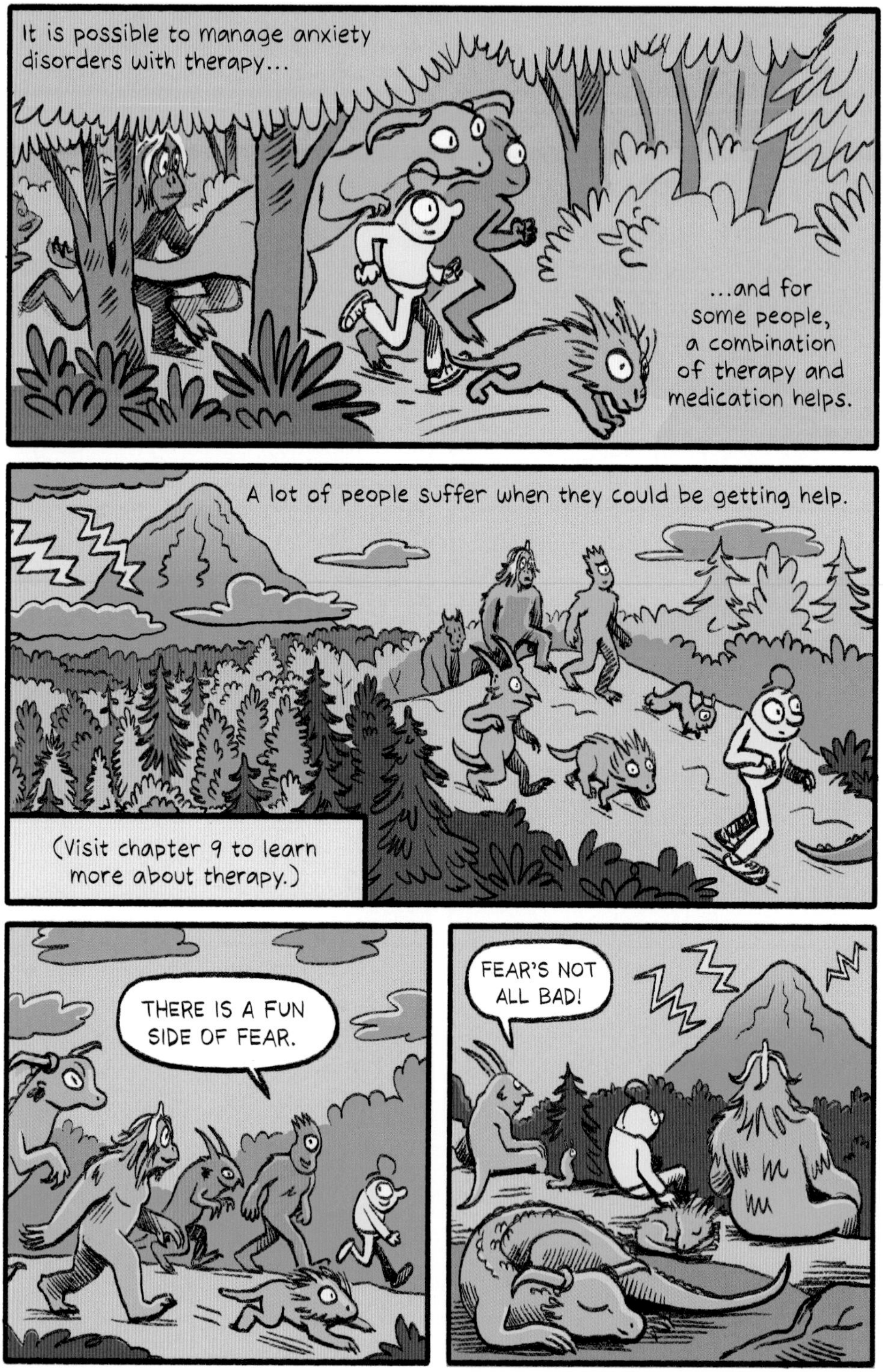
It is possible to manage anxiety disorders with therapy...
...and for some people, a combination of therapy and medication helps.
A lot of people suffer when they could be getting help.
(Visit chapter 9 to learn more about therapy.)
THERE IS A FUN SIDE OF FEAR.
FEAR'S NOT ALL BAD!

FEAR FUN

Let's take a moment to think about the playful side of fear.

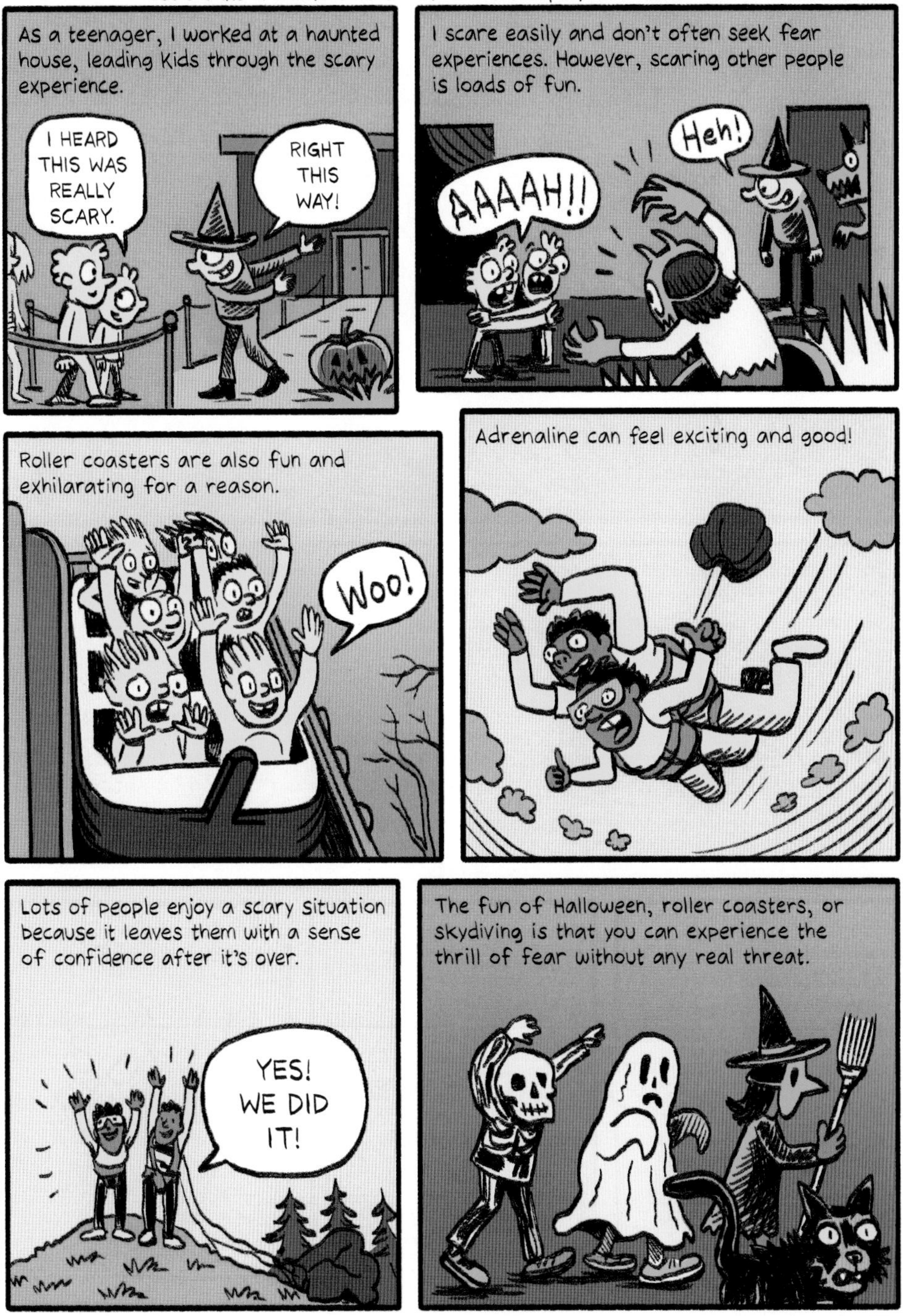

As a teenager, I worked at a haunted house, leading kids through the scary experience.
I HEARD THIS WAS REALLY SCARY.
RIGHT THIS WAY!
I scare easily and don't often seek fear experiences. However, scaring other people is loads of fun.
AAAAH!!
Heh!
Roller coasters are also fun and exhilarating for a reason.
Woo!
Adrenaline can feel exciting and good!
Lots of people enjoy a scary situation because it leaves them with a sense of confidence after it's over.
YES! WE DID IT!
The fun of Halloween, roller coasters, or skydiving is that you can experience the thrill of fear without any real threat.

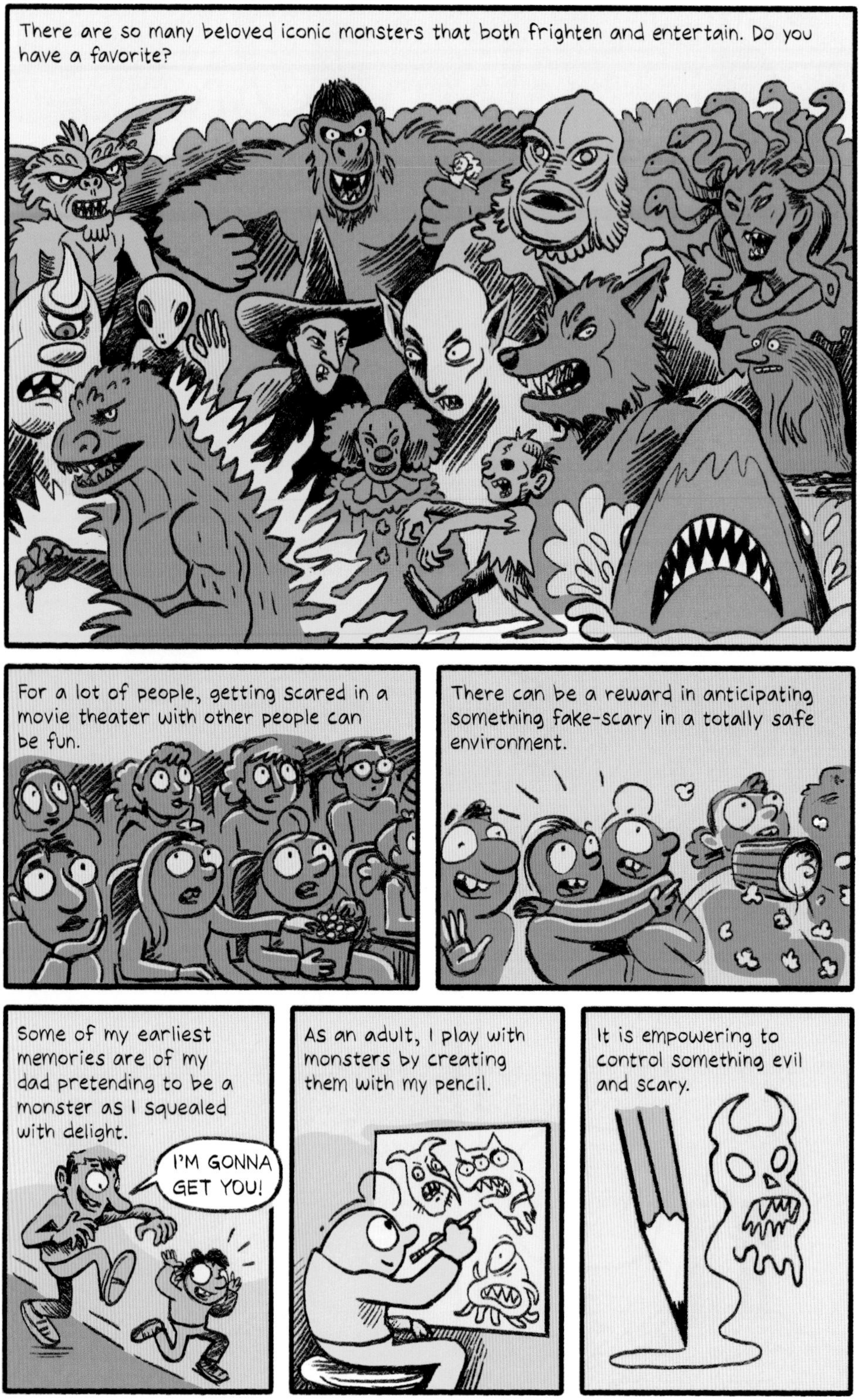
There are so many beloved iconic monsters that both frighten and entertain. Do you have a favorite?
For a lot of people, getting scared in a movie theater with other people can be fun.
There can be a reward in anticipating something fake-scary in a totally safe environment.
Some of my earliest memories are of my dad pretending to be a monster as I squealed with delight.
I'M GONNA GET YOU!
As an adult, I play with monsters by creating them with my pencil.
It is empowering to control something evil and scary.

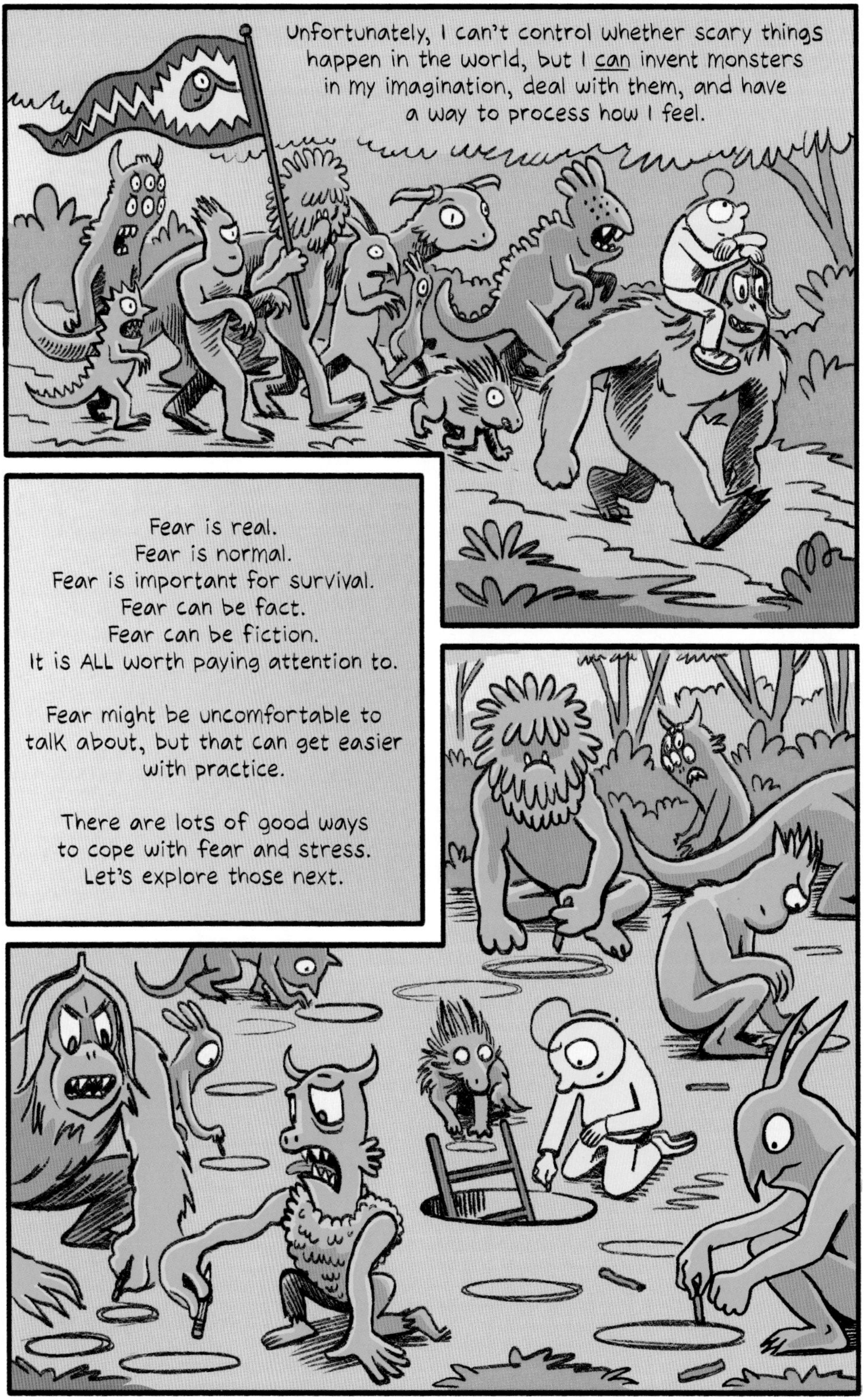
Unfortunately, I can't control whether scary things happen in the world, but I can invent monsters in my imagination, deal with them, and have a way to process how I feel.
Fear is real.
Fear is normal.
Fear is important for survival.
Fear can be fact.
Fear can be fiction.
It is ALL worth paying attention to.
Fear might be uncomfortable to talk about, but that can get easier with practice.
There are lots of good ways to cope with fear and stress. Let's explore those next.

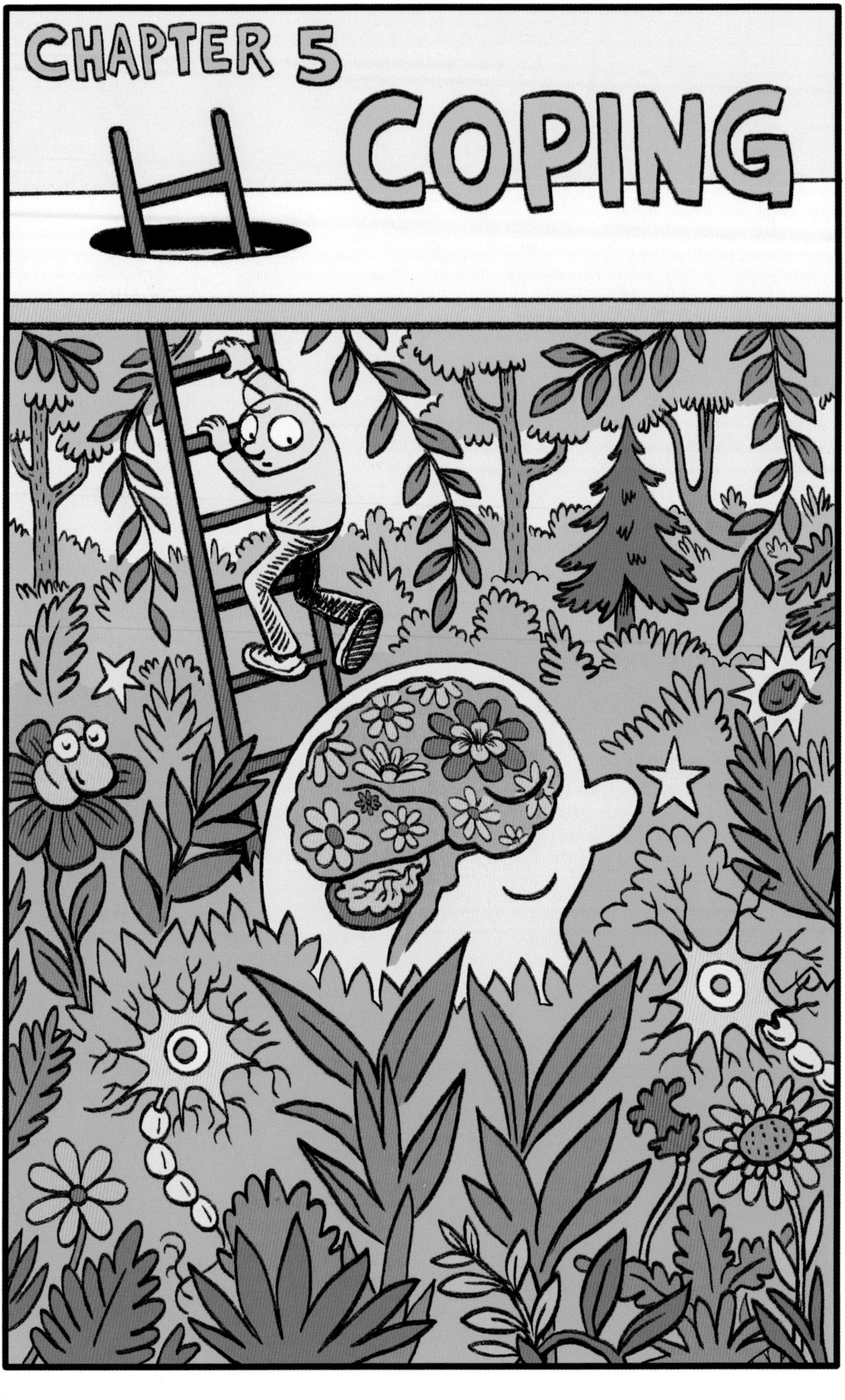
CHAPTER 5
COPING

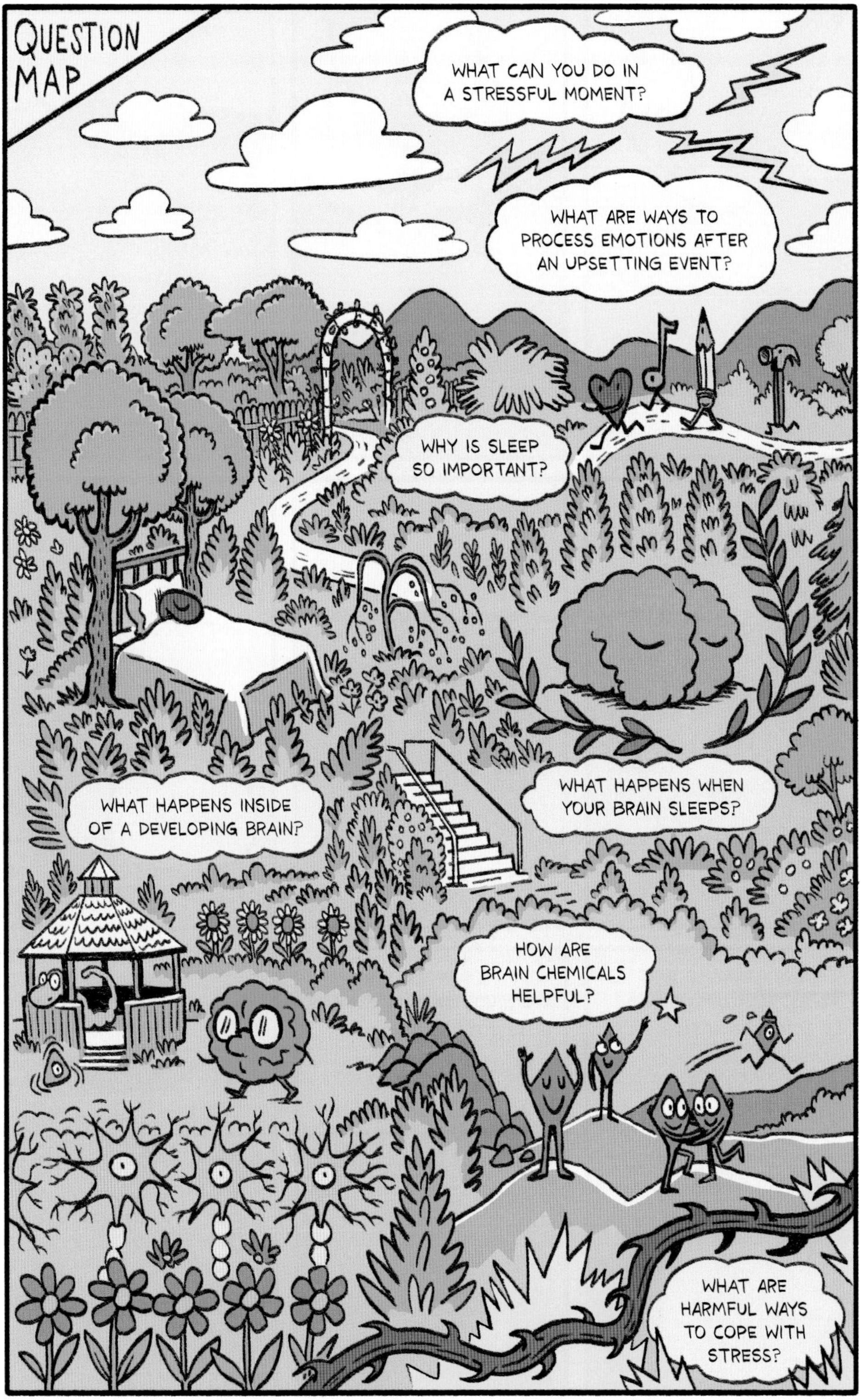
QUESTION MAP
WHAT CAN YOU DO IN A STRESSFUL MOMENT?
WHAT ARE WAYS TO PROCESS EMOTIONS AFTER AN UPSETTING EVENT?
WHY IS SLEEP SO IMPORTANT?
WHAT HAPPENS INSIDE OF A DEVELOPING BRAIN?
WHAT HAPPENS WHEN YOUR BRAIN SLEEPS?
HOW ARE BRAIN CHEMICALS HELPFUL?
WHAT ARE HARMFUL WAYS TO COPE WITH STRESS?

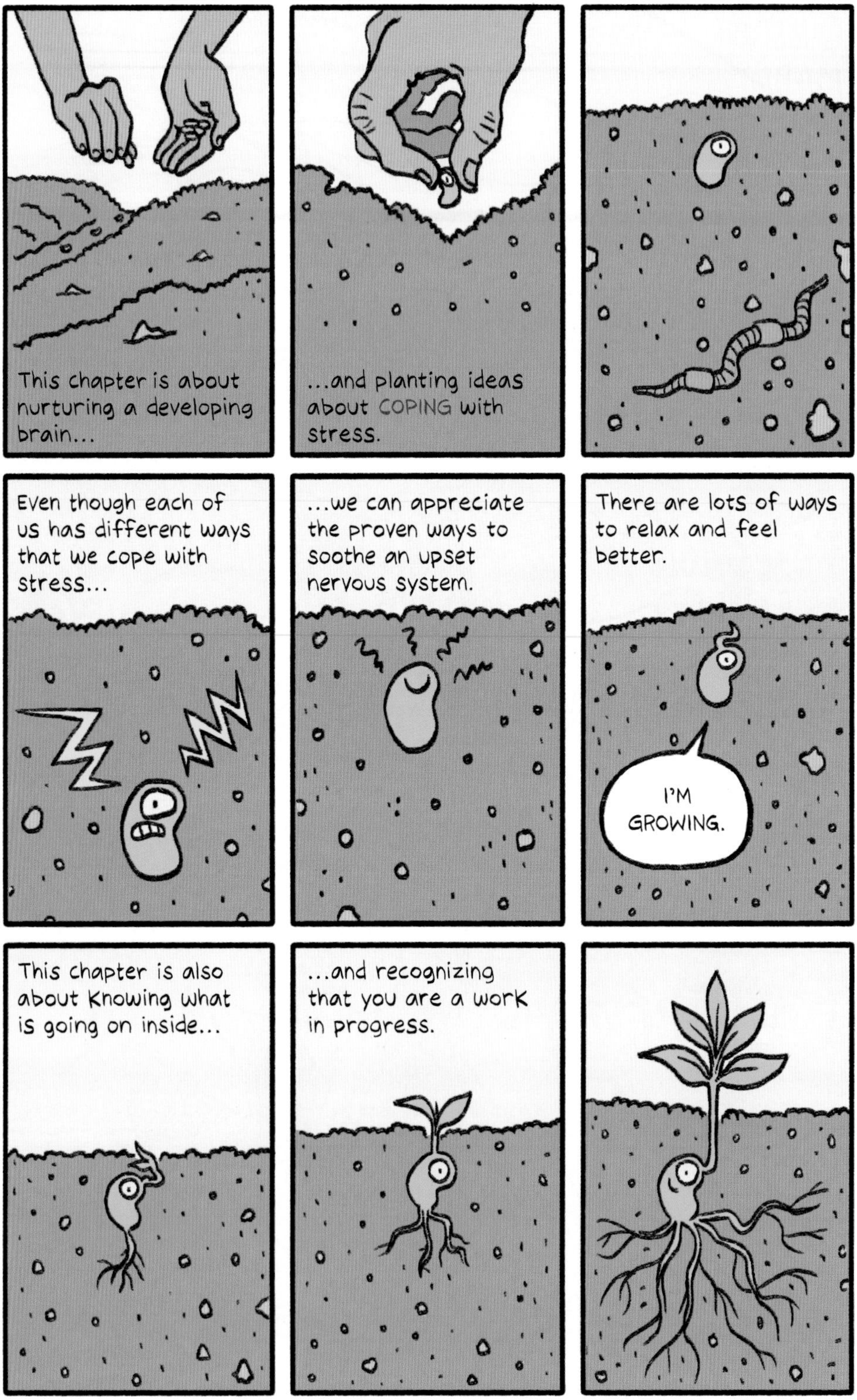
This chapter is about nurturing a developing brain...
...and planting ideas about COPING with stress.
Even though each of us has different ways that we cope with stress...
...we can appreciate the proven ways to soothe an upset nervous system.
There are lots of ways to relax and feel better.
I'M GROWING.
This chapter is also about knowing what is going on inside...
...and recognizing that you are a work in progress.

THERE ARE MANY REASONS WE NEED TO COPE

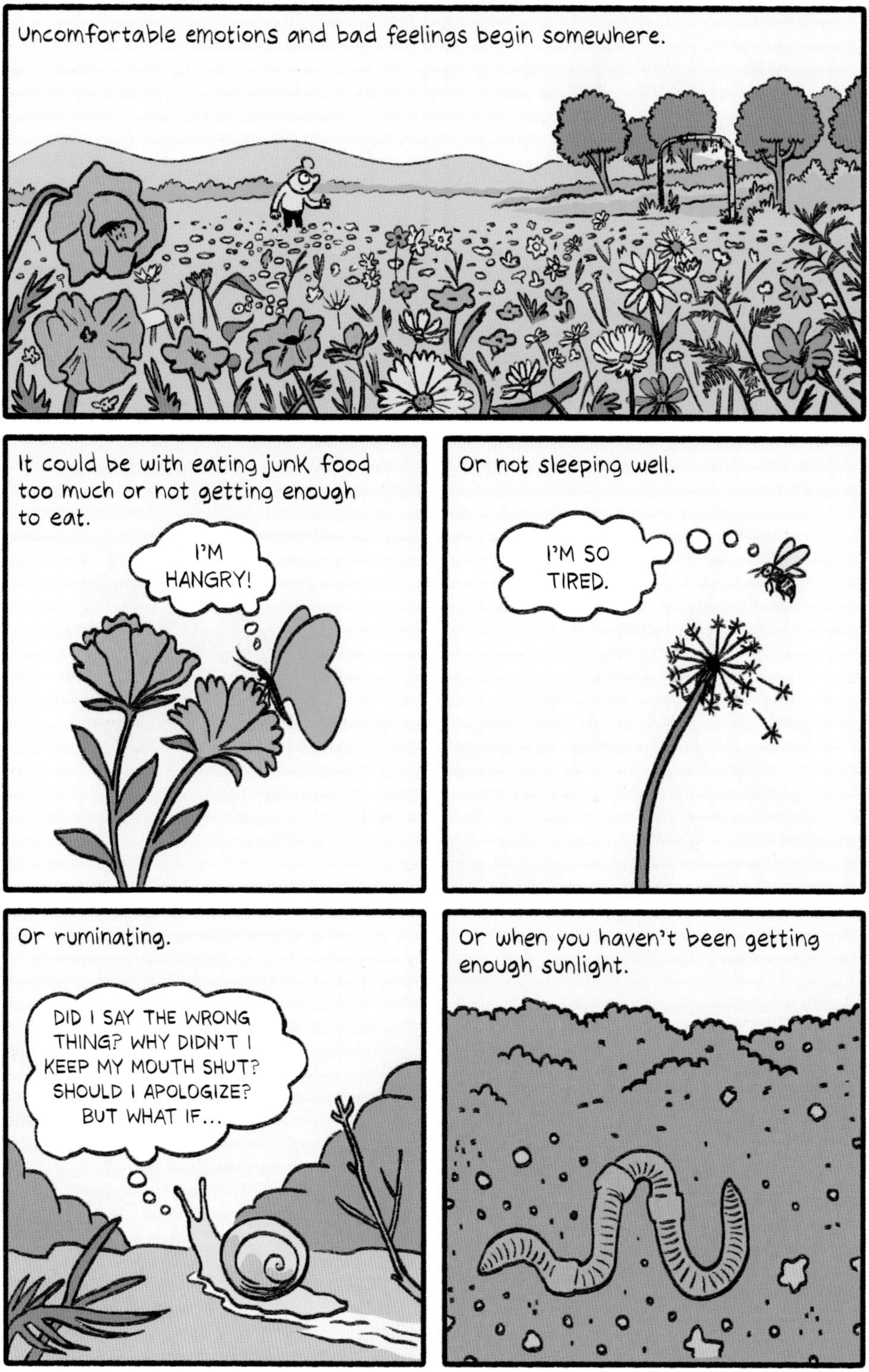
Uncomfortable emotions and bad feelings begin somewhere.
It could be with eating junk food too much or not getting enough to eat.
I'M HANGRY!
Or not sleeping well.
I'M SO TIRED.
Or ruminating.
DID I SAY THE WRONG THING? WHY DIDN'T I KEEP MY MOUTH SHUT? SHOULD I APOLOGIZE? BUT WHAT IF...
Or when you haven't been getting enough sunlight.

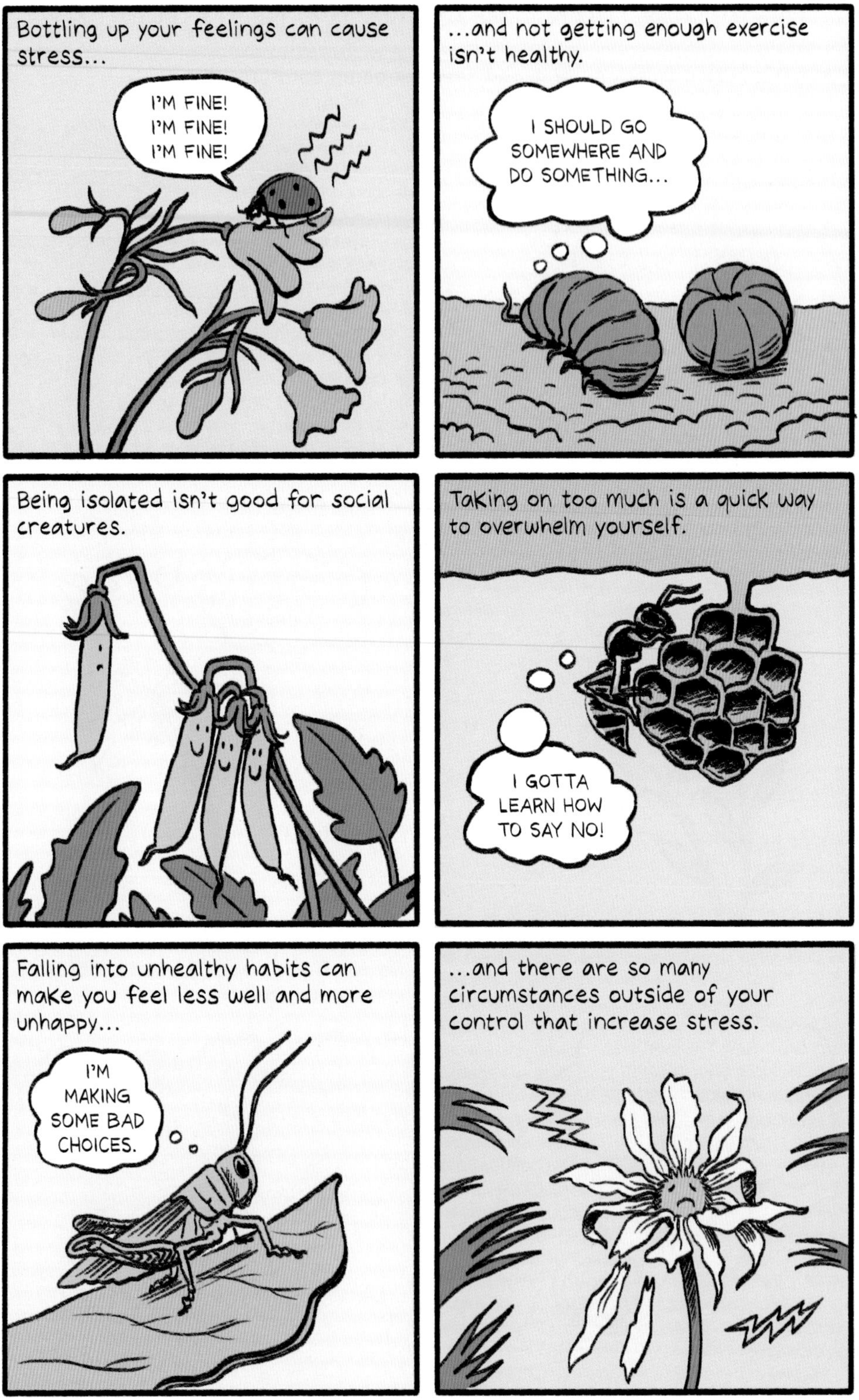
Bottling up your feelings can cause stress...
I'M FINE! I'M FINE! I'M FINE!
...and not getting enough exercise isn't healthy.
I SHOULD GO SOMEWHERE AND DO SOMETHING...
Being isolated isn't good for social creatures.
Taking on too much is a quick way to overwhelm yourself.
I GOTTA LEARN HOW TO SAY NO!
Falling into unhealthy habits can make you feel less well and more unhappy...
I'M MAKING SOME BAD CHOICES.
...and there are so many circumstances outside of your control that increase stress.

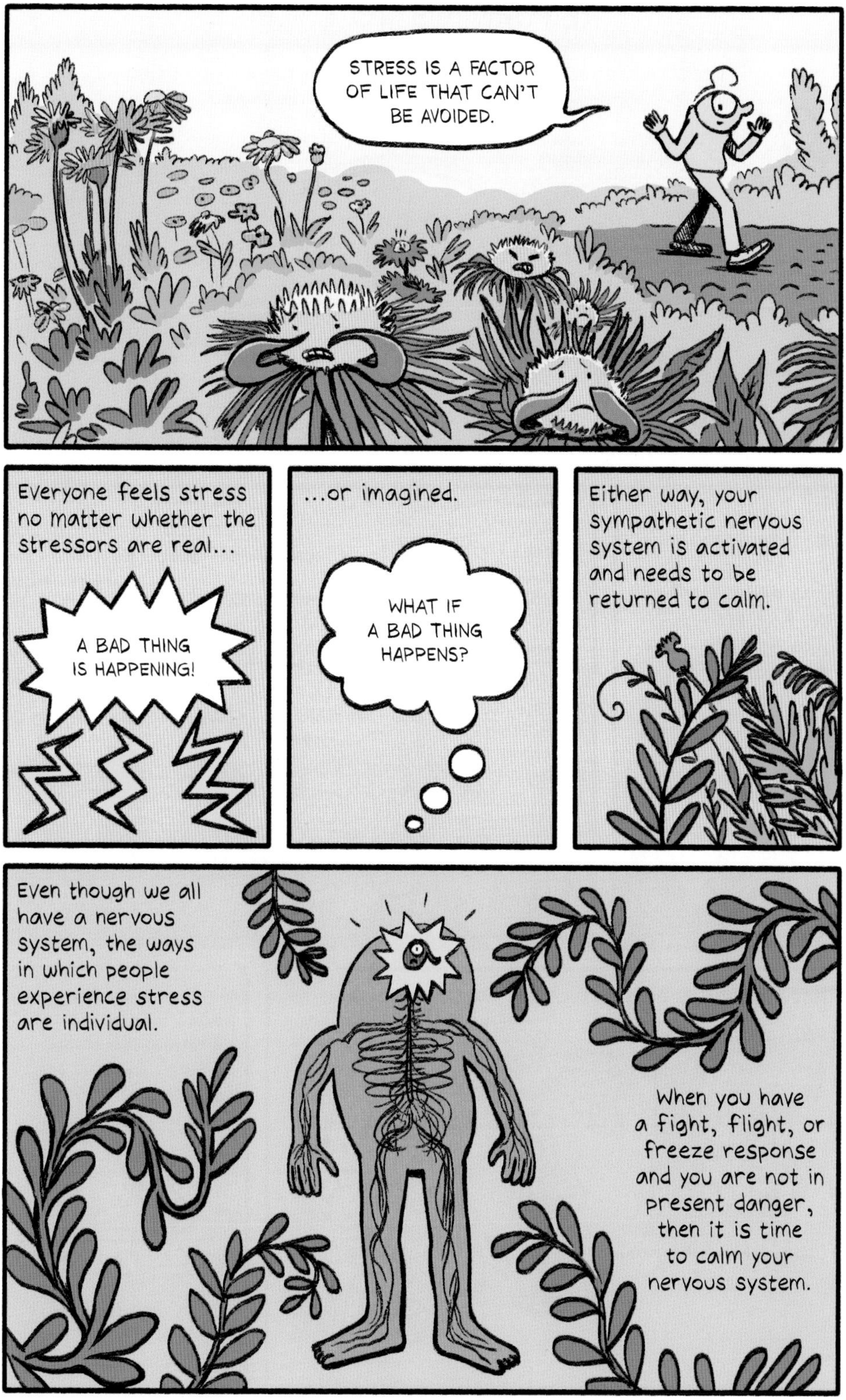
STRESS IS A FACTOR OF LIFE THAT CAN'T BE AVOIDED.
Everyone feels stress no matter whether the stressors are real...
A BAD THING IS HAPPENING!
...or imagined.
WHAT IF A BAD THING HAPPENS?
Either way, your sympathetic nervous system is activated and needs to be returned to calm.
Even though we all have a nervous system, the ways in which people experience stress are individual.
When you have a fight, flight, or freeze response and you are not in present danger, then it is time to calm your nervous system.

RETURNING TO CALM

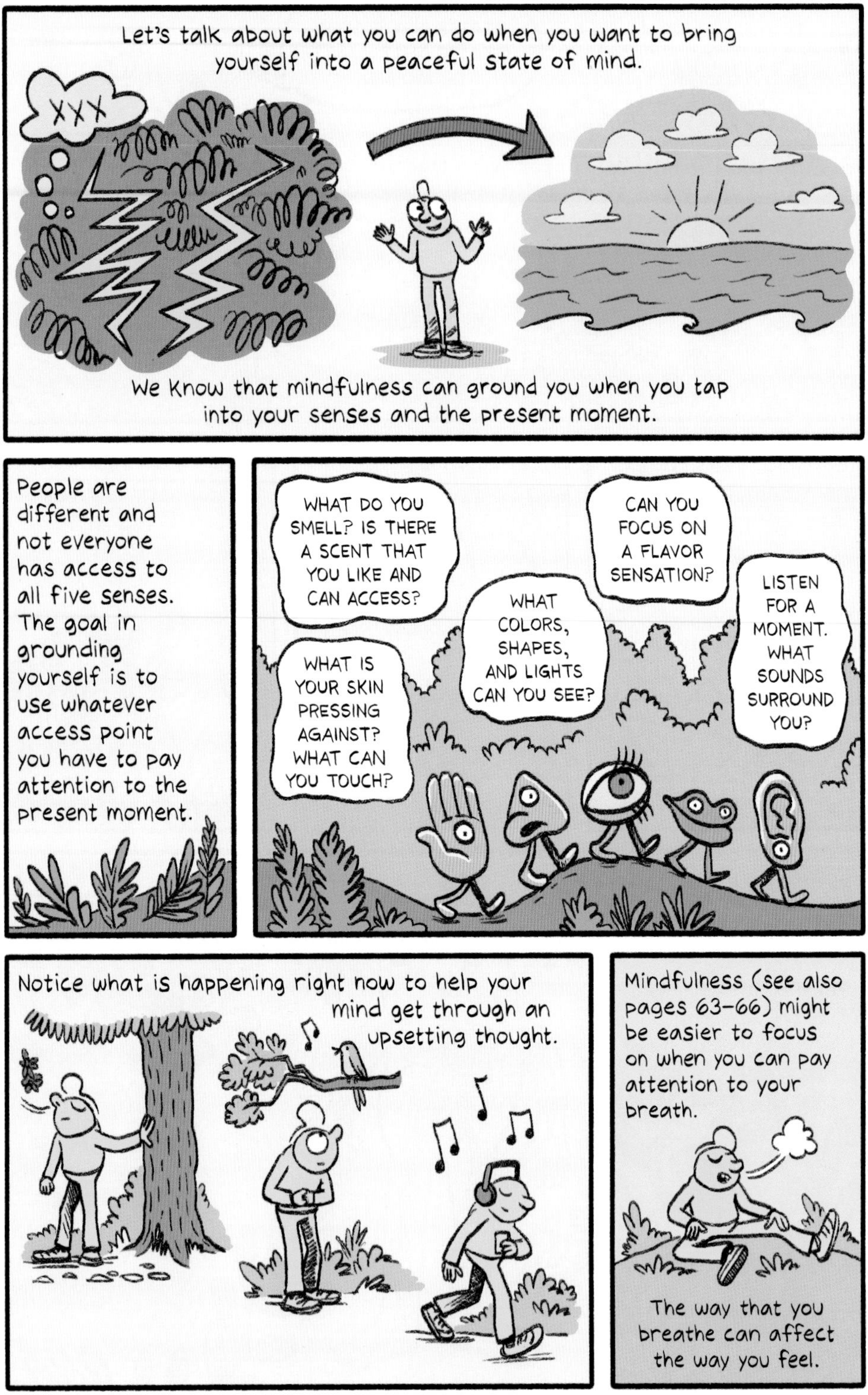

Let's talk about what you can do when you want to bring yourself into a peaceful state of mind.
XXX
We know that mindfulness can ground you when you tap into your senses and the present moment.
People are different and not everyone has access to all five senses. The goal in grounding yourself is to use whatever access point you have to pay attention to the present moment.
WHAT IS YOUR SKIN PRESSING AGAINST? WHAT CAN YOU TOUCH?
WHAT DO YOU SMELL? IS THERE A SCENT THAT YOU LIKE AND CAN ACCESS?
WHAT COLORS, SHAPES, AND LIGHTS CAN YOU SEE?
CAN YOU FOCUS ON A FLAVOR SENSATION?
LISTEN FOR A MOMENT. WHAT SOUNDS SURROUND YOU?
Notice what is happening right now to help your mind get through an upsetting thought.
Mindfulness (see also pages 63–66) might be easier to focus on when you can pay attention to your breath.
The way that you breathe can affect the way you feel.

THE POWER OF BREATHING

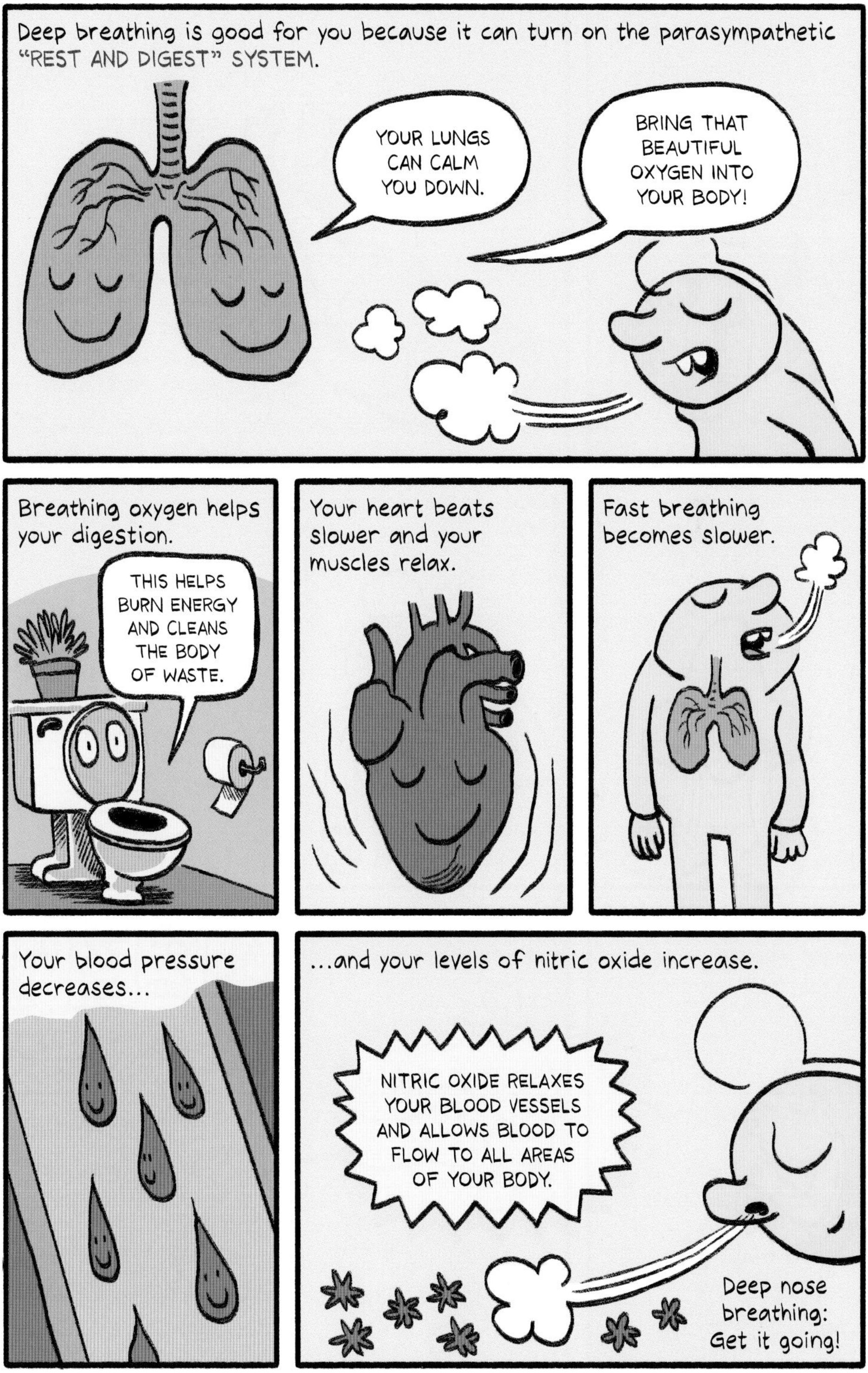

Deep breathing is good for you because it can turn on the parasympathetic "REST AND DIGEST" SYSTEM.
YOUR LUNGS CAN CALM YOU DOWN.
BRING THAT BEAUTIFUL OXYGEN INTO YOUR BODY!
Breathing oxygen helps your digestion.
THIS HELPS BURN ENERGY AND CLEANS THE BODY OF WASTE.
Your heart beats slower and your muscles relax.
Fast breathing becomes slower.
Your blood pressure decreases...
...and your levels of nitric oxide increase.
NITRIC OXIDE RELAXES YOUR BLOOD VESSELS AND ALLOWS BLOOD TO FLOW TO ALL AREAS OF YOUR BODY.
Deep nose breathing: Get it going!

TRY THIS BELLY BREATHING EXERCISE

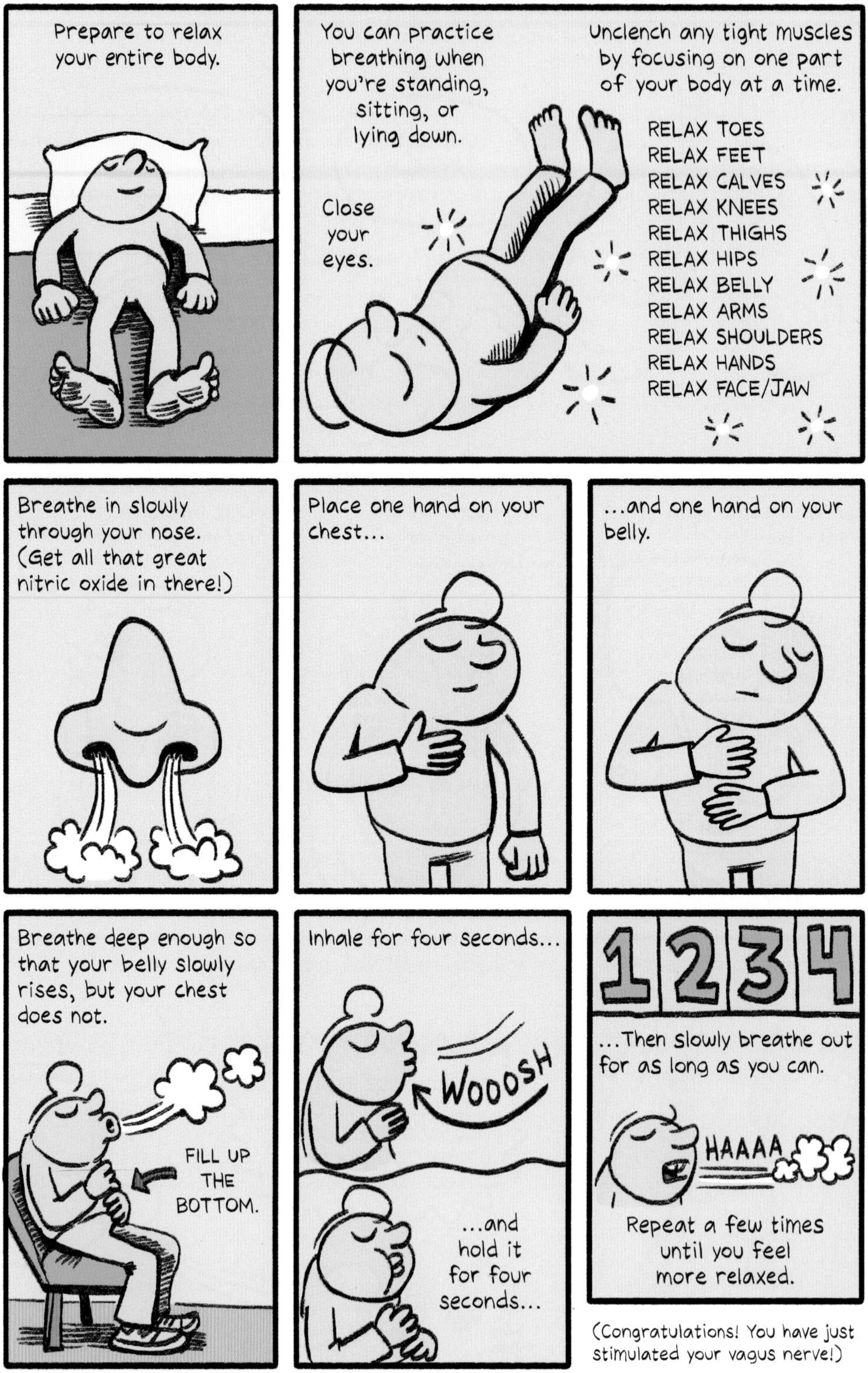

Prepare to relax your entire body.
You can practice breathing when you're standing, sitting, or lying down.
Close your eyes.
Unclench any tight muscles by focusing on one part of your body at a time.
RELAX TOES
RELAX FEET
RELAX CALVES
RELAX KNEES
RELAX THIGHS
RELAX HIPS
RELAX BELLY
RELAX ARMS
RELAX SHOULDERS
RELAX HANDS
RELAX FACE/JAW
Breathe in slowly through your nose. (Get all that great nitric oxide in there!)
Place one hand on your chest...
...and one hand on your belly.
Breathe deep enough so that your belly slowly rises, but your chest does not.
FILL UP THE BOTTOM.
Inhale for four seconds...
WOOOSH
...and hold it for four seconds...
1 2 3 4
...Then slowly breathe out for as long as you can.
HAAAA
Repeat a few times until you feel more relaxed.
(Congratulations! You have just stimulated your vagus nerve!)

MEET YOUR VAGUS NERVE

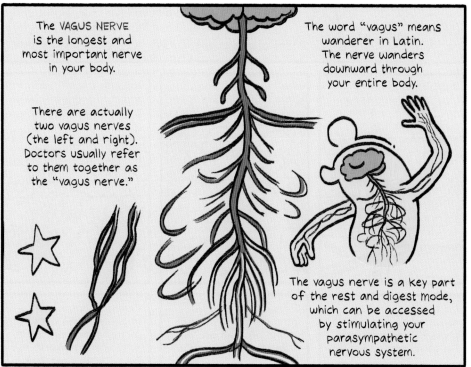

The VAGUS NERVE is the longest and most important nerve in your body.

There are actually two vagus nerves (the left and right). Doctors usually refer to them together as the "vagus nerve."

The word "vagus" means wanderer in Latin. The nerve wanders downward through your entire body.

The vagus nerve is a key part of the rest and digest mode, which can be accessed by stimulating your parasympathetic nervous system.

MORE WAYS TO STIMULATE YOUR VAGUS NERVE:

VOCAL CORDS

-SINGING

-HUMMING

-CHANTING

-GARGLING

-LAUGHING

(THE VAGUS NERVE IS CONNECTED TO YOUR VOCAL CORDS AND THE MUSCLES AT THE BACK OF THE THROAT.)

COLD EXPOSURE

-TAKING A COLD SHOWER

-DUNKING YOUR FACE IN ICE WATER

-DRINKING A COLD DRINK

-BEING BRIEFLY OUTSIDE IN THE COLD

MASSAGE

-VERY GENTLE PRESSURE ON THE RIGHT SIDE OF YOUR NECK, THEN UP BEHIND THE EAR, THEN BACK DOWN THE NECK

-MASSAGING VERY GENTLY AROUND YOUR EARS WITH YOUR FINGERTIPS

(CHECK WITH YOUR DOCTOR TO SEE IF THIS IS OKAY FOR YOUR BODY.)

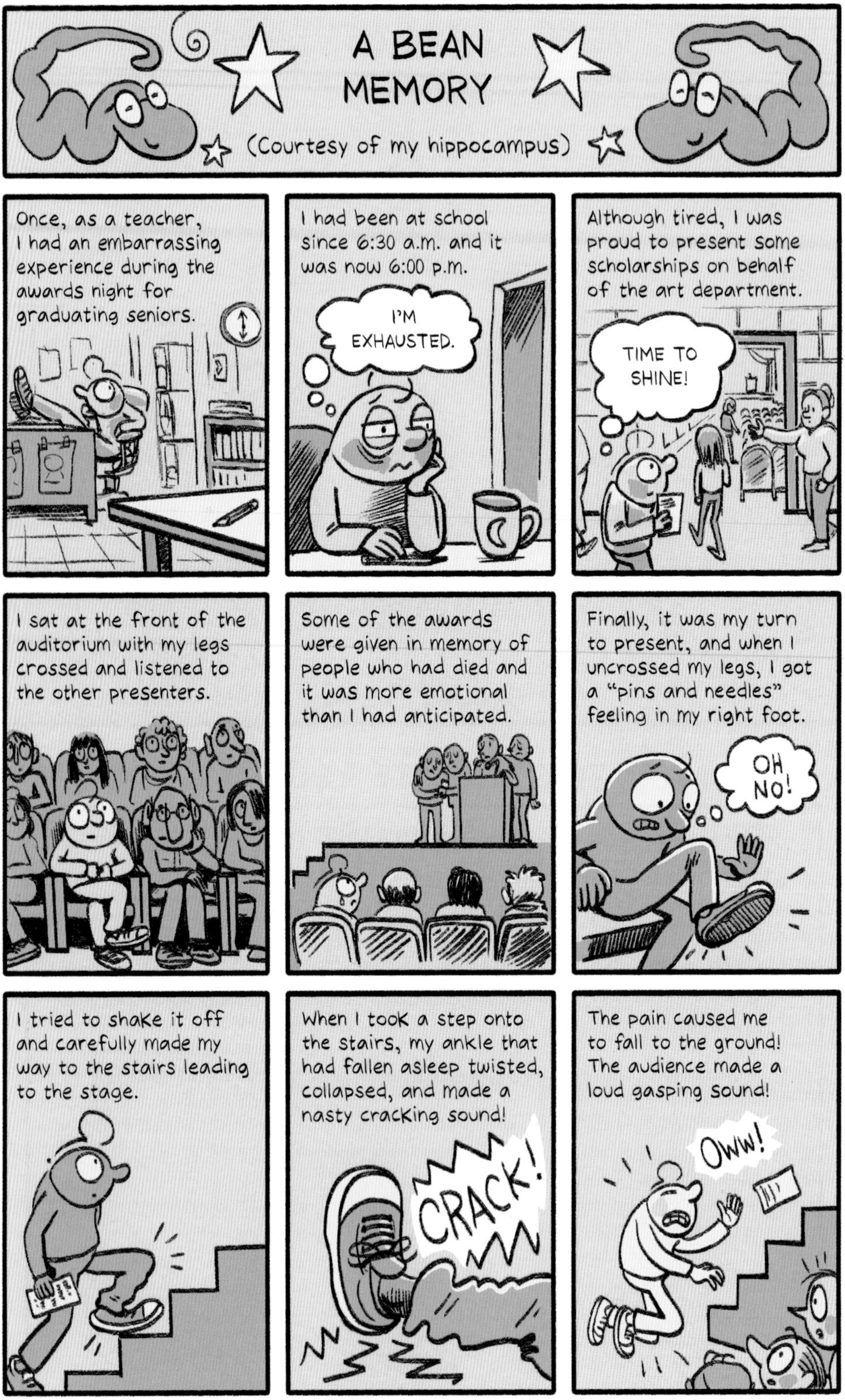
A BEAN MEMORY
(Courtesy of my hippocampus)
Once, as a teacher, I had an embarrassing experience during the awards night for graduating seniors.
I had been at school since 6:30 a.m. and it was now 6:00 p.m.
I'M EXHAUSTED.
Although tired, I was proud to present some scholarships on behalf of the art department.
TIME TO SHINE!
I sat at the front of the auditorium with my legs crossed and listened to the other presenters.
Some of the awards were given in memory of people who had died and it was more emotional than I had anticipated.
Finally, it was my turn to present, and when I uncrossed my legs, I got a "pins and needles" feeling in my right foot.
OH NO!
I tried to shake it off and carefully made my way to the stairs leading to the stage.
When I took a step onto the stairs, my ankle that had fallen asleep twisted, collapsed, and made a nasty cracking sound!
CRACK!
The pain caused me to fall to the ground! The audience made a loud gasping sound!
OWW!

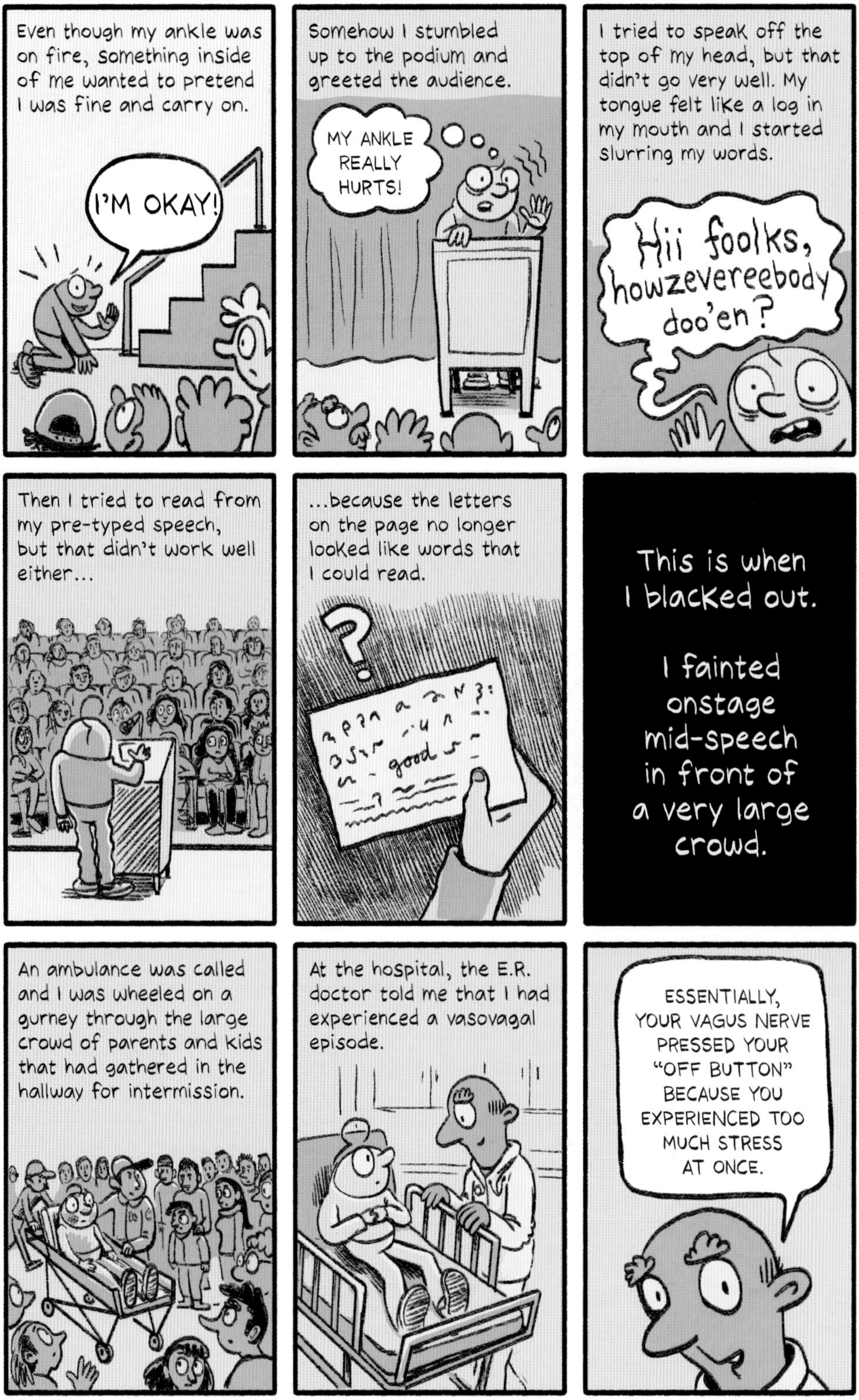
Even though my ankle was on fire, something inside of me wanted to pretend I was fine and carry on.
I'M OKAY!
Somehow I stumbled up to the podium and greeted the audience.
MY ANKLE REALLY HURTS!
I tried to speak off the top of my head, but that didn't go very well. My tongue felt like a log in my mouth and I started slurring my words.
Hii foolks, howzevereebody doo'en?
Then I tried to read from my pre-typed speech, but that didn't work well either...
...because the letters on the page no longer looked like words that I could read.
?
good
This is when I blacked out.
I fainted onstage mid-speech in front of a very large crowd.
An ambulance was called and I was wheeled on a gurney through the large crowd of parents and kids that had gathered in the hallway for intermission.
At the hospital, the E.R. doctor told me that I had experienced a vasovagal episode.
ESSENTIALLY, YOUR VAGUS NERVE PRESSED YOUR "OFF BUTTON" BECAUSE YOU EXPERIENCED TOO MUCH STRESS AT ONCE.

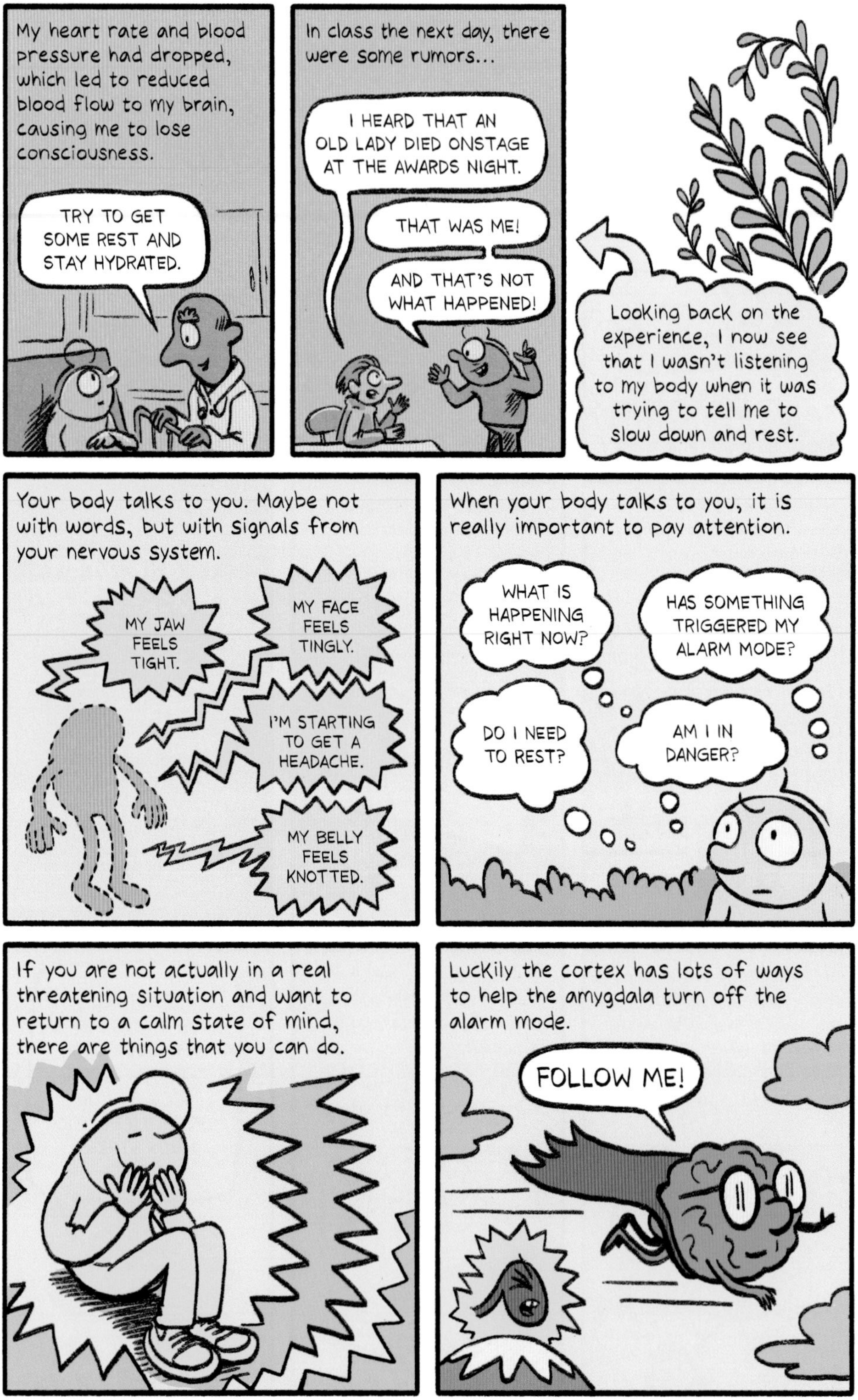
My heart rate and blood pressure had dropped, which led to reduced blood flow to my brain, causing me to lose consciousness.
TRY TO GET SOME REST AND STAY HYDRATED.
In class the next day, there were some rumors...
I HEARD THAT AN OLD LADY DIED ONSTAGE AT THE AWARDS NIGHT.
THAT WAS ME!
AND THAT'S NOT WHAT HAPPENED!
Looking back on the experience, I now see that I wasn't listening to my body when it was trying to tell me to slow down and rest.
Your body talks to you. Maybe not with words, but with signals from your nervous system.
MY JAW FEELS TIGHT.
MY FACE FEELS TINGLY.
I'M STARTING TO GET A HEADACHE.
MY BELLY FEELS KNOTTED.
When your body talks to you, it is really important to pay attention.
WHAT IS HAPPENING RIGHT NOW?
HAS SOMETHING TRIGGERED MY ALARM MODE?
DO I NEED TO REST?
AM I IN DANGER?
If you are not actually in a real threatening situation and want to return to a calm state of mind, there are things that you can do.
Luckily the cortex has lots of ways to help the amygdala turn off the alarm mode.
FOLLOW ME!

WHAT CAN YOU DO TO DISTRACT YOURSELF DURING A STRESSFUL MOMENT?

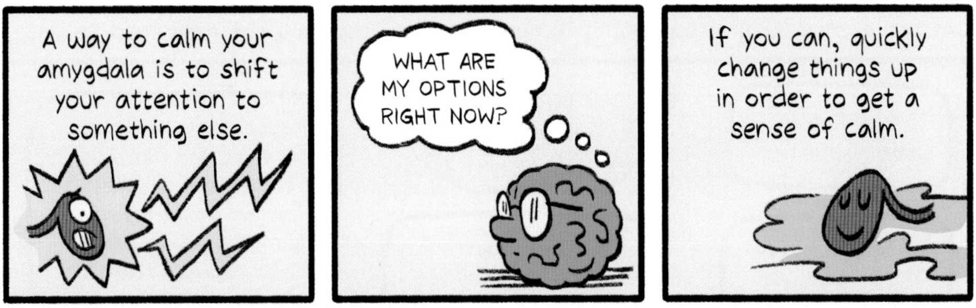

A way to calm your amygdala is to shift your attention to something else.
WHAT ARE MY OPTIONS RIGHT NOW?
If you can, quickly change things up in order to get a sense of calm.

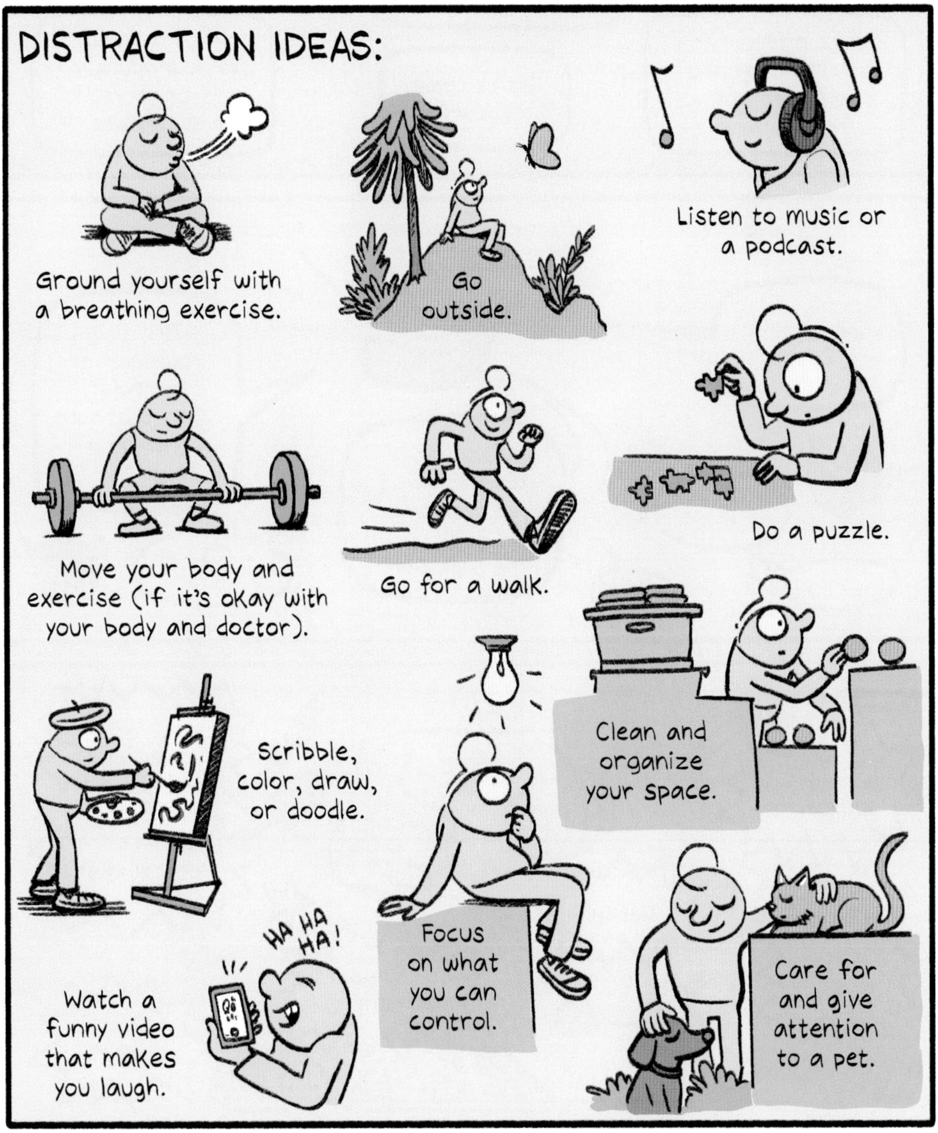

DISTRACTION IDEAS:
Ground yourself with a breathing exercise.
Go outside.
Listen to music or a podcast.
Move your body and exercise (if it's okay with your body and doctor).
Go for a walk.
Do a puzzle.
Scribble, color, draw, or doodle.
Clean and organize your space.
Focus on what you can control.
HA HA HA!
Watch a funny video that makes you laugh.
Care for and give attention to a pet.

WHAT ARE WAYS TO PROCESS EMOTIONS AFTER AN UPSETTING EVENT?

After a stressful situation, it is helpful to reflect on what happened to you.

WRITE

Journal about what happened.

Release all your hurt feelings.

Write a letter to a person you are angry at and then rip it up.

Write down something that you like about yourself.

Write some poetry.

Record your impulses and what you are hoping to get out of them. Then jot down ideas for something you can do to replace them.

Write a letter to your younger self or yourself in the future.

TALK

Call or text a friend.

Chat with a trusted adult to get some clarity on the situation.

Talk to a counselor or therapist. (More about therapy in chapter 9.)

!

?

CREATE

Build something.

Make music.

Dance.

Bake something.

Make art:
- drawing
- painting
- sculpture
- collage
- installation

Cook a meal.

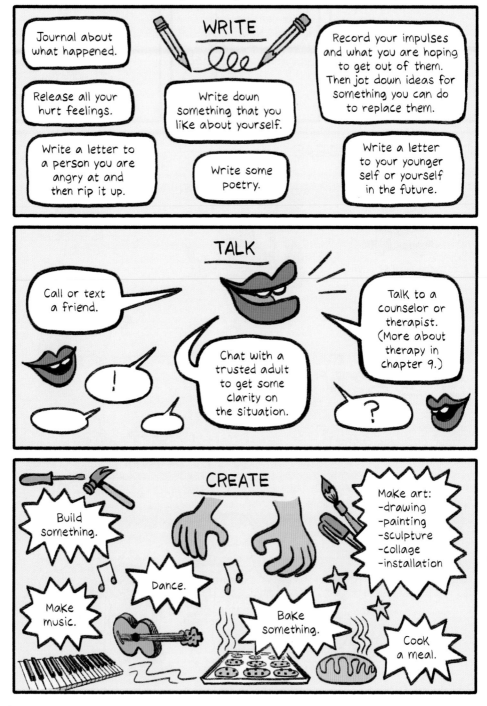

WHY IS SLEEP SO IMPORTANT FOR THE BRAIN?

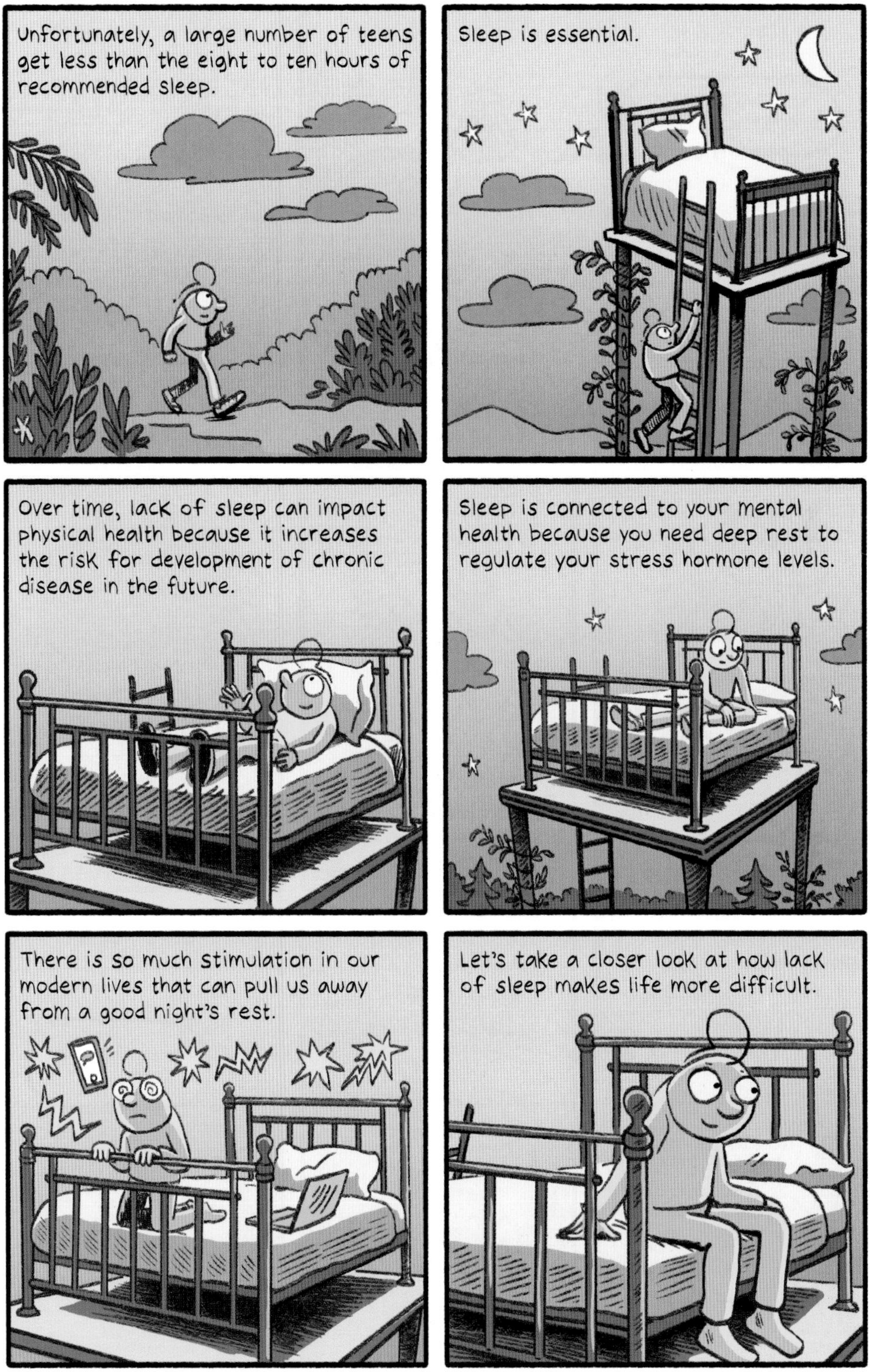
Unfortunately, a large number of teens get less than the eight to ten hours of recommended sleep.
Sleep is essential.
Over time, lack of sleep can impact physical health because it increases the risk for development of chronic disease in the future.
Sleep is connected to your mental health because you need deep rest to regulate your stress hormone levels.
There is so much stimulation in our modern lives that can pull us away from a good night's rest.
Let's take a closer look at how lack of sleep makes life more difficult.

THE STORY OF THE SLEEP-DEPRIVED BRAIN

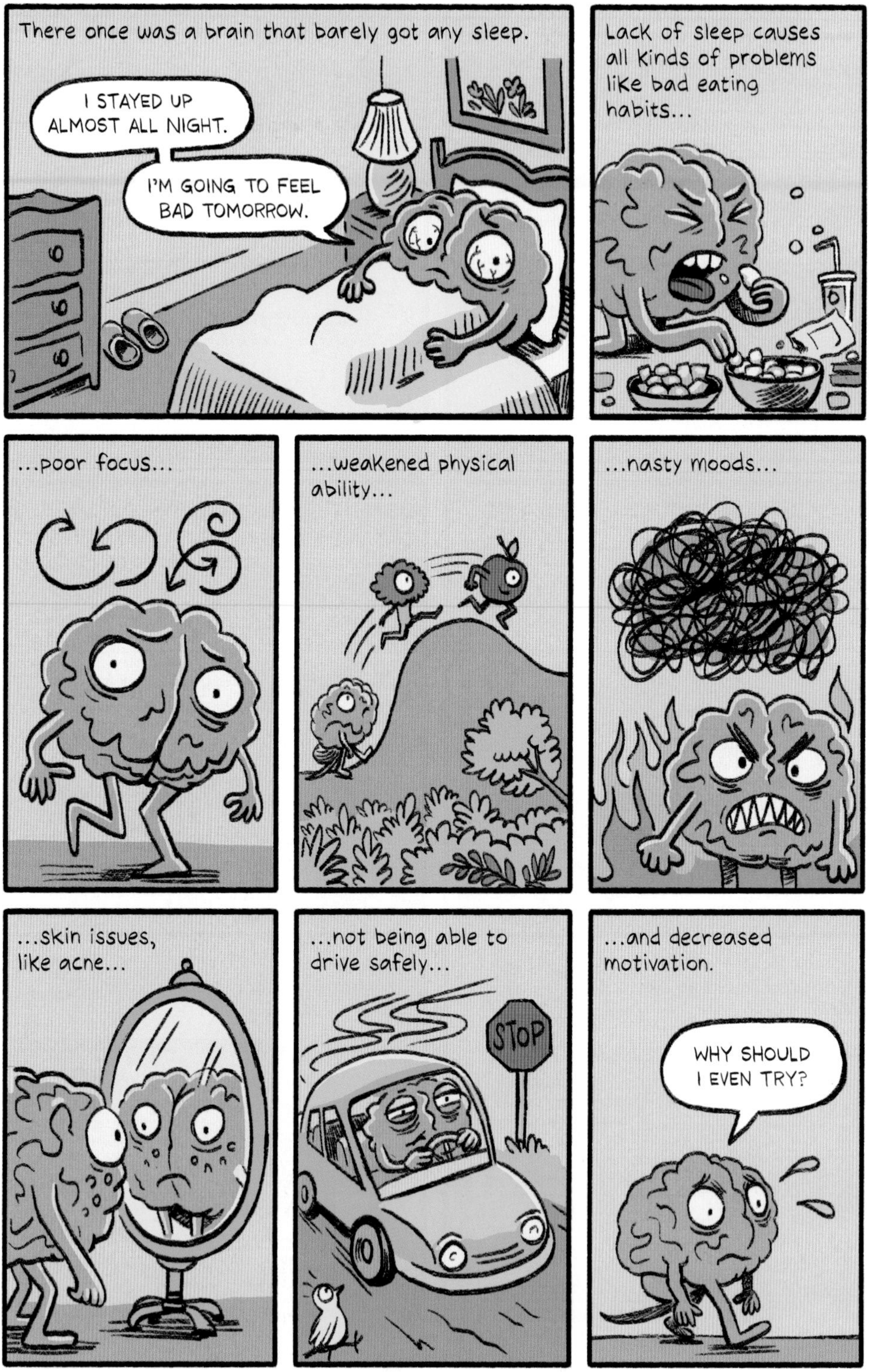
There once was a brain that barely got any sleep.
I STAYED UP ALMOST ALL NIGHT.
I'M GOING TO FEEL BAD TOMORROW.
Lack of sleep causes all kinds of problems like bad eating habits...
...poor focus...
...weakened physical ability...
...nasty moods...
...skin issues, like acne...
...not being able to drive safely...
STOP
...and decreased motivation.
WHY SHOULD I EVEN TRY?

WHAT HAPPENS INSIDE THE BRAIN WHILE YOU SLEEP?

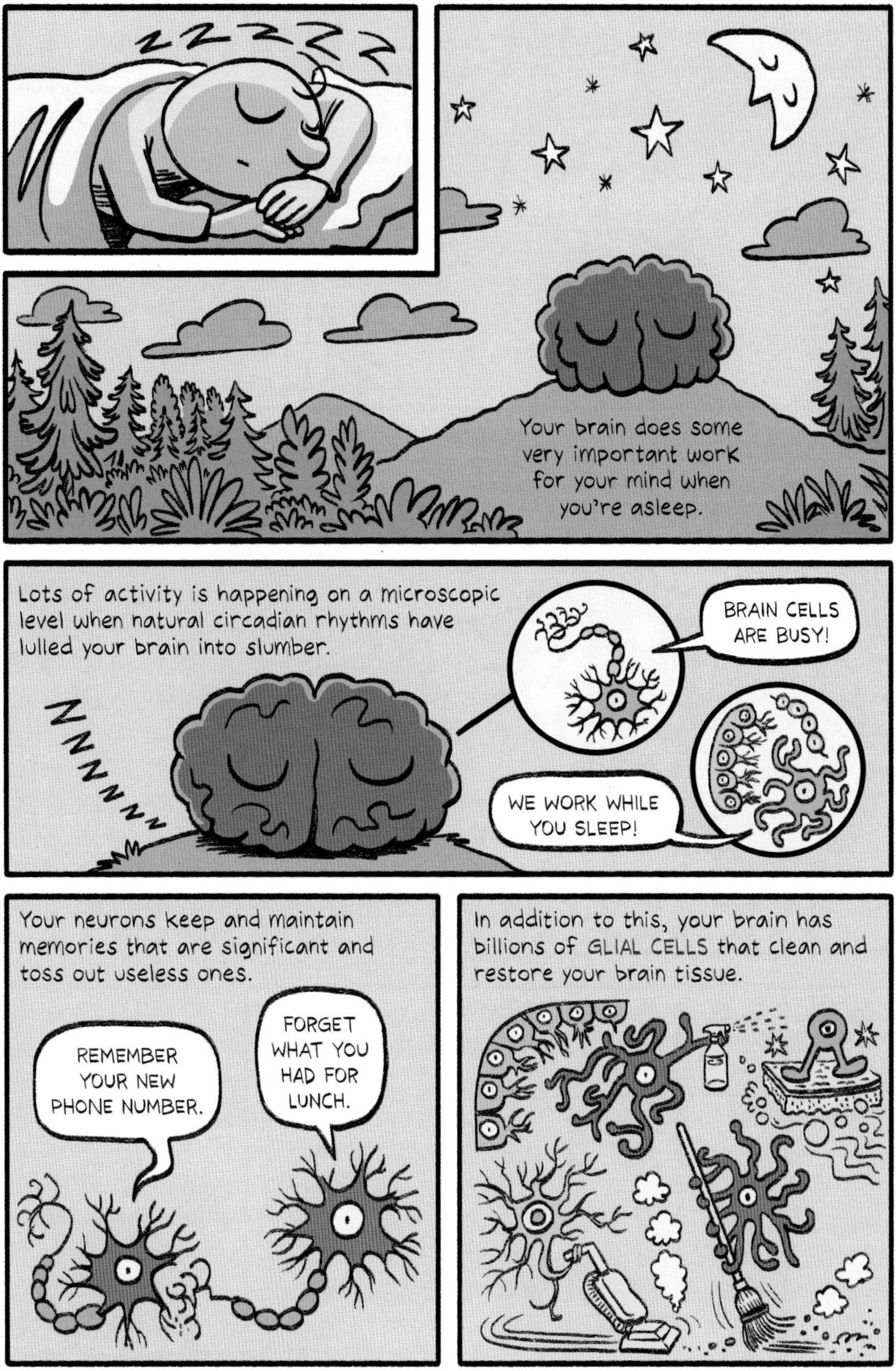
ZZZZZZ
Your brain does some very important work for your mind when you're asleep.
Lots of activity is happening on a microscopic level when natural circadian rhythms have lulled your brain into slumber.
NNNNNN
BRAIN CELLS ARE BUSY!
WE WORK WHILE YOU SLEEP!
Your neurons keep and maintain memories that are significant and toss out useless ones.
REMEMBER YOUR NEW PHONE NUMBER.
FORGET WHAT YOU HAD FOR LUNCH.
In addition to this, your brain has billions of GLIAL CELLS that clean and restore your brain tissue.

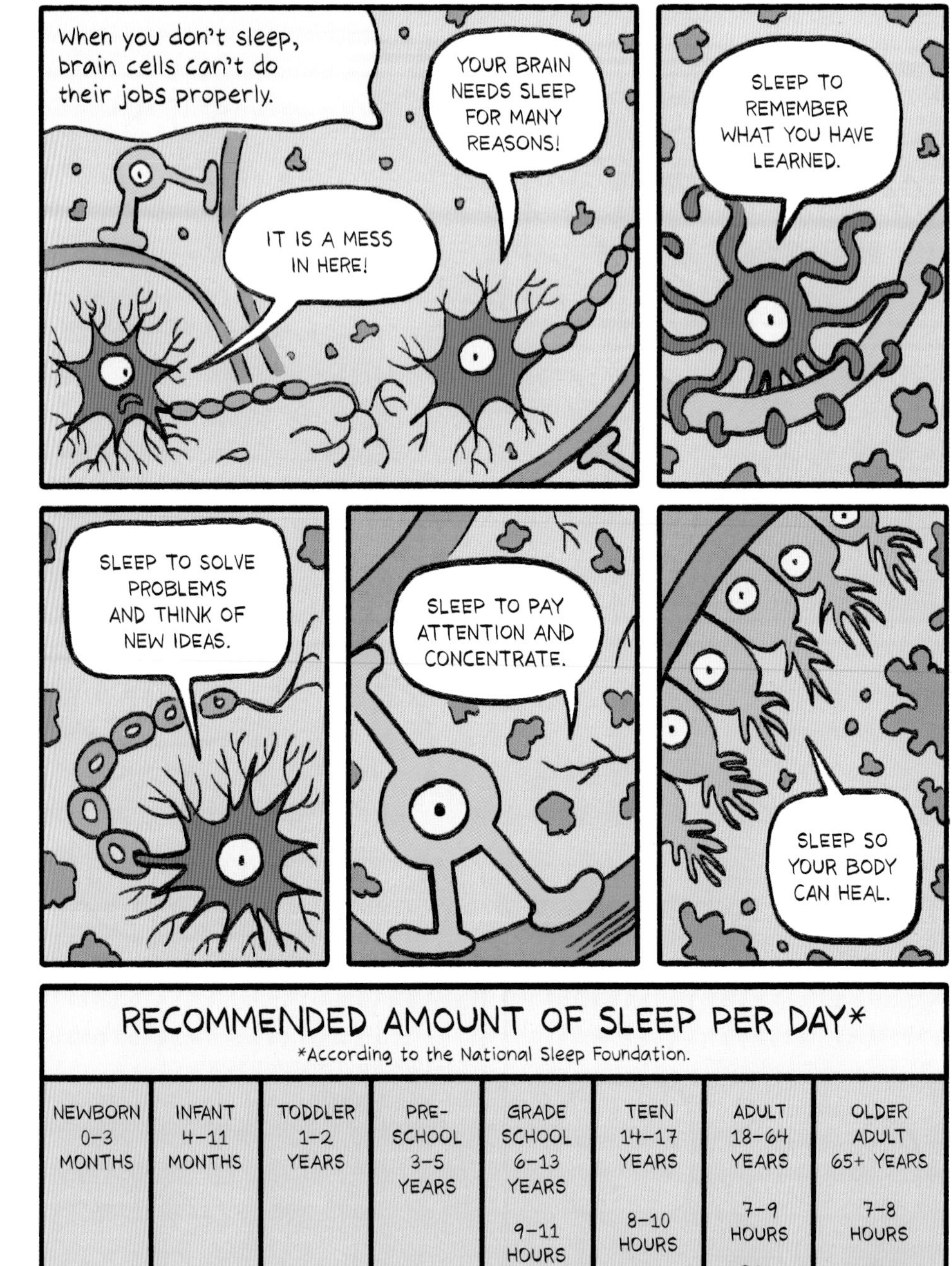
When you don't sleep, brain cells can't do their jobs properly.
IT IS A MESS IN HERE!
YOUR BRAIN NEEDS SLEEP FOR MANY REASONS!
SLEEP TO REMEMBER WHAT YOU HAVE LEARNED.
SLEEP TO SOLVE PROBLEMS AND THINK OF NEW IDEAS.
SLEEP TO PAY ATTENTION AND CONCENTRATE.
SLEEP SO YOUR BODY CAN HEAL.

RECOMMENDED AMOUNT OF SLEEP PER DAY*

*According to the National Sleep Foundation.

NEWBORN 0–3 MONTHS	INFANT 4–11 MONTHS	TODDLER 1–2 YEARS	PRE-SCHOOL 3–5 YEARS	GRADE SCHOOL 6–13 YEARS	TEEN 14–17 YEARS	ADULT 18–64 YEARS	OLDER ADULT 65+ YEARS
14–17 HOURS	12–15 HOURS	11–14 HOURS	10–13 HOURS	9–11 HOURS	8–10 HOURS	7–9 HOURS	7–8 HOURS

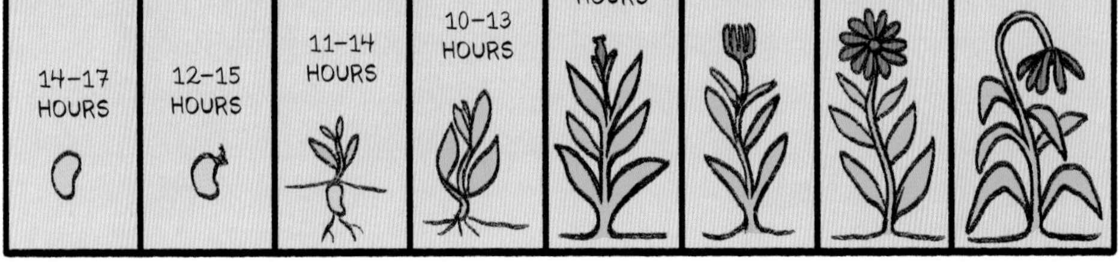

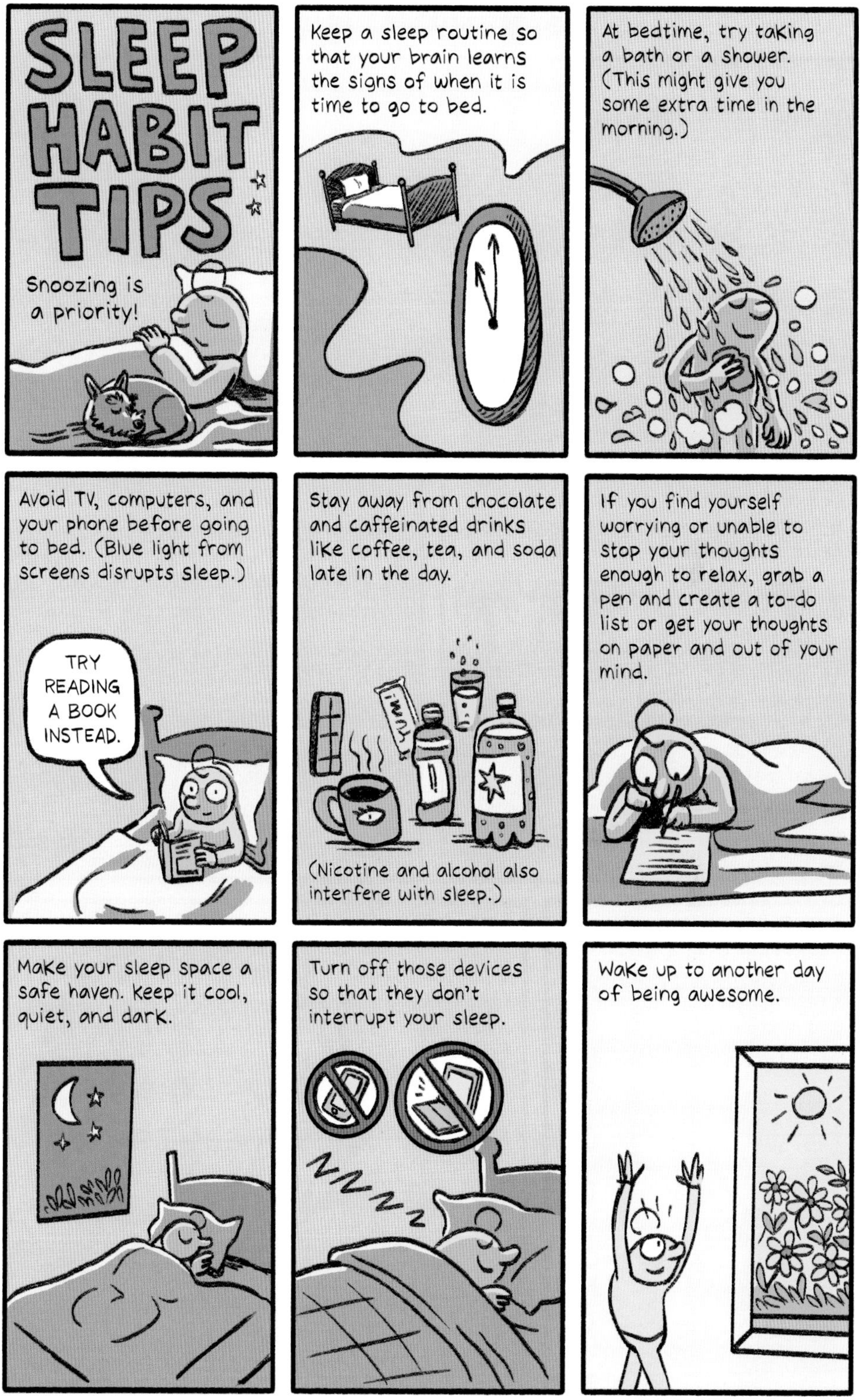
SLEEP HABIT TIPS
Snoozing is a priority!
Keep a sleep routine so that your brain learns the signs of when it is time to go to bed.
At bedtime, try taking a bath or a shower. (This might give you some extra time in the morning.)
Avoid TV, computers, and your phone before going to bed. (Blue light from screens disrupts sleep.)
TRY READING A BOOK INSTEAD.
Stay away from chocolate and caffeinated drinks like coffee, tea, and soda late in the day.
YUM!
(Nicotine and alcohol also interfere with sleep.)
If you find yourself worrying or unable to stop your thoughts enough to relax, grab a pen and create a to-do list or get your thoughts on paper and out of your mind.
Make your sleep space a safe haven. Keep it cool, quiet, and dark.
Turn off those devices so that they don't interrupt your sleep.
ZZZZZ
Wake up to another day of being awesome.

YOUR BRAIN IS A GARDEN THAT IS ALWAYS GROWING.

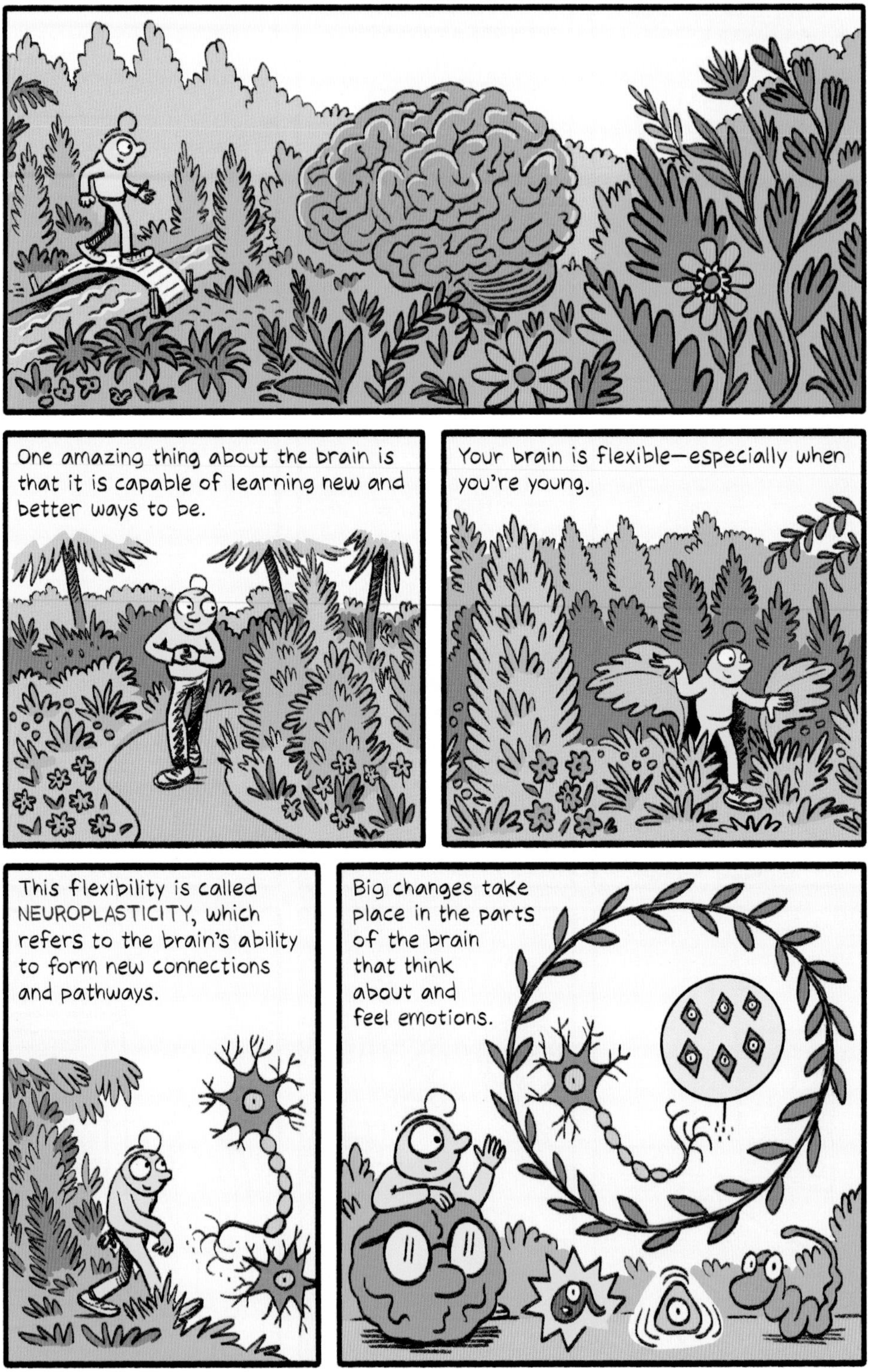
One amazing thing about the brain is that it is capable of learning new and better ways to be.
Your brain is flexible—especially when you're young.
This flexibility is called NEUROPLASTICITY, which refers to the brain's ability to form new connections and pathways.
Big changes take place in the parts of the brain that think about and feel emotions.

TEND THE GARDEN OF YOUR MIND

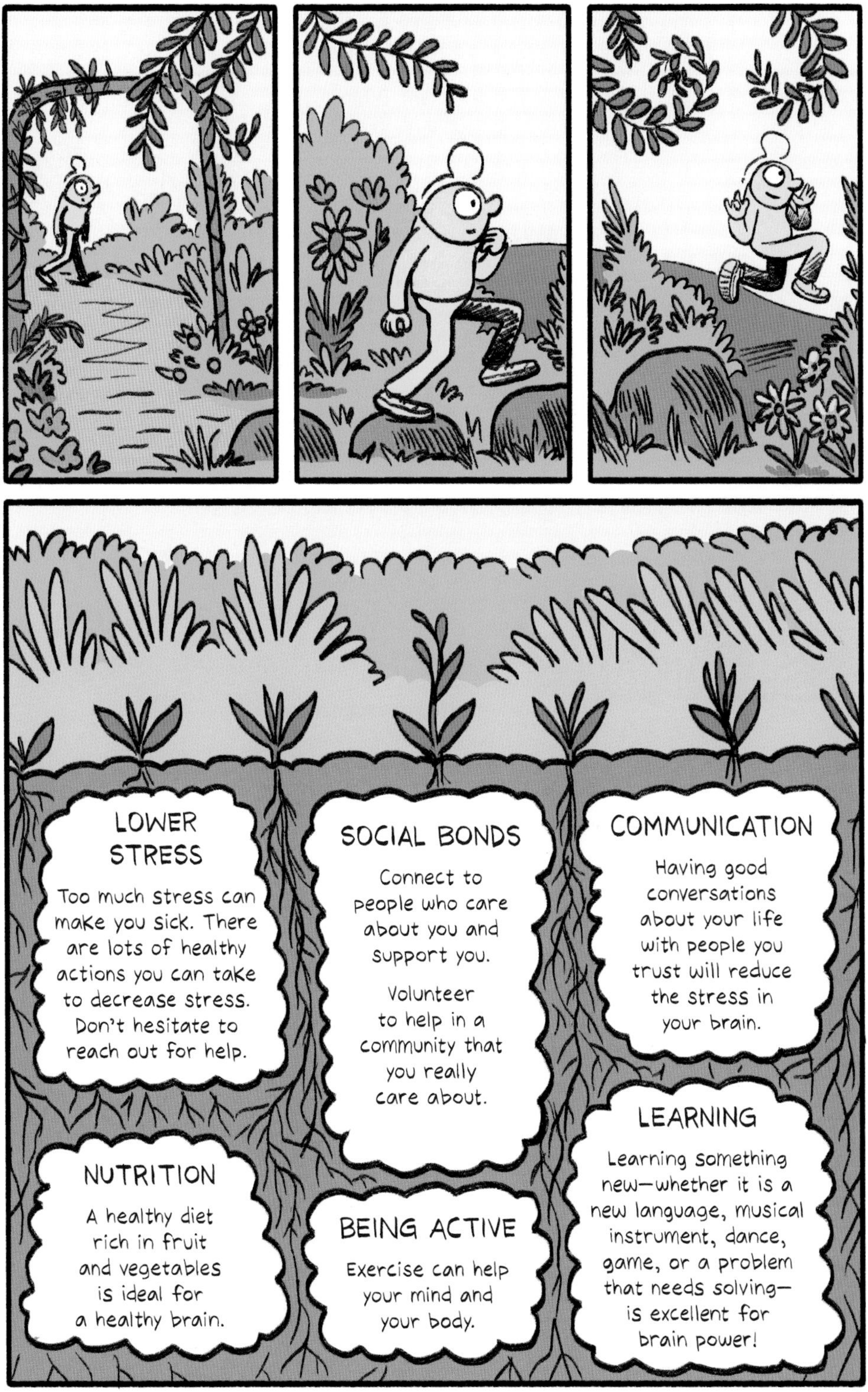
LOWER STRESS
Too much stress can make you sick. There are lots of healthy actions you can take to decrease stress. Don't hesitate to reach out for help.
SOCIAL BONDS
Connect to people who care about you and support you.
Volunteer to help in a community that you really care about.
COMMUNICATION
Having good conversations about your life with people you trust will reduce the stress in your brain.
NUTRITION
A healthy diet rich in fruit and vegetables is ideal for a healthy brain.
BEING ACTIVE
Exercise can help your mind and your body.
LEARNING
Learning something new—whether it is a new language, musical instrument, dance, game, or a problem that needs solving—is excellent for brain power!

WHAT HAPPENS INSIDE A DEVELOPING BRAIN?

There are big changes that take place in the brain during adolescence that impact emotions!

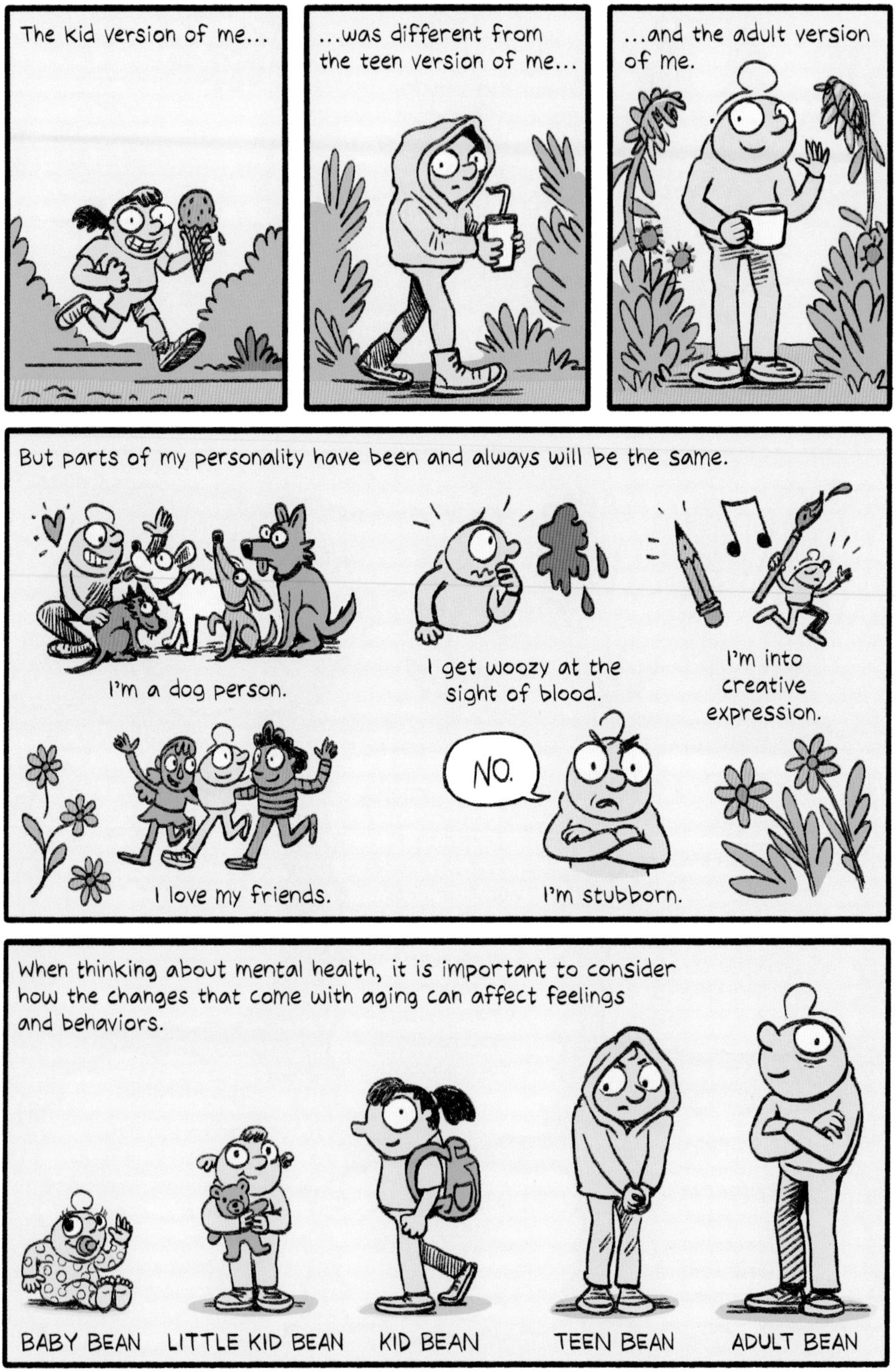
The kid version of me...
...was different from the teen version of me...
...and the adult version of me.
But parts of my personality have been and always will be the same.
I'm a dog person.
I get woozy at the sight of blood.
I'm into creative expression.
I love my friends.
NO.
I'm stubborn.
When thinking about mental health, it is important to consider how the changes that come with aging can affect feelings and behaviors.
BABY BEAN
LITTLE KID BEAN
KID BEAN
TEEN BEAN
ADULT BEAN

THE TEEN BRAIN IS INTENSE!

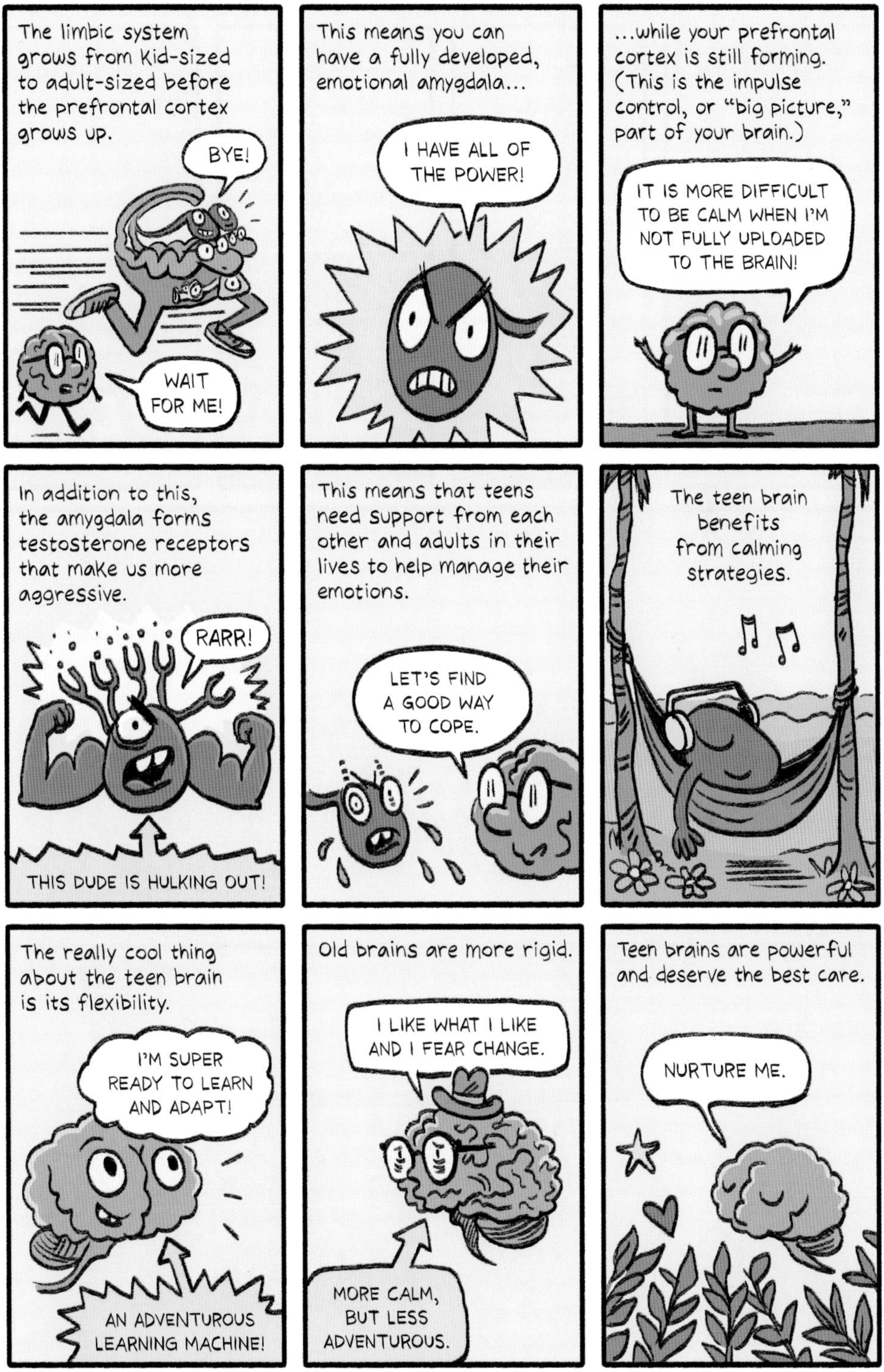
The limbic system grows from kid-sized to adult-sized before the prefrontal cortex grows up.
BYE!
WAIT FOR ME!
This means you can have a fully developed, emotional amygdala...
I HAVE ALL OF THE POWER!
...while your prefrontal cortex is still forming. (This is the impulse control, or "big picture," part of your brain.)
IT IS MORE DIFFICULT TO BE CALM WHEN I'M NOT FULLY UPLOADED TO THE BRAIN!
In addition to this, the amygdala forms testosterone receptors that make us more aggressive.
RARR!
THIS DUDE IS HULKING OUT!
This means that teens need support from each other and adults in their lives to help manage their emotions.
LET'S FIND A GOOD WAY TO COPE.
The teen brain benefits from calming strategies.
The really cool thing about the teen brain is its flexibility.
I'M SUPER READY TO LEARN AND ADAPT!
AN ADVENTUROUS LEARNING MACHINE!
Old brains are more rigid.
I LIKE WHAT I LIKE AND I FEAR CHANGE.
MORE CALM, BUT LESS ADVENTUROUS.
Teen brains are powerful and deserve the best care.
NURTURE ME.

HOW DO BRAIN CHEMICALS HELP?

Remember those neurotransmitters we mentioned in chapter 2? Each of those chemicals produces a slightly different experience.

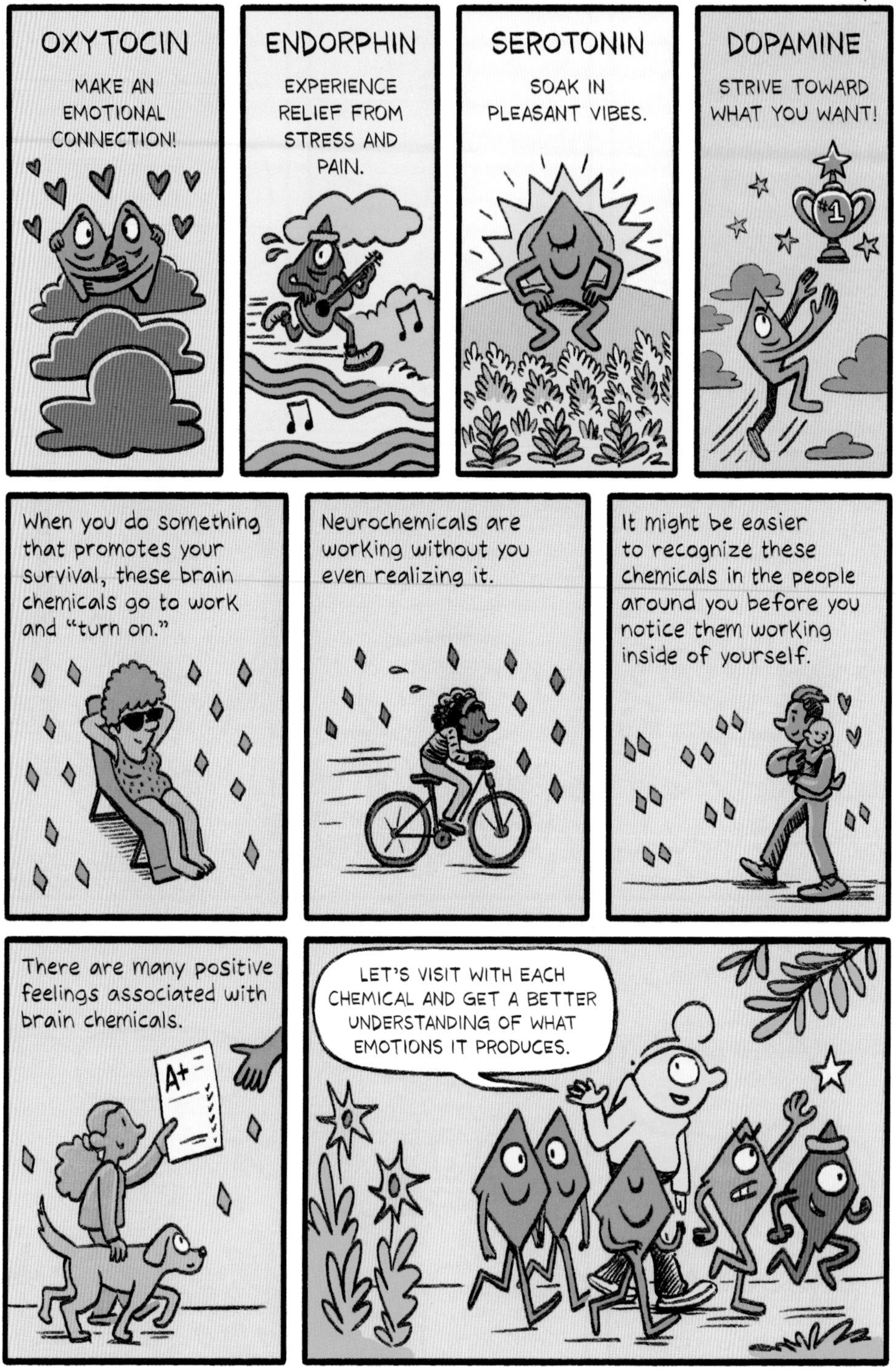
OXYTOCIN
MAKE AN EMOTIONAL CONNECTION!
ENDORPHIN
EXPERIENCE RELIEF FROM STRESS AND PAIN.
SEROTONIN
SOAK IN PLEASANT VIBES.
DOPAMINE
STRIVE TOWARD WHAT YOU WANT!
#1
When you do something that promotes your survival, these brain chemicals go to work and "turn on."
Neurochemicals are working without you even realizing it.
It might be easier to recognize these chemicals in the people around you before you notice them working inside of yourself.
There are many positive feelings associated with brain chemicals.
A+
LET'S VISIT WITH EACH CHEMICAL AND GET A BETTER UNDERSTANDING OF WHAT EMOTIONS IT PRODUCES.

OXYTOCIN

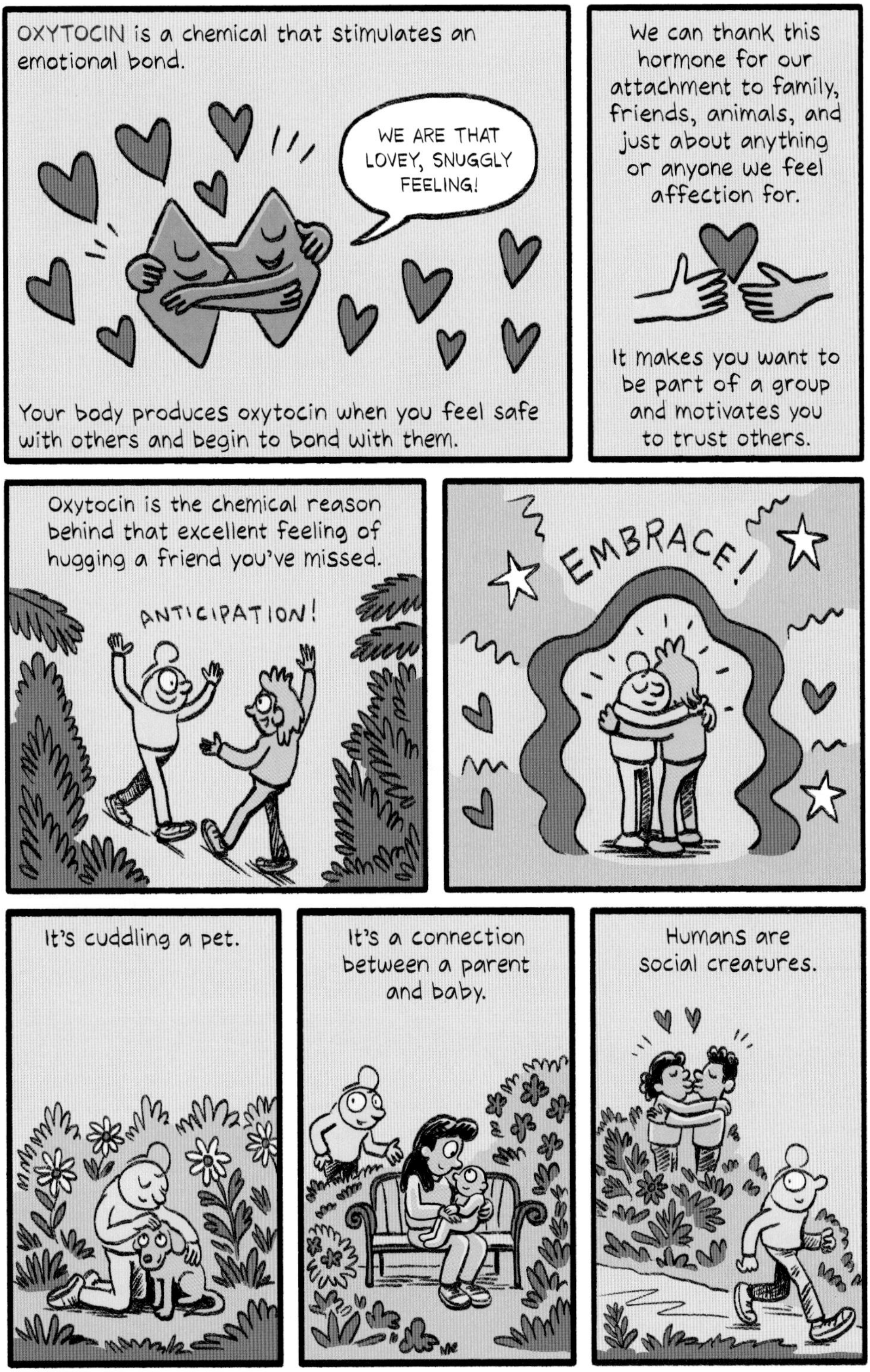

OXYTOCIN is a chemical that stimulates an emotional bond.
WE ARE THAT LOVEY, SNUGGLY FEELING!
Your body produces oxytocin when you feel safe with others and begin to bond with them.
We can thank this hormone for our attachment to family, friends, animals, and just about anything or anyone we feel affection for.
It makes you want to be part of a group and motivates you to trust others.
Oxytocin is the chemical reason behind that excellent feeling of hugging a friend you've missed.
ANTICIPATION!
EMBRACE!
It's cuddling a pet.
It's a connection between a parent and baby.
Humans are social creatures.

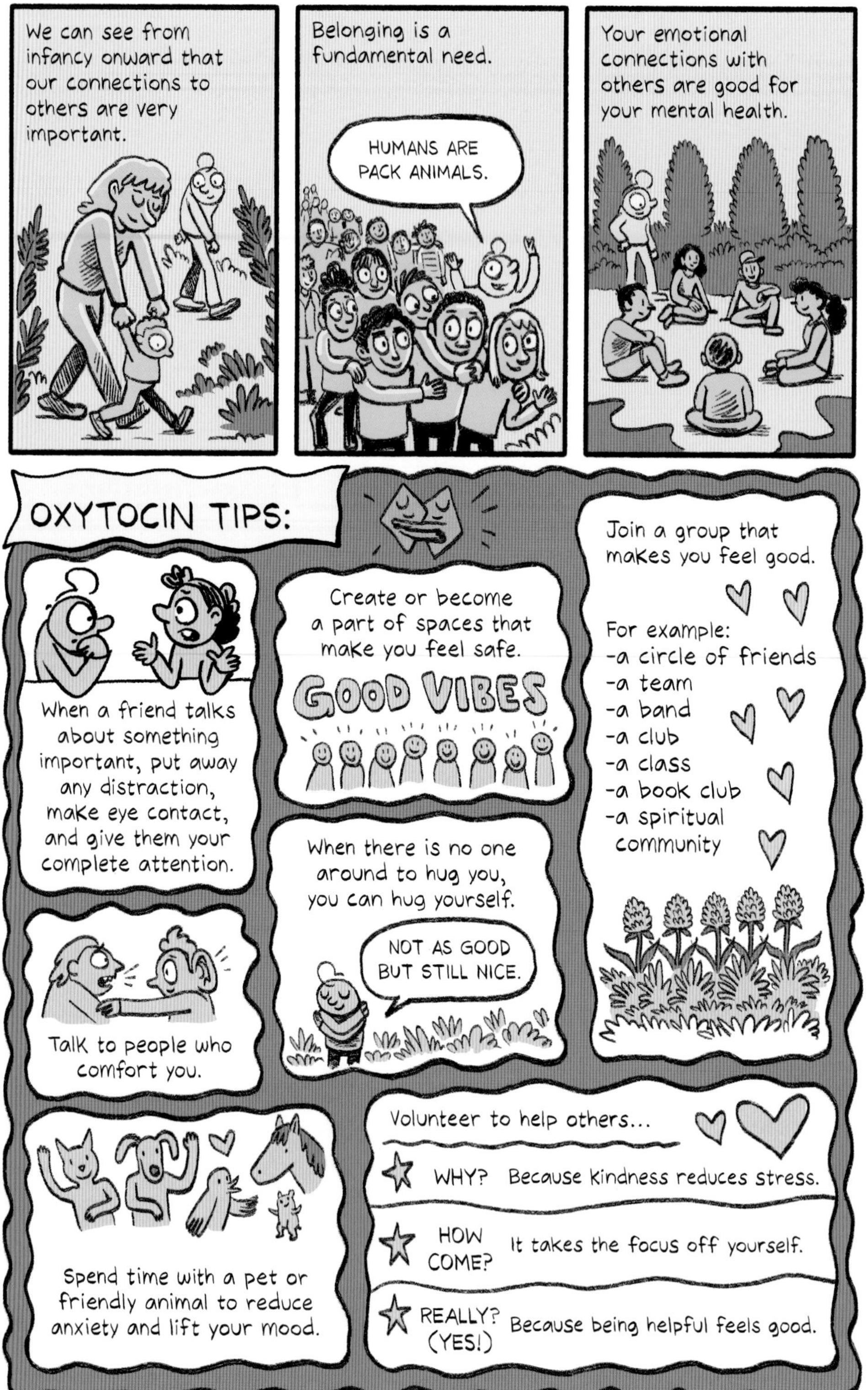
We can see from infancy onward that our connections to others are very important.
Belonging is a fundamental need.
HUMANS ARE PACK ANIMALS.
Your emotional connections with others are good for your mental health.
OXYTOCIN TIPS:
When a friend talks about something important, put away any distraction, make eye contact, and give them your complete attention.
Create or become a part of spaces that make you feel safe.
GOOD VIBES
Join a group that makes you feel good.
For example:
-a circle of friends
-a team
-a band
-a club
-a class
-a book club
-a spiritual community
When there is no one around to hug you, you can hug yourself.
NOT AS GOOD BUT STILL NICE.
Talk to people who comfort you.
Spend time with a pet or friendly animal to reduce anxiety and lift your mood.
Volunteer to help others...
WHY? Because kindness reduces stress.
HOW COME? It takes the focus off yourself.
REALLY? (YES!) Because being helpful feels good.

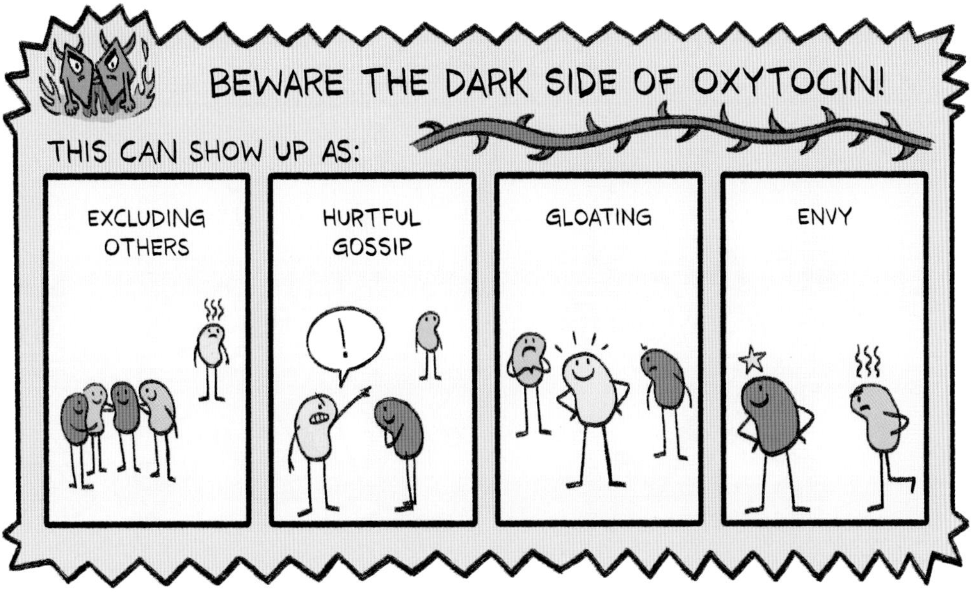
BEWARE THE DARK SIDE OF OXYTOCIN!
THIS CAN SHOW UP AS:
EXCLUDING OTHERS
HURTFUL GOSSIP
!
GLOATING
ENVY

HOW DO YOUR FRIENDS MAKE YOU FEEL?

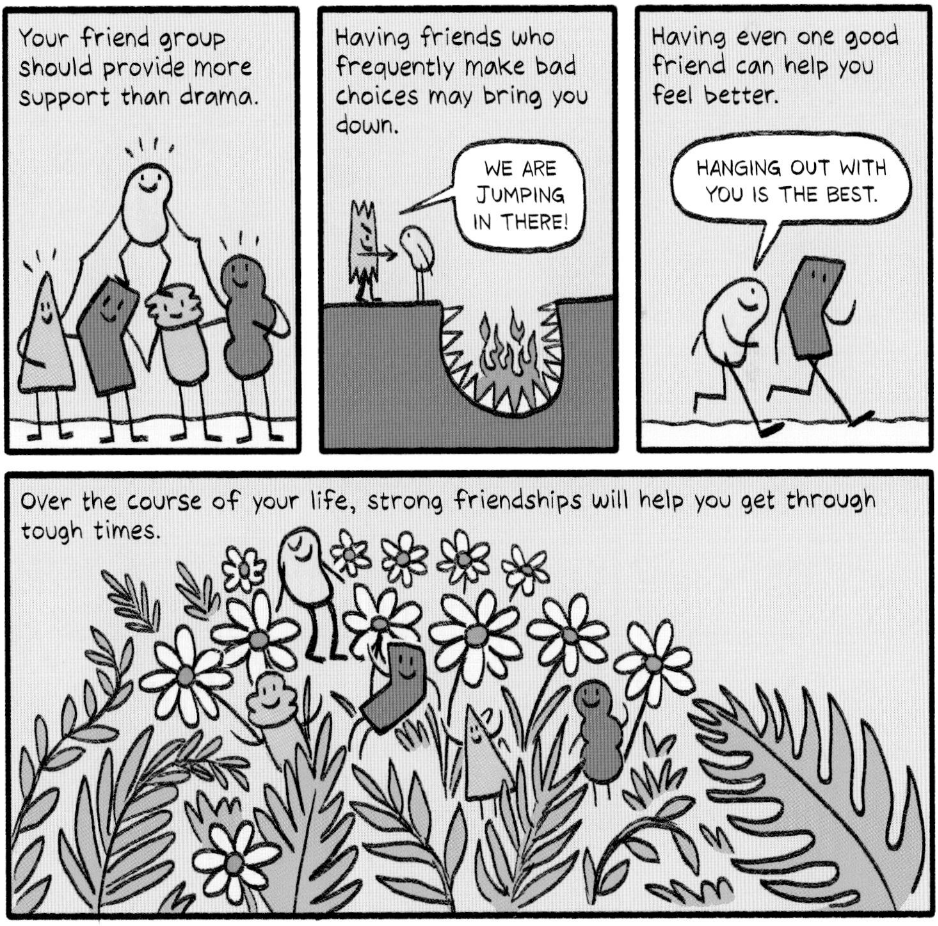
Your friend group should provide more support than drama.
Having friends who frequently make bad choices may bring you down.
WE ARE JUMPING IN THERE!
Having even one good friend can help you feel better.
HANGING OUT WITH YOU IS THE BEST.
Over the course of your life, strong friendships will help you get through tough times.

ENDORPHINS

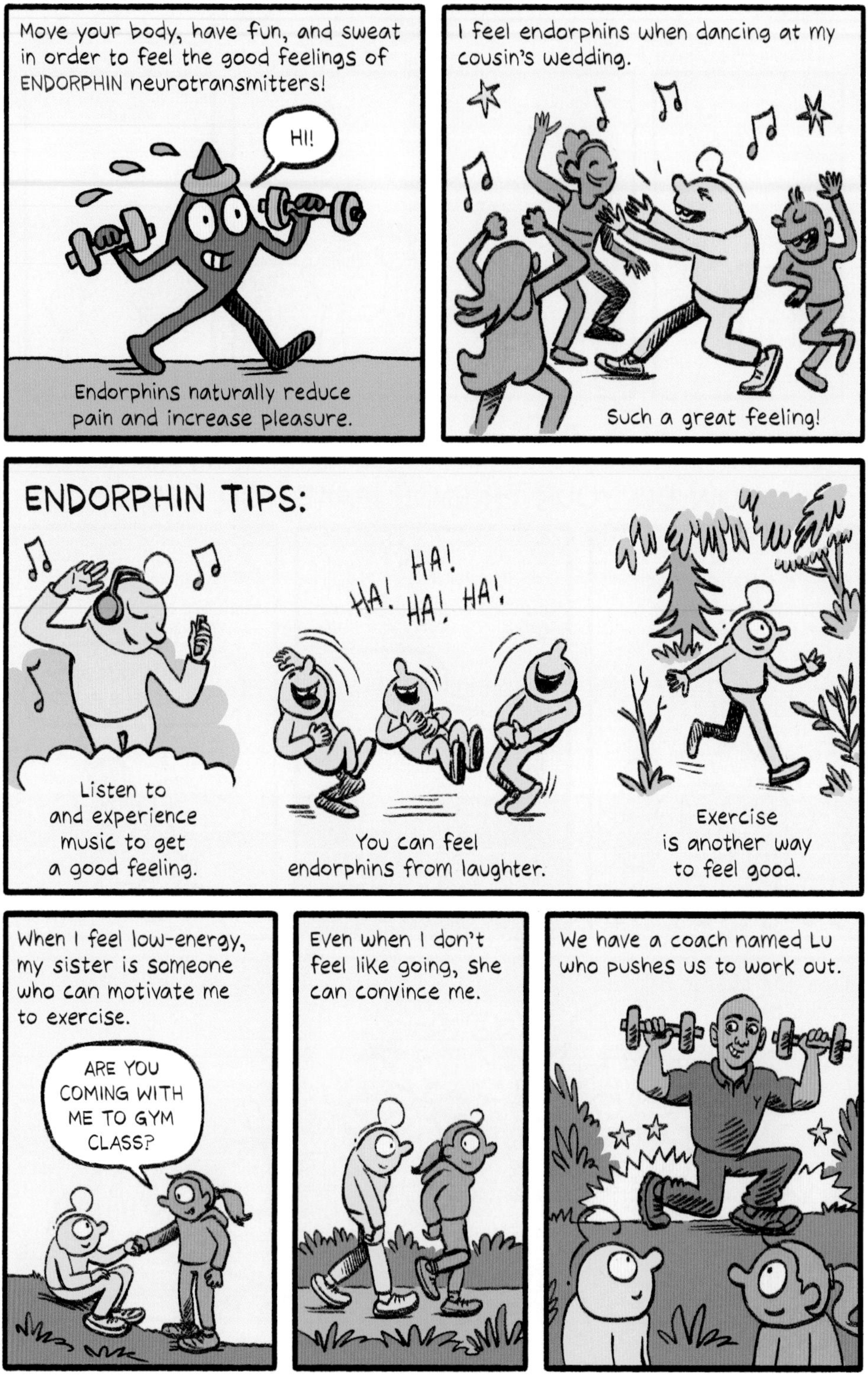

Move your body, have fun, and sweat in order to feel the good feelings of ENDORPHIN neurotransmitters!
HI!
Endorphins naturally reduce pain and increase pleasure.
I feel endorphins when dancing at my cousin's wedding.
Such a great feeling!
ENDORPHIN TIPS:
Listen to and experience music to get a good feeling.
HA! HA! HA! HA!
You can feel endorphins from laughter.
Exercise is another way to feel good.
When I feel low-energy, my sister is someone who can motivate me to exercise.
ARE YOU COMING WITH ME TO GYM CLASS?
Even when I don't feel like going, she can convince me.
We have a coach named Lu who pushes us to work out.

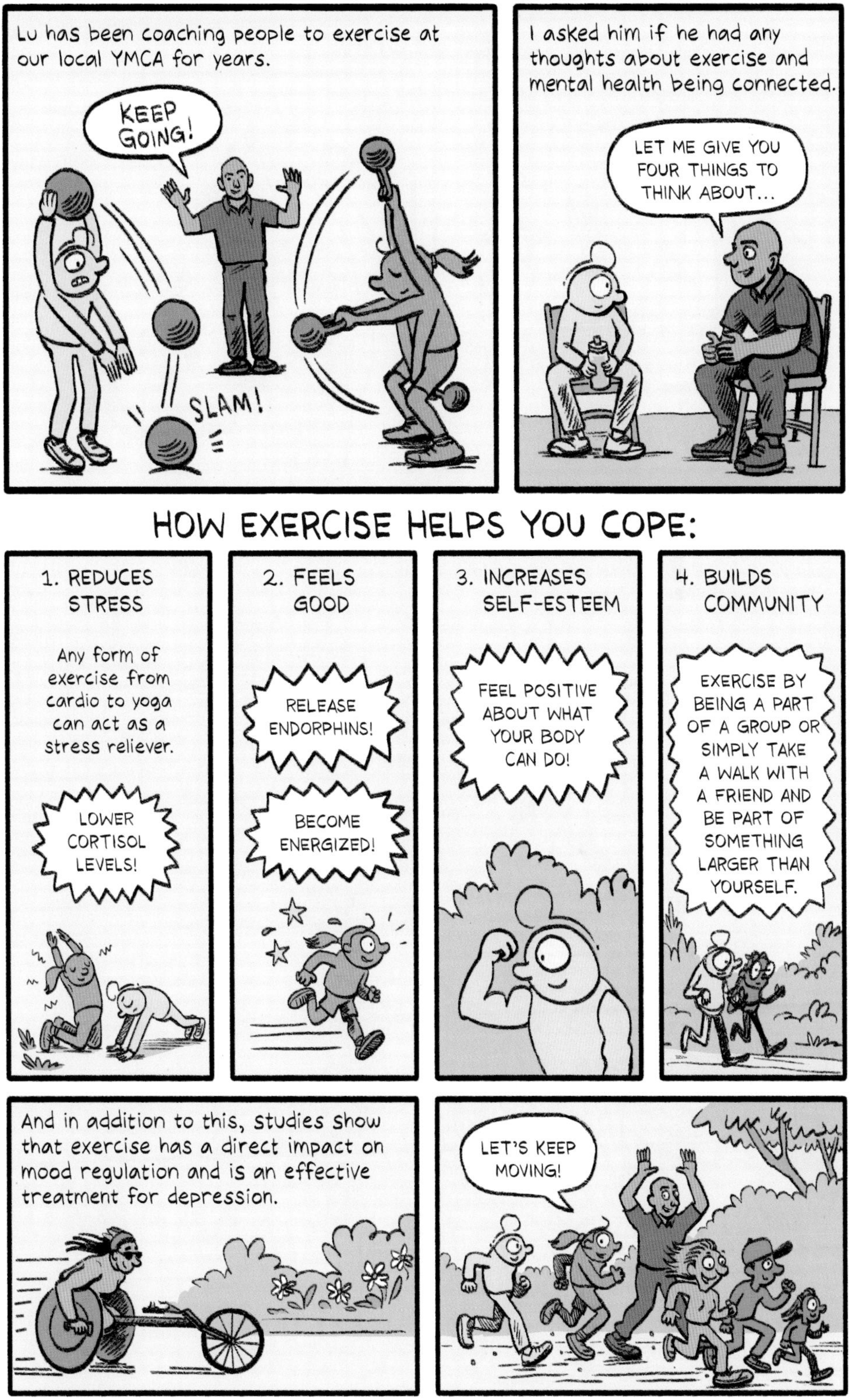
Lu has been coaching people to exercise at our local YMCA for years.
KEEP GOING!
SLAM!
I asked him if he had any thoughts about exercise and mental health being connected.
LET ME GIVE YOU FOUR THINGS TO THINK ABOUT...
HOW EXERCISE HELPS YOU COPE:
1. REDUCES STRESS
Any form of exercise from cardio to yoga can act as a stress reliever.
LOWER CORTISOL LEVELS!
2. FEELS GOOD
RELEASE ENDORPHINS!
BECOME ENERGIZED!
3. INCREASES SELF-ESTEEM
FEEL POSITIVE ABOUT WHAT YOUR BODY CAN DO!
4. BUILDS COMMUNITY
EXERCISE BY BEING A PART OF A GROUP OR SIMPLY TAKE A WALK WITH A FRIEND AND BE PART OF SOMETHING LARGER THAN YOURSELF.
And in addition to this, studies show that exercise has a direct impact on mood regulation and is an effective treatment for depression.
LET'S KEEP MOVING!

SEROTONIN

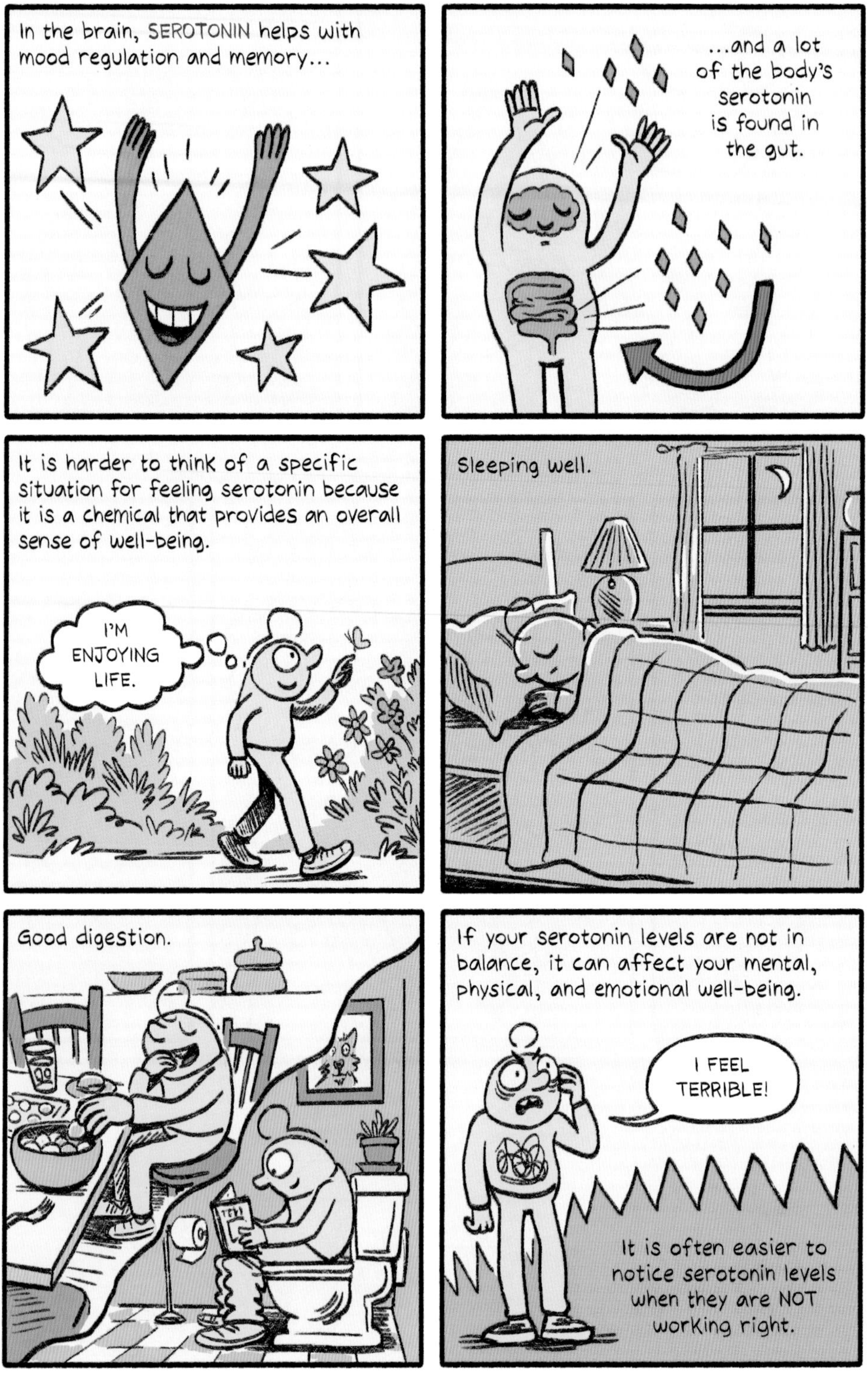
In the brain, SEROTONIN helps with mood regulation and memory...
...and a lot of the body's serotonin is found in the gut.
It is harder to think of a specific situation for feeling serotonin because it is a chemical that provides an overall sense of well-being.
I'M ENJOYING LIFE.
Sleeping well.
Good digestion.
If your serotonin levels are not in balance, it can affect your mental, physical, and emotional well-being.
I FEEL TERRIBLE!
It is often easier to notice serotonin levels when they are NOT working right.

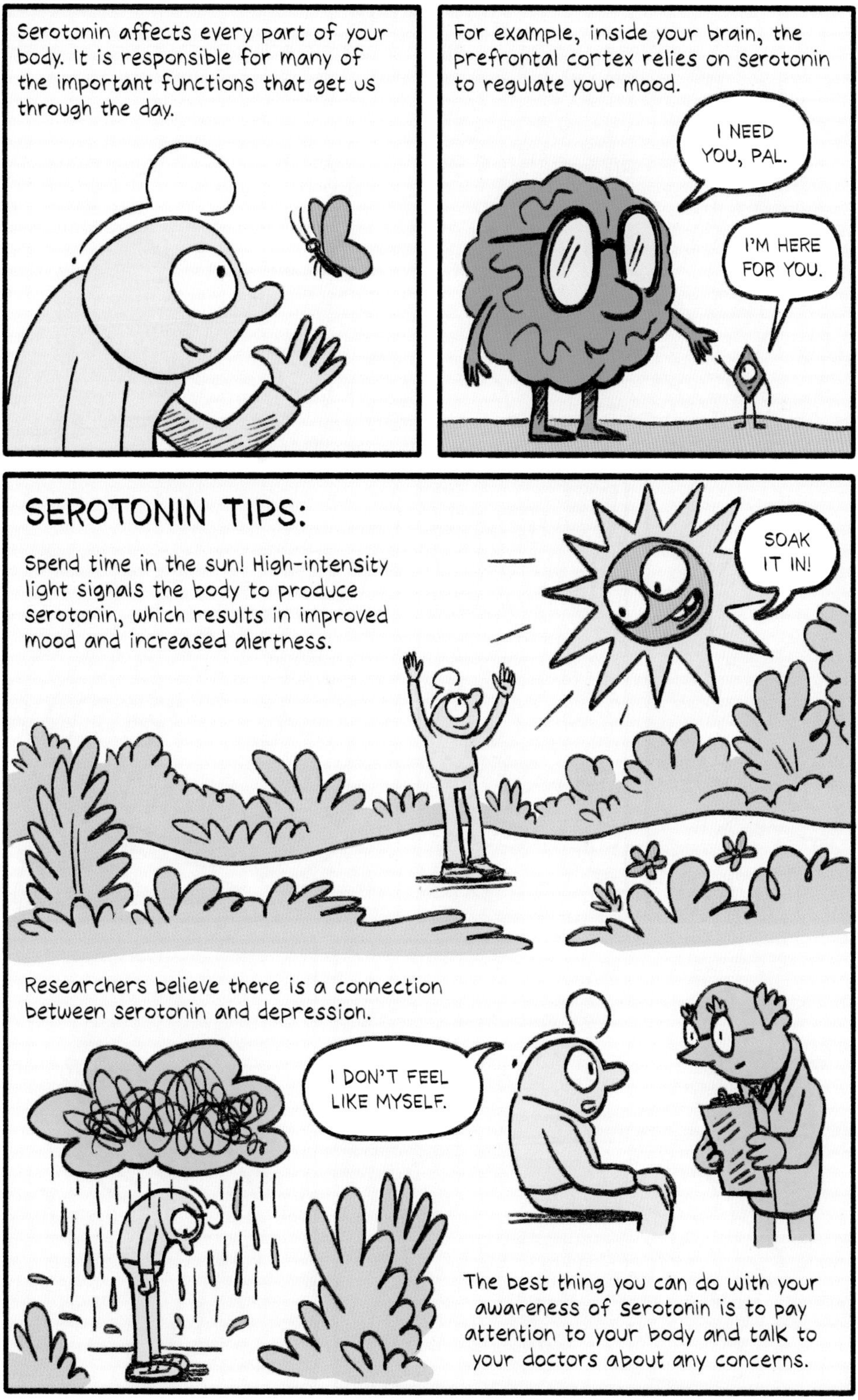
Serotonin affects every part of your body. It is responsible for many of the important functions that get us through the day.
For example, inside your brain, the prefrontal cortex relies on serotonin to regulate your mood.
I NEED YOU, PAL.
I'M HERE FOR YOU.
SEROTONIN TIPS:
Spend time in the sun! High-intensity light signals the body to produce serotonin, which results in improved mood and increased alertness.
SOAK IT IN!
Researchers believe there is a connection between serotonin and depression.
I DON'T FEEL LIKE MYSELF.
The best thing you can do with your awareness of serotonin is to pay attention to your body and talk to your doctors about any concerns.

DOPAMINE

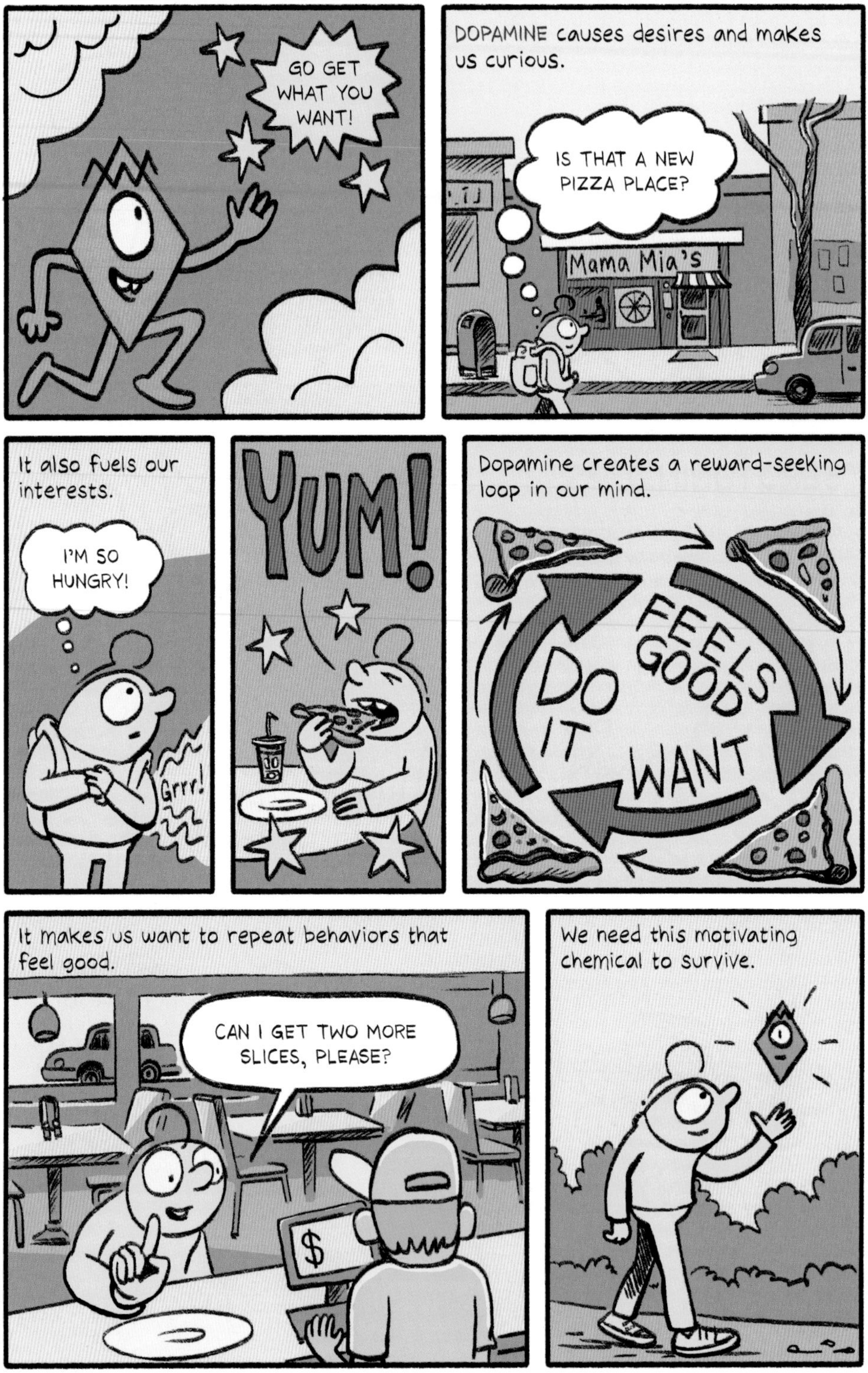
GO GET WHAT YOU WANT!
DOPAMINE causes desires and makes us curious.
IS THAT A NEW PIZZA PLACE?
Mama Mia's
It also fuels our interests.
I'M SO HUNGRY!
Grrr!
YUM!
Dopamine creates a reward-seeking loop in our mind.
FEELS GOOD
WANT
DO IT
It makes us want to repeat behaviors that feel good.
CAN I GET TWO MORE SLICES, PLEASE?
$
We need this motivating chemical to survive.

DOPAMINE IN THE TEEN BRAIN

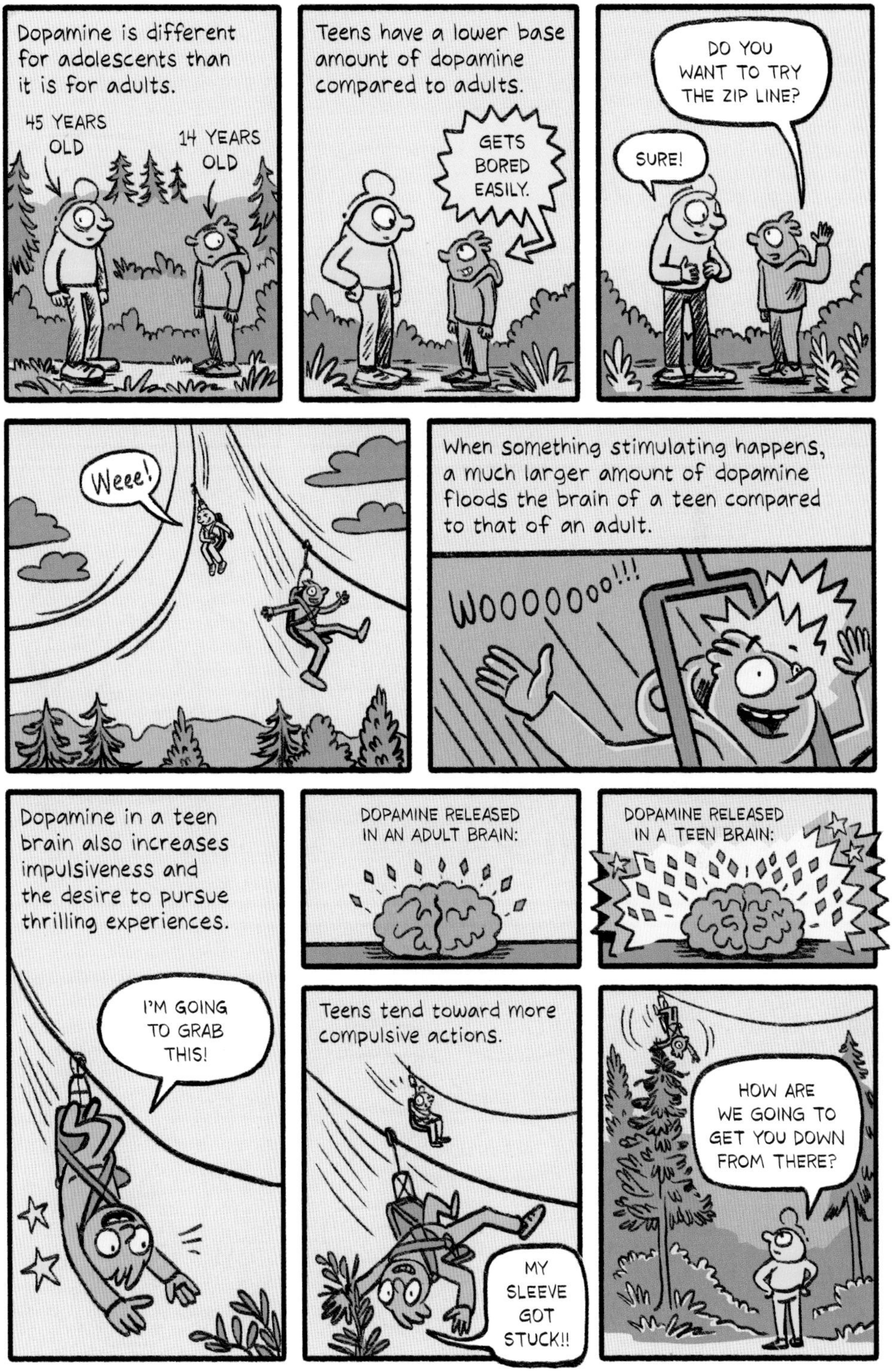

Dopamine is different for adolescents than it is for adults.
45 YEARS OLD
14 YEARS OLD
Teens have a lower base amount of dopamine compared to adults.
GETS BORED EASILY.
DO YOU WANT TO TRY THE ZIP LINE?
SURE!
Weee!
When something stimulating happens, a much larger amount of dopamine floods the brain of a teen compared to that of an adult.
WOOOOOOoo!!!
Dopamine in a teen brain also increases impulsiveness and the desire to pursue thrilling experiences.
I'M GOING TO GRAB THIS!
DOPAMINE RELEASED IN AN ADULT BRAIN:
DOPAMINE RELEASED IN A TEEN BRAIN:
Teens tend toward more compulsive actions.
MY SLEEVE GOT STUCK!!
HOW ARE WE GOING TO GET YOU DOWN FROM THERE?

THE DOWNSIDE OF DOPAMINE

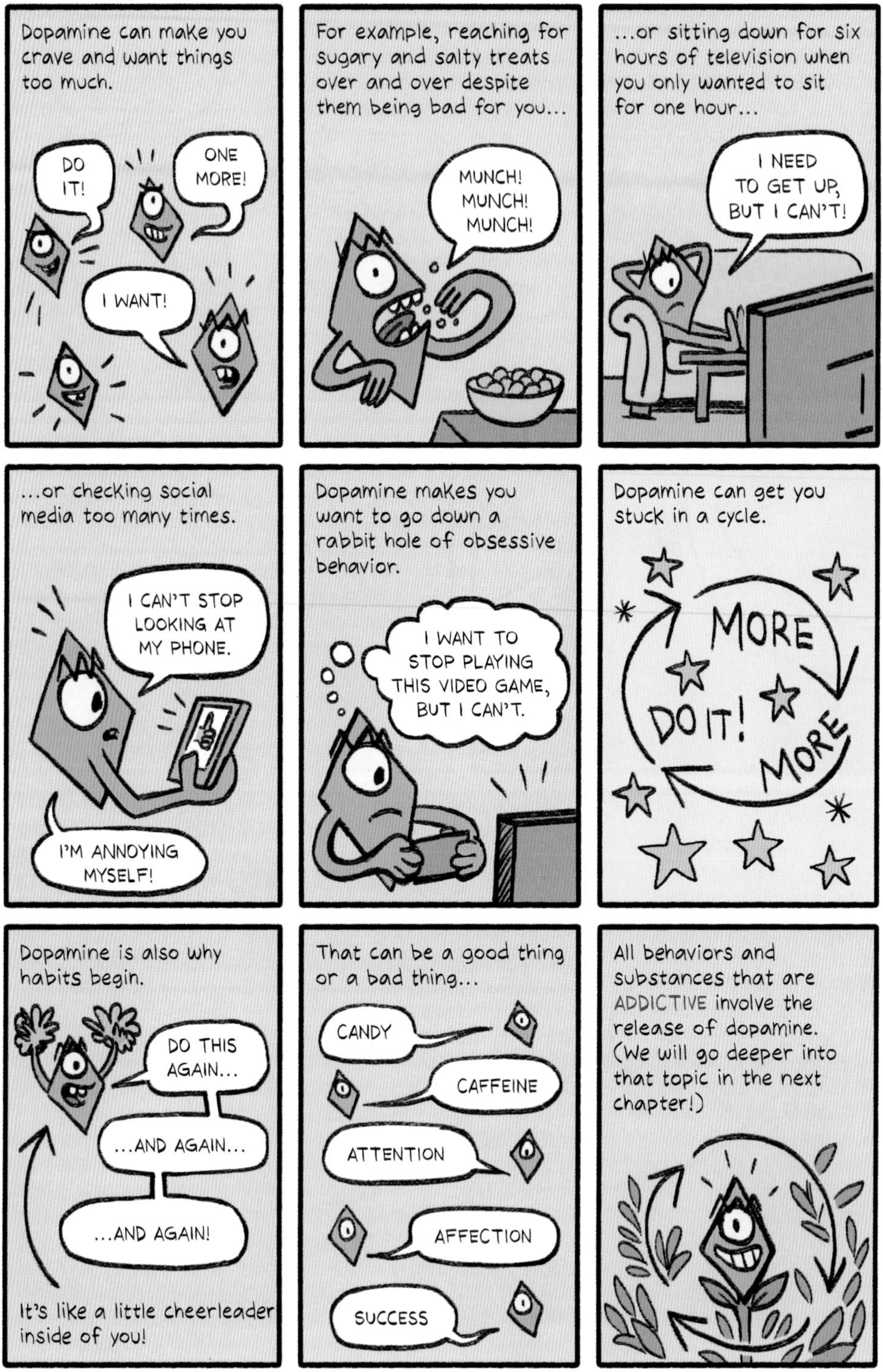

Dopamine can make you crave and want things too much.
DO IT!
ONE MORE!
I WANT!
For example, reaching for sugary and salty treats over and over despite them being bad for you...
MUNCH! MUNCH! MUNCH!
...or sitting down for six hours of television when you only wanted to sit for one hour...
I NEED TO GET UP, BUT I CAN'T!
...or checking social media too many times.
I CAN'T STOP LOOKING AT MY PHONE.
I'M ANNOYING MYSELF!
Dopamine makes you want to go down a rabbit hole of obsessive behavior.
I WANT TO STOP PLAYING THIS VIDEO GAME, BUT I CAN'T.
Dopamine can get you stuck in a cycle.
MORE
DO IT!
MORE
Dopamine is also why habits begin.
DO THIS AGAIN...
...AND AGAIN...
...AND AGAIN!
It's like a little cheerleader inside of you!
That can be a good thing or a bad thing...
CANDY
CAFFEINE
ATTENTION
AFFECTION
SUCCESS
All behaviors and substances that are ADDICTIVE involve the release of dopamine. (We will go deeper into that topic in the next chapter!)

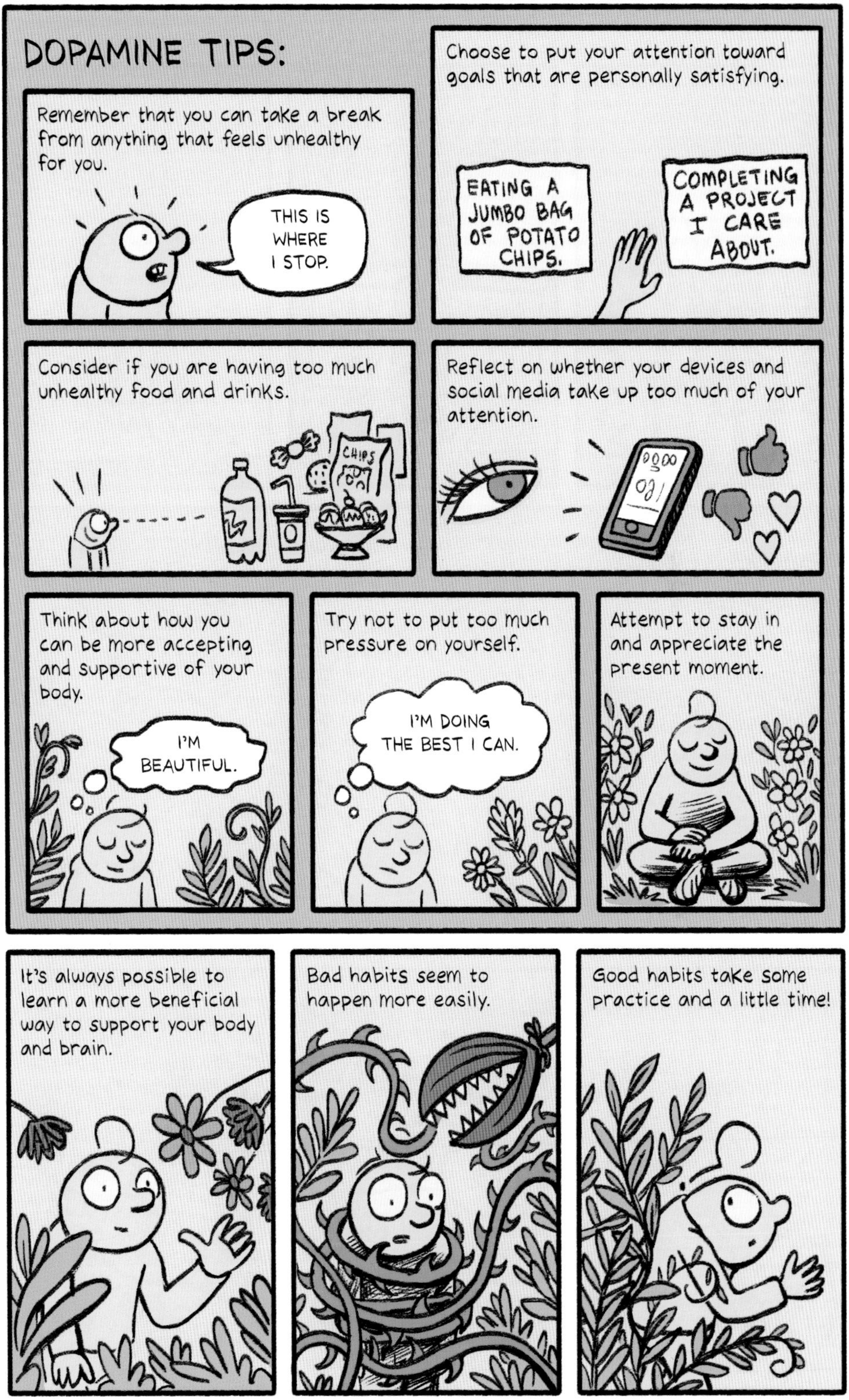
DOPAMINE TIPS:
Remember that you can take a break from anything that feels unhealthy for you.
THIS IS WHERE I STOP.
Choose to put your attention toward goals that are personally satisfying.
EATING A JUMBO BAG OF POTATO CHIPS.
COMPLETING A PROJECT I CARE ABOUT.
Consider if you are having too much unhealthy food and drinks.
CHIPS
Reflect on whether your devices and social media take up too much of your attention.
Think about how you can be more accepting and supportive of your body.
I'M BEAUTIFUL.
Try not to put too much pressure on yourself.
I'M DOING THE BEST I CAN.
Attempt to stay in and appreciate the present moment.
It's always possible to learn a more beneficial way to support your body and brain.
Bad habits seem to happen more easily.
Good habits take some practice and a little time!

HARMFUL COPING

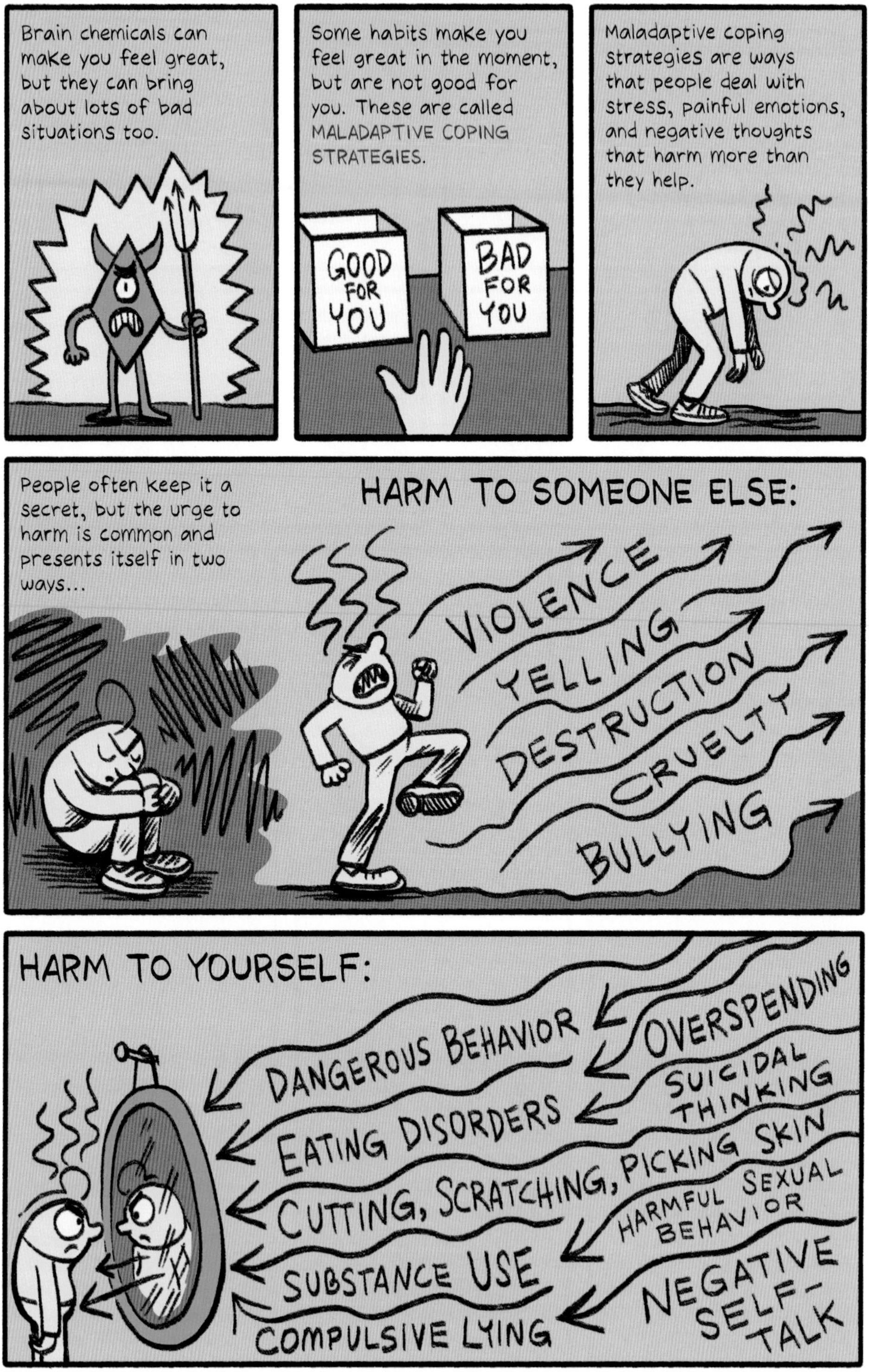

Brain chemicals can make you feel great, but they can bring about lots of bad situations too.
Some habits make you feel great in the moment, but are not good for you. These are called MALADAPTIVE COPING STRATEGIES.
GOOD FOR YOU
BAD FOR YOU
Maladaptive coping strategies are ways that people deal with stress, painful emotions, and negative thoughts that harm more than they help.
People often keep it a secret, but the urge to harm is common and presents itself in two ways...
HARM TO SOMEONE ELSE:
VIOLENCE
YELLING
DESTRUCTION
CRUELTY
BULLYING
HARM TO YOURSELF:
DANGEROUS BEHAVIOR
OVERSPENDING
EATING DISORDERS
SUICIDAL THINKING
CUTTING, SCRATCHING, PICKING SKIN
HARMFUL SEXUAL BEHAVIOR
SUBSTANCE USE
NEGATIVE SELF-TALK
COMPULSIVE LYING

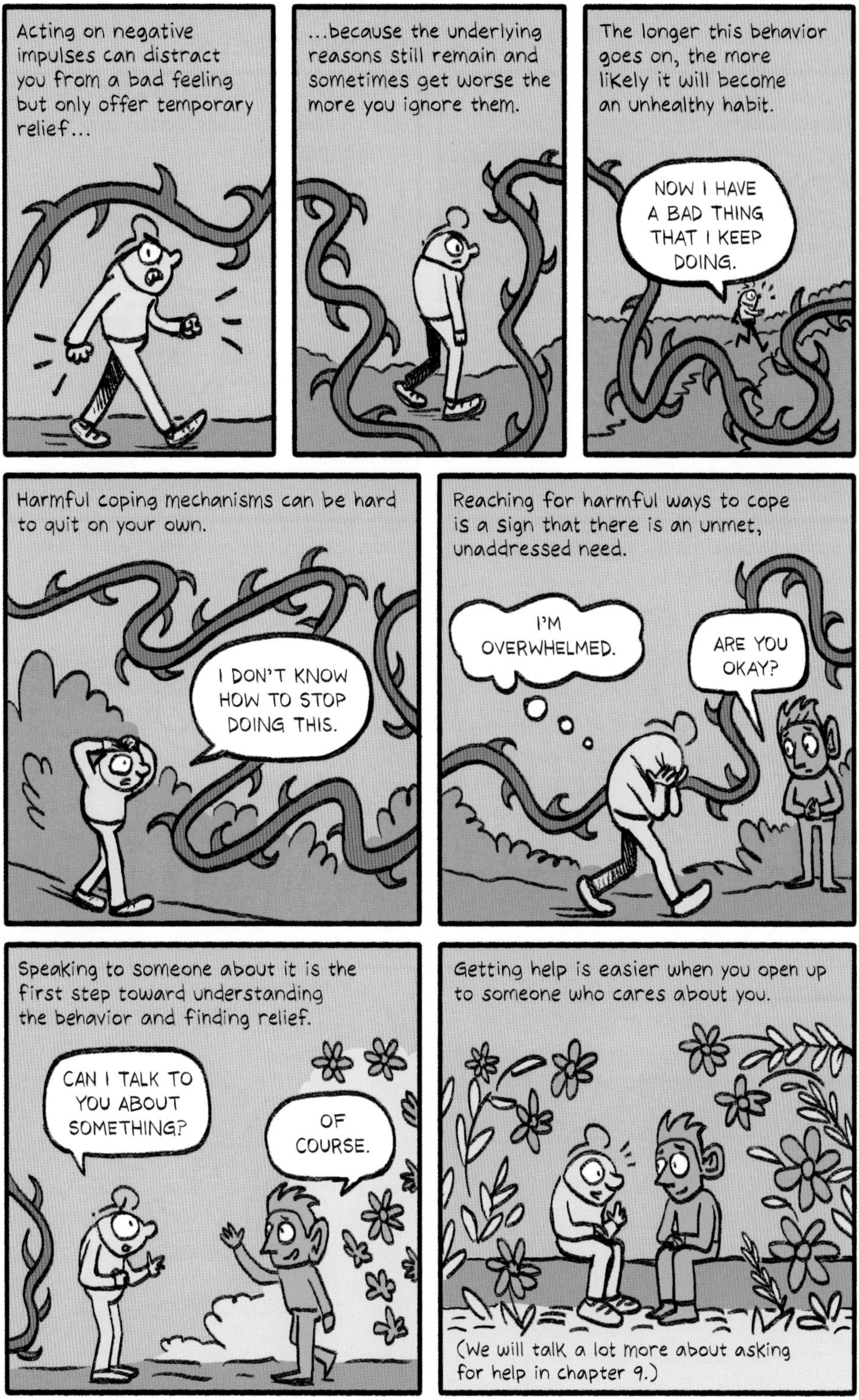
Acting on negative impulses can distract you from a bad feeling but only offer temporary relief...
...because the underlying reasons still remain and sometimes get worse the more you ignore them.
The longer this behavior goes on, the more likely it will become an unhealthy habit.
NOW I HAVE A BAD THING THAT I KEEP DOING.
Harmful coping mechanisms can be hard to quit on your own.
I DON'T KNOW HOW TO STOP DOING THIS.
Reaching for harmful ways to cope is a sign that there is an unmet, unaddressed need.
I'M OVERWHELMED.
ARE YOU OKAY?
Speaking to someone about it is the first step toward understanding the behavior and finding relief.
CAN I TALK TO YOU ABOUT SOMETHING?
OF COURSE.
Getting help is easier when you open up to someone who cares about you.
(We will talk a lot more about asking for help in chapter 9.)

COPING WITH STRESS AND CARING FOR YOUR BRAIN IS A LIFELONG PROCESS

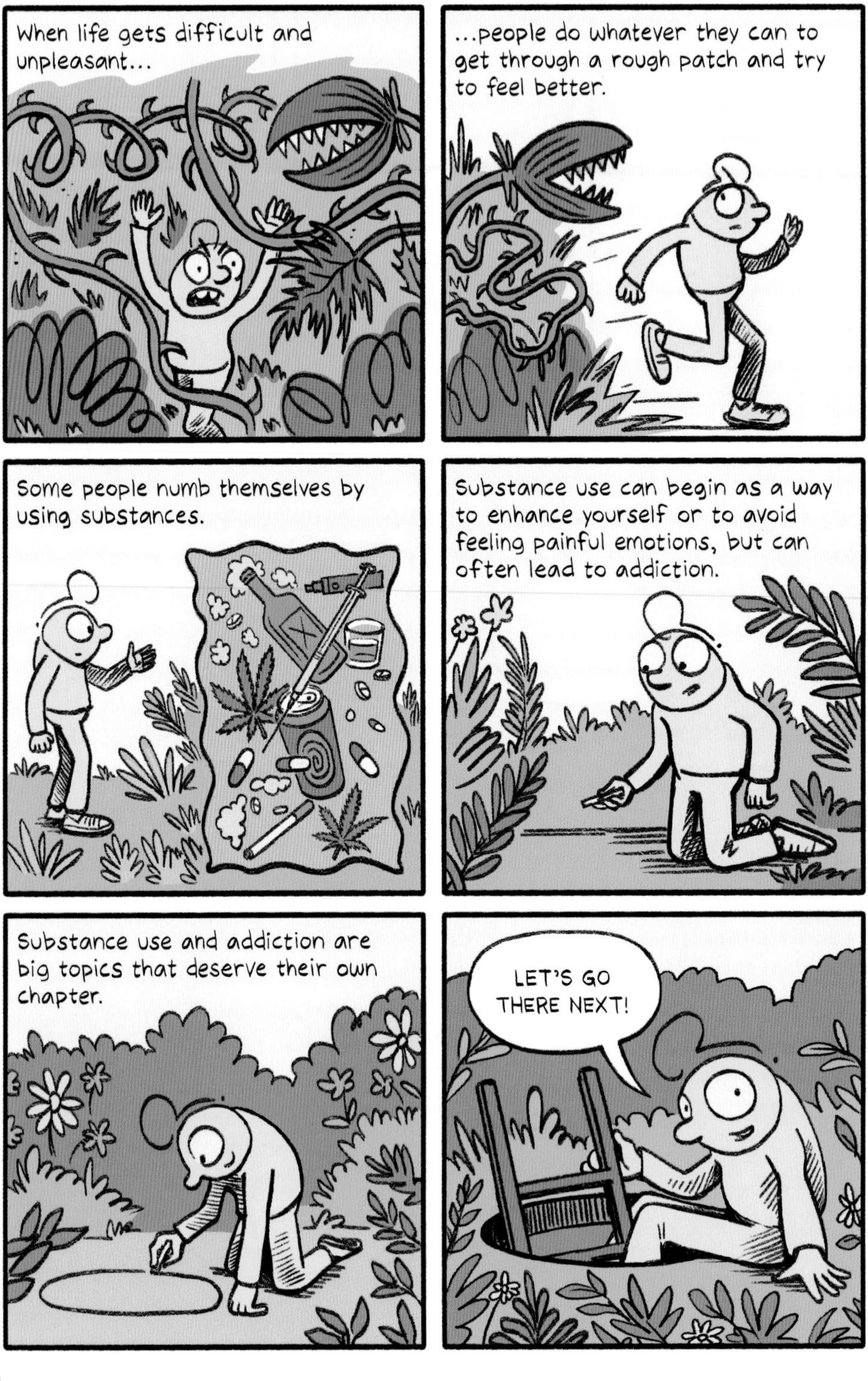
When life gets difficult and unpleasant...
...people do whatever they can to get through a rough patch and try to feel better.
Some people numb themselves by using substances.
Substance use can begin as a way to enhance yourself or to avoid feeling painful emotions, but can often lead to addiction.
Substance use and addiction are big topics that deserve their own chapter.
LET'S GO THERE NEXT!

CHAPTER 6 SUBSTANCE USE & ADDICTION

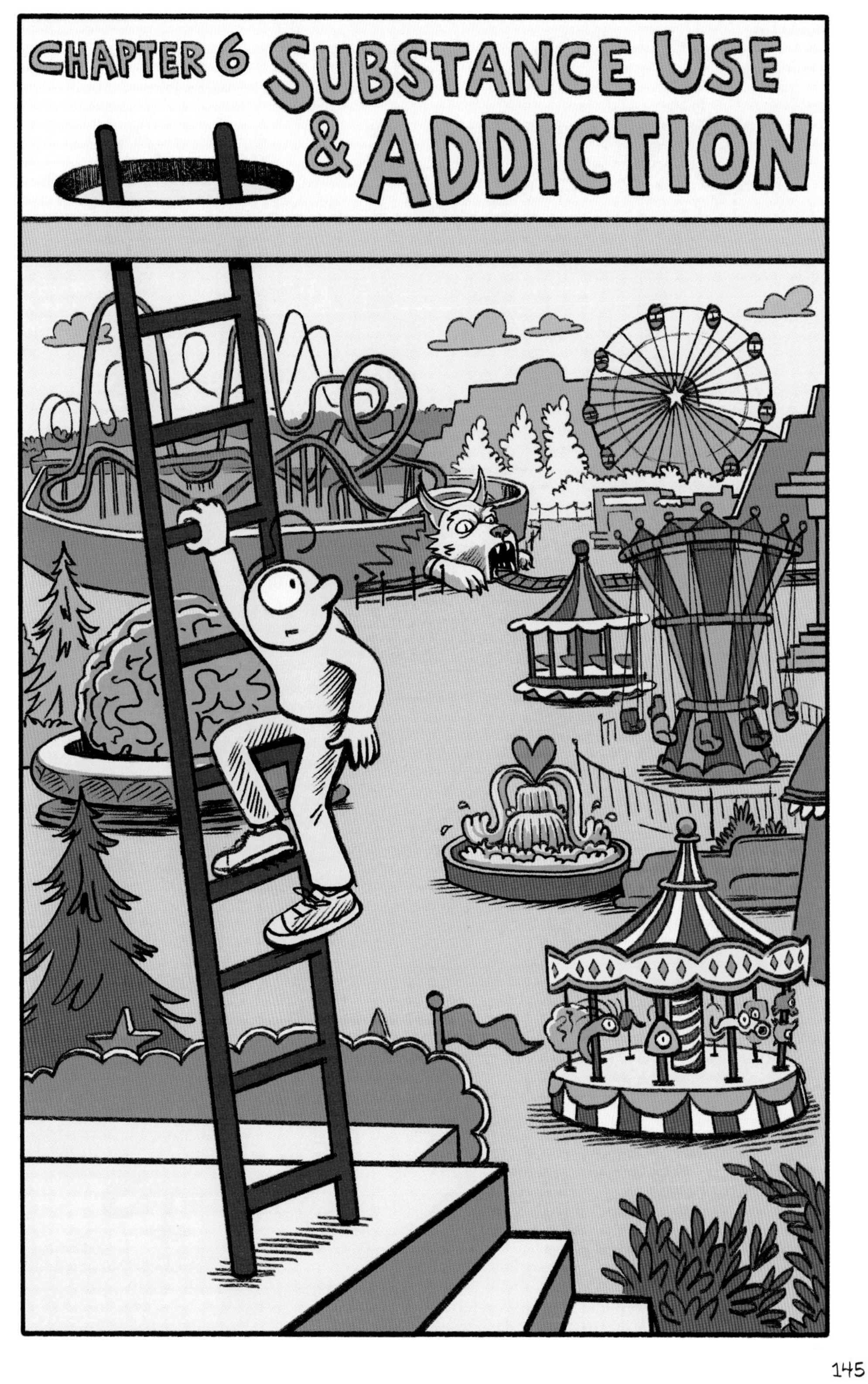

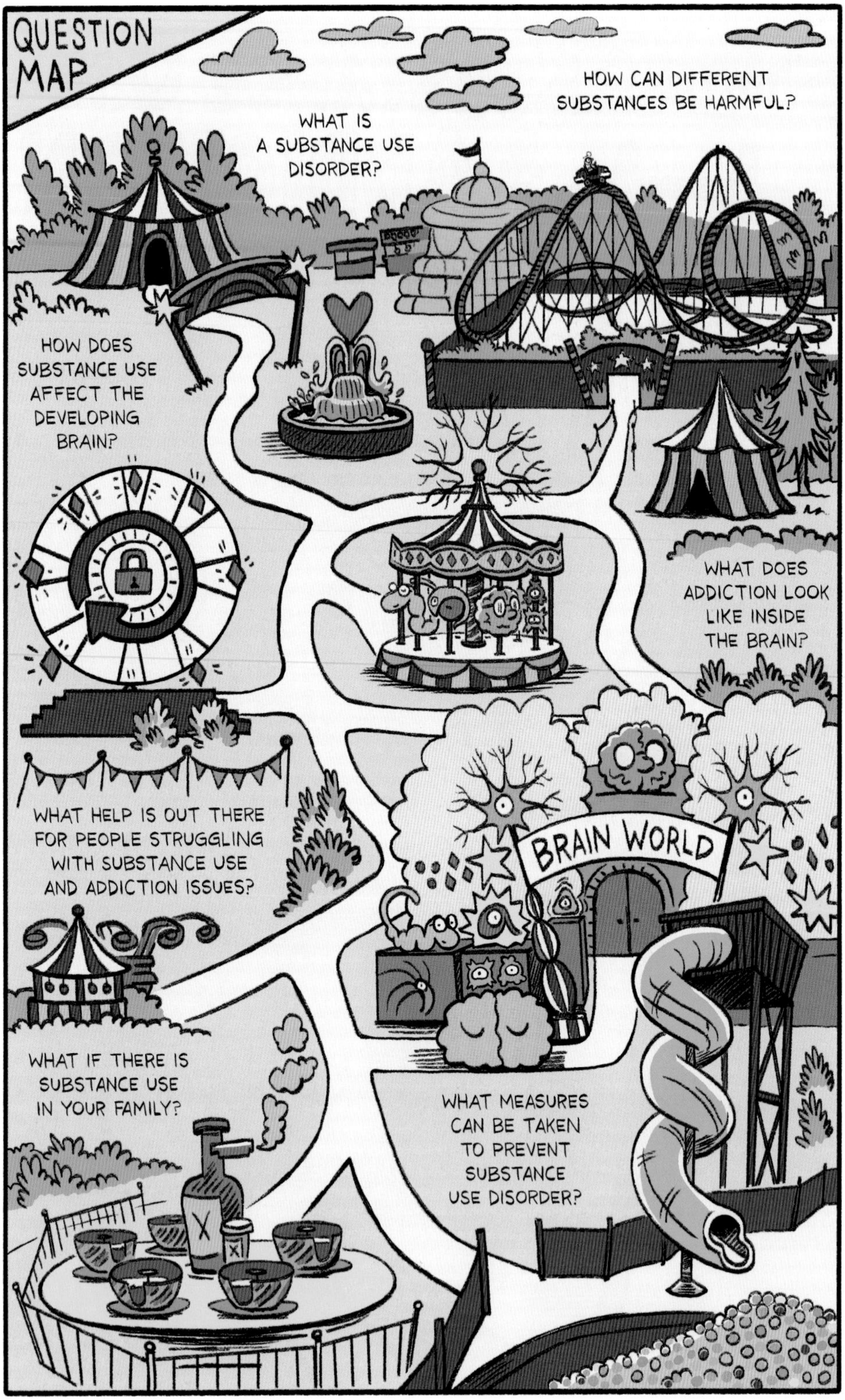
QUESTION MAP
WHAT IS A SUBSTANCE USE DISORDER?
HOW CAN DIFFERENT SUBSTANCES BE HARMFUL?
HOW DOES SUBSTANCE USE AFFECT THE DEVELOPING BRAIN?
WHAT DOES ADDICTION LOOK LIKE INSIDE THE BRAIN?
WHAT HELP IS OUT THERE FOR PEOPLE STRUGGLING WITH SUBSTANCE USE AND ADDICTION ISSUES?
BRAIN WORLD
WHAT IF THERE IS SUBSTANCE USE IN YOUR FAMILY?
WHAT MEASURES CAN BE TAKEN TO PREVENT SUBSTANCE USE DISORDER?

MEDICATION HELPS PEOPLE

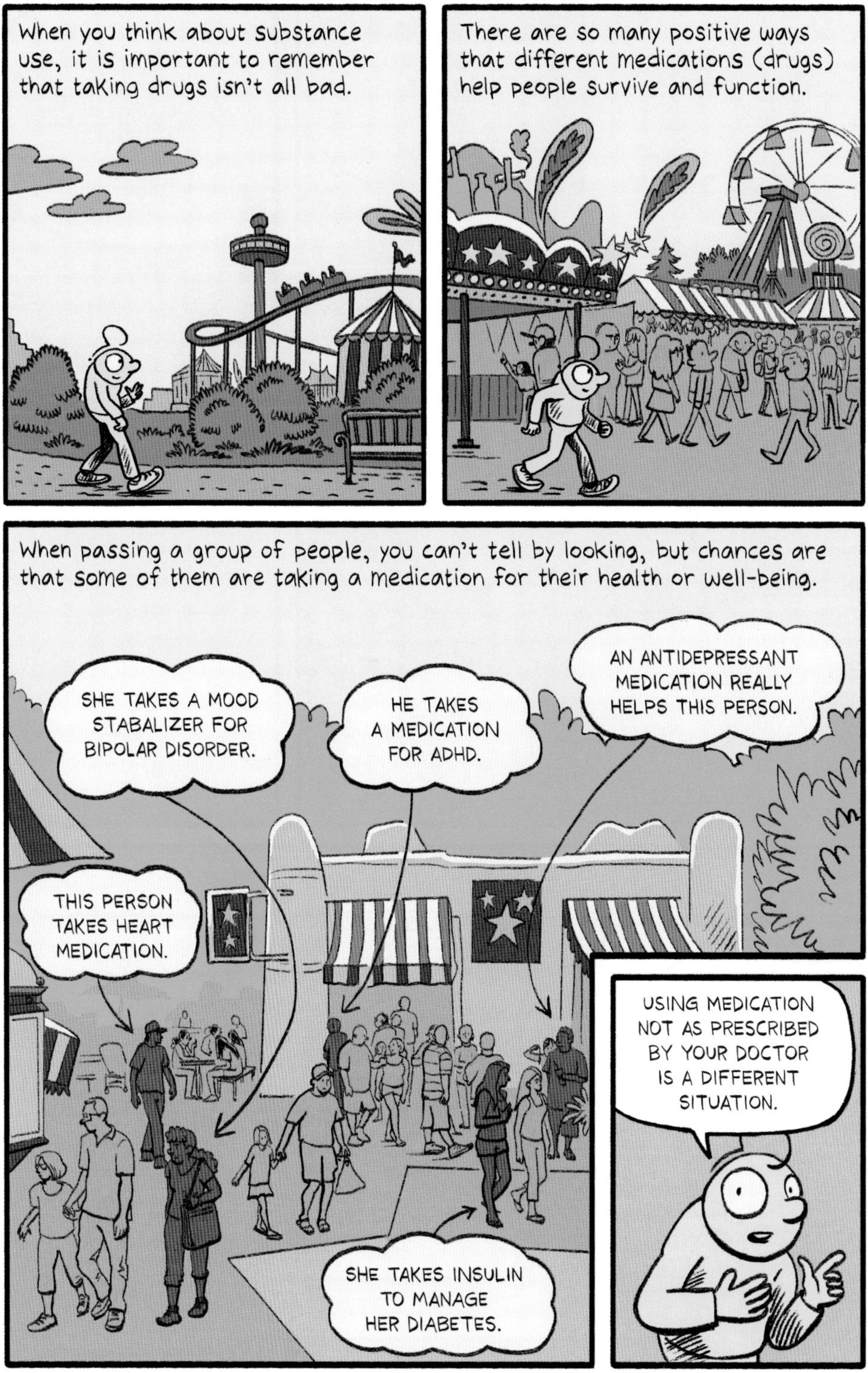
When you think about substance use, it is important to remember that taking drugs isn't all bad.
There are so many positive ways that different medications (drugs) help people survive and function.
When passing a group of people, you can't tell by looking, but chances are that some of them are taking a medication for their health or well-being.
SHE TAKES A MOOD STABALIZER FOR BIPOLAR DISORDER.
HE TAKES A MEDICATION FOR ADHD.
AN ANTIDEPRESSANT MEDICATION REALLY HELPS THIS PERSON.
THIS PERSON TAKES HEART MEDICATION.
SHE TAKES INSULIN TO MANAGE HER DIABETES.
USING MEDICATION NOT AS PRESCRIBED BY YOUR DOCTOR IS A DIFFERENT SITUATION.

ADDICTION IS COMPLICATED

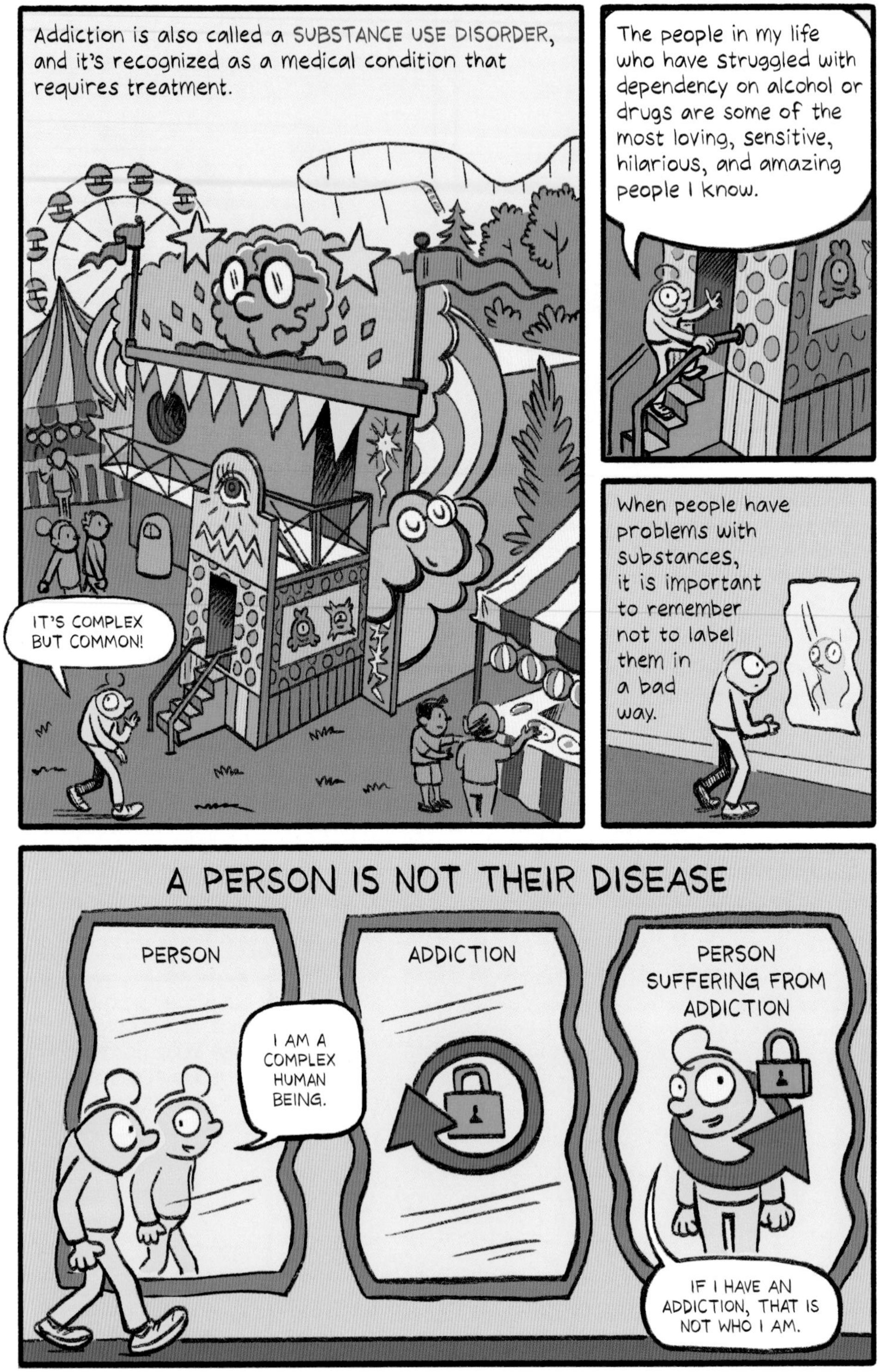
Addiction is also called a SUBSTANCE USE DISORDER, and it's recognized as a medical condition that requires treatment.
IT'S COMPLEX BUT COMMON!
The people in my life who have struggled with dependency on alcohol or drugs are some of the most loving, sensitive, hilarious, and amazing people I know.
When people have problems with substances, it is important to remember not to label them in a bad way.
A PERSON IS NOT THEIR DISEASE
PERSON
I AM A COMPLEX HUMAN BEING.
ADDICTION
PERSON SUFFERING FROM ADDICTION
IF I HAVE AN ADDICTION, THAT IS NOT WHO I AM.

LANGUAGE MATTERS

DON'T:
DO:

DON'T:	DO:
USE LABELS OR DESCRIPTIONS THAT HAVE A NEGATIVE CONNOTATION (LIKE "DIRTY" OR "LESS THAN")	USE LANGUAGE THAT CENTERS ON THE PERSON AHEAD OF THE DISORDER
SAY "SUBSTANCE ABUSE DISORDER" (ABUSE SOUNDS BAD)	SAY "SUBSTANCE USE DISORDER" (THIS IS THE OFFICIAL TERM)
SAY "RELAPSE" OR "OFF THE WAGON" (CONFUSING)	SAY "RECURRENCE OF USE" (SIMPLE TRUTH)

SOME USEFUL VOCABULARY:

BEHAVIORS are your actions.

Behaviors are the things that you do.

HABITS become a pattern or routine.

Repeated behaviors become habits.

ADDICTION is also called a substance use disorder.

Sometimes a habit can become an addiction, especially when chemical substances like alcohol and drugs are involved.

WITHDRAWAL causes highly unpleasant symptoms that are both physical AND in the mind.

When a person is addicted, they can experience withdrawal when they cannot do their habit.

RECOVERY is a place to get help with substance use or any harmful habits.

UNLOCK!

People can go into recovery to learn to manage their addiction.

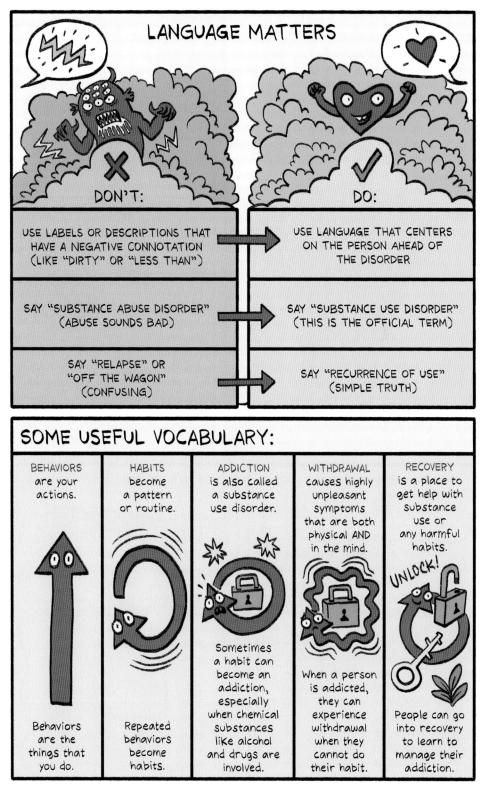

ADDICTION AFFECTS ALL MEMBERS OF A FAMILY

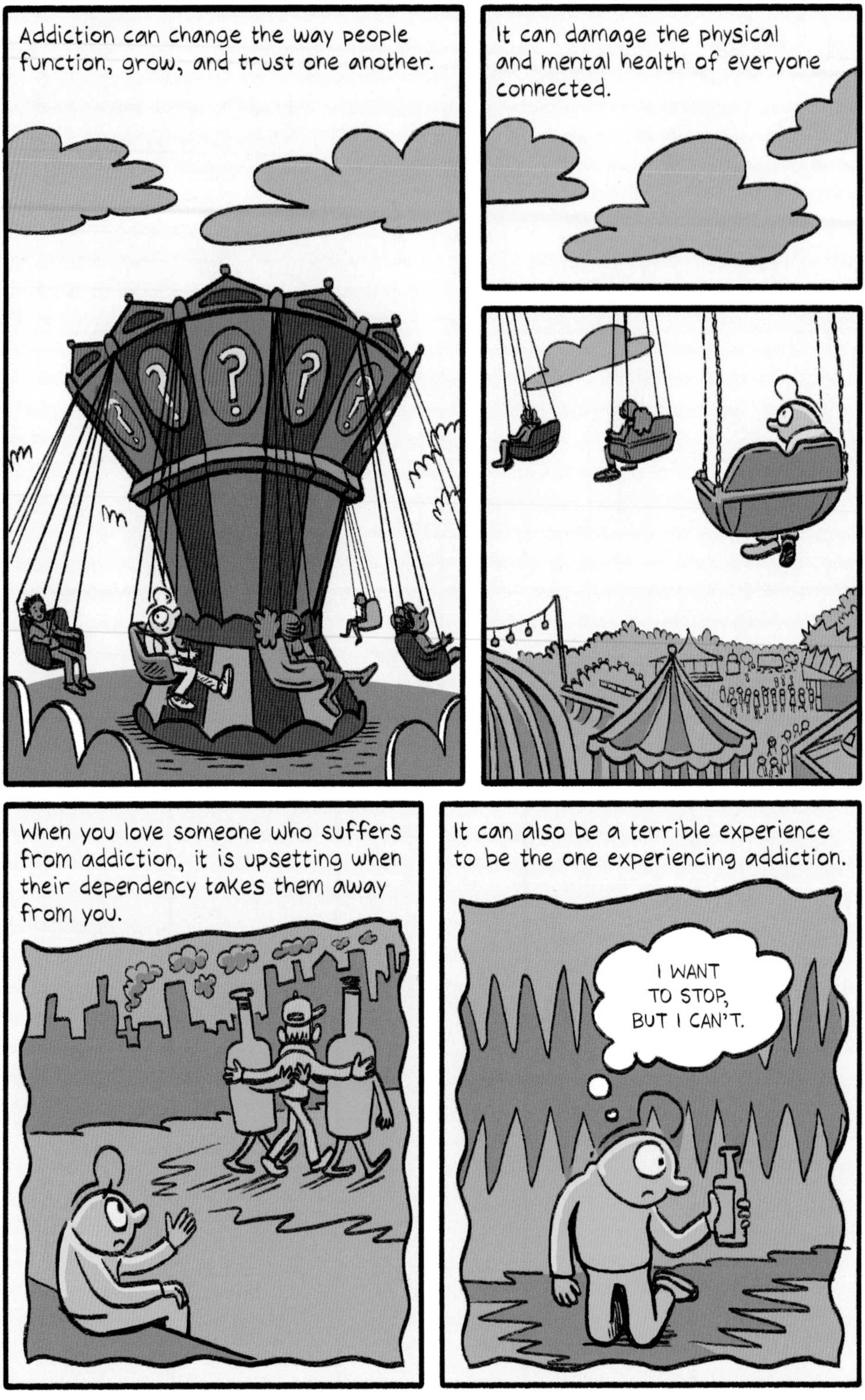
Addiction can change the way people function, grow, and trust one another.
It can damage the physical and mental health of everyone connected.
When you love someone who suffers from addiction, it is upsetting when their dependency takes them away from you.
It can also be a terrible experience to be the one experiencing addiction.
I WANT TO STOP, BUT I CAN'T.

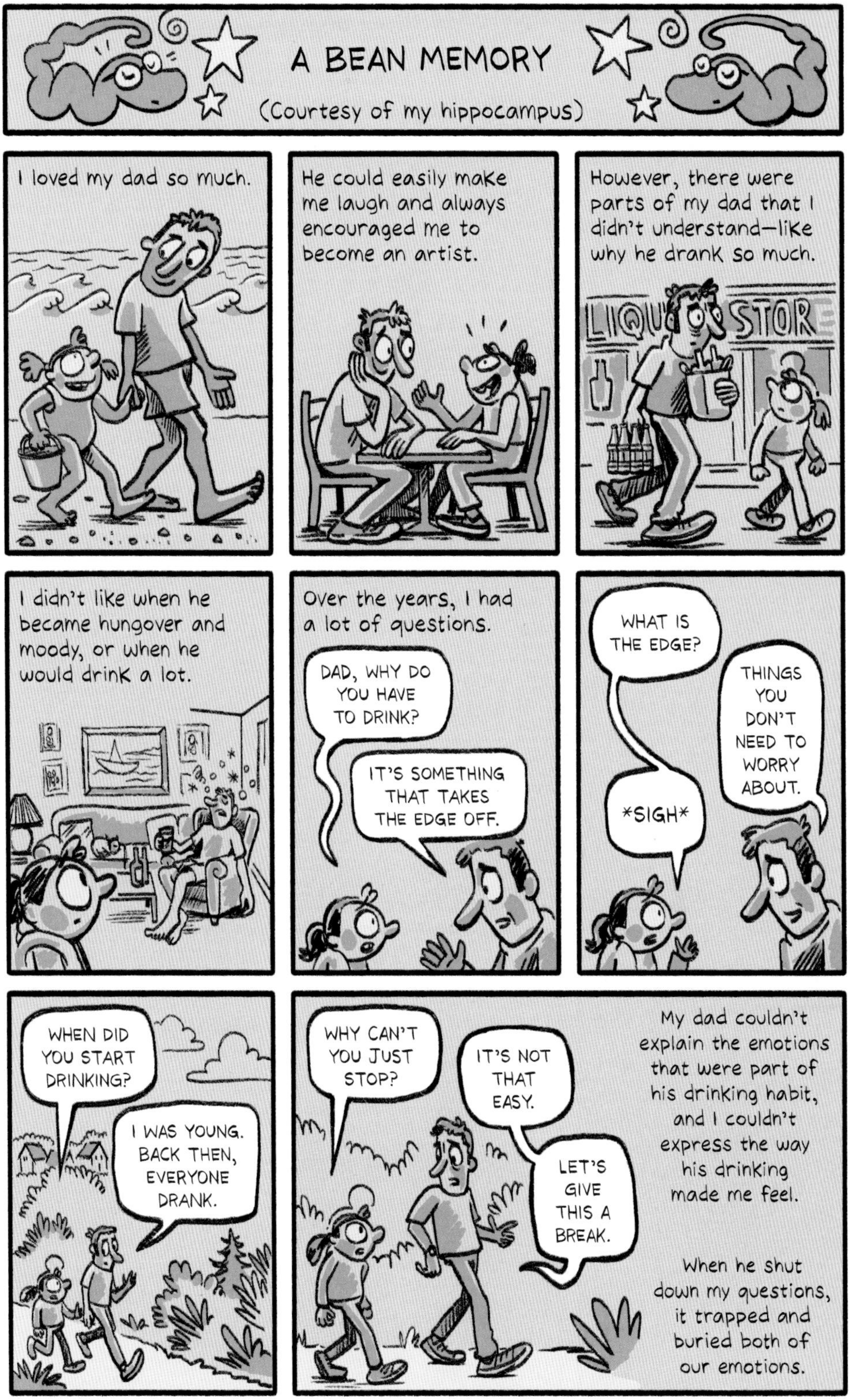
A BEAN MEMORY
(Courtesy of my hippocampus)
I loved my dad so much.
He could easily make me laugh and always encouraged me to become an artist.
However, there were parts of my dad that I didn't understand—like why he drank so much.
LIQU STOR
I didn't like when he became hungover and moody, or when he would drink a lot.
Over the years, I had a lot of questions.
DAD, WHY DO YOU HAVE TO DRINK?
IT'S SOMETHING THAT TAKES THE EDGE OFF.
WHAT IS THE EDGE?
SIGH
THINGS YOU DON'T NEED TO WORRY ABOUT.
WHEN DID YOU START DRINKING?
I WAS YOUNG. BACK THEN, EVERYONE DRANK.
WHY CAN'T YOU JUST STOP?
IT'S NOT THAT EASY.
LET'S GIVE THIS A BREAK.
My dad couldn't explain the emotions that were part of his drinking habit, and I couldn't express the way his drinking made me feel.
When he shut down my questions, it trapped and buried both of our emotions.

EMOTIONS HAVE A PURPOSE

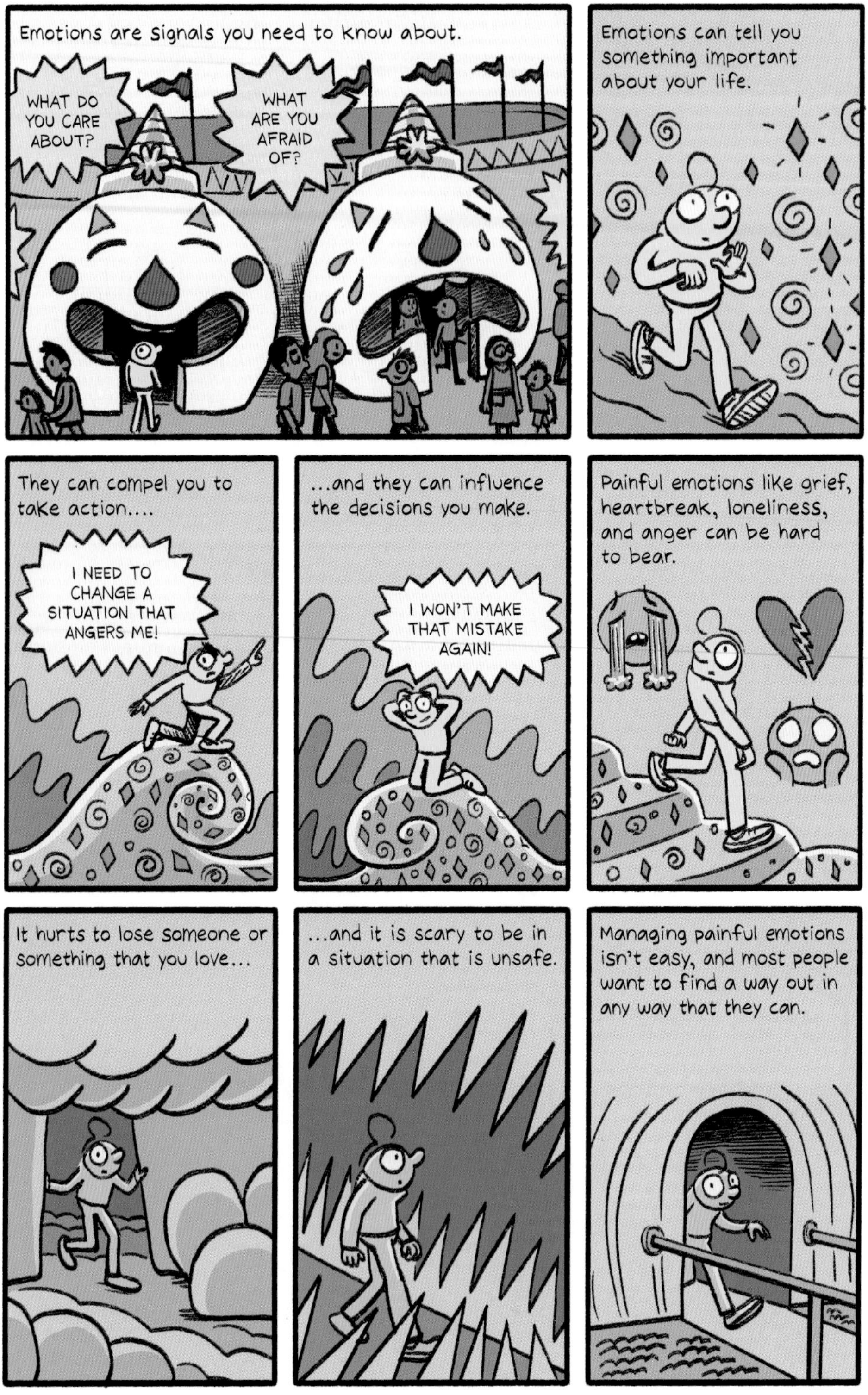
Emotions are signals you need to know about.
WHAT DO YOU CARE ABOUT?
WHAT ARE YOU AFRAID OF?
Emotions can tell you something important about your life.
They can compel you to take action....
I NEED TO CHANGE A SITUATION THAT ANGERS ME!
...and they can influence the decisions you make.
I WON'T MAKE THAT MISTAKE AGAIN!
Painful emotions like grief, heartbreak, loneliness, and anger can be hard to bear.
It hurts to lose someone or something that you love...
...and it is scary to be in a situation that is unsafe.
Managing painful emotions isn't easy, and most people want to find a way out in any way that they can.

USING SUBSTANCES TO NUMB EMOTIONS

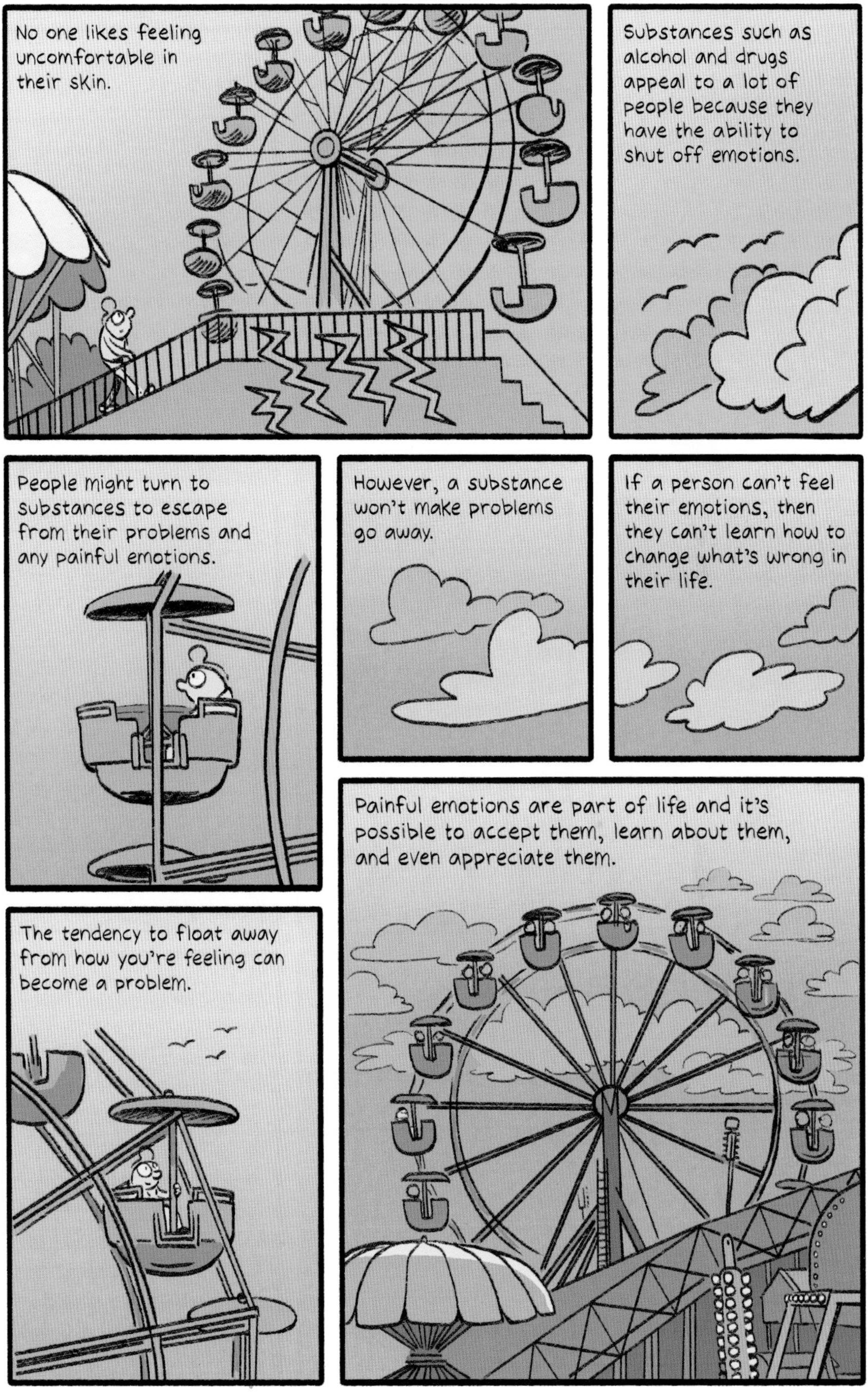

No one likes feeling uncomfortable in their skin.
Substances such as alcohol and drugs appeal to a lot of people because they have the ability to shut off emotions.
People might turn to substances to escape from their problems and any painful emotions.
However, a substance won't make problems go away.
If a person can't feel their emotions, then they can't learn how to change what's wrong in their life.
The tendency to float away from how you're feeling can become a problem.
Painful emotions are part of life and it's possible to accept them, learn about them, and even appreciate them.

THE RISKS OF SUBSTANCE USE

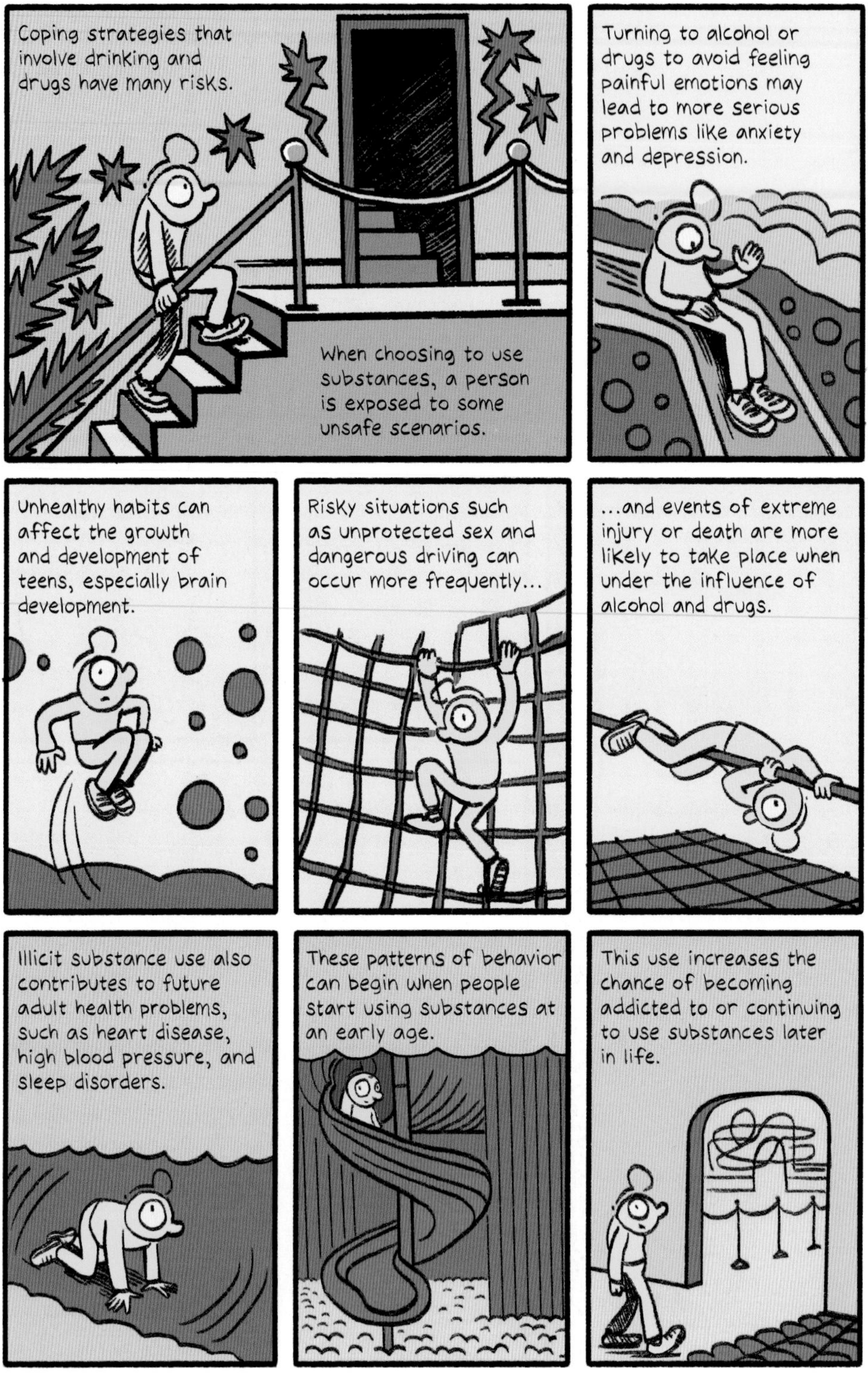
Coping strategies that involve drinking and drugs have many risks.
When choosing to use substances, a person is exposed to some unsafe scenarios.
Turning to alcohol or drugs to avoid feeling painful emotions may lead to more serious problems like anxiety and depression.
Unhealthy habits can affect the growth and development of teens, especially brain development.
Risky situations such as unprotected sex and dangerous driving can occur more frequently...
...and events of extreme injury or death are more likely to take place when under the influence of alcohol and drugs.
Illicit substance use also contributes to future adult health problems, such as heart disease, high blood pressure, and sleep disorders.
These patterns of behavior can begin when people start using substances at an early age.
This use increases the chance of becoming addicted to or continuing to use substances later in life.

WHAT ARE THE REASONS PEOPLE START USING SUBSTANCES?

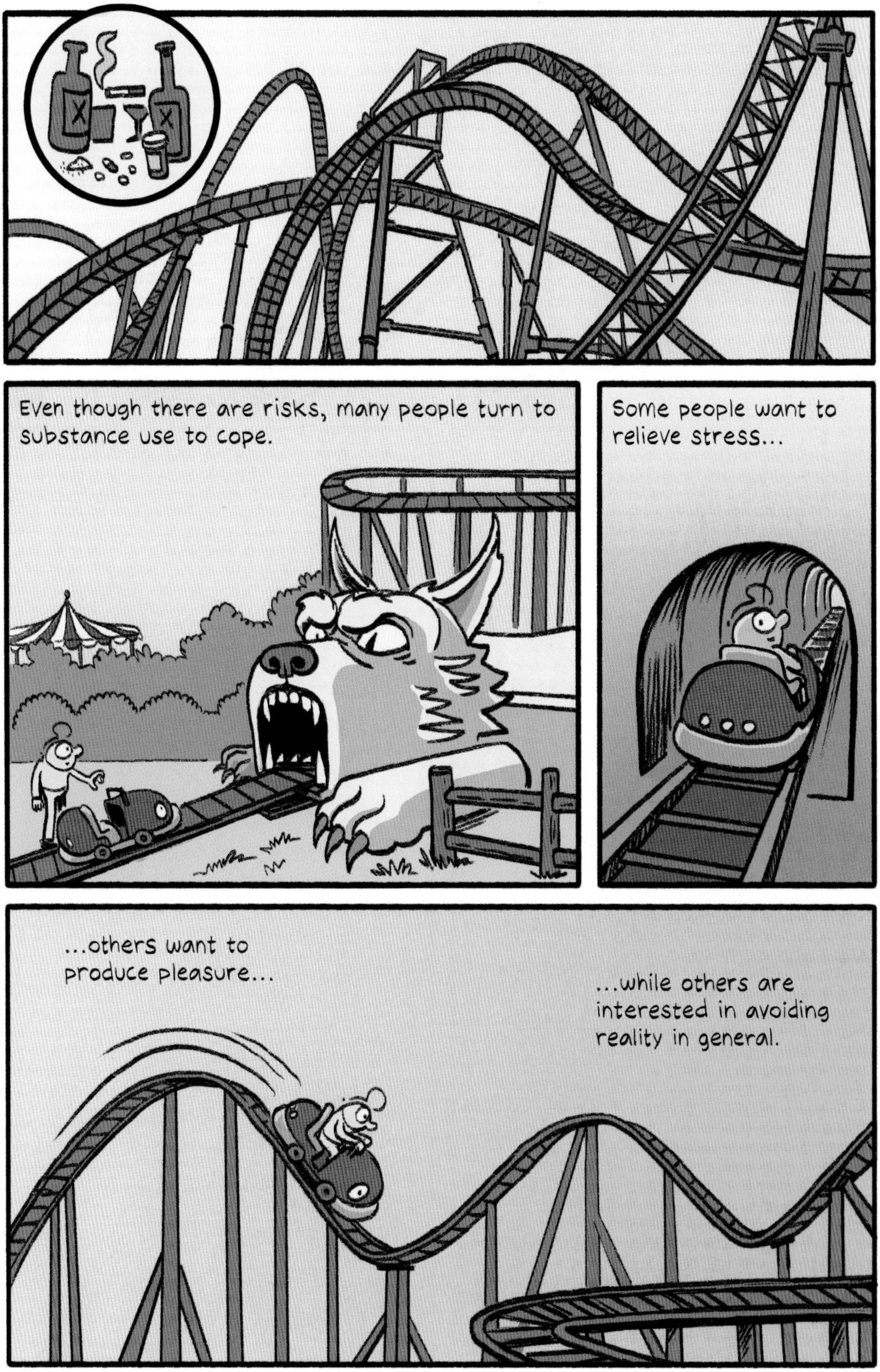
Even though there are risks, many people turn to substance use to cope.
Some people want to relieve stress...
...others want to produce pleasure...
...while others are interested in avoiding reality in general.

WHO WILL DEVELOP A SUBSTANCE USE DISORDER OR ADDICTION?

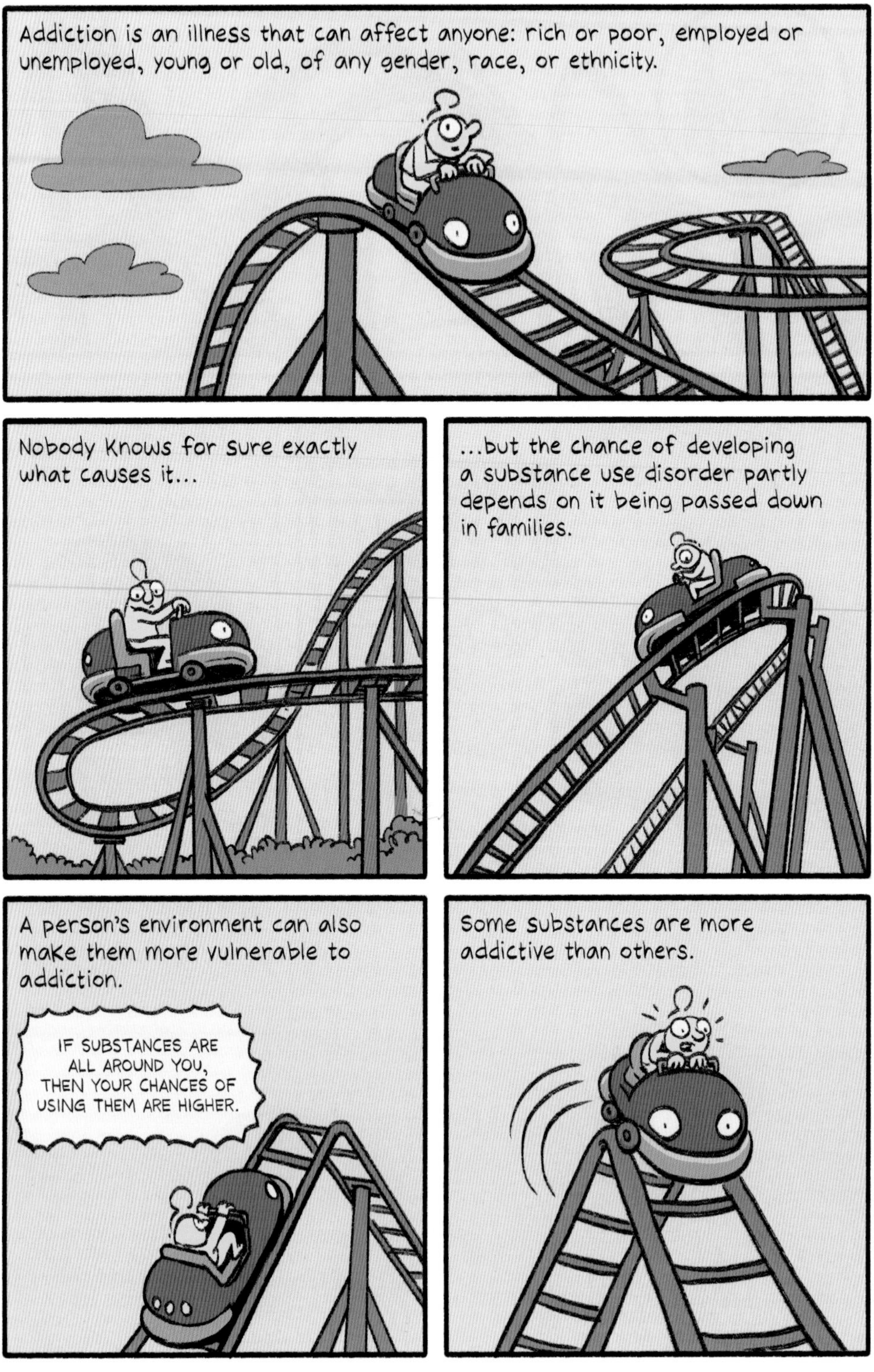
Addiction is an illness that can affect anyone: rich or poor, employed or unemployed, young or old, of any gender, race, or ethnicity.
Nobody knows for sure exactly what causes it...
...but the chance of developing a substance use disorder partly depends on it being passed down in families.
A person's environment can also make them more vulnerable to addiction.
IF SUBSTANCES ARE ALL AROUND YOU, THEN YOUR CHANCES OF USING THEM ARE HIGHER.
Some substances are more addictive than others.

HOW DO DIFFERENT KINDS OF SUBSTANCES ACT IN THE BRAIN AND BODY?

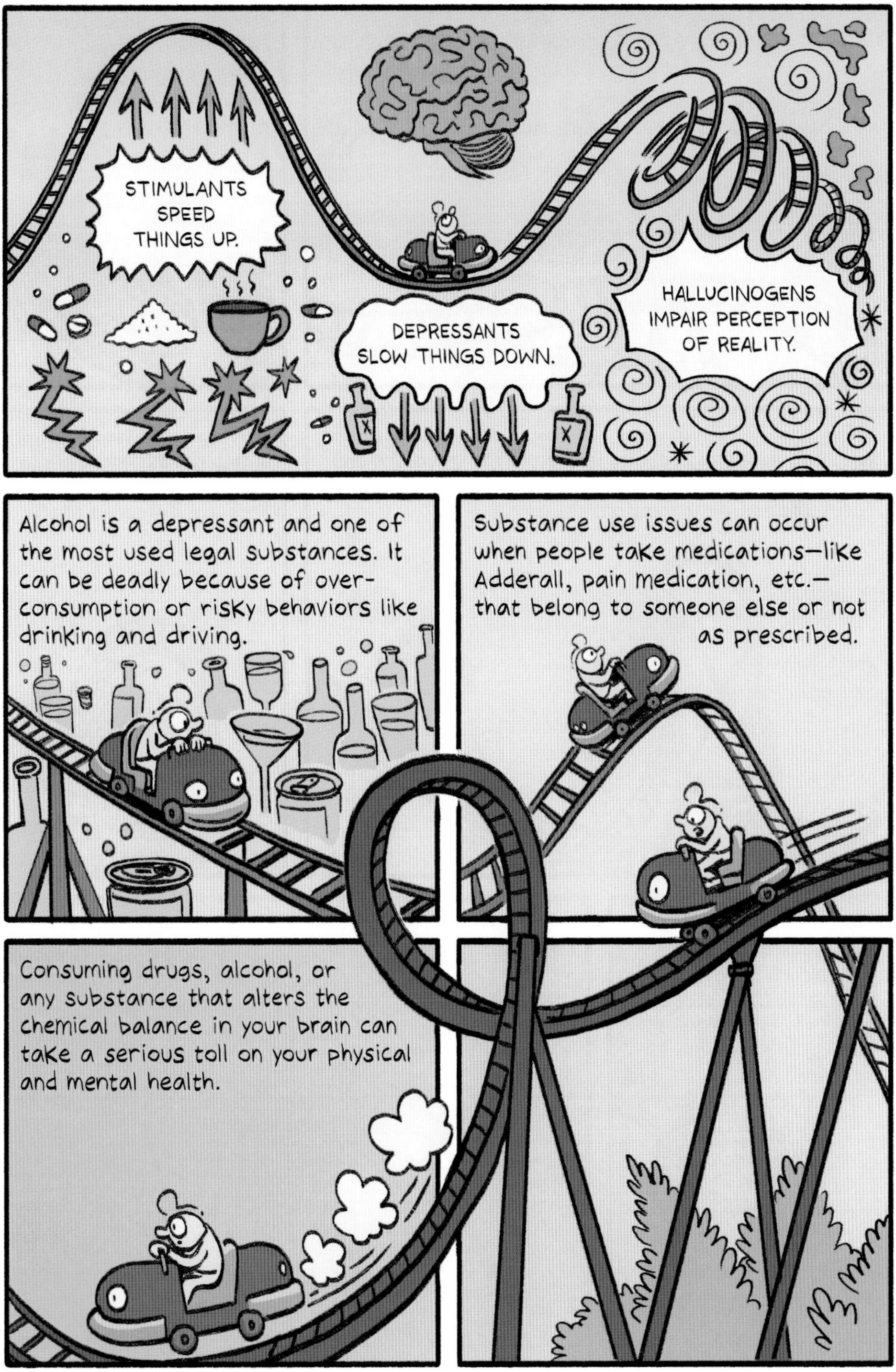
STIMULANTS SPEED THINGS UP.
DEPRESSANTS SLOW THINGS DOWN.
HALLUCINOGENS IMPAIR PERCEPTION OF REALITY.
Alcohol is a depressant and one of the most used legal substances. It can be deadly because of over-consumption or risky behaviors like drinking and driving.
Substance use issues can occur when people take medications—like Adderall, pain medication, etc.—that belong to someone else or not as prescribed.
Consuming drugs, alcohol, or any substance that alters the chemical balance in your brain can take a serious toll on your physical and mental health.

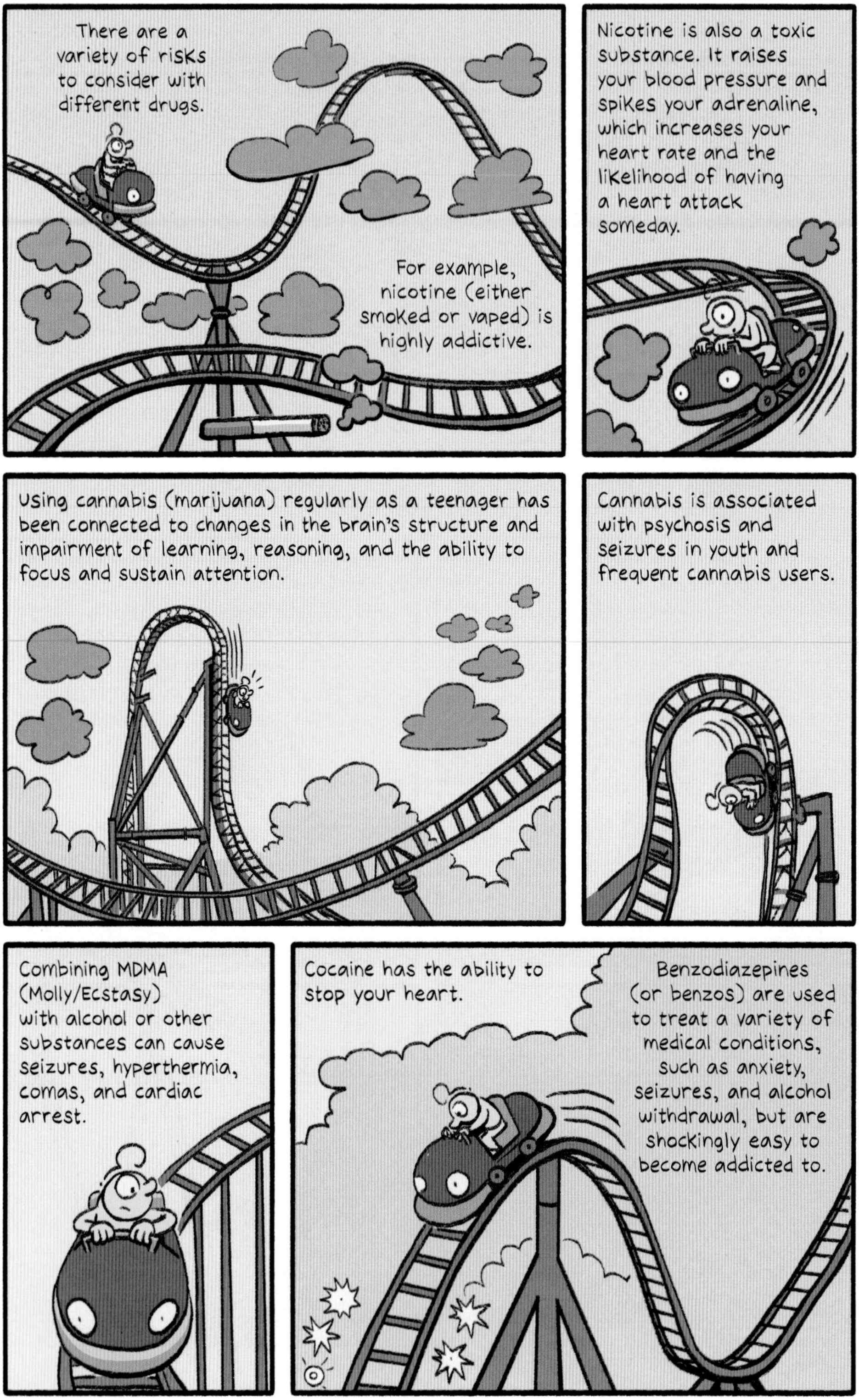
There are a variety of risks to consider with different drugs.
For example, nicotine (either smoked or vaped) is highly addictive.
Nicotine is also a toxic substance. It raises your blood pressure and spikes your adrenaline, which increases your heart rate and the likelihood of having a heart attack someday.
Using cannabis (marijuana) regularly as a teenager has been connected to changes in the brain's structure and impairment of learning, reasoning, and the ability to focus and sustain attention.
Cannabis is associated with psychosis and seizures in youth and frequent cannabis users.
Combining MDMA (Molly/Ecstasy) with alcohol or other substances can cause seizures, hyperthermia, comas, and cardiac arrest.
Cocaine has the ability to stop your heart.
Benzodiazepines (or benzos) are used to treat a variety of medical conditions, such as anxiety, seizures, and alcohol withdrawal, but are shockingly easy to become addicted to.

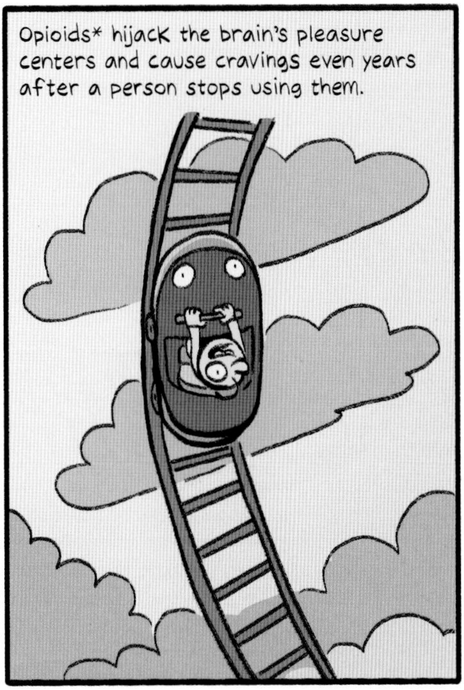
Opioids* hijack the brain's pleasure centers and cause cravings even years after a person stops using them.

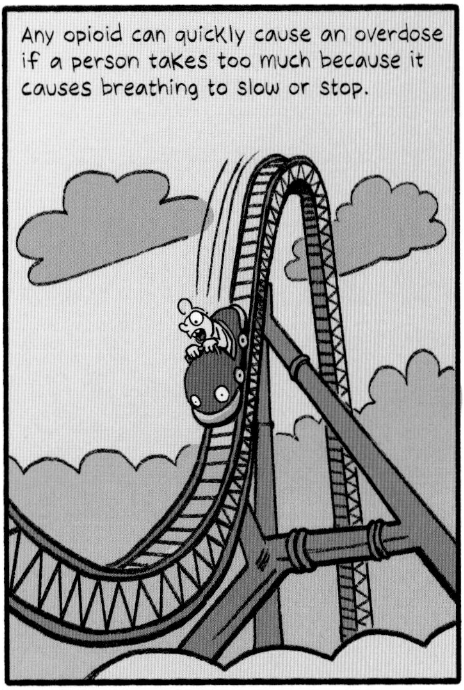
Any opioid can quickly cause an overdose if a person takes too much because it causes breathing to slow or stop.

There is a very intense opioid called fentanyl that is made in a lab. It is up to 50 times stronger than heroin and 100 times stronger than morphine.

Drug dealers can mix the cheaper fentanyl with other drugs like heroin, cocaine, MDMA, and methamphetamine to increase their profits.

Being arrested and serving prison time for illegal drugs is a big risk too!

With or without a conviction, a person's future can be impacted by societal roadblocks to travel, education, and employment.

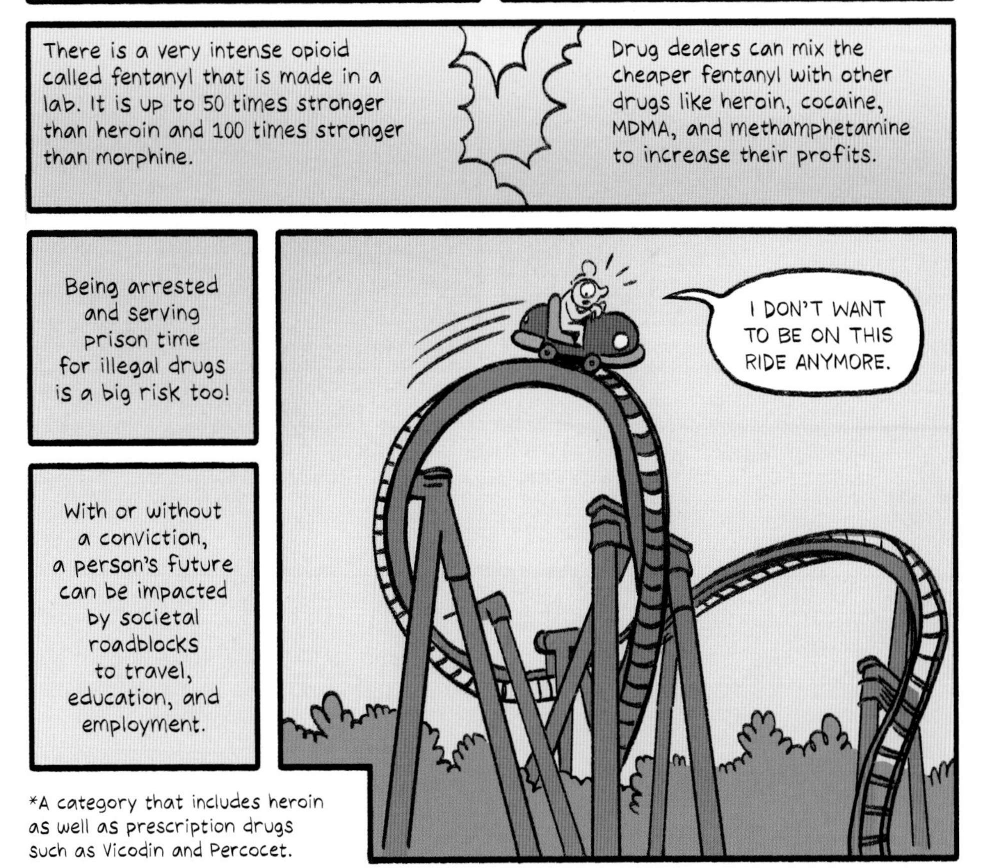
I DON'T WANT TO BE ON THIS RIDE ANYMORE.

*A category that includes heroin as well as prescription drugs such as Vicodin and Percocet.

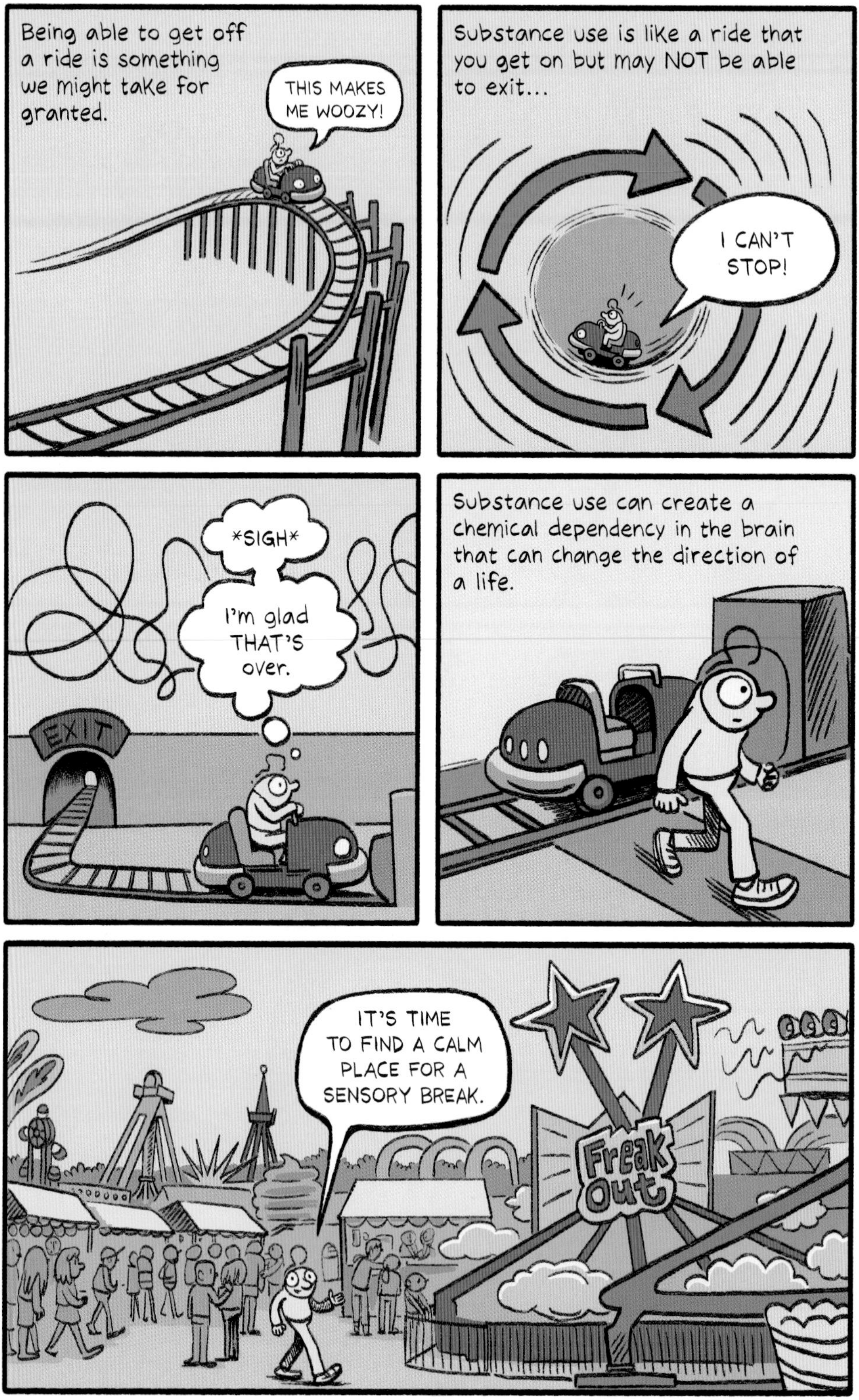
Being able to get off a ride is something we might take for granted.
THIS MAKES ME WOOZY!
Substance use is like a ride that you get on but may NOT be able to exit...
I CAN'T STOP!
SIGH
I'm glad THAT'S over.
EXIT
Substance use can create a chemical dependency in the brain that can change the direction of a life.
IT'S TIME TO FIND A CALM PLACE FOR A SENSORY BREAK.
Freak Out

IS THERE A CURE FOR ADDICTION?

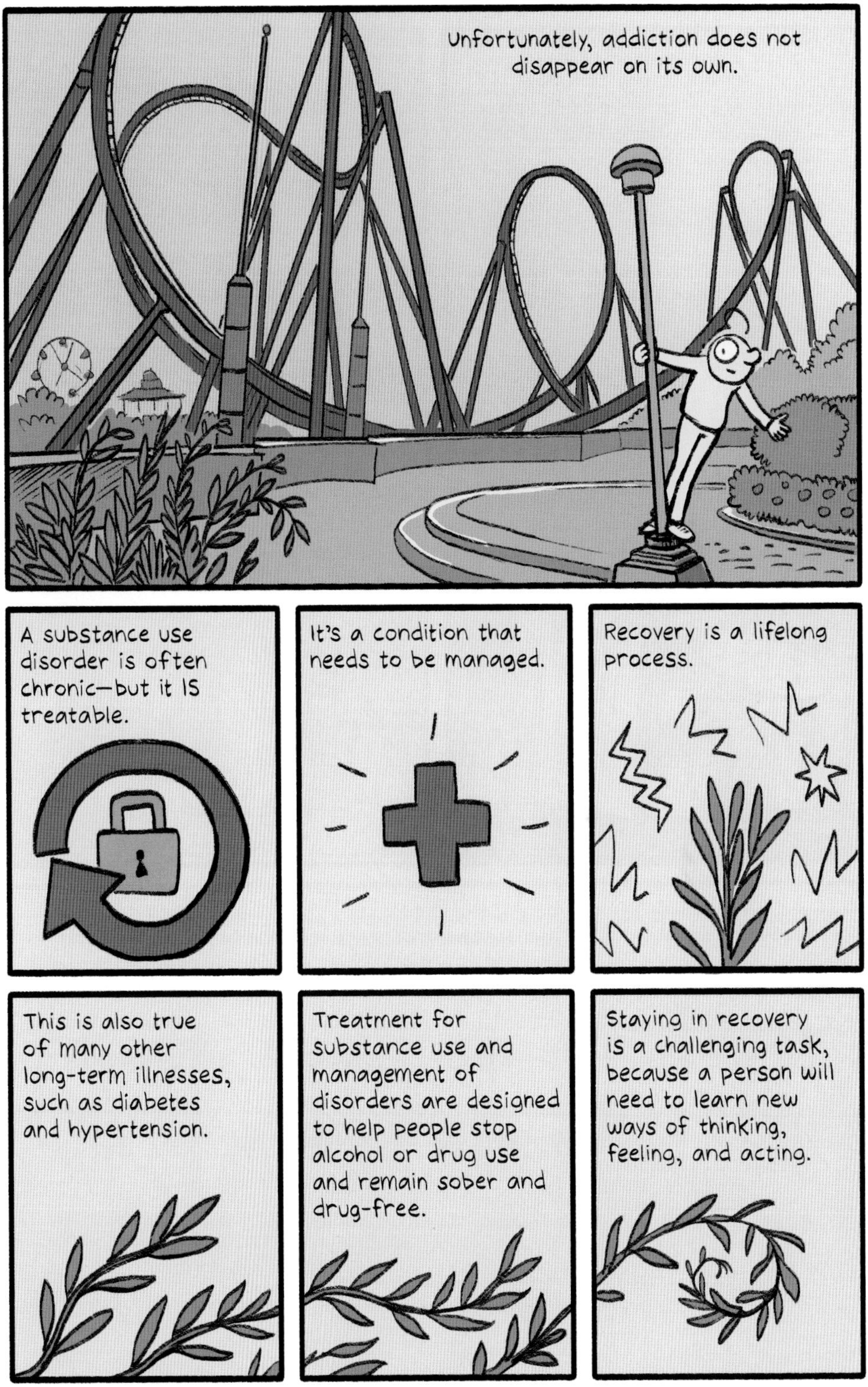
Unfortunately, addiction does not disappear on its own.
A substance use disorder is often chronic—but it IS treatable.
It's a condition that needs to be managed.
Recovery is a lifelong process.
This is also true of many other long-term illnesses, such as diabetes and hypertension.
Treatment for substance use and management of disorders are designed to help people stop alcohol or drug use and remain sober and drug-free.
Staying in recovery is a challenging task, because a person will need to learn new ways of thinking, feeling, and acting.

ENTRYWAY TO ADDICTION

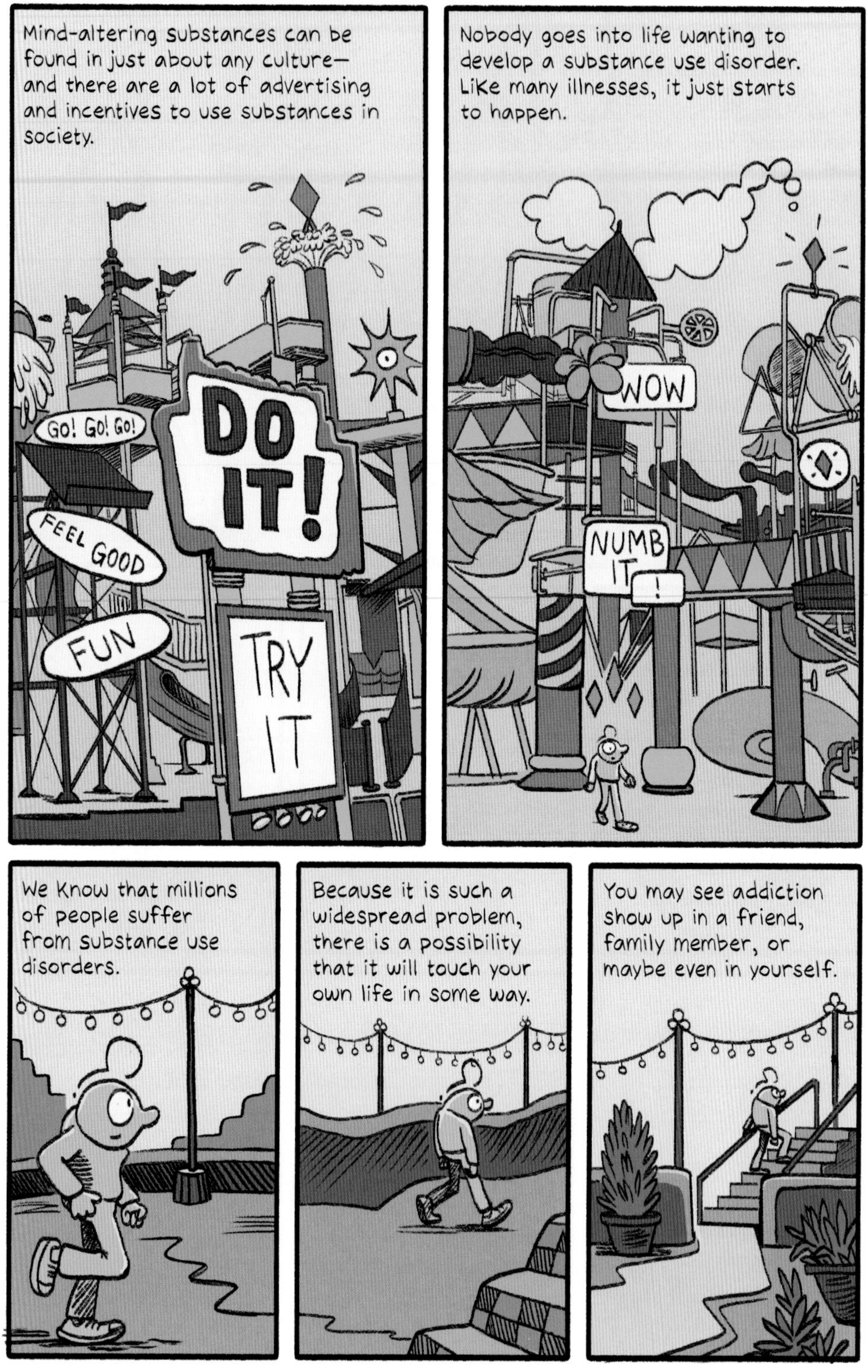
Mind-altering substances can be found in just about any culture—and there are a lot of advertising and incentives to use substances in society.
GO! GO! GO!
DO IT!
FEEL GOOD
FUN
TRY IT
Nobody goes into life wanting to develop a substance use disorder. Like many illnesses, it just starts to happen.
WOW
NUMB IT
!
We know that millions of people suffer from substance use disorders.
Because it is such a widespread problem, there is a possibility that it will touch your own life in some way.
You may see addiction show up in a friend, family member, or maybe even in yourself.

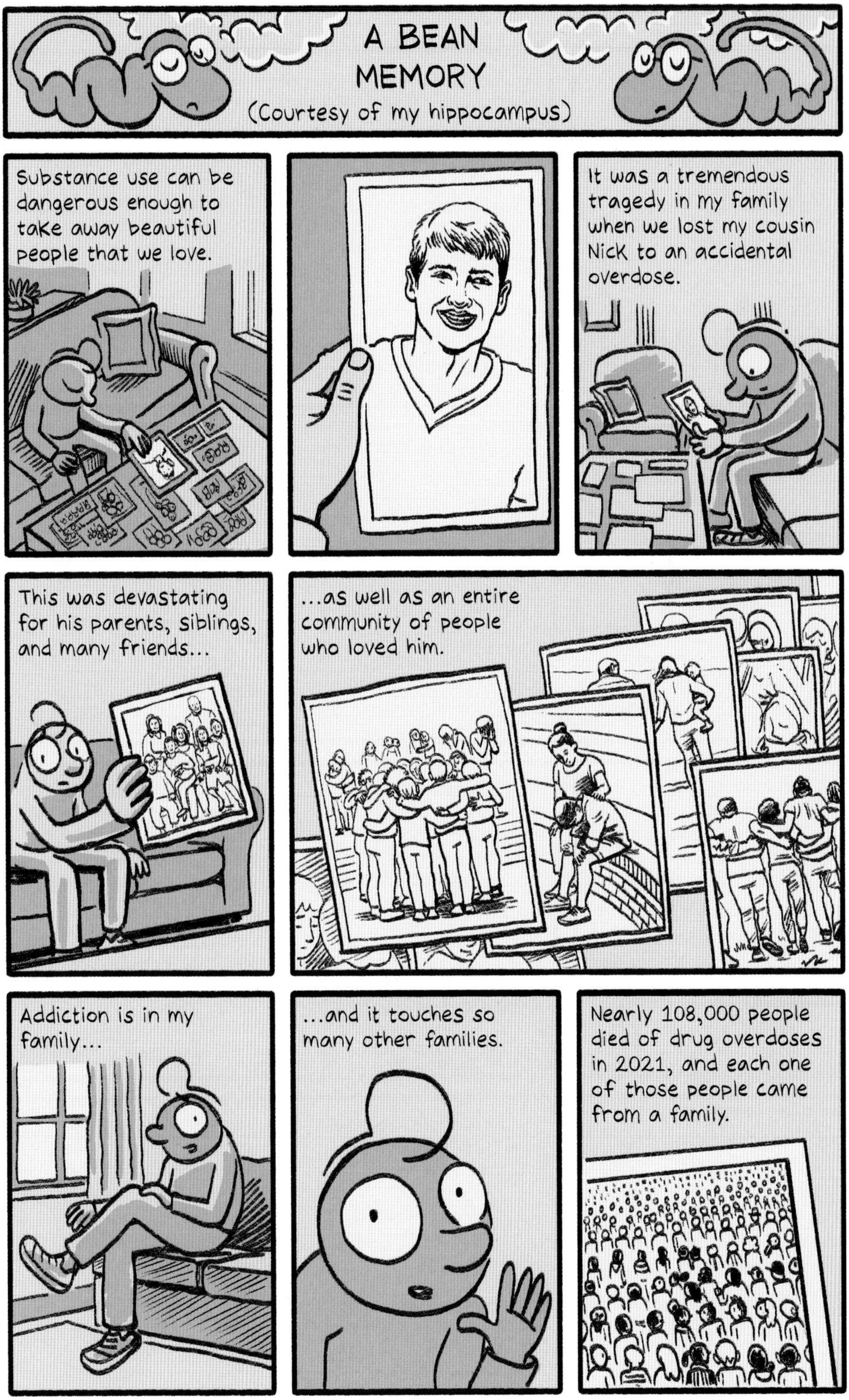
A BEAN MEMORY
(Courtesy of my hippocampus)
Substance use can be dangerous enough to take away beautiful people that we love.
It was a tremendous tragedy in my family when we lost my cousin Nick to an accidental overdose.
This was devastating for his parents, siblings, and many friends...
...as well as an entire community of people who loved him.
Addiction is in my family...
...and it touches so many other families.
Nearly 108,000 people died of drug overdoses in 2021, and each one of those people came from a family.

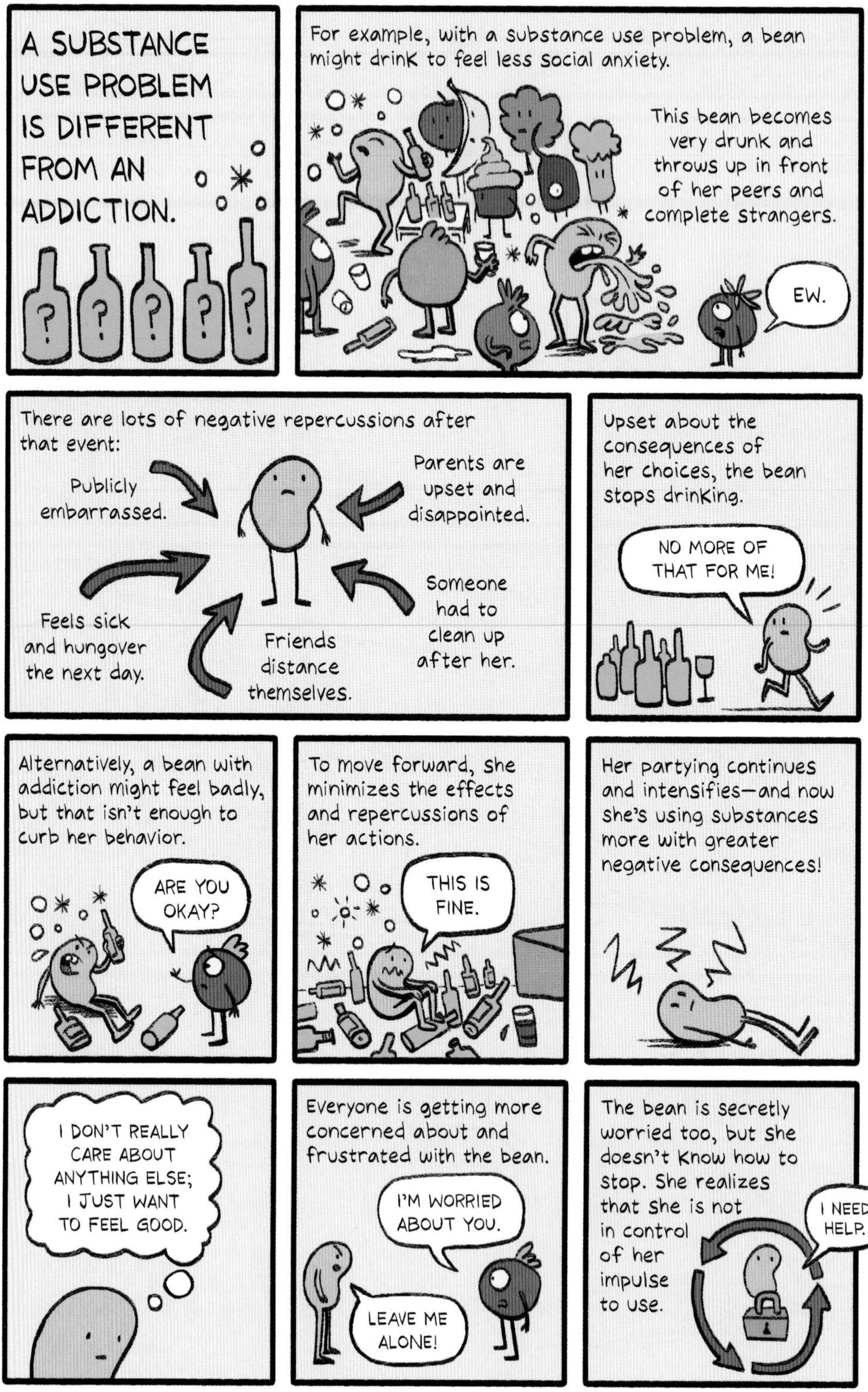
A SUBSTANCE USE PROBLEM IS DIFFERENT FROM AN ADDICTION.
?
?
?
?
?
For example, with a substance use problem, a bean might drink to feel less social anxiety.
This bean becomes very drunk and throws up in front of her peers and complete strangers.
EW.
There are lots of negative repercussions after that event:
Publicly embarrassed.
Parents are upset and disappointed.
Feels sick and hungover the next day.
Friends distance themselves.
Someone had to clean up after her.
Upset about the consequences of her choices, the bean stops drinking.
NO MORE OF THAT FOR ME!
Alternatively, a bean with addiction might feel badly, but that isn't enough to curb her behavior.
ARE YOU OKAY?
To move forward, she minimizes the effects and repercussions of her actions.
THIS IS FINE.
Her partying continues and intensifies—and now she's using substances more with greater negative consequences!
I DON'T REALLY CARE ABOUT ANYTHING ELSE; I JUST WANT TO FEEL GOOD.
Everyone is getting more concerned about and frustrated with the bean.
I'M WORRIED ABOUT YOU.
LEAVE ME ALONE!
The bean is secretly worried too, but she doesn't know how to stop. She realizes that she is not in control of her impulse to use.
I NEED HELP.

BEHAVIORS CAN BECOME ADDICTIVE TOO

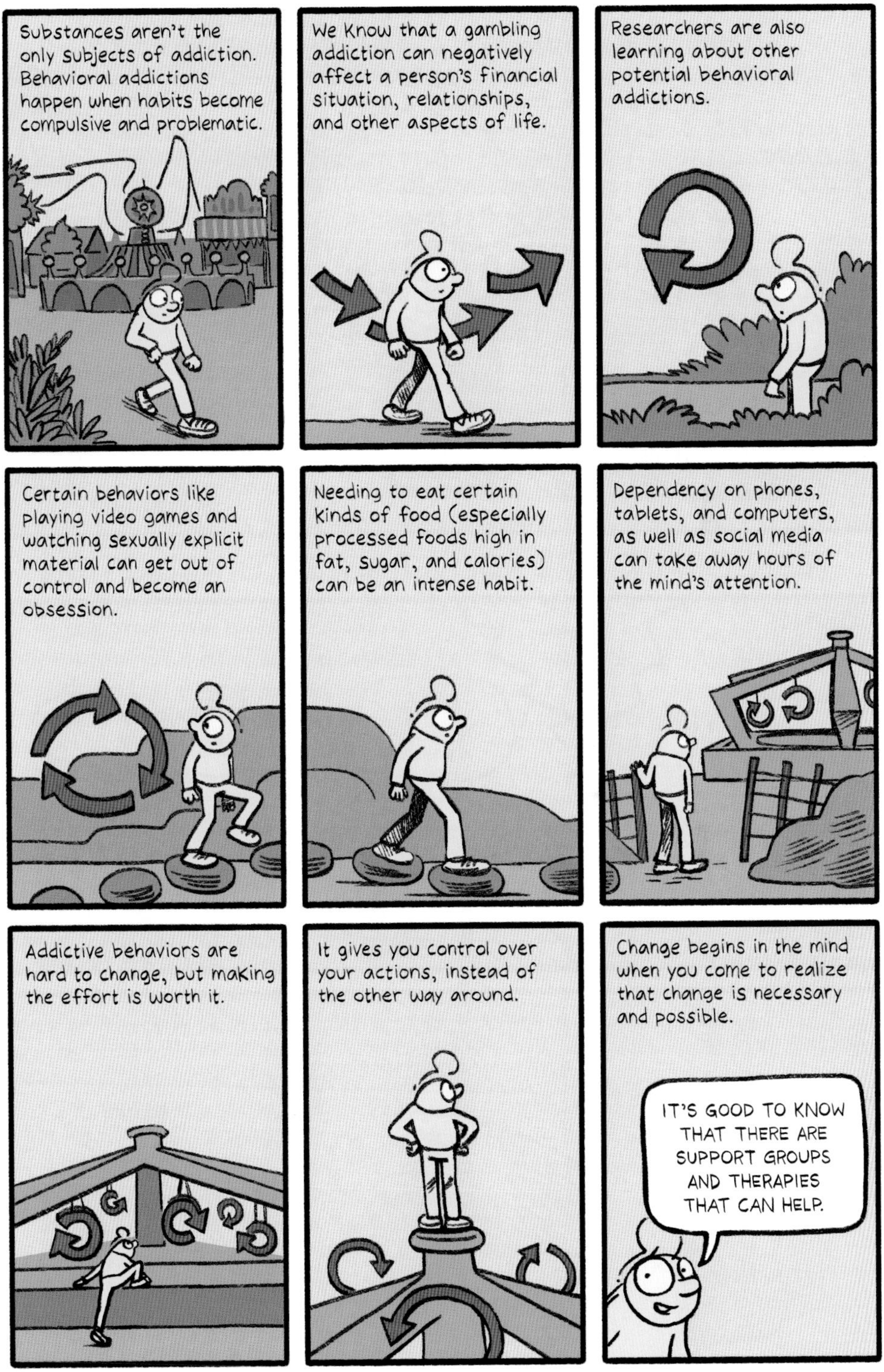

Substances aren't the only subjects of addiction. Behavioral addictions happen when habits become compulsive and problematic.
We know that a gambling addiction can negatively affect a person's financial situation, relationships, and other aspects of life.
Researchers are also learning about other potential behavioral addictions.
Certain behaviors like playing video games and watching sexually explicit material can get out of control and become an obsession.
Needing to eat certain kinds of food (especially processed foods high in fat, sugar, and calories) can be an intense habit.
Dependency on phones, tablets, and computers, as well as social media can take away hours of the mind's attention.
Addictive behaviors are hard to change, but making the effort is worth it.
It gives you control over your actions, instead of the other way around.
Change begins in the mind when you come to realize that change is necessary and possible.
IT'S GOOD TO KNOW THAT THERE ARE SUPPORT GROUPS AND THERAPIES THAT CAN HELP.

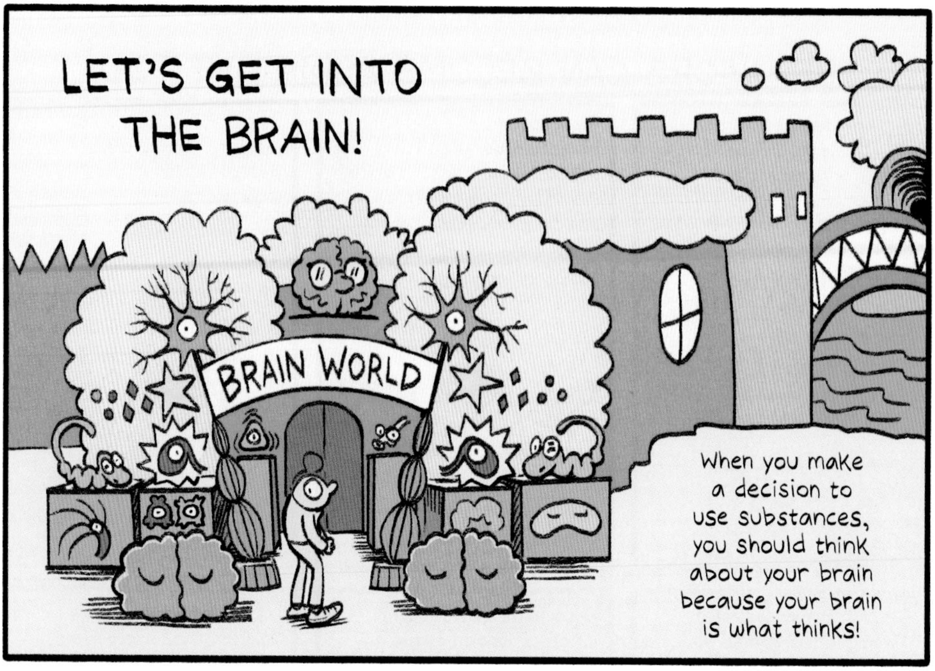
LET'S GET INTO THE BRAIN!
BRAIN WORLD
When you make a decision to use substances, you should think about your brain because your brain is what thinks!

TEEN BRAINS ARE VULNERABLE TO ADDICTION

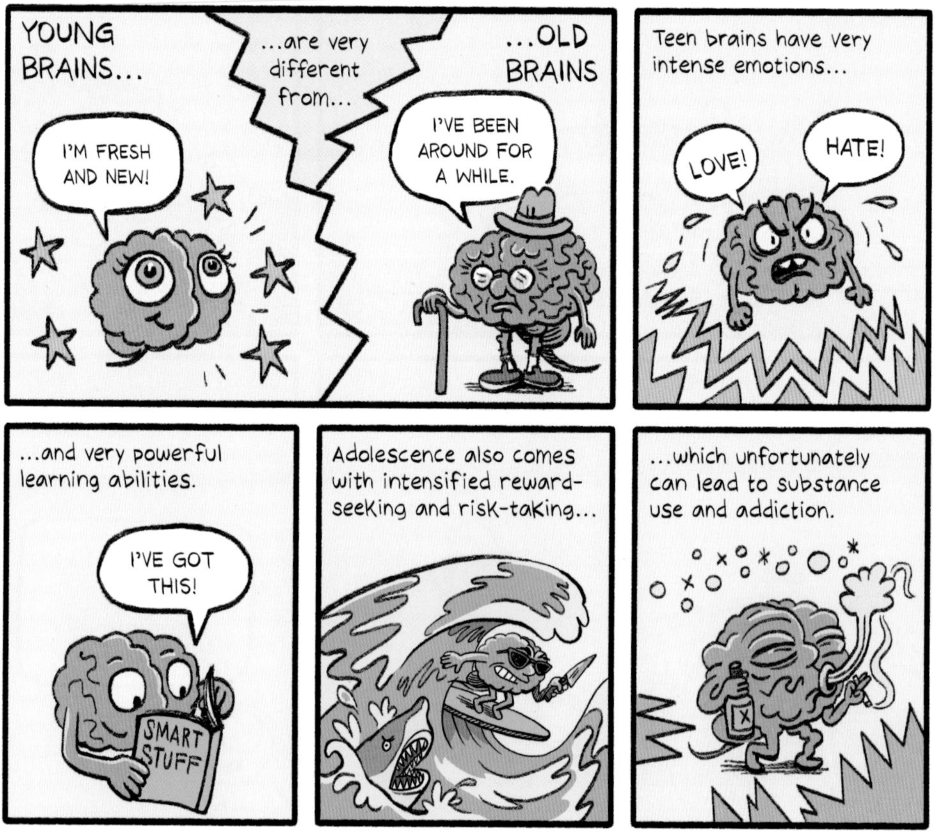
YOUNG BRAINS...
...are very different from...
...OLD BRAINS
I'M FRESH AND NEW!
I'VE BEEN AROUND FOR A WHILE.
Teen brains have very intense emotions...
LOVE!
HATE!
...and very powerful learning abilities.
I'VE GOT THIS!
SMART STUFF
Adolescence also comes with intensified reward-seeking and risk-taking...
...which unfortunately can lead to substance use and addiction.

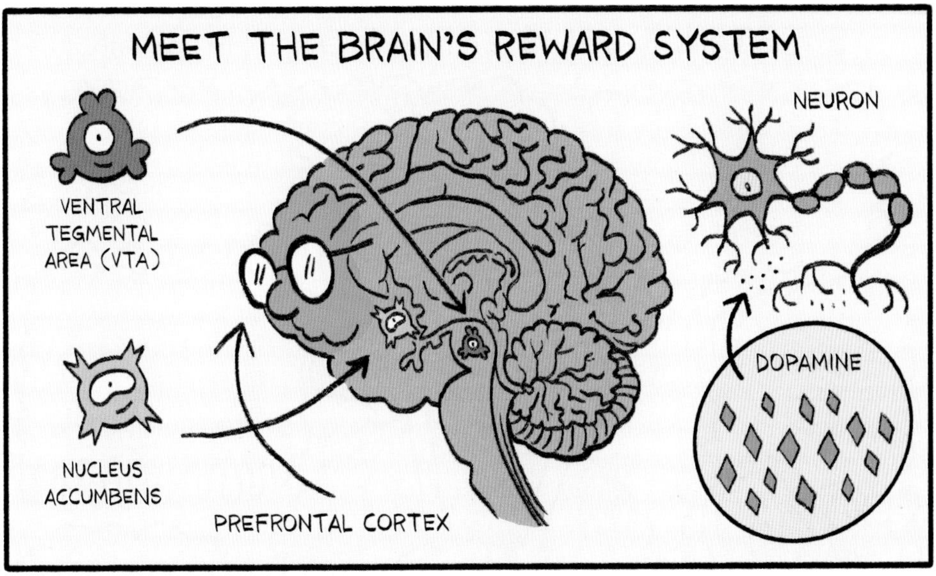
MEET THE BRAIN'S REWARD SYSTEM
VENTRAL TEGMENTAL AREA (VTA)
NUCLEUS ACCUMBENS
PREFRONTAL CORTEX
NEURON
DOPAMINE

HOW DOES THE BRAIN EXPERIENCE DRUGS?

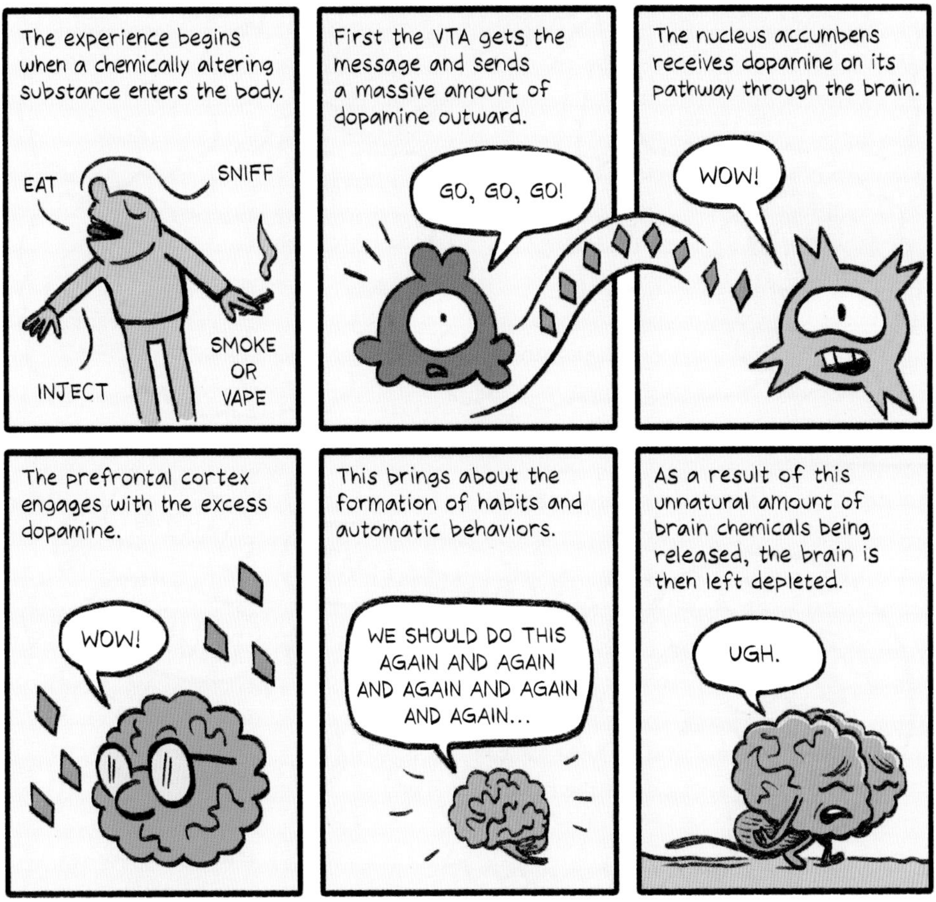
The experience begins when a chemically altering substance enters the body.
EAT
SNIFF
INJECT
SMOKE OR VAPE
First the VTA gets the message and sends a massive amount of dopamine outward.
GO, GO, GO!
The nucleus accumbens receives dopamine on its pathway through the brain.
WOW!
The prefrontal cortex engages with the excess dopamine.
WOW!
This brings about the formation of habits and automatic behaviors.
WE SHOULD DO THIS AGAIN AND AGAIN AND AGAIN AND AGAIN AND AGAIN...
As a result of this unnatural amount of brain chemicals being released, the brain is then left depleted.
UGH.

SUBSTANCE USE'S EFFECT ON THE BRAIN

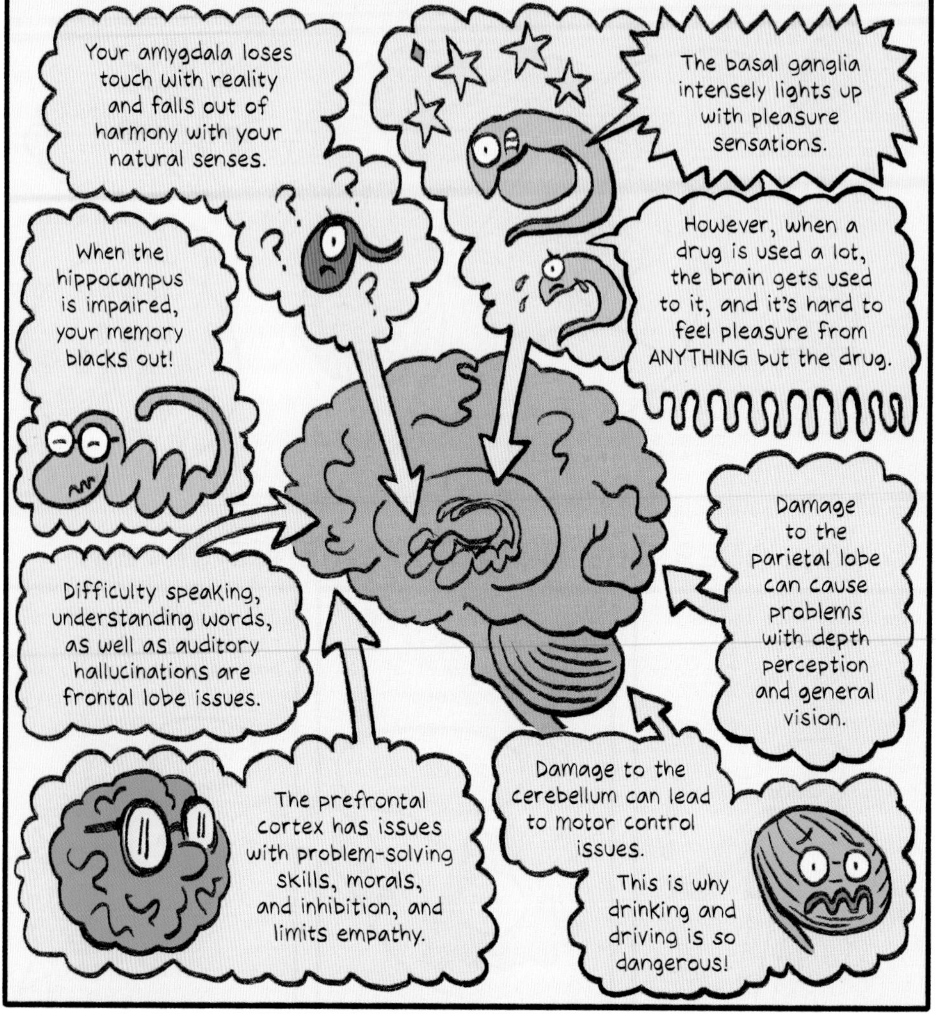
Your amygdala loses touch with reality and falls out of harmony with your natural senses.
The basal ganglia intensely lights up with pleasure sensations.
However, when a drug is used a lot, the brain gets used to it, and it's hard to feel pleasure from ANYTHING but the drug.
When the hippocampus is impaired, your memory blacks out!
Damage to the parietal lobe can cause problems with depth perception and general vision.
Difficulty speaking, understanding words, as well as auditory hallucinations are frontal lobe issues.
The prefrontal cortex has issues with problem-solving skills, morals, and inhibition, and limits empathy.
Damage to the cerebellum can lead to motor control issues.
This is why drinking and driving is so dangerous!

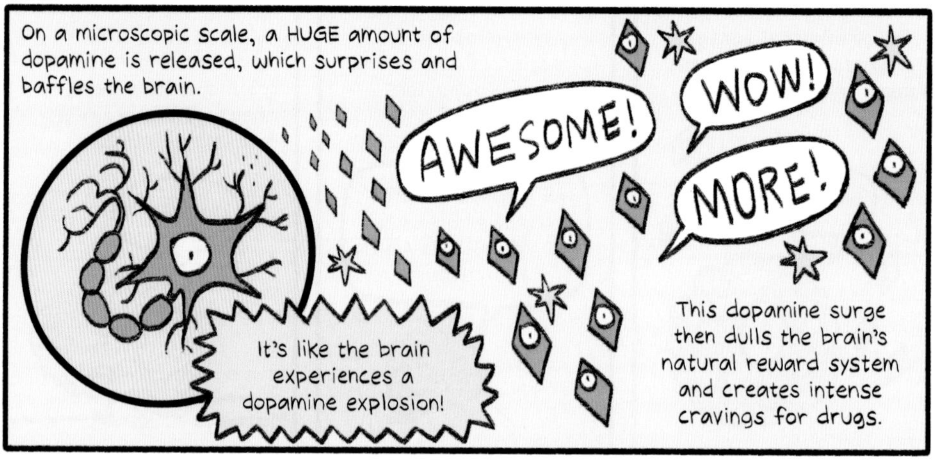
On a microscopic scale, a HUGE amount of dopamine is released, which surprises and baffles the brain.
AWESOME!
WOW!
MORE!
It's like the brain experiences a dopamine explosion!
This dopamine surge then dulls the brain's natural reward system and creates intense cravings for drugs.

HOW DOES SUBSTANCE USE DAMAGE THE BRAIN?

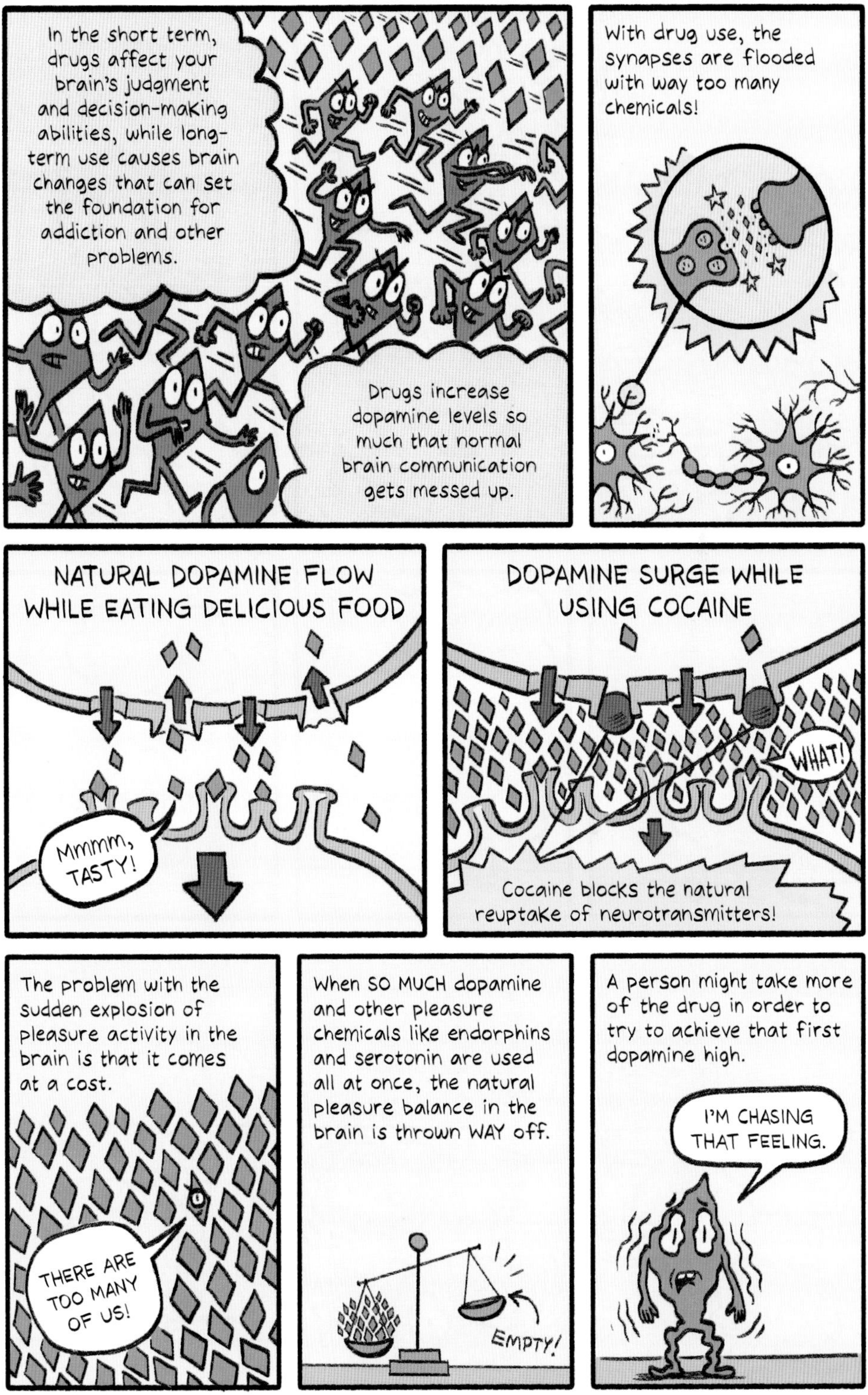
In the short term, drugs affect your brain's judgment and decision-making abilities, while long-term use causes brain changes that can set the foundation for addiction and other problems.
Drugs increase dopamine levels so much that normal brain communication gets messed up.
With drug use, the synapses are flooded with way too many chemicals!
NATURAL DOPAMINE FLOW WHILE EATING DELICIOUS FOOD
MMMM, TASTY!
DOPAMINE SURGE WHILE USING COCAINE
WHAT!
Cocaine blocks the natural reuptake of neurotransmitters!
The problem with the sudden explosion of pleasure activity in the brain is that it comes at a cost.
THERE ARE TOO MANY OF US!
When SO MUCH dopamine and other pleasure chemicals like endorphins and serotonin are used all at once, the natural pleasure balance in the brain is thrown WAY off.
EMPTY!
A person might take more of the drug in order to try to achieve that first dopamine high.
I'M CHASING THAT FEELING.

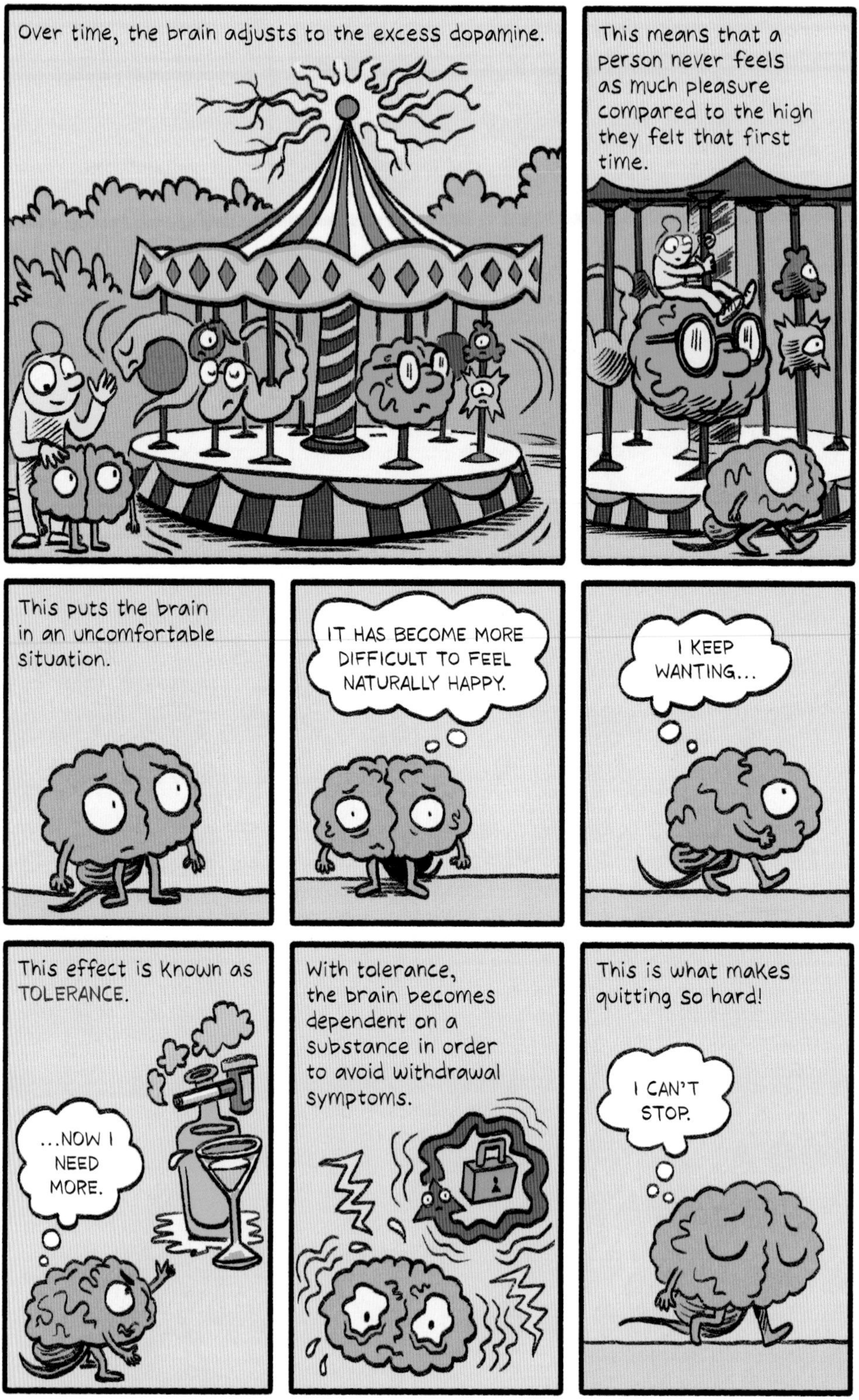
Over time, the brain adjusts to the excess dopamine.
This means that a person never feels as much pleasure compared to the high they felt that first time.
This puts the brain in an uncomfortable situation.
IT HAS BECOME MORE DIFFICULT TO FEEL NATURALLY HAPPY.
I KEEP WANTING...
This effect is known as TOLERANCE.
...NOW I NEED MORE.
With tolerance, the brain becomes dependent on a substance in order to avoid withdrawal symptoms.
This is what makes quitting so hard!
I CAN'T STOP.

THE PROGRESSION OF ADDICTION

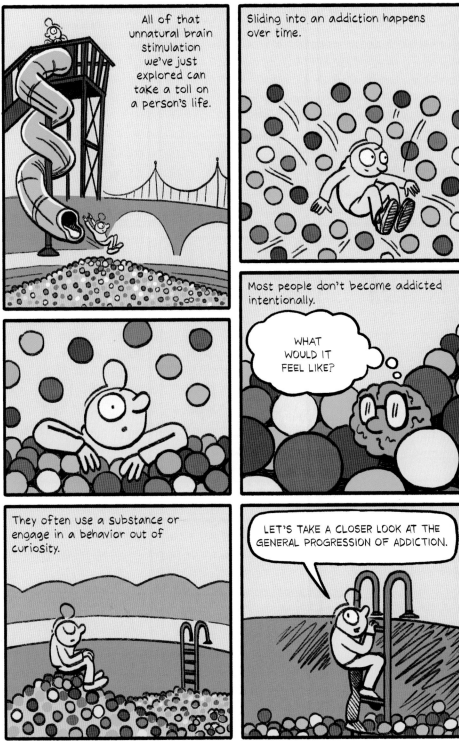

All of that unnatural brain stimulation we've just explored can take a toll on a person's life.

Sliding into an addiction happens over time.

Most people don't become addicted intentionally.

WHAT WOULD IT FEEL LIKE?

They often use a substance or engage in a behavior out of curiosity.

LET'S TAKE A CLOSER LOOK AT THE GENERAL PROGRESSION OF ADDICTION.

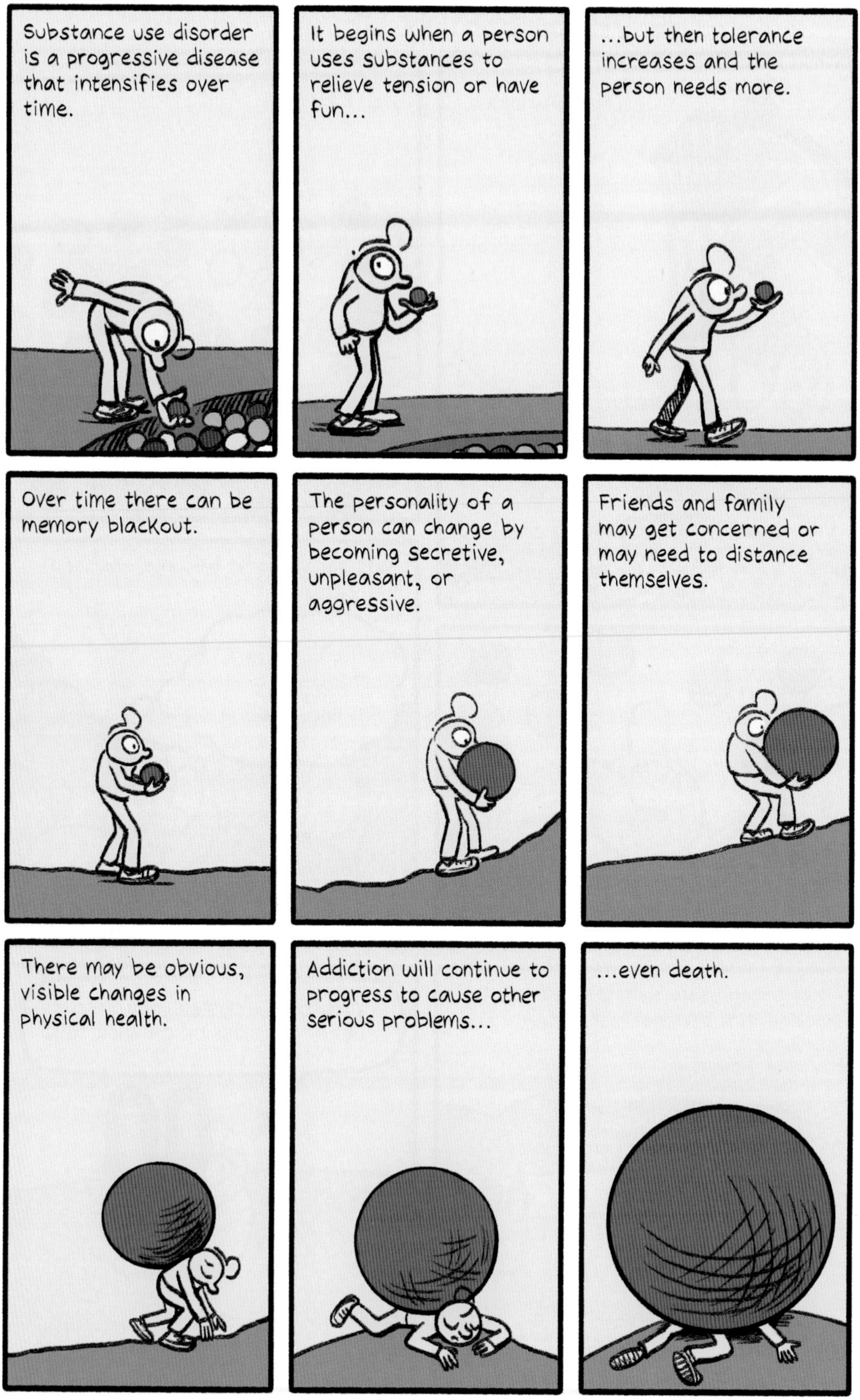
Substance use disorder is a progressive disease that intensifies over time.
It begins when a person uses substances to relieve tension or have fun...
...but then tolerance increases and the person needs more.
Over time there can be memory blackout.
The personality of a person can change by becoming secretive, unpleasant, or aggressive.
Friends and family may get concerned or may need to distance themselves.
There may be obvious, visible changes in physical health.
Addiction will continue to progress to cause other serious problems...
...even death.

ABOUT DEADLY SUBSTANCE USE

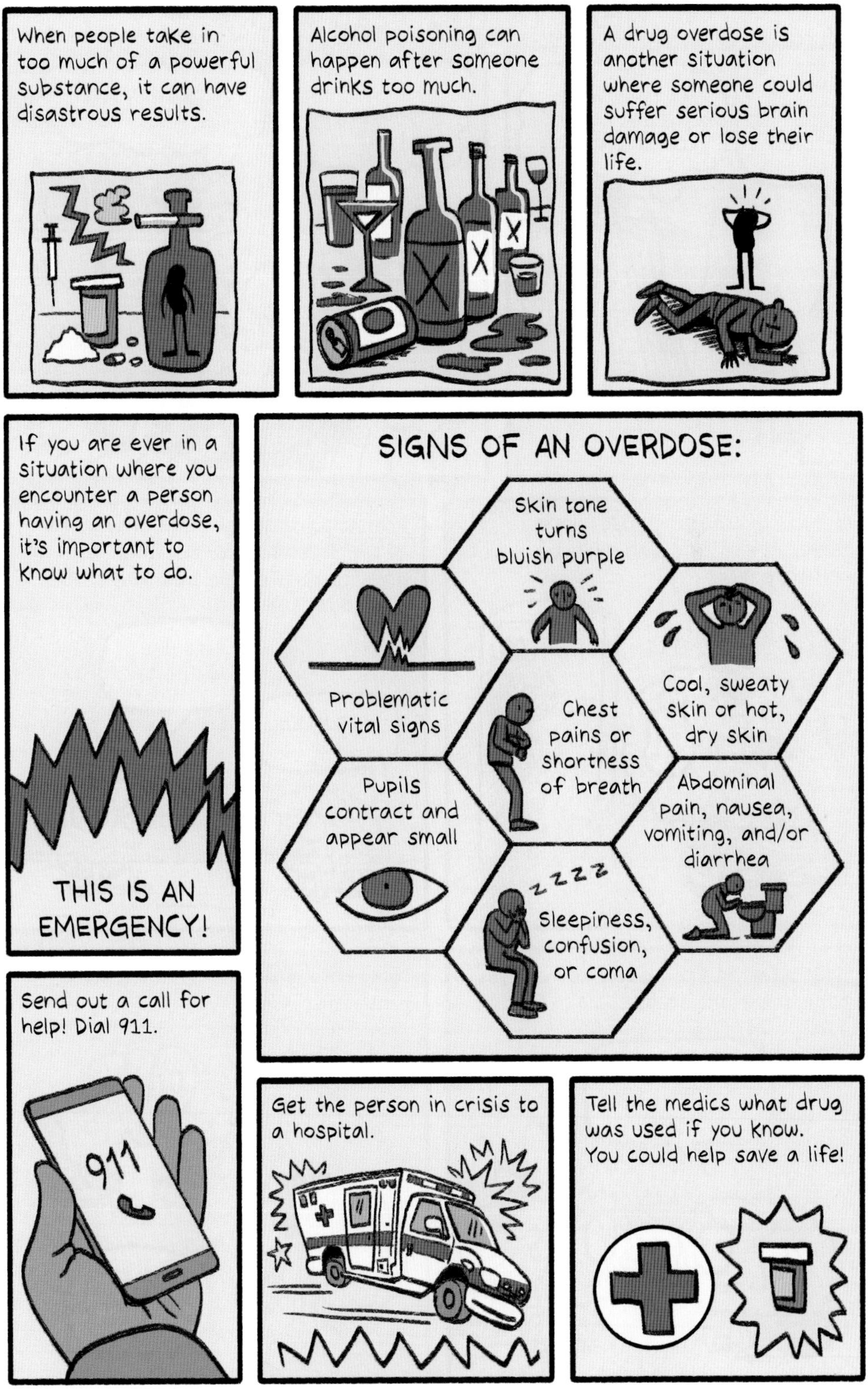

When people take in too much of a powerful substance, it can have disastrous results.
Alcohol poisoning can happen after someone drinks too much.
A drug overdose is another situation where someone could suffer serious brain damage or lose their life.
If you are ever in a situation where you encounter a person having an overdose, it's important to know what to do.
THIS IS AN EMERGENCY!
SIGNS OF AN OVERDOSE:
Skin tone turns bluish purple
Problematic vital signs
Cool, sweaty skin or hot, dry skin
Chest pains or shortness of breath
Pupils contract and appear small
Abdominal pain, nausea, vomiting, and/or diarrhea
ZZZZ
Sleepiness, confusion, or coma
Send out a call for help! Dial 911.
911
Get the person in crisis to a hospital.
Tell the medics what drug was used if you know. You could help save a life!

WHAT IF YOU NEED HELP?

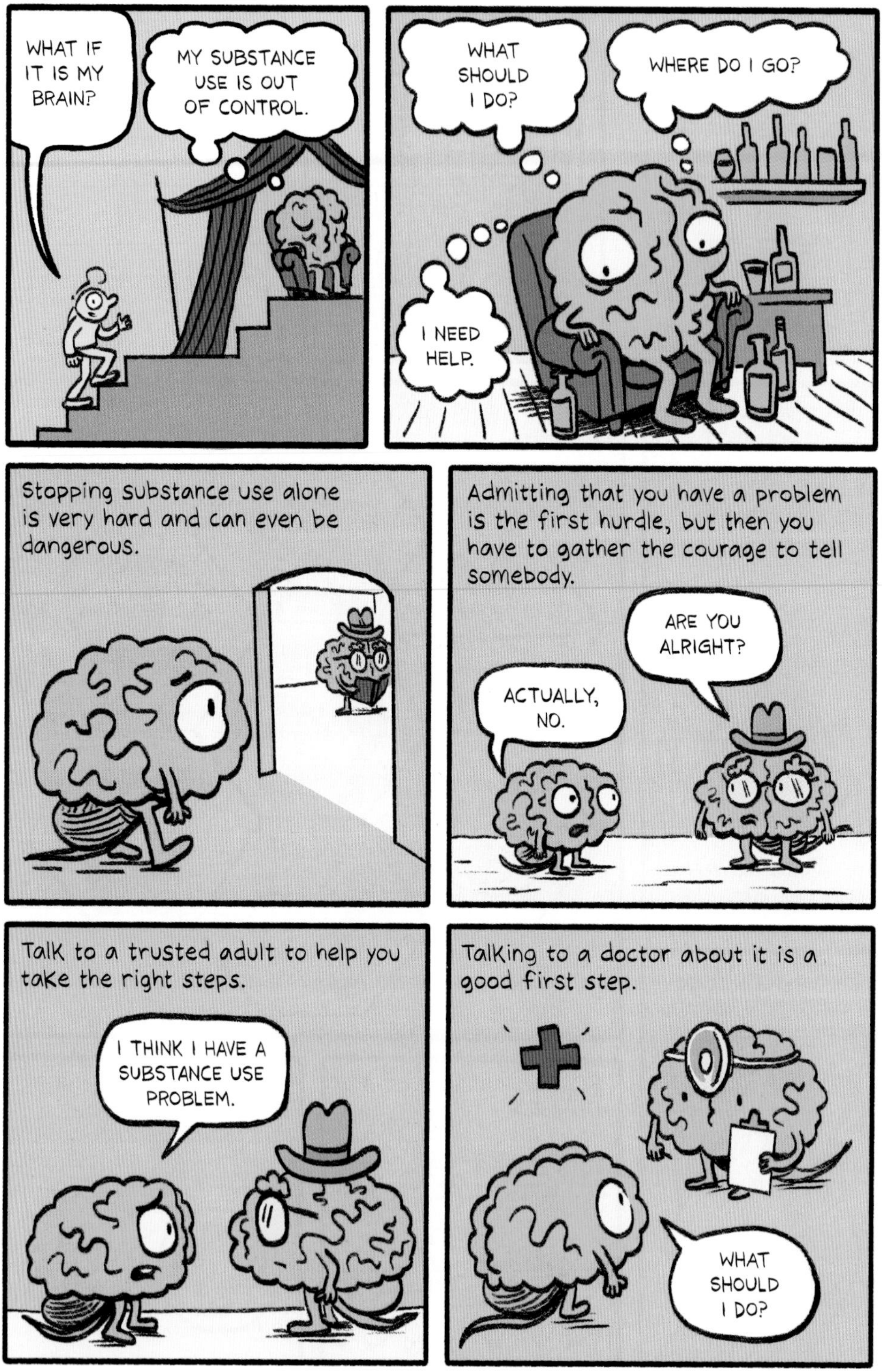
WHAT IF IT IS MY BRAIN?
MY SUBSTANCE USE IS OUT OF CONTROL.
WHAT SHOULD I DO?
WHERE DO I GO?
I NEED HELP.
Stopping substance use alone is very hard and can even be dangerous.
Admitting that you have a problem is the first hurdle, but then you have to gather the courage to tell somebody.
ARE YOU ALRIGHT?
ACTUALLY, NO.
Talk to a trusted adult to help you take the right steps.
I THINK I HAVE A SUBSTANCE USE PROBLEM.
Talking to a doctor about it is a good first step.
WHAT SHOULD I DO?

WHAT ARE SOME TREATMENTS FOR SUBSTANCE USE DISORDERS?

Drug addiction is treatable and can be successfully managed!

A doctor can recommend treatment programs such as online therapy or support groups as part of the recovery process.

SPEAKING TO A THERAPIST TO ADDRESS ANY UNDERLYING EMOTIONAL PAIN IS A GREAT WAY TO GAIN SUPPORT AND STRENGTH.

There are different ways people access help for a substance use disorder:

MEDICATION-ASSISTED TREATMENT	REHAB HOSPITALIZATION AND SHORT-TERM TREATMENT	SUPPORT GROUPS	MAINTENANCE AND LONG-TERM TREATMENT
Some medication helps people stop craving a drug and can be lifesaving.	People may need to go to an overnight facility for detoxification and rehabilitation services.	There are many free groups that meet to support one another in recovery like Alcoholics Anonymous and Narcotics Anonymous.	People can make a commitment to continuing with medical care, therapy, and a treatment program to remain sober.

LOVING SOMEONE WITH ADDICTION CAN BE HARD

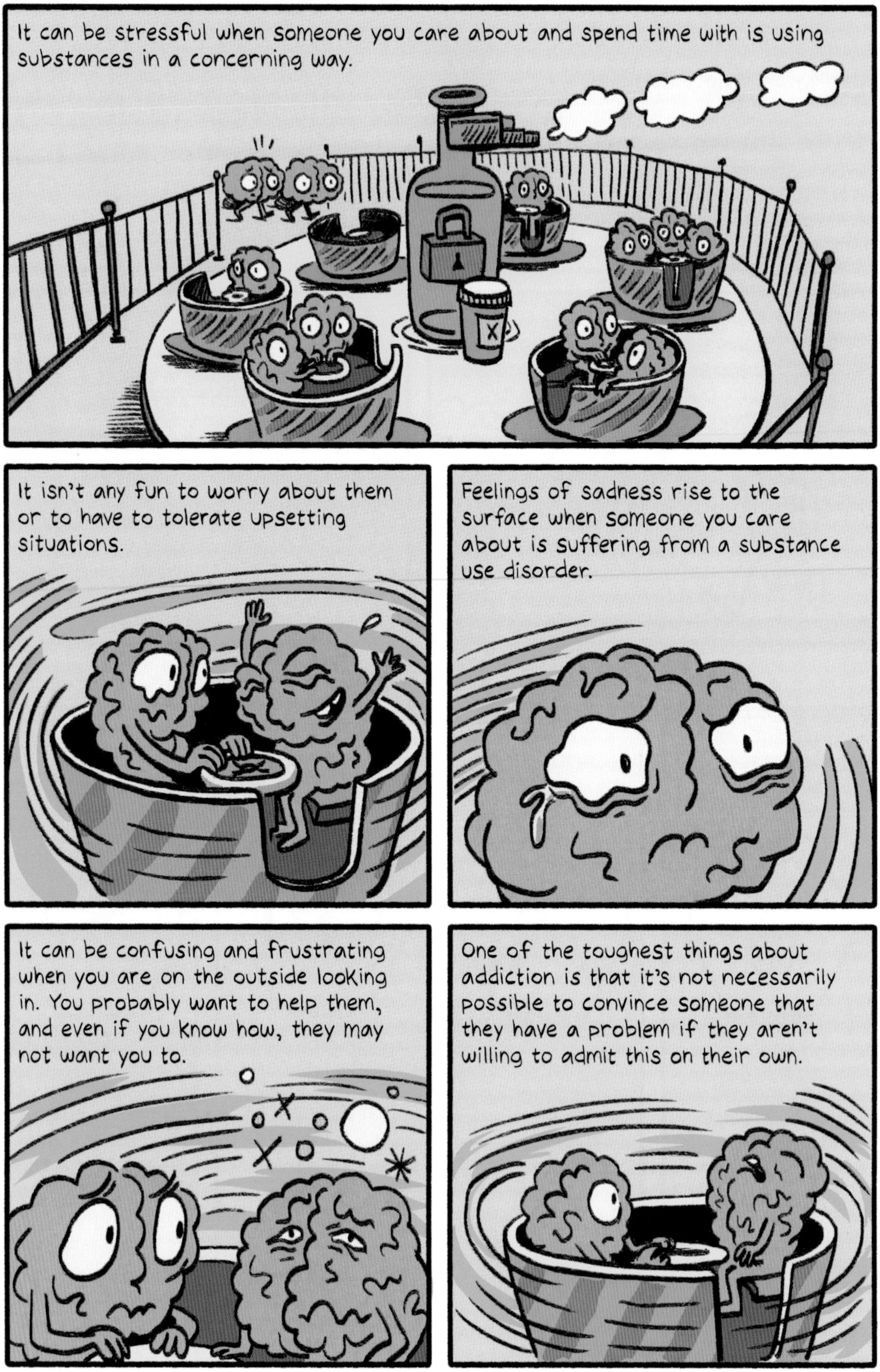
It can be stressful when someone you care about and spend time with is using substances in a concerning way.
It isn't any fun to worry about them or to have to tolerate upsetting situations.
Feelings of sadness rise to the surface when someone you care about is suffering from a substance use disorder.
It can be confusing and frustrating when you are on the outside looking in. You probably want to help them, and even if you know how, they may not want you to.
One of the toughest things about addiction is that it's not necessarily possible to convince someone that they have a problem if they aren't willing to admit this on their own.

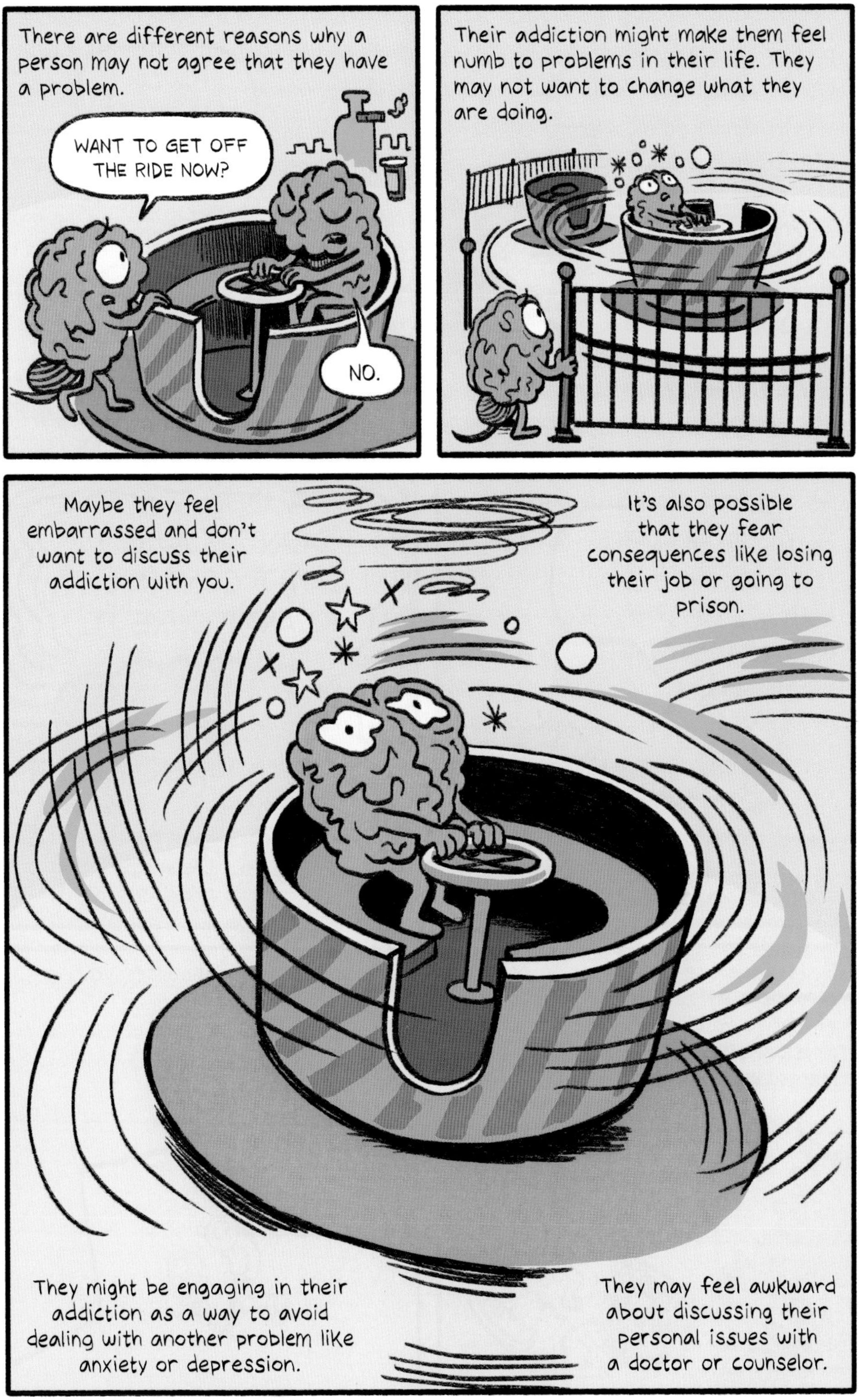
There are different reasons why a person may not agree that they have a problem.
WANT TO GET OFF THE RIDE NOW?
NO.
Their addiction might make them feel numb to problems in their life. They may not want to change what they are doing.
Maybe they feel embarrassed and don't want to discuss their addiction with you.
It's also possible that they fear consequences like losing their job or going to prison.
They might be engaging in their addiction as a way to avoid dealing with another problem like anxiety or depression.
They may feel awkward about discussing their personal issues with a doctor or counselor.

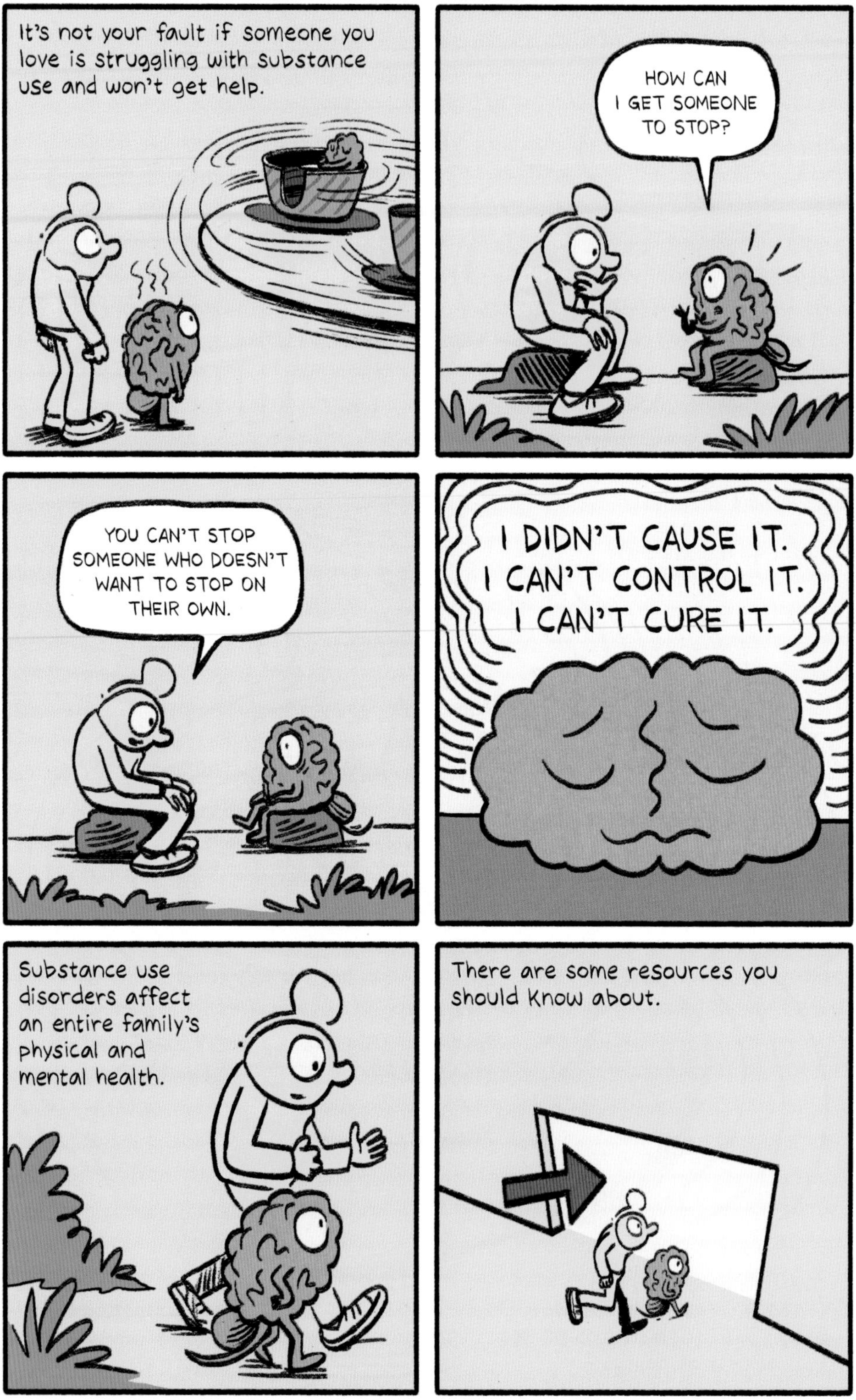
It's not your fault if someone you love is struggling with substance use and won't get help.
HOW CAN I GET SOMEONE TO STOP?
YOU CAN'T STOP SOMEONE WHO DOESN'T WANT TO STOP ON THEIR OWN.
I DIDN'T CAUSE IT. I CAN'T CONTROL IT. I CAN'T CURE IT.
Substance use disorders affect an entire family's physical and mental health.
There are some resources you should know about.

SUPPORT GROUPS FOR FAMILIES AND FRIENDS

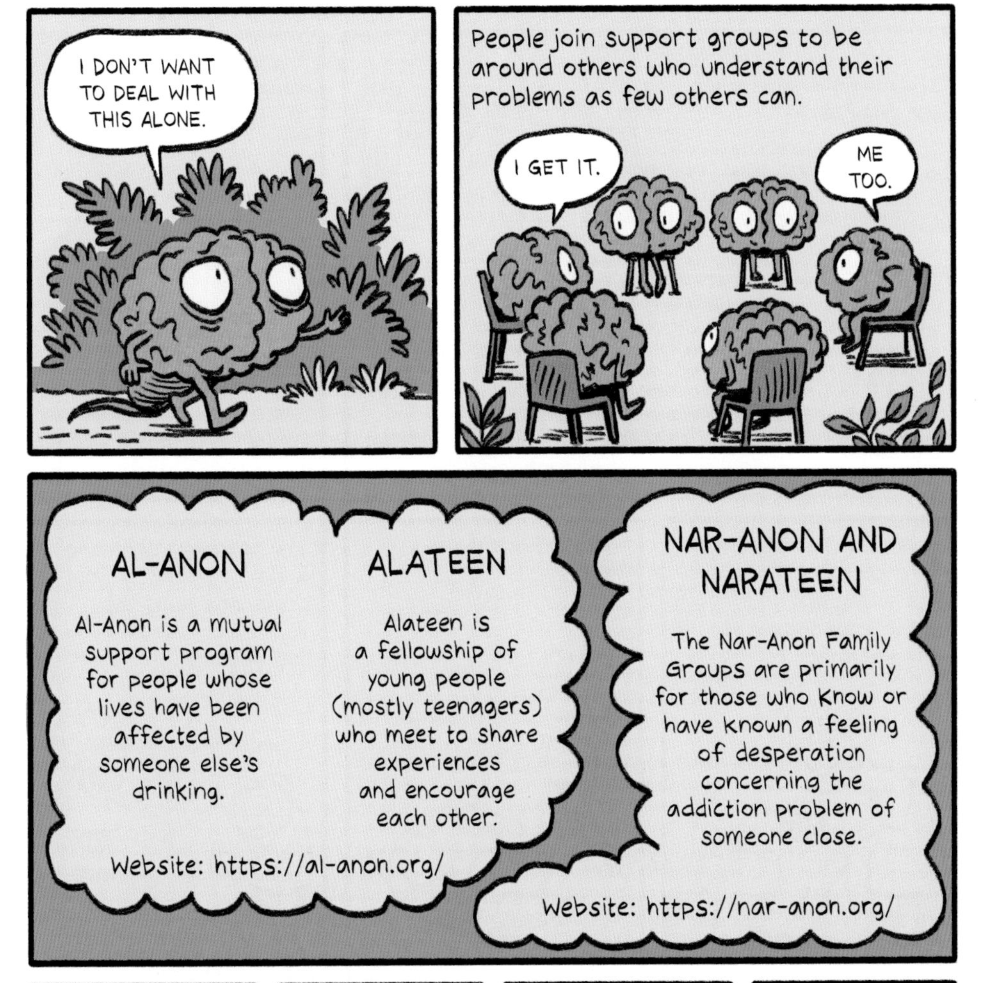
I DON'T WANT TO DEAL WITH THIS ALONE.
People join support groups to be around others who understand their problems as few others can.
I GET IT.
ME TOO.

AL-ANON

Al-Anon is a mutual support program for people whose lives have been affected by someone else's drinking.

ALATEEN

Alateen is a fellowship of young people (mostly teenagers) who meet to share experiences and encourage each other.

Website: https://al-anon.org/

NAR-ANON AND NARATEEN

The Nar-Anon Family Groups are primarily for those who know or have known a feeling of desperation concerning the addiction problem of someone close.

Website: https://nar-anon.org/

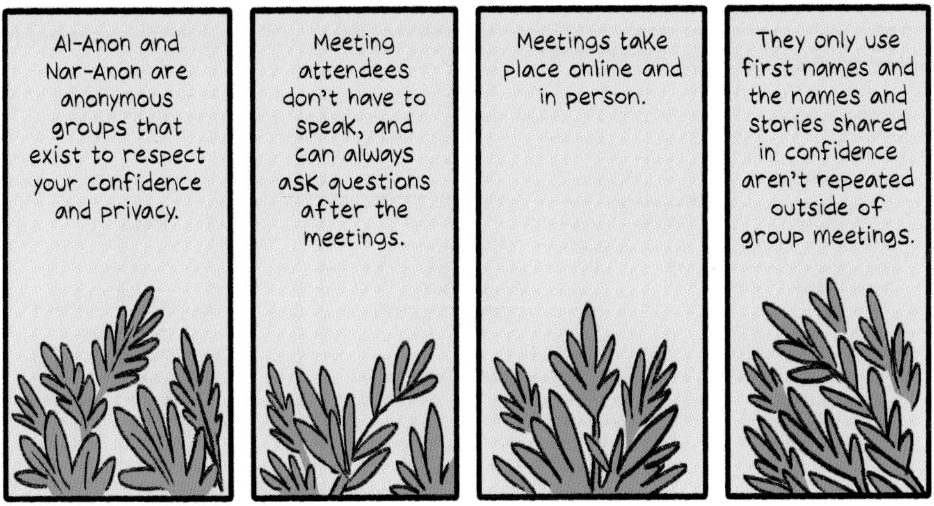
Al-Anon and Nar-Anon are anonymous groups that exist to respect your confidence and privacy.
Meeting attendees don't have to speak, and can always ask questions after the meetings.
Meetings take place online and in person.
They only use first names and the names and stories shared in confidence aren't repeated outside of group meetings.

ARE THERE WAYS TO PREVENT A SUBSTANCE USE DISORDER?

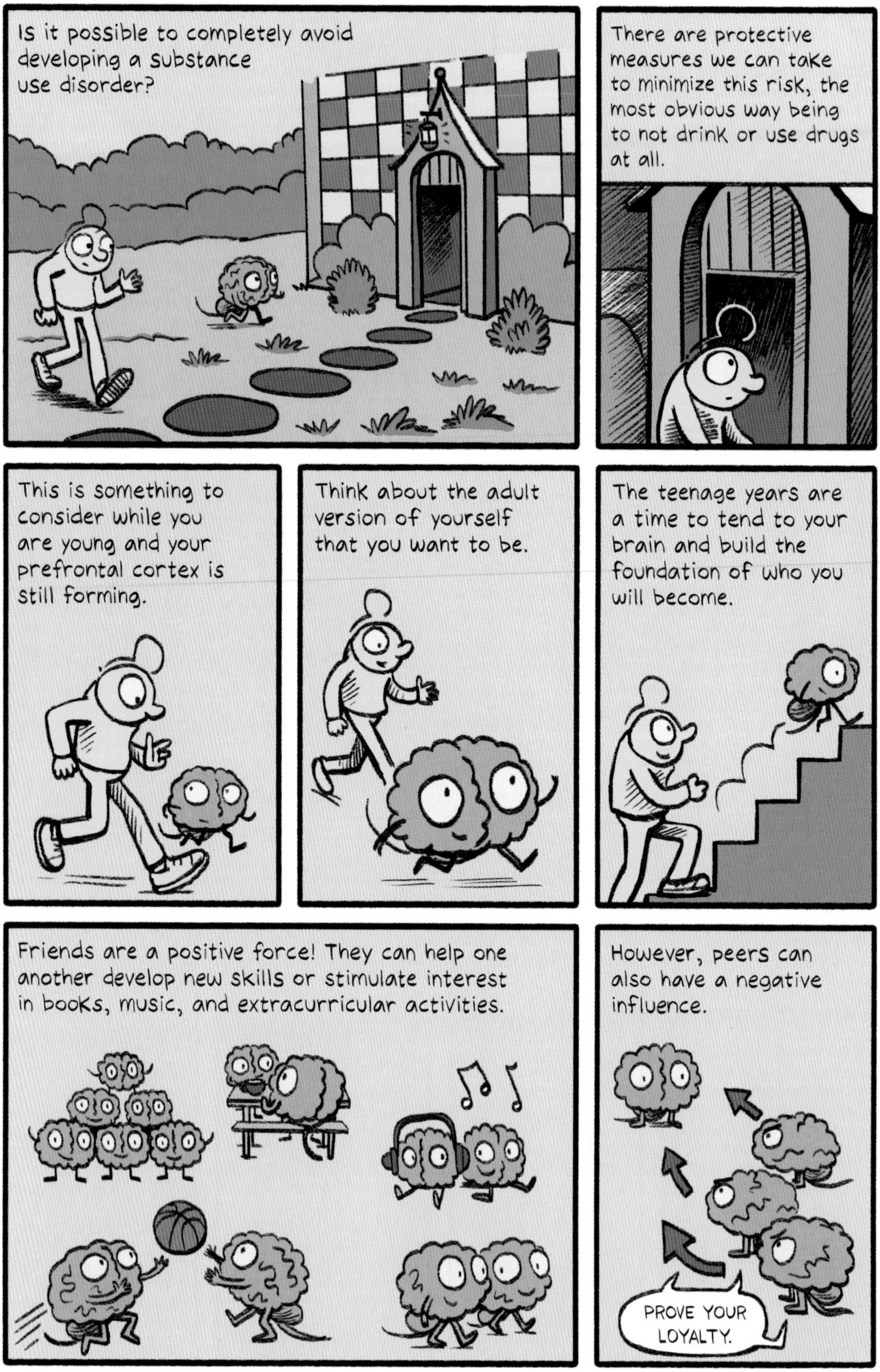
Is it possible to completely avoid developing a substance use disorder?
There are protective measures we can take to minimize this risk, the most obvious way being to not drink or use drugs at all.
This is something to consider while you are young and your prefrontal cortex is still forming.
Think about the adult version of yourself that you want to be.
The teenage years are a time to tend to your brain and build the foundation of who you will become.
Friends are a positive force! They can help one another develop new skills or stimulate interest in books, music, and extracurricular activities.
However, peers can also have a negative influence.
PROVE YOUR LOYALTY.

PEER PRESSURE IMPACTS YOUNGER BRAINS

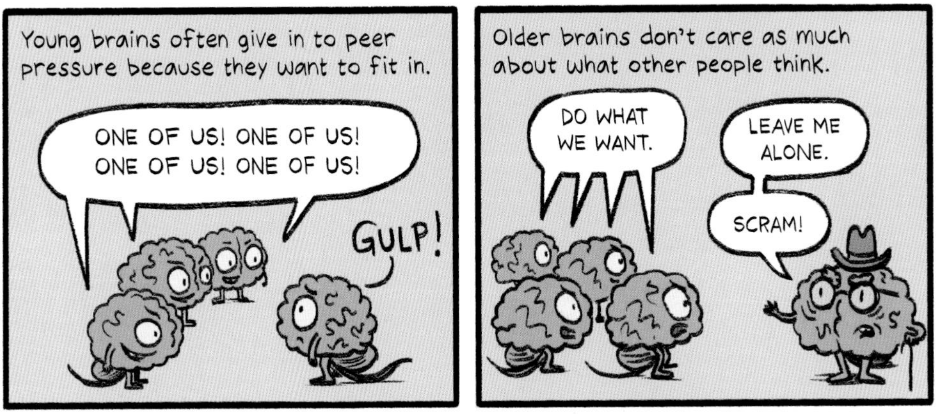
Young brains often give in to peer pressure because they want to fit in.
ONE OF US! ONE OF US! ONE OF US! ONE OF US!
GULP!
Older brains don't care as much about what other people think.
DO WHAT WE WANT.
LEAVE ME ALONE.
SCRAM!

The majority of teens with substance use problems began using drugs or alcohol as a result of peer pressure. It's natural to want to be liked and to worry about being left out or being made fun of.

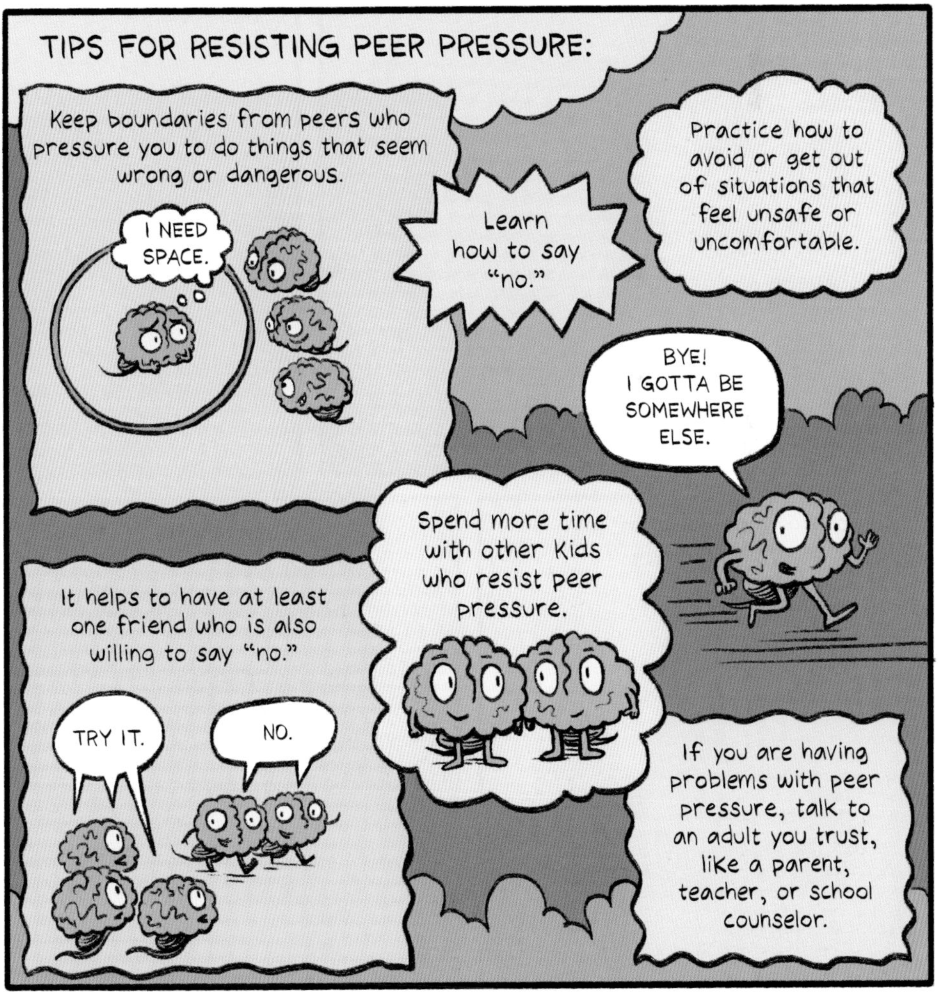
TIPS FOR RESISTING PEER PRESSURE:
Keep boundaries from peers who pressure you to do things that seem wrong or dangerous.
I NEED SPACE.
Learn how to say "no."
Practice how to avoid or get out of situations that feel unsafe or uncomfortable.
BYE! I GOTTA BE SOMEWHERE ELSE.
It helps to have at least one friend who is also willing to say "no."
TRY IT.
NO.
Spend more time with other kids who resist peer pressure.
If you are having problems with peer pressure, talk to an adult you trust, like a parent, teacher, or school counselor.

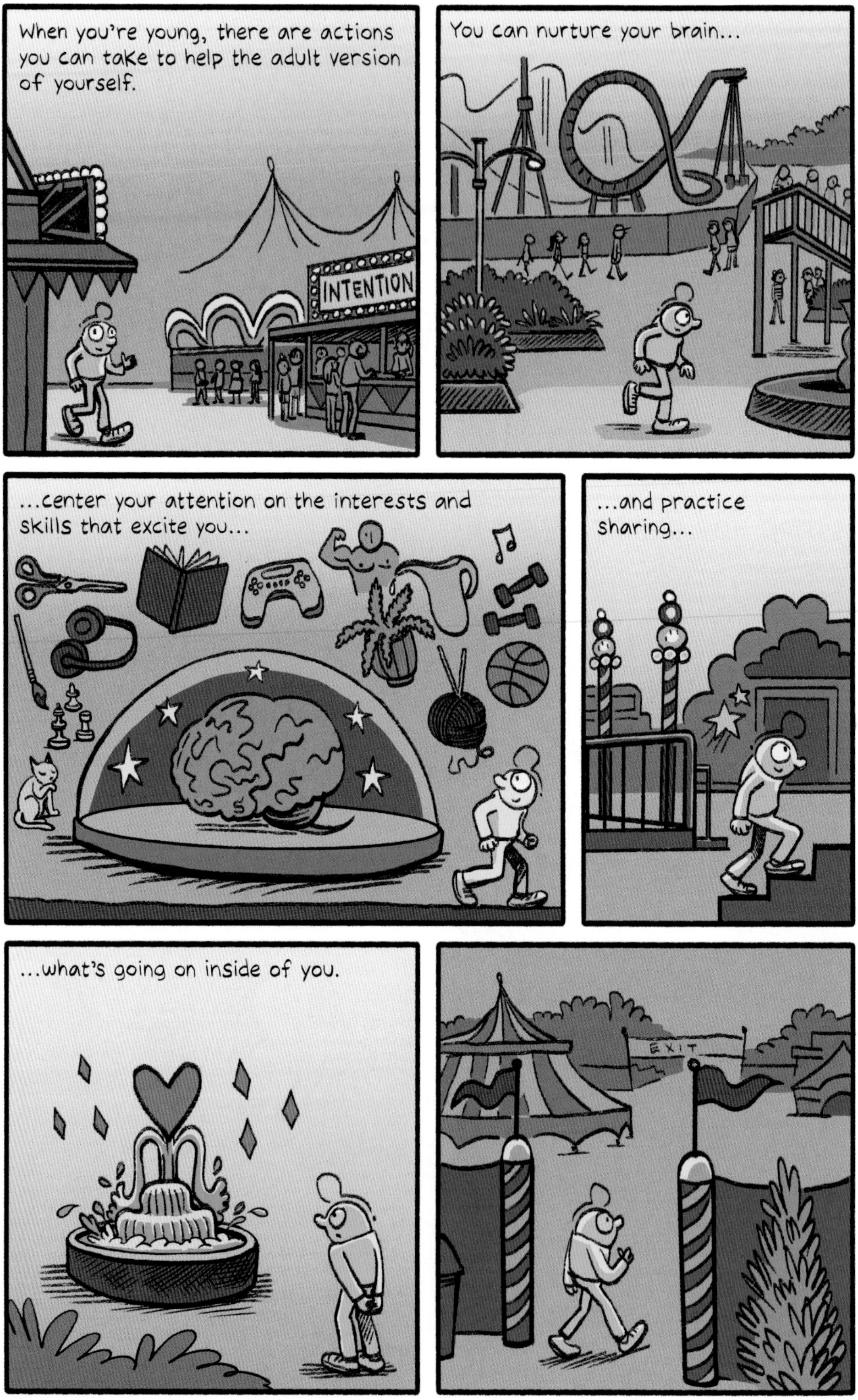
When you're young, there are actions you can take to help the adult version of yourself.
INTENTION
You can nurture your brain...
...center your attention on the interests and skills that excite you...
...and practice sharing...
...what's going on inside of you.
EXIT

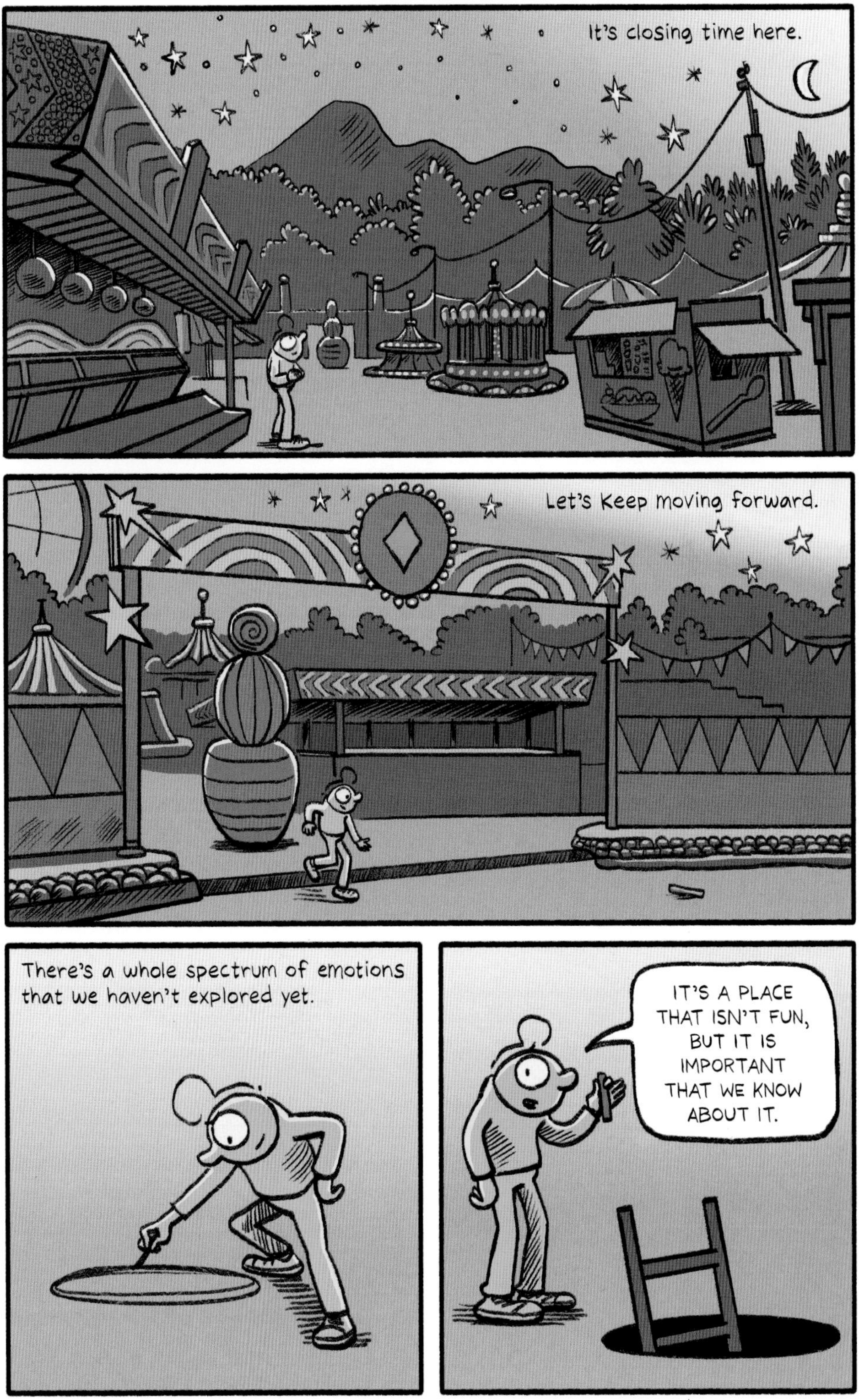
It's closing time here.
Let's keep moving forward.
There's a whole spectrum of emotions that we haven't explored yet.
IT'S A PLACE THAT ISN'T FUN, BUT IT IS IMPORTANT THAT WE KNOW ABOUT IT.

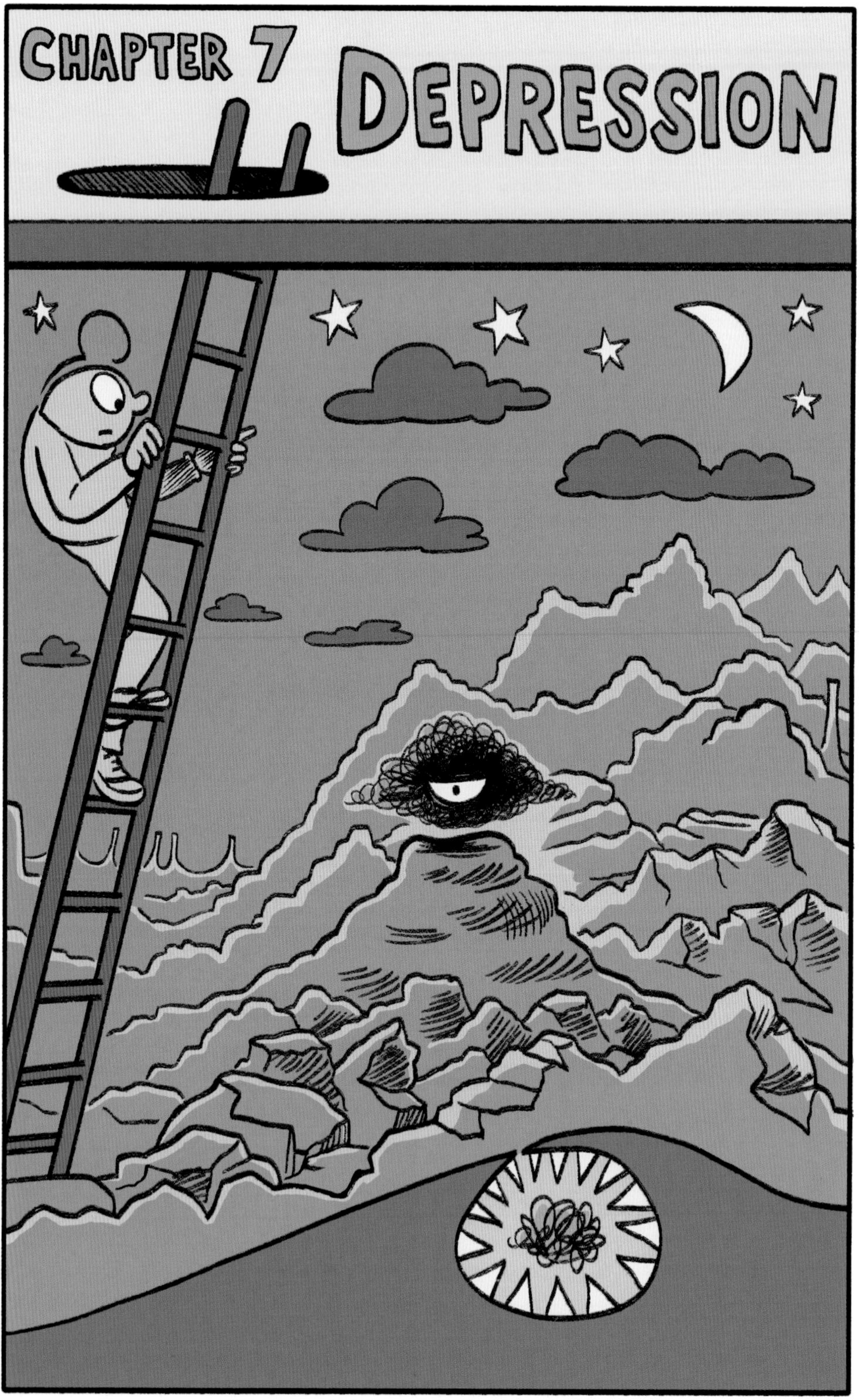
CHAPTER 7
DEPRESSION

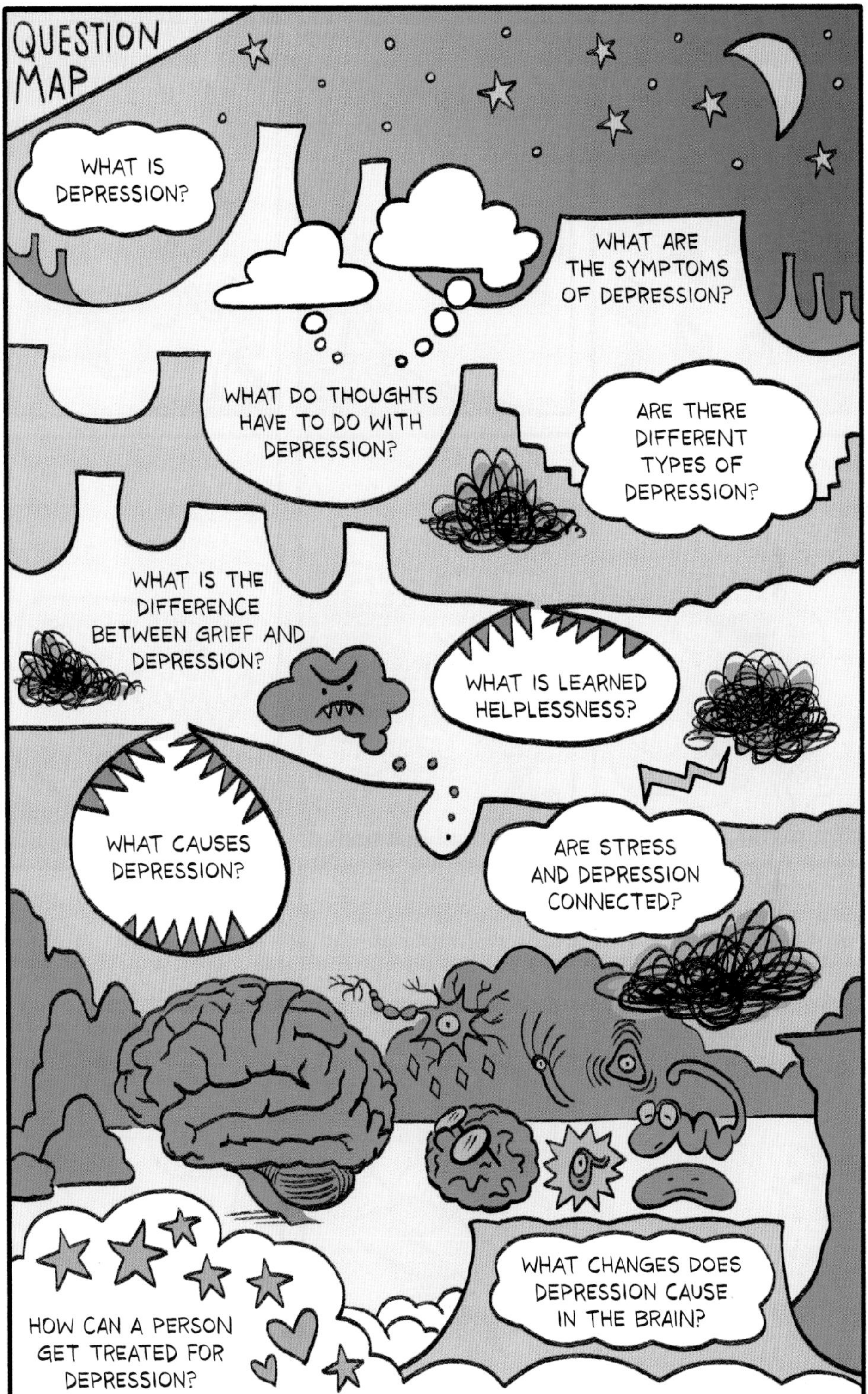
QUESTION MAP
WHAT IS DEPRESSION?
WHAT ARE THE SYMPTOMS OF DEPRESSION?
WHAT DO THOUGHTS HAVE TO DO WITH DEPRESSION?
ARE THERE DIFFERENT TYPES OF DEPRESSION?
WHAT IS THE DIFFERENCE BETWEEN GRIEF AND DEPRESSION?
WHAT IS LEARNED HELPLESSNESS?
WHAT CAUSES DEPRESSION?
ARE STRESS AND DEPRESSION CONNECTED?
HOW CAN A PERSON GET TREATED FOR DEPRESSION?
WHAT CHANGES DOES DEPRESSION CAUSE IN THE BRAIN?

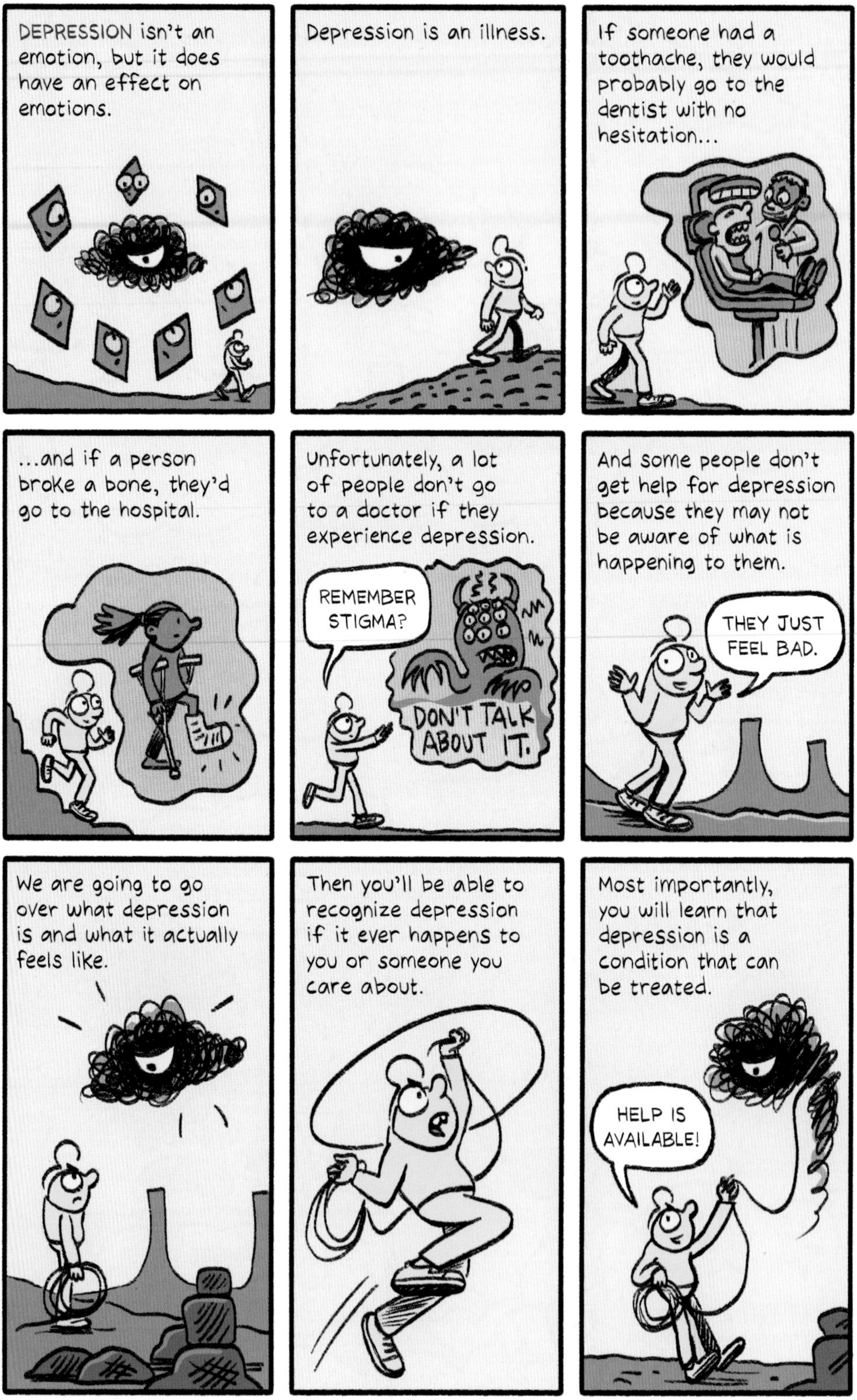
DEPRESSION isn't an emotion, but it does have an effect on emotions.
Depression is an illness.
If someone had a toothache, they would probably go to the dentist with no hesitation...
...and if a person broke a bone, they'd go to the hospital.
Unfortunately, a lot of people don't go to a doctor if they experience depression.
REMEMBER STIGMA?
DON'T TALK ABOUT IT.
And some people don't get help for depression because they may not be aware of what is happening to them.
THEY JUST FEEL BAD.
We are going to go over what depression is and what it actually feels like.
Then you'll be able to recognize depression if it ever happens to you or someone you care about.
Most importantly, you will learn that depression is a condition that can be treated.
HELP IS AVAILABLE!

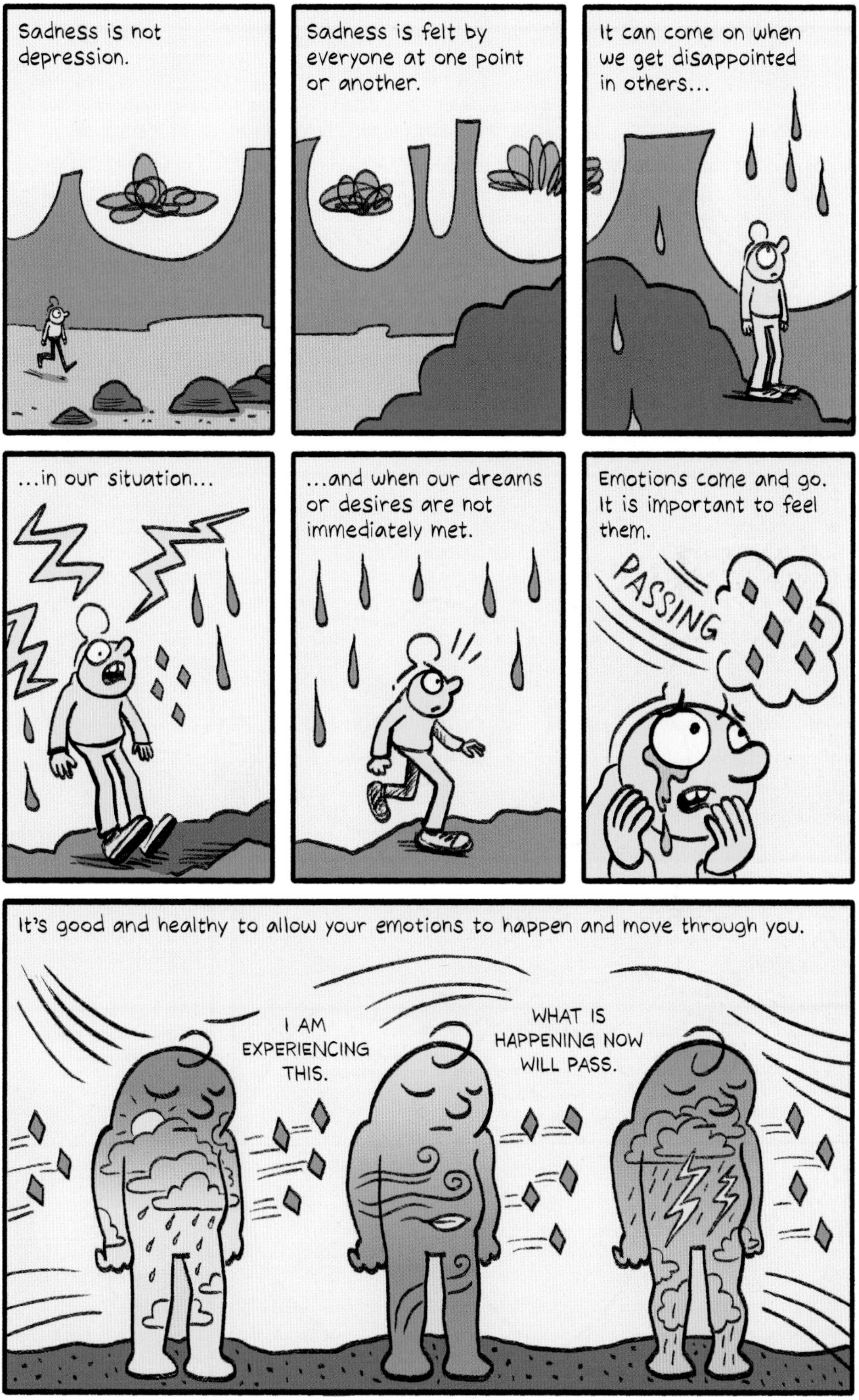
Sadness is not depression.
Sadness is felt by everyone at one point or another.
It can come on when we get disappointed in others...
...in our situation...
...and when our dreams or desires are not immediately met.
Emotions come and go. It is important to feel them.
PASSING
It's good and healthy to allow your emotions to happen and move through you.
I AM EXPERIENCING THIS.
WHAT IS HAPPENING NOW WILL PASS.

A WORD ABOUT GRIEF

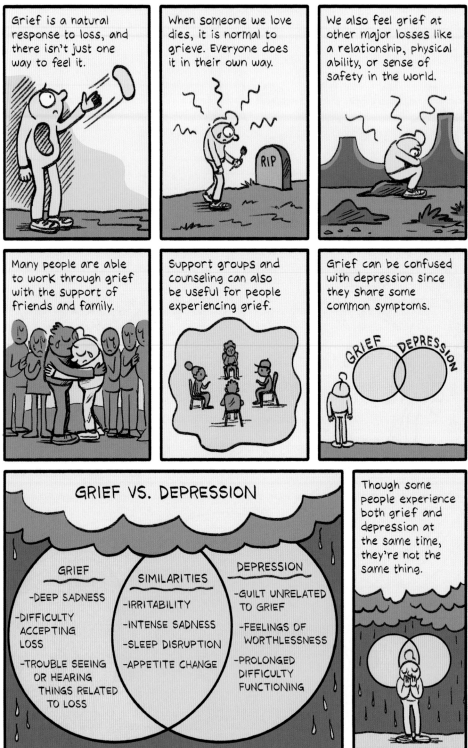

Grief is a natural response to loss, and there isn't just one way to feel it.

When someone we love dies, it is normal to grieve. Everyone does it in their own way.

We also feel grief at other major losses like a relationship, physical ability, or sense of safety in the world.

Many people are able to work through grief with the support of friends and family.

Support groups and counseling can also be useful for people experiencing grief.

Grief can be confused with depression since they share some common symptoms.

GRIEF DEPRESSION

GRIEF VS. DEPRESSION

GRIEF
- DEEP SADNESS
- DIFFICULTY ACCEPTING LOSS
- TROUBLE SEEING OR HEARING THINGS RELATED TO LOSS

SIMILARITIES
- IRRITABILITY
- INTENSE SADNESS
- SLEEP DISRUPTION
- APPETITE CHANGE

DEPRESSION
- GUILT UNRELATED TO GRIEF
- FEELINGS OF WORTHLESSNESS
- PROLONGED DIFFICULTY FUNCTIONING

Though some people experience both grief and depression at the same time, they're not the same thing.

WHAT IS DEPRESSION?

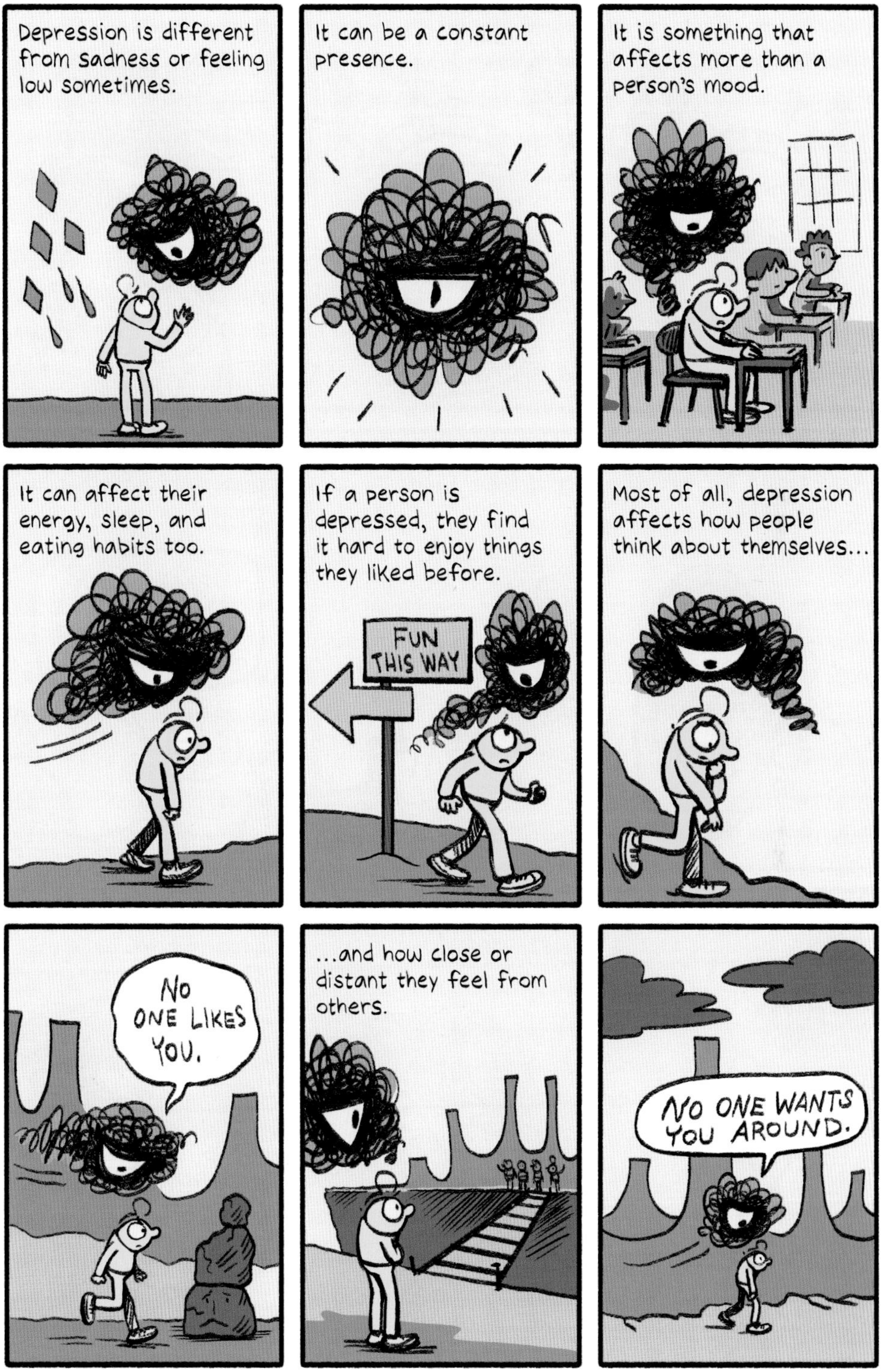
Depression is different from sadness or feeling low sometimes.
It can be a constant presence.
It is something that affects more than a person's mood.
It can affect their energy, sleep, and eating habits too.
If a person is depressed, they find it hard to enjoy things they liked before.
FUN THIS WAY
Most of all, depression affects how people think about themselves...
NO ONE LIKES YOU.
...and how close or distant they feel from others.
NO ONE WANTS YOU AROUND.

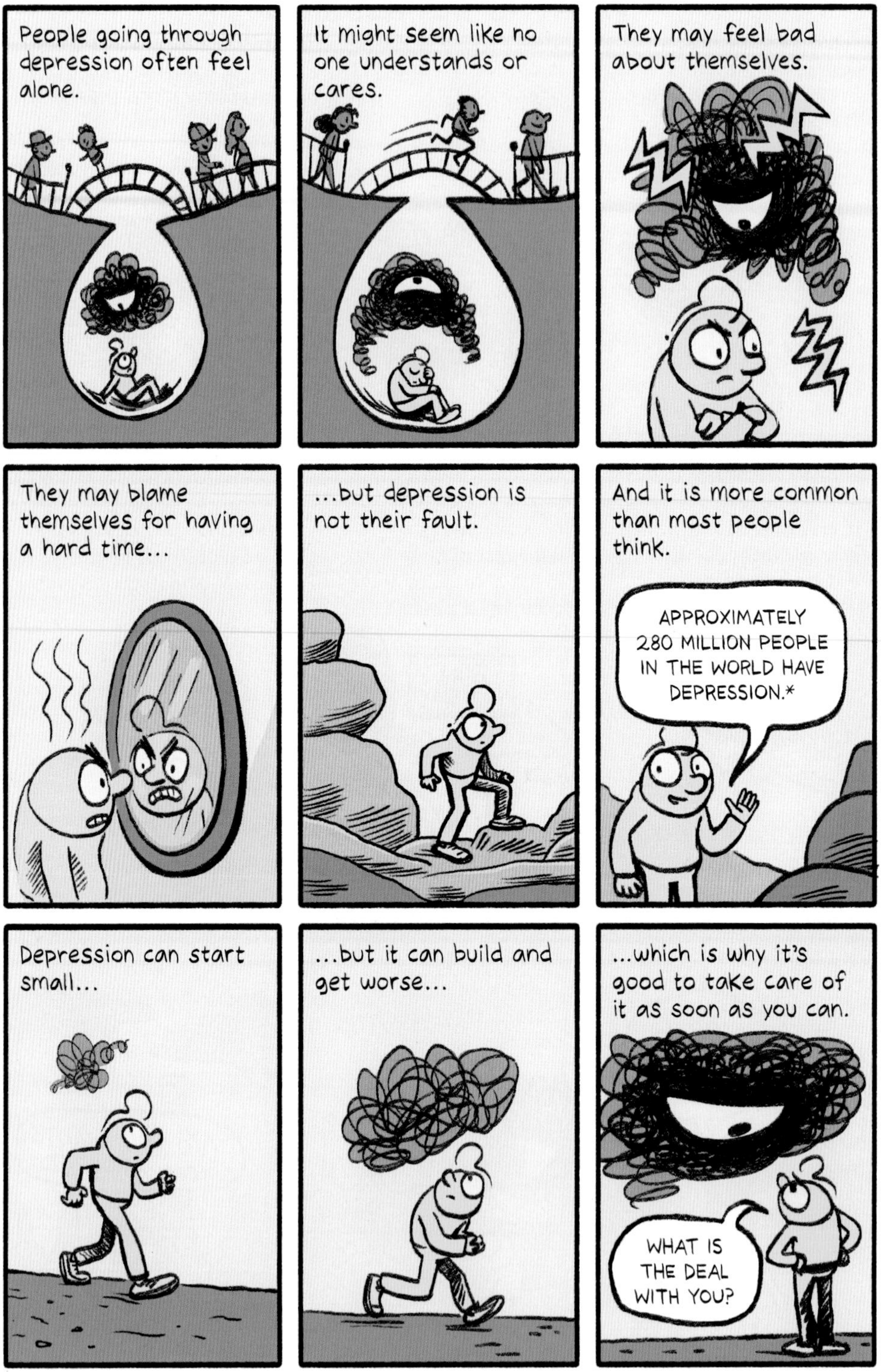
People going through depression often feel alone.
It might seem like no one understands or cares.
They may feel bad about themselves.
They may blame themselves for having a hard time...
...but depression is not their fault.
And it is more common than most people think.
APPROXIMATELY 280 MILLION PEOPLE IN THE WORLD HAVE DEPRESSION.*
Depression can start small...
...but it can build and get worse...
...which is why it's good to take care of it as soon as you can.
WHAT IS THE DEAL WITH YOU?

*According to the Institute of Health Metrics and Evaluation, Global Health Data Exchange (2021).

SYMPTOMS OF DEPRESSION

For a person to get a diagnosis for a MAJOR DEPRESSIVE DISORDER, they need to have had at least four of these symptoms for at least a two-week period:

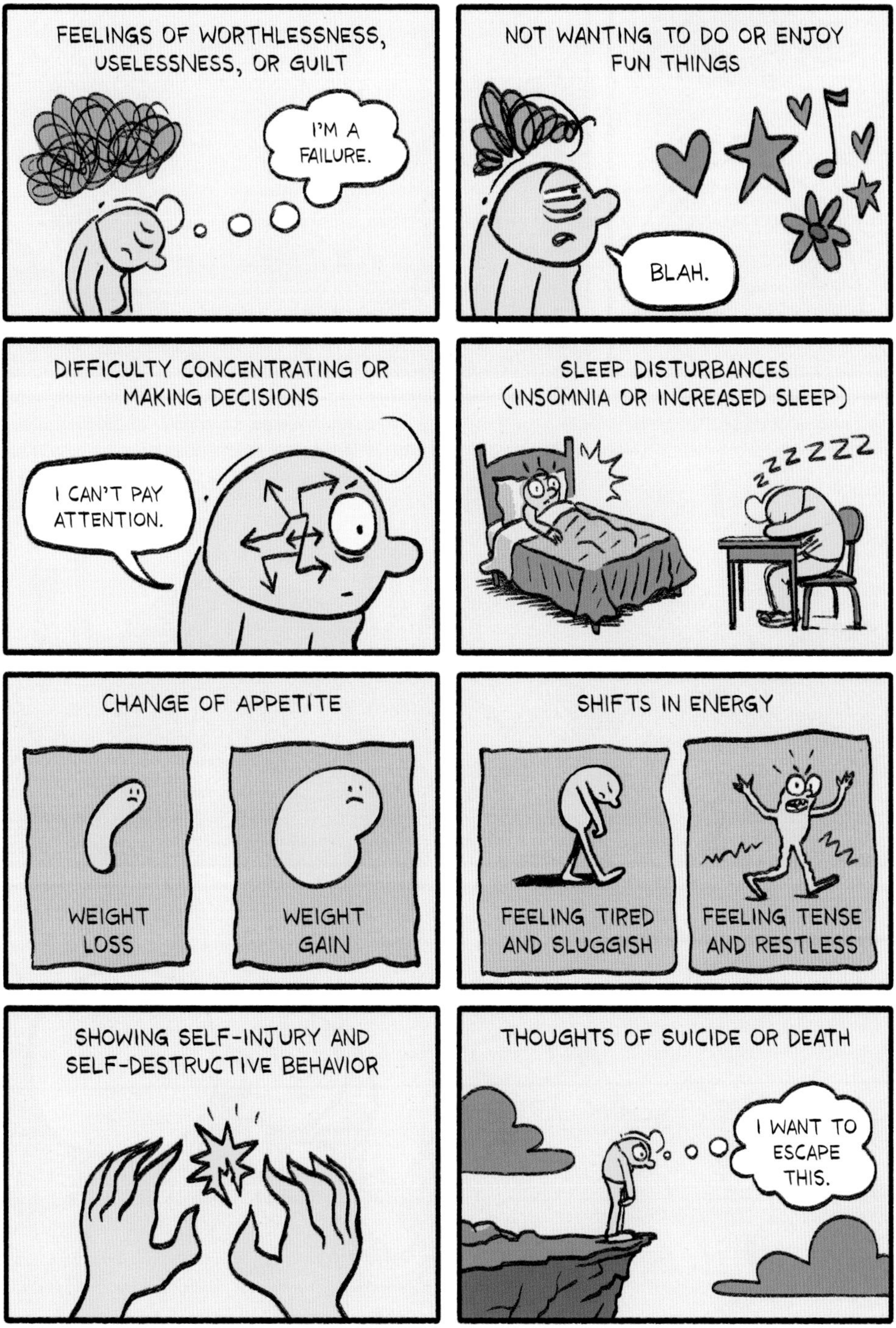
FEELINGS OF WORTHLESSNESS, USELESSNESS, OR GUILT
I'M A FAILURE.
NOT WANTING TO DO OR ENJOY FUN THINGS
BLAH.
DIFFICULTY CONCENTRATING OR MAKING DECISIONS
I CAN'T PAY ATTENTION.
SLEEP DISTURBANCES (INSOMNIA OR INCREASED SLEEP)
ZZZZZZ
CHANGE OF APPETITE
WEIGHT LOSS
WEIGHT GAIN
SHIFTS IN ENERGY
FEELING TIRED AND SLUGGISH
FEELING TENSE AND RESTLESS
SHOWING SELF-INJURY AND SELF-DESTRUCTIVE BEHAVIOR
THOUGHTS OF SUICIDE OR DEATH
I WANT TO ESCAPE THIS.

DEPRESSION INSIDE THE BRAIN

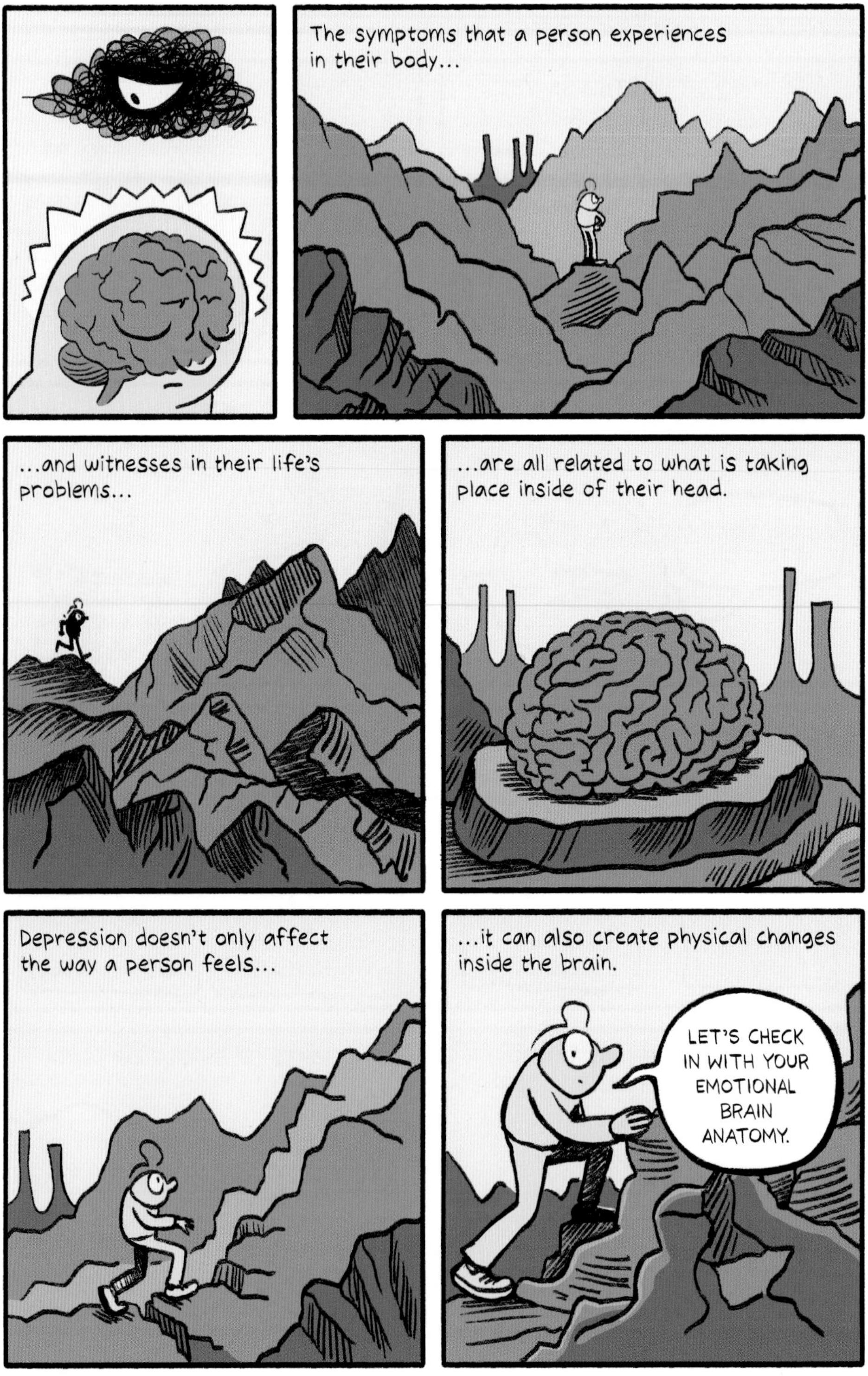
The symptoms that a person experiences in their body...
...and witnesses in their life's problems...
...are all related to what is taking place inside of their head.
Depression doesn't only affect the way a person feels...
...it can also create physical changes inside the brain.
LET'S CHECK IN WITH YOUR EMOTIONAL BRAIN ANATOMY.

HOW BRAIN AREAS EXPERIENCE DEPRESSION

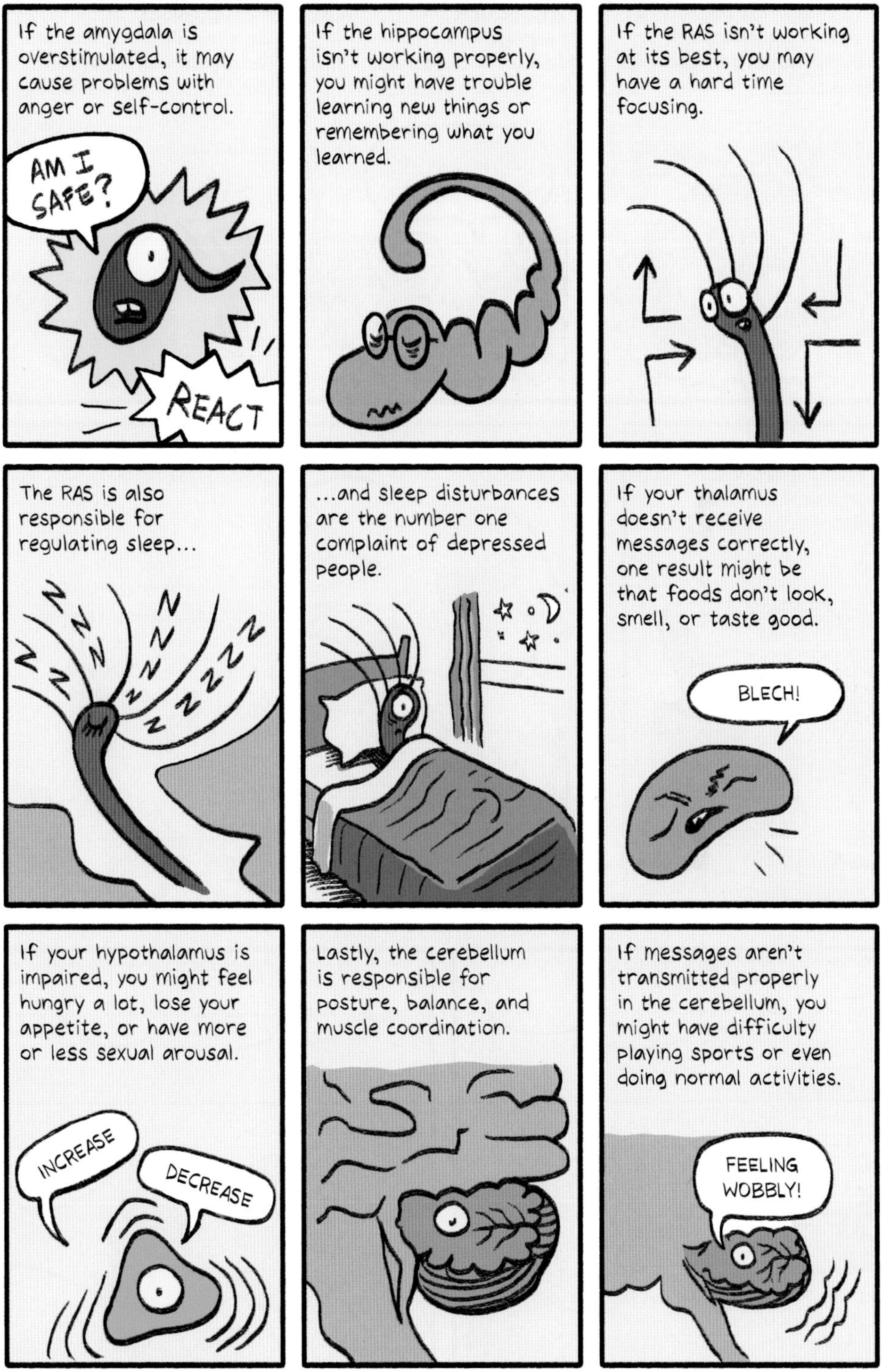
If the amygdala is overstimulated, it may cause problems with anger or self-control.
AM I SAFE?
REACT
If the hippocampus isn't working properly, you might have trouble learning new things or remembering what you learned.
If the RAS isn't working at its best, you may have a hard time focusing.
The RAS is also responsible for regulating sleep...
...and sleep disturbances are the number one complaint of depressed people.
If your thalamus doesn't receive messages correctly, one result might be that foods don't look, smell, or taste good.
BLECH!
If your hypothalamus is impaired, you might feel hungry a lot, lose your appetite, or have more or less sexual arousal.
INCREASE
DECREASE
Lastly, the cerebellum is responsible for posture, balance, and muscle coordination.
If messages aren't transmitted properly in the cerebellum, you might have difficulty playing sports or even doing normal activities.
FEELING WOBBLY!

A MICROSCOPIC VIEW OF DEPRESSION

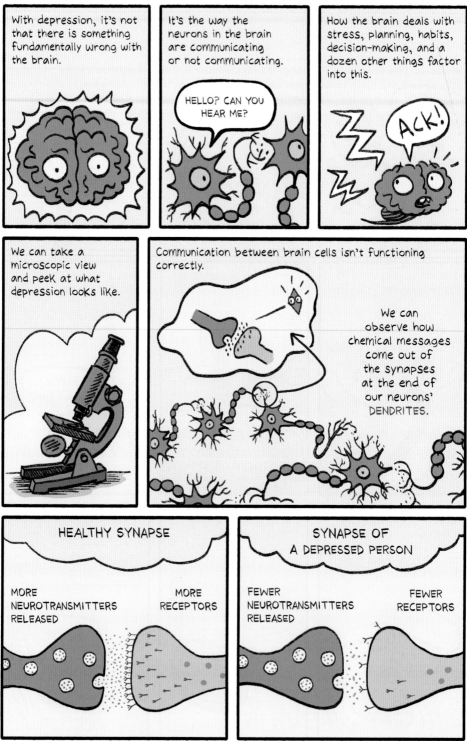

With depression, it's not that there is something fundamentally wrong with the brain.

It's the way the neurons in the brain are communicating or not communicating.

HELLO? CAN YOU HEAR ME?

How the brain deals with stress, planning, habits, decision-making, and a dozen other things factor into this.

ACK!

We can take a microscopic view and peek at what depression looks like.

Communication between brain cells isn't functioning correctly.

We can observe how chemical messages come out of the synapses at the end of our neurons' DENDRITES.

HEALTHY SYNAPSE

MORE NEUROTRANSMITTERS RELEASED

MORE RECEPTORS

SYNAPSE OF A DEPRESSED PERSON

FEWER NEUROTRANSMITTERS RELEASED

FEWER RECEPTORS

Looking inside the brain is interesting, but it doesn't paint a complete picture of what depression feels like to the many people who experience it.

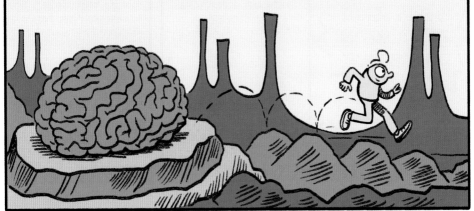

With depression, people don't feel like the healthy version of themselves anymore.

It's Kind of an invisible thing going on inside, and that's why it's useful to invent symbols for the feeling.

So what does this experience of depression feel like?

What can it be compared to?

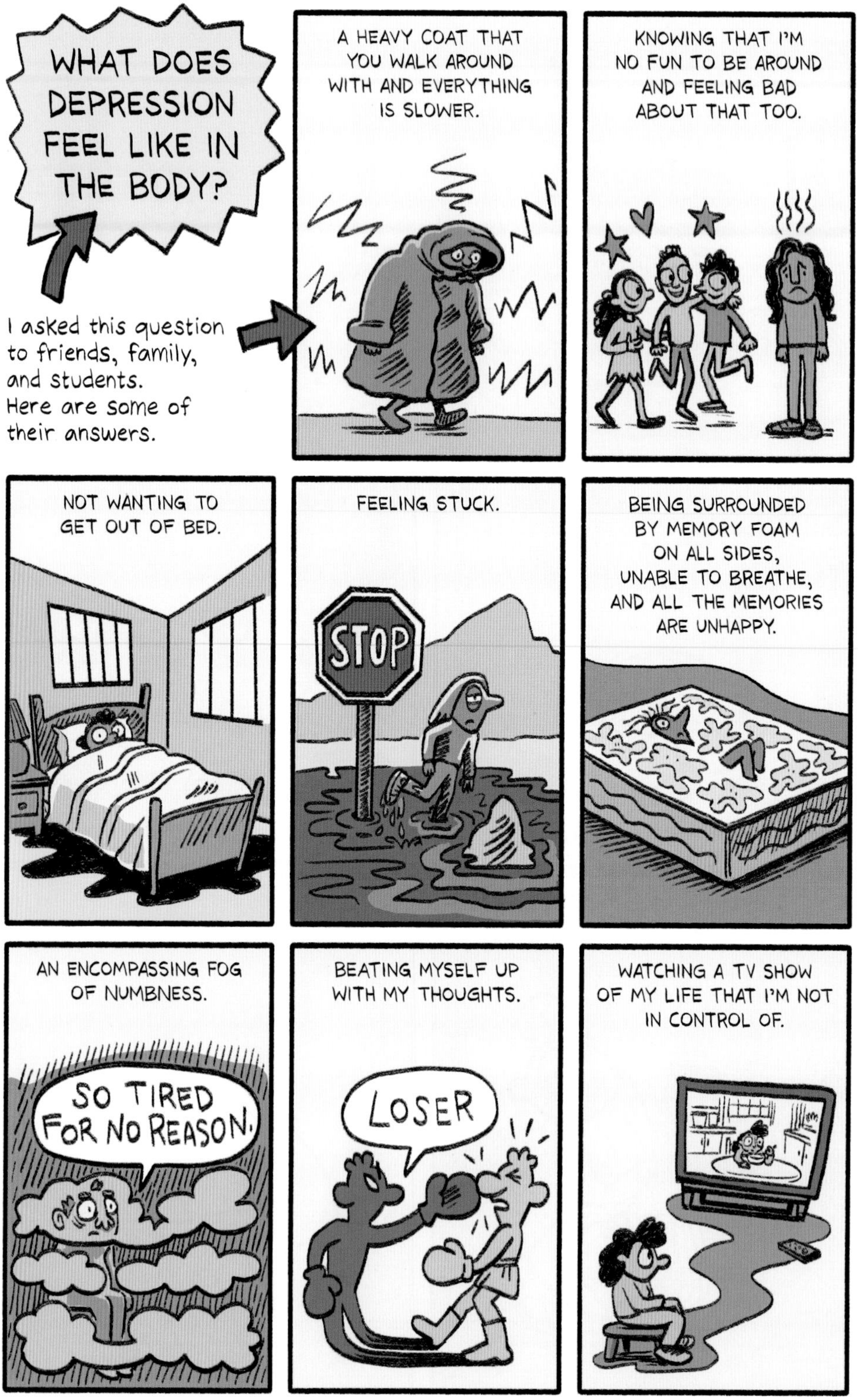
WHAT DOES DEPRESSION FEEL LIKE IN THE BODY?
I asked this question to friends, family, and students. Here are some of their answers.
A HEAVY COAT THAT YOU WALK AROUND WITH AND EVERYTHING IS SLOWER.
KNOWING THAT I'M NO FUN TO BE AROUND AND FEELING BAD ABOUT THAT TOO.
NOT WANTING TO GET OUT OF BED.
FEELING STUCK.
STOP
BEING SURROUNDED BY MEMORY FOAM ON ALL SIDES, UNABLE TO BREATHE, AND ALL THE MEMORIES ARE UNHAPPY.
AN ENCOMPASSING FOG OF NUMBNESS.
SO TIRED FOR NO REASON.
BEATING MYSELF UP WITH MY THOUGHTS.
LOSER
WATCHING A TV SHOW OF MY LIFE THAT I'M NOT IN CONTROL OF.

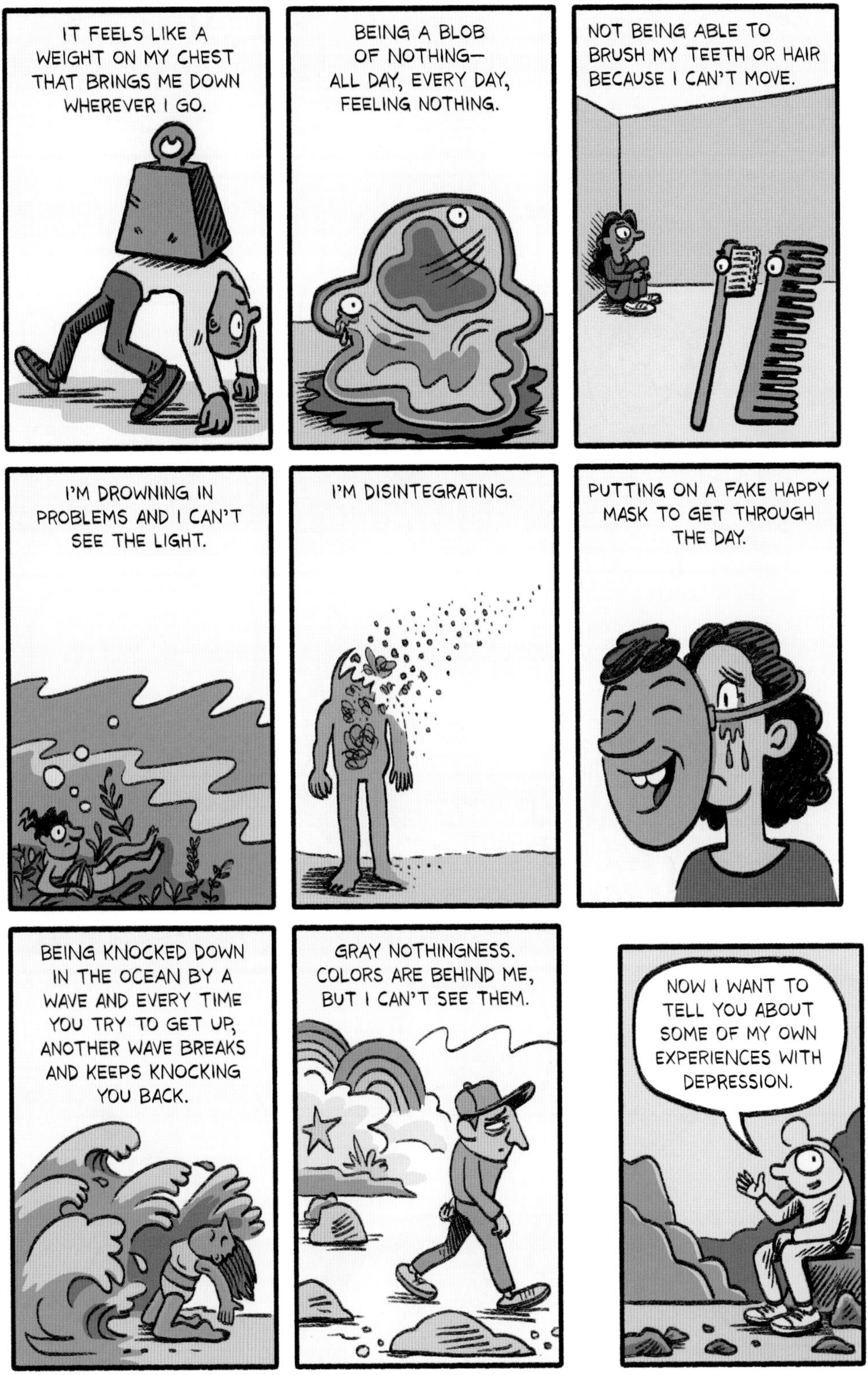
IT FEELS LIKE A WEIGHT ON MY CHEST THAT BRINGS ME DOWN WHEREVER I GO.
BEING A BLOB OF NOTHING— ALL DAY, EVERY DAY, FEELING NOTHING.
NOT BEING ABLE TO BRUSH MY TEETH OR HAIR BECAUSE I CAN'T MOVE.
I'M DROWNING IN PROBLEMS AND I CAN'T SEE THE LIGHT.
I'M DISINTEGRATING.
PUTTING ON A FAKE HAPPY MASK TO GET THROUGH THE DAY.
BEING KNOCKED DOWN IN THE OCEAN BY A WAVE AND EVERY TIME YOU TRY TO GET UP, ANOTHER WAVE BREAKS AND KEEPS KNOCKING YOU BACK.
GRAY NOTHINGNESS. COLORS ARE BEHIND ME, BUT I CAN'T SEE THEM.
NOW I WANT TO TELL YOU ABOUT SOME OF MY OWN EXPERIENCES WITH DEPRESSION.

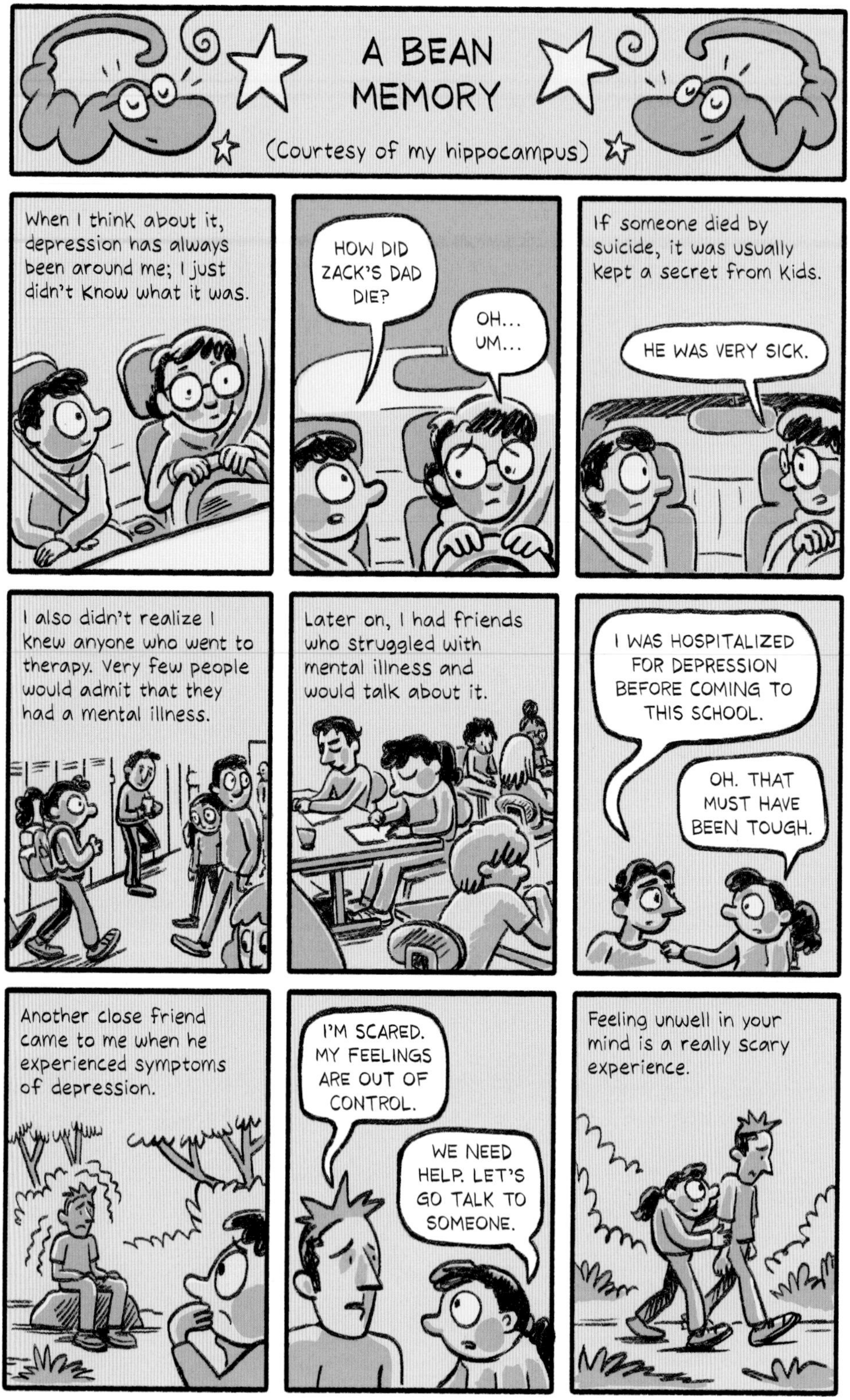
A BEAN MEMORY
(Courtesy of my hippocampus)
When I think about it, depression has always been around me; I just didn't know what it was.
HOW DID ZACK'S DAD DIE?
OH... UM...
If someone died by suicide, it was usually kept a secret from kids.
HE WAS VERY SICK.
I also didn't realize I knew anyone who went to therapy. Very few people would admit that they had a mental illness.
Later on, I had friends who struggled with mental illness and would talk about it.
I WAS HOSPITALIZED FOR DEPRESSION BEFORE COMING TO THIS SCHOOL.
OH. THAT MUST HAVE BEEN TOUGH.
Another close friend came to me when he experienced symptoms of depression.
I'M SCARED. MY FEELINGS ARE OUT OF CONTROL.
WE NEED HELP. LET'S GO TALK TO SOMEONE.
Feeling unwell in your mind is a really scary experience.

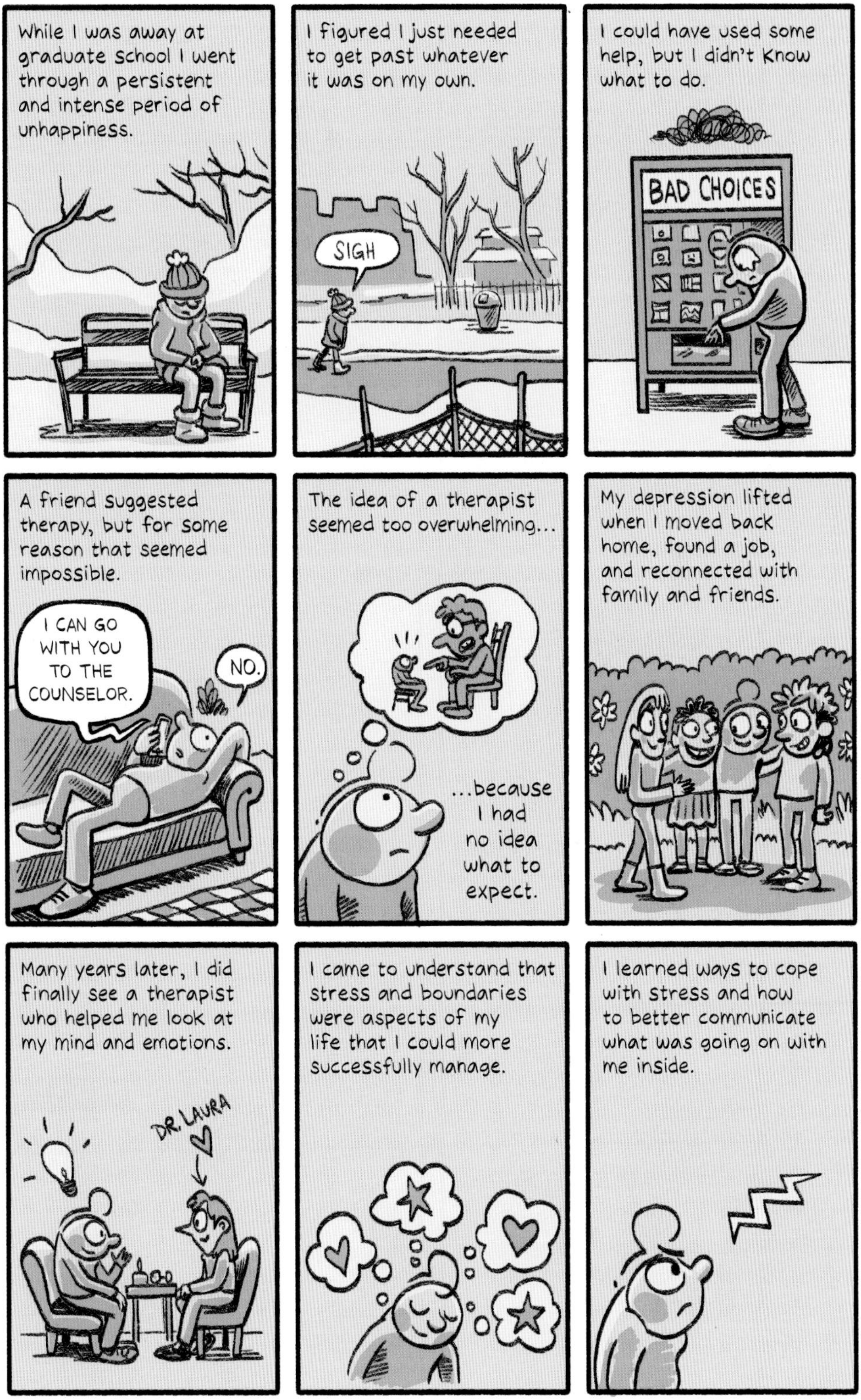
While I was away at graduate school I went through a persistent and intense period of unhappiness.
I figured I just needed to get past whatever it was on my own.
SIGH
I could have used some help, but I didn't know what to do.
BAD CHOICES
A friend suggested therapy, but for some reason that seemed impossible.
I CAN GO WITH YOU TO THE COUNSELOR.
NO.
The idea of a therapist seemed too overwhelming...
...because I had no idea what to expect.
My depression lifted when I moved back home, found a job, and reconnected with family and friends.
Many years later, I did finally see a therapist who helped me look at my mind and emotions.
DR. LAURA
I came to understand that stress and boundaries were aspects of my life that I could more successfully manage.
I learned ways to cope with stress and how to better communicate what was going on with me inside.

DEPRESSION CAN BE DIFFERENT

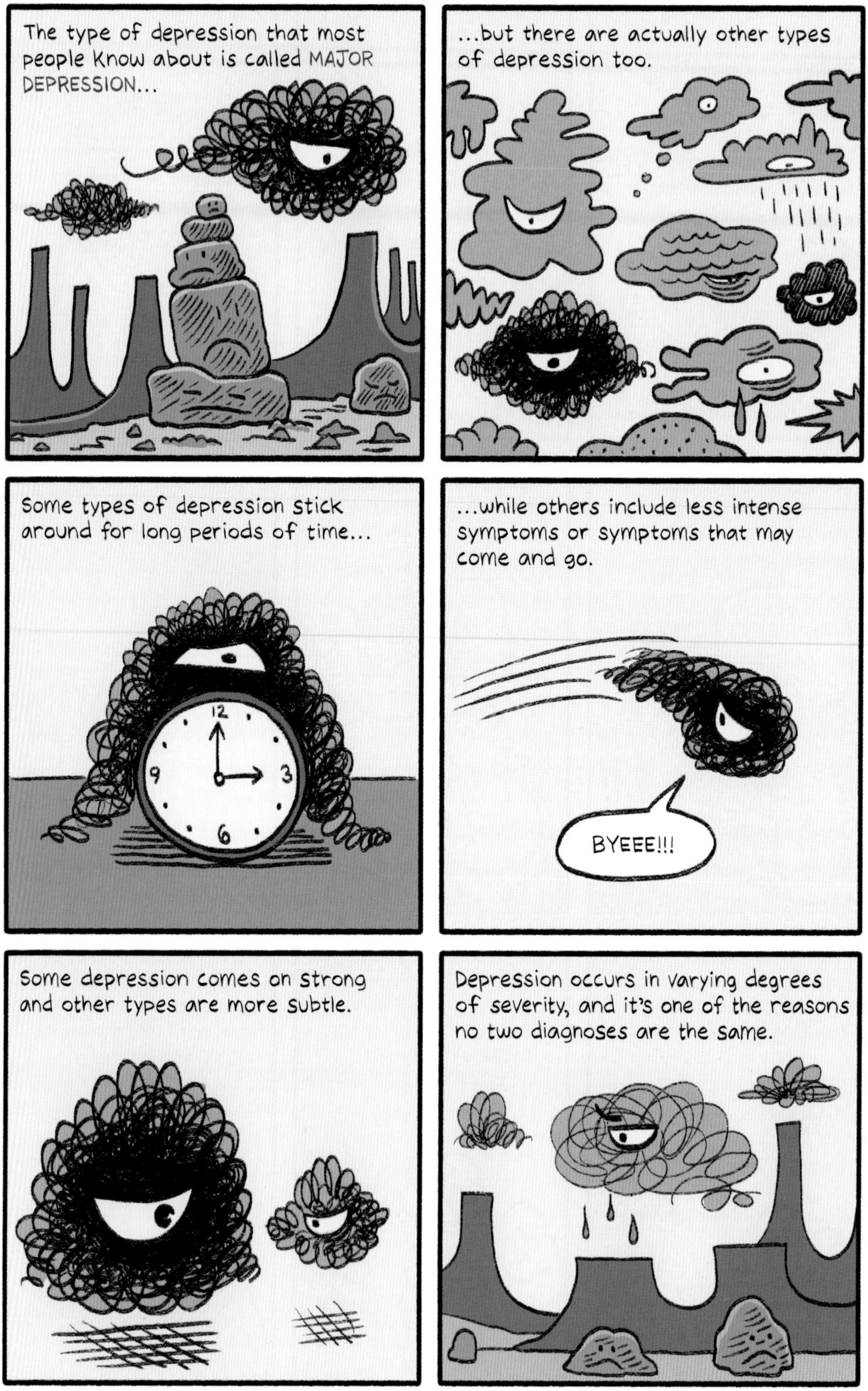
The type of depression that most people know about is called MAJOR DEPRESSION...
...but there are actually other types of depression too.
Some types of depression stick around for long periods of time...
12
3
6
9
...while others include less intense symptoms or symptoms that may come and go.
BYEEE!!!
Some depression comes on strong and other types are more subtle.
Depression occurs in varying degrees of severity, and it's one of the reasons no two diagnoses are the same.

DEPRESSION TYPES

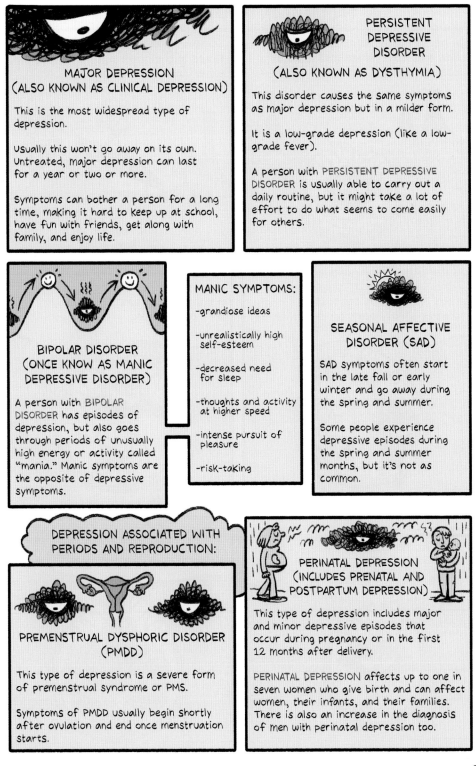

MAJOR DEPRESSION
(ALSO KNOWN AS CLINICAL DEPRESSION)

This is the most widespread type of depression.

Usually this won't go away on its own. Untreated, major depression can last for a year or two or more.

Symptoms can bother a person for a long time, making it hard to keep up at school, have fun with friends, get along with family, and enjoy life.

PERSISTENT DEPRESSIVE DISORDER
(ALSO KNOWN AS DYSTHYMIA)

This disorder causes the same symptoms as major depression but in a milder form.

It is a low-grade depression (like a low-grade fever).

A person with PERSISTENT DEPRESSIVE DISORDER is usually able to carry out a daily routine, but it might take a lot of effort to do what seems to come easily for others.

BIPOLAR DISORDER
(ONCE KNOW AS MANIC DEPRESSIVE DISORDER)

A person with BIPOLAR DISORDER has episodes of depression, but also goes through periods of unusually high energy or activity called "mania." Manic symptoms are the opposite of depressive symptoms.

MANIC SYMPTOMS:

-grandiose ideas

-unrealistically high self-esteem

-decreased need for sleep

-thoughts and activity at higher speed

-intense pursuit of pleasure

-risk-taking

SEASONAL AFFECTIVE DISORDER (SAD)

SAD symptoms often start in the late fall or early winter and go away during the spring and summer.

Some people experience depressive episodes during the spring and summer months, but it's not as common.

DEPRESSION ASSOCIATED WITH PERIODS AND REPRODUCTION:

PREMENSTRUAL DYSPHORIC DISORDER (PMDD)

This type of depression is a severe form of premenstrual syndrome or PMS.

Symptoms of PMDD usually begin shortly after ovulation and end once menstruation starts.

PERINATAL DEPRESSION (INCLUDES PRENATAL AND POSTPARTUM DEPRESSION)

This type of depression includes major and minor depressive episodes that occur during pregnancy or in the first 12 months after delivery.

PERINATAL DEPRESSION affects up to one in seven women who give birth and can affect women, their infants, and their families. There is also an increase in the diagnosis of men with perinatal depression too.

FALLING INTO DEPRESSION

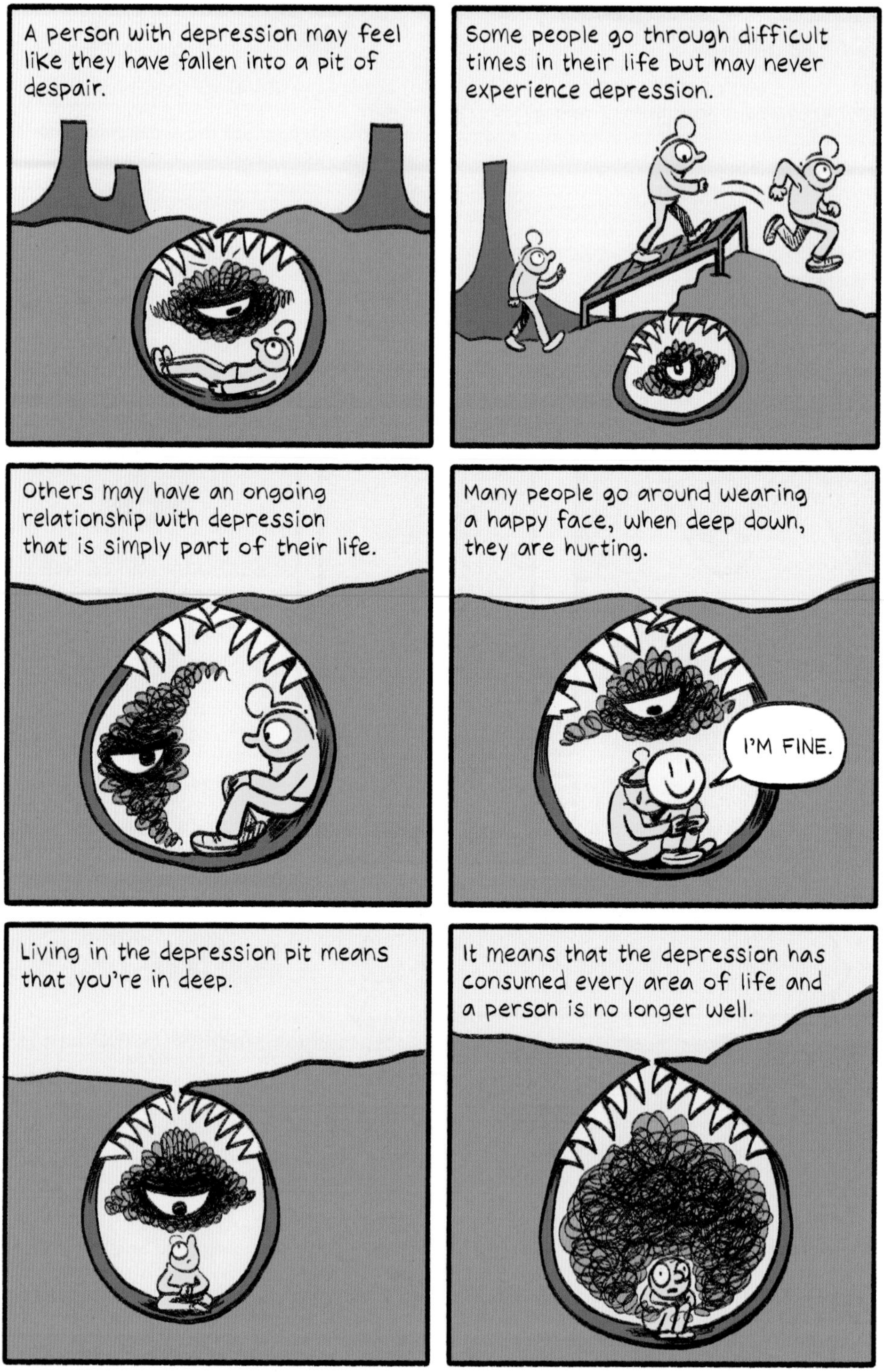
A person with depression may feel like they have fallen into a pit of despair.
Some people go through difficult times in their life but may never experience depression.
Others may have an ongoing relationship with depression that is simply part of their life.
Many people go around wearing a happy face, when deep down, they are hurting.
I'M FINE.
Living in the depression pit means that you're in deep.
It means that the depression has consumed every area of life and a person is no longer well.

WHAT CAUSES DEPRESSION?

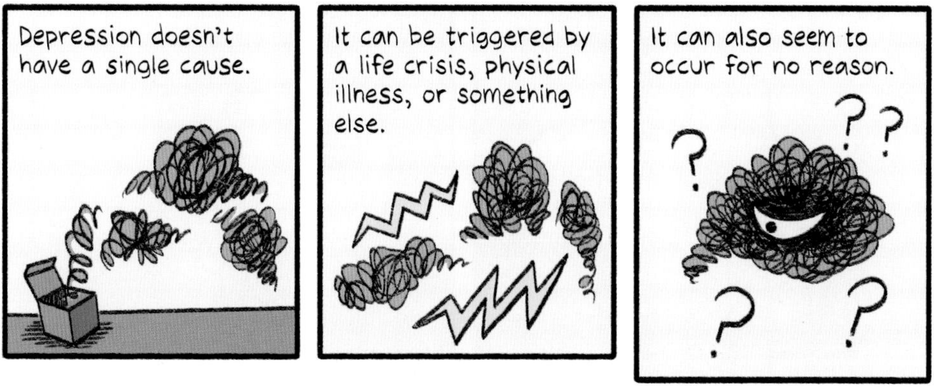
Depression doesn't have a single cause.
It can be triggered by a life crisis, physical illness, or something else.
It can also seem to occur for no reason.

WHAT ARE SOME FACTORS THAT COULD CONTRIBUTE TO DEVELOPING DEPRESSION?

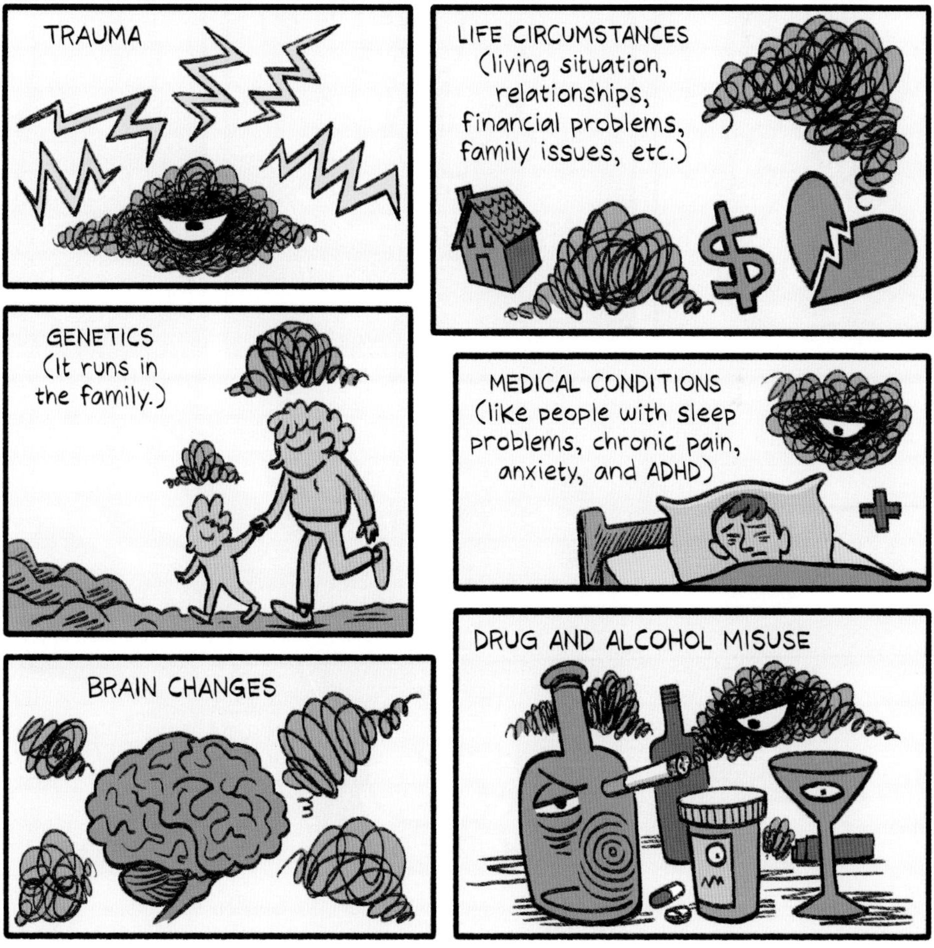
TRAUMA
LIFE CIRCUMSTANCES (living situation, relationships, financial problems, family issues, etc.)
GENETICS (It runs in the family.)
MEDICAL CONDITIONS (like people with sleep problems, chronic pain, anxiety, and ADHD)
BRAIN CHANGES
DRUG AND ALCOHOL MISUSE

DEPRESSION AND STRESS

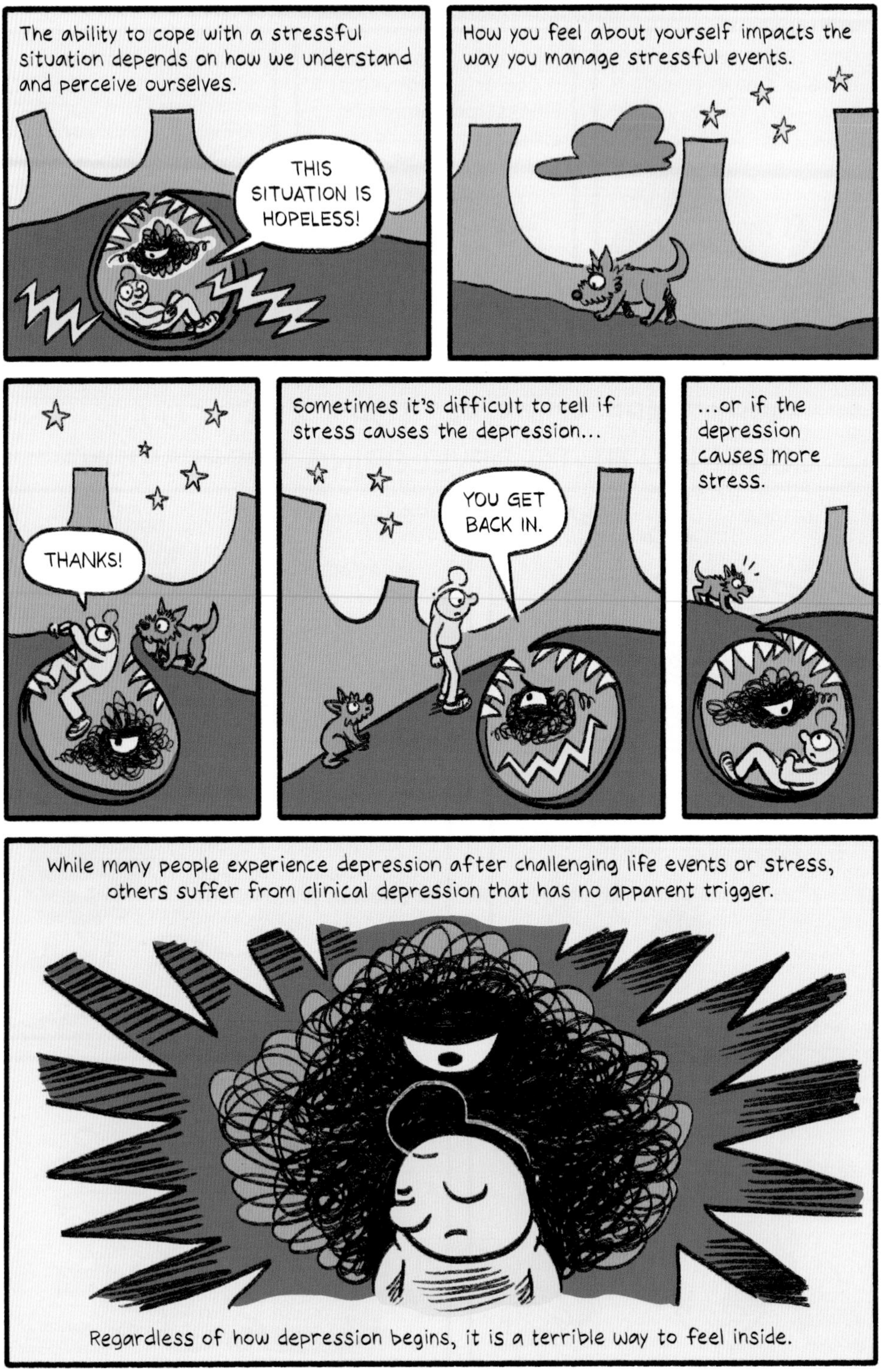
The ability to cope with a stressful situation depends on how we understand and perceive ourselves.
THIS SITUATION IS HOPELESS!
How you feel about yourself impacts the way you manage stressful events.
THANKS!
Sometimes it's difficult to tell if stress causes the depression...
YOU GET BACK IN.
...or if the depression causes more stress.
While many people experience depression after challenging life events or stress, others suffer from clinical depression that has no apparent trigger.
Regardless of how depression begins, it is a terrible way to feel inside.

HELPLESS FEELINGS

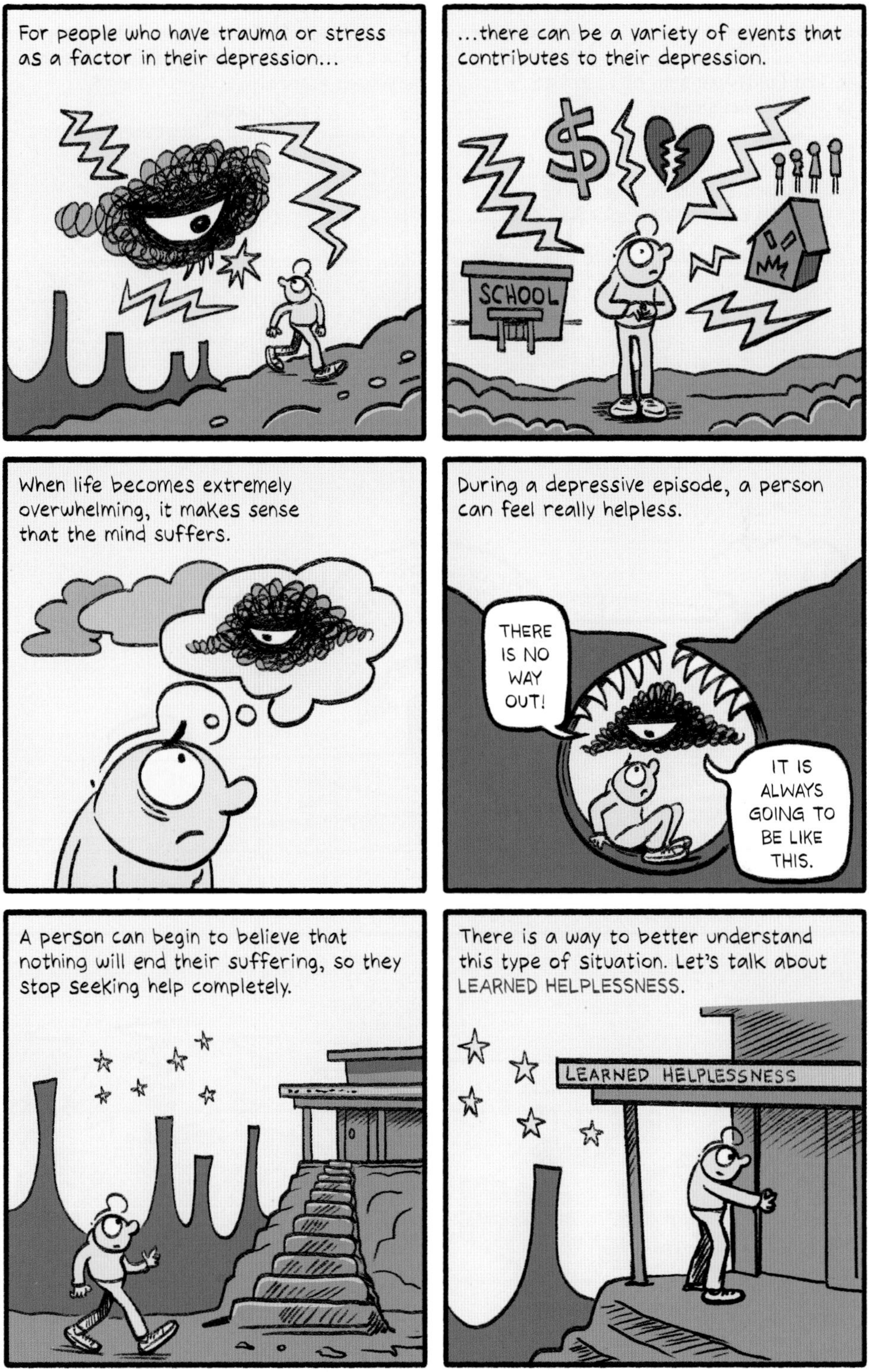
For people who have trauma or stress as a factor in their depression...
...there can be a variety of events that contributes to their depression.
SCHOOL
When life becomes extremely overwhelming, it makes sense that the mind suffers.
During a depressive episode, a person can feel really helpless.
THERE IS NO WAY OUT!
IT IS ALWAYS GOING TO BE LIKE THIS.
A person can begin to believe that nothing will end their suffering, so they stop seeking help completely.
There is a way to better understand this type of situation. Let's talk about LEARNED HELPLESSNESS.
LEARNED HELPLESSNESS

WHAT IS LEARNED HELPLESSNESS?

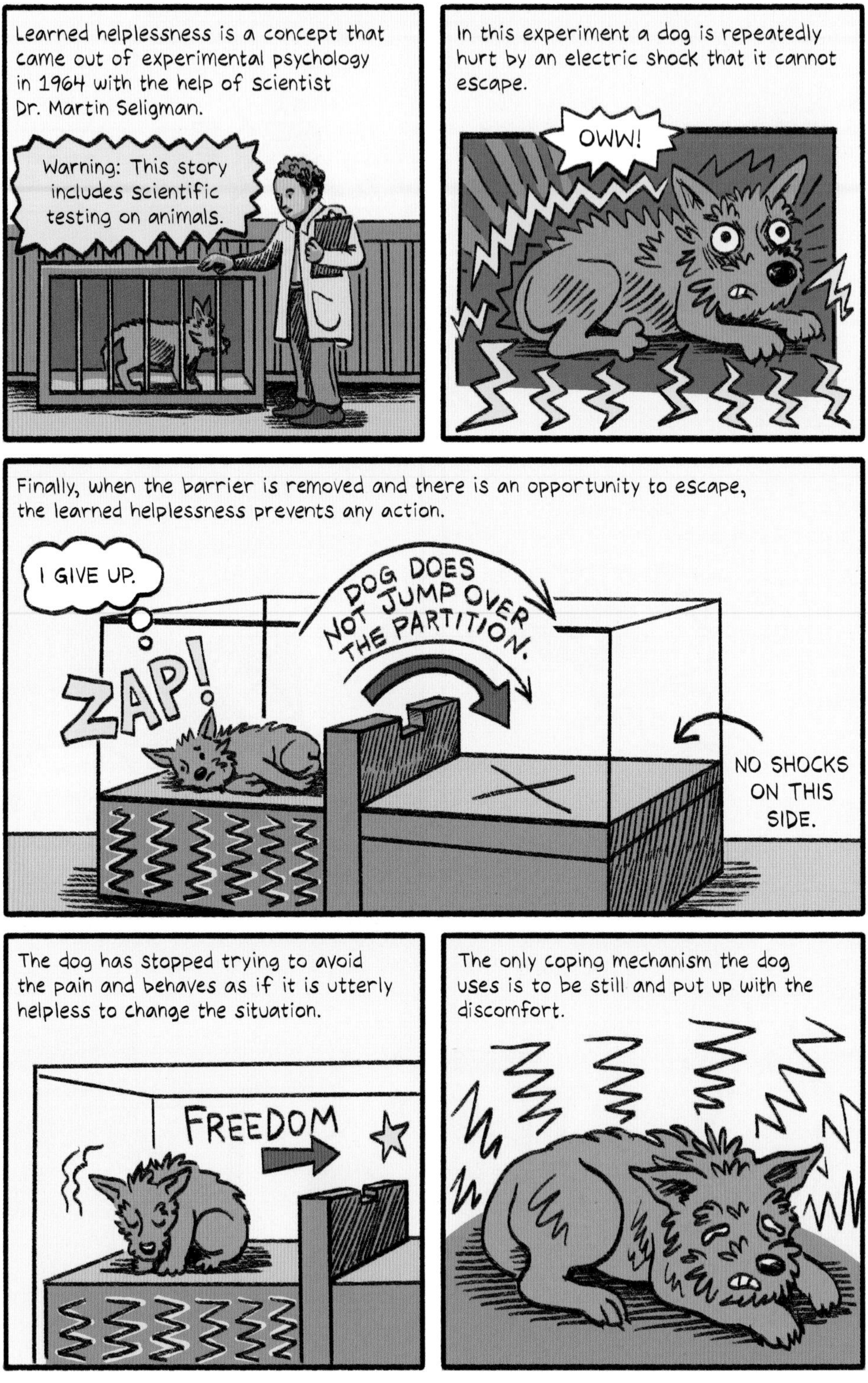
Learned helplessness is a concept that came out of experimental psychology in 1964 with the help of scientist Dr. Martin Seligman.
Warning: This story includes scientific testing on animals.
In this experiment a dog is repeatedly hurt by an electric shock that it cannot escape.
OWW!
Finally, when the barrier is removed and there is an opportunity to escape, the learned helplessness prevents any action.
I GIVE UP.
DOG DOES NOT JUMP OVER THE PARTITION.
ZAP!
NO SHOCKS ON THIS SIDE.
The dog has stopped trying to avoid the pain and behaves as if it is utterly helpless to change the situation.
FREEDOM
The only coping mechanism the dog uses is to be still and put up with the discomfort.

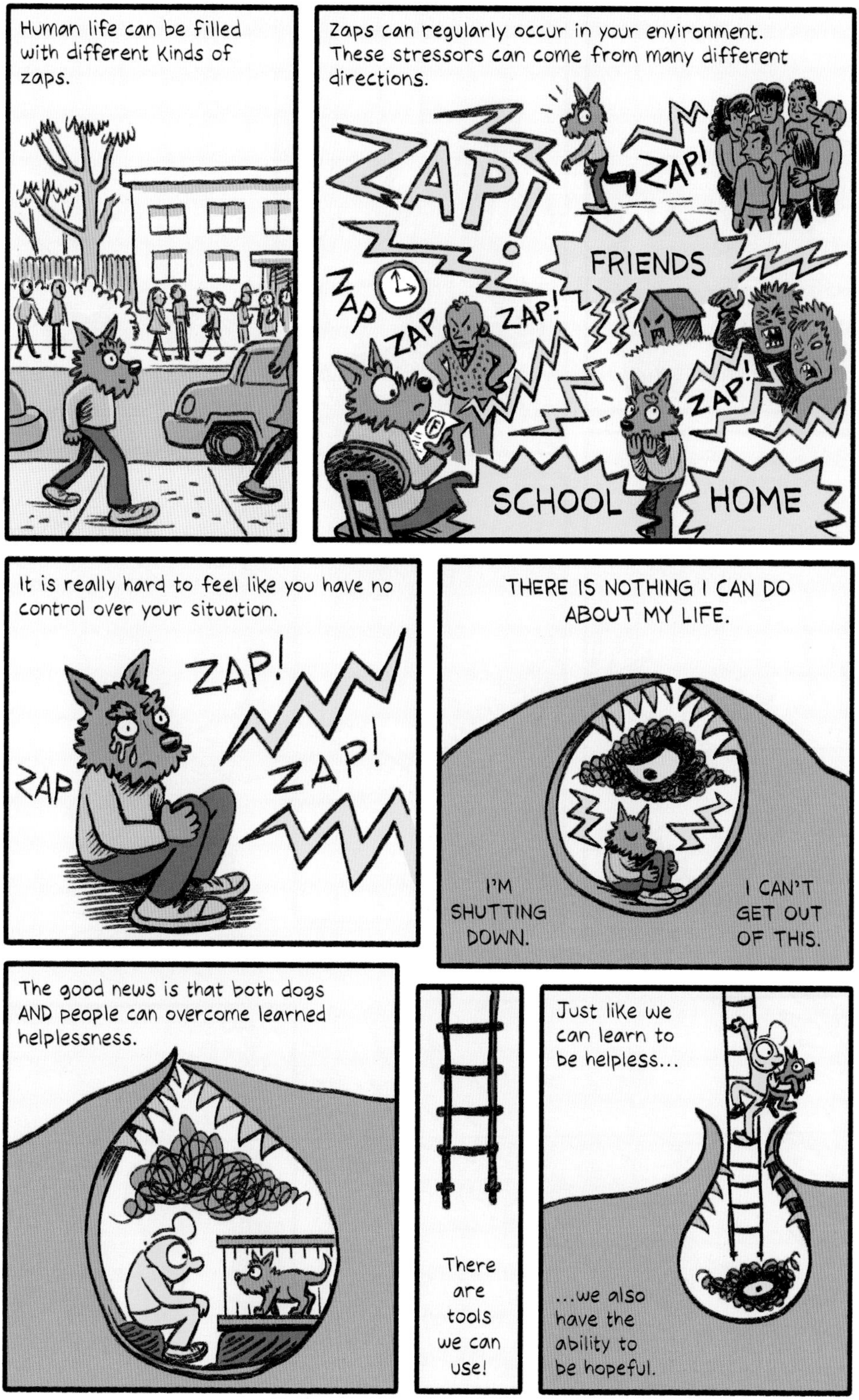
Human life can be filled with different kinds of zaps.
Zaps can regularly occur in your environment. These stressors can come from many different directions.
ZAP!
ZAP!
FRIENDS
ZAP
ZAP
ZAP!
ZAP!
SCHOOL
HOME
It is really hard to feel like you have no control over your situation.
ZAP!
ZAP!
ZAP
THERE IS NOTHING I CAN DO ABOUT MY LIFE.
I'M SHUTTING DOWN.
I CAN'T GET OUT OF THIS.
The good news is that both dogs AND people can overcome learned helplessness.
There are tools we can use!
Just like we can learn to be helpless...
...we also have the ability to be hopeful.

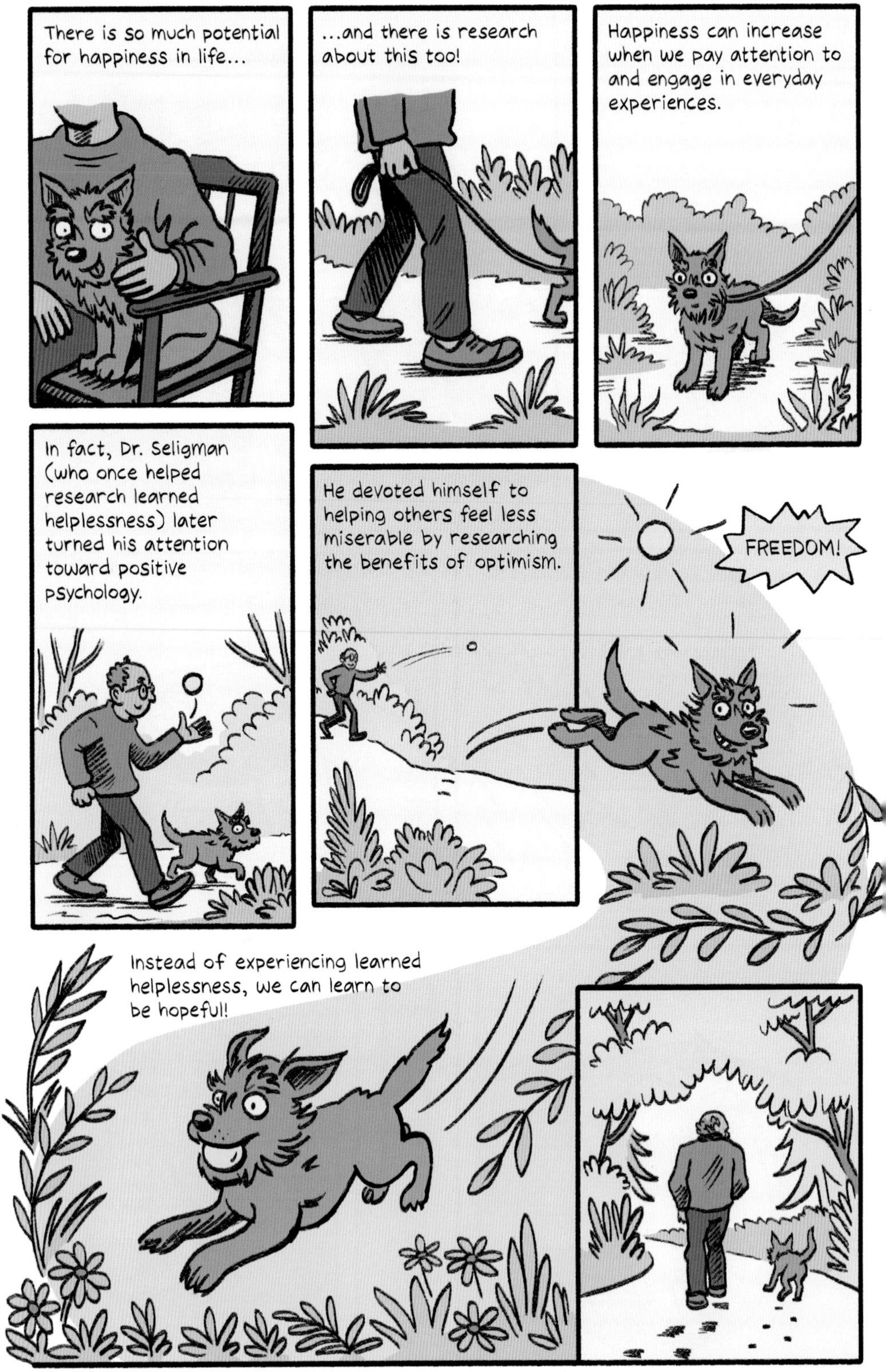
There is so much potential for happiness in life...
...and there is research about this too!
Happiness can increase when we pay attention to and engage in everyday experiences.
In fact, Dr. Seligman (who once helped research learned helplessness) later turned his attention toward positive psychology.
He devoted himself to helping others feel less miserable by researching the benefits of optimism.
FREEDOM!
Instead of experiencing learned helplessness, we can learn to be hopeful!

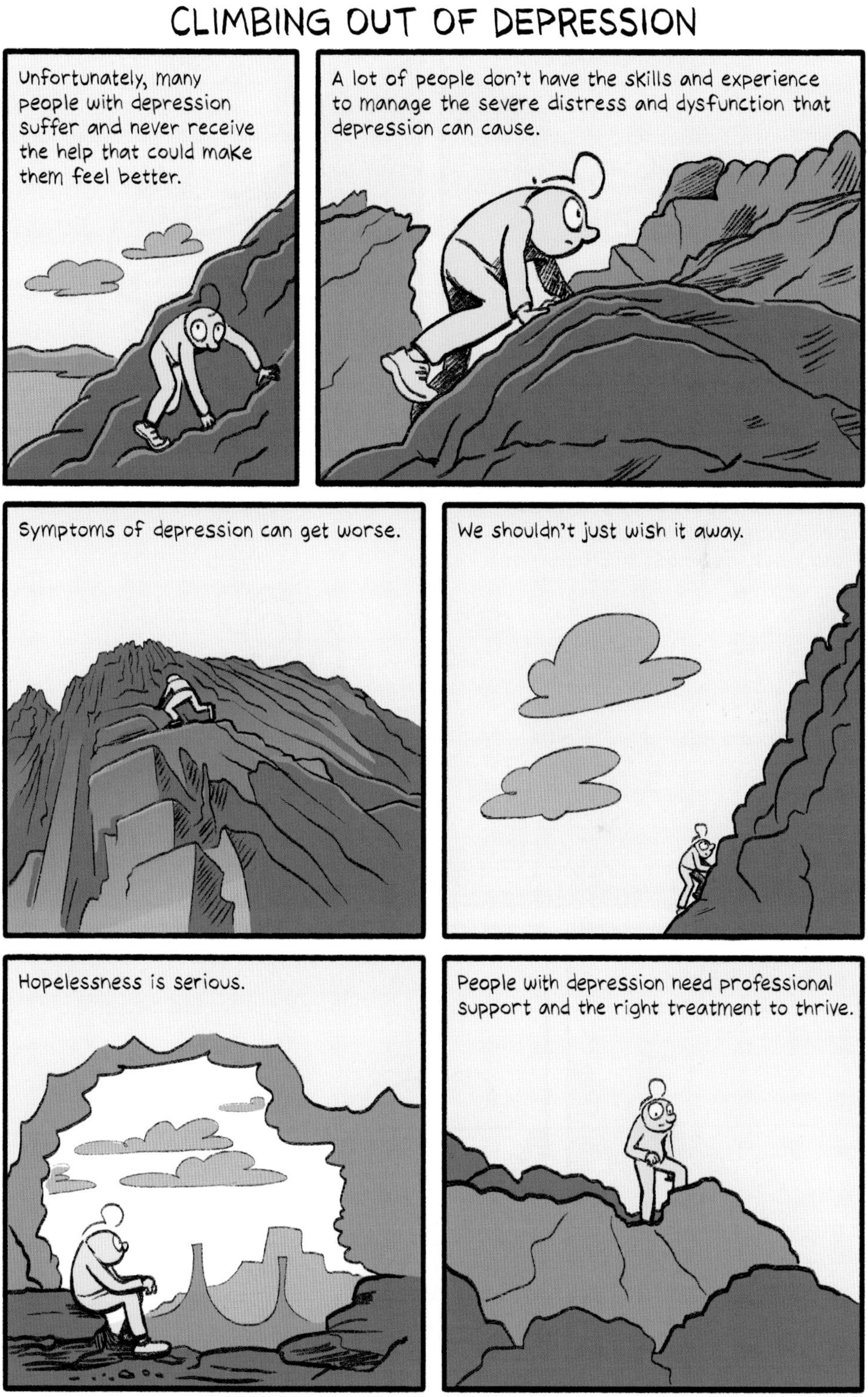

CLIMBING OUT OF DEPRESSION
Unfortunately, many people with depression suffer and never receive the help that could make them feel better.
A lot of people don't have the skills and experience to manage the severe distress and dysfunction that depression can cause.
Symptoms of depression can get worse.
We shouldn't just wish it away.
Hopelessness is serious.
People with depression need professional support and the right treatment to thrive.

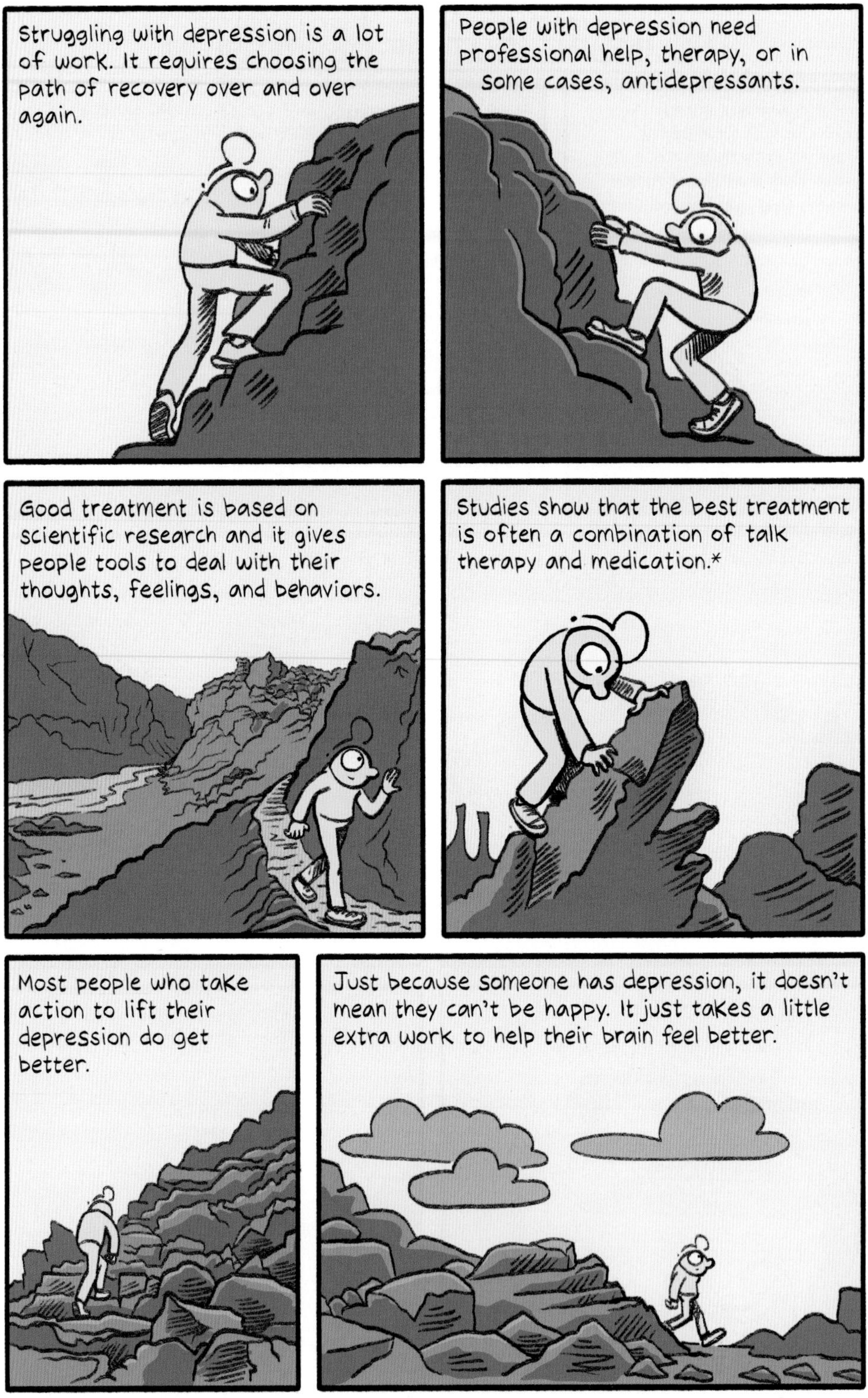
Struggling with depression is a lot of work. It requires choosing the path of recovery over and over again.
People with depression need professional help, therapy, or in some cases, antidepressants.
Good treatment is based on scientific research and it gives people tools to deal with their thoughts, feelings, and behaviors.
Studies show that the best treatment is often a combination of talk therapy and medication.*
Most people who take action to lift their depression do get better.
Just because someone has depression, it doesn't mean they can't be happy. It just takes a little extra work to help their brain feel better.

*We will explore more about treatment for mental health disorders in chapter 9.

DEPRESSION AND THOUGHTS

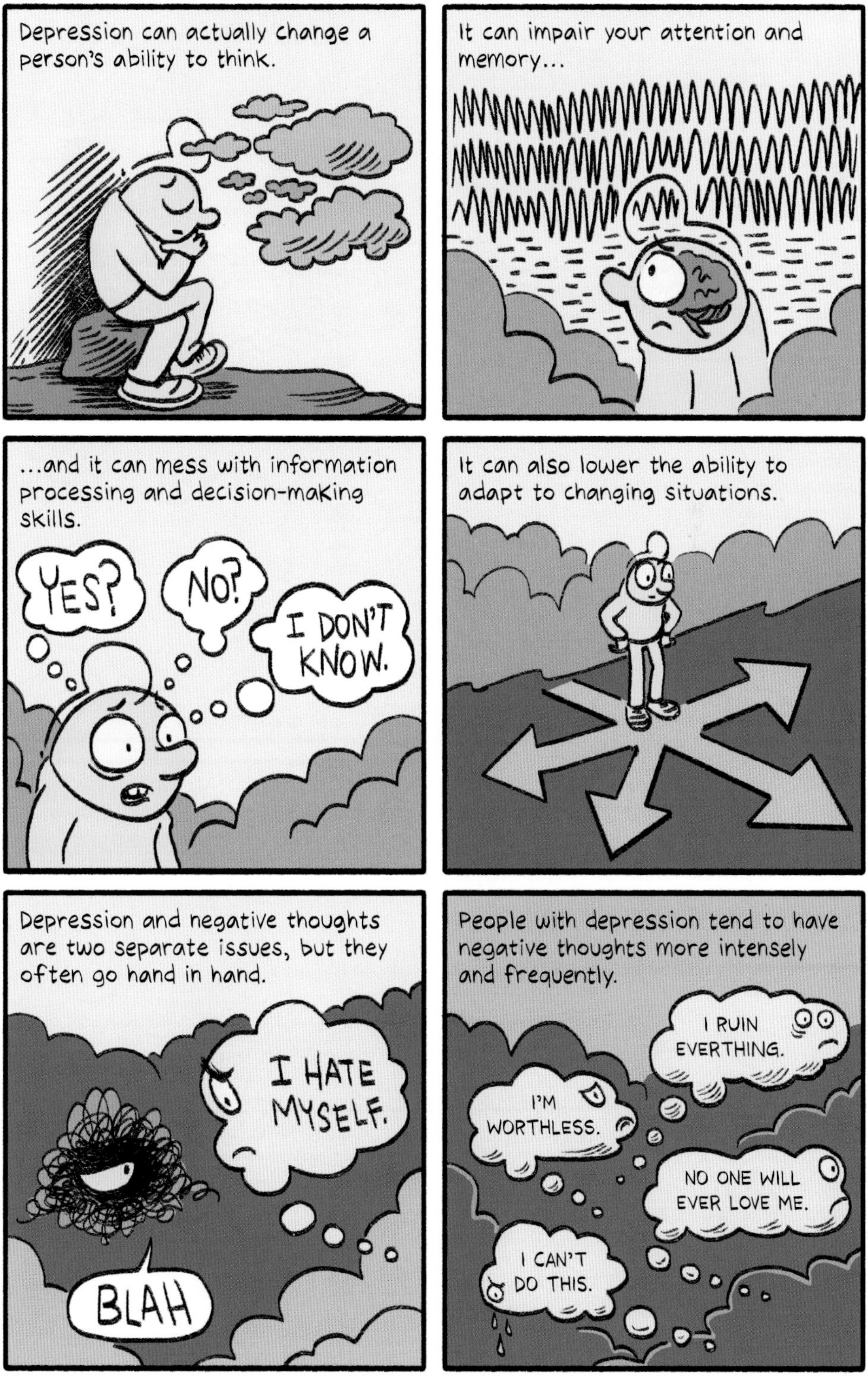
Depression can actually change a person's ability to think.
It can impair your attention and memory...
...and it can mess with information processing and decision-making skills.
YES?
NO?
I DON'T KNOW.
It can also lower the ability to adapt to changing situations.
Depression and negative thoughts are two separate issues, but they often go hand in hand.
I HATE MYSELF.
BLAH
People with depression tend to have negative thoughts more intensely and frequently.
I RUIN EVERTHING.
I'M WORTHLESS.
NO ONE WILL EVER LOVE ME.
I CAN'T DO THIS.

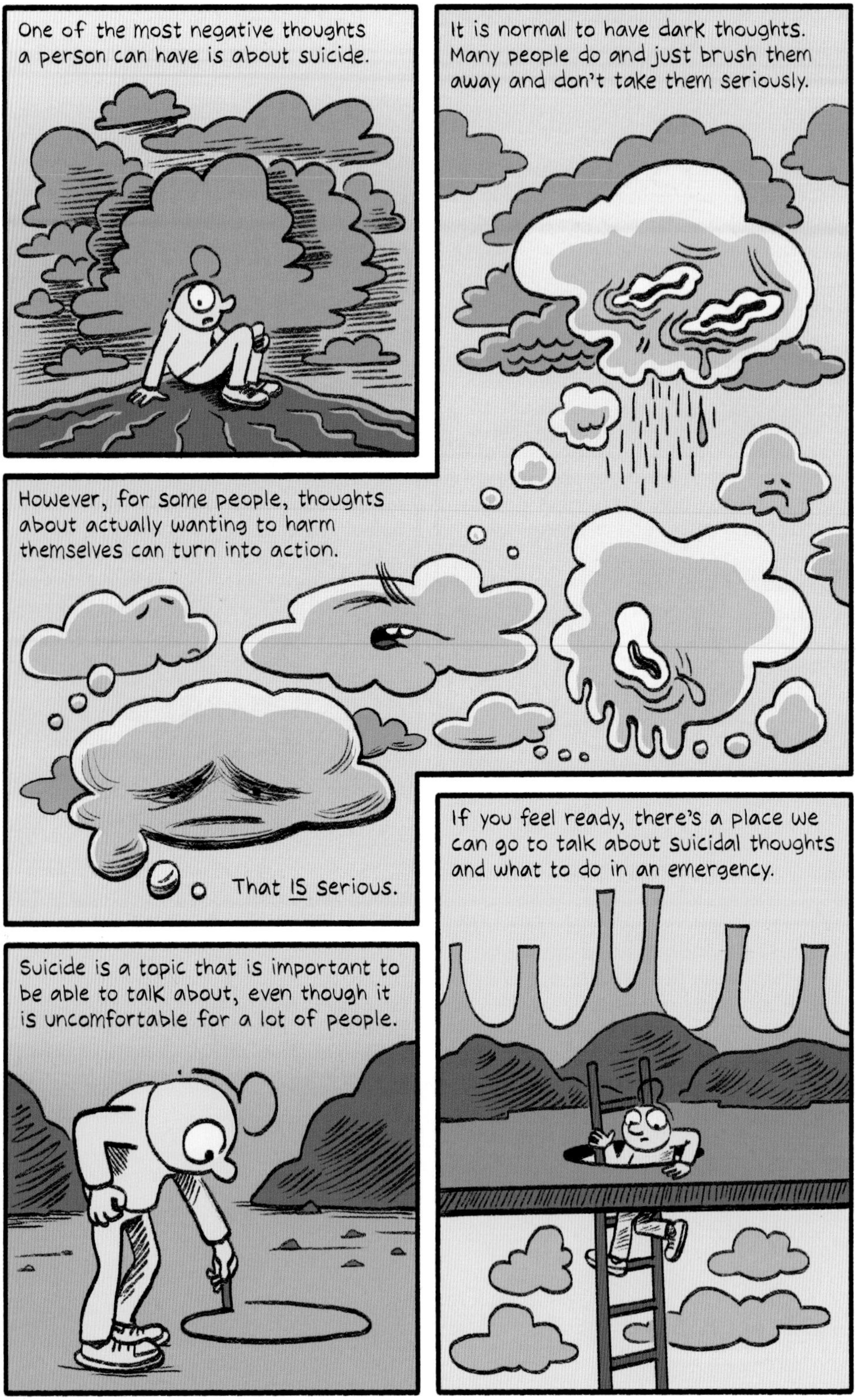
One of the most negative thoughts a person can have is about suicide.
It is normal to have dark thoughts. Many people do and just brush them away and don't take them seriously.
However, for some people, thoughts about actually wanting to harm themselves can turn into action.
That IS serious.
If you feel ready, there's a place we can go to talk about suicidal thoughts and what to do in an emergency.
Suicide is a topic that is important to be able to talk about, even though it is uncomfortable for a lot of people.

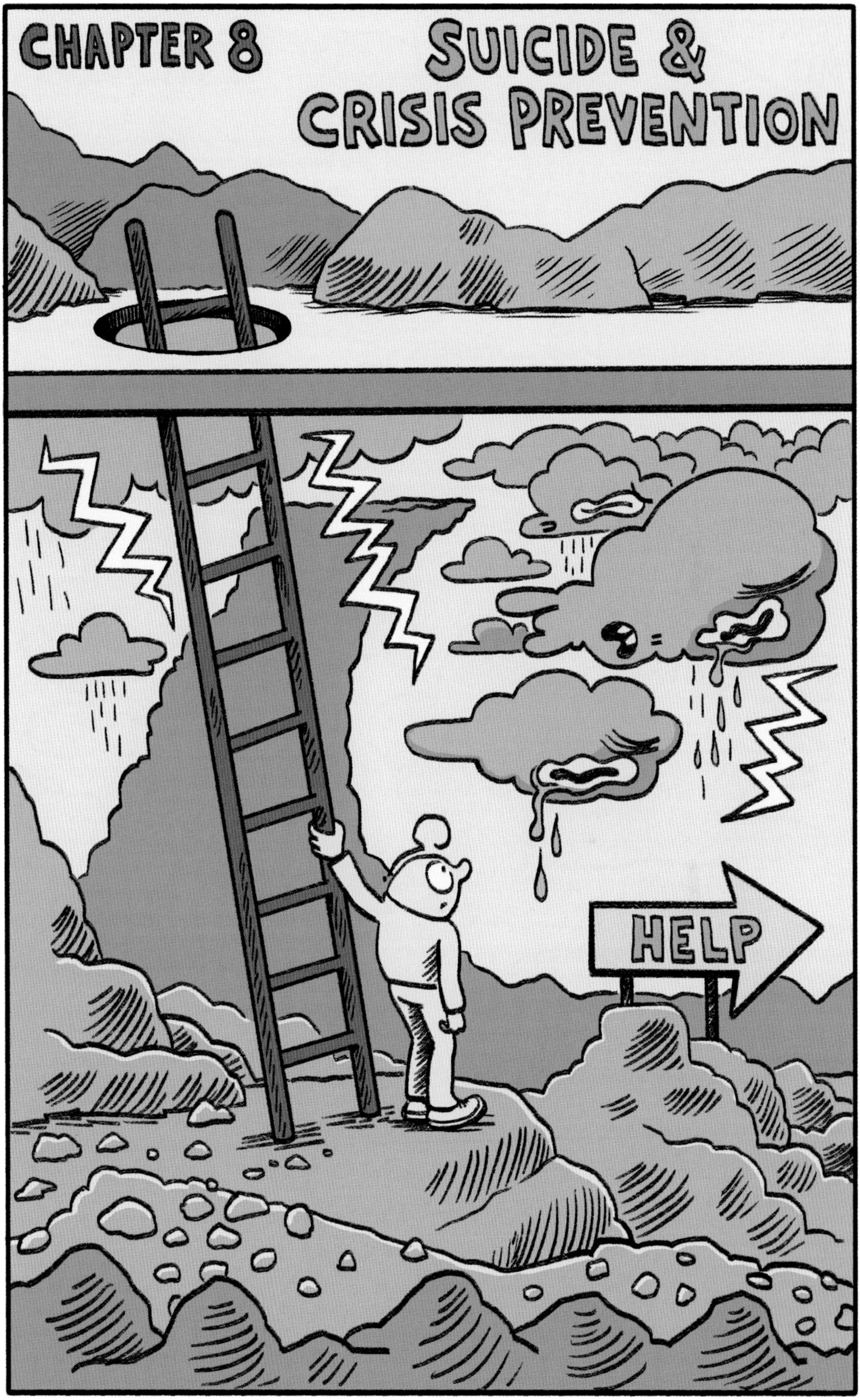
CHAPTER 8
SUICIDE & CRISIS PREVENTION
HELP

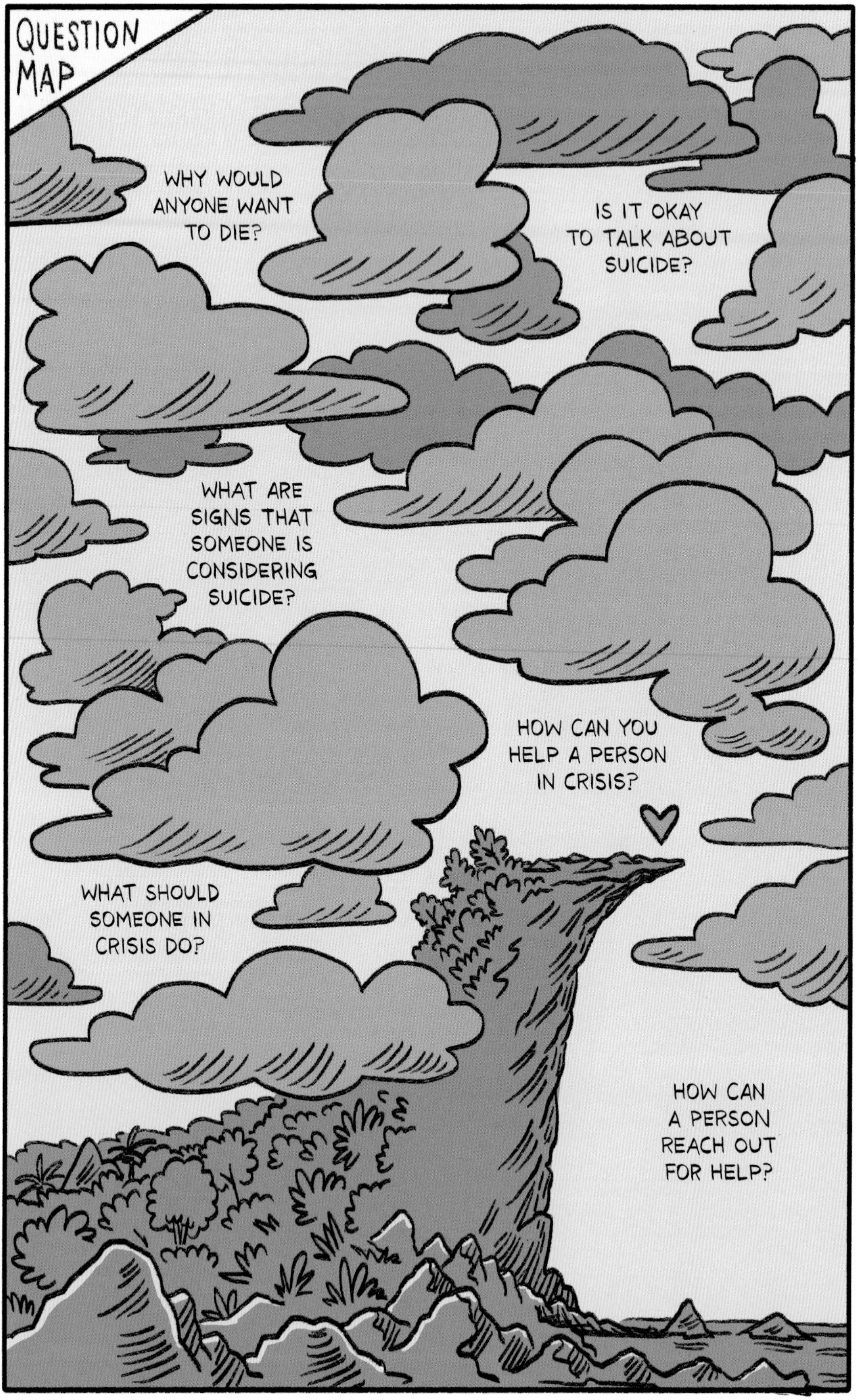
QUESTION MAP
WHY WOULD ANYONE WANT TO DIE?
IS IT OKAY TO TALK ABOUT SUICIDE?
WHAT ARE SIGNS THAT SOMEONE IS CONSIDERING SUICIDE?
HOW CAN YOU HELP A PERSON IN CRISIS?
WHAT SHOULD SOMEONE IN CRISIS DO?
HOW CAN A PERSON REACH OUT FOR HELP?

THOUGHTS ABOUT ENDING LIFE

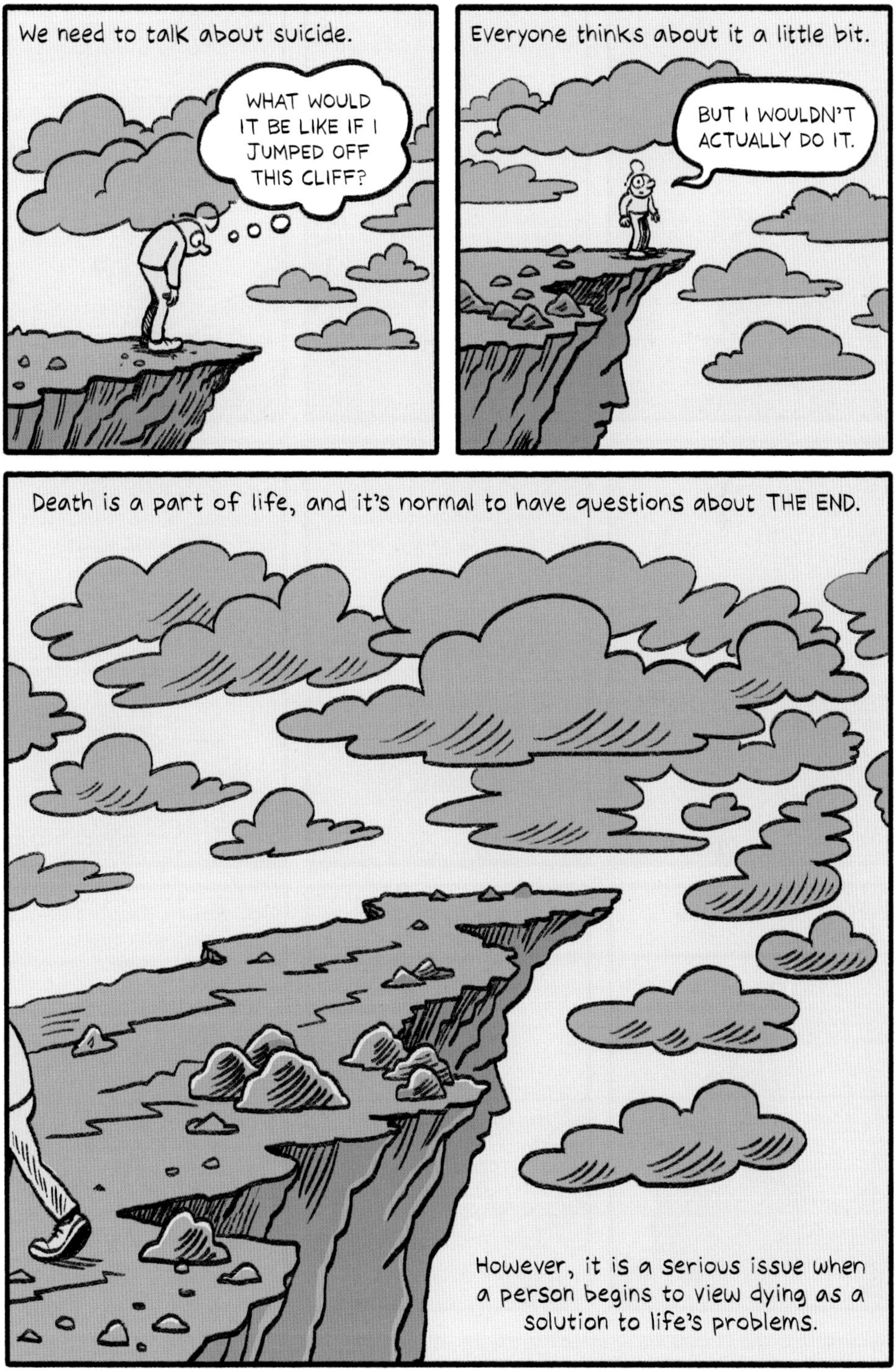
We need to talk about suicide.
WHAT WOULD IT BE LIKE IF I JUMPED OFF THIS CLIFF?
Everyone thinks about it a little bit.
BUT I WOULDN'T ACTUALLY DO IT.
Death is a part of life, and it's normal to have questions about THE END.
However, it is a serious issue when a person begins to view dying as a solution to life's problems.

ABOUT SUICIDE

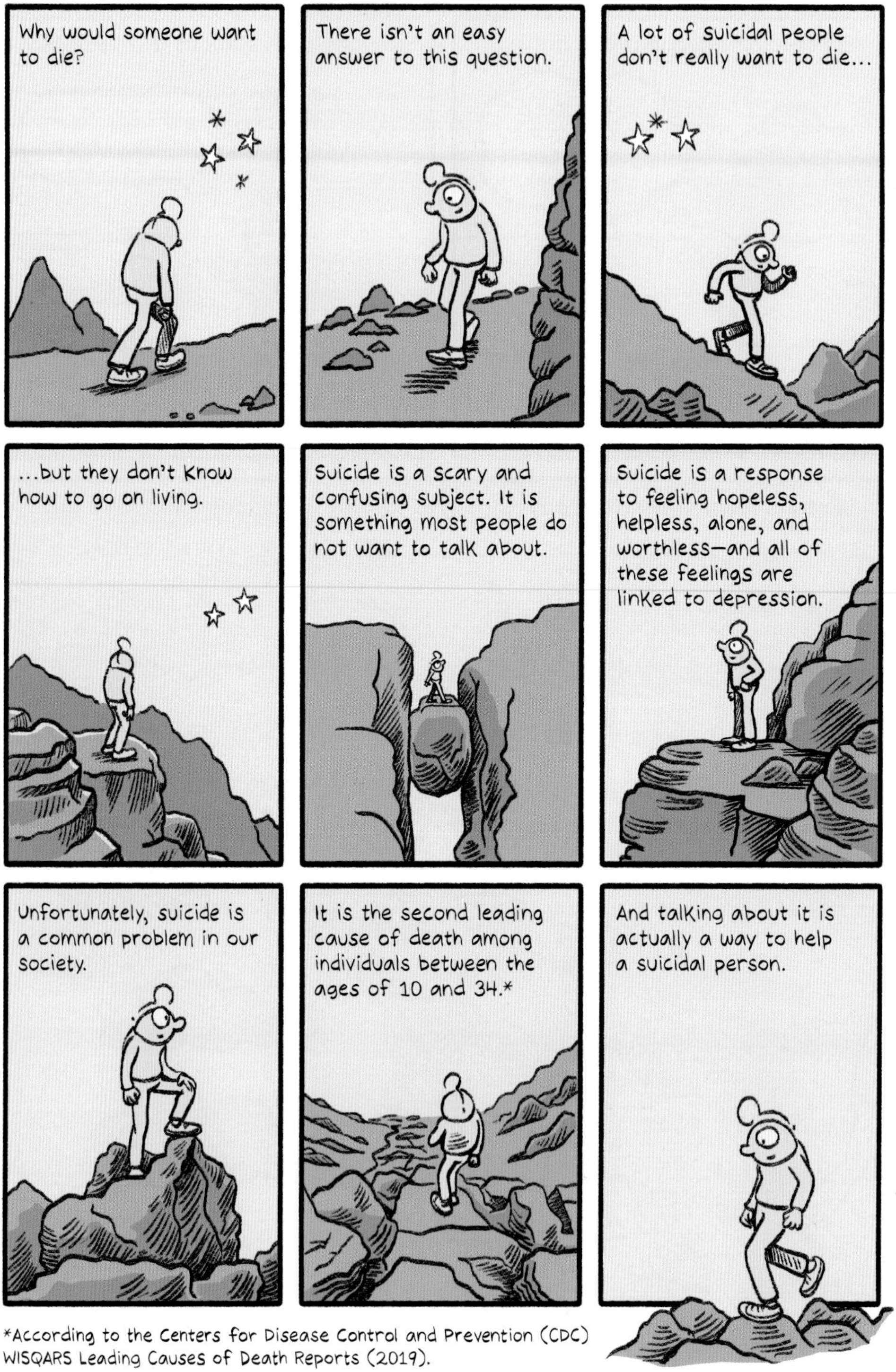
Why would someone want to die?
There isn't an easy answer to this question.
A lot of suicidal people don't really want to die...
...but they don't know how to go on living.
Suicide is a scary and confusing subject. It is something most people do not want to talk about.
Suicide is a response to feeling hopeless, helpless, alone, and worthless—and all of these feelings are linked to depression.
Unfortunately, suicide is a common problem in our society.
It is the second leading cause of death among individuals between the ages of 10 and 34.*
And talking about it is actually a way to help a suicidal person.

*According to the Centers for Disease Control and Prevention (CDC) WISQARS Leading Causes of Death Reports (2019).

WHEN DOES A NEGATIVE THOUGHT BECOME DANGEROUS?

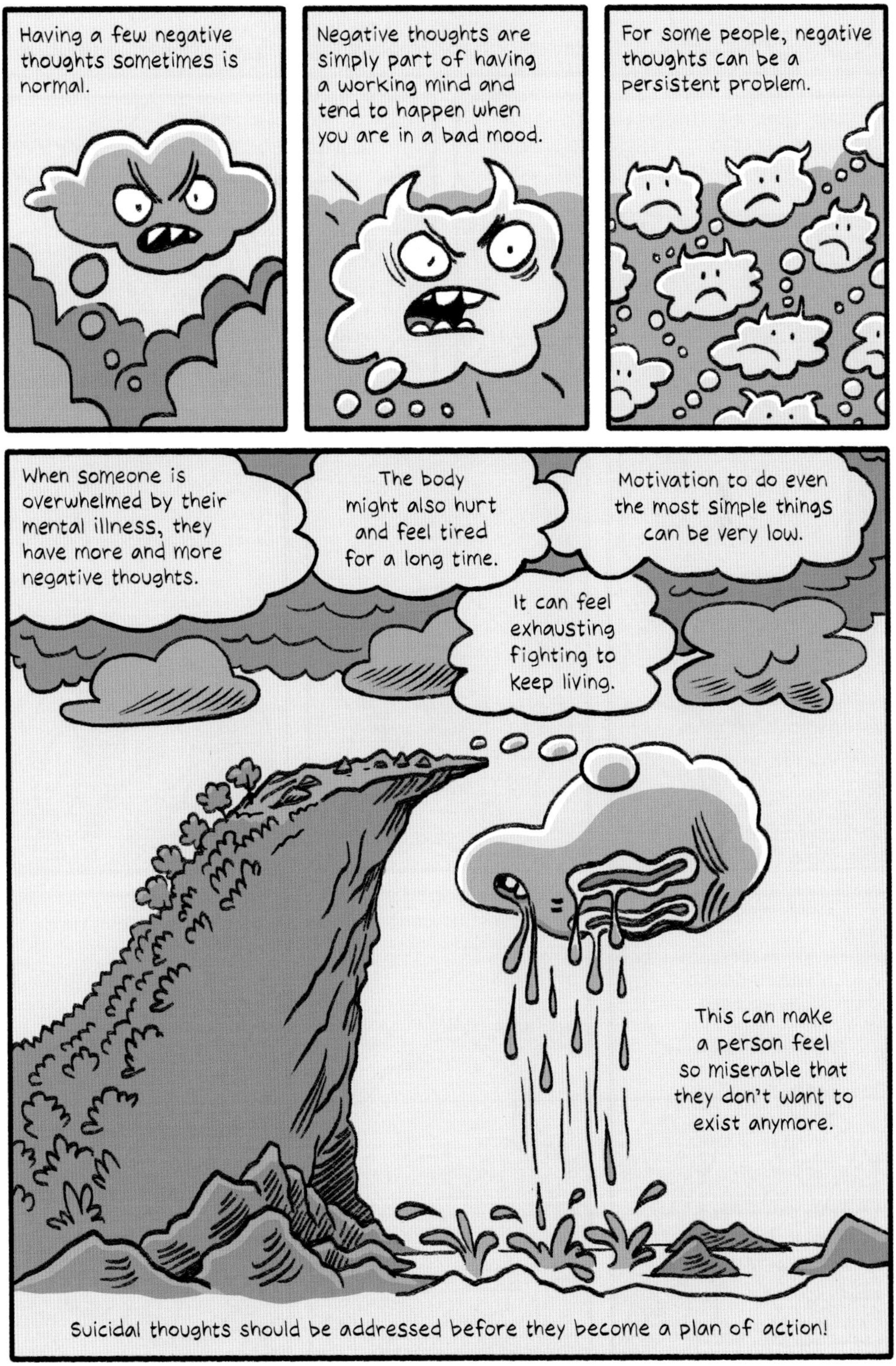
Having a few negative thoughts sometimes is normal.
Negative thoughts are simply part of having a working mind and tend to happen when you are in a bad mood.
For some people, negative thoughts can be a persistent problem.
When someone is overwhelmed by their mental illness, they have more and more negative thoughts.
The body might also hurt and feel tired for a long time.
Motivation to do even the most simple things can be very low.
It can feel exhausting fighting to keep living.
This can make a person feel so miserable that they don't want to exist anymore.
Suicidal thoughts should be addressed before they become a plan of action!

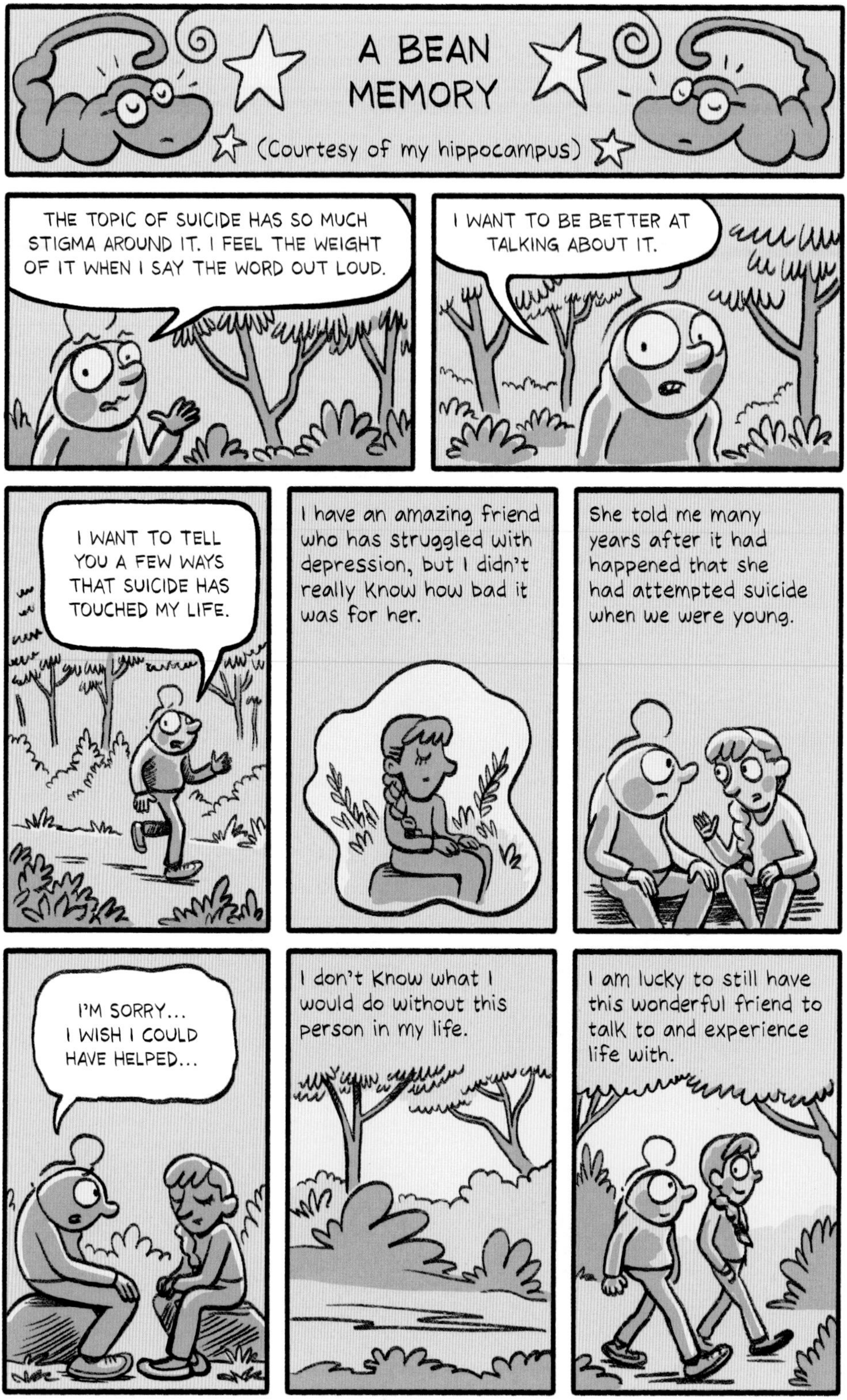
A BEAN MEMORY
(Courtesy of my hippocampus)
THE TOPIC OF SUICIDE HAS SO MUCH STIGMA AROUND IT. I FEEL THE WEIGHT OF IT WHEN I SAY THE WORD OUT LOUD.
I WANT TO BE BETTER AT TALKING ABOUT IT.
I WANT TO TELL YOU A FEW WAYS THAT SUICIDE HAS TOUCHED MY LIFE.
I have an amazing friend who has struggled with depression, but I didn't really know how bad it was for her.
She told me many years after it had happened that she had attempted suicide when we were young.
I'M SORRY... I WISH I COULD HAVE HELPED...
I don't know what I would do without this person in my life.
I am lucky to still have this wonderful friend to talk to and experience life with.

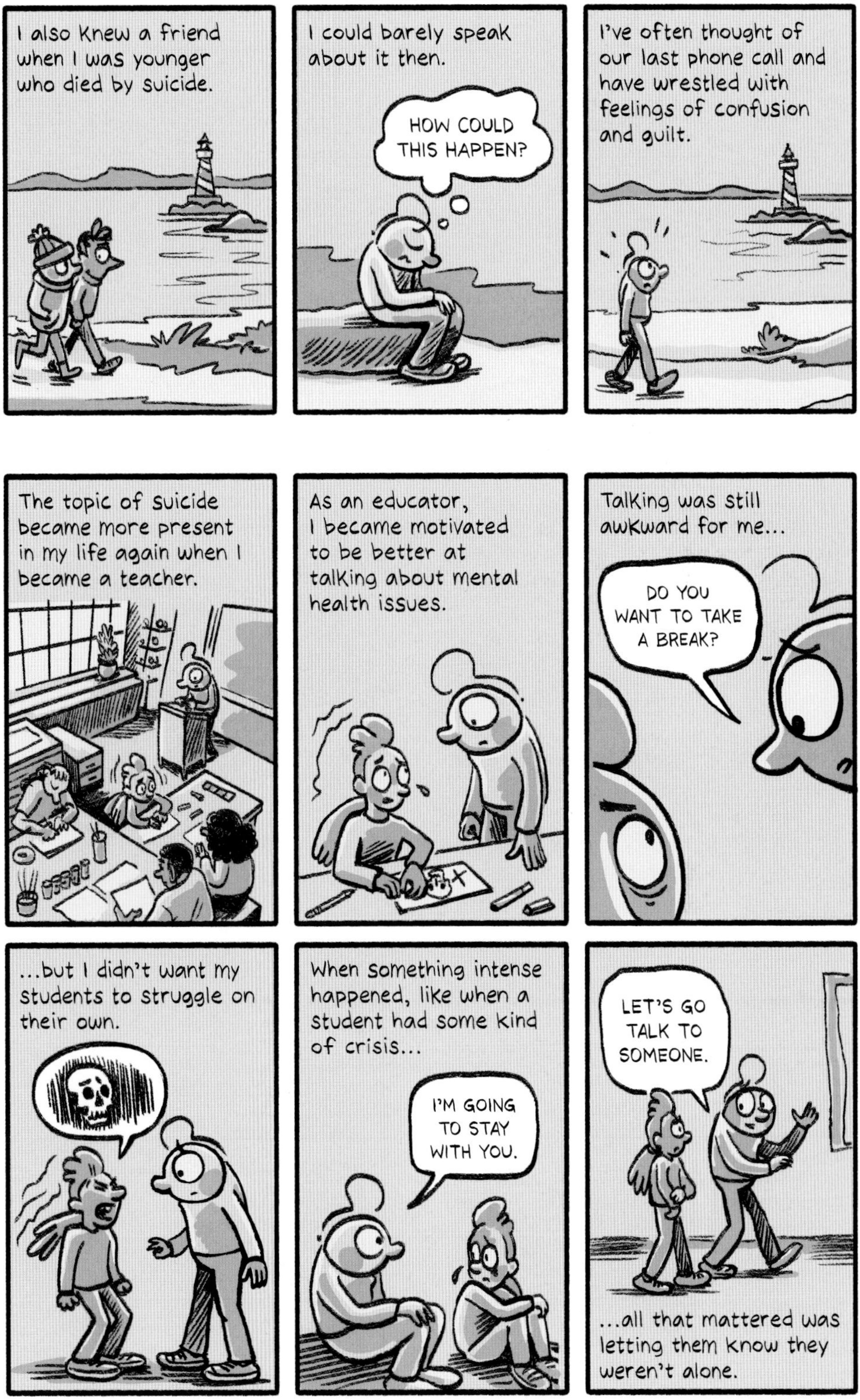
I also knew a friend when I was younger who died by suicide.
I could barely speak about it then.
HOW COULD THIS HAPPEN?
I've often thought of our last phone call and have wrestled with feelings of confusion and guilt.
The topic of suicide became more present in my life again when I became a teacher.
As an educator, I became motivated to be better at talking about mental health issues.
Talking was still awkward for me...
DO YOU WANT TO TAKE A BREAK?
...but I didn't want my students to struggle on their own.
When something intense happened, like when a student had some kind of crisis...
I'M GOING TO STAY WITH YOU.
LET'S GO TALK TO SOMEONE.
...all that mattered was letting them know they weren't alone.

KEEPING EACH OTHER SAFE

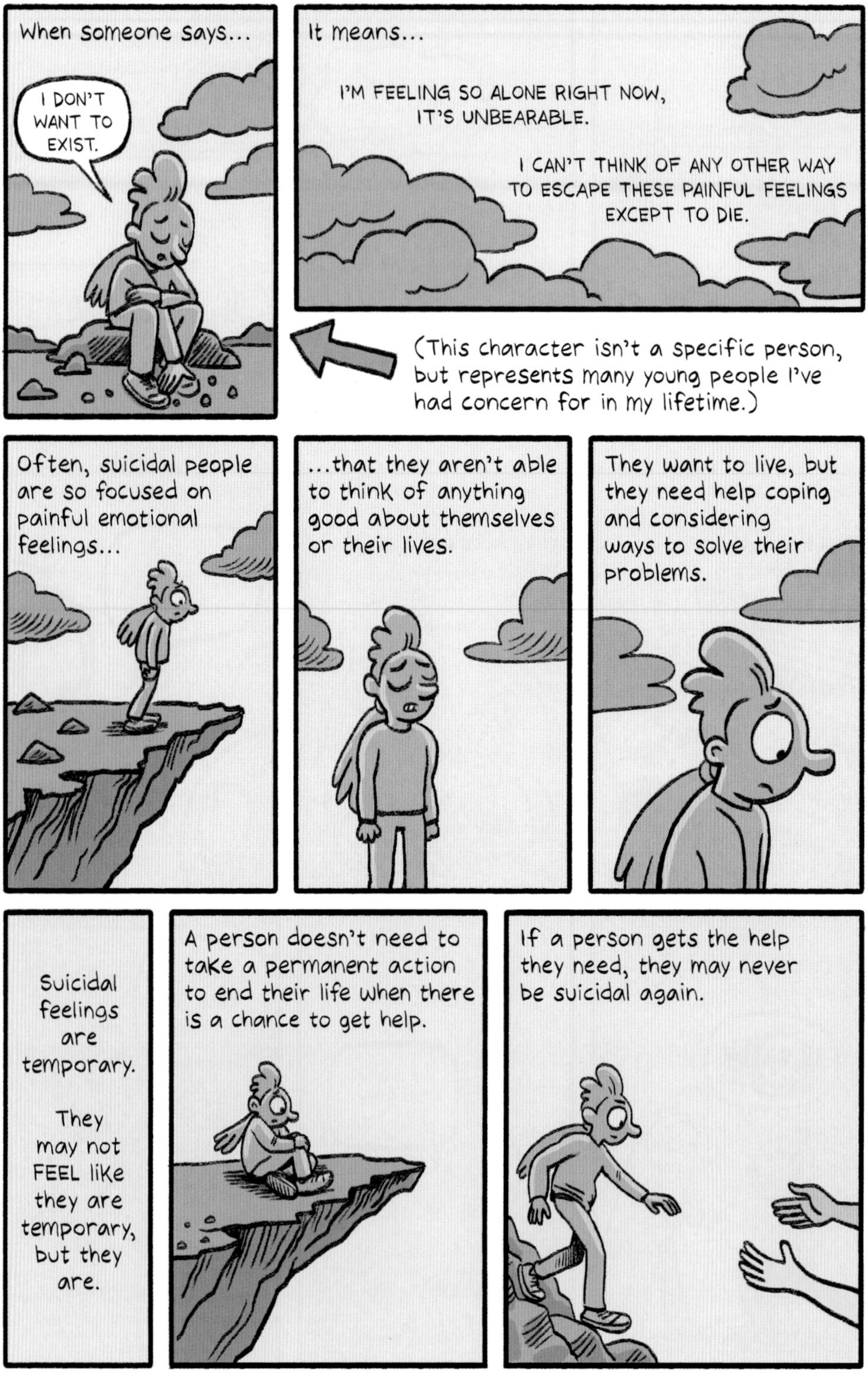

When someone says...
I DON'T WANT TO EXIST.
It means...
I'M FEELING SO ALONE RIGHT NOW, IT'S UNBEARABLE.
I CAN'T THINK OF ANY OTHER WAY TO ESCAPE THESE PAINFUL FEELINGS EXCEPT TO DIE.
(This character isn't a specific person, but represents many young people I've had concern for in my lifetime.)
Often, suicidal people are so focused on painful emotional feelings...
...that they aren't able to think of anything good about themselves or their lives.
They want to live, but they need help coping and considering ways to solve their problems.
Suicidal feelings are temporary.
They may not FEEL like they are temporary, but they are.
A person doesn't need to take a permanent action to end their life when there is a chance to get help.
If a person gets the help they need, they may never be suicidal again.

WHAT ARE THE WARNING SIGNS OF SUICIDE?

Here are some clues to pay attention to if you believe that someone you care about could be considering suicide.

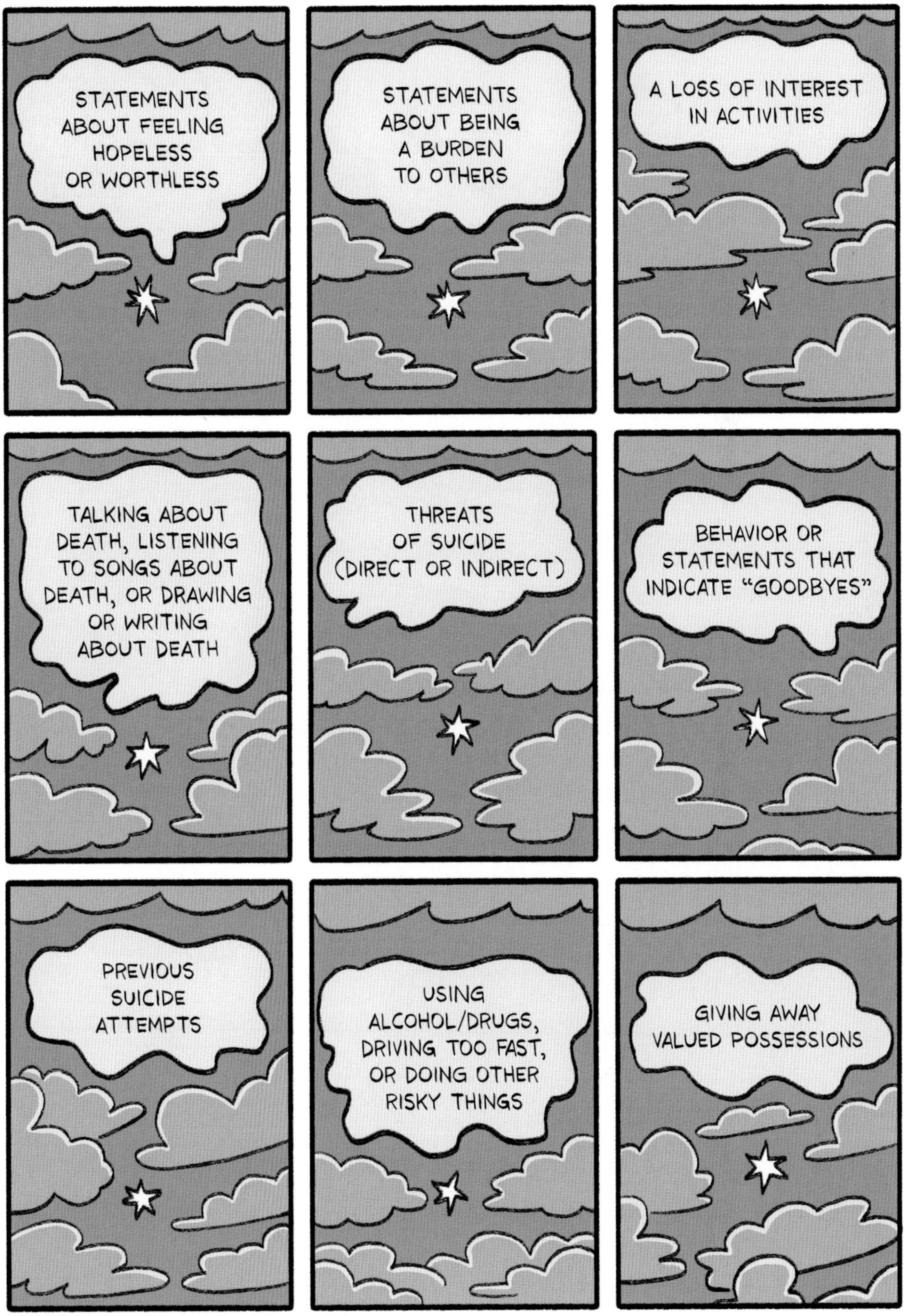
STATEMENTS ABOUT FEELING HOPELESS OR WORTHLESS
STATEMENTS ABOUT BEING A BURDEN TO OTHERS
A LOSS OF INTEREST IN ACTIVITIES
TALKING ABOUT DEATH, LISTENING TO SONGS ABOUT DEATH, OR DRAWING OR WRITING ABOUT DEATH
THREATS OF SUICIDE (DIRECT OR INDIRECT)
BEHAVIOR OR STATEMENTS THAT INDICATE "GOODBYES"
PREVIOUS SUICIDE ATTEMPTS
USING ALCOHOL/DRUGS, DRIVING TOO FAST, OR DOING OTHER RISKY THINGS
GIVING AWAY VALUED POSSESSIONS

SOME SECRETS ARE NOT GOOD TO KEEP

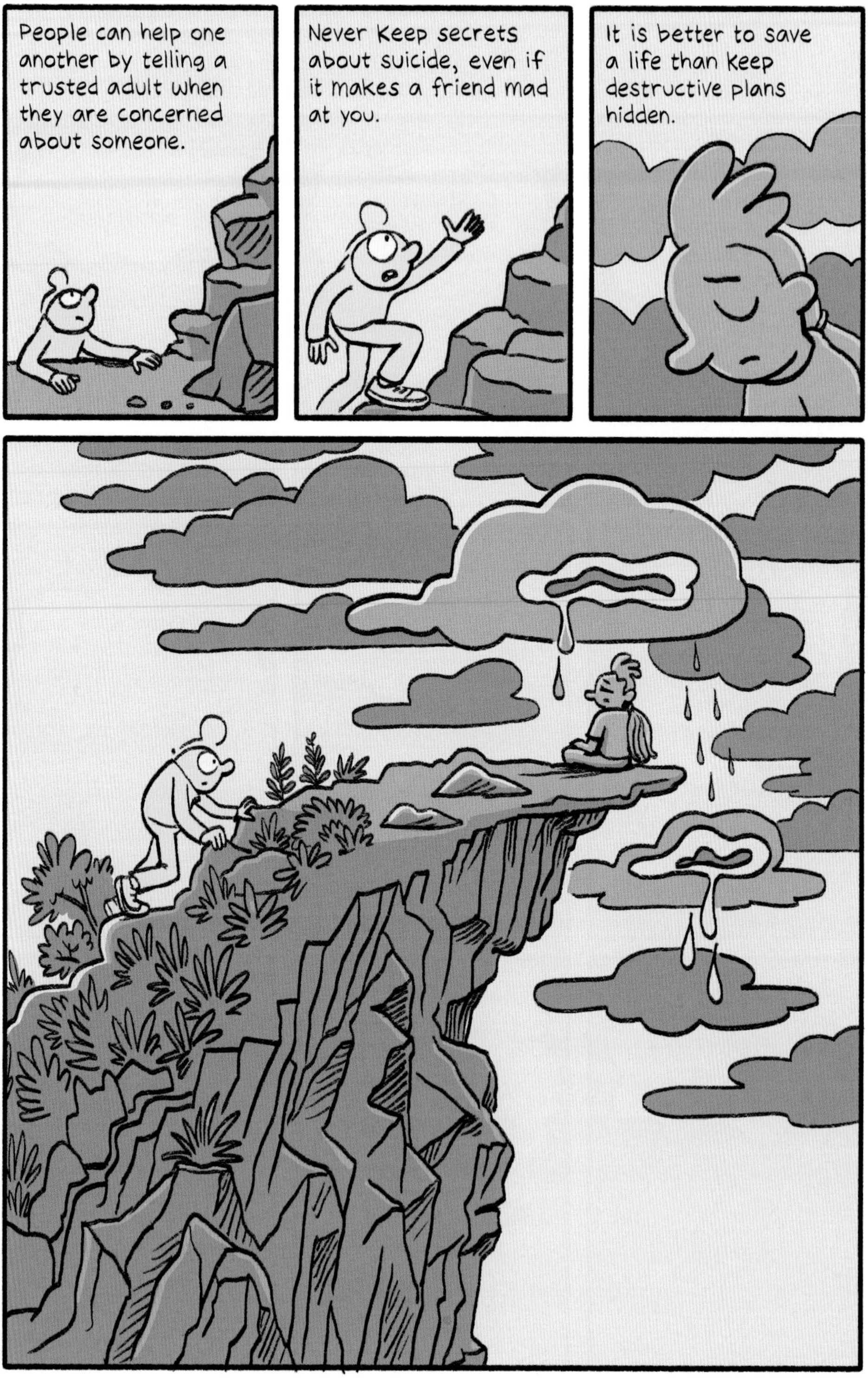
People can help one another by telling a trusted adult when they are concerned about someone.
Never keep secrets about suicide, even if it makes a friend mad at you.
It is better to save a life than keep destructive plans hidden.

WHAT TO DO IF SOMEONE THREATENS SUICIDE

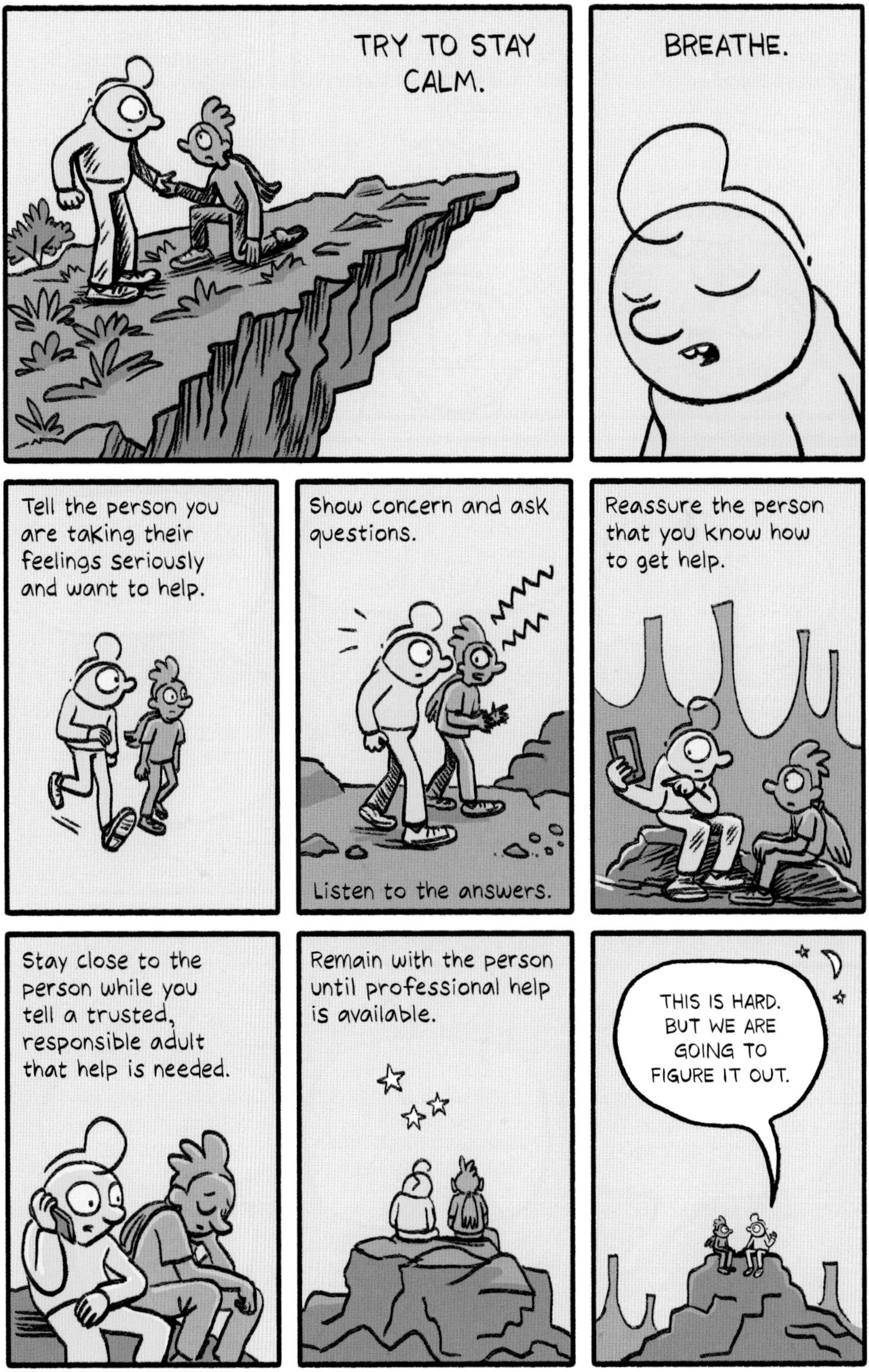
TRY TO STAY CALM.
BREATHE.
Tell the person you are taking their feelings seriously and want to help.
Show concern and ask questions.
Listen to the answers.
Reassure the person that you know how to get help.
Stay close to the person while you tell a trusted, responsible adult that help is needed.
Remain with the person until professional help is available.
THIS IS HARD. BUT WE ARE GOING TO FIGURE IT OUT.

DON'T TAKE ON A CRISIS BY YOURSELF

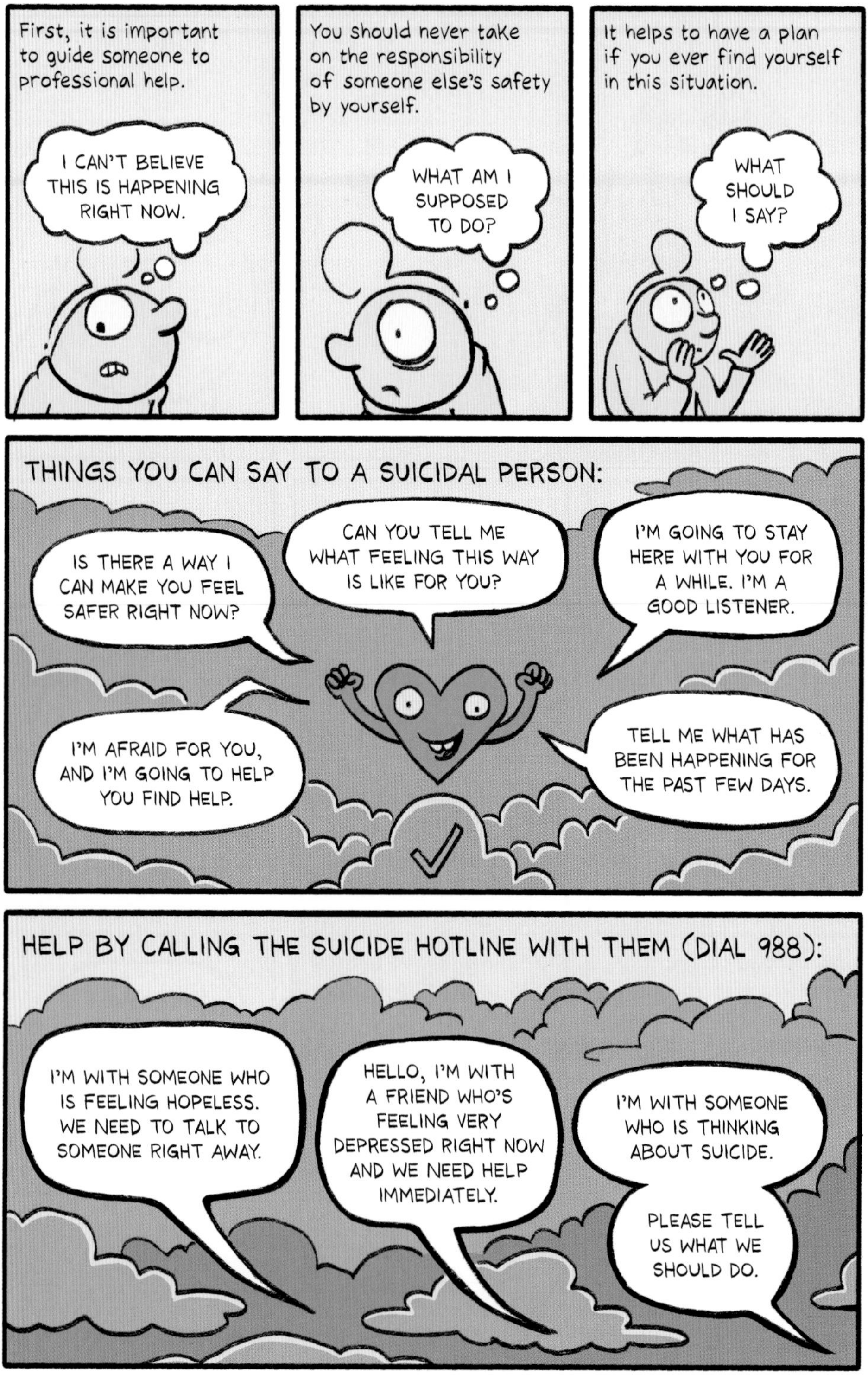
First, it is important to guide someone to professional help.
I CAN'T BELIEVE THIS IS HAPPENING RIGHT NOW.
You should never take on the responsibility of someone else's safety by yourself.
WHAT AM I SUPPOSED TO DO?
It helps to have a plan if you ever find yourself in this situation.
WHAT SHOULD I SAY?
THINGS YOU CAN SAY TO A SUICIDAL PERSON:
IS THERE A WAY I CAN MAKE YOU FEEL SAFER RIGHT NOW?
CAN YOU TELL ME WHAT FEELING THIS WAY IS LIKE FOR YOU?
I'M GOING TO STAY HERE WITH YOU FOR A WHILE. I'M A GOOD LISTENER.
I'M AFRAID FOR YOU, AND I'M GOING TO HELP YOU FIND HELP.
TELL ME WHAT HAS BEEN HAPPENING FOR THE PAST FEW DAYS.
HELP BY CALLING THE SUICIDE HOTLINE WITH THEM (DIAL 988):
I'M WITH SOMEONE WHO IS FEELING HOPELESS. WE NEED TO TALK TO SOMEONE RIGHT AWAY.
HELLO, I'M WITH A FRIEND WHO'S FEELING VERY DEPRESSED RIGHT NOW AND WE NEED HELP IMMEDIATELY.
I'M WITH SOMEONE WHO IS THINKING ABOUT SUICIDE.
PLEASE TELL US WHAT WE SHOULD DO.

LANGUAGE MATTERS

WHAT NOT TO DO IF SOMEONE THREATENS SUICIDE

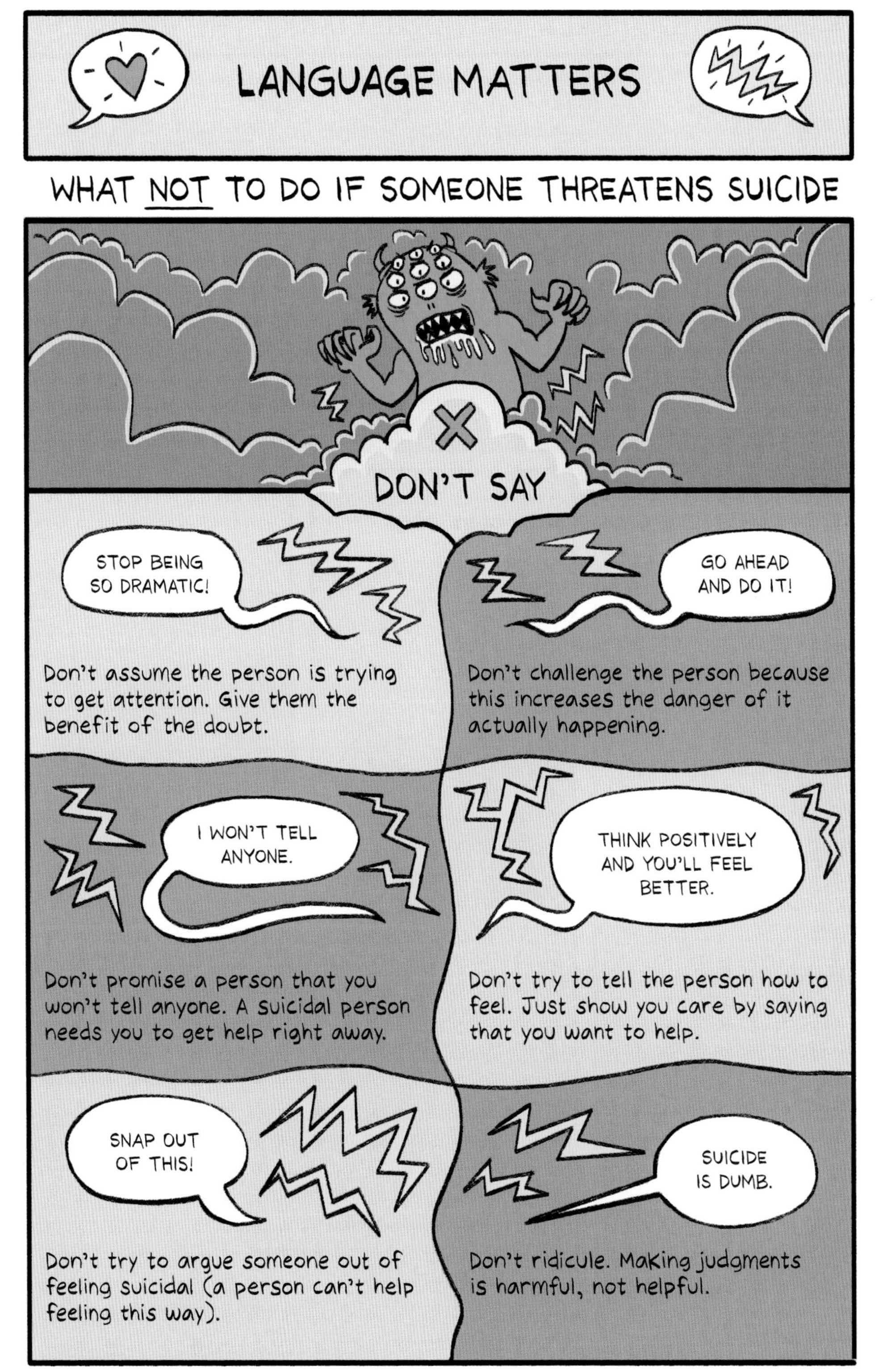
DON'T SAY
STOP BEING SO DRAMATIC!
Don't assume the person is trying to get attention. Give them the benefit of the doubt.
GO AHEAD AND DO IT!
Don't challenge the person because this increases the danger of it actually happening.
I WON'T TELL ANYONE.
Don't promise a person that you won't tell anyone. A suicidal person needs you to get help right away.
THINK POSITIVELY AND YOU'LL FEEL BETTER.
Don't try to tell the person how to feel. Just show you care by saying that you want to help.
SNAP OUT OF THIS!
Don't try to argue someone out of feeling suicidal (a person can't help feeling this way).
SUICIDE IS DUMB.
Don't ridicule. Making judgments is harmful, not helpful.

A FRIEND CAN HELP WITHOUT FIXING THE PROBLEM

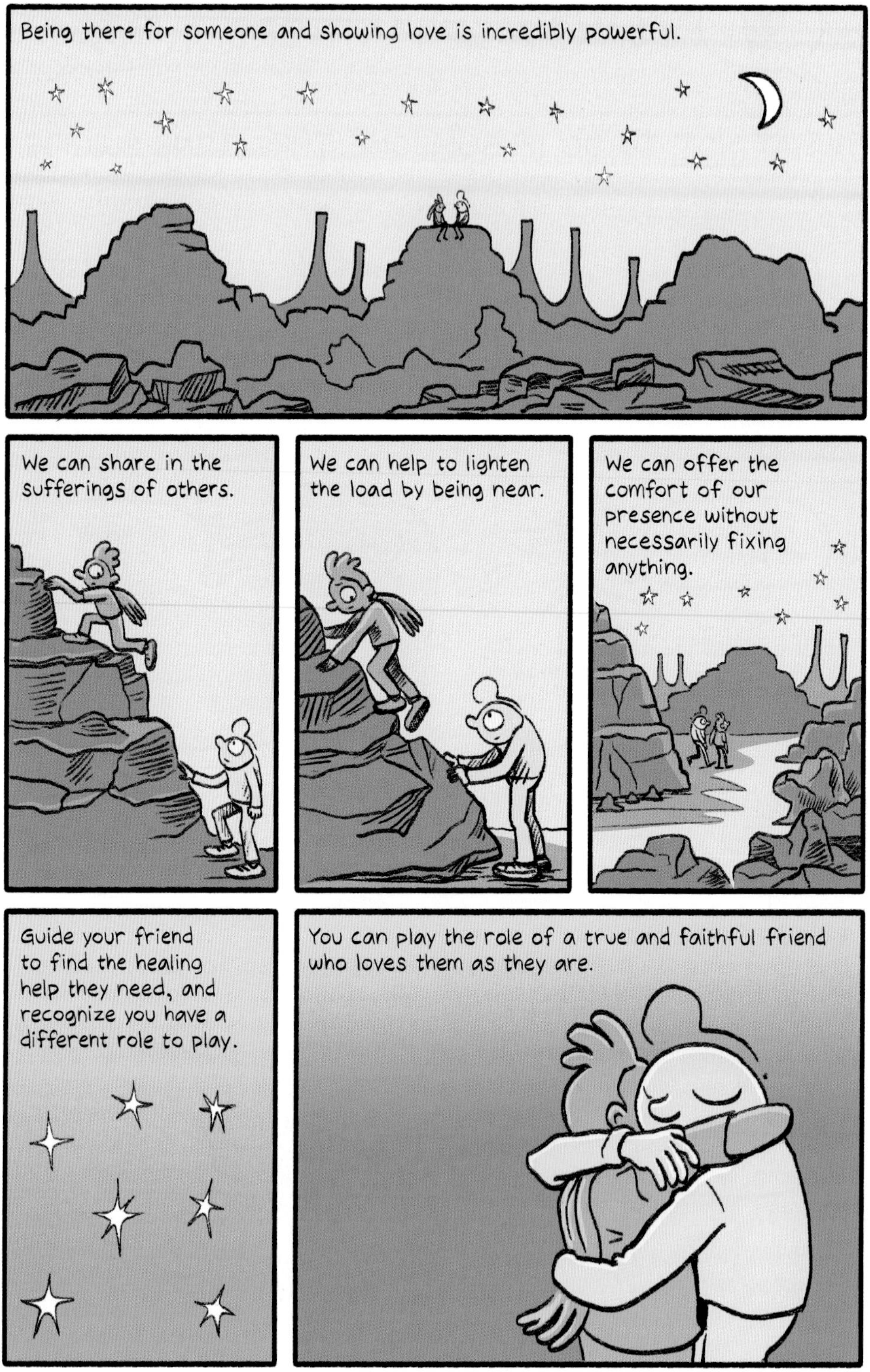
Being there for someone and showing love is incredibly powerful.
We can share in the sufferings of others.
We can help to lighten the load by being near.
We can offer the comfort of our presence without necessarily fixing anything.
Guide your friend to find the healing help they need, and recognize you have a different role to play.
You can play the role of a true and faithful friend who loves them as they are.

GUIDE YOUR FRIEND TO A TRUSTED ADULT

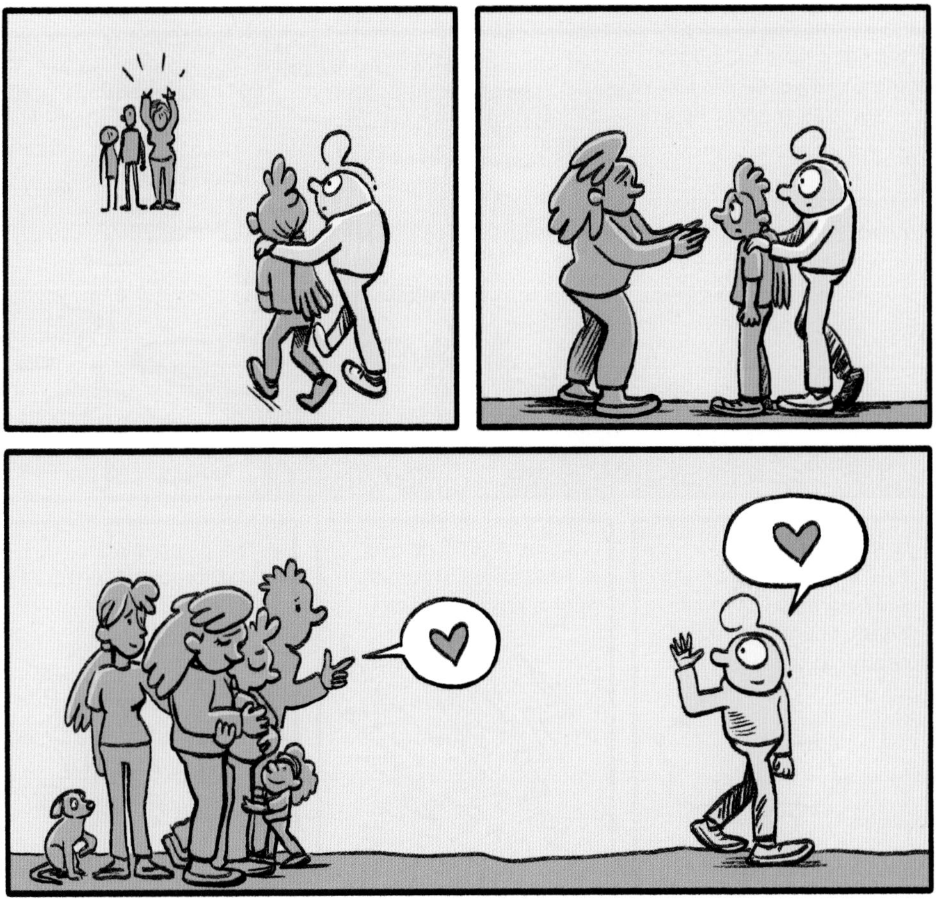

CHECK IN WITH YOURSELF

When you give a lot of your energy to support someone else, you may not be paying attention to your own needs.

It is always a good idea to take a quiet moment to yourself and see how you are doing.

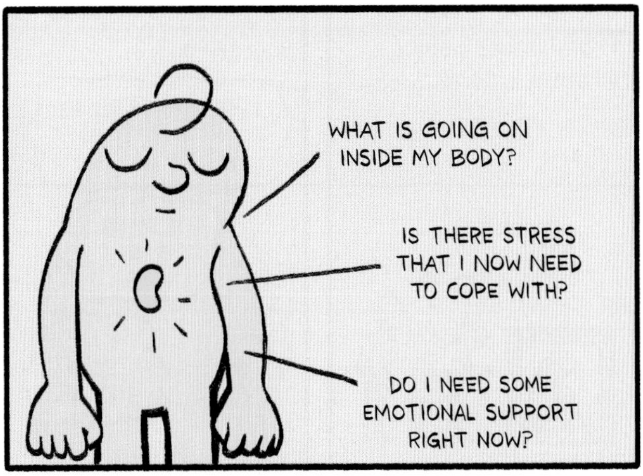
WHAT IS GOING ON INSIDE MY BODY?
IS THERE STRESS THAT I NOW NEED TO COPE WITH?
DO I NEED SOME EMOTIONAL SUPPORT RIGHT NOW?

WHAT IF YOU ARE THE ONE IN A CRISIS?

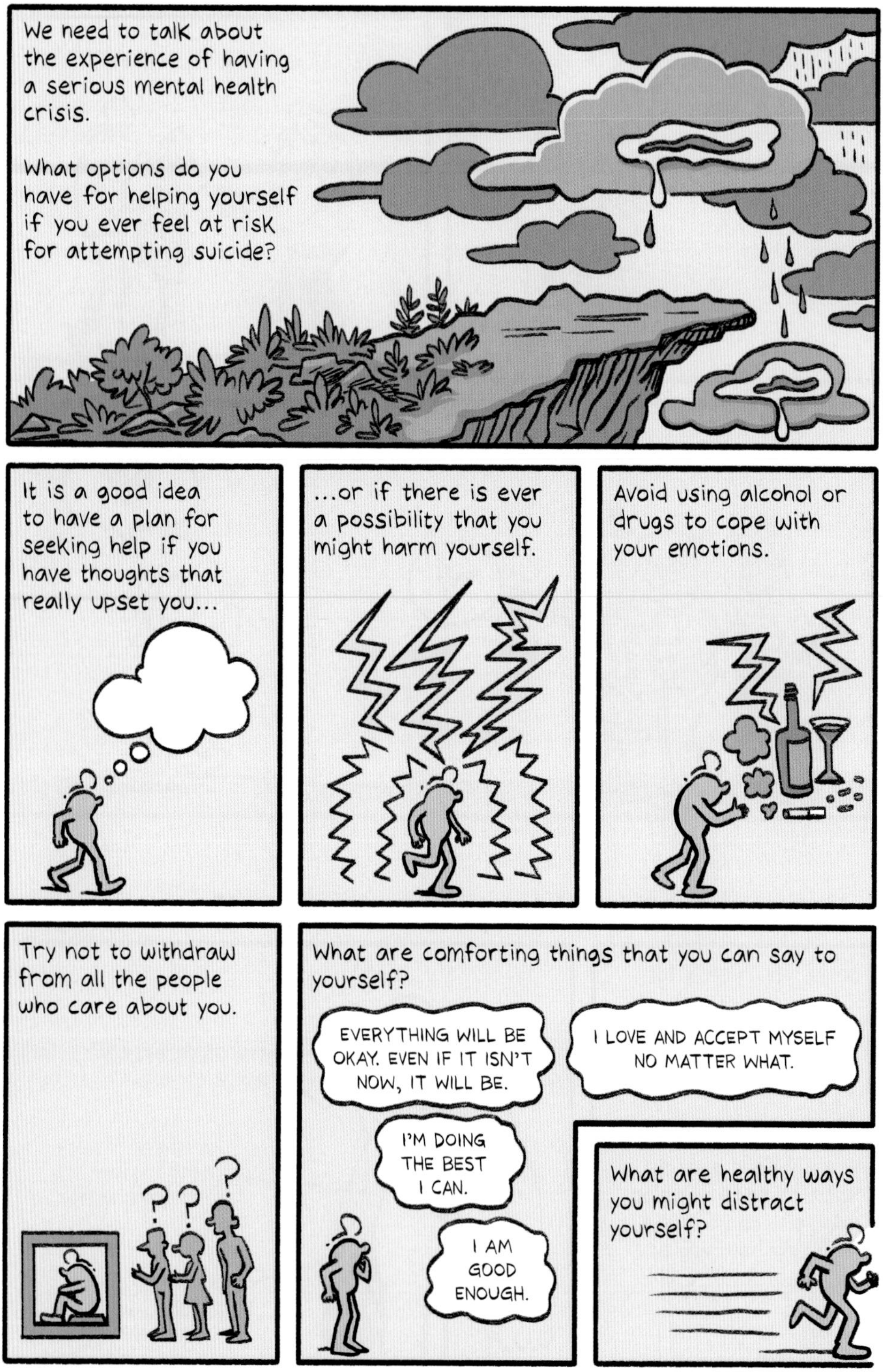
We need to talk about the experience of having a serious mental health crisis.
What options do you have for helping yourself if you ever feel at risk for attempting suicide?
It is a good idea to have a plan for seeking help if you have thoughts that really upset you...
...or if there is ever a possibility that you might harm yourself.
Avoid using alcohol or drugs to cope with your emotions.
Try not to withdraw from all the people who care about you.
What are comforting things that you can say to yourself?
EVERYTHING WILL BE OKAY. EVEN IF IT ISN'T NOW, IT WILL BE.
I LOVE AND ACCEPT MYSELF NO MATTER WHAT.
I'M DOING THE BEST I CAN.
I AM GOOD ENOUGH.
What are healthy ways you might distract yourself?

REMEMBER YOUR GOOD COPING SKILLS

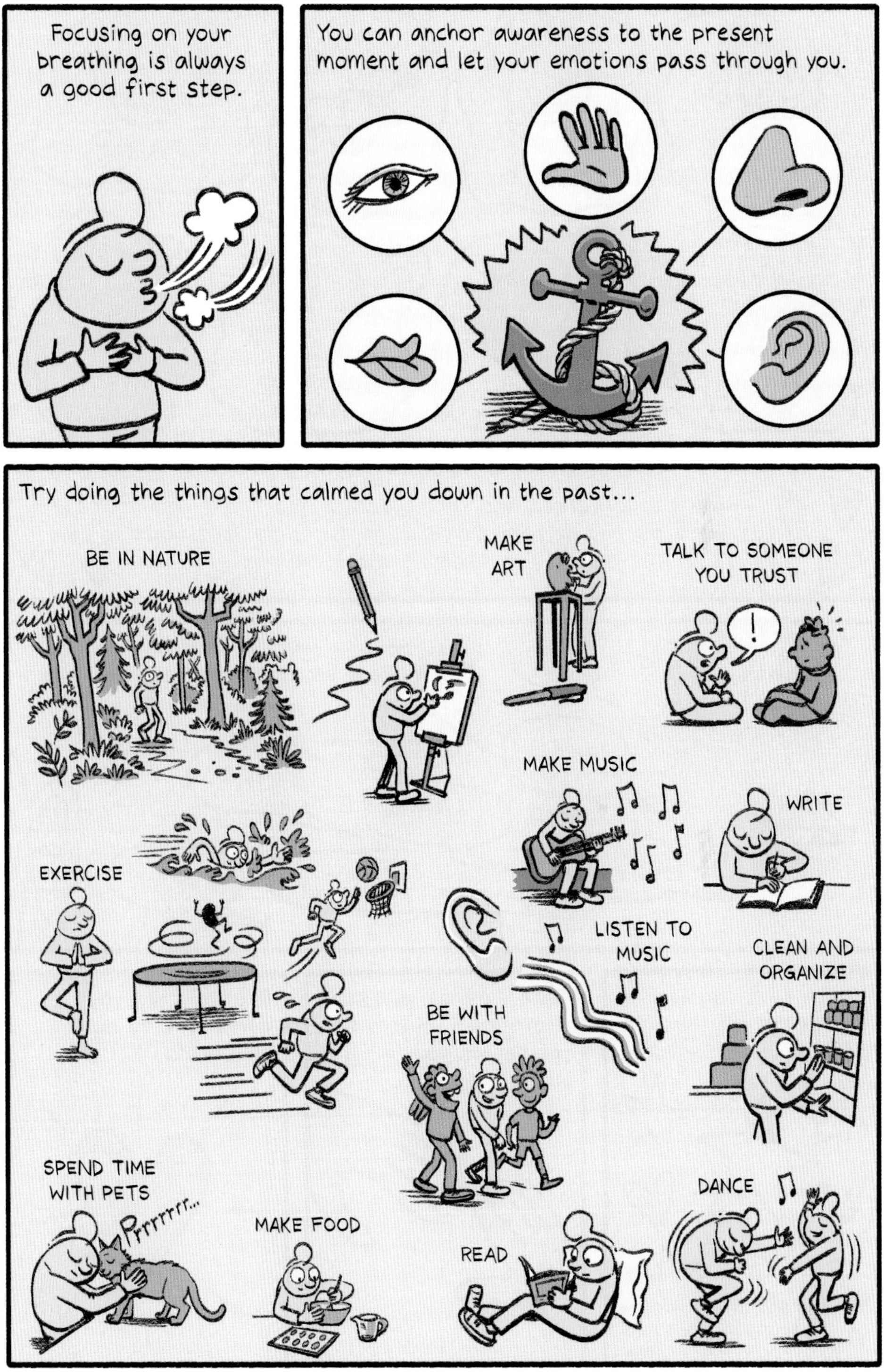

Focusing on your breathing is always a good first step.
You can anchor awareness to the present moment and let your emotions pass through you.
Try doing the things that calmed you down in the past...
BE IN NATURE
MAKE ART
TALK TO SOMEONE YOU TRUST
!
MAKE MUSIC
WRITE
EXERCISE
LISTEN TO MUSIC
CLEAN AND ORGANIZE
BE WITH FRIENDS
SPEND TIME WITH PETS
Prrrrrrr...
MAKE FOOD
READ
DANCE

WHO IS AN ADULT THAT YOU TRUST AND CAN TALK TO?

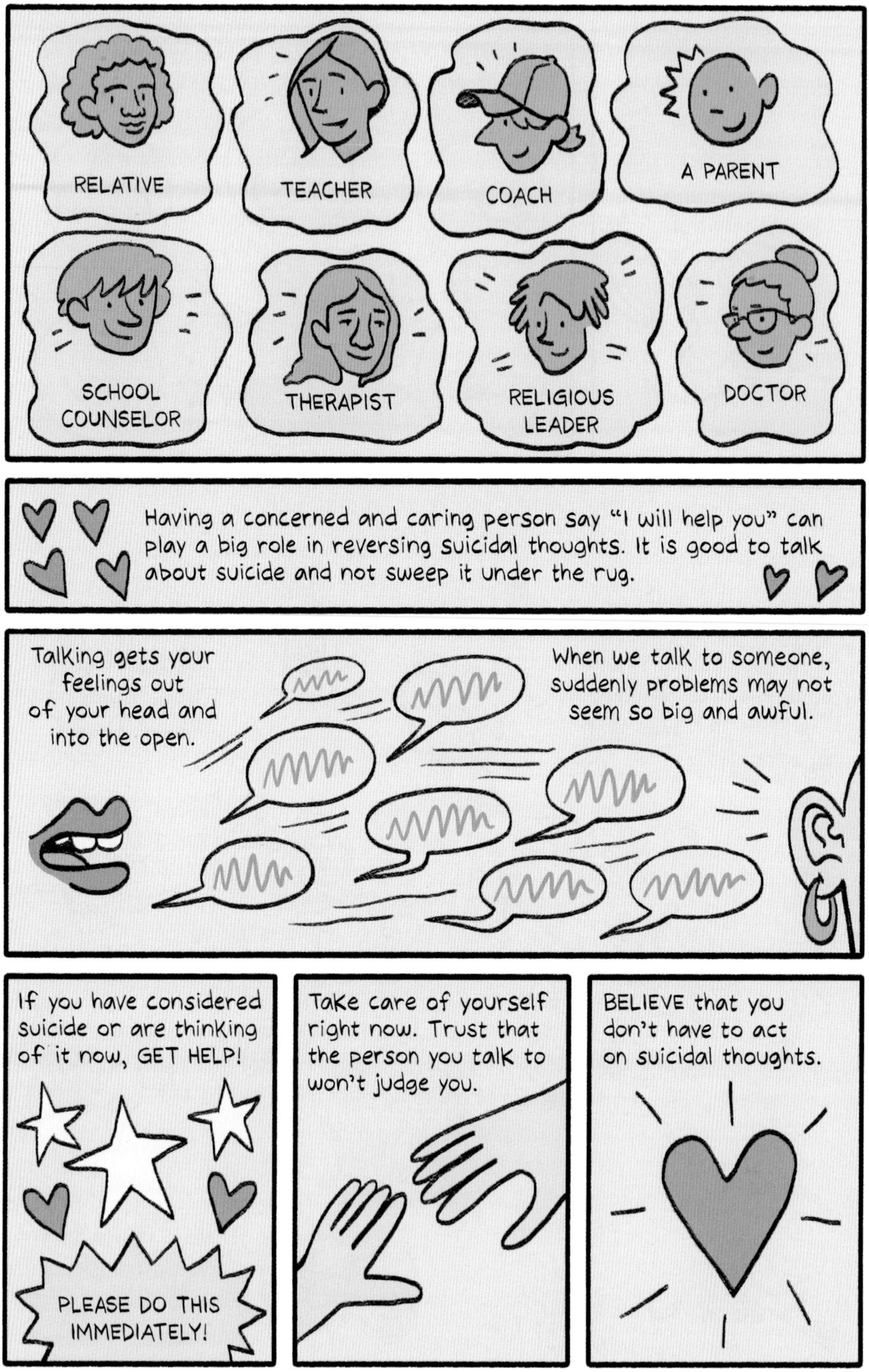
RELATIVE
TEACHER
COACH
A PARENT
SCHOOL COUNSELOR
THERAPIST
RELIGIOUS LEADER
DOCTOR
Having a concerned and caring person say "I will help you" can play a big role in reversing suicidal thoughts. It is good to talk about suicide and not sweep it under the rug.
Talking gets your feelings out of your head and into the open.
When we talk to someone, suddenly problems may not seem so big and awful.
If you have considered suicide or are thinking of it now, GET HELP!
PLEASE DO THIS IMMEDIATELY!
Take care of yourself right now. Trust that the person you talk to won't judge you.
BELIEVE that you don't have to act on suicidal thoughts.

START THE AWKWARD CONVERSATION

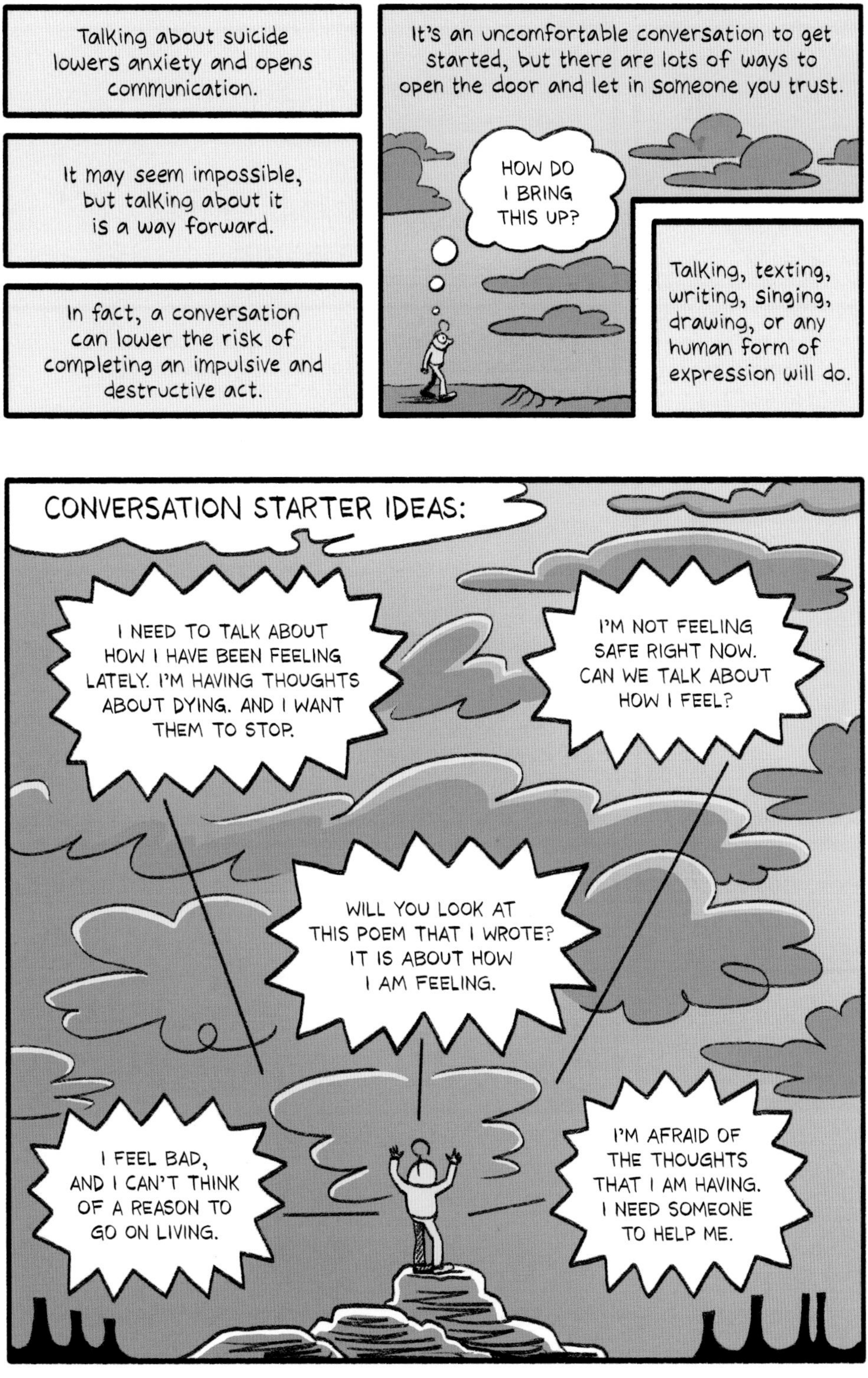
Talking about suicide lowers anxiety and opens communication.
It may seem impossible, but talking about it is a way forward.
In fact, a conversation can lower the risk of completing an impulsive and destructive act.
It's an uncomfortable conversation to get started, but there are lots of ways to open the door and let in someone you trust.
HOW DO I BRING THIS UP?
Talking, texting, writing, singing, drawing, or any human form of expression will do.
CONVERSATION STARTER IDEAS:
I NEED TO TALK ABOUT HOW I HAVE BEEN FEELING LATELY. I'M HAVING THOUGHTS ABOUT DYING. AND I WANT THEM TO STOP.
I'M NOT FEELING SAFE RIGHT NOW. CAN WE TALK ABOUT HOW I FEEL?
WILL YOU LOOK AT THIS POEM THAT I WROTE? IT IS ABOUT HOW I AM FEELING.
I FEEL BAD, AND I CAN'T THINK OF A REASON TO GO ON LIVING.
I'M AFRAID OF THE THOUGHTS THAT I AM HAVING. I NEED SOMEONE TO HELP ME.

CRISIS RESOURCES

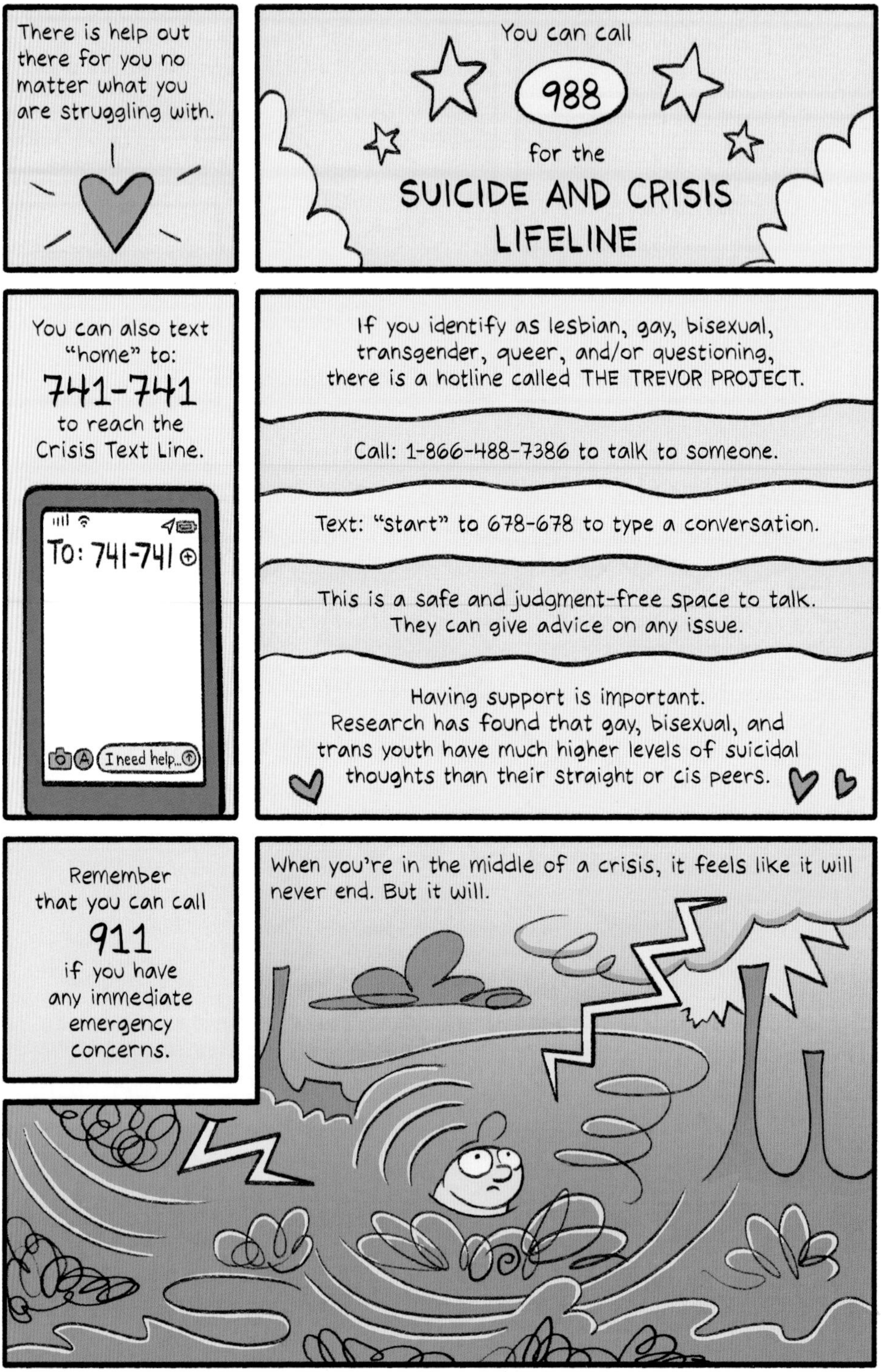
There is help out there for you no matter what you are struggling with.
You can call
988
for the
SUICIDE AND CRISIS LIFELINE
You can also text "home" to:
741-741
to reach the Crisis Text Line.
TO: 741-741
I need help...
If you identify as lesbian, gay, bisexual, transgender, queer, and/or questioning, there is a hotline called THE TREVOR PROJECT.
Call: 1-866-488-7386 to talk to someone.
Text: "start" to 678-678 to type a conversation.
This is a safe and judgment-free space to talk. They can give advice on any issue.
Having support is important. Research has found that gay, bisexual, and trans youth have much higher levels of suicidal thoughts than their straight or cis peers.
Remember that you can call
911
if you have any immediate emergency concerns.
When you're in the middle of a crisis, it feels like it will never end. But it will.

CLIMBING OUT TO A BETTER PLACE

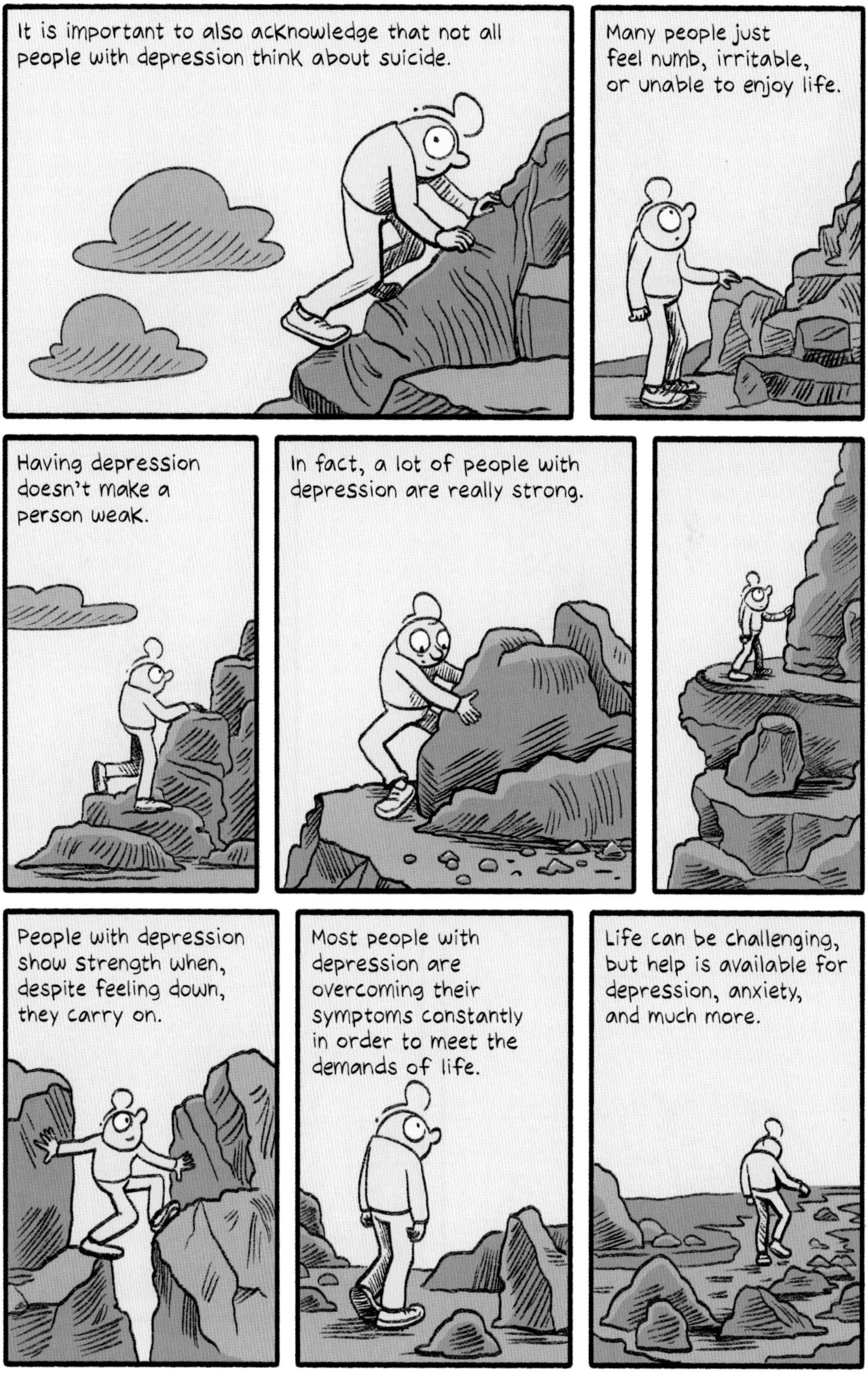
It is important to also acknowledge that not all people with depression think about suicide.
Many people just feel numb, irritable, or unable to enjoy life.
Having depression doesn't make a person weak.
In fact, a lot of people with depression are really strong.
People with depression show strength when, despite feeling down, they carry on.
Most people with depression are overcoming their symptoms constantly in order to meet the demands of life.
Life can be challenging, but help is available for depression, anxiety, and much more.

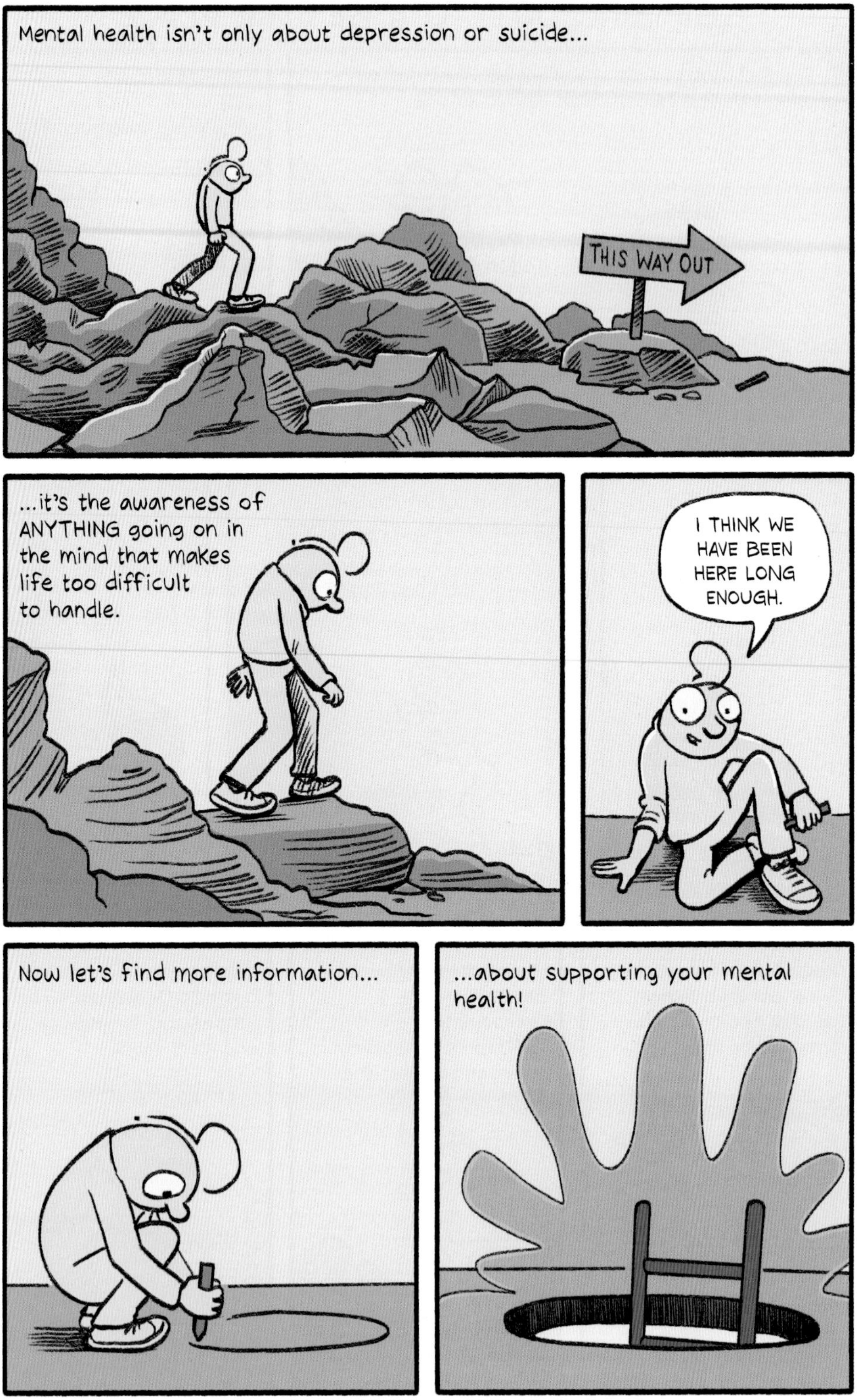
Mental health isn't only about depression or suicide...
THIS WAY OUT
...it's the awareness of ANYTHING going on in the mind that makes life too difficult to handle.
I THINK WE HAVE BEEN HERE LONG ENOUGH.
Now let's find more information...
...about supporting your mental health!

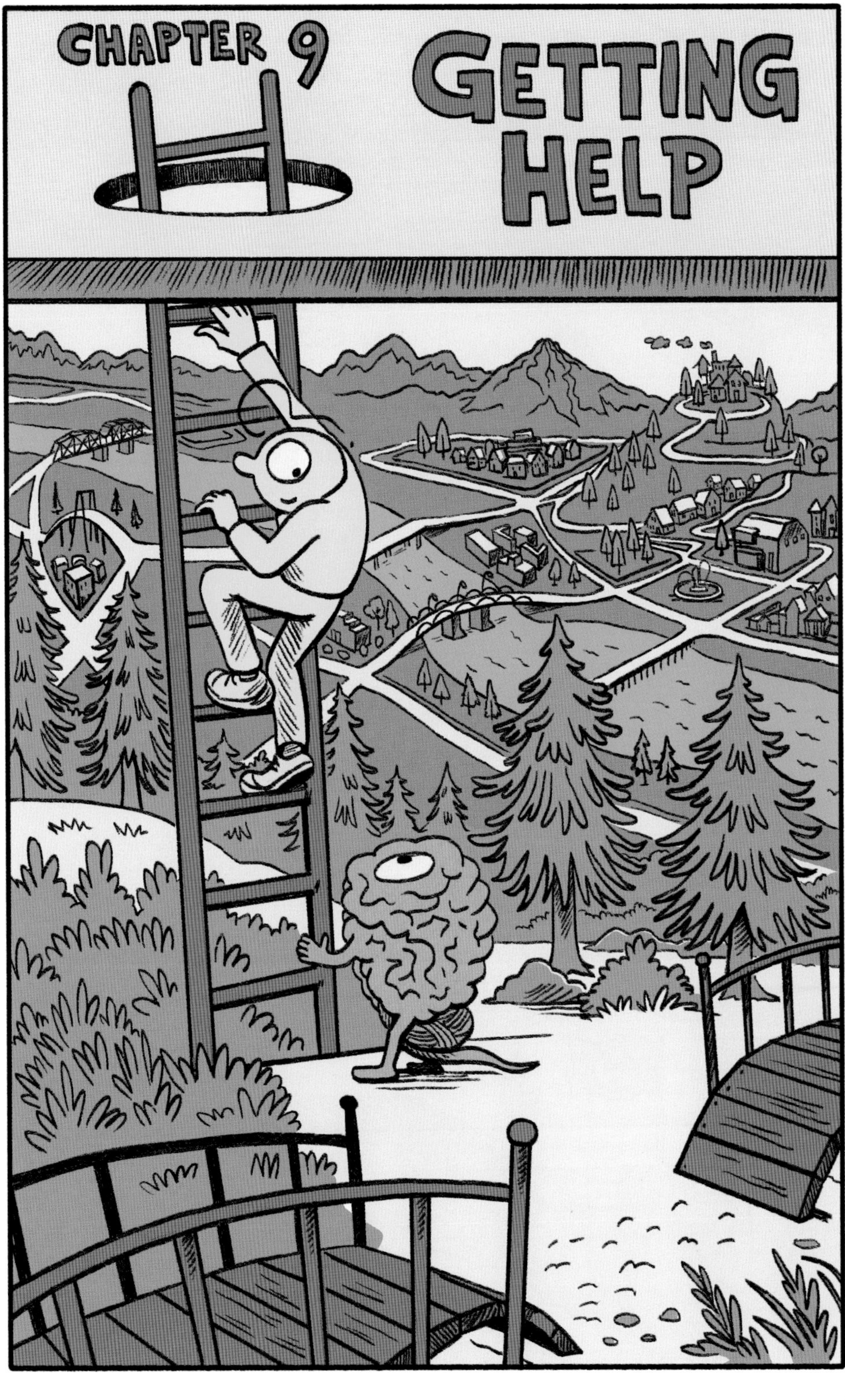
CHAPTER 9
GETTING HELP

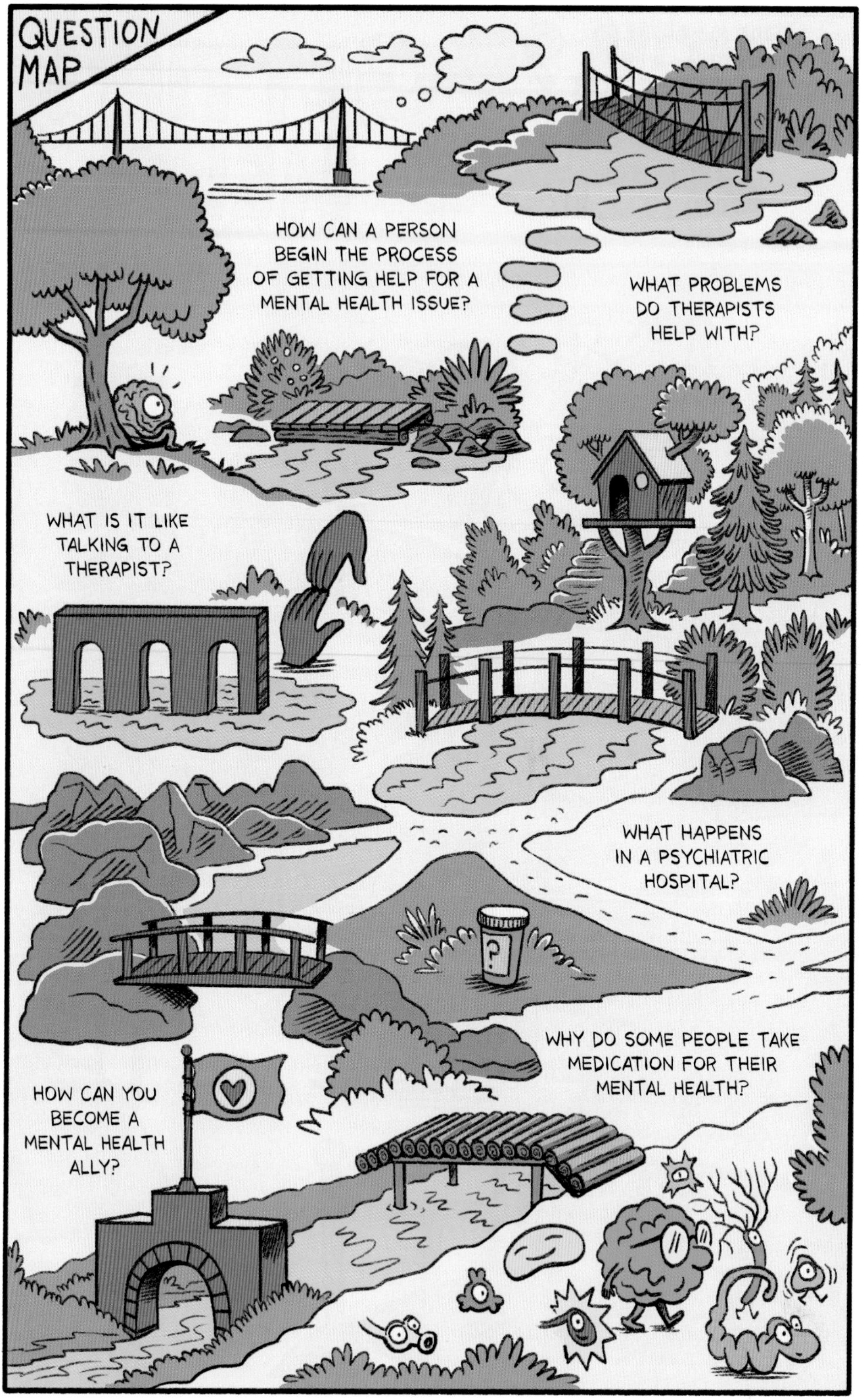
QUESTION MAP
HOW CAN A PERSON BEGIN THE PROCESS OF GETTING HELP FOR A MENTAL HEALTH ISSUE?
WHAT PROBLEMS DO THERAPISTS HELP WITH?
WHAT IS IT LIKE TALKING TO A THERAPIST?
WHAT HAPPENS IN A PSYCHIATRIC HOSPITAL?
WHY DO SOME PEOPLE TAKE MEDICATION FOR THEIR MENTAL HEALTH?
HOW CAN YOU BECOME A MENTAL HEALTH ALLY?

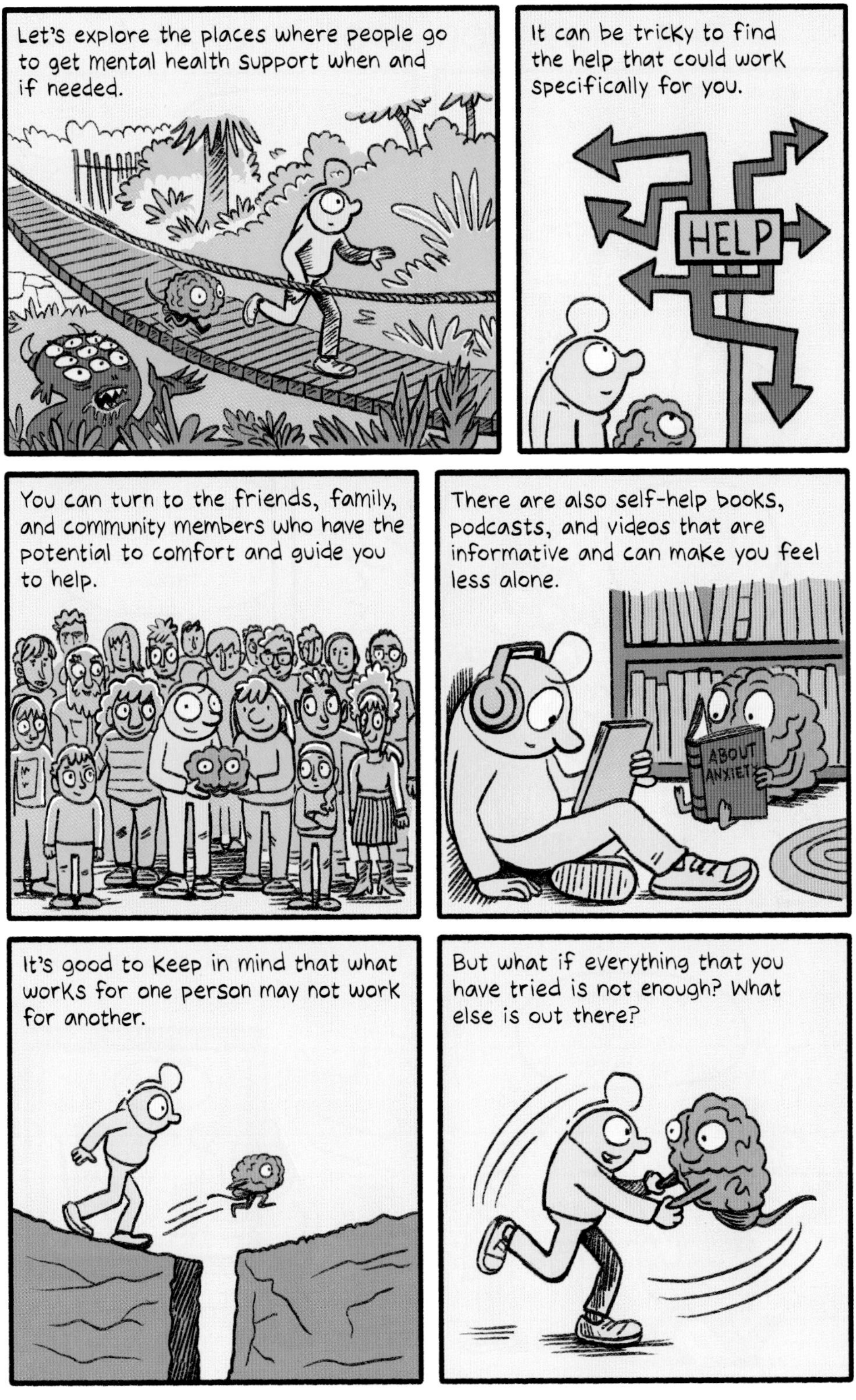
Let's explore the places where people go to get mental health support when and if needed.
It can be tricky to find the help that could work specifically for you.
HELP
You can turn to the friends, family, and community members who have the potential to comfort and guide you to help.
There are also self-help books, podcasts, and videos that are informative and can make you feel less alone.
ABOUT ANXIETY
It's good to keep in mind that what works for one person may not work for another.
But what if everything that you have tried is not enough? What else is out there?

THE WIDE WORLD OF THERAPY

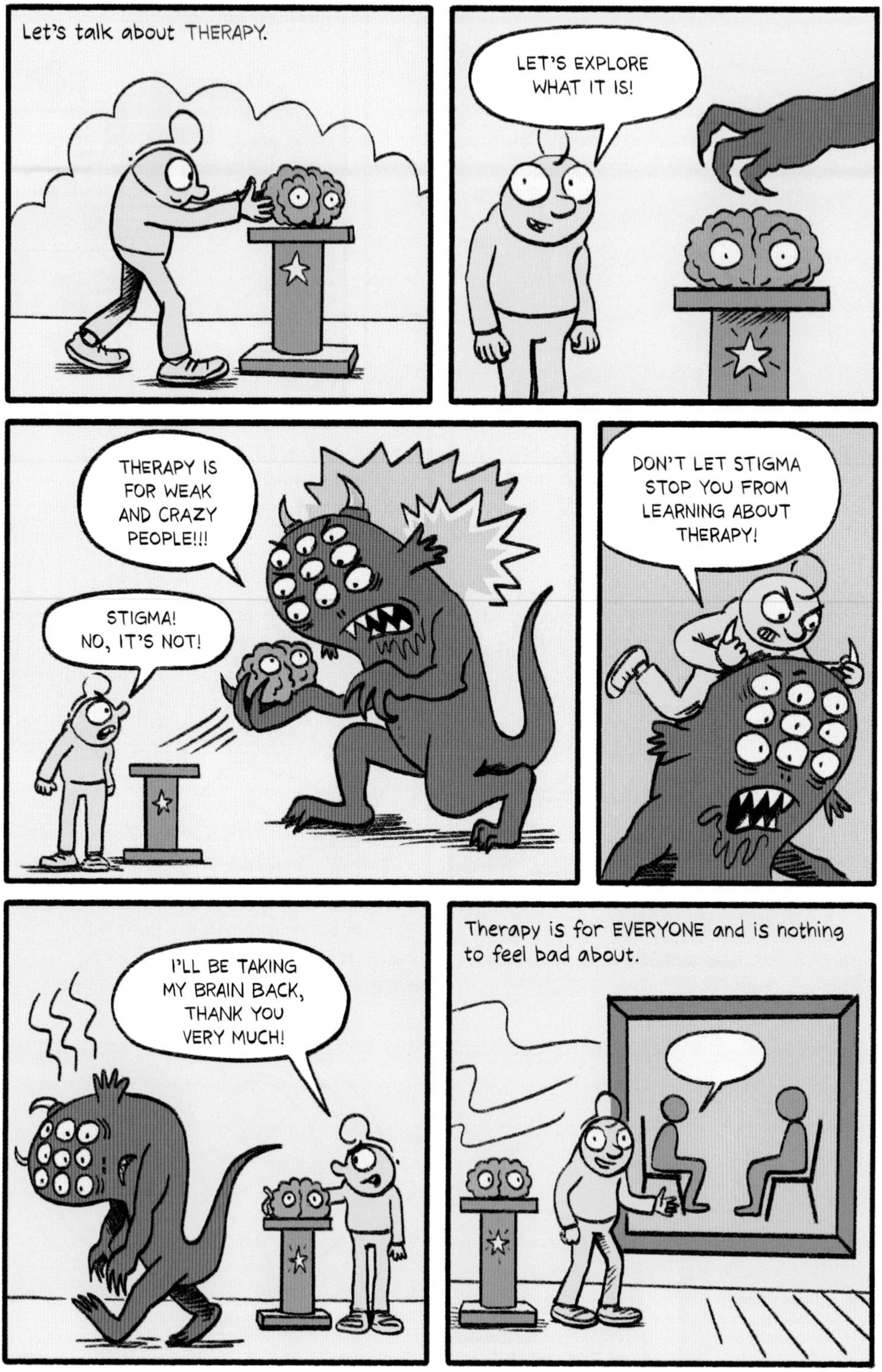

Let's talk about THERAPY.
LET'S EXPLORE WHAT IT IS!
THERAPY IS FOR WEAK AND CRAZY PEOPLE!!!
STIGMA! NO, IT'S NOT!
DON'T LET STIGMA STOP YOU FROM LEARNING ABOUT THERAPY!
I'LL BE TAKING MY BRAIN BACK, THANK YOU VERY MUCH!
Therapy is for EVERYONE and is nothing to feel bad about.

Did you know that one in six youths (ages 6 to 17) experience a mental health disorder each year?*

THAT'S MILLIONS OF PEOPLE!

Mental health disorders are treatable.

PEOPLE CAN RECOVER.

People in any culture can experience mental health disorder symptoms, though they might think about mental health or describe their symptoms differently.

If treatment is needed, talking with a THERAPIST who understands your culture might be helpful.

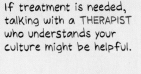

All therapists are different. They work in different specialties that serve the many reasons people go to therapy.

The important thing is to get the help that is right for you.

*According to the report *The Comprehensive Community Mental Health Services for Children and Their Families, Evaluation Findings,* written by the U.S. Department of Health & Human Services agency SAMHSA and delivered to Congress in 2011.

WHAT CAN THERAPISTS HELP WITH?

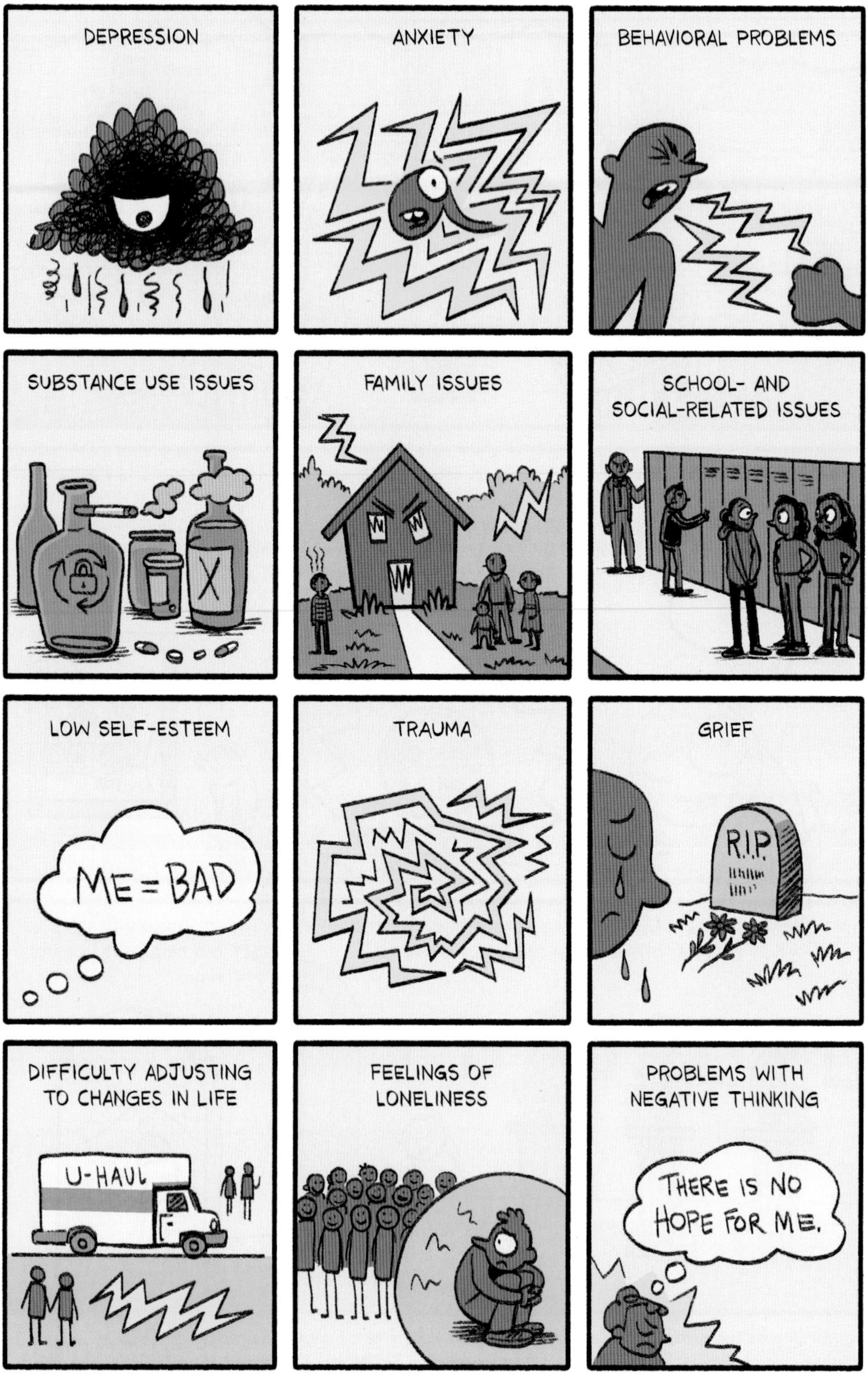
DEPRESSION
ANXIETY
BEHAVIORAL PROBLEMS
SUBSTANCE USE ISSUES
FAMILY ISSUES
SCHOOL- AND SOCIAL-RELATED ISSUES
LOW SELF-ESTEEM
ME = BAD
TRAUMA
GRIEF
R.I.P.
DIFFICULTY ADJUSTING TO CHANGES IN LIFE
U-HAUL
FEELINGS OF LONELINESS
PROBLEMS WITH NEGATIVE THINKING
THERE IS NO HOPE FOR ME.

WHAT OTHER ISSUES CAN THERAPISTS HELP WITH?

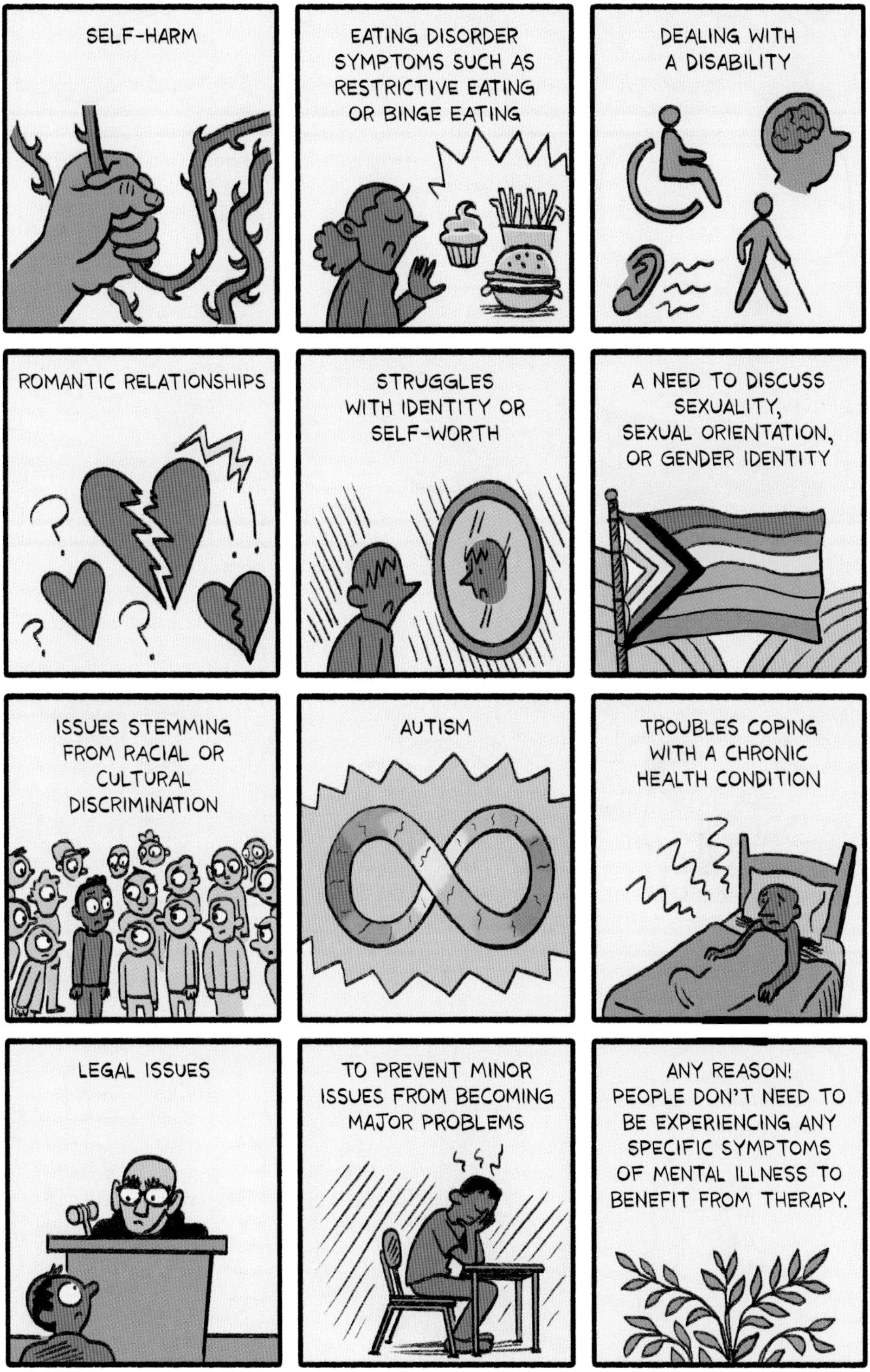
SELF-HARM
EATING DISORDER SYMPTOMS SUCH AS RESTRICTIVE EATING OR BINGE EATING
DEALING WITH A DISABILITY
ROMANTIC RELATIONSHIPS
STRUGGLES WITH IDENTITY OR SELF-WORTH
A NEED TO DISCUSS SEXUALITY, SEXUAL ORIENTATION, OR GENDER IDENTITY
ISSUES STEMMING FROM RACIAL OR CULTURAL DISCRIMINATION
AUTISM
TROUBLES COPING WITH A CHRONIC HEALTH CONDITION
LEGAL ISSUES
TO PREVENT MINOR ISSUES FROM BECOMING MAJOR PROBLEMS
ANY REASON! PEOPLE DON'T NEED TO BE EXPERIENCING ANY SPECIFIC SYMPTOMS OF MENTAL ILLNESS TO BENEFIT FROM THERAPY.

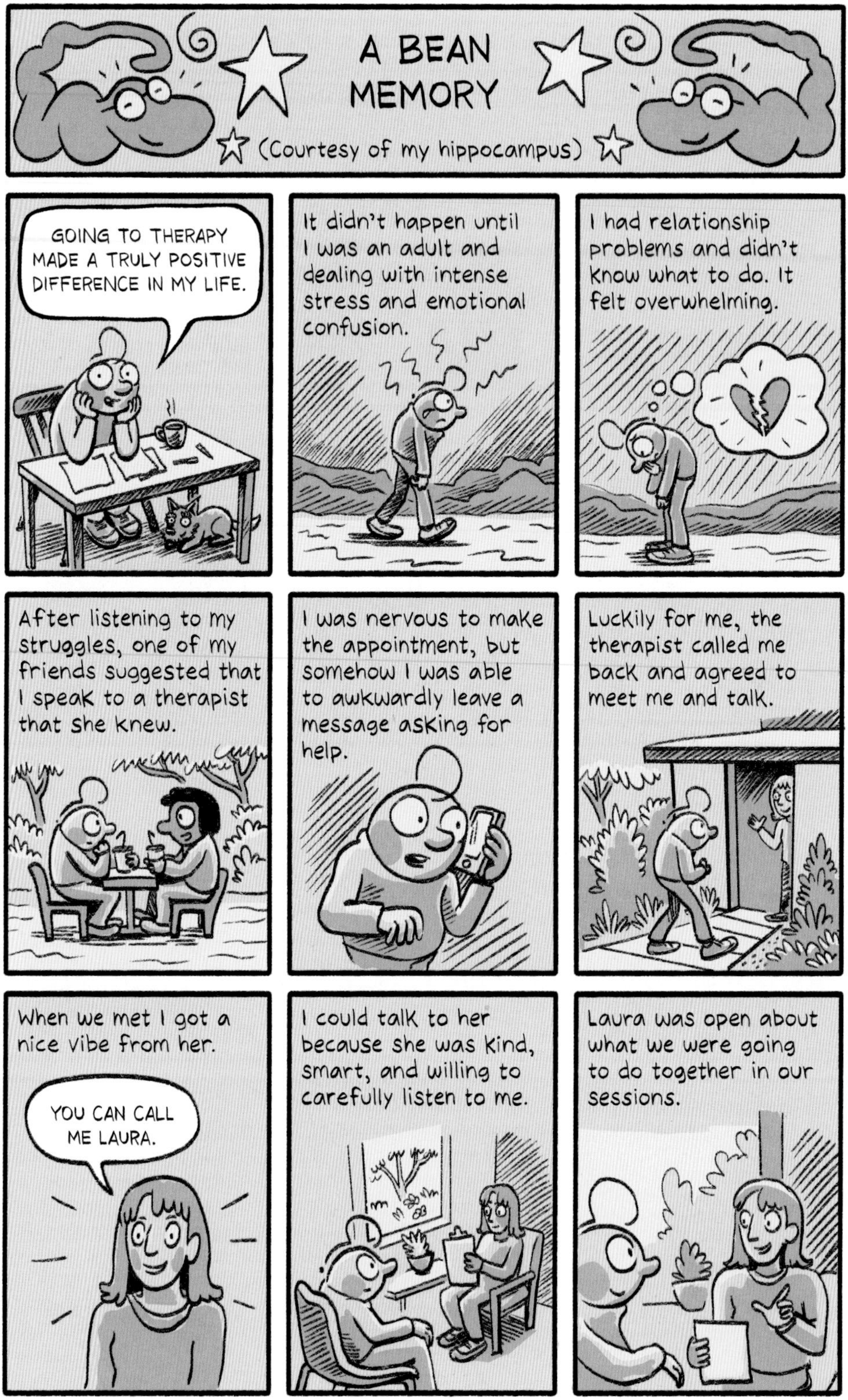
A BEAN MEMORY
(Courtesy of my hippocampus)
GOING TO THERAPY MADE A TRULY POSITIVE DIFFERENCE IN MY LIFE.
It didn't happen until I was an adult and dealing with intense stress and emotional confusion.
I had relationship problems and didn't know what to do. It felt overwhelming.
After listening to my struggles, one of my friends suggested that I speak to a therapist that she knew.
I was nervous to make the appointment, but somehow I was able to awkwardly leave a message asking for help.
Luckily for me, the therapist called me back and agreed to meet me and talk.
When we met I got a nice vibe from her.
YOU CAN CALL ME LAURA.
I could talk to her because she was kind, smart, and willing to carefully listen to me.
Laura was open about what we were going to do together in our sessions.

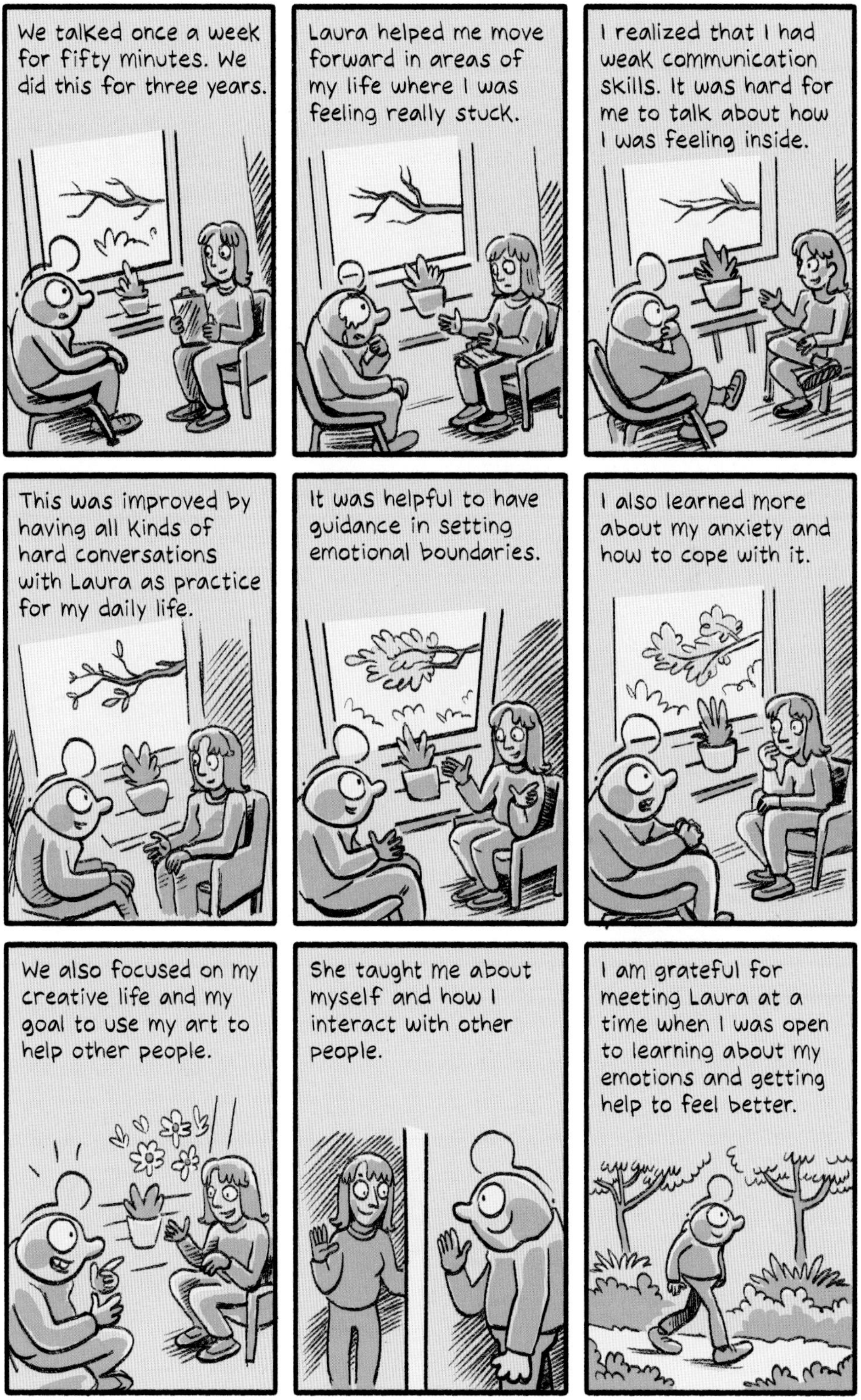
We talked once a week for fifty minutes. We did this for three years.
Laura helped me move forward in areas of my life where I was feeling really stuck.
I realized that I had weak communication skills. It was hard for me to talk about how I was feeling inside.
This was improved by having all kinds of hard conversations with Laura as practice for my daily life.
It was helpful to have guidance in setting emotional boundaries.
I also learned more about my anxiety and how to cope with it.
We also focused on my creative life and my goal to use my art to help other people.
She taught me about myself and how I interact with other people.
I am grateful for meeting Laura at a time when I was open to learning about my emotions and getting help to feel better.

CAN WE TALK ABOUT TALK THERAPY?

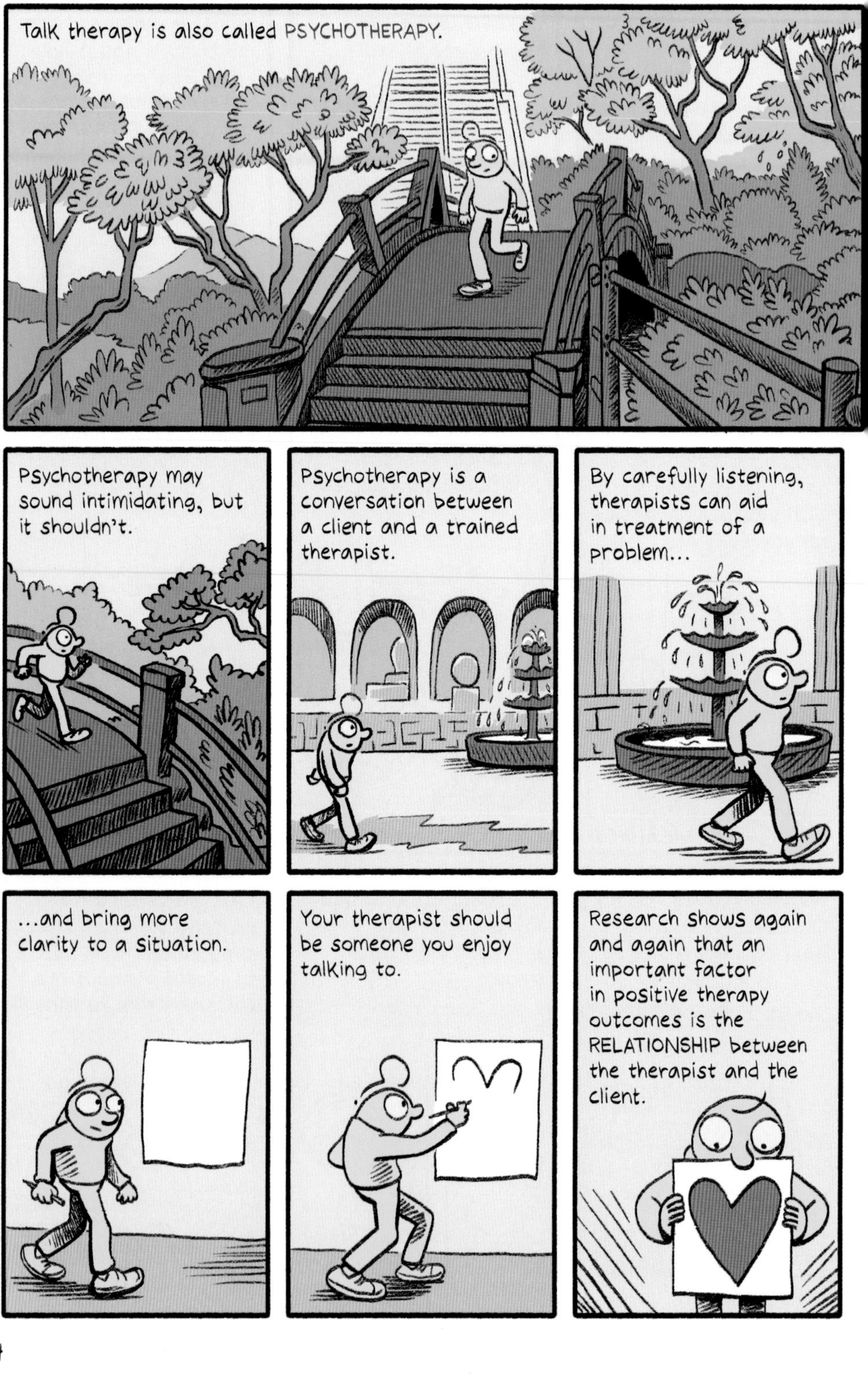
Talk therapy is also called PSYCHOTHERAPY.
Psychotherapy may sound intimidating, but it shouldn't.
Psychotherapy is a conversation between a client and a trained therapist.
By carefully listening, therapists can aid in treatment of a problem...
...and bring more clarity to a situation.
Your therapist should be someone you enjoy talking to.
Research shows again and again that an important factor in positive therapy outcomes is the RELATIONSHIP between the therapist and the client.

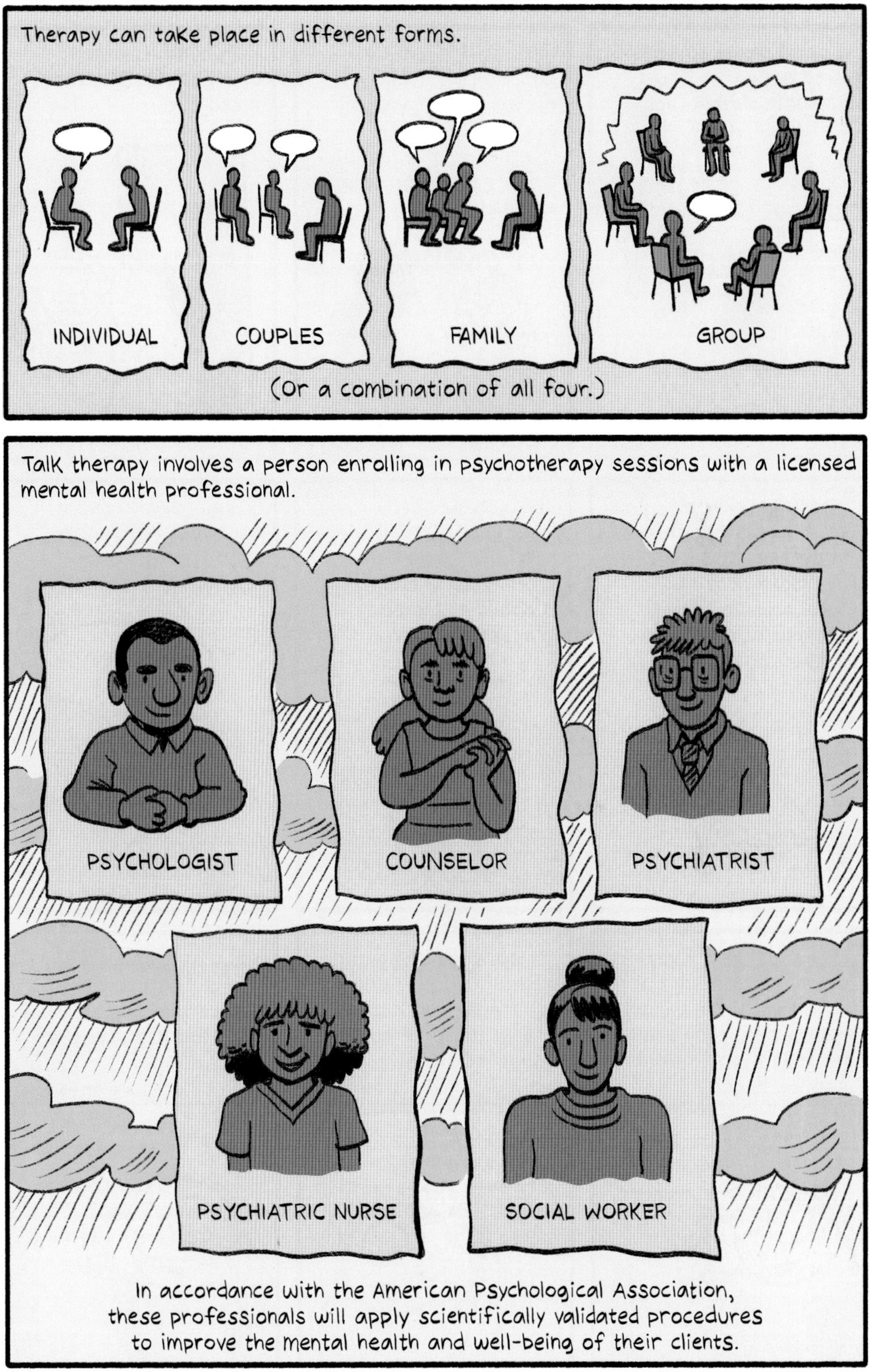
Therapy can take place in different forms.
INDIVIDUAL
COUPLES
FAMILY
GROUP
(Or a combination of all four.)
Talk therapy involves a person enrolling in psychotherapy sessions with a licensed mental health professional.
PSYCHOLOGIST
COUNSELOR
PSYCHIATRIST
PSYCHIATRIC NURSE
SOCIAL WORKER
In accordance with the American Psychological Association, these professionals will apply scientifically validated procedures to improve the mental health and well-being of their clients.

HOW DO I BEGIN THE PROCESS OF THERAPY?

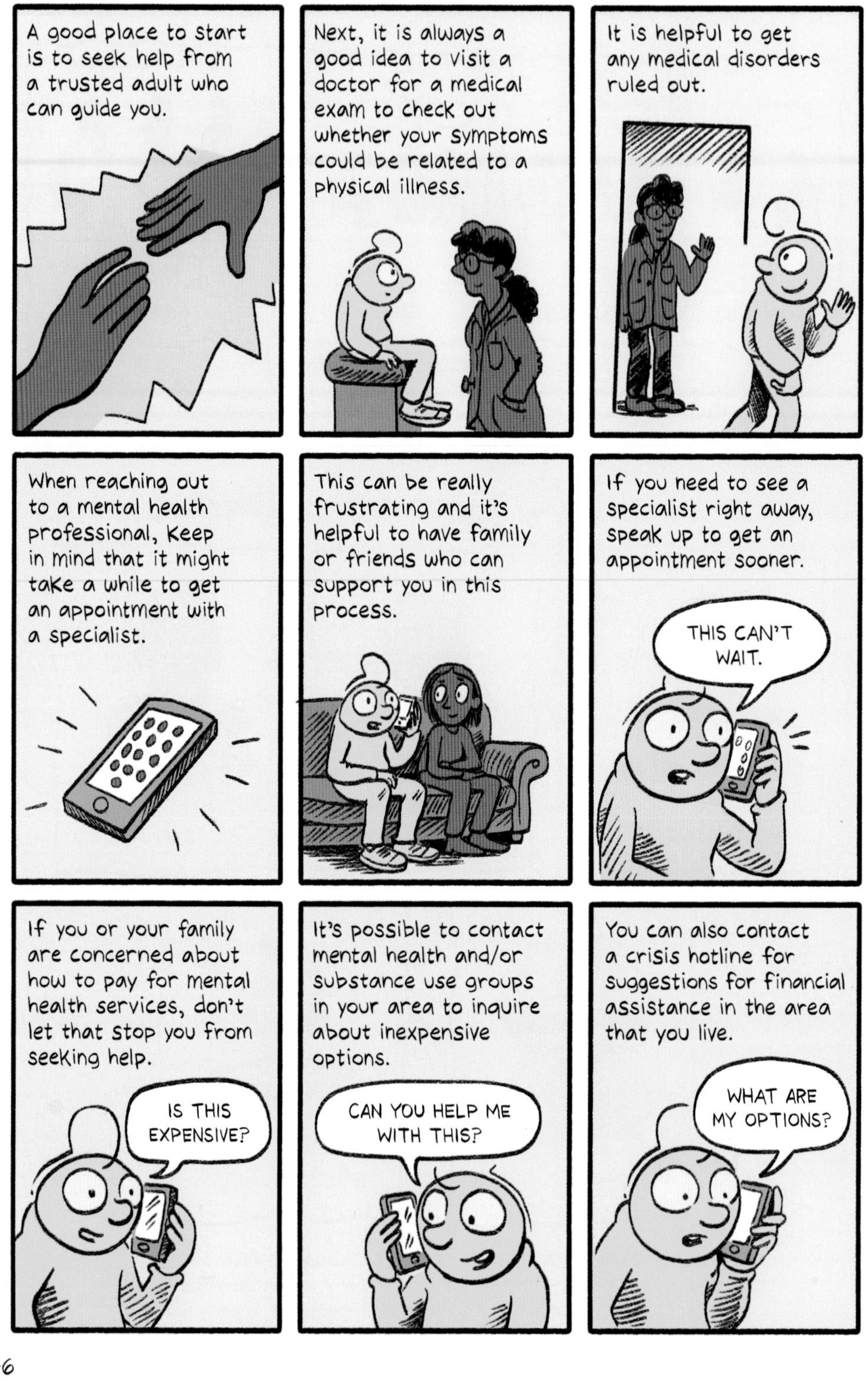
A good place to start is to seek help from a trusted adult who can guide you.
Next, it is always a good idea to visit a doctor for a medical exam to check out whether your symptoms could be related to a physical illness.
It is helpful to get any medical disorders ruled out.
When reaching out to a mental health professional, keep in mind that it might take a while to get an appointment with a specialist.
This can be really frustrating and it's helpful to have family or friends who can support you in this process.
If you need to see a specialist right away, speak up to get an appointment sooner.
THIS CAN'T WAIT.
If you or your family are concerned about how to pay for mental health services, don't let that stop you from seeking help.
IS THIS EXPENSIVE?
It's possible to contact mental health and/or substance use groups in your area to inquire about inexpensive options.
CAN YOU HELP ME WITH THIS?
You can also contact a crisis hotline for suggestions for financial assistance in the area that you live.
WHAT ARE MY OPTIONS?

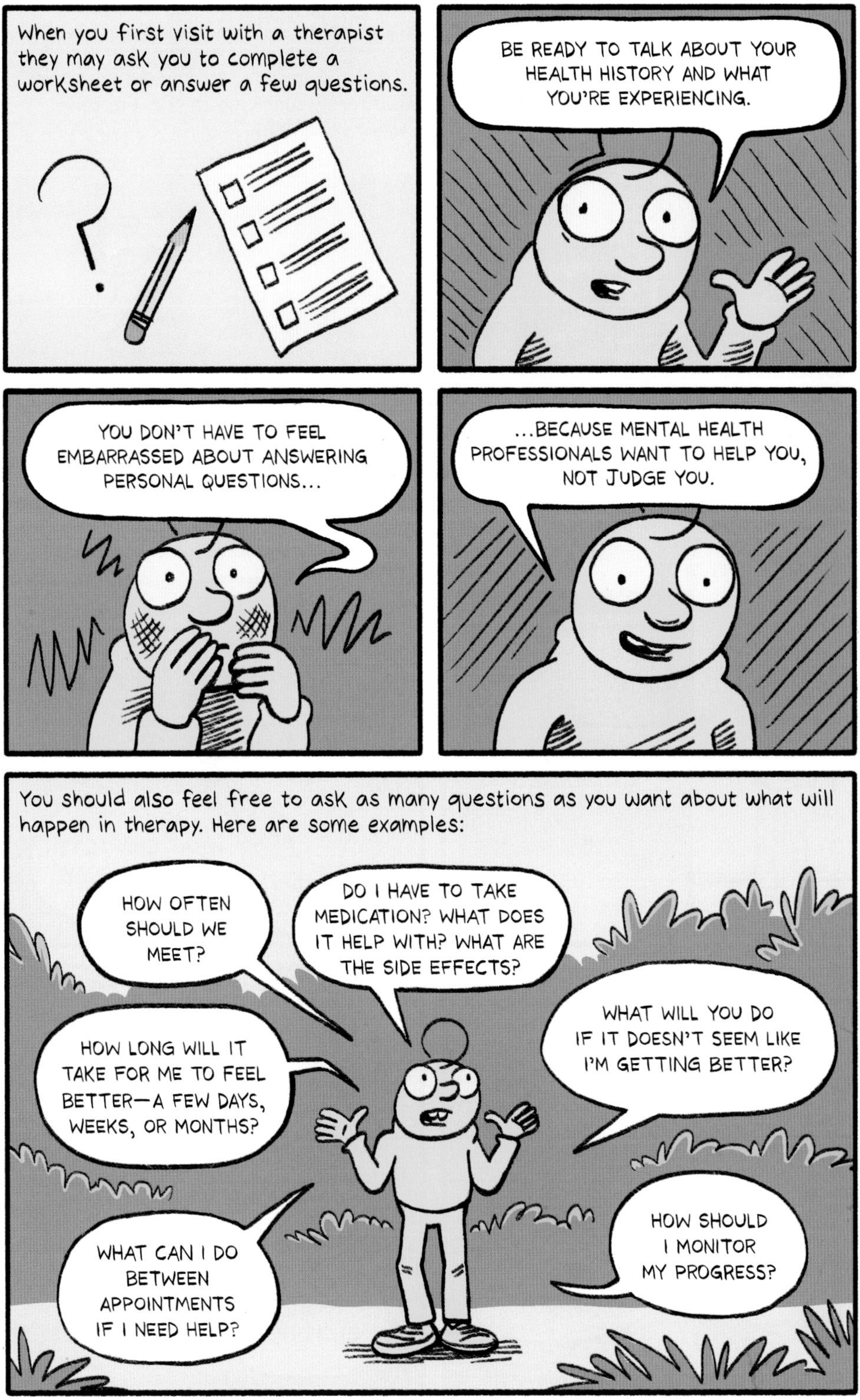
When you first visit with a therapist they may ask you to complete a worksheet or answer a few questions.
BE READY TO TALK ABOUT YOUR HEALTH HISTORY AND WHAT YOU'RE EXPERIENCING.
YOU DON'T HAVE TO FEEL EMBARRASSED ABOUT ANSWERING PERSONAL QUESTIONS...
...BECAUSE MENTAL HEALTH PROFESSIONALS WANT TO HELP YOU, NOT JUDGE YOU.
You should also feel free to ask as many questions as you want about what will happen in therapy. Here are some examples:
HOW OFTEN SHOULD WE MEET?
DO I HAVE TO TAKE MEDICATION? WHAT DOES IT HELP WITH? WHAT ARE THE SIDE EFFECTS?
HOW LONG WILL IT TAKE FOR ME TO FEEL BETTER—A FEW DAYS, WEEKS, OR MONTHS?
WHAT WILL YOU DO IF IT DOESN'T SEEM LIKE I'M GETTING BETTER?
WHAT CAN I DO BETWEEN APPOINTMENTS IF I NEED HELP?
HOW SHOULD I MONITOR MY PROGRESS?

TALKING TO A THERAPIST

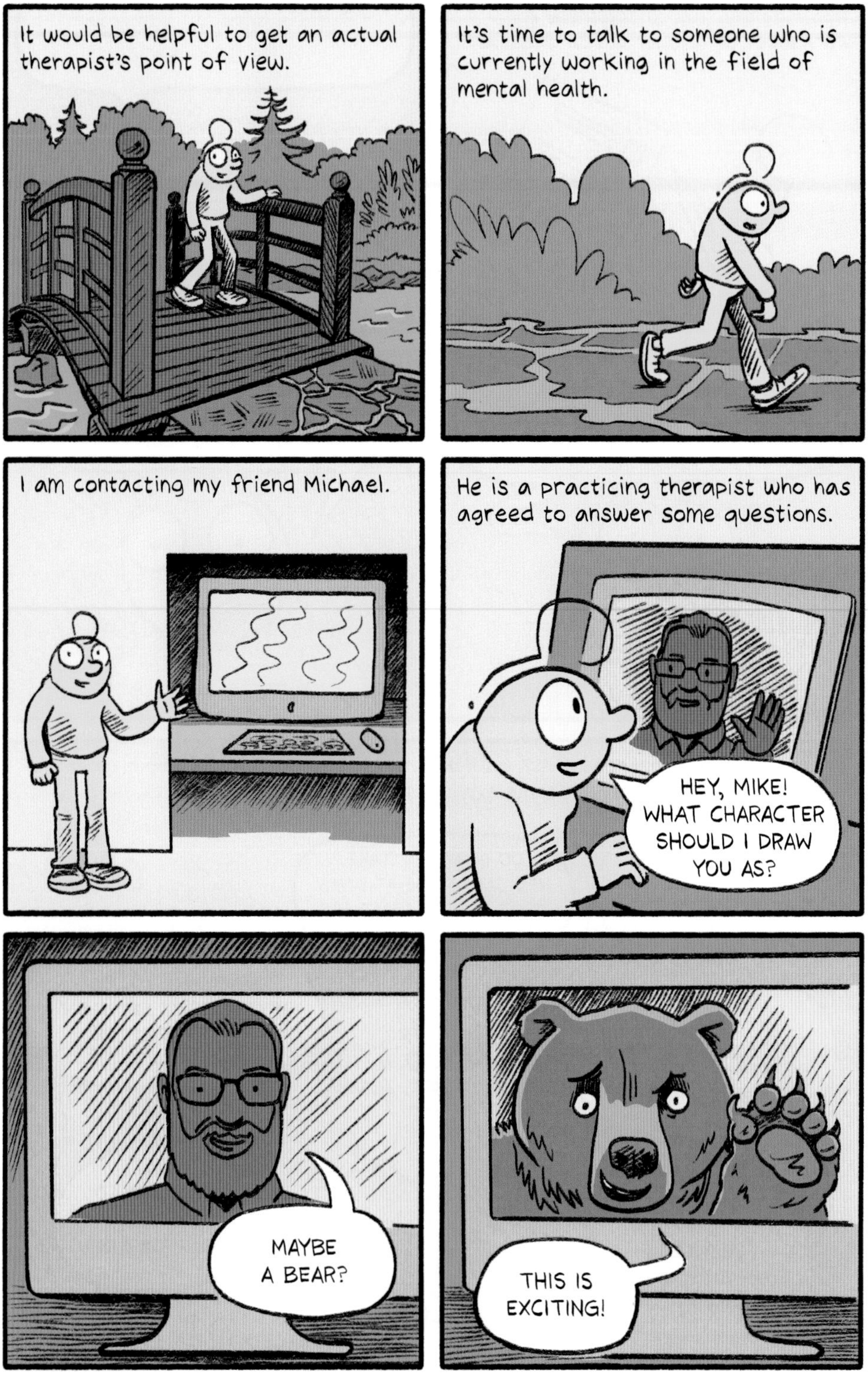
It would be helpful to get an actual therapist's point of view.
It's time to talk to someone who is currently working in the field of mental health.
I am contacting my friend Michael.
He is a practicing therapist who has agreed to answer some questions.
HEY, MIKE! WHAT CHARACTER SHOULD I DRAW YOU AS?
MAYBE A BEAR?
THIS IS EXCITING!

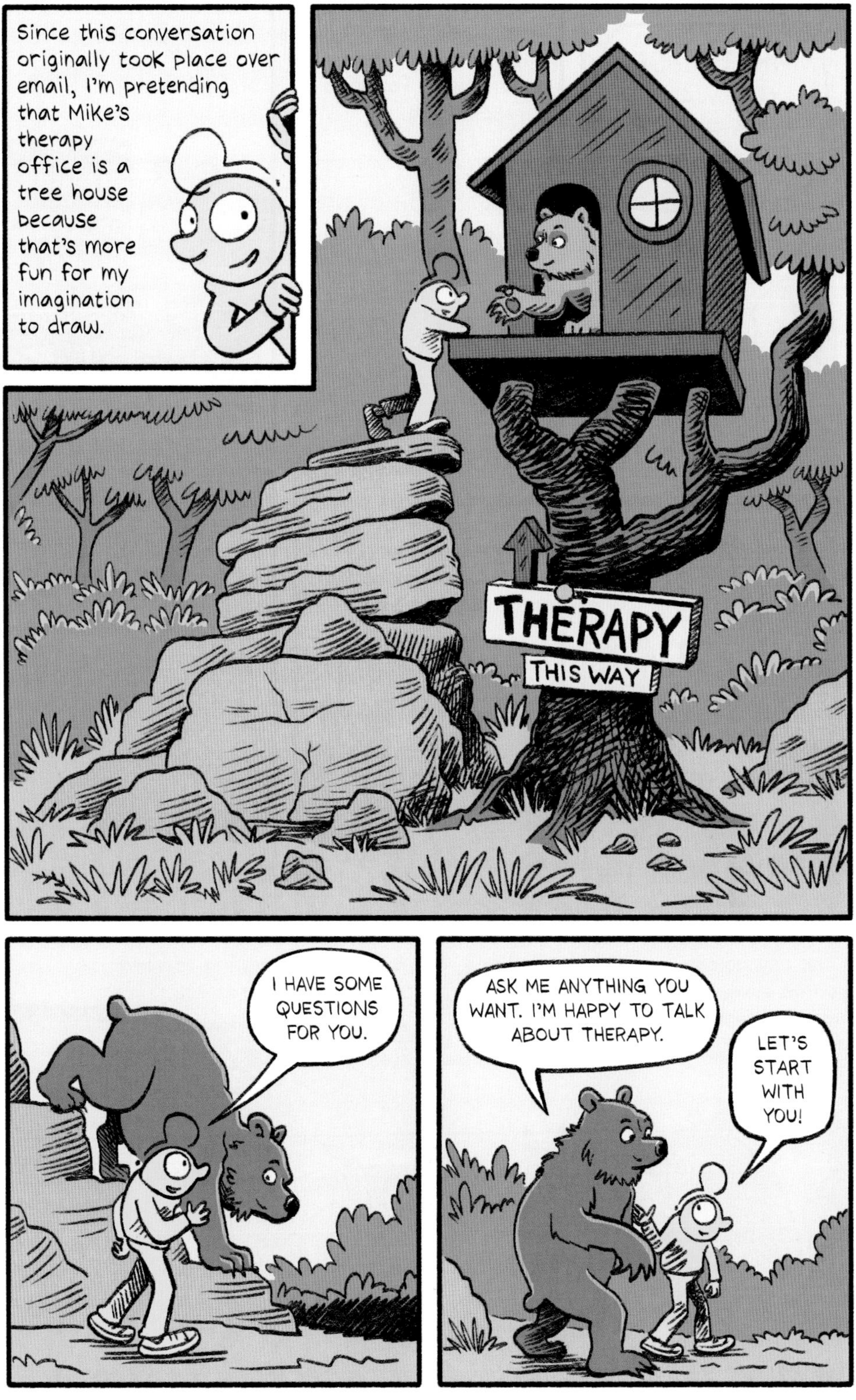
Since this conversation originally took place over email, I'm pretending that Mike's therapy office is a tree house because that's more fun for my imagination to draw.
THERAPY
THIS WAY
I HAVE SOME QUESTIONS FOR YOU.
ASK ME ANYTHING YOU WANT. I'M HAPPY TO TALK ABOUT THERAPY.
LET'S START WITH YOU!

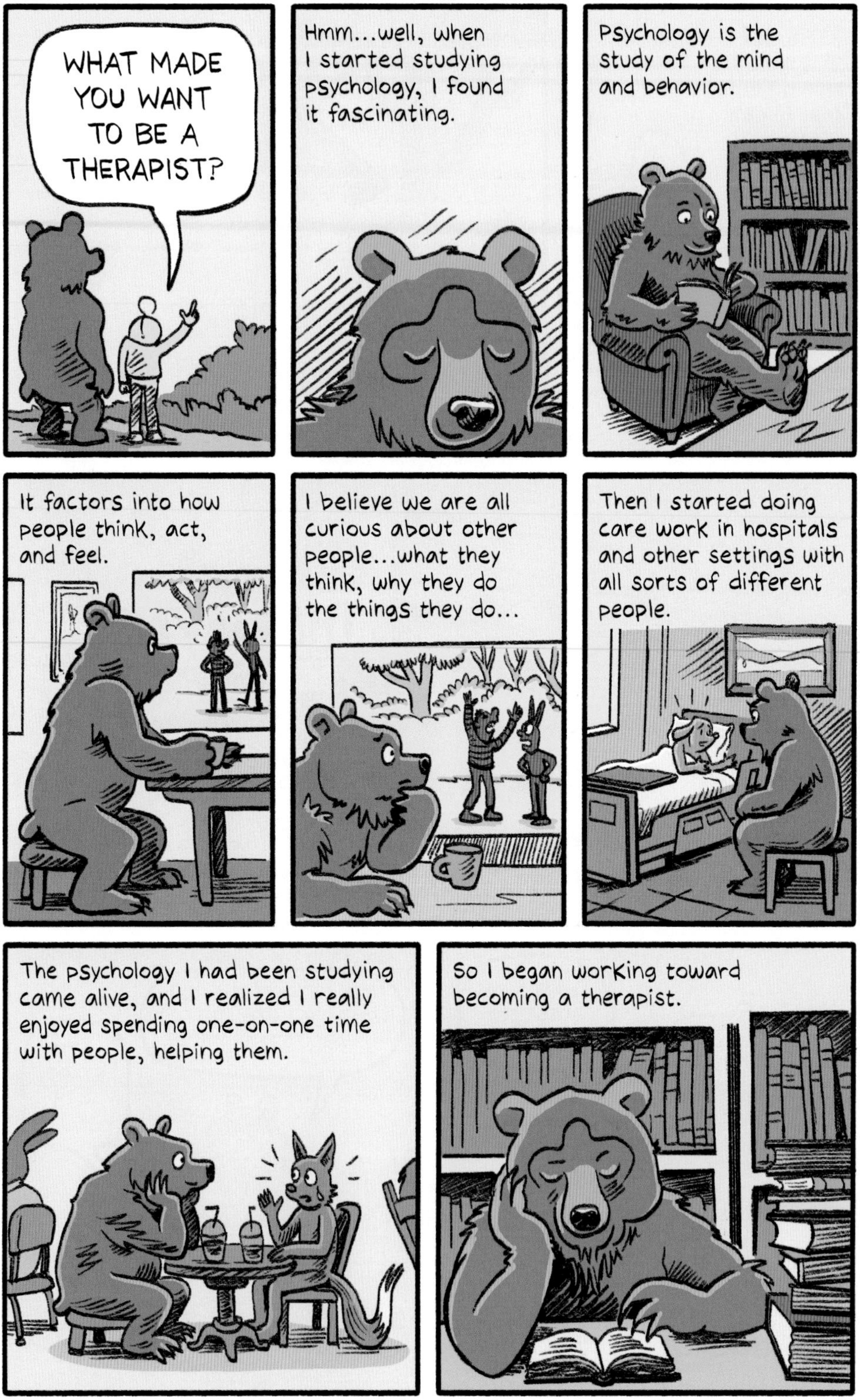
WHAT MADE YOU WANT TO BE A THERAPIST?
Hmm...well, when I started studying psychology, I found it fascinating.
Psychology is the study of the mind and behavior.
It factors into how people think, act, and feel.
I believe we are all curious about other people...what they think, why they do the things they do...
Then I started doing care work in hospitals and other settings with all sorts of different people.
The psychology I had been studying came alive, and I realized I really enjoyed spending one-on-one time with people, helping them.
So I began working toward becoming a therapist.

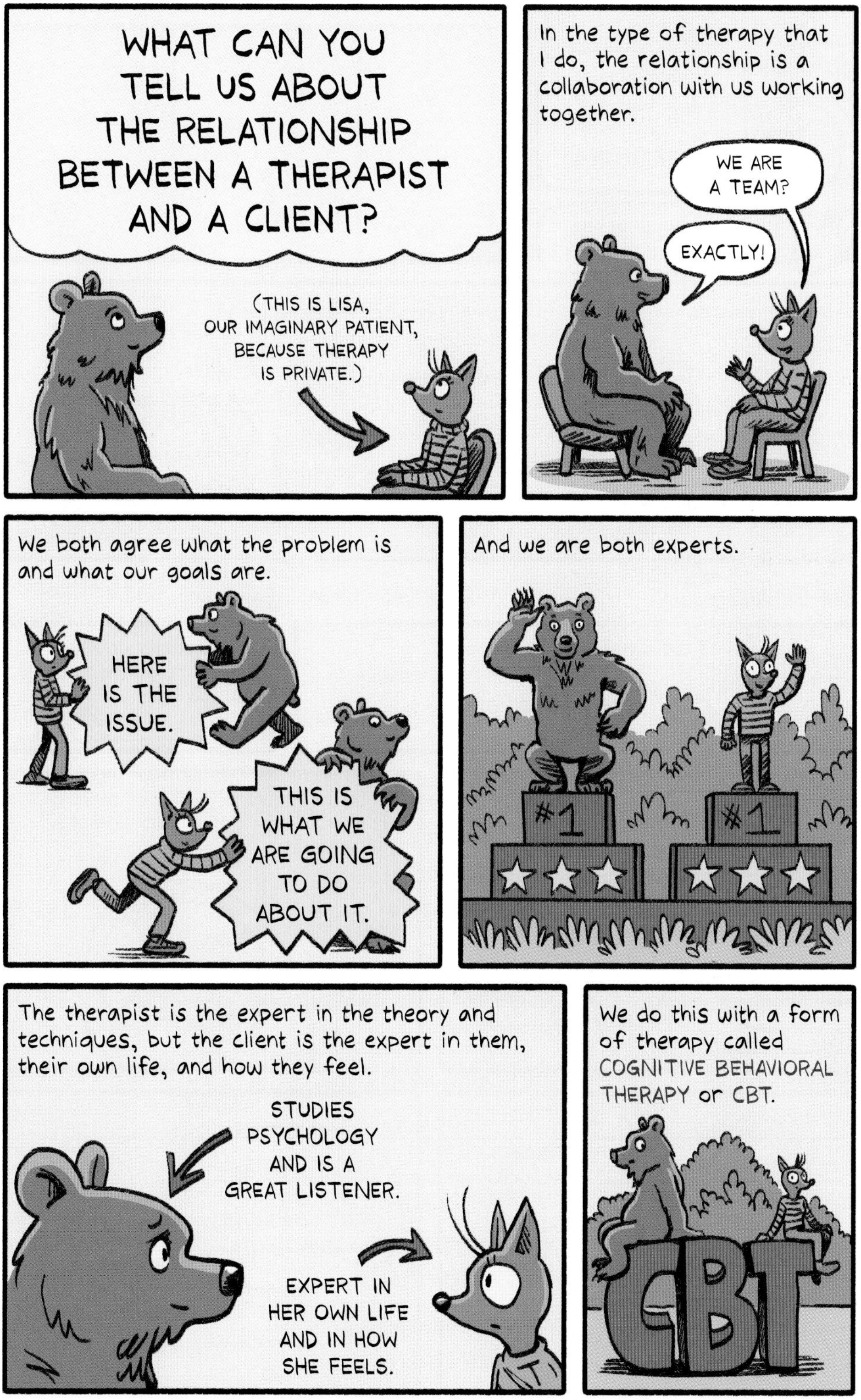
WHAT CAN YOU TELL US ABOUT THE RELATIONSHIP BETWEEN A THERAPIST AND A CLIENT?
(THIS IS LISA, OUR IMAGINARY PATIENT, BECAUSE THERAPY IS PRIVATE.)
In the type of therapy that I do, the relationship is a collaboration with us working together.
WE ARE A TEAM?
EXACTLY!
We both agree what the problem is and what our goals are.
HERE IS THE ISSUE.
THIS IS WHAT WE ARE GOING TO DO ABOUT IT.
And we are both experts.
#1
#1
The therapist is the expert in the theory and techniques, but the client is the expert in them, their own life, and how they feel.
STUDIES PSYCHOLOGY AND IS A GREAT LISTENER.
EXPERT IN HER OWN LIFE AND IN HOW SHE FEELS.
We do this with a form of therapy called COGNITIVE BEHAVIORAL THERAPY or CBT.
CBT

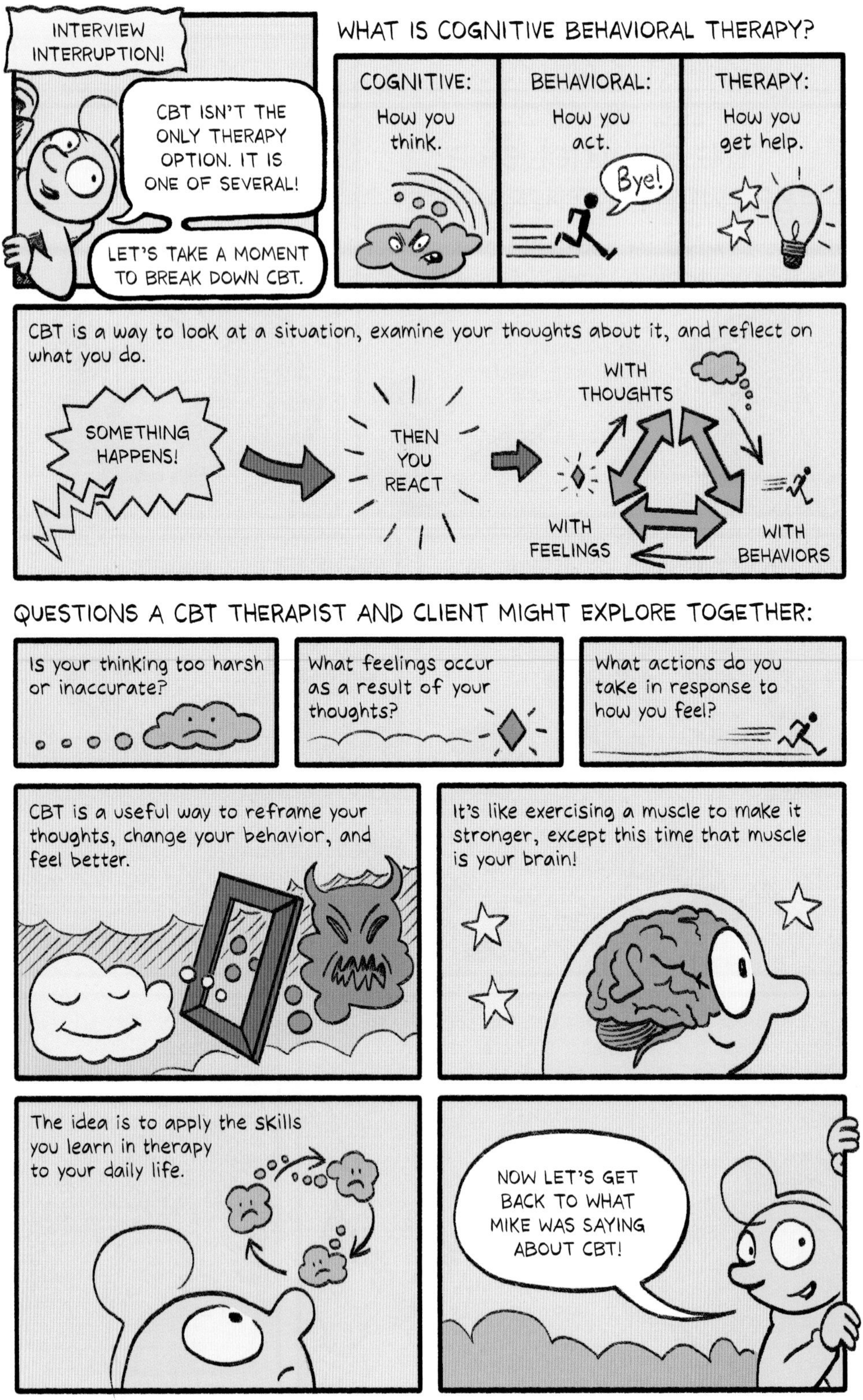
INTERVIEW INTERRUPTION!
CBT ISN'T THE ONLY THERAPY OPTION. IT IS ONE OF SEVERAL!
LET'S TAKE A MOMENT TO BREAK DOWN CBT.
WHAT IS COGNITIVE BEHAVIORAL THERAPY?
COGNITIVE: How you think.
BEHAVIORAL: How you act.
Bye!
THERAPY: How you get help.
CBT is a way to look at a situation, examine your thoughts about it, and reflect on what you do.
SOMETHING HAPPENS!
THEN YOU REACT
WITH THOUGHTS
WITH FEELINGS
WITH BEHAVIORS
QUESTIONS A CBT THERAPIST AND CLIENT MIGHT EXPLORE TOGETHER:
Is your thinking too harsh or inaccurate?
What feelings occur as a result of your thoughts?
What actions do you take in response to how you feel?
CBT is a useful way to reframe your thoughts, change your behavior, and feel better.
It's like exercising a muscle to make it stronger, except this time that muscle is your brain!
The idea is to apply the skills you learn in therapy to your daily life.
NOW LET'S GET BACK TO WHAT MIKE WAS SAYING ABOUT CBT!

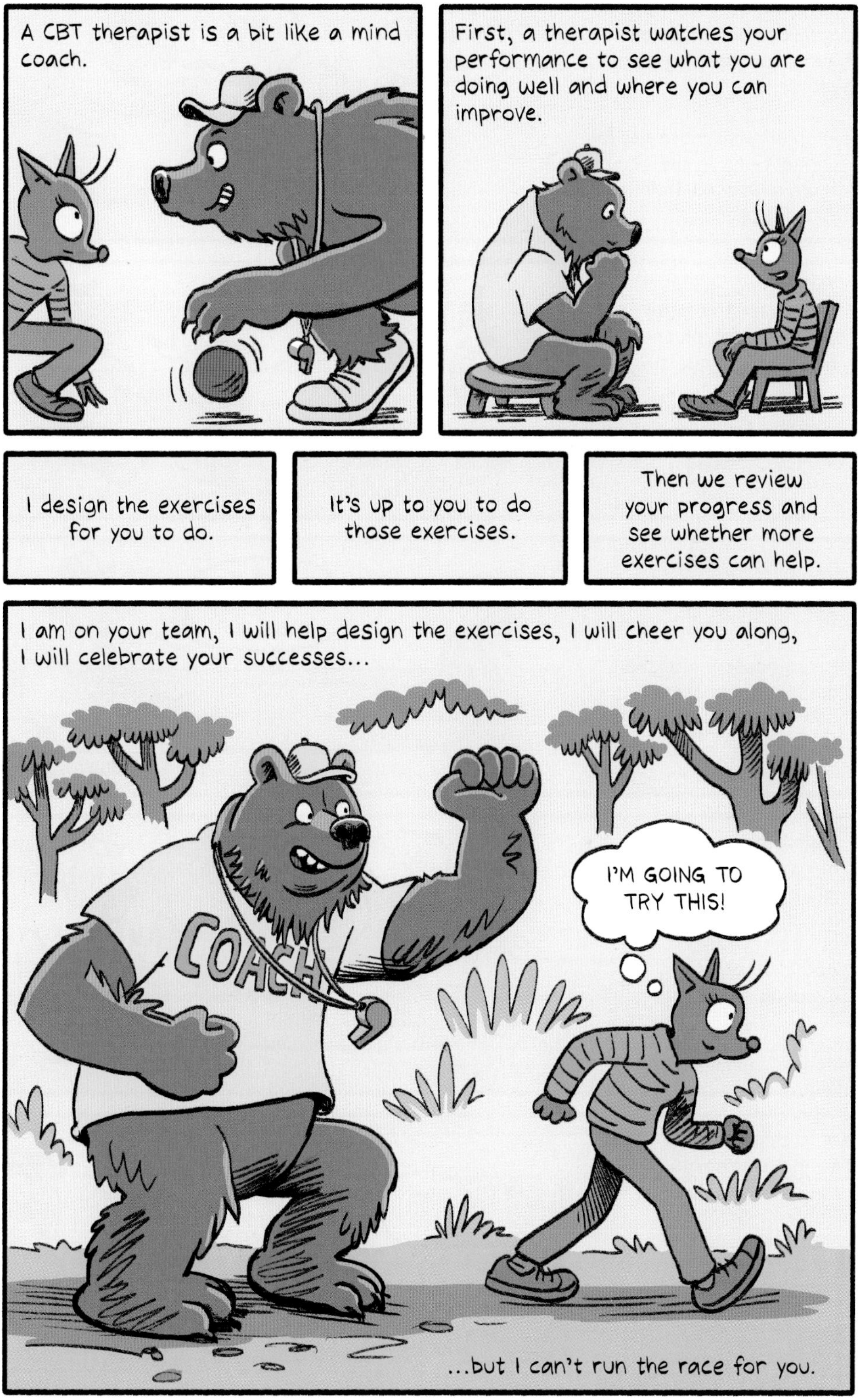
A CBT therapist is a bit like a mind coach.
First, a therapist watches your performance to see what you are doing well and where you can improve.
I design the exercises for you to do.
It's up to you to do those exercises.
Then we review your progress and see whether more exercises can help.
I am on your team, I will help design the exercises, I will cheer you along, I will celebrate your successes...
COACH
I'M GOING TO TRY THIS!
...but I can't run the race for you.

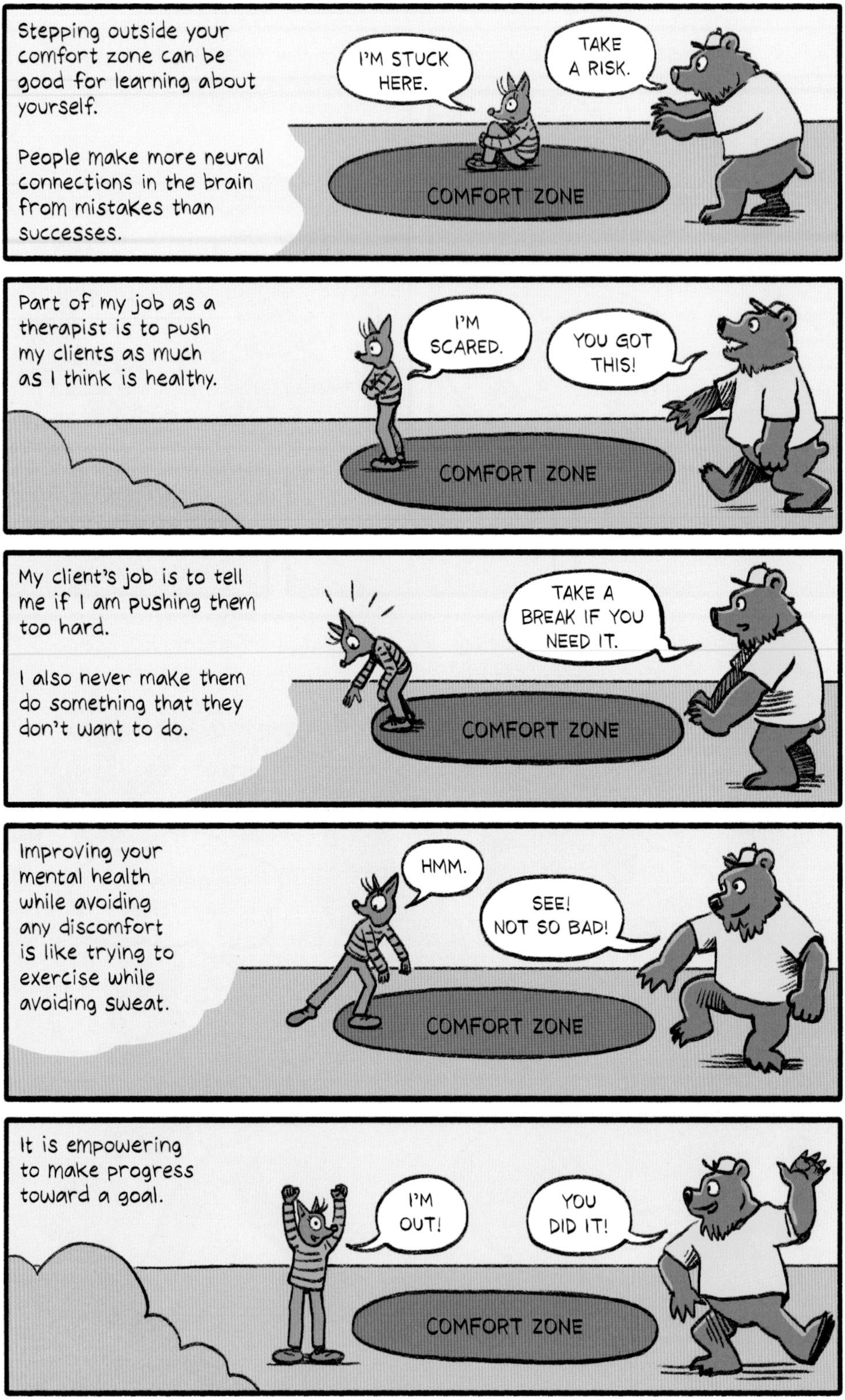
Stepping outside your comfort zone can be good for learning about yourself.
People make more neural connections in the brain from mistakes than successes.
I'M STUCK HERE.
TAKE A RISK.
COMFORT ZONE
Part of my job as a therapist is to push my clients as much as I think is healthy.
I'M SCARED.
YOU GOT THIS!
COMFORT ZONE
My client's job is to tell me if I am pushing them too hard.
I also never make them do something that they don't want to do.
TAKE A BREAK IF YOU NEED IT.
COMFORT ZONE
Improving your mental health while avoiding any discomfort is like trying to exercise while avoiding sweat.
HMM.
SEE! NOT SO BAD!
COMFORT ZONE
It is empowering to make progress toward a goal.
I'M OUT!
YOU DID IT!
COMFORT ZONE

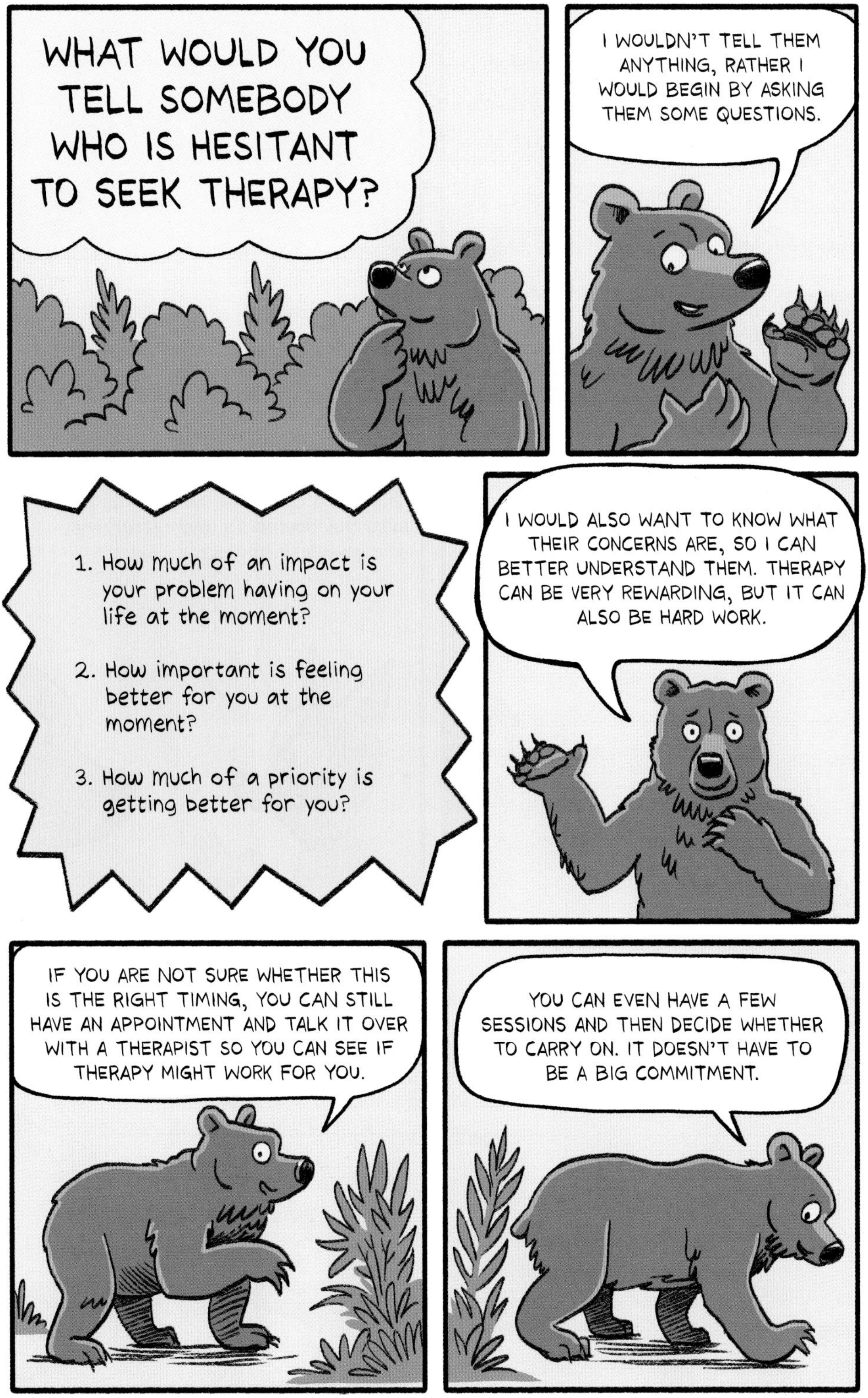
WHAT WOULD YOU TELL SOMEBODY WHO IS HESITANT TO SEEK THERAPY?
I WOULDN'T TELL THEM ANYTHING, RATHER I WOULD BEGIN BY ASKING THEM SOME QUESTIONS.
1. How much of an impact is your problem having on your life at the moment?
2. How important is feeling better for you at the moment?
3. How much of a priority is getting better for you?
I WOULD ALSO WANT TO KNOW WHAT THEIR CONCERNS ARE, SO I CAN BETTER UNDERSTAND THEM. THERAPY CAN BE VERY REWARDING, BUT IT CAN ALSO BE HARD WORK.
IF YOU ARE NOT SURE WHETHER THIS IS THE RIGHT TIMING, YOU CAN STILL HAVE AN APPOINTMENT AND TALK IT OVER WITH A THERAPIST SO YOU CAN SEE IF THERAPY MIGHT WORK FOR YOU.
YOU CAN EVEN HAVE A FEW SESSIONS AND THEN DECIDE WHETHER TO CARRY ON. IT DOESN'T HAVE TO BE A BIG COMMITMENT.

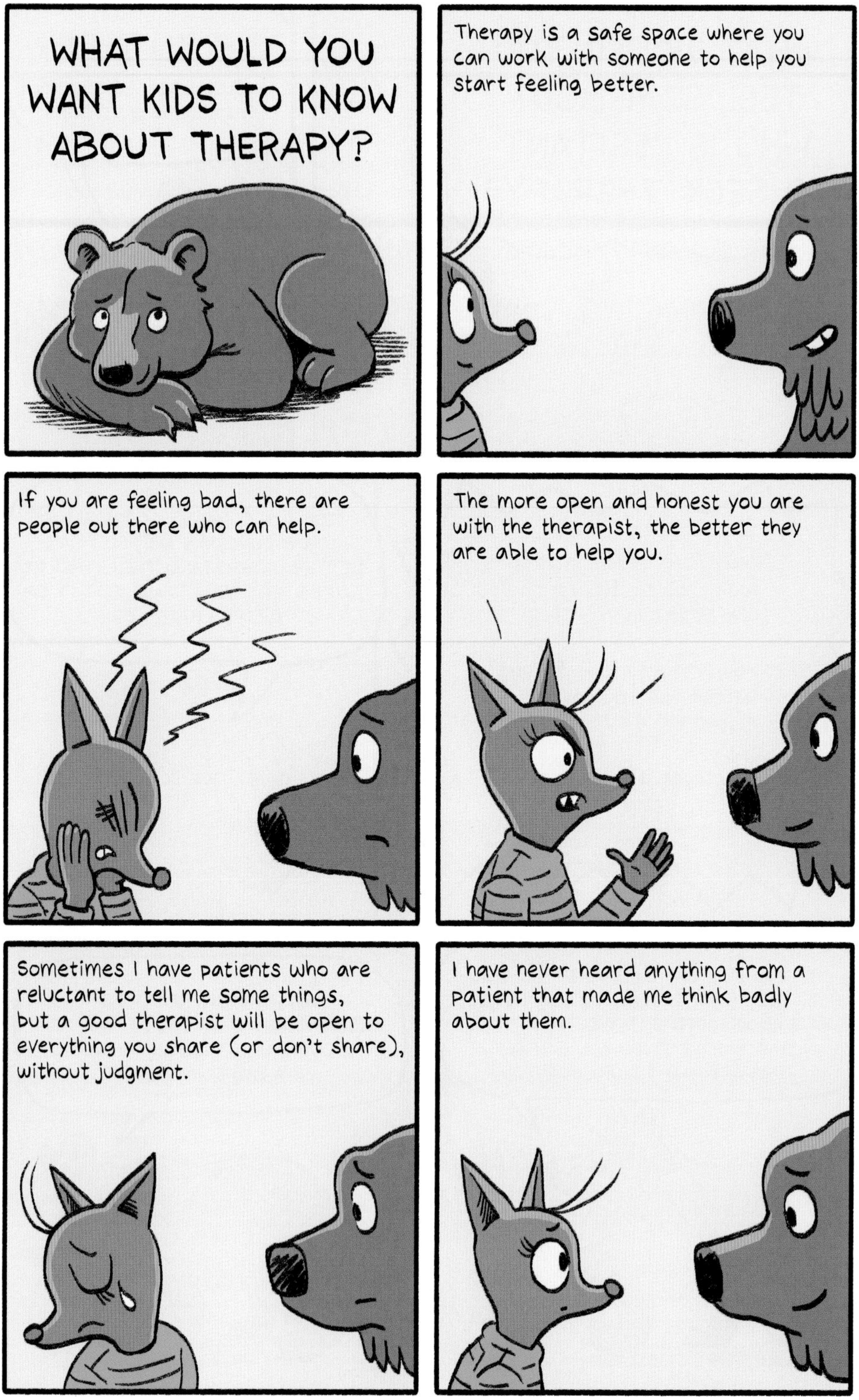
WHAT WOULD YOU WANT KIDS TO KNOW ABOUT THERAPY?
Therapy is a safe space where you can work with someone to help you start feeling better.
If you are feeling bad, there are people out there who can help.
The more open and honest you are with the therapist, the better they are able to help you.
Sometimes I have patients who are reluctant to tell me some things, but a good therapist will be open to everything you share (or don't share), without judgment.
I have never heard anything from a patient that made me think badly about them.

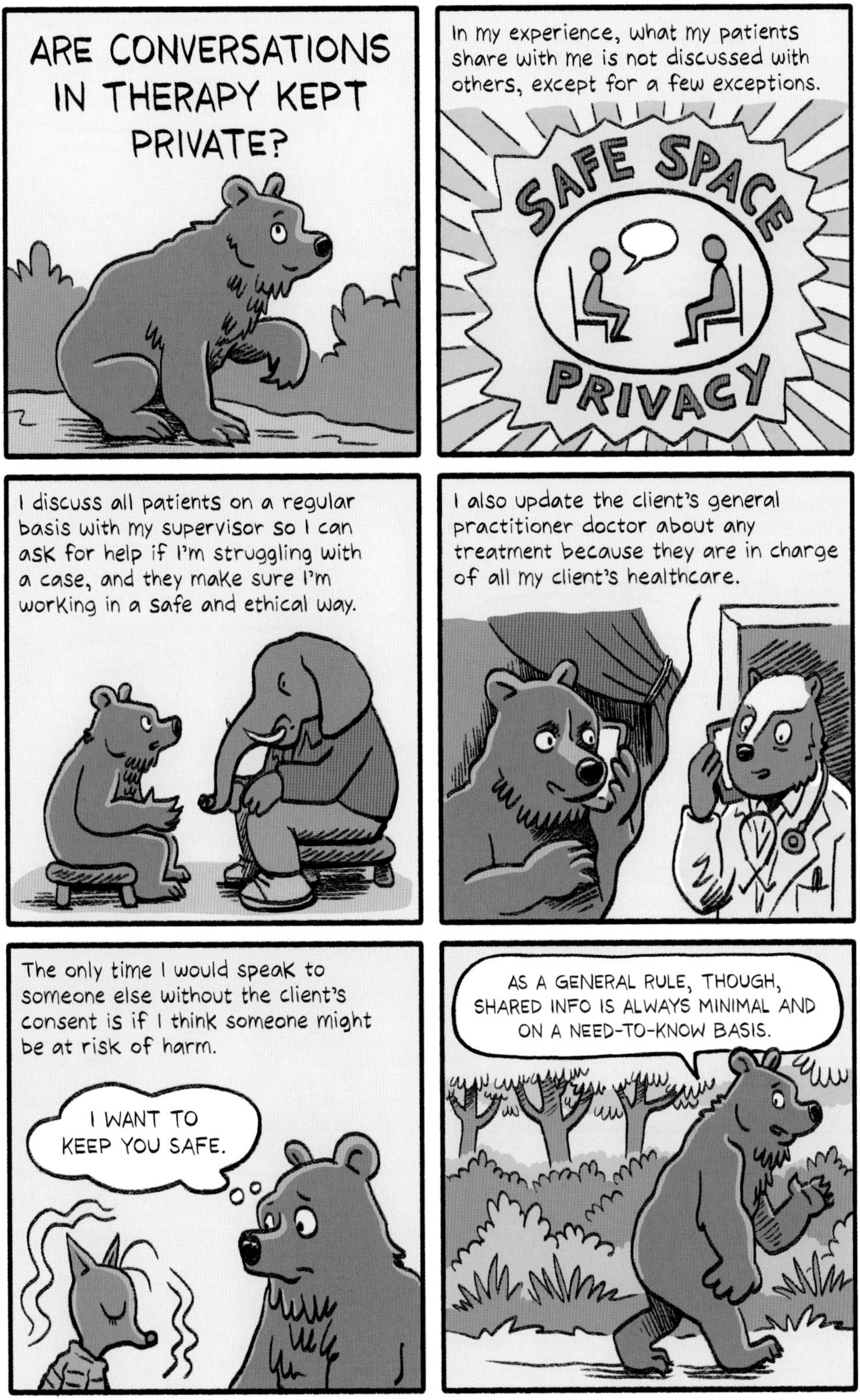
ARE CONVERSATIONS IN THERAPY KEPT PRIVATE?
In my experience, what my patients share with me is not discussed with others, except for a few exceptions.
SAFE SPACE
PRIVACY
I discuss all patients on a regular basis with my supervisor so I can ask for help if I'm struggling with a case, and they make sure I'm working in a safe and ethical way.
I also update the client's general practitioner doctor about any treatment because they are in charge of all my client's healthcare.
The only time I would speak to someone else without the client's consent is if I think someone might be at risk of harm.
I WANT TO KEEP YOU SAFE.
AS A GENERAL RULE, THOUGH, SHARED INFO IS ALWAYS MINIMAL AND ON A NEED-TO-KNOW BASIS.

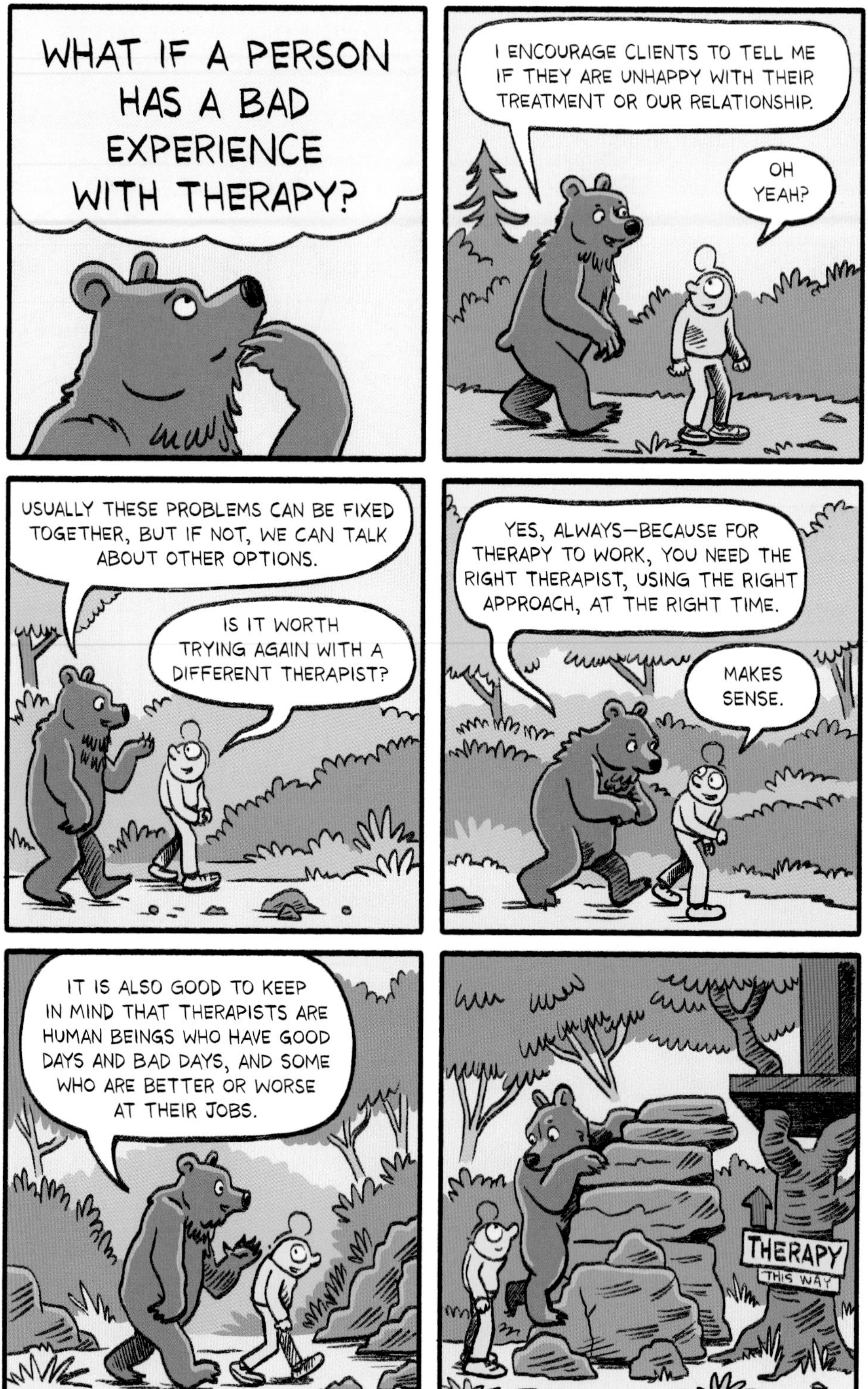
WHAT IF A PERSON HAS A BAD EXPERIENCE WITH THERAPY?
I ENCOURAGE CLIENTS TO TELL ME IF THEY ARE UNHAPPY WITH THEIR TREATMENT OR OUR RELATIONSHIP.
OH YEAH?
USUALLY THESE PROBLEMS CAN BE FIXED TOGETHER, BUT IF NOT, WE CAN TALK ABOUT OTHER OPTIONS.
IS IT WORTH TRYING AGAIN WITH A DIFFERENT THERAPIST?
YES, ALWAYS—BECAUSE FOR THERAPY TO WORK, YOU NEED THE RIGHT THERAPIST, USING THE RIGHT APPROACH, AT THE RIGHT TIME.
MAKES SENSE.
IT IS ALSO GOOD TO KEEP IN MIND THAT THERAPISTS ARE HUMAN BEINGS WHO HAVE GOOD DAYS AND BAD DAYS, AND SOME WHO ARE BETTER OR WORSE AT THEIR JOBS.
THERAPY
THIS WAY

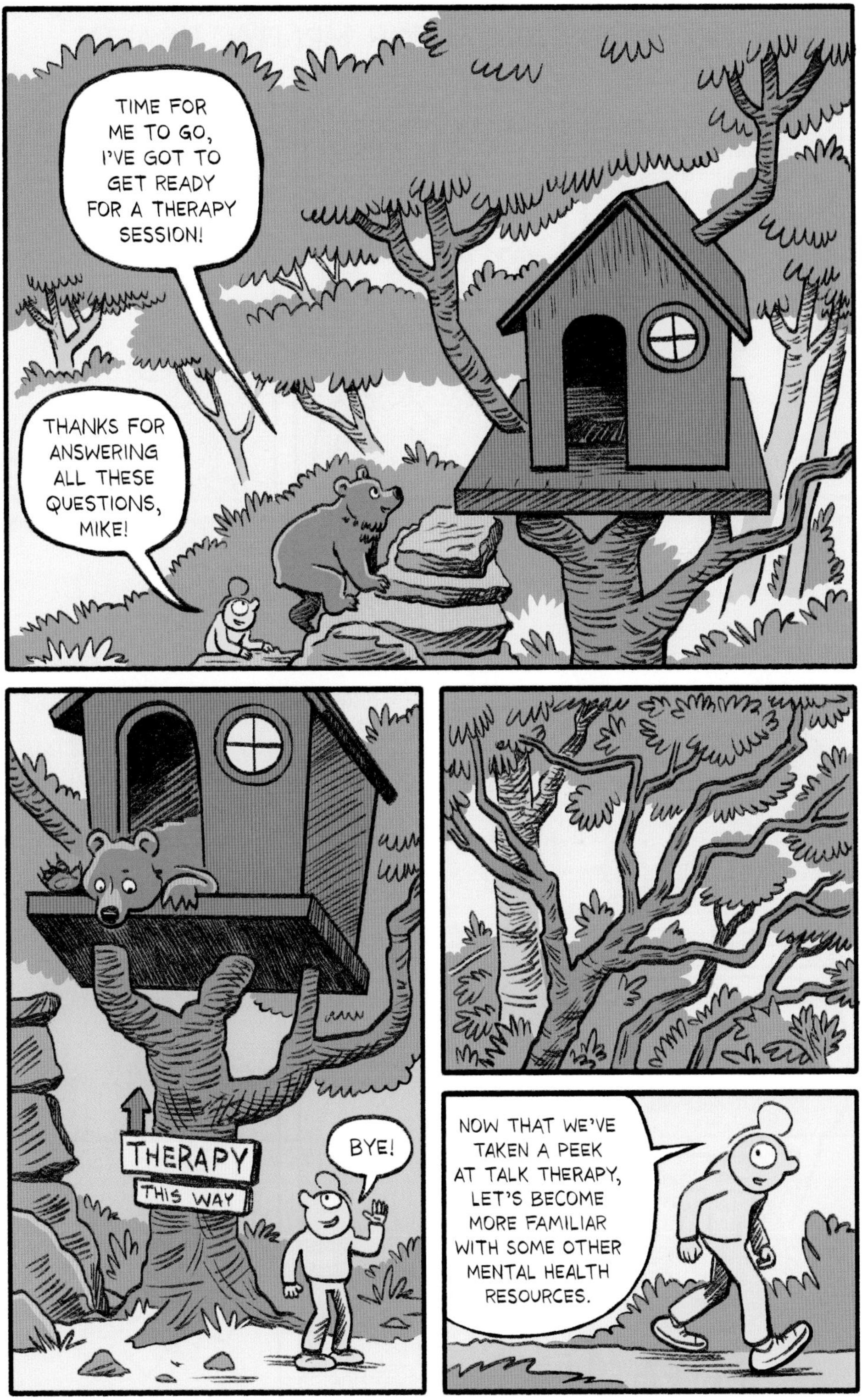
TIME FOR ME TO GO, I'VE GOT TO GET READY FOR A THERAPY SESSION!
THANKS FOR ANSWERING ALL THESE QUESTIONS, MIKE!
THERAPY
THIS WAY
BYE!
NOW THAT WE'VE TAKEN A PEEK AT TALK THERAPY, LET'S BECOME MORE FAMILIAR WITH SOME OTHER MENTAL HEALTH RESOURCES.

ABOUT MEDICATION FOR MENTAL HEALTH

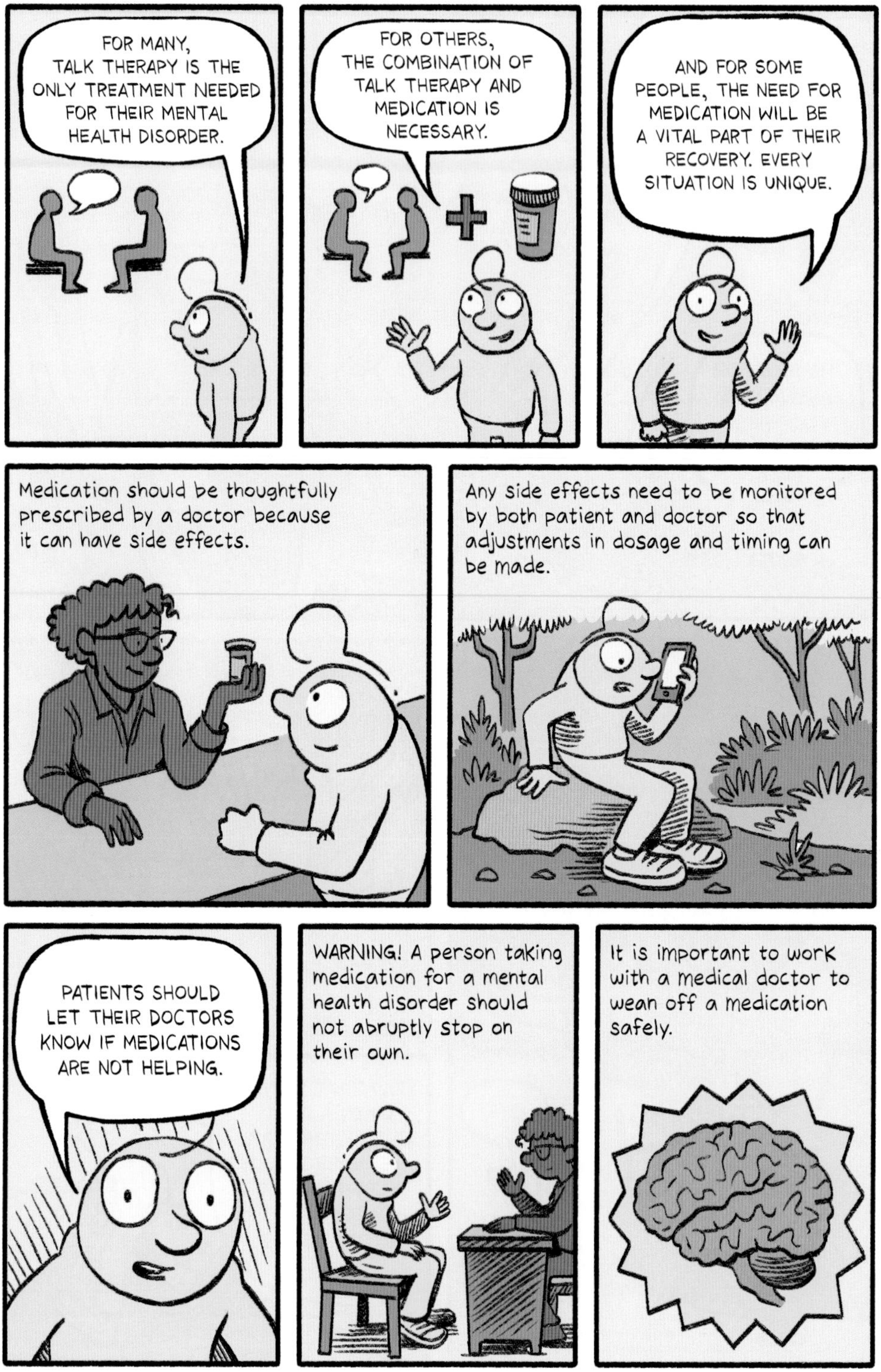

FOR MANY, TALK THERAPY IS THE ONLY TREATMENT NEEDED FOR THEIR MENTAL HEALTH DISORDER.
FOR OTHERS, THE COMBINATION OF TALK THERAPY AND MEDICATION IS NECESSARY.
AND FOR SOME PEOPLE, THE NEED FOR MEDICATION WILL BE A VITAL PART OF THEIR RECOVERY. EVERY SITUATION IS UNIQUE.
Medication should be thoughtfully prescribed by a doctor because it can have side effects.
Any side effects need to be monitored by both patient and doctor so that adjustments in dosage and timing can be made.
PATIENTS SHOULD LET THEIR DOCTORS KNOW IF MEDICATIONS ARE NOT HELPING.
WARNING! A person taking medication for a mental health disorder should not abruptly stop on their own.
It is important to work with a medical doctor to wean off a medication safely.

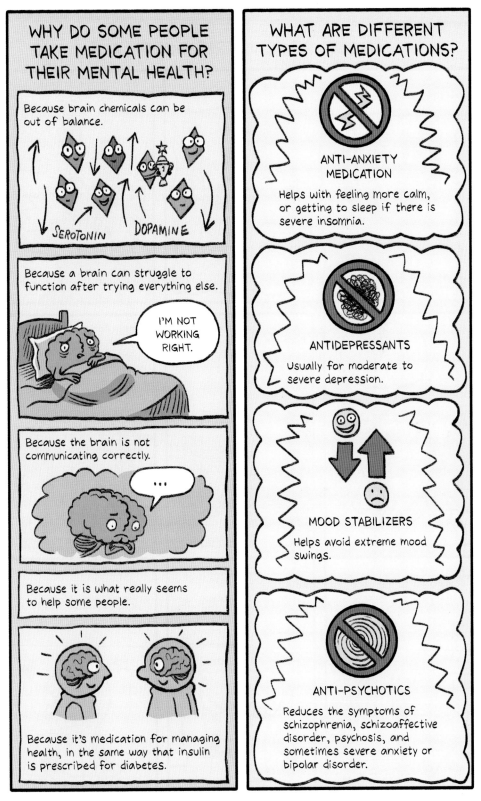

WHY DO SOME PEOPLE TAKE MEDICATION FOR THEIR MENTAL HEALTH?

Because brain chemicals can be out of balance.

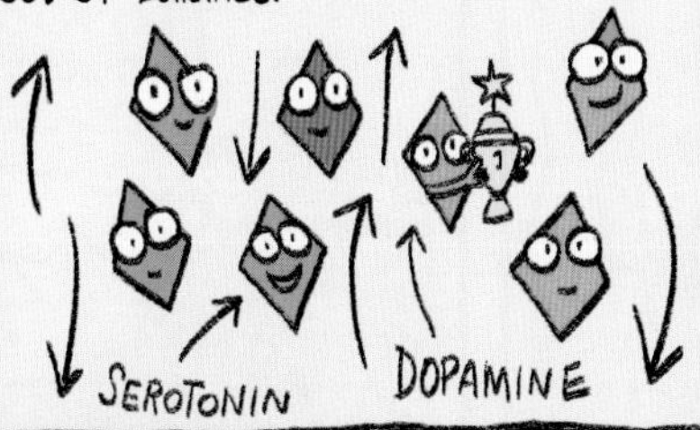
SEROTONIN
DOPAMINE

Because a brain can struggle to function after trying everything else.

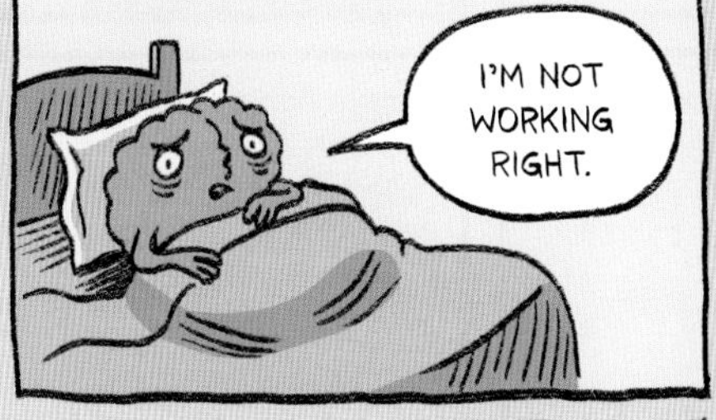
I'M NOT WORKING RIGHT.

Because the brain is not communicating correctly.

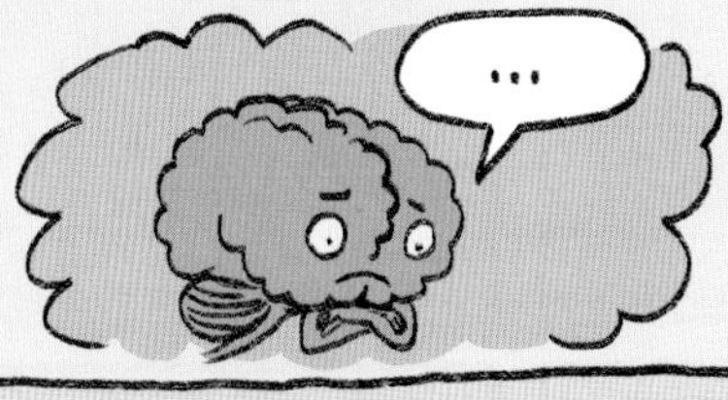
...

Because it is what really seems to help some people.

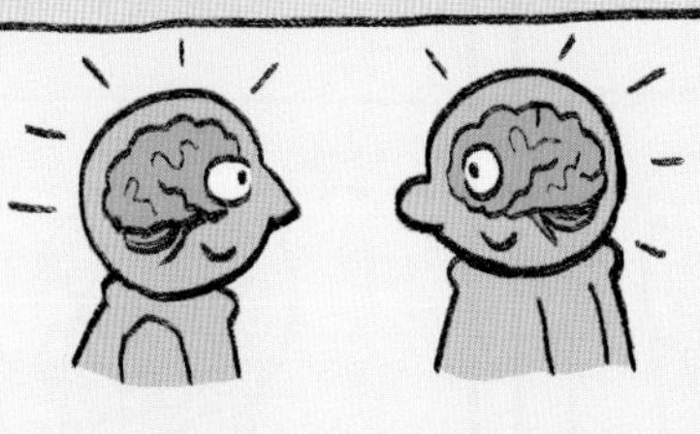

Because it's medication for managing health, in the same way that insulin is prescribed for diabetes.

WHAT ARE DIFFERENT TYPES OF MEDICATIONS?

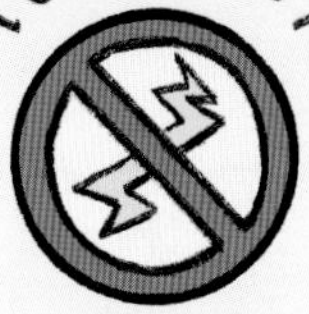

ANTI-ANXIETY MEDICATION

Helps with feeling more calm, or getting to sleep if there is severe insomnia.

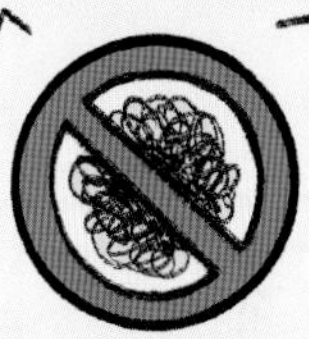

ANTIDEPRESSANTS

Usually for moderate to severe depression.

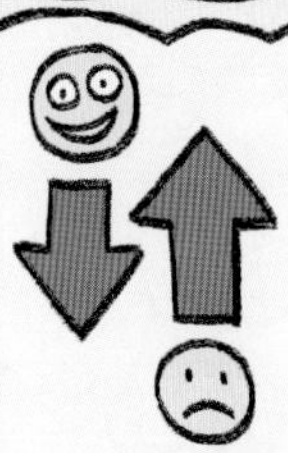

MOOD STABILIZERS

Helps avoid extreme mood swings.

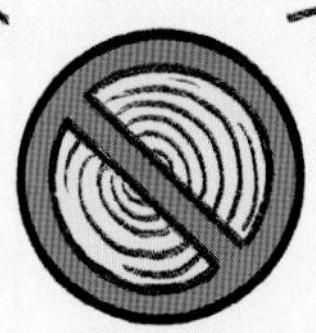

ANTI-PSYCHOTICS

Reduces the symptoms of schizophrenia, schizoaffective disorder, psychosis, and sometimes severe anxiety or bipolar disorder.

ABOUT PSYCHIATRIC HOSPITALS

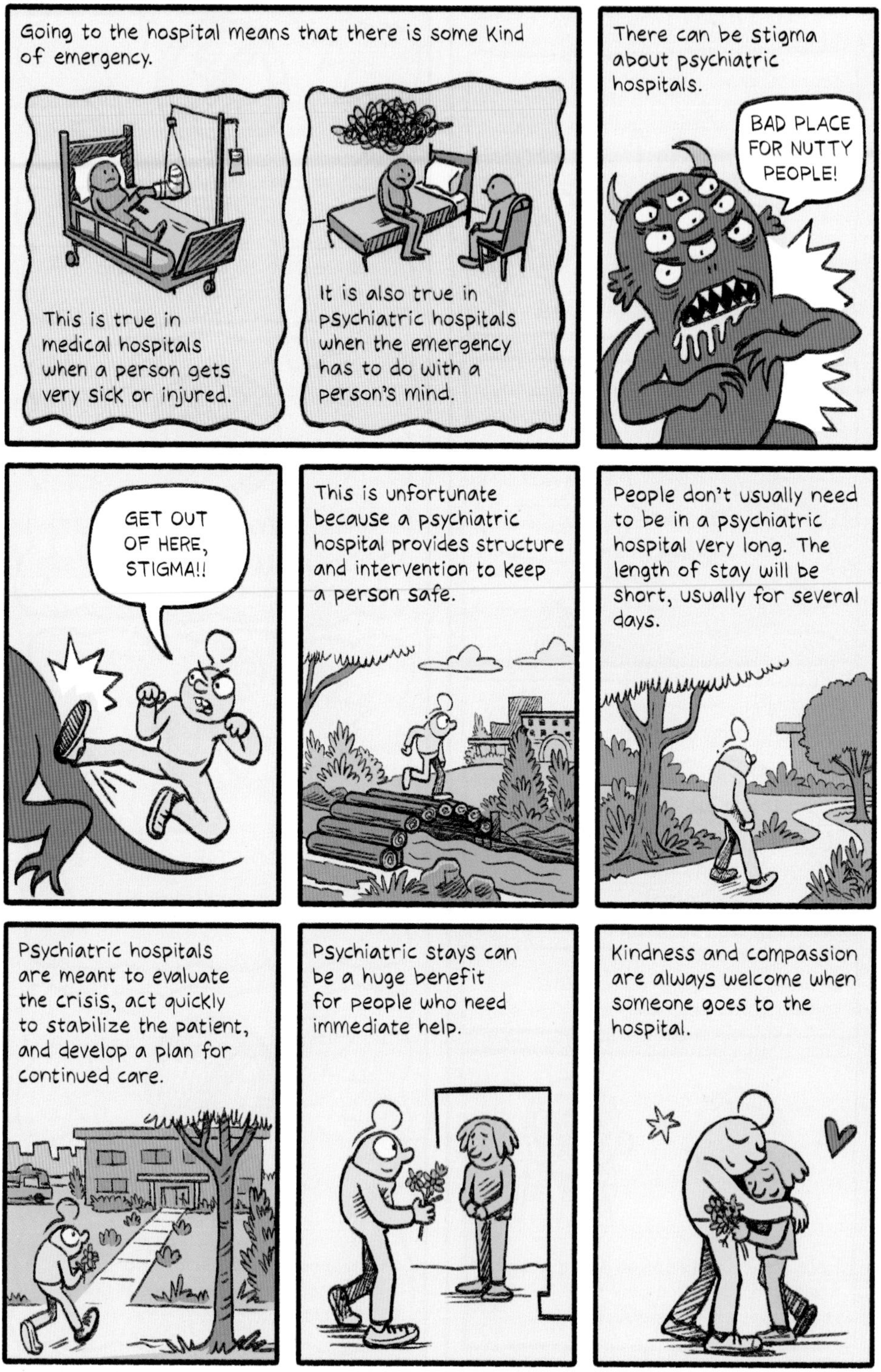
Going to the hospital means that there is some kind of emergency.
This is true in medical hospitals when a person gets very sick or injured.
It is also true in psychiatric hospitals when the emergency has to do with a person's mind.
There can be stigma about psychiatric hospitals.
BAD PLACE FOR NUTTY PEOPLE!
GET OUT OF HERE, STIGMA!!
This is unfortunate because a psychiatric hospital provides structure and intervention to keep a person safe.
People don't usually need to be in a psychiatric hospital very long. The length of stay will be short, usually for several days.
Psychiatric hospitals are meant to evaluate the crisis, act quickly to stabilize the patient, and develop a plan for continued care.
Psychiatric stays can be a huge benefit for people who need immediate help.
Kindness and compassion are always welcome when someone goes to the hospital.

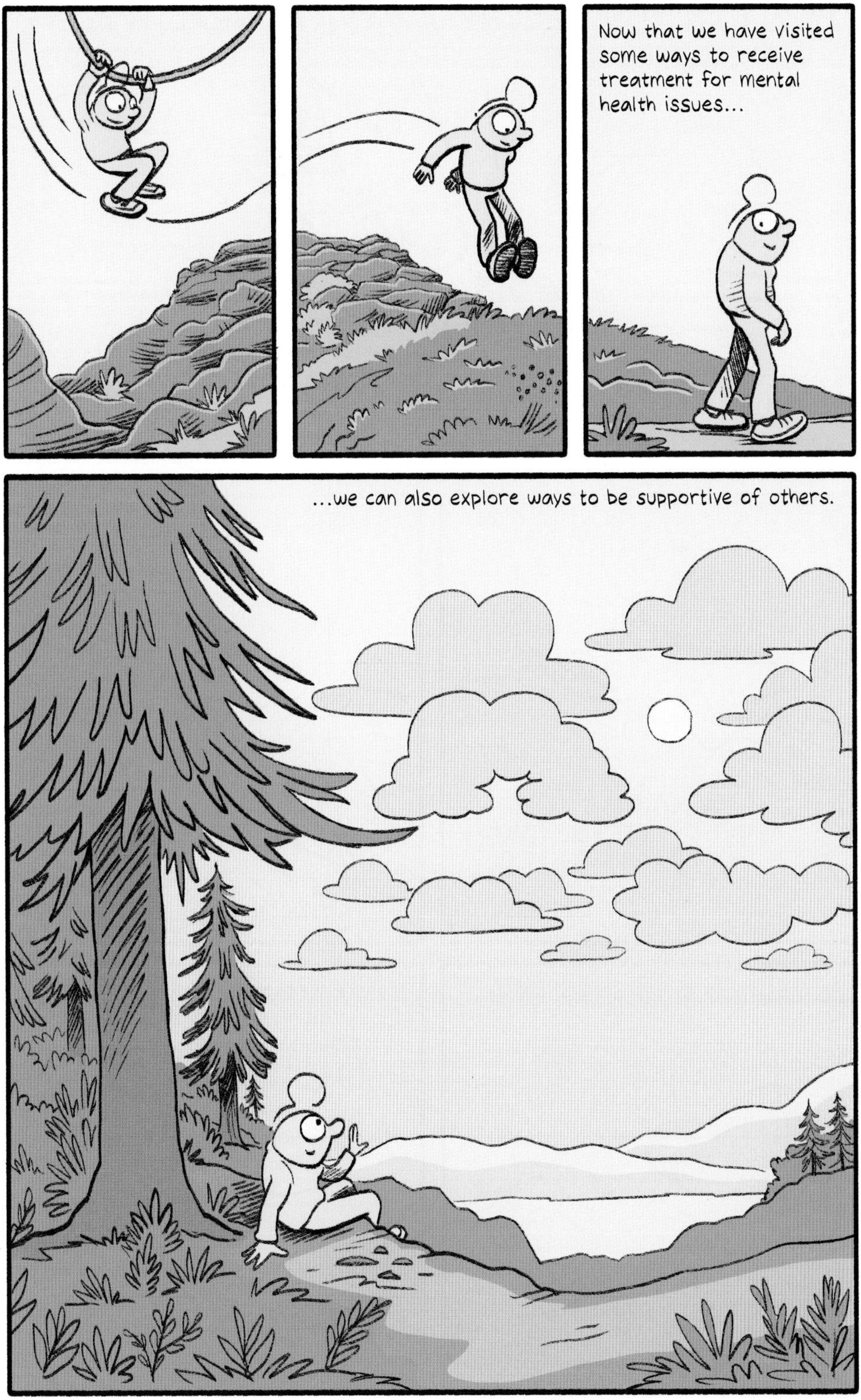
Now that we have visited some ways to receive treatment for mental health issues...
...we can also explore ways to be supportive of others.

HOW CAN YOU BECOME A MENTAL HEALTH ALLY?

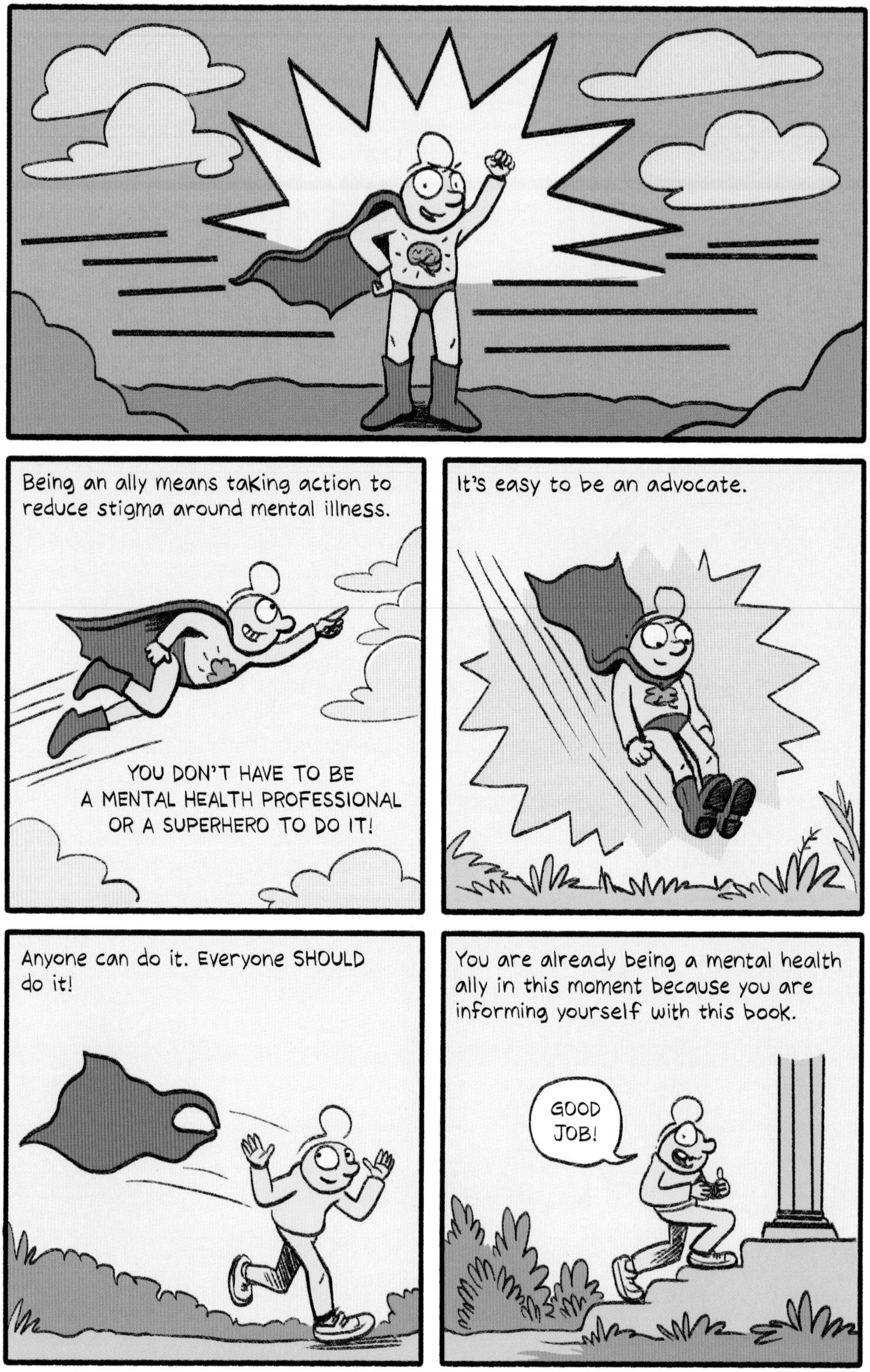
Being an ally means taking action to reduce stigma around mental illness.
YOU DON'T HAVE TO BE A MENTAL HEALTH PROFESSIONAL OR A SUPERHERO TO DO IT!
It's easy to be an advocate.
Anyone can do it. Everyone SHOULD do it!
You are already being a mental health ally in this moment because you are informing yourself with this book.
GOOD JOB!

One simple way to be a mental health ally is to be more thoughtful with your words.

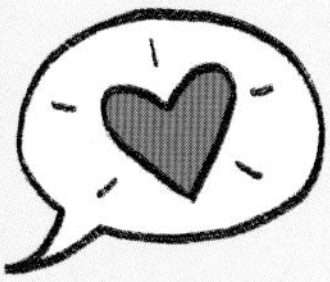

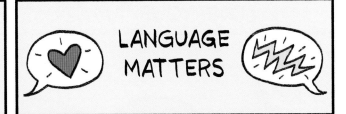

LANGUAGE MATTERS

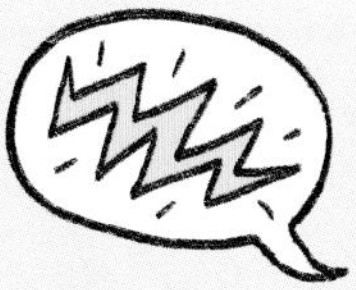

Mental disorders are not ways to describe how people feel or act. Words associated with mental health should be used when discussing, treating, and celebrating mental health.

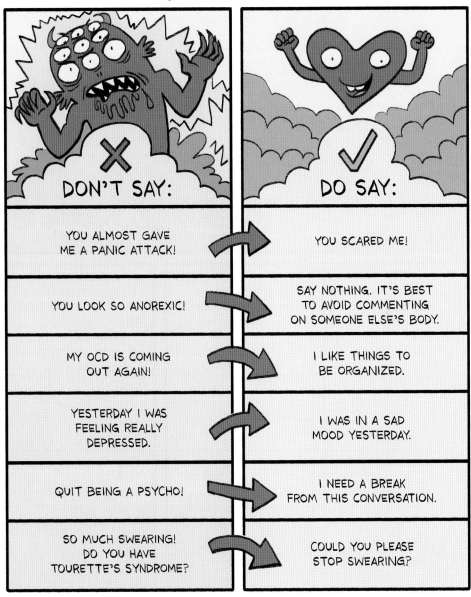

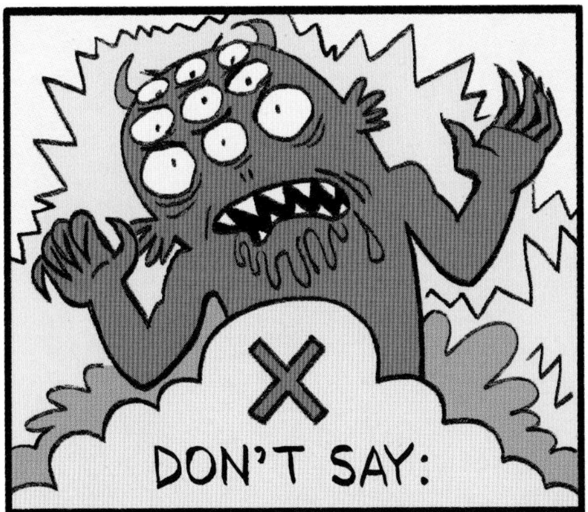
DON'T SAY:

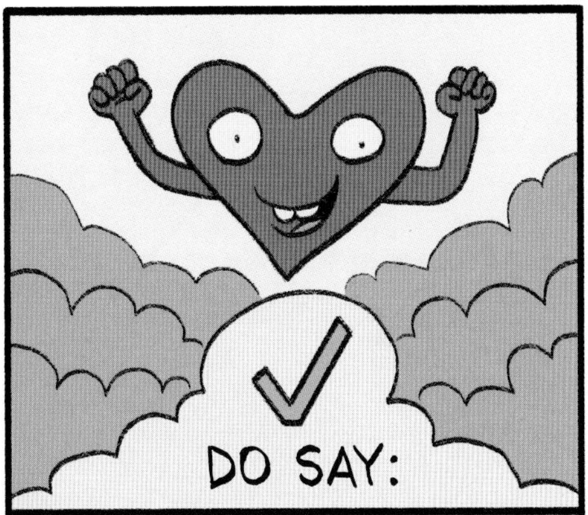
DO SAY:

YOU ALMOST GAVE ME A PANIC ATTACK!	YOU SCARED ME!
YOU LOOK SO ANOREXIC!	SAY NOTHING. IT'S BEST TO AVOID COMMENTING ON SOMEONE ELSE'S BODY.
MY OCD IS COMING OUT AGAIN!	I LIKE THINGS TO BE ORGANIZED.
YESTERDAY I WAS FEELING REALLY DEPRESSED.	I WAS IN A SAD MOOD YESTERDAY.
QUIT BEING A PSYCHO!	I NEED A BREAK FROM THIS CONVERSATION.
SO MUCH SWEARING! DO YOU HAVE TOURETTE'S SYNDROME?	COULD YOU PLEASE STOP SWEARING?

LOVE YOUR AMAZING BRAIN

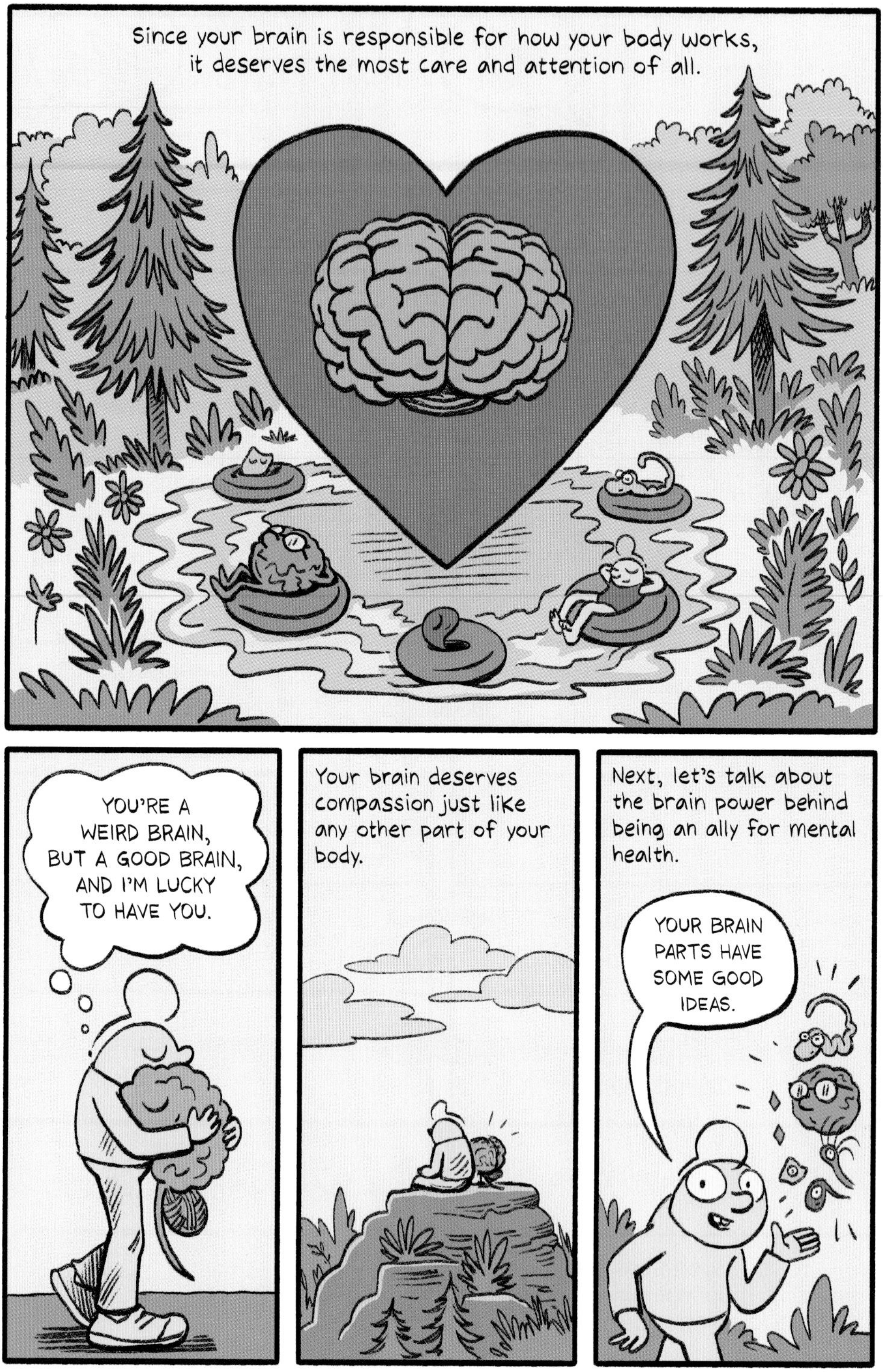
Since your brain is responsible for how your body works, it deserves the most care and attention of all.
YOU'RE A WEIRD BRAIN, BUT A GOOD BRAIN, AND I'M LUCKY TO HAVE YOU.
Your brain deserves compassion just like any other part of your body.
Next, let's talk about the brain power behind being an ally for mental health.
YOUR BRAIN PARTS HAVE SOME GOOD IDEAS.

SHOW AMYGDALA AWARENESS

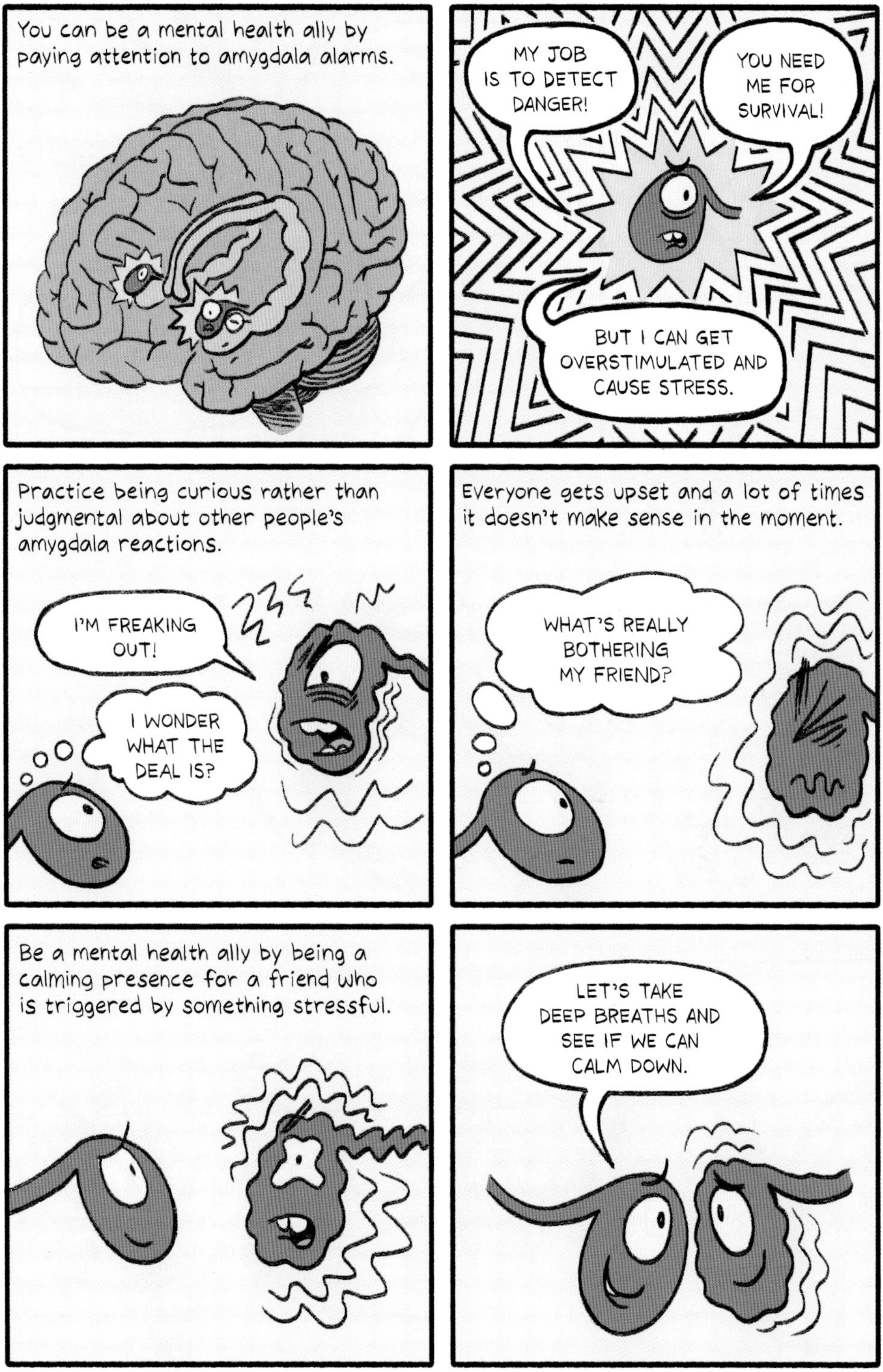
You can be a mental health ally by paying attention to amygdala alarms.
MY JOB IS TO DETECT DANGER!
YOU NEED ME FOR SURVIVAL!
BUT I CAN GET OVERSTIMULATED AND CAUSE STRESS.
Practice being curious rather than judgmental about other people's amygdala reactions.
I'M FREAKING OUT!
I WONDER WHAT THE DEAL IS?
Everyone gets upset and a lot of times it doesn't make sense in the moment.
WHAT'S REALLY BOTHERING MY FRIEND?
Be a mental health ally by being a calming presence for a friend who is triggered by something stressful.
LET'S TAKE DEEP BREATHS AND SEE IF WE CAN CALM DOWN.

RESPECT YOUR RAS

(Reticular Activating System)

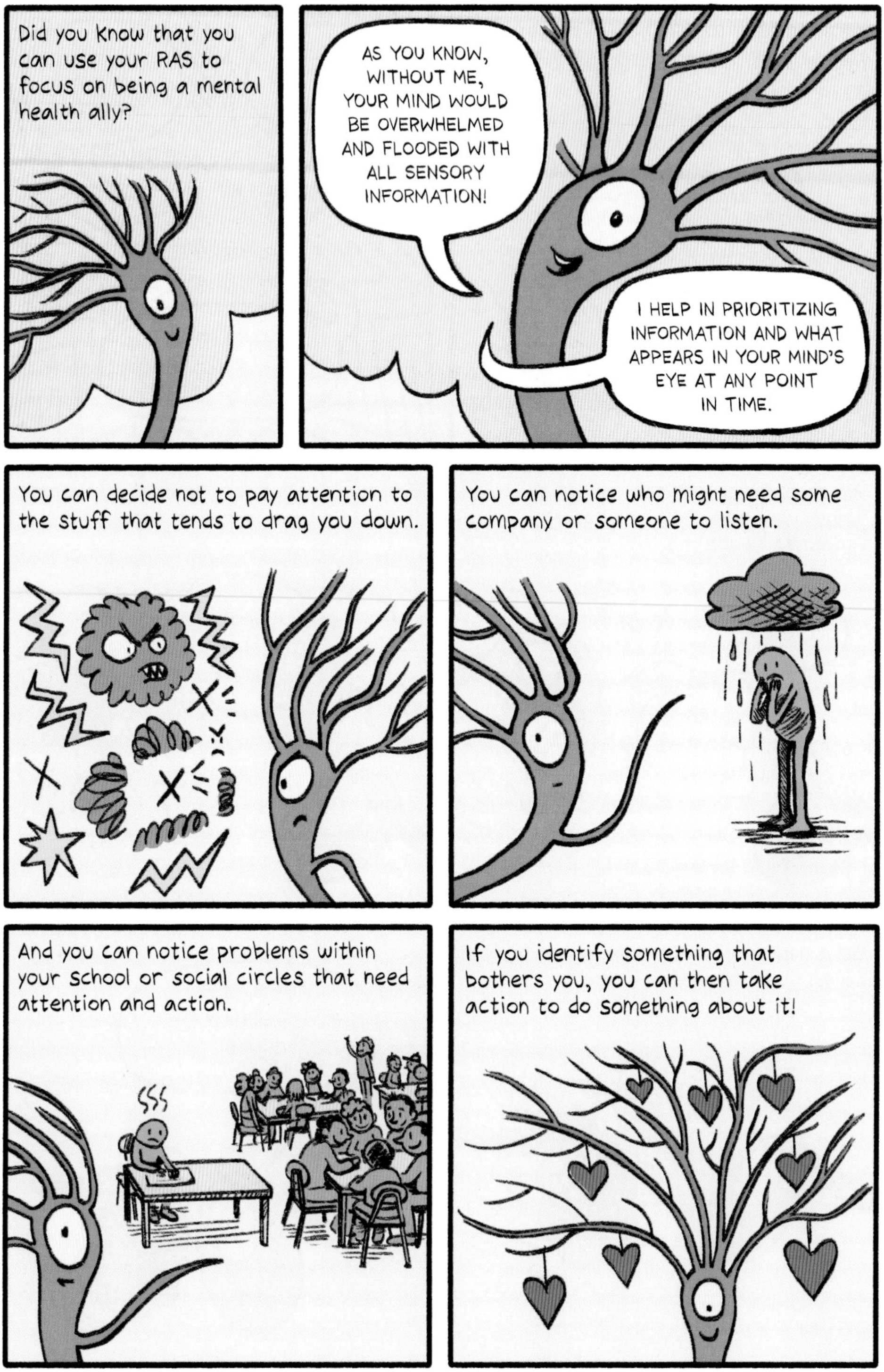
Did you know that you can use your RAS to focus on being a mental health ally?
AS YOU KNOW, WITHOUT ME, YOUR MIND WOULD BE OVERWHELMED AND FLOODED WITH ALL SENSORY INFORMATION!
I HELP IN PRIORITIZING INFORMATION AND WHAT APPEARS IN YOUR MIND'S EYE AT ANY POINT IN TIME.
You can decide not to pay attention to the stuff that tends to drag you down.
You can notice who might need some company or someone to listen.
And you can notice problems within your school or social circles that need attention and action.
If you identify something that bothers you, you can then take action to do something about it!

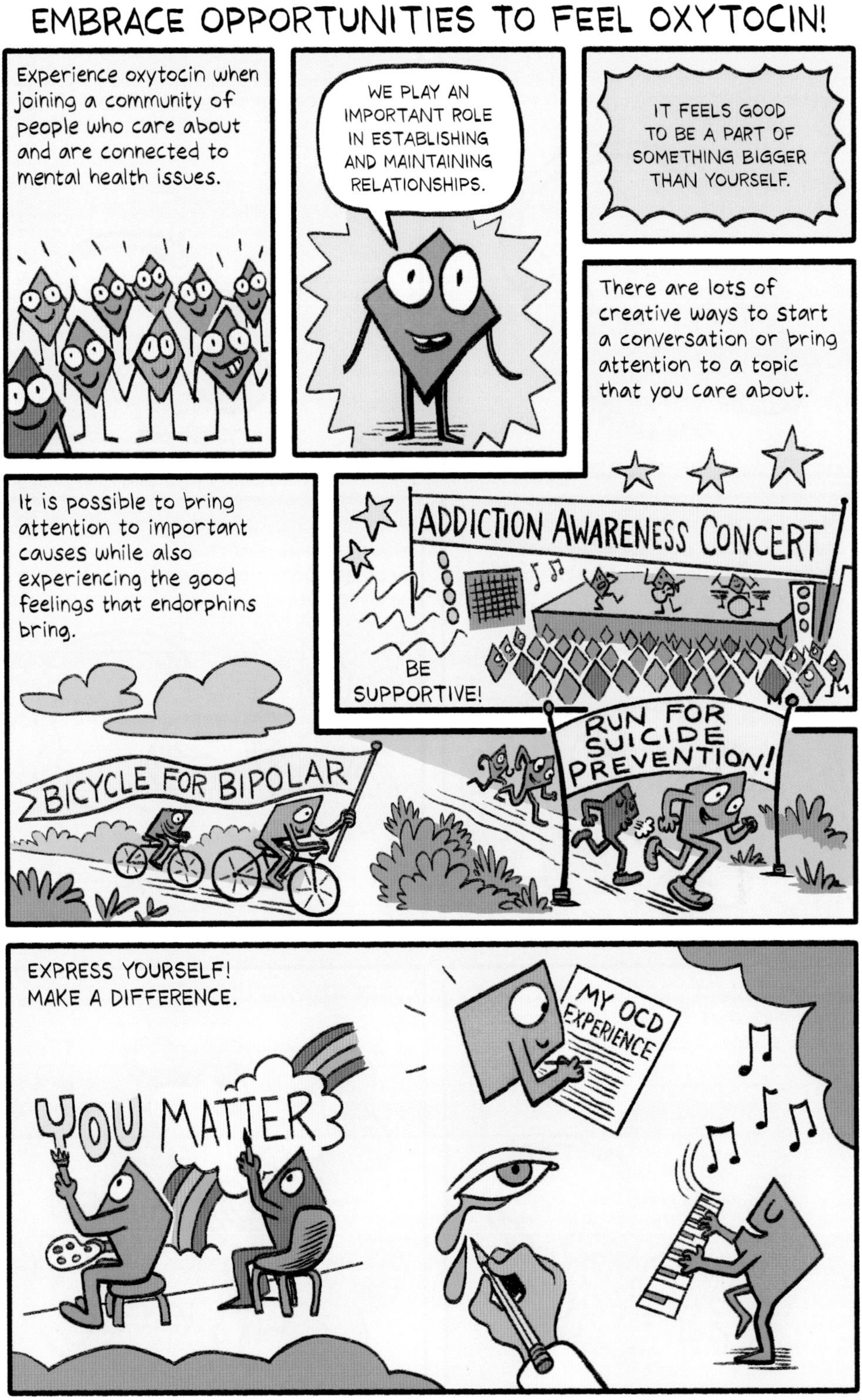
EMBRACE OPPORTUNITIES TO FEEL OXYTOCIN!
Experience oxytocin when joining a community of people who care about and are connected to mental health issues.
WE PLAY AN IMPORTANT ROLE IN ESTABLISHING AND MAINTAINING RELATIONSHIPS.
IT FEELS GOOD TO BE A PART OF SOMETHING BIGGER THAN YOURSELF.
There are lots of creative ways to start a conversation or bring attention to a topic that you care about.
It is possible to bring attention to important causes while also experiencing the good feelings that endorphins bring.
ADDICTION AWARENESS CONCERT
BE SUPPORTIVE!
BICYCLE FOR BIPOLAR
RUN FOR SUICIDE PREVENTION!
EXPRESS YOURSELF! MAKE A DIFFERENCE.
MY OCD EXPERIENCE
YOU MATTER

PROTECT YOUR HIPPOCAMPUS

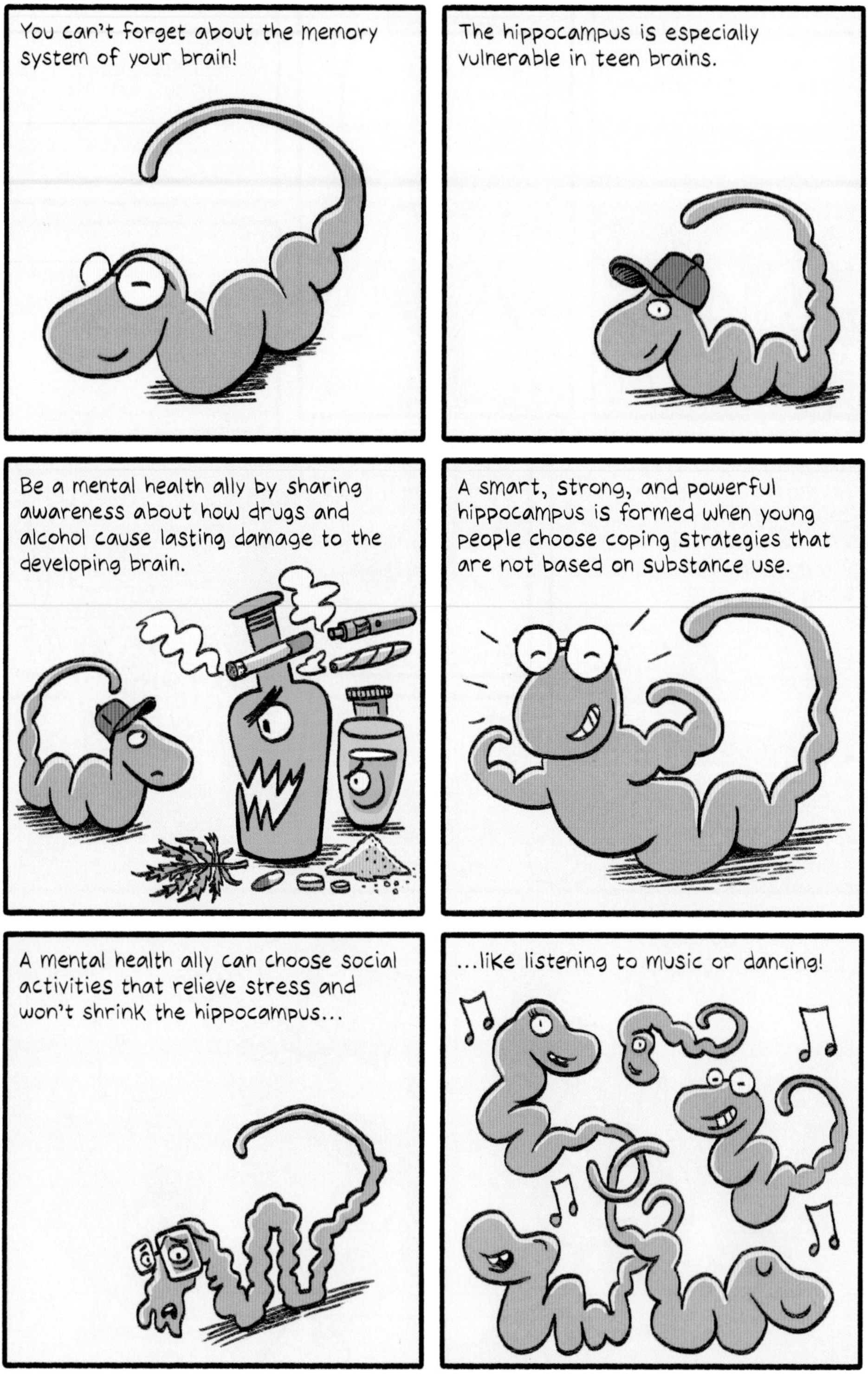
You can't forget about the memory system of your brain!
The hippocampus is especially vulnerable in teen brains.
Be a mental health ally by sharing awareness about how drugs and alcohol cause lasting damage to the developing brain.
A smart, strong, and powerful hippocampus is formed when young people choose coping strategies that are not based on substance use.
A mental health ally can choose social activities that relieve stress and won't shrink the hippocampus...
...like listening to music or dancing!

BE PATIENT WITH YOUR PREFRONTAL CORTEX

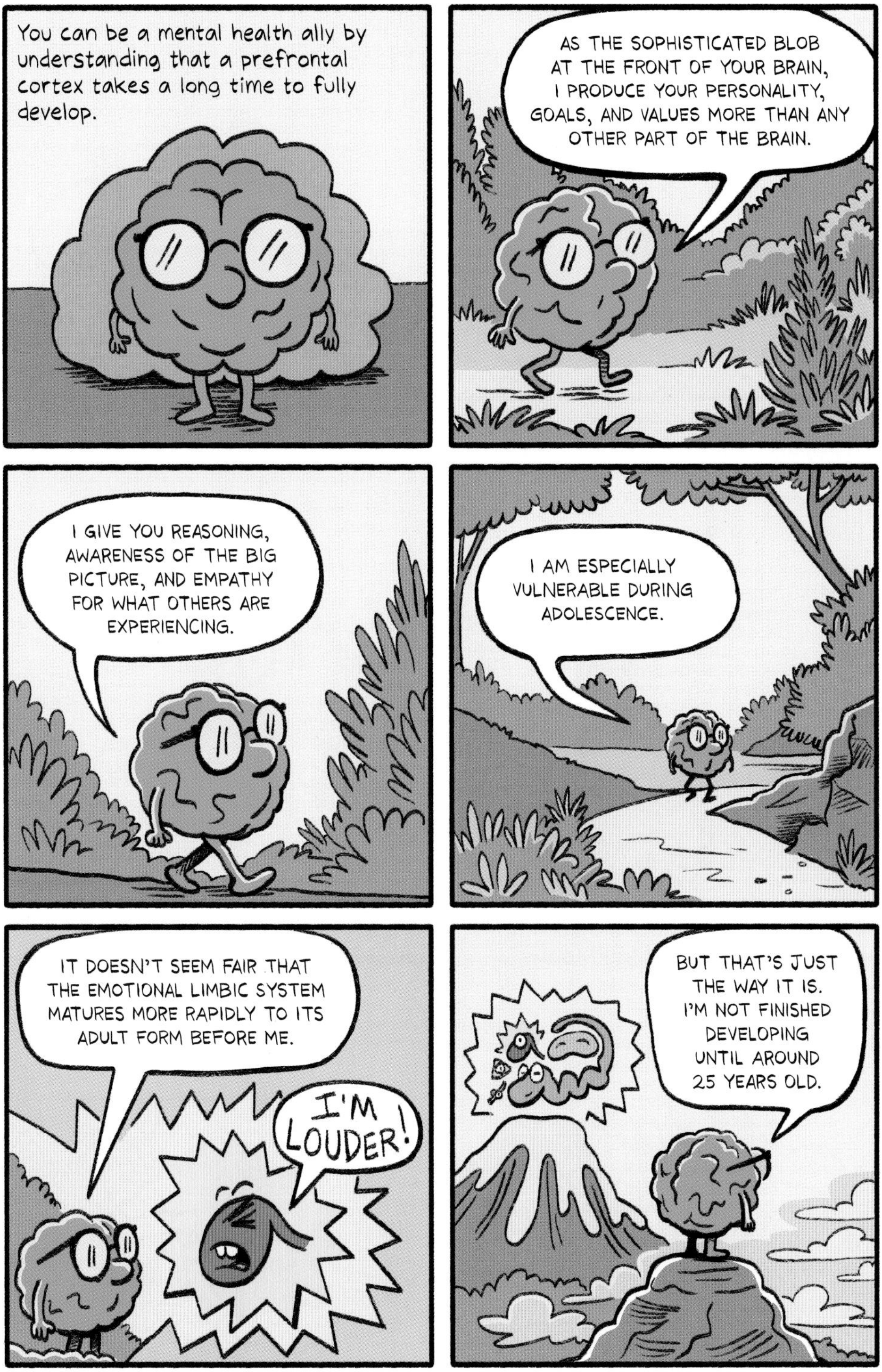

You can be a mental health ally by understanding that a prefrontal cortex takes a long time to fully develop.
AS THE SOPHISTICATED BLOB AT THE FRONT OF YOUR BRAIN, I PRODUCE YOUR PERSONALITY, GOALS, AND VALUES MORE THAN ANY OTHER PART OF THE BRAIN.
I GIVE YOU REASONING, AWARENESS OF THE BIG PICTURE, AND EMPATHY FOR WHAT OTHERS ARE EXPERIENCING.
I AM ESPECIALLY VULNERABLE DURING ADOLESCENCE.
IT DOESN'T SEEM FAIR THAT THE EMOTIONAL LIMBIC SYSTEM MATURES MORE RAPIDLY TO ITS ADULT FORM BEFORE ME.
I'M LOUDER!
BUT THAT'S JUST THE WAY IT IS. I'M NOT FINISHED DEVELOPING UNTIL AROUND 25 YEARS OLD.

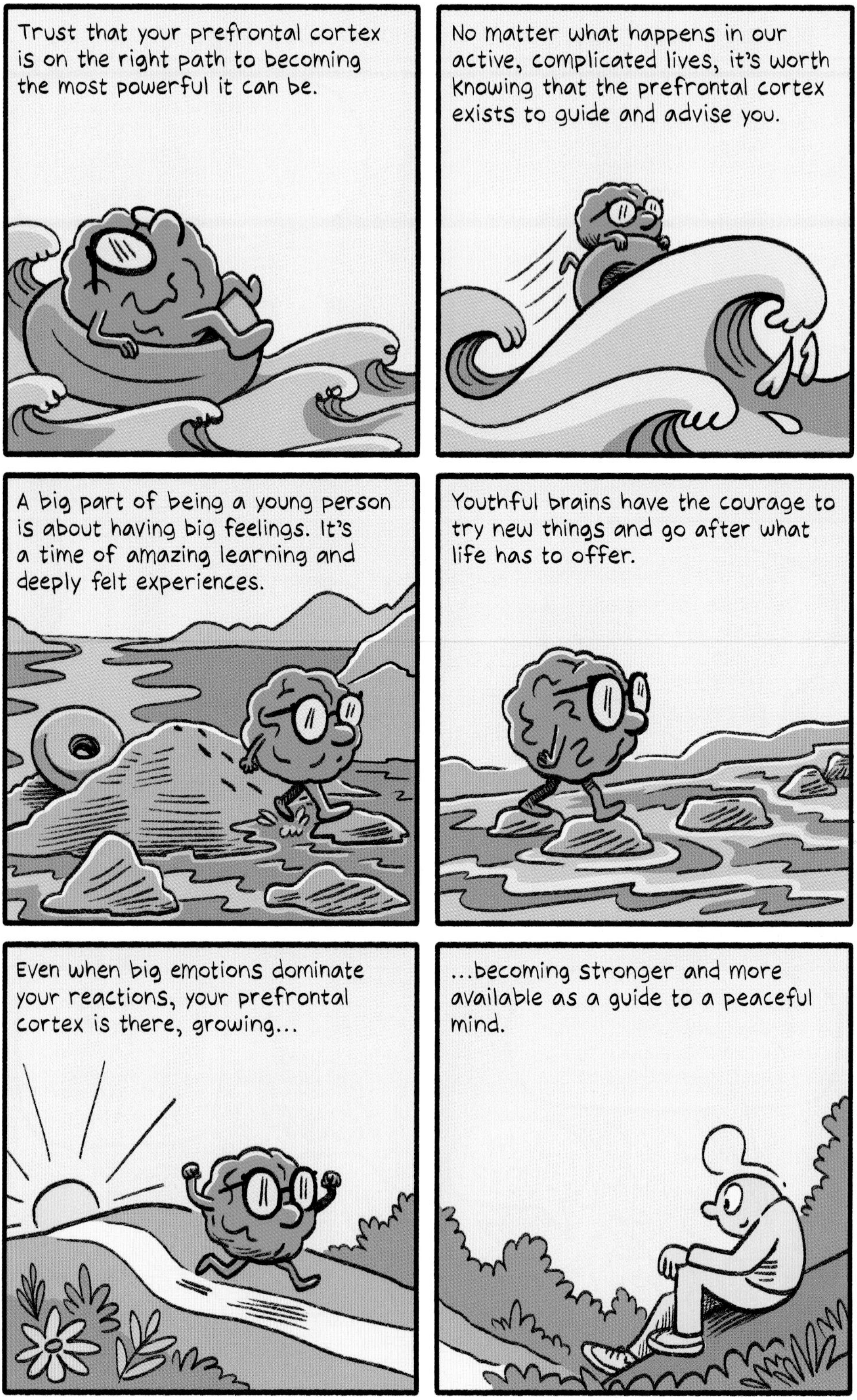
Trust that your prefrontal cortex is on the right path to becoming the most powerful it can be.
No matter what happens in our active, complicated lives, it's worth knowing that the prefrontal cortex exists to guide and advise you.
A big part of being a young person is about having big feelings. It's a time of amazing learning and deeply felt experiences.
Youthful brains have the courage to try new things and go after what life has to offer.
Even when big emotions dominate your reactions, your prefrontal cortex is there, growing...
...becoming stronger and more available as a guide to a peaceful mind.

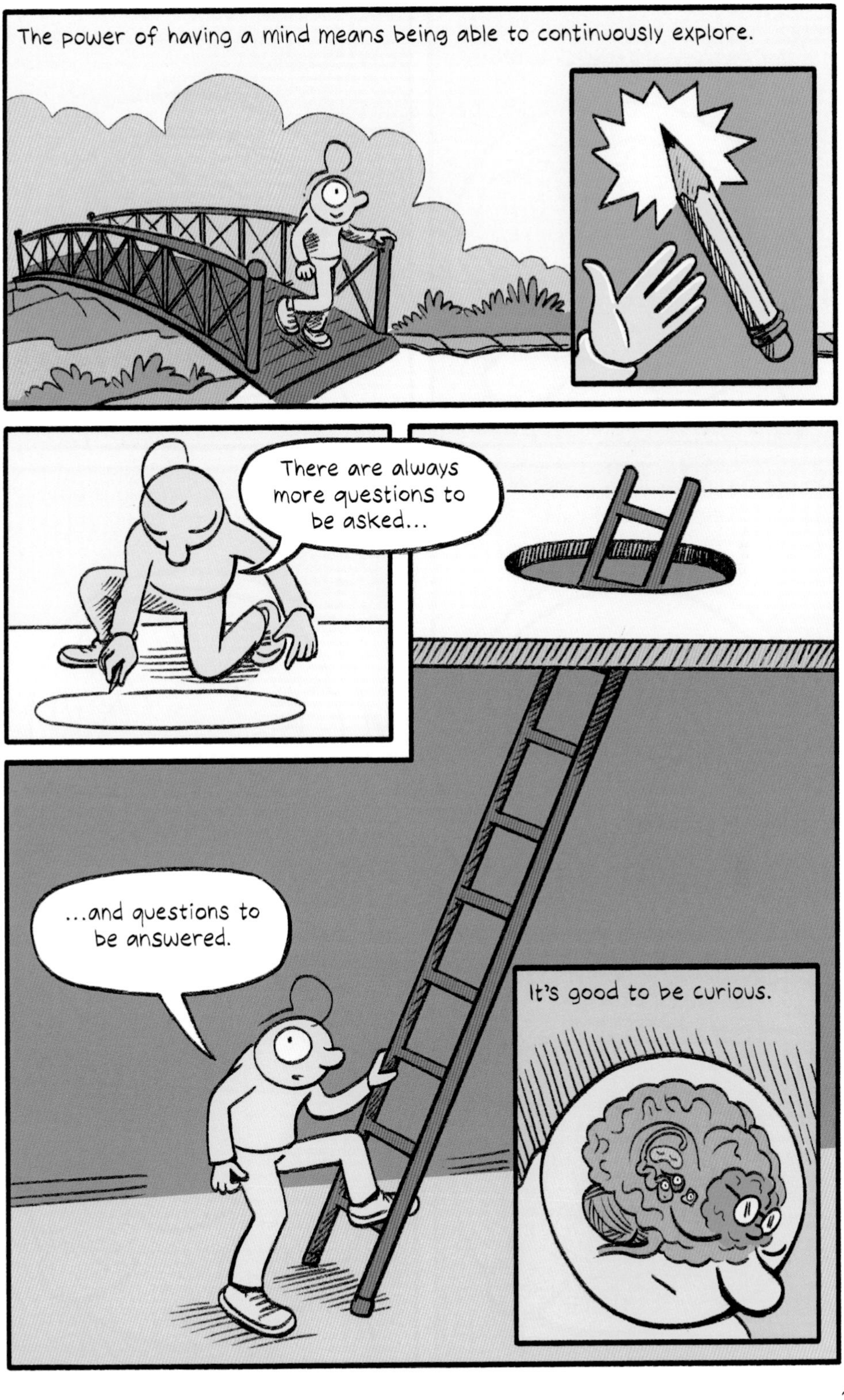
The power of having a mind means being able to continuously explore.
There are always more questions to be asked...
...and questions to be answered.
It's good to be curious.

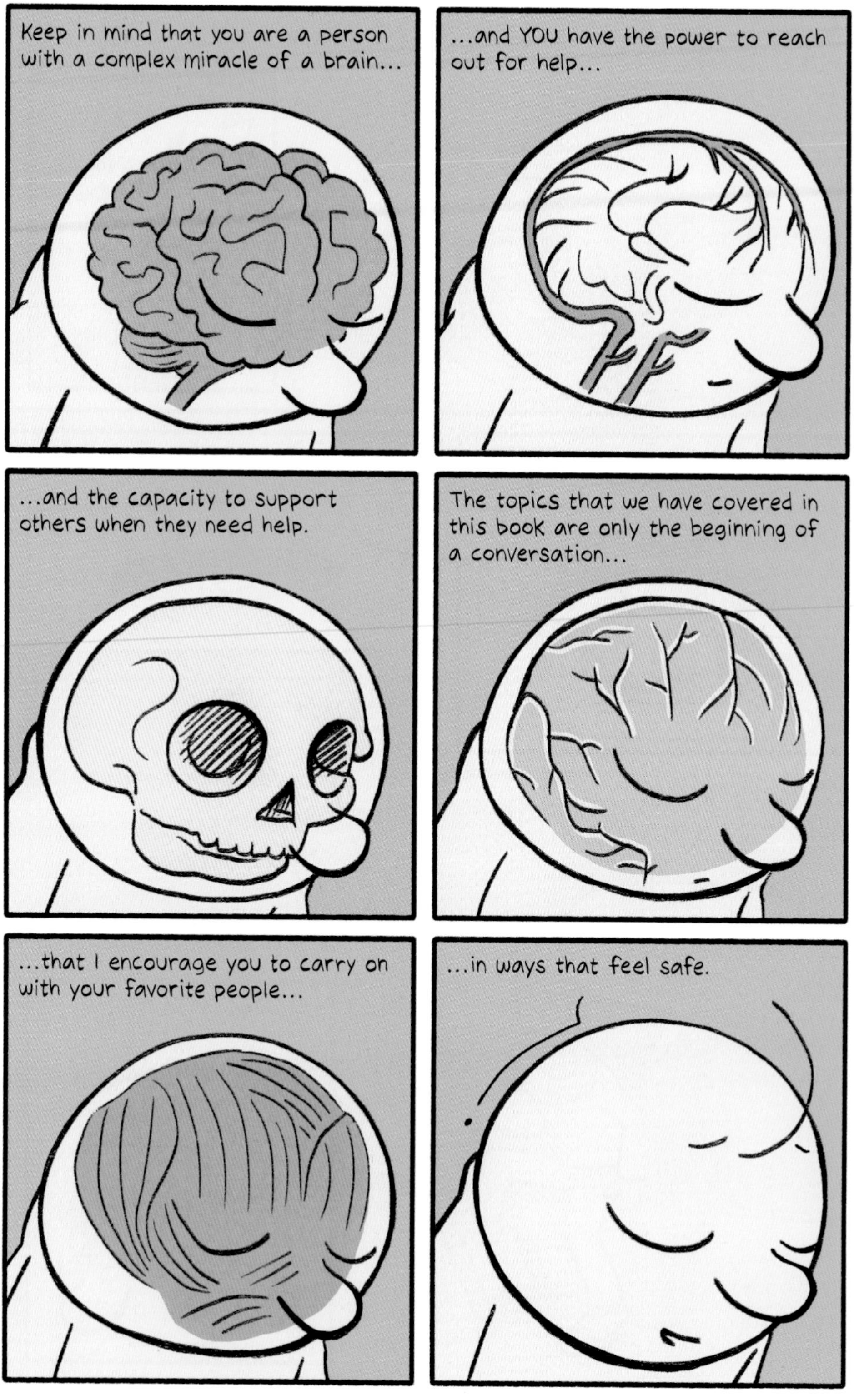
Keep in mind that you are a person with a complex miracle of a brain...
...and YOU have the power to reach out for help...
...and the capacity to support others when they need help.
The topics that we have covered in this book are only the beginning of a conversation...
...that I encourage you to carry on with your favorite people...
...in ways that feel safe.

GLOSSARY

addiction: A medical condition where a habit of consuming a substance like alcohol or drugs leads to dependence on the substance. Also known as a substance use disorder.

addictive: A substance or activity likely to cause someone to become dependent on it.

adrenal glands: Glands located on top of the kidneys that secrete reaction hormones like adrenaline and cortisol.

adrenaline: A hormone that makes the heart beat faster, increases blood flow to the brain and muscles, and stimulates the body to make sugar for fuel. Also known as epinephrine.

amygdala: A part of the limbic system that functions as the brain's emotional alarm system.

anxiety: When a person suffers from persistent and excessive worries that don't go away even without a stressor.

avoidance: When a person stays away from a potentially stressful situation because they anticipate negative consequences or associate anxious feelings with the situation.

behaviors: A person's actions or the things they do.

bipolar disorder: A mood disorder characterized by episodes of depression as well as periods of unusually high energy or activity called mania.

brain: An organ inside the skull that controls all the body functions in a human being.

central nervous system: The part of the nervous system made up of the brain and spinal cord.

circulatory system: The system that circulates blood through the body via the heart and blood vessels.

Cognitive Behavioral Therapy (CBT): A type of psychotherapy that challenges a client's negative thought patterns, encourages them to reframe the way they look at situations, then helps them to change their behaviors and thoughts to healthier ones.

conscious mind: The surface level of the mind where one is aware of their thoughts, actions, and speech.

coping: Managing difficult or stressful situations, usually with mental or physical strategies.

cortex: A wrinkly outer area of the brain that is the source of complex thoughts and behaviors. The cortex is the largest part of the brain.

cortisol: A hormone that is released into the body during a stress response.

dendrite: A branching extension of a neuron where the synapses are located and neurotransmitters are sent and received.

depression: A negative state of being that can affect a person's mood, energy, sleep, eating habits, thoughts, self-esteem, relationships, and enjoyment of social activities.

dopamine: Neurotransmitters that produce pleasure when a person does something that feels good. This creates a reward-seeking loop in the mind that encourages repeated behaviors that feel good.

emotions: Chemical signals that happen in the brain and nervous system and are expressed as thoughts, feelings, behaviors, and changes in the body.

endorphins: Neurotransmitters that are produced during physical activity like dancing, running, and laughing. They provide relief from stress and pain and increase pleasure.

enteric nervous system: The area of the nervous system located around the intestines and associated with a person's instincts. There, the brain can affect the gut and the gut can send messages to the brain.

fawn response: An aspect of the freeze response that involves merging with the wishes, needs, and demands of others so that they will cooperate. It may be used to calm a tense situation or avoid conflict.

fear: An intense emotion triggered when a person detects a threat that produces an alarm reaction in the body to mobilize and protect them from the threat.

fear fact: Fear that is a result of a real threat to one's body or survival.

fear fiction: Fear that is a result of an imagined threat. It often happens when a person is not thinking about what is happening in the here and now.

fight response: An automatic defensive reaction the body makes when faced with a stressful or frightening situation. The fight response can show up as anger, shouting, large movements, clenched muscles, and other displays of aggression.

flight response: An automatic defensive reaction the body makes when faced with a stressful or frightening situation. The flight response can show up as avoiding threats, escaping from the situation, procrastinating, and seeking distraction.

freeze response: An automatic defensive reaction the body makes when faced with a stressful or frightening situation. The freeze response includes reactions like being unable to move, playing dead, feeling detached, and zoning out.

Generalized Anxiety Disorder (GAD): An anxiety disorder exhibited through chronic, difficult to control anxiety, worry, and nervousness.

glial cells: Cells that play a supportive role in protecting and maintaining brain tissue.

habit: A repeated behavior that becomes a pattern or routine.

hindbrain: The lower area of the brain that initiates basic survival functions like breathing, swallowing, heartbeat, and movement. Also known as the rhombencephalon.

hippocampus: A part in the brain's limbic system that plays a role in learning and memory.

hormones: Chemical messengers that come out of glands and travel to tissues or organs via the bloodstream.

hypothalamus: A part in the brain's limbic system that controls the body's physical responses like sweat, hunger, fatigue, and energy levels.

learned helplessness: A situation that occurs when someone is repeatedly exposed to stressors they cannot control and they stop seeking help completely.

limbic system: The part of the brain that creates emotions and forms memories.

major depression: See Major Depressive Disorder.

Major Depressive Disorder: A depressive disorder with symptoms including persistent sadness, feelings of worthlessness, listlessness, difficulty concentrating, disturbed sleep, change of appetite, shifts in energy, self-

destructive behavior, and thoughts of suicide or death. A person must have had at least four of these symptoms for at least two weeks to receive a diagnosis.

maladaptive coping strategies: Habits that people use to deal with stress, painful emotions, and negative thoughts that make them feel good in the moment but are not good in the long run.

mind: A person's consciousness. The mind is what enables a person to be aware of the world around them, think about their experiences, feel emotions, explore memories, and make choices.

mindfulness: Having an awareness of one's mind and what is going on inside of it.

mindset: The type of thoughts a person has. Having a positive mindset means being optimistic about the world; having a negative mindset means being pessimistic about the world.

mixed anxiety and substance use: When a person uses a substance like alcohol or drugs to treat their anxiety, which then has negative effects on the person's health and relationships.

nervous system: The network of nerve cells that transmits chemical signals, or messages, throughout the body. It controls automatic functions like thought, heartbeat, breath, and balance, as well as voluntary functions like movement and speech.

neurons: Nerve cells that receive chemical messages from the body and send messages out from the brain using neurotransmitters. Neurons are the basic unit of the nervous system.

neuroplasticity: The brain's ability to form new connections and pathways.

neurotransmitters: Chemical messengers that send information, or chemical signals, from neuron to neuron.

nucleus accumbens: A part of the limbic system that works with the ventral tegmental area in the reward system of the brain, using dopamine neurons.

Obsessive Compulsive Disorder (OCD): An anxiety disorder characterized by a cycle of recurring intrusive thoughts, or obsessions, that make a person perform rituals, or compulsions.

oxytocin: A neurotransmitter that produces emotional connections with loved ones, motivates trust in others, and makes people want to be social.

panic attack: A sudden episode of intense fear that triggers physical reactions when there is no real danger or apparent cause.

panic disorder: An anxiety disorder characterized by repeating, sudden panic attacks that are sometimes caused by the fear of having a panic attack.

parasympathetic nervous system: The area of the nervous system that relaxes and calms the body down with a "rest and digest" response.

perinatal depression: A type of depression with symptoms of major and minor depressive episodes that occurs during pregnancy or in the first twelve months after childbirth. Includes prenatal and postpartum depression.

peripheral nervous system: The part of the nervous system containing all the nerves in the body other than the brain and the spinal cord.

Persistent Depressive Disorder: A depressive disorder that causes the same symptoms as major depression but in a milder form. Also known as dysthymia.

phobia: An anxiety disorder characterized by an overwhelming fear of a specific thing, where the imagined threat is greater than any actual danger.

pituitary gland: A part in the brain's limbic system that is connected to the hypothalamus and releases chemical messages.

Post-Traumatic Stress Disorder (PTSD): An anxiety disorder seen in people who continue to have persistent stress responses long after a traumatic event.

prefrontal cortex: A part of the brain located in the frontmost part of the cortex's frontal lobe. This part of the brain influences a person's personality, goals, and values, as well as helps them to predict consequences, control impulses, focus, and feel empathy.

Premenstrual Dysphoric Disorder (PMDD): A severe form of premenstrual syndrome (PMS) with symptoms of depression, anxiety, feelings of helplessness, and lowered interest in activities. Symptoms begin shortly after ovulation and end once menstruation starts.

psychologist: An expert in psychology. Psychologists can help individuals, athletic teams, and businesses, as well as conduct research.

psychology: The study of the mind and behavior. It focuses on how people think, act, and feel.

psychotherapy: A conversation between a client and a licensed mental health professional that uses communication to treat mental health problems and bring clarity to complicated situations. Also known as talk therapy.

recovery: A place where someone can go to get help with managing their addiction or stopping harmful habits.

rest and digest system: Another name for the parasympathetic nervous system, this system helps the body relax and calm down. When the rest and digest system takes over, heart rate slows, breathing slows, muscles relax, blood pressure decreases, and more.

reticular activating system (RAS): A part in the brain's limbic system that filters the information entering the brain. It helps you pay attention to important things and discard unneeded information.

ruminating: Thinking about something over and over again until it takes command of all one's focus and drains them of energy.

Seasonal Affective Disorder (SAD): A mood disorder characterized by episodes of depression that usually start in the fall or winter and go away during the spring or summer.

serotonin: A neurotransmitter that helps with mood regulation and memory, producing good moods and an overall sense of well-being.

stigma: An invisible mark of disgrace on a person that makes people think of something negative. Stigma happens when society forms a set of negative or unfair beliefs about a person, a group, or characteristics associated with them.

stress: A state of worry or tension caused by a difficult situation, challenge, or threat.

stressors: Activities, events, or other stimuli that cause stress.

substance use disorder: See addiction.

sympathetic nervous system: The area of the nervous system that activates the body's "fight or flight" response.

synapse: A junction between two neurons, located at the end of the neurons' dendrites, that sends chemical messages (neurotransmitters) from one neuron to another.

thalamus: A part in the brain's limbic system that helps pass along sensory signals from the cortex.

therapist: A mental health professional who has been trained in and practices therapy to improve the mental health and well-being of their clients.

therapy: See psychotherapy.

thoughts: Ideas and opinions produced by thinking, or that occur suddenly in the mind.

tolerance: A condition that occurs when a person uses a drug so much that the drug has less of an effect. When the person is dependent on that substance, they must increase the dose of the drug in order to avoid withdrawal symptoms.

trauma: A stressful and disturbing experience that causes intense, persistent fear and the feeling of being very unsafe or out of control. Traumatic events can create long-term symptoms that affect a person physically, socially, and emotionally.

unconscious mind: The lower level of the mind where ideas, sensory information, and memories exist, even when a person is not paying attention to them.

vagus nerve: A nerve in the parasympathetic nervous system that helps regulate body functions like breath, heartbeat, digestion, and blood pressure.

ventral tegmental area: A part of the limbic system that works with the nucleus accumbens in the reward system of the brain, using dopamine neurons.

withdrawal: Occurs when someone who is addicted to something cannot do their habit, causing highly unpleasant physical and mental symptoms.

RESOURCES

ORGANIZATIONS

National Alliance for Mental Health (NAMI)
nami.org
This organization focusing on mental health provides information, resources, advocacy, and more, with local and state chapters offering support groups and other services.

National Institute on Drug Abuse (NIDA)
teens.drugabuse.gov
NIDA is the leading federal agency for scientific research on drug use and addiction. The section of their website for adolescents, their caregivers, and educators includes videos, blog posts, and drug facts. NIDA for Teens provides a wealth of knowledge and resources including easy-to-read guides.

Society for Adolescent Health and Medicine (SAHM)
adolescenthealth.org
Their "Substance Use Resources for Adolescents and Young Adults" page provides resources aimed specifically at young people.

RESOURCES FOR HELP

988 Suicide & Crisis Lifeline
Call 988 or 800-273-TALK (8255)
en Español (888-628-9454)
TTY (800-799-4889)
988lifeline.org
The Lifeline provides 24/7 free and confidential support for people in distress, prevention and crisis resources, and a guide to best practices for improving mental health in the United States.

Boys Town National Hotline (serves girls too)
Text VOICE to 20121 · Call 800-448-3000
Email hotline@boystown.org
boystown.org/hotline
This 24/7 hotline, staffed by specially trained counselors, supports parents, teens, and families across a range of issues including abuse, anger, depression, school issues, bullying, and so on.

Continued on next page

National Crisis Text Line
Text HOME to 741741
crisistextline.org

This 24/7 service provides live, trained crisis counselors who receive each text and respond via a secure online platform. The volunteer counselors are trained to help you move from "a hot moment to a cool calm."

National Eating Disorders Association (NEDA)
nationaleatingdisorders.org/help-support
NEDA provides support, resources, and treatment options for yourself or a loved one who is struggling with an eating disorder.

notOK App
notokapp.com
The notOK App is a free digital panic button to get you immediate support via text, phone call, or GPS location when you're struggling to reach out.

Substance Use and Mental Health Services (SAMSA) Drug Abuse Treatment Locator
Call 800-662-HELP (4357)
findtreatment.gov

Through this 24/7 resource for people seeking treatment for mental and substance use disorders in the United States and its territories you can search for substance use and mental health facilities, health care centers, buprenorphine practitioners, and opioid treatment providers.

Teen Line
Text TEEN to 839863 · Call 800-852-8336
teenline.org

Teen Line provides a hotline of professionally trained teen counselors and outreach programs that destigmatize and normalize mental health. Check their website for current hours.

Trans Lifeline
Call 877-565-8860 (U.S.) or 877-330-6366 (Canada)
translifeline.org

This 24/7 hotline (available in English and Spanish) for transgender people is peer-focused, and staffed by and for transgender people.

The Trevor Project
Text START to 678678 · Call 866-488-7386
thetrevorproject.org/get-help

The Trevor Project is the leading national organization providing peer support, research, advocacy, education, and 24/7 crisis intervention and support (via phone, text, or chat) for lesbian, gay, bisexual, transgender, queer, and questioning (LGBTQ) young people under 25.

ADDITIONAL RESOURCES FOR INFORMATION

Active Minds
activeminds.org

This nonprofit organization is dedicated to promoting mental health, especially among young adults, via peer-to-peer dialogue and interaction.

Society for the Prevention of Teen Suicide
sptsusa.org

This organization is dedicated to increasing awareness, saving lives, and reducing the stigma of suicide through specialized training programs and resources that empower teens, parents, and educational leaders with the skills needed to help youth build a life of resiliency.

StopBullying
stopbullying.gov

This site provides information from various government agencies on what bullying is, what cyberbullying is, who is at risk, and how to prevent and respond to bullying.

Suicide Prevention Lifeline, Youth section
988lifeline.org/help-yourself/youth

This is a youth-focused section within the 988 Suicide & Crisis Lifeline that centers the emotional and mental health of youth and provides related resources and care.

Youth Suicide Warning Signs
youthsuicidewarningsigns.org/youth

This site shares youth suicide warning signs from the American Association of Suicidology (AAS) and the National Center for the Prevention of Youth Suicide (NCPYS).

ACKNOWLEDGMENTS

This book would not be possible without many people's enthusiasm, intelligence, guidance, and emotional support.

Thank you to my editors: Traci Todd—for believing in this book when it was only an idea; Chris Duffy—for helping me relax and make comics; Katie Campbell, for nurturing me throughout the entire process; and Megan Nicolay, for uncovering the title of the book and heroically and enthusiastically bringing this book to the finish line.

I'm fortunate to have had wonderful advisors: Dr. Mandi White-Ajmani—for writing the foreword and for your valuable feedback; Dr. Monica Berlanga—for graciously reviewing the neuroscience information; Michael Safranek—for being the first reader of the depression and suicide chapters and for becoming a favorite character in this book; and Dr. Margaret A. Smith—for your wisdom on the substance use and addiction chapter.

I'm so grateful to my Workman/Hachette collaborators: Sara Corbett, art director—for your beautiful bookmaking skills; Molly Magnell and Sam Pun, designers—for laboring over and organizing so many files; Keirsten Geise, associate art director—for your cover image idea; Catherine Weening, production editor—for your intelligent eyes; Barbara Peragine, typesetter—for your expertise and attention to detail; Stacy Lellos, publisher—for your confidence and discernment; Moira Kerrigan, director of marketing—for your guidance toward readers; Rebecca Carlisle, VP of marketing and publicity—for your work toward making this book accessible; Diana Griffin, assistant director of publicity and marketing—for spreading the word; Laura Lutz, marketing manager—for getting my book in front of librarians and teachers; and Shawn Foster and Danielle Cantarella, sales directors—for helping to place my book into the hands of readers.

I could not have done this without my creative community: Oulu Comics Center and The Liminka School of Art—for welcoming me to Finland at the beginning of this book's journey; the Cornish Residency and Harry Bliss—for providing me a special place to wrestle with ideas; the Center for Cartoon Studies, James Sturm and Michelle Ollie—for your encouragement and opportunities; K Space—for providing an open, creative space to work in Texas; Patreon Supporters—for providing your attention and suggestions; MICE, Graphic Medicine, CXC, and SPX—for producing comic events that have inspired me; my teachers, librarians, and counselors—for your important work with kids; Neil Brideau—for sharing my comics and being my pal; Ellen Forney—for being my mental health comics inspiration; Jonathan Hill—for being my Clip Studio coach; and Alec Longstreth—for your digital coloring lesson.

The love of my friends and family means the world to me: Rebecca, Jason, and Robin—for being your caring selves; Mary—for our walks and your advice; Jen D., Jenn M., Kara, Kathleen, and Leah—for being loyal squirrels; Anne, Amanda, Erica, Jenn H., Lisa, Meighan, and Jennifer M.—for our childhood and adulthood friendship; Beans, Cantys, and Reads—for being my people; Mom and Dad—for encouraging me to pursue art; Jackie, Jonathan, Howie, and Elena—for always lending a helping hand; and Matt—for hiking through every moment of this book and believing in me when I doubted.

ABOUT THE AUTHOR

PHOTO BY STEPHANIE GEORGIA

CARA BEAN is a cartoonist and art educator living in Massachusetts with her husband and their dog, Raisin. She is the author of *Draw 500 Funny Faces and Features*. *Here I Am, I Am Me* is her first book for adolescents. Her favorite ways to feel calm are walking in the woods, floating in the water, snuggling with pets, feeling cozy with a cup of tea, and laughing with loved ones. Cara is passionate about drawing and enjoys admiring other people's sketchbooks, especially kids' sketchbooks! Find her online at carabeancomics.com.